Focused Issues in Family Therapy

Series Editor

D. Russell Crane, Brigham Young University, Provo, UT, USA

More information about this series at http://www.springer.com/series/13372

Jacob D. Christenson · Ashley N. Merritts
Editors

Family Therapy
with Adolescents
in Residential Treatment

Intervention and Research

Springer

Editors
Jacob D. Christenson
Mount Mercy University
Cedar Rapids, IA
USA

Ashley N. Merritts
Mount Mercy University
Cedar Rapids, IA
USA

ISSN 2520-1190   ISSN 2520-1204   (electronic)
Focused Issues in Family Therapy
ISBN 978-3-319-51746-9   ISBN 978-3-319-51747-6   (eBook)
DOI 10.1007/978-3-319-51747-6

Library of Congress Control Number: 2017933435

Printed on acid-free paper

This Springer imprint is published by Springer Nature
The registered company is Springer International Publishing AG
The registered company address is: Gewerbestrasse 11, 6330 Cham, Switzerland

I dedicate this book to my wife Vanessa, who has always supported me and without whom none of this would have been possible. I also dedicate this book to my kids, Nathan, Ryan, Kyle, and Katie. My hope is that each of you will do greater things than I could have ever dreamed of.

—Jacob D. Christenson

I'd like to thank my parents, Scott and Diane, for instilling in me a love of learning and teaching, my husband, Sean, for encouraging me to achieve my goals and to set them high, and my boys, Manning and Madden. Always remember you can do anything you set your minds to.

—Ashley N. Merritts

Foreword

I was walking in the desert of Utah in the early summer of 1997 with a 15-year old young man named *Timmy* and we were opining about the state of the world, girls, life, and how lucky we were that it was such a nice day. He was a really cool kid. Brilliant even, probably to his detriment, based on his stories of trying to navigate the hallowed halls of his large suburban high school without standing out too much. His goal, he told me, was to remain invisible, speak up only if asked, and never come off as knowing too much or too little. If he seemed too smart, he said he would get harassed; not smart enough and he would get singled out by his teachers. "Right down the middle" he said, that was his goal. He had hauled his diagnosed ADHD around those halls like a ball and chain his whole life, never feeling like he could be free from the constant threat that he would miss an assignment, get confused about his schedule, or impulsively tell one of the upper classmen to *bug off* if he was getting picked on. That happened once and he wasn't about to have it happen again. He said it was different out here, plodding along in the desert. He felt free, which was ironic, he said, given that he didn't really want to be there, and wouldn't be there if his parents (divorced) hadn't strongly suggested he attend the program after his recent raw and violent outbursts toward his poor undeserving mother. He said he just couldn't hold it in any longer, and it just exploded out of him. It frightened him and his mother. His father and stepmother (*step monster* as he referred to her) also weighed in on the episode and wondered when their turn would be to feel his wrath. Every other weekend he switched, he said, and hated the visitation schedule. As a researcher spending 14 days in the field with this group, I had become a steady confidante of Timmy's, trusted to hold some of his deepest secrets and incipient goals that he had begun to think about to get his situation turned around. The therapist and leaders said I should run with it, as Timmy was reluctant to get close to people and trust others because of how many times he had been let him down in his life.

The family system, which Timmy said he was merely trying *survive*, was the topic of many of our conversations on the trail. The perfect older brother with straight A's and a sparkling athletic future; the quiet little sister who could do no wrong and always did what she was told; the distraught mother coping with her husband's infidelity, new wife, and her own loneliness; and the over-bearing father who never had the time or patience to listen to anything Timmy ever said. Timmy and I were in agreement that the whole family should be out there on the trail with us, and in many ways they were. Timmy's situation was a central case study in my research during this period, as I also interviewed Timmy's mother and father to gain their perspective. The therapist and leaders centered Timmy's treatment plan and goals on finding strategic ways for Timmy to begin deconstructing his family system and finding ways that Timmy could learn to thrive, not just survive, in this complicated web of relationships he was born into. The therapist also spent an inordinate amount of time working with each parent, from the beginning family sessions, to weekly conversations about Timmy's progress in treatment, and their role in helping Timmy reintegrate back into the system when he was finished with the program. The therapist said that Timmy was the easy part; he was doing well and thriving in the program. Timmy was slowly discovering the beautiful young man that had been suppressed through years of building up walls around him to traverse the divide between his ADHD, self-awareness and worth, and his family that always seemed to be working against him. It was the parents and family system that were the tough part.

This text is a critical contribution to the field of residential treatment for adolescents, as well as wilderness and adventure therapy, and can help practitioners, researchers, parents, educational consultants, and mental health professionals understand the critical role that families play in the treatment of adolescents. Virtually all adolescent and young adult treatment programs, to varying degrees, approach treatment from a family systems perspective. The editors have done a wonderful job weaving research and practical advice into the volume that forms a perfect complement to existing texts in the field. This book is literally a treasure trove of perspectives, strategies, and novel approaches to working with families in traditional residential treatment settings and Outdoor Behavioral Healthcare programs. The book and chapters herein tell a story that is both compelling and informative, and is a must read for professionals and stakeholders in the field.

Keith C. Russell, Ph.D.
Professor and Chair
Department of Health and Human Development
Western Washington University, Bellingham, USA

Acknowledgments

When we started this process more than a year ago, we had hoped to be able to garner enough enthusiasm to produce a book of 10–15 chapters. However, as we moved forward the response was overwhelming and allowed us to produce a comprehensive overview of family therapy with adolescents in residential settings. This work would not have been possible without the help of a number of individuals who are certainly worthy of our acknowledgement. Amanda Glunz and Amber Miller were there from the beginning and both were instrumental in reaching out to potential authors and beginning the process of selecting contributors. Caitlin Ledin worked closely with us as well and assisted in formatting chapter submissions and reviewing references. Steve DeMille, Troy Faddis, Tristan Morgan, Christine Norton, and Phil Scoville volunteered to review manuscripts and make suggestions that would help strengthen the final product. The work of all of these individuals has helped to strengthen this book, and for that we are very thankful. Finally, we would also like to thank Dr. Russ Crane for the opportunity to work on a special issue of *Contemporary Family Therapy*, which laid a foundation on which we were able to build this book. His helpful advice and feedback as we put this project together has been appreciated.

Contents

About the Editors

Jacob D. Christenson, Ph.D., LMFT is Assistant Professor of Marriage and Family Therapy at Mount Mercy University. Dr. Christenson received his Bachelor degree in Psychology from California Polytechnic State University. He then completed his Master's degree and doctorate in Marriage and Family Therapy from Brigham Young University. Before coming to Mount Mercy University, Dr. Christenson worked for 4 years at Aspen Achievement Academy in Loa, UT as a Field Therapist. As a Field Therapist, Dr. Christenson experienced firsthand the challenge of being a systemic marriage and family therapist in the world of residential care.

Over the course of his career Dr. Christenson has consistently been involved in academic research and publication. In addition to numerous presentations at national and international conferences, Dr. Christenson has published a number of articles in peer-reviewed journals such as the Journal of Marital and Family Therapy, Contemporary Family Therapy, and the American Journal of Family Therapy. Dr. Christenson also serves as an editorial board member for the Journal of Marital and Family Therapy and Contemporary Family Therapy.

Dr. Christenson teaches a number of courses at Mount Mercy University. The courses he has taught include Parents and Children, Micro-counseling, Medical Family Therapy, and Research Methods. Dr. Christenson is also an AAMFT Approved Supervisor, which has enabled him to provide supervision in practicum courses. Dr. Christenson also serves as the Clinical Director for the Gerald and Audrey Olson Marriage and Family Therapy Clinic, which is attached to the Marriage and Family Therapy program at Mount Mercy University. In addition to his work as a professor, Dr. Christenson provides therapy in private practice and is the founder of Covenant Family Solutions, an outpatient therapy group practice in Cedar Rapids, Iowa. When not working, Dr. Christenson enjoys spending time with his family and being active in his community.

Ashley N. Merritts, Ph.D., LMFT is Assistant Professor of Marriage and Family Therapy program at Mount Mercy University. Dr. Merritts received her BS degree from the University of Iowa in Psychology, with a minor in Human Relations. After graduating from the University of Iowa, Dr. Merritts continued her education and has a Ph.D. in Human Development and Family Studies and a Master of Science degree in the same major, both from Iowa State University. In her Master's degree program, Dr. Merritts specialized in couple and family therapy and is now a licensed Marital and Family Therapist.

Dr. Merritts has extensive clinical training and has worked with a wide variety of problems in clinical settings. She specializes in working with distressed couples and has advanced training in Trauma Focused Cognitive Behavior Therapy as well. Dr. Merritt's has worked with adolescents in residential settings during her career and understands the unique needs of this population. Here clinical interests also include working with childhood behavioral problems, families in crisis, co-parenting and divorce, individual healing, and affairs.

Dr. Merritts is Clinical Fellow and Approved Supervisor with the American Association for Marriage and Family Therapy. She has also served as a board member for the Iowa Association for Marriage and Family Therapy. Dr. Merritts has published her work in the International Journal of Disability, Development and Education. She has also published in, and has served as a reviewer for Contemporary Family Therapy: An International Journal. Dr. Merritts' research interests include relationship quality in African American couples and the impact of adverse childhood experiences on parent–child attachment.

Chapter 1
Introduction to Family Therapy with Adolescents in Residential Settings: Intervention and Research

Jacob D. Christenson and Ashley N. Merritts

Chapter Highlights

- The need for family involvement in the treatment of adolescents in residential settings is well understood. However, providers are often unsure of how to best meet this need.
- The purpose of the book is to provide foundational information for conducting family therapy in adolescent residential treatment settings, which providers can draw on to increase their effectiveness.
- The cost of treatment is considered and the implications for therapists and healthcare systems are discussed.
- General definitions and terminology used throughout the book are presented to orient the reader.
- The chapter concludes with a discussion of the rational for the organization of the book and highlights some of the commonalities across chapters.

Most counselors and therapists would agree that engaging the whole family and working with the entire system locally is the preferred approach when working with children and adolescents. Nevertheless, families with a troubled adolescent or young adult may find themselves in a position where community-based outpatient treatment has failed and they are in need of additional support. When this is the case, families and social agencies may turn to inpatient treatment to address contributing factors. Adolescents and young adults in residential treatment present with significant mental health concerns, including conduct disorder, oppositional behavior, depression and anxiety, drug and alcohol abuse, and eating disorders, to

J.D. Christenson (✉) · A.N. Merritts
Mount Mercy University, 1330 Elmhurst Dr. NE, Cedar Rapids, IA 52402, USA
e-mail: jchristenson@mtmercy.edu

A.N. Merritts
e-mail: amerritts@mtmercy.edu

© Springer International Publishing AG 2017   1
J.D. Christenson and A.N. Merritts (eds.), *Family Therapy with Adolescents in Residential Treatment*, Focused Issues in Family Therapy,
DOI 10.1007/978-3-319-51747-6_1

name a few. Parents may fear that without some type of out-of-home placement the child will end up in repeated psychiatric hospitalizations, or worse, incarcerated. Even though the problems may be severe, making the choice to send a child away to a program is often a heart wrenching decision and parents may be susceptible to guilt as a result (Frensch and Cameron 2002).

Families who place their child in a residential program will need support from therapists at home and in the program as they struggle to navigate the challenges that will arise while their child is placed in treatment. Although there is some disagreement concerning what exactly constitutes *residential treatment* (e.g., Lee and Barth 2011) parents are able to choose from a variety of programs with different structures, purposes, and methods. Among the options are emotional growth schools, therapeutic boarding schools, and residential treatment centers. Given the various approaches to treatment, it is important for parents to research and understand the different options. When this process is overwhelming, it may be helpful to enlist the help of an Educational Consultant that specializes in matching individuals with treatment options. Educational Consults spend a considerable amount of time learning about various program options so that they can be effective in helping families make decisions that will best address the needs of the child.

Once the adolescent is in treatment, therapists within the program are tasked with engaging the family in therapeutic activities. For some time now it has been recognized that children do better in residential care when their family is involved in the treatment process (e.g., Jenson and Whittaker 1987). Accordingly, it is now recognized within the industry that programs must have family involvement and work to modify the home environment that the child will eventually return to after discharge. Although this is understood, the separation between the child and parents makes it difficult to deliver traditional family therapy. This creates unique challenges for practitioners working in these settings. They must become proficient in working directly with the individual in treatment, as well as with the family, both directly and indirectly. Often family members are hundreds of miles away and may only be available by phone or for brief family visits a few times during the entire course of the program. Even when families live near the program, practitioners may find there are other barriers, such as a lack of motivation, abandonment of the child, and lengthy stays in residential programs (Burns et al. 1999) that make conjoint treatment difficult. Family therapists are often required to be creative and find unique ways of engaging the family. Once treatment is completed in a particular program, aftercare plans must be created and families will need help in determining what type of follow-on care is needed and how to modify family life to regulate the environment for the returning adolescent.

As will be seen throughout this book, significant efforts have been made to overcome the challenges inherent in delivering family therapy in these settings and a number of specific interventions have been developed to better involve the family. However, there remains a need to establish the effectiveness of those interventions and models, which has become increasingly apparent over time. Historically, the research in this field has been criticized for being limited to descriptive data or correlational analysis, without reliable measures or longitudinal data (e.g., Hattie et al. 1997). Although more rigorous methods have been used recently, the majority of the research continues to be concerned with program evaluation that is focused on the individual, rather than on determining what specific assessment methods and treatments approaches are effective with this population (McLendon et al. 2012). This leaves the field vulnerable to reproach from those who see residential placements as less effective and ignores the importance of the family in the process. Accordingly, more research is needed to strengthen the place of family therapy in residential settings for adolescents and young adults. The purpose of this chapter is to show how the book addresses the concerns and challenges outlined above in a comprehensive manner.

Cost of Treatment

Before delving into the contents of the book, some background information on costs is warranted to provide needed context. Demonstrating the effectiveness of family therapy services in adolescent residential treatment is only the beginning of what will be needed to solidify this treatment option in the marketplace. Over the last two decades the cost of health care has become a significant concern (e.g., Crane 1995) and efforts have consistently been made to improve care while also containing costs. A number of authors in the field of marriage and family therapy have called for greater integration of cost evaluations when conducting family therapy research (e.g., Christenson and Crane 2014). This will be especially important for those who research treatment in residential settings since the cost of this type of treatment is exponentially higher than community-based programs and interventions. This is true for both privately and publically funded institutions.

As noted in Chap. 20 of this book, there is a significance difference between private and public residential facilities in terms of type and quality of care (Behrens and Satterfield 2006; Lee and Barth 2011); however, the per day cost is not necessarily significantly different. Therefore, since more information is available for the cost of private programs, data concerning such programs will be used in this discussion. The Envoy Group (2016) provides some cost data on residential programs and show that residential treatment centers cost between $1500 and $3500 per month. They also show that a therapeutic boarding school will cost between $2500 and $10,000 per month, while short term intensive programs cost between $10,000 and $12,000 per month. The first author of this chapter worked at short-term intensive program for a number of years where the typical cost per week was approximately $5000. If an adolescent were to stay in a program like this for 2 months, the total cost would approach $40,000.

Given the high costs of these types of programs it begs the question of who pays for this type of treatment. Again, the type of program (i.e., private versus public) plays a significant role in answering this question. For private institutions, there are basically three options: (a) out-of-pocket private pay; (b) private insurance; and, (c) healthcare loans (The Envoy Group 2016). Out-of-pocket private pay is self-explanatory, but may involve contributions from family, friends, and co-workers. Some healthcare loans are available directly to the individual through insurance companies (e.g., www.unitedmedicalcredit.com) and others are available through enrolled provider organizations (e.g., www.prosperhealthcare.com). These services can be used to provide the funding up front, but of course, have to be paid back.

The third option mentioned above is private insurance, which can involve a number of complex systems and transactions. Some policies have a provision for inpatient treatment, but most insurance companies will not pay for private residential treatment outright, though they may be willing to pay for the discrete individual and family therapy services delivered within these settings. One option, sometimes taken advantage of by programs, is to provide the family with a claim for the therapy services provided to the child, which they can then give to their insurance company in the hopes of obtaining reimbursement. However, because private programs do not typically credential directly with any insurance companies there is no guarantee of payment. Some high-end so-called *Cadillac* insurance plans may cover private residential treatment, but this is the exception and not the rule.

The other type of program mentioned above is public residential programs. As implied in the title, these programs are usually funded by the government. Most often Medicaid funds are applied to pay for this type of treatment. However, adolescents may enter a public residential program through a number of mechanisms, including the juvenile justice system and organization that provide child services (e.g., foster care programs). Because of the high cost of this type of treatment, it will be essential for those in this field to demonstrate the cost effectiveness of their services, and to date little to no work has been done in this regard. Accordingly, in Chap. 20 there is a significant focus placed on cost evaluations and the need for more research in this area. Given the importance of this topic for the field we felt it prudent to emphasize it again here. The purpose and placement of the other chapters in the book is described more fully below.

Definitions and Consistency Across Chapters

Before moving on to a description of the contents of the book, a word is needed about the use of definitions used throughout the text. One thing that characterizes the work in the field of adolescent treatment is the unique terms and descriptions individuals use to describe the treatment setting and/or the interventions they use. In fact, it is not uncommon to hear people use the same term for very different programs and interventions. However, throughout this book every effort has been made to be consistent in the definitions used. A useful example can be seen in the field of *wilderness therapy*. Some people will apply this term to any program that involves the therapeutic use of the outdoors, while in reality there are two very distinct forms of this type of intervention. In the text, we use the term *therapeutic wilderness program* to denote wilderness programs without professional clinical support, while the terms wilderness therapy and *Outdoor Behavioral Healthcare* (OBH) refer to programs with licensed clinical staff and formal mental healthcare. These definitions are clearly identified in the chapters for which they apply. We have also made efforts to provide some consistency across chapters in the form of *chapter highlights*. Each author provided approximately five brief statements that offer an overview of the contents of the chapter. This was intended to give the reader a way to quickly evaluate the information contained in the chapters and determine whether what is presented meets their needs at any given moment.

Chapter Contents and Organization

The background information provided in this chapter reveals a number of areas that need to be considered when detailing adolescent residential treatment in a comprehensive manner. These include

- The decision to initiate treatment
- Supporting the family during the process
- Engaging the family in treatment
- Therapy while the family is separated
- Onsite family therapy
- Aftercare decisions
- Research on treatment.

Each of the bullets points are intentionally and thoroughly covered in the material selected to be included in this book. However, for the purpose of organizing the book, these seven areas were further delineated into three broad categories, and the book is divided up into parts, each of which covers one broad category. Some of the chapters may touch on more than one category, but all chapters fall solidly within at least one of the three parts of the book, which are (1) Family Therapy during Separation;   (2) Onsite Family Therapy; and, (3) Research and Outcomes. What follows below is a brief overview of the chapters that make up each of these three parts of the book.

Family Therapy During Separation

The section on family therapy during separation contains nine chapters and covers a variety of topics relevant to this type of work. The first chapter in this section, Chap. 2, has useful information for providers about how to employ family focused letter writing while the adolescent is in treatment. The authors of this chapter show how impact and accountability letters can be used to help adolescents engage in the treatment process and begin to change the family system. In Chap. 3, the authors describe their use of Narrative Therapy to help a struggling youth shed his problem saturated story and engage in constructing a new story with the help of his family. This chapter provides a detailed description of the intervention and sample questions providers can use to engage in this kind of work in their own practice. Chapters 4 and 5 introduce the topic of video game addiction, which is rapidly becoming a core presenting problem in residential treatment. In Chap. 4, the author lays the groundwork for understanding the addictive nature of video games, which is crucial for designing an effective treatment approach. In Chap. 5, the author extends this conversation to the implications for family therapy while the adolescent is in residential treatment. Practical suggestions are made for assessment and intervention when this is a primary concern. In Chap. 6, the reader will find a first person account of the decision making process for sending a child to residential treatment, what it is like to participate in these programs, as well as some information about their own experience with outcomes. This is accomplished through a modified case study approach in which the participants were also the authors. The chapter also includes a substantial amount of information about Educational Consultants and how therapist can work effectively with them. Chapter 7 introduces the idea of a parallel process, meaning that the parents need to be engaging in their own concurrent therapeutic work while the child is in treatment. A sample treatment plan is provided for those who are interested in working with parents still at home. Chapter 8 contains a discussion of some of the factors that should be considered when making the decision to send a child to treatment. Along with Chap. 6, this chapter can be used by providers to gather helpful information that will empower them to support parents who are struggling to make this decision. Chapter 9 discusses aftercare planning, which is a crucial task when a child approaches the end of their stay in a program. As can be seen in the description above the contents of this section, there are a number of tasks and techniques therapists should be aware of to be effective in delivering therapeutic services. However, in residential settings therapists are often expected to do more than just provide therapy; generally, they are also expected to lead the treatment team. Accordingly, Chap. 10 was included to provide some guidance on how therapists can be effect in this crucial role.

Onsite Family Therapy

The section of the book about onsite family therapy begins with a chapter on the emerging models of family therapy that are being used in adolescent residential treatment (Chap. 11). The author reviews both those models that have been effectively used already and a number of approaches that could be adapted to work with adolescents in residential treatment. In addition to treatment models, there has also been some focus in the literature on how adolescents arrive at treatment (e.g., Tucker et al. 2015). Accordingly, Chap. 12 was included to give the reader information on *Interventions* as a mechanism to encourage an adolescent or young adult to enter treatment. Interventions have grown in popularity and are usually facilitated by an individual trained in a particular model. Interventions involve as much of the family as possible and the process is described in this chapter. Chapter 13 provides a description of fundamental aspects of addiction that all practitioners working with substance abusing adolescents should know. The chapter also includes a review of some of the major models of substance abuse treatment used with adolescents and how these can be adapted for use in residential settings. Regardless of the specific type of setting, most therapists who work in this type of environment will experience resistance from both the adolescent and the child's parents and/or guardians. Accordingly, it is important to know how to help people move toward engagement in treatment. Chapter 14 addresses this issue and provides a framework for how to engage parents using a *stages of change* approach. In Chap. 15, the authors discuss how to engage the family in Outdoor Behavioral Healthcare and touch on the utility of adventure therapy in helping adolescents to change. This chapter would have also fit in the first part of the book, but it was included here because of its discussion of the overall process of working with families, including selecting a program with a home therapist and onsite work once the adolescent has been placed. Chapter 16 provides the reader with information about the use of family sculptures and reflecting teams. This type of activity can be used effectively during family workshops, which are discussed more fully in Chap. 17. Chapters 18 and 19 are both brief chapters that describe models of family involvement as used in two different programs. These descriptions are intended to help therapists gain a better understanding of the options available to them when it comes to family involvement and onsite family therapy. Chapter 18 also provides a research-based argument for how research on family involvement should be structured in the future.

Research and Outcomes

As will be evident as one actually reads the chapters outlined above, while there are a number of ways to integrate family therapy into adolescent residential treatment, there has been little effectiveness research conducted to support the use of any specific model, despite the basic understanding that family involvement improves outcomes (Hair 2005). Accordingly, this last part of the book was included to promote research in this field and support those who might be interested in participating in such an endeavor. The first chapter of this section describes qualitative, quantitative, and mixed methods and outlines a number of studies that could be conducted to promote family therapy in residential settings (Chap. 20). This chapter also discusses the importance of investigating the cost-effectiveness of family therapy in this field, which given the high cost of treatment will be needed to justify the place of adolescent residential programs in the marketplace. The next few chapters provide actual examples of the types of studies outlined in Chap. 20, along with practical suggestions for being effective in using each of the three methods. Chapter 21 contains a description of a mixed methods study that looked at outcomes related to the use of clinical consultation within the REStArT model. Chapter 22 details a quantitative study that surveyed youth about coping strategies they use, and the authors provide a number of suggestions for how family therapists can use the results of their study. Chapter 23 is based on the results of a qualitative study that looked at communication patterns in families before and after participation in a therapeutic wilderness program. Chapter 24 completes this part of the book with a discussion of program evaluation. These authors describe the major components of program evaluation and factors that need to be taken in account to ensure the results are useful to families and stakeholders. The final chapter of the book, Chap. 25, is intended to provide a synthesis of the material presented in the book and discuss how well the objectives of writing the book were met. As noted above, there are many challenges associated with working with adolescents in residential settings and our purpose was to provide practical information that will help individuals and organizations to provide quality services that benefit the family.

Conclusion

Overall, the chapters included in this book provide detailed information, beyond what is available in the literature currently, about how to work with adolescents in residential placements. Those who read these chapters will gain a greater understanding of the importance of research in establishing the place of family therapy in these settings and improve their ability to deliver services. They will also learn how to navigate some of the challenges associated with providing care to these clients and gain specific knowledge about interventions that can be used to promote change in the identified patient and family. This type of information has historically been learned piecemeal as a therapist gains experience in treatment over months and years. Accordingly, it is hoped that this book will help speed up this process and provide a foundation that therapists can use to build their clinical skill. Although this information should be immediately useful to those in this field, as always, the information presented herein should be seen as groundwork that can be used to further inquiry and research focused on these settings.

References

Behrens, E., & Satterfield, K. (2006). Report of findings from a multi-center study of youth outcomes in private residential treatment. In *Proceedings of the Annual Convention of the American Psychological Association* (pp. 1–21). New Orleans, LA: American Psychological Association.

Burns, B. J., Hoagwood, K., & Mrazek, P. (1999). Effective treatment for mental disorders in children and adolescents. *Clinical Child and Family Psychology Review, 2,* 199–254. doi:10.1023/A:1021826216025

Christenson, J. D., & Crane, D. R. (2014). Integrating costs into marriage and family therapy research. In R. B. Miller & L. N. Johnson (Eds.), *Advanced methods in family therapy research: A focus on validity and change* (pp. 420–436). New York: Routledge.

Crane, D. R. (1995). Health care reform in the United States: Implications for training and practice in marriage and family therapy. *Journal of Marital and Family Therapy, 21*(2), 115–125. doi:10.1111/j.1752-0606.1995.tb00146.x

Frensch, K. M., & Cameron, G. (2002). Treatment of choice or a last resort? A review of residential mental health placements for children and youth. *Child & Youth Care Forum, 31*(5), 307–339. doi:10.1023/A:1016826627406

Hair, H. J. (2005). Outcomes for children and adolescents after residential treatment: A review of research from 1993 to 2003. *Journal of Child and Family Studies, 14*(4), 551–575. doi:10. 1007/s10826-005-7188-9

Hattie, J., Marsh, H. W., Neill, J. T., & Richards, G. E. (1997). Adventure education and outward bound: Out-of-class experiences that make a lasting difference. *Review of Educational Research, 67*(1), 43–87. doi:10.3102/00346543067001043

Jenson, J. M., & Whittaker, J. K. (1987). Parental involvement in children's residential treatment. *Children and Youth Services Review, 9,* 81–100. doi:10.1016/0190-7409(87)90011-9

Lee, B. R., & Barth, R. P. (2011). Defining group care programs: An index of reporting standards. *Child & Youth Care Forum, 40,* 253–266. doi:10.1007/s10566-011-9143-9

McLendon, T., McLendon, D., & Hatch, L. (2012). Engaging families in the residential treatment process utilizing family-directed structural therapy. *Residential Treatment for Children & Youth, 29*(1), 66–77.

The Envoy Group (2016). *How much do therapeutic boarding schools cost?* Retrieved from: http://www.theenvoygroup.com/parents/therapeutic-boarding-school-cost/

Tucker, A. R., Bettmann, J. E., Norton, C. L., & Comart, C. (2015). The role of transport use in adolescent wilderness treatment: Its relationship to readiness to change and outcomes. *Child and Youth Care Forum, 44*(1). doi:10.1007/s10566-015-9301-6

Author Biographies

Jacob D. Christenson, Ph.D., LMFT is an assistant professor of marriage and family therapy at Mount Mercy University. Dr. Christenson received his Bachelor degree in Psychology from California Polytechnic State University. He then completed his Master's degree and doctorate in Marriage and Family Therapy from Brigham Young University. Before coming to Mount Mercy University Dr. Christenson worked for 4 years at Aspen Achievement Academy in Loa, UT as a Field Therapist. As a Field Therapist, Dr. Christenson experienced firsthand the challenge of being a systemic marriage and family therapist in the world of residential care. Over the course of his career, Dr. Christenson has consistently been involved in academic research and publication. In addition to numerous presentations at national and international conferences, Dr. Christenson has published a number of articles in peer-reviewed journals such as the Journal of Marital and Family Therapy, Contemporary Family Therapy, and the American Journal of Family Therapy. Dr. Christenson also serves as an editorial board member for the Journal of Marital and Family Therapy and Contemporary Family Therapy. Dr. Christenson teaches a number of course at Mount Mercy University. The courses he is taught have included, Parents and Children, Micro-counselling, Medical Family Therapy, and Research Methods. Dr. Christenson is also an AAMFT Approved Supervisor, which has enabled him to provide supervision in practicum courses. Dr. Christenson also serves as the Clinical Director for the Gerald and Audrey Olson Marriage and Family Therapy Clinic, which is attached to the marriage and family therapy program at Mount Mercy University. In addition to his work as a professor, Dr. Christenson provides therapy in private practice and is the founder of Covenant Family Solutions, an outpatient therapy group practice in Cedar Rapids, Iowa. When not working, Dr. Christenson enjoys spending time with his family and being active in his community.

Ashley N. Merritts, Ph.D., LMFT is an assistant professor in the marriage and family therapy program at Mount Mercy University. Dr. Merritts received her BS degree from the University of Iowa in Psychology, with a minor in Human Relations. After graduating from the University of Iowa, Dr. Merritts continued her education and has a Ph.D. in Human Development and Family Studies and a Master of Science degree in the same major, both from Iowa State University. In her Master's degree program, Dr. Merritts specialized in couple and family therapy and is now a Licensed Marital and Family Therapist. Dr. Merritts has extensive clinical training and has worked with a wide variety of problems in clinical settings. She specializes in working with distressed couples and has advanced training in Trauma Focused Cognitive Behavior Therapy as well. Dr. Merritt's has worked with adolescents in residential settings during her career and understands the unique needs of this population. Here clinical interests also include working with childhood behavioral problems, families in crisis, co-parenting and divorce, individual healing, and affairs. Dr. Merritts is a Clinical Fellow and Approved Supervisor with the American Association for Marriage and Family Therapy. She has also served as a board member for the Iowa Association for Marriage and Family Therapy. Dr. Merritts has published her work in the International Journal of Disability, Development and Education. She has also published in, and has served as a reviewer for, Contemporary Family Therapy: An International Journal. Dr. Merritts' research interests include relationship quality in African American couples and the impact of adverse childhood experiences on parent–child attachment.

Part I
Family Therapy During Separation

Chapter 2
The Use of Letters to Create Movement in Residential Settings with Adolescents and Their Parents

Jacob D. Christenson and Amber L. Runkel

Chapter Highlights

- Therapeutic letter writing has been used to promote change within the client and family system for some time.
- The use of specific letter writing assignments with an adolescent in residential care allows the therapist to work systemically on specific patterns of interaction within the family.
- Letters writing techniques are described that provide opportunities for adolescents to be confronted with their behaviors, while also giving them space to accept responsibility and embrace the need to change.
- Some possible outcomes from using such assignments include moving individuals and families through the stages of change, promoting a systemic view, slowing down the conversation, teaching communication skills, increasing nurturance, and repairing attachment injuries.

The use of written communication in psychotherapy can be found in the literature as early as the 1960s (e.g., Pearson 1965). Since that time nonsystemic approaches have made use of therapist-authored letters for a number of purposes. For example, Omer (1991) described the use of letters to follow-up after therapy that ended badly, and Allan and Bertoia (1992) explained how therapist-authored letters can be used within a Jungian approach to promote healing in children. Likewise, there have been a number of movements within the field of family

J.D. Christenson (✉)
Mount Mercy University, 1330 Elmhurst Dr. NE, Cedar Rapids, IA 52402, USA
e-mail: jchristenson@mtmercy.edu

A.L. Runkel
Sampson Family Therapy, 309 Court Avenue, Suite 241, 5th Floor,
Des Moines, IA 50309, USA
e-mail: amberm1171@gmail.com

© Springer International Publishing AG 2017
J.D. Christenson and A.N. Merritts (eds.), *Family Therapy with Adolescents in Residential Treatment*, Focused Issues in Family Therapy,
DOI 10.1007/978-3-319-51747-6_2

therapy focused on letter writing as a means of creating a context for change. For example, in the 1970s the Milan group wrote about the use of therapeutic letters as part of a paradoxical intervention (Selvini Palazzoli et al. 1978), and in the 1990s David Epston and Michael White wrote extensively about the use of letters to clients within a narrative approach (e.g., Epston 1994; White 1995; White and Epston 1990).

In addition to therapist-authored letters, client-authored letters have been used to promote change within clients (e.g., Diamond 2000; Nau 1997; Tubman et al. 2001). A good example of the use of client-authored letters is the recent work of Pennebaker and Evans (2014). These authors described the use of transactional letters, meaning that they follow the format of a typical letter and are addressed to another person, though that person may sometimes be another version of the client (e.g., a future self). These letters are then used to offer such things as compassion, gratitude, and forgiveness. Similarly, Tubman et al. (2001) encouraged clients to write a *goodbye* letter to their problem, which was intended to help the client to externalize the issue and move forward. Frequently, these types of letters are written without the requirement that they be delivered directly to another person (Pennebaker and Evan 2014); however, if the letter is given to another person, the clinician is careful to prepare the client for a negative reaction from the recipient.

Although much has been written about the use of letters in therapy, much less frequently defined has been the use of letters between family members as part of the therapeutic process. One exception to this can be seen in the work of Gordon et al. (2004) who detailed the use of letter writing in the treatment of extramarital affairs. One of the interventions used in their integrated approach consists of therapeutic guidance to help the partners in writing and exchanging letters about how the affair impacted their feelings and perceptions. Despite the work of Gordon et al. (2004) there remains a significant lack of information within the literature about how to effectively use letter writing between family members to promote systemic change. Given the impracticality of conjoint sessions when an adolescent is placed in residential treatment, letter writing can serve as an important adjunct to the work done separately with the parent system and adolescent. Within some programs, letters serve as the primary form of communication for the duration of the adolescent's stay, as is the case in wilderness therapy. Therefore, the purpose of this chapter is to outline how letters can be effectively and powerfully used to promote change in the family system. Recently in the literature there has been some debate about the age range that represents adolescence, with some authors arguing that adolescence may continue up until age 25 (e.g., Arnone 2014). For the sake of simplicity, the term *adolescent* as used in this article should be understood to mean an individual between the ages of 12 and 25 years old. Likewise, the term *parent* will be used to represent parents, primary caregivers, and legal guardians. The plural *parents* will be used, though it is understood that often adolescents may have only one parent participating in the process.

Adolescents in therapeutic residential placements present in a unique manner and bring with them unique challenges. Those who work with adolescents in long-term residential settings understand most of them do not come willingly and may be prepared to push limits as far as possible to prematurely exit the program (e.g., Gorske et al. 2003). Accordingly, it is important for clinicians to be prepared to meet them where they are at and help them to move toward a more productive stance that will facilitate treatment and increase the likelihood of a positive outcome. Having a basic understanding of the stages of change, as detailed in the transtheoretical model (Prochaska and Velicer 1997), can be very helpful in this effort. As would be expected from the transtheoretical model (Prochaska and Velicer 1997), the majority of adolescents who are placed in a residential program will be in the precontemplation stage, which is characterized by not seeing their behaviors as a problem and blaming others for any problems they do recognize. Other stages in the transtheoretical model include contemplation, preparation, action, maintenance, and termination. Chapter 14 in this book provides a detailed description of each of these stages of change and should be referenced by those who are unfamiliar with this model.

Impact Letters

One of the first therapeutic tasks in many programs for families is the creation of impact letters. Impact letters have their origins in intervention letters used by those confronting a loved one struggling with drug and alcohol addiction. Because emotions can run high during an intervention, it is often recommended for family members to write out their thoughts and feelings before the actual intervention (Jay 2013). Over the years this process has been modified and adapted to work within residential settings. Letters are typically requested from both parents when possible, and they may be requested from siblings or other family members that are important in the youth's life. With regard to sibling letters, these are generally not required unless the sibling is old enough to write it themselves and they are able to articulate ways they have been impacted by the adolescent's behavior. If the parents want a sibling or another adult to write an impact letter, therapists should consider inviting that person to participate in a phone call to ask a few questions about their relationship with the adolescent and how they have been impacted to determine if they have sufficient understanding and maturity to complete the task appropriately. In cases where it is clear that a sibling lacks the necessary maturity, therapists will need to carefully advise the parents against including a sibling letter. A poorly crafted letter can become a distraction and lessen the impact of the experience.

The actual letters "...cover topics including, but not limited to, the history of the family's or the participant's problems, how these problems affected various family members or the participant, positive feelings and hopes for the future" (Blanchette 2010, p. 200). According to Blanchette, those working with adolescents in programs see a number of therapeutic benefits from impact letters. Among these potential benefits are that it (a) provides the adolescent with an opportunity to reflect on their behaviors, increase accountability, and accept responsibility; (b) helps make their behaviors more *real* and allows them to see the way they have affected others; and (c) encourages greater family involvement while allowing for the expression of previously unsaid thoughts and feelings. In addition to the benefits for the adolescent, impact letters also provide parents with an opportunity to begin to move away from their problem saturated view of the child. As will be discussed more fully below, this occurs as the therapist guides the process and helps the parents to focus on the underlying emotions they have experienced as they have witnessed their child's behavior. This process can set the stage for parents to notice exceptions to the dominate narrative that has developed around the adolescent.

Though the potential benefits are numerous, this is only possible when the letters are well constructed and appropriate. Just like adolescents in treatment, their family members are often in the precontemplation stage themselves and are prone to see the child as a problem that someone else needs to fix (e.g., Slesnick et al. 2009). Families may be resistant to expressing feelings or allowing themselves to be vulnerable to a counter attack by the adolescent. Nevertheless, in order for impact letters to be effective, the therapist must help the family move from a position of blame to vulnerability and open expression of emotion. Often the first draft of an impact letter will consist of little more than numerous instances of *bad behavior* and a detailing of the destruction that was left behind. If parents actually do talk about emotions, they will usually stick to secondary emotions such as anger and frustration. Therapists working with parents to craft impact letters should help them be factual about the behaviors that occurred and follow each of these with a primary emotion that resulted from that behavior. An example might be a parent who describes a time when they picked up the adolescent from the police department followed by a description of their feelings of sadness and failure they experienced as a result.

Additionally, it can be helpful to encourage the parents to outline some things that the adolescent might not be aware of because of their preoccupation with their own needs and wants. For example, parents might talk about how the adolescent's siblings are being made fun of at school because of their brother or sister's behaviors. The first author once worked with a set of parents who revealed that another one of their children had been seriously injured when she used the eye drops her sibling had left behind when he entered the program. After this incident they learned that the sibling had replaced the eye drops with chlorine, which he used to tamper with drug tests when they would administer one at home. The adolescent was indifferent as he read the letter until the parents described this incident, after which he broke down into tears and realized, maybe for the first time, the damage his drug use was causing. Parents may not come up with these sorts of examples on their own, so the therapist needs to be prepared to help them to explore their experiences and label the emotions that have arisen as a result. An extremely useful intervention in this phase is empathic conjecture, wherein the therapist listens to the content of the parent's experience and then attributes a feeling word to their description (Johnson 2012). Once the feeling has been identified and labeled, the therapist helps the family to incorporate it into the letter.

Finally, it is important for the parent(s) to devote a portion of the letter to the good things about their child and positive things they have done. It is not uncommon for this section to actually have the most impact since families are usually severely polarized by this point, and as described by Sells (2001), they are stuck in a cycle of escalating negative behavior and punishment. Hearing something positive from a parent is unexpected and breaks through the adolescent's defenses.

Typically, impact letters will go through more than one revision before they are ready to be delivered to the youth in residential treatment. When the letters are completed they are delivered to the adolescent by the therapist in a group therapy setting and read verbatim. Adolescents are given the instruction to read each word in the letter out loud and without stopping. They are further instructed that they are not allowed to add commentary that rationalizes, justifies, or minimizes their behavior while reading the letter. After the adolescent has read the letters the group is provided with an opportunity to provide feedback about what they heard in the letters, as well as some of their reactions. This provides the adolescent who is the focus of the letter with an opportunity to hear about their behavior from a perspective that is outside of their family of origin.

Furthermore, other adolescents in the group are able to hear an unfiltered representation of the issues that brought the adolescent to treatment. Group members are instructed that they should remain focused on reflecting the content of the letters, as opposed to defending the adolescent who has read them. If done properly impact letters set the stage for the adolescent to move from precontemplation to contemplation and for the family members to begin the process of improving communication and repairing attachment injuries. It should also be noted that impact letters can be used at other times beyond the beginning of treatment and in various ways. For example, it might be helpful to revisit the impact letters after the adolescent has moved out of precontemplation for the purpose of identifying exceptions to the problem behaviors listed in the letters.

Response to Impact Letters

After the adolescent has read the letters, they are tasked with responding to those who provided the content. Although the impact letter can be useful in breaking through defenses and helping the adolescent to take responsibility for their behavior, it is not unusual for those defenses to return by the time the adolescent is asked to provide a written response. In cases where defensiveness is high, it is imperative that the therapist help the adolescent work on understanding and effectively using listener skills (e.g., Markman et al. 2010). This can be done by having them take each feeling and reflect it back using the "I hear you feel..." prompt. Ideally the therapist will take time beforehand to work with the adolescent in such a way that they are genuinely able to accept the impact they had on others and feel some level of responsibility or even remorse for the effects of their behavior. It may be helpful to have the adolescent read through the letters more than once or reflect on the content for a period of time before responding.

If the first draft of the response letter is filled with justification, rationalization, and minimization the therapist should provide feedback and have the adolescent make revisions or start over if needed. The adolescent may need time to work on hearing the content and responding appropriately. This can be very similar to the process of helping parents move away from blaming the adolescent, as described above, in that the therapist may need to help the adolescent identify primary emotions they experienced while reading the letters. For programs that foster a positive-peer environment, it may also be useful to have the adolescent read their responses to a group of peers and receive feedback. Those who are farther along in the treatment process can serve as a resource to the staff and therapist and help call out attempts to avoid responsibility and justify negative behavior. It is interesting to note that it is sometimes the adolescent's peers that have the most direct and constructive feedback to offer about the response to impact letters. They are often much better able to see the defensiveness in the writing of their peers than when the focus is on themselves. Nevertheless, this can be channeled into a positive by a therapist who uses the momentum of *positive peer pressure* to work through an adolescent's defenses.

Ideally, the adolescent will be able to fully integrate the information provided by their parents and experience a change in their perspective. When this occurs it is important that they extend their response beyond merely reflecting the content and express this new perspective in their response to impact letters. One example of how they might accomplish this is to express what it was like for them to read the impact letter. The youth might describe how they were feeling right before reading it and what thoughts went through their head as they processed the content. The therapist can encourage this type of reflection and ask process questions to help the youth develop insight into what might be appropriate to include. When the response to impact letters is well done it has the potential to reaffirm the therapeutic benefits the parents got from writing the letters and promote increased open dialogue.

One note of caution is warranted before continuing forward. Although the adolescent may be contrite and openly express primary emotions in their response, some parents will not take it at face value and will instead see their child's effort as an attempt to placate, or worse, to be manipulative. When this type of response is observed the therapist should validate the parent's concerns, but also make every effort to help them to accept the response at face value. Ideally the therapist will have joined with the family enough by this point such that they can take some leadership in their interactions (Minuchin and Fishman 1981) and challenge the family's reality in a productive manner. Even if the parents are correct about the child's intent it does not help the therapeutic process when they respond with contempt or criticism (Katz et al. 1998). On the contrary, when they respond from a place of defensiveness it can shut down the conversation and cause regression to old negative behaviors on both sides. Accordingly, it might be helpful for the therapist to ask the parents to send their next few letters to them for review when they have a difficult time accepting the response from their child. On the other hand, those who prefer a strategic approach may let a letter with parental defensiveness *slip* through to the child, knowing that the adolescent will have a negative reaction.

This can be particularly useful for pointing out weaknesses in the preparation of adolescents who believes they are ready to go home after little to no second-order change has occurred.

Reversing the Process

Typically, accountability letters, as described below, would sequentially follow the impact letter, but before moving forward a word on reversing the process is warranted. After the adolescent has demonstrated the ability to be accountable for their behavior and appropriately describe the behavior of their family members, it may be fitting to have them write impact letters to their parents or other important family members. Systemic therapists recognize the reciprocal nature of family interactions and look for opportunities to promote accountability in all members of the family, thereby increasing the likelihood of second-order change (Golann 1998). When working with the adolescent to construct impact letters to parents many of the recommendations outlined above apply. The adolescent should be helped to remain factual and focus on their emotional reactions to the events they detail. During this process the adolescent may outline events and feelings that the therapist was not aware of and that have had a powerful impact on the development of problems within the family system.

Although one might expect parents to be more capable of reading an impact letter from their child with less defensiveness and more insight, quite the opposite is usually true. Family members are often very reactive to the way they have been characterized by their child and the blame that has been placed on them as well. Sometimes without their own therapy the family gets stuck in the problem saturated view. This home-based therapy is necessary because the family members do not have the benefit of group feedback and are not participating in daily treatment related activities (see Chap. 7). Likewise, parents may be highly invested in their child being the identified patient and reluctant to abandon this perspective (Minuchin and Fishman 1981). Because of this, it is essential that the therapist join with the parents and help them to sincerely listen to what their child is saying and accept responsibility for their own behaviors that contributed to the problem.

During this process Miller and Rollnick (2012) concept of *rolling with resistance* can be used effectively to promote problem recognition. When a therapist rolls with resistance they acknowledge the parent's perspective without judgment. They focus on being non-argumentative and provide for the possibility that the parent may not be ready to hear the adolescent's perspective. Sometimes parents simply need some time to process the content of the letters, and therapists who give them space to do so may find that they are able to achieve a positive outcome much quicker than when they continue to struggle to get the parent to *hear* the adolescent's perspective. After the parents are able to hear what their child is saying they are then asked to construct a response to the impact letter. As is true when the adolescent writes the response, family members should be helped to make sure these are appropriate by the therapist before they are delivered to the adolescent.

Accountability Letters

The concept of writing an accountability letter has its roots in steps eight and nine of 12-step recovery models. In these two steps individuals make a list of those who they have harmed and make amends for any damage they have done (Alcoholics Anonymous 2002). This process requires being honest with oneself and taking full responsibility for past behaviors. In more recent years accountability letters have become popular in the treatment of domestic violence and drug abuse treatment models (e.g., Hernández et al. 2005; Parker 2009) as well. Regardless of the model in which they are employed, accountability letters are used to help an individual demonstrate a willingness to accept full responsibility for their behavior and the effect it has had on other people. Writing an accountability letter sets the stage for amends by identifying areas where an apology might be appropriate or where restitution can be made. As an example, the first author of this article once worked with a man who indicated that he could not make amends because most of the damage his verbal abuse had caused was manifest in the deteriorating mental health of his spouse. Through writing an accountability letter he was able to recognize an opportunity to make amends by being patient, kind, and encouraging as she engaged in her own recovery work.

Within the context of residential settings for adolescents, the accountability letter usually occurs somewhere between the contemplation and action stage. Accordingly, the assignment to write this type of letter is not usually introduced until the adolescent has already begun to demonstrate some level of accountability for their ongoing behavior problems in the current placement. Some signs that an adolescent may be ready for this exercise are that they are able to be confronted about their negative behavior without significant defensives, or that they begin to bring up negative behavior they feel responsible for without prompting from the therapist or staff. One place to look for this type of response is in process groups where the adolescent is allowed to share their thoughts and perspectives openly and without judgement. For programs that use a level system it may be effective to have a requirement of completing an accountability letter before being able to advance to one of the higher levels. This instills the idea of completing such a letter before the adolescent is confronted with the task, which may help them to mentally prepare for completing the letter at a later date. However, therapists and staff should exercise caution when taking this approach and make sure the adolescents are sincere in their effort and not just trying to *check a box* to advance to a higher level. A daily focus by the therapist and program staff on accountability and responsibility for behavior also aids in this process.

In terms of composing the letter, the adolescent is asked to explain their negative behaviors in detail and to demonstrate they accept full responsibility for the choices they made. Additionally, they are asked to acknowledge in detail how their behaviors affected other people and express their feelings about the damage they have caused. If the adolescent has difficulty coming up with example of negative behavior, the parents and family members can be asked to provide a list the therapist can use to prompt self-reflection. The adolescent can also be encouraged to disclose things that the parents are not aware of about their past or make apologies for things they have done in the letter. It can be helpful in this process to stress that being accountable for one's behavior does not imply that the development of problems are *all their fault*. Conversely, they are being asked to just focus on their part of the problem, since that is the only part they have control over.

The adolescent's willingness to be completely open and honest provides a good indicator of how genuinely ready they are to change. The process of writing an accountability letter is difficult for most adolescents in residential treatment. Ruminating on one's negative behaviors in detail can trigger deep feelings of disgust with oneself and self-loathing (Gilbert 2015). Therefore, it is important for the therapist to lay the groundwork by helping the adolescent to understand the freedom that comes with accountability (e.g., De Cremer et al. 2001) and provide opportunities for them to reaffirm their worth and value. Given that this is a difficult task, sufficient time should be allotted for the adolescent to complete the letter. Additional drafts may be needed, especially if the adolescent easily slips into blaming or justifying their behavior.

Once the letter is completed it is sent to parents and they are given an opportunity to process the content. As is true for the response to impact letters, parents may be initially doubtful or hesitate to accept what their child has said. Additionally, they may become angry if the child discloses something the parent did not know about, or that is offensive to their values and beliefs. Again, it is the responsibility of the therapist to help them to process their reactions and to soften their responses. Once they are able to take in the content of the accountability letter appropriately, the parents should be asked to write a response. One suggestion that can be made is to write the response letter from a place of gratitude for their child's willingness to be open and honest. Another possibility would be to offer forgiveness to their child for the misdeeds that were outlined in the letter. If parents are unable to complete these types of higher level responses they can be asked to focus on first reflecting back the content to make sure the adolescent at least feels heard.

As was true for the impact letters, the process of the accountability letter can also be reversed. Therapists should typically have the adolescent write the first letter in each sequence as their infractions are frequently more obvious and dramatic (e.g., running away, drug use, violence, etc.). However, after the adolescent has done the work required of them parents should be invited to demonstrate accountability as well through their own letters. The same suggestions outlined above for the adolescent are applicable to the parents, with the exception of divulging details of their life that the adolescent does not already know about. It is not necessary for parents and family members to detail every misdeed from their life, though it might be appropriate to discuss things related to the child. For example, a parent might admit that they had been checking the child's phone, even though they repeatedly denied having done so while the child was home. This type of honesty and openness can set the stage for the repair of attachment injuries as well.

Purposes and Desired Outcomes

Letter writing in residential settings serves a number of purposes, among which are moving individuals and families through the stages of change, teaching communication skills, promoting a systemic view, increasing nurturance, slowing down the conversation, and repairing attachment injuries. In terms of the stages of change, as noted, adolescents most often come to long-term residential settings seeing everyone else as the problem. If they are allowed to remain in this state, residential treatment would serve little purpose beyond containing the adolescent's behavior. Accordingly, interventions must be utilized that help the adolescent move toward planning, action, and maintenance. Letter writing as outlined in this article accomplishes this purpose by providing opportunities for adolescents to be confronted with their behaviors while also giving them space to accept responsibility and embrace the need to change. Likewise, parents are held accountable for their behaviors and helped through nonconfrontive means to change their approach to working with their child.

Another purpose of using transactional letters within residential settings is to maintain a systemic perspective in treatment. Historically, one of the biggest criticisms of residential treatment programs has been that they do not work on changing the family (Henggeler and Lee 2003), leaving the child to return to the same system that they left, which contributes to them returning to old behavior patterns. The effective use of letters between the family and the adolescent provides the opportunity for the therapist to work on specific patterns of interaction within the family. In particular, the therapist is able to target family processes such as patterns of criticism and contempt, ruptured attachment, and communication skills directly and deliberately. In conjunction with other program offerings (see Chap. 19), therapeutic letter writing helps to addresses this traditional limitation of residential therapy.

Sometimes the only way to create a context for change in a family system is to have physical distance between family members. This is especially true when the family members have low levels of differentiation and cannot effectively work on their issues in conjoint sessions (see Chap. 8). Residential treatment provides such an environment by limiting interaction between the two sides for an extended period of time. In this way, the limited interaction inherent in residential works as a strength of the approach, since parents and adolescents are able to deliver a large amount of highly charged emotional content quickly, and then are allowed time to process it thoroughly and generate an appropriate response. Therapists are available to prepare the individuals who will be receiving the letters, similar to the approach outlined by Gordon et al. (2004). The therapist is also there to help the individual members of the systems to process information that is difficult for them to hear after the letter has been read. Throughout this process the therapist is responsible for teaching and modeling effective communication skills to all members of the family.

On a deeper level, impact letters and accountability letters have the potential to restore nurturance and heal attachment injuries. Johnson et al. (2001) describe attachment injuries as occurring in a couple's relationship when one partner experiences an event as a betrayal or violation, and the other partner fails to respond by offering reassurance or comfort. This leads to a rupture in the trust between partners and intimacy is damaged. Likewise, in parent–child relationships, when a child misbehaves the parent may perceive this as an affront and react harshly. This leads the child to perceive the parent as unsafe and unavailable. As these types of interactions escalate over time the parent–child relationship no longer serves as a secure base or a safe haven and attachment is damaged.

Although such ruptures are problematic, Johnson (2002) argues that attachment injuries can be repaired (in part) by the expression of disowned needs and blocked emotions. Impact letters and accountability letters, as described above, provide the adolescent and parents with an opportunity to express deep feelings that they have suppressed, and to meet each other's needs by being accountable for their behavior and making amends. By doing so they are afforded an opportunity to move from a position of blame and attack to one of soft love (Sells 2001) and seeing the other person as human and like themselves, instead of seeing them as irrelevant, an obstacle, or an object (Arbinger Institute 2008). The process of healing attachment injuries also provides opportunities to restore lost nurturance through the expression of positive thoughts and feelings as well as efforts to connect lovingly with each other.

While the process of transactional letter writing in and of itself is important to discuss, outcomes are the greatest indicator of utility. As can be inferred from the information above, the desired outcome is for families to move through the stages of change, improve communication skills, and strengthen bonds. If used correctly, impact letters and accountability letters should result in both the adolescent and parent being more open to change and motivated to work on their part in the problem. Moreover, they would be expected to employ better communication skills in their interactions, or at least be able to pick up on speaker-listener techniques more readily when introduced to them as part of the family reunion process, weekly phone calls, or other family visits. Finally, and probably most importantly, these types of letters provide fertile ground for healing attachment injuries and reestablishing nurturance, which should result in greater family satisfaction and decreased conflict.

Future Directions

Letter writing has long been an accepted intervention for working with families and should continue to be used frequently by both inpatient and outpatient therapists (e.g., Rombach 2003). There is a need to continue to develop methods for using letter writing in creative ways that encourages stronger family ties. DeMille and Montgomery (2016) detailed one such effort in their description of using letter writing as part of the process of integrating narrative family therapy in an outdoor residential program. In their case study, DeMille and Montgomery described working with a particular adolescent in an egalitarian manner for a number of sessions to first help prepare him for the narrative work with his family. Once the adolescent had softened and was prepared to engage, they used a form of parallel letter writing to help create a new story that contrasted the problem saturated narrative. They initially asked the adolescent questions that "...included 'what did your home look like as a child?' 'What did it take to live in your home?' 'Who was in charge in your home and what did it take to be in charge?' 'What were the most fearful events in your childhood?'" (p. 8). The answers to these questions were labeled as the adolescent's *autobiography*. The parents were asked to reflect and write on questions that mirrored those provided to the adolescent. Once the adolescent was ready to share, the autobiography and the parent's narrative was read in front of the group, and space was given to cocreate a new narrative that enabled greater progress and a more positive view of the adolescent. This process was repeated over a number of weeks and the authors demonstrated how this provided the adolescent and family with an opportunity to expand their understanding of each other and experience a more positive outcome.

Similar to the work of DeMille and Montgomery (2016) some therapists assign a *strengths letter*, wherein the parents highlight the positive qualities and characteristics they see in their child, which is done to encourage a focus on strengths during the treatment process. Another possibility is to modify letter writing assignments given for individual development in such a way that it also addresses family concerns. For example, toward the end of an adolescent's stay in a residential program they are commonly given the assignment to write to their future self and share things they either think in the present that will be important to remember, or things that they hope the future self has accomplished or experienced. This assignment could be modified to include a letter to their family members in the future. A possibility would be to write positive things their family should remember about them if the adolescent relapses or returns to old behavior. Although this is just one example there are, of course, numerous opportunities for creative assignments and activities that could merge letter writing and family therapy. The key factor in applying this creativity is to keep the focus on relationship patterns and processes. When this is prioritized a number of possibilities and opportunities become evident. As a final example, an adolescent or parent could initiate a discussion via letters about successes and challenges they are having in applying principles from program materials. They could also discuss positive qualities they see in each other or ask for support in different areas of functioning. This could provide an opportunity for a positive conversation about the process of change and increase empathy for both parties.

Conclusion

One of the most common difficulties in teaching effective communication skills is keeping people in a state of mind where they can accept what the other person is saying and integrate new information into their world view. Therapeutic letter writing provides the opportunity for adolescents and their parents to slow down the conversation and to see each other as human beings like themselves who struggle, feel shame, and aspire for acceptance. Through writing and sharing letters, adolescents and parents can feel less alone in their struggles and feel a greater sense of empowerment against the problem (Hoffman et al. 2010). Families can act as their own audience for the ways in which they gain stability and work collaboratively to develop a cohesive unit. Because of the many benefits, programs should include therapeutic letter writing within their conceptualization of best practices. By doing so, programs will demonstrate an understanding of the systemic nature of adolescent behavior problems, which would have a positive effective on posttreatment outcomes.

References

Alcoholics Anonymous. (2002). *Twelve steps and twelve traditions.* New York: Author.

Allan, J., & Bertoia, J. (1992). *Written paths to healing: Education and Jungian child counseling.* Dallas, TX: Spring.

Arbinger Institute. (2008). *The anatomy of peace: Resolving the heart of conflict.* Oakland, CA: Berrett-Koehler Publishers.

Arnone, J. M. (2014). Adolescents may be older than we think: Today 25 is the new 18, or is it? *International Journal of Celiac Disease, 2*(2), 47–48. doi:10.12691/ijcd-2-2-4

Blanchette, A. W. (2010). *The clinical theory and practice of outdoor behavioral healthcare* (Unpublished doctoral dissertation). Regent University, Virginia Beach, VA.

De Cremer, D., Snyder, M., & Dewitte, S. (2001). The less I trust, the less I contribute (or not): The effects of trust, accountability and self-monitoring in social dilemmas. *European Journal of Social Psychology, 31*(1), 93–107.

DeMille, S. M., & Montgomery, M. (2016). Integrating narrative family therapy in an outdoor behavioral healthcare program: A case study. *Contemporary Family Therapy, 38*(1), 3–13. doi:10.1007/s10591-015-9362-6

Diamond, J. (2000). *Narrative means to sober ends: Treating addiction and its aftermath.* New York: Guilford Press.

Epston, D. (1994). Extending the conversation. *Family Therapy Networker, 18,* 30–37.

Gilbert, P. (2015). Self-disgust, self-hatred, and compassion focused therapy. In P. A. Powell, P. G. Overton, & J. Simpson (Eds.), *The revolting self: Perspectives on the psychological, social, and clinical implications of self-directed disgust* (pp. 223–242). London: Karnac Books.

Golann, S. (1988). On second-order family therapy. *Family Process, 27*(1), 51–65. doi:10.1111/j.1545-5300.1988.00051.x

Gordon, K. C., Baucom, D. H., & Snyder, D. K. (2004). An integrative intervention for promoting recovery from extramarital affairs. *Journal of Marital and Family Therapy, 30,* 213–232. doi:10.1111/j.1752-0606.2004.tb01235.x

Gorske, T. T., Srebalus, D. J., & Walls, R. T. (2003). Adolescents in residential centers: Characteristics and treatment outcome. *Children and Youth Services Review, 25*(4), 317–326. doi:10.1016/S0190-7409(03)00014-8

Henggeler, S. W., & Lee, T. (2003). Multisystemic treatment of serious clinical problems. In A. E. Kazdin & J. R. Weisz (Eds.), *Evidence-based psychotherapies for children and adolescents* (pp. 301–322). New York: Guilford Press.

Hernández, P., Almeida, R., & Vecchio, D. D. (2005). Critical consciousness, accountability, and empowerment: Key processes for helping families heal. *Family Process, 44*(1), 105–119. doi:10.1111/j.1545-5300.2005.00045.x

Hoffman, R., Hinkle, M. G., & Kress, V. W. (2010). Letter writing as an intervention in family therapy with adolescents who engage in nonsuicidal self-injury. *The Family Journal: Counseling and Therapy for Couples and Families, 18*(1), 24–30. doi:10.1177/1066480709355039

Jay, J. (2013). *Love first: A family's guide to intervention.* Center City, MN: Hazelden Publishing.

Johnson, S. M. (2002). *Emotionally focused couple therapy with trauma survivors: Strengthening attachment bonds.* New York: Guilford Press.

Johnson, S. M. (2012). *Practice of emotionally focused couple therapy: Creating connection.* New York: Routledge.

Johnson, S. M., Makinen, J. A., & Millikin, J. W. (2001). Attachment injuries in couple relationships: A new perspective on impasses in couples therapy. *Journal of Marital and Family Therapy, 27*(2), 145–155. doi:10.1111/j.1752-0606.2001.tb01152.x

Katz, L. F., Wilson, B., & Gottman, J. M. (1998). Meta-emotion philosophy and family adjustment: Making an emotional connection. In M. J. Cox & J. Brooks-Gunn (Eds.), *Conflict and cohesion in families: Causes and consequences* (pp. 131–166). New York: Routledge.

Markman, H. J., Stanley, S. M., & Blumberg, S. L. (2010). *Fighting for your marriage.* Hoboken, NJ: Wiley.

Miller, W. R., & Rollnick, S. (2012). *Motivational interviewing: Helping people change.* New York: Guilford Press.

Minuchin, S., & Fishman, H. C. (1981). *Family therapy techniques.* Cambridge, MA: Harvard University Press.

Nau, D. S. (1997). Andy writes to his amputated leg: Utilizing letter writing as an interventive technique in brief family therapy. *Journal of Family Psychotherapy, 8,* 1–12.

Omer, H. (1991). Writing a post-scriptum to a badly ended therapy. *Psychotherapy, 28,* 483–492.

Parker, L. (2009). Disrupting power and privilege in couples therapy. *Clinical Social Work Journal, 37*(3), 248–255. doi:10.1007/s10615-009-0211-7

Pearson, L. (1965). *Written communications in psychotherapy.* Springfield, IL: Charles C. Thomas.

Pennebaker, J. W., & Evans, J. F. (2014). *Expressive writing: Words that heal.* Enumclaw, WA: Idyl Arbor Inc.

Prochaska, J. O., & Velicer, W. F. (1997). The transtheoretical model of health behavior change. *American Journal of Health Promotion, 12*(1), 38–48.

Rombach, M. A. M. (2003). An invitation to therapeutic letter writing. *Journal of Systemic Therapies, 22*(1), 15–32. doi:10.1521/jsyt.22.1.15.24097

Sells, S. P. (2001). *Parenting your out-of-control teenager: 7 steps to reestablish authority and reclaim love.* New York: St. Martin's Press.

Selvini Palazzoli, M., Boscolo, L., Cecchin, G., & Prata, G. (1978). *Paradox and counterparadox.* New York: Jason Aronson.

Slesnick, N., Bartle-Haring, S., Erdem, G., Budde, H., Letcher, A., Bantchevska, D., et al. (2009). Troubled parents, motivated adolescents: Predicting motivation to change substance use among runaways. *Addictive Behaviors, 34*(8), 675–684. doi:10.1016/j.addbeh.2009.04.002

Tubman, J. G., Montgomery, M. J., & Wagner, E. E. (2001). Letter writing as a tool to increase client motivation to change: Application to an inpatient crisis unit. *Journal of Mental Health Counseling, 23,* 295–311.

White, M. (1995). *Re-authoring lives: Interviews and essays.* Adelaide, South Australia: Dulwich Centre.

White, M., & Epston, D. (1990). *Narrative means to therapeutic ends.* New York: W.W. Norton.

Author Biographies

Jacob D. Christenson, Ph.D., LMFT is an assistant professor of marriage and family therapy at Mount Mercy University. Dr. Christenson received his Bachelor degree in Psychology from California Polytechnic State University. He then completed his Master's degree and doctorate in Marriage and Family Therapy from Brigham Young University. Before coming to Mount Mercy University, Dr. Christenson worked for 4 years at Aspen Achievement Academy in Loa, UT as a Field Therapist. As a Field Therapist, Dr. Christenson experienced firsthand the challenge of being a systemic marriage and family therapist in the world of residential care. Over the course of his career Dr. Christenson has consistently been involved in academic research and publication. In addition to numerous presentations at national and international conferences, Dr. Christenson has published a number of articles in peer-reviewed journals such as the Journal of Marital and Family Therapy, Contemporary Family Therapy, and the American Journal of Family Therapy. Dr. Christenson also serves as an editorial board member for the Journal of Marital and Family Therapy and Contemporary Family Therapy. Dr. Christenson teaches a number of course at Mount Mercy University. The courses he taught have included, Parents and Children, Micro-counseling, Medical Family Therapy, and Research Methods. Dr. Christenson is also an AAMFT Approved Supervisor, which has enabled him to provide supervision in practicum courses. Dr. Christenson also serves as the Clinical Director for the Gerald and Audrey Olson Marriage and Family Therapy Clinic, which is attached to the marriage and family therapy program at Mount Mercy University. In addition to his work as a professor, Dr. Christenson provides therapy in private practice and is the founder of Covenant Family Solutions, an outpatient therapy group practice in Cedar Rapids, Iowa. When not working, Dr. Christenson enjoys spending time with his family and being active in his community.

Amber L. Runkel, MA, TLMFT works as a provisionally licensed marital and family therapist in a private practice in downtown Des Moines, IA. She specializes in individual, couple, and family therapy, and she strives to help clients gain self-awareness and acceptance, increase mindfulness, and heal wounds that hinder daily functioning, relationships, and life goals. Amber is also a preclinical fellow of the American Association for Marriage and Family Therapy and the Iowa Association for Marriage and Family Therapy. Amber received her Master of Arts degree in Marriage and Family Therapy from Mount Mercy University in Cedar Rapids, Iowa, and her Bachelor of Science degree in Psychology at Iowa State University in Ames, Iowa. Amber has published articles in Contemporary Family Therapy as well.

Chapter 3
A Case Study of Narrative Family Therapy in an Outdoor Treatment Program with a Struggling Adolescent

Steven M. DeMille and Marilyn J. Montgomery

Chapter Highlights

- Outdoor Behavioral Healthcare (OBH) is a flexible treatment modality, supported by a growing body of research.
- Narrative family therapy offers flexible tools that can be adapted for many kinds of clients including adolescents and their families.
- Narrative family therapy can be integrated flexibly into an OBH program and provides a way to link families and teens that are separated by treatment.
- A case study with specific examples illustrates how letter writing can be used to change the teen's and the family's story.
- Suggestions for therapists working with families in OBH and residential settings are offered.

Adolescent mental health is a growing societal concern in the United States. Diagnosable mental health disorders are reported at rates of 10–20% among children and adolescents (Kieling et al. 2011), with an even greater number of adolescents who experience personal and interpersonal distress that do not meet diagnostic criteria (O'Connell et al. 2009). Diagnosable disorders and other interpersonal problems are concerning as they interfere with the accomplishment of normal developmental tasks; this includes developing healthy interpersonal relationships, social relationships, success in school, and transitioning into the

S.M. DeMille (✉)
Clinical Department, RedCliff Ascent, Wilderness Therapy Program,
709 E Main St., Enterprise, UT 84725, USA
e-mail: steved@redcliffascent.com

M.J. Montgomery
Clinical Mental Health Counseling Program, Northwest Christian University,
755 E 11th Ave, Eugene, OR 97401, USA
e-mail: mmontgomery@nwcu.edu

© Springer International Publishing AG 2017
J.D. Christenson and A.N. Merritts (eds.), *Family Therapy with Adolescents in Residential Treatment*, Focused Issues in Family Therapy,
DOI 10.1007/978-3-319-51747-6_3

workforce (O'Connell, Boat, and Warner). If not appropriately addressed, they may lead to adult health (Brown et al. 2009) and mental health problems (Belfer 2008).

Adolescent problems with mental health also negatively affect the lives of family and friends (O'Connell et al. 2009). The impact of adolescent mental health problems on the family system often drives families to seek professional help. According to the Substance Abuse and Mental Health Services Administration [SAMHSA] (2012), approximately 2.9 million youth are receiving professional services for emotional and behavioral problems. However, when conventional practices do not work, families often seek alternatives such as out-of-home treatments. For example, of those estimated 2.9 million youth who received services in 2012, nearly 600,000 received inpatient treatment (hospital, residential treatment, and foster care), and approximately 80,000 more received long-term (defined as more than 25 days) inpatient treatment (SAMHSA 2012). Some estimates of youth receiving treatment are even higher, suggesting that there may be as many as 375,000 youth treated in residential treatment settings each year (Russell and Gillis 2010). It is unknown how many of these settings systematically engage in theory-based innovation or program evaluation that advances our understanding of effectiveness of out-of-home approaches for troubled adolescents and their families. Even less is known about the effectiveness of the specific efforts made by these programs to deliberately and directly involving the family in the treatment process with the adolescent.

However, several studies support the importance of family involvement in the treatment of adolescents (Cottrell and Boston 2002; Diamond et al. 1996; Fauber and Long 1991) and specifically, adolescents in residential care (Safran et al. 2009). Hair (2005) reviewed 18 studies and found evidence that frequent family visits and participation in family therapy are associated with successful outcomes. In one study, when an adolescent participated in family therapy while in residential care, the odds were eight to one that they would transition to a less restrictive environment. In contrast, adolescents who experienced parent abandonment at the onset of treatment were more likely to be discharged to juvenile detention or a psychiatric hospital (Stage 1998). Similarly, Leichtman et al. (2001) found that family and community involvement predicted successful maintenance of gains post psychiatric inpatient treatment. These findings were corroborated by the national Building Bridges Initiative (2007), which identified family support as a predictor of post-treatment success for adolescents in residential care. In sum, there is a growing body of literature that indicates family involvement and family therapy is a significant indicator of posttreatment success in residential care for adolescents.

Most of the research mentioned above on family involvement has been conducted in traditional residential settings for adolescents. While still useful and informative, these results are limited because of the wide range of treatment options available to families currently (e.g., emotional growth schools). Because of the many options available to families, parents and guardians now have the opportunity to select a program designed to best fit their particular child's needs. OBH is one of the available options and is a promising alternative to traditional residential care for struggling adolescents. OBH builds upon an established tradition of using the wilderness as a therapeutic setting with unique opportunities for fostering change (Russell and Hendee 2000), such as what is described in Chap. 23 of this book. As an out-of-home treatment alternative, OBH is growing in popularity and accruing evidence of effectiveness (DeMille 2015). In a survey by Russell et al. (2008) approximately 10,000 youth received services annually in programs that identify as OBH. As an emerging and contemporary approach, OBH is receiving attention in the professional literature and conferences (e.g., Outdoor Behavioral Healthcare Research Cooperative; OBHRC 2015), in professional magazines (Bray 2014; DeAngelis 2013) and in the popular media (Telep 2014).

While most OBH research has focused on its general effectiveness for struggling adolescents, some investigators have explored the integration of aspects of family therapy in OBH (DeMille and Burdick 2015; DeMille and Montgomery 2016; Faddis and Bettmann 2010) and evaluated family change resulting from OBH participation (Harper and Russell 2008; Harper et al. 2007). Although the ideal role and quantity of family involvement in OBH treatment is currently unclear in the literature (Becker 2010), family involvement will likely be identified as a predictor of posttreatment outcome, as in other studies of family involvement in adolescent treatment and residential care. To add to what is known about the impact of family involvement on OBH treatment outcomes, this chapter illustrates how narrative family therapy techniques can be integrated in an OBH setting and their impact on one adolescent in treatment and his family. Despite its focus on application, this chapter can also be used by providers to learn techniques and methods that can help them to integrate a narrative approach into their work with adolescents in an OBH setting.

Outdoor Behavioral Healthcare

The outdoors has been used for centuries as a stage for change and healing (White 2011). In modern times, the outdoors has been used to foster personal growth, character development, and to build traits believed to be necessary for healthy functioning (Cason and Gillis 1994; White 2011). Walsh and Golins (1976) were some of the first authors to describe the role of the outdoors in fostering change; asserting that the outdoors provides the individual with a contrasting environment to see aspects of themselves that are often overlooked in a familiar environment. In other words, the outdoors provides a contrast for an individual to gain a new perspective on old patterns that occurred in their familiar environment. Walsh and Golins (1976) argued that this is the first step in helping an individual reorganize the meaning and direction of their experience. Additionally, these authors argue that the outdoors is particularly useful as a contrasting environment because it is a highly stimulating environment with much to see, hear and touch, while also providing a sense of uncertainty and risk. At the same time, the outdoors is a neutral environment. Rules exist in nature that are not arbitrary and which must be respected—there are no human buffers to protect individuals from nature, the elements, and the consequences that can ensue from taking unwise risks. Individuals must take on an awareness of their context and responsibility for their actions to a higher degree in an outdoor setting than typically required in other settings (Walsh and Golins 1976).

OBH, a contemporary and systematic provider of outdoor therapeutic environments, has made significant strides as a profession in the last decade. In 1996, a small group of programs formed the Outdoor Behavioral Healthcare Industry Council (OBHIC; now call the Outdoor Behavioral Healthcare Council or OBHC), which was formed to promote program standards and excellence in OBH (OBHC 2015). The council has grown and currently has 20 member programs. In addition, an Outdoor Behavioral Healthcare Center was established at the University of New Hampshire in 2015 with the mission to "advance the OBH field through the development of best practices, effective treatments, and evidence-based research" (OBHC 2015). The growth of OBH has led to the development of accreditation standards, managed by the Association of Experiential Educations (AEE; AEE 2015).

Although various definitions of OBH and wilderness therapy have been proposed, the OBH Accreditation Manual describes OBH as the "the prescriptive use of wilderness experiences by licensed mental health professionals to meet the therapeutic needs of clients" (Gass et al. 2014, p. 1). Specifically, OHB has been described as consisting of the following:

(a) Extended backcountry travel and wilderness living experiences long enough to allow for clinical assessment, establishment of treatment goals, and a reasonable course of treatment not to exceed the productive impact of the experience.
(b) Active and direct use of clients' participation and responsibility in their therapeutic process.
(c) Continuous group-living and regular formal group therapy sessions to foster teamwork and social interactions (excluding solo experiences).
(d) Individual therapy sessions, which may be supported by the inclusion of family therapy.
(e) Adventure experiences utilized to appropriately enhance treatment by fostering the development of eustress (i.e., the positive use of stress) as a beneficial element in the therapeutic experience.
(f) The use of nature in reality as well as a metaphor within the therapeutic process.
(g) A strong ethic of care and support throughout the therapeutic experience (Gass et al. 2014, p. 1).

Russell and Hendee (2000) provide a briefer description of OBH as a therapeutic program or modality that uses outdoor settings and counseling interventions to assess, diagnosis, and treat clients. A common feature of OBH programs is the immersion of a client in an unfamiliar environment, where they engage in group living with peers and guides. Participants also engage in individual and group therapy overseen by a licensed mental health professional and an educational curriculum designed to foster changes that clients can integrate into their lives upon returning home. As mentioned above, this type of program is growing in popularity, and examples of the type of work done in these programs can also been seen in Chaps. 6, 8, 15, 16, and 18 of this book. The reader is referred to those chapters for additional information on this powerful modality.

General effectiveness research on OBH has provided promising evidence of positive outcomes for struggling adolescents who receive treatment, indicating that adolescents with emotional, behavioral, and substance related disorders improve during the course of treatment and these improvements are maintained post-discharge (Bettmann et al. 2012; Clark et al. 2004; Lewis 2013; Magle-Haberek et al. 2012; Norton 2008, 2010a, b; Russell 2003, 2005a, b, 2008; Russell and Farnum 2004; Russell and Sibthorp 2004; Tucker et al. 2011, 2014; Zelov et al. 2013). Positive physiological outcomes have also been found (DeMille et al. 2014; Tucker et al. 2016). In addition, OBH appears to be effective for a variety of populations and problems, including adolescents in the Juvenile Justice system (Jones et al. 2004; Russell 2006; Wright 1983), adolescent sex offenders (Gillis and Gass 2010; Lambie et al. 2000), and adolescents with various diagnosable disorders (Clark et al. 2004; Russell 2006).

Many residential treatment programs for individuals claim to improve family functioning. In OBH, the family has received some research attention which has supported this claim. In one study, Harper et al. (2007) developed a questionnaire to measure adolescent and family outcomes in an OBH program. The 60-item questionnaire contained five subscales; (a) Family Functioning; (b) Adolescent Mental Health; (c) Adolescent Behavior; (d) School Success; and, (e) Positive Social Relations. These authors found numerous improvements in family functioning at 2 months post-discharge, with the exception of family arguments which increased at 2 months post treatment. Another study by Harper and Russell (2008) also found a positive trend toward improvements in family functions post OBH treatment. These authors noted that families reported a stabilizing effect and a generally rewarding experience from the wilderness treatment process.

Narrative Family Therapy

Narrative approaches to therapy have grown in popularity, particularly in the field of family therapy (Carr 1998). This is in large part due to the efforts of Michael White and David Epston (Epston and White 1992; White 1989), who describe their approach to therapy as based on principles rather than methods. Narrative therapy grew out of the postmodern perspective, which is reflected in its principles: (a) there is not one universal reality but reality is socially constructed; (b) language constructs reality; (c) reality is maintained through narratives; and (d) not all narratives are equal (Freedman and Combs 1996). From those foundations, narrative family therapy views human problems as arising and being maintained by oppressive stories that dominate a person's life. Problems occur when individual stories do not fit with their lived experience. According to the narrative perspective, treatment is a process of re-authoring personal narratives by providing a new and different perspective on a problem-saturated narrative. Re-authoring a narrative is done through a process of helping the client: (a) externalize the problem(s) they are experiencing; (b) deconstructing problem-saturated narratives through questioning; (c) identifying unique outcomes or times when a person was not oppressed by their problem; (d) linking unique outcomes to future and providing an alternative and preferred narrative; (e) inviting members of a person's social network to witness the new narrative; and (f) documenting new knowledge (Carr 1998; O'Connor et al. 1997).

Because postmodern perspectives place emphasis on principles rather than techniques, formal techniques are limited in narrative therapy. However, some authors have identified practices that are useful in assisting a person in re-authoring a personal story such as the *telling and retelling of story*, letter writing, and documentation (Carr 1998). For example, letter writing has been used in individual, family and group therapy to address a variety of issues including improving family communication, trauma, grief and loss, identity development, and crisis management (Christenson and Miller 2016; Riordan 1996; Tubman et al. 2001). In addition, Christenson and Miller (2016) describe ways letter writing can be used clinically to promote movement through the stages of change, promote a systemic view of issues, teach communication skills, and repair attachment injuries in residential treatment programs. Particularly useful from the narrative perspective, the authors describe letter writing as a means for families to slow down their interactions to provide the family space for reflections. By slowing the conversation, the family is able to begin the process of re-authoring problem-saturated narratives through externalizing problems, deconstructing problem-saturated narratives through questioning, and identifying unique outcomes to their problem.

Narrative Family Therapy in an Outdoor Behavioral Healthcare Setting

Narrative therapy has been used extensively in outpatient settings, but it has also been minimally applied to inpatient settings, including OBH. For example, Faddis and Cobb (2016) described the use of family sculptures and narrative techniques in an OBH program. Family sculptures originated from the work of David Kantor and his colleagues. Family sculptures are used as an experiential way to externalize family dynamics and the roles of family members. Family sculptures are used by Faddis and Cobb (2016) as a way to illuminate relational dynamics and creates empathy and understanding among family members. In addition, sculptures create witnesses of the family members and other observers of the family sculpture. Additionally, Faddis and Cobb (2016) describe the use of reflection teams in an OBH setting. The authors describe a process of using field staff and other families as part of a reflection team. The reflection team observes the session and at the end is asked specific questions based on their observations of the session. The reflecting team model and family sculptures offer the potential for family involvement in the therapeutic process, but present logistical challenges that prevent it from being broadly implemented.

Narrative family therapy provides some structural advantages that can be useful in an OBH setting. As noted above, OBH consists of "extended backcountry travel and wilderness living experiences long enough to allow for clinical assessment, establishment of treatment goals, and a reasonable course of treatment" (Gass et al. 2014, p. 1). Immersion in the backcountry and wilderness living brings many logistical challenges for families who wish to be actively involved in the treatment process. Wilderness programs are often located in rural and difficult to access locations. Thus, significant travel is required for most adolescents and families in order to participant in OBH, and the necessary investment of time and money is prohibitive for many families. Additionally, the backcountry environment limits the potential for electronic communication between the adolescent and family. Some programs have attempted to increase contact with the family while the child is in the backcountry through satellite communications, but the effectiveness and practicality of this approach is debated. Therefore, communication between a family and adolescent in an OBH program most often occurs through letter writing (see Chap. 2).

As a result of the limitations to conducting family therapy in an OBH setting, creative approaches to implementing family therapy are needed. Narrative family therapy provides potential advantages that compensate for some of these limitations. Narrative therapists often work alone with a client, or flexibly, as Anderson described, "with individuals, parts of families, and members of the larger system" (1997, pp. 66–67). Freedman and Combs (1996) noted that they prefer to "interact with one person in the family while the others listen" (p. 187). This process makes family members an audience to each other and their personal narratives. The telling and retelling of the story occurs with the family as an audience to the story. This approach is useful in an OBH setting, as adaptation can be made to tell and retell the narratives through writing, a common feature of OBH programs. Family members who are distant can still be involved in the process through being asked to reflect on stories that are being told (Freedman and Combs 1996).

This *distance* approach to family therapy creates some limitations. For example, the lack of observation of interpersonal patterns among the family members has been criticized (Minuchin 1998). However, the use of letter writing as a ways for families to tell, retell, and reflect on stories has great potential as a means of integrating the family during the entire treatment, even when the adolescent is in the backcountry. The following case study illustrates the application of narrative family therapy techniques in an OBH setting.

Case Study

Case studies provide an in-depth understanding of a new or innovative approach and have a long history of use in the field of psychology and medicine, and are particularly useful in documenting, evaluating, and disseminating new approaches or new applications of an approach (McLeod 2010). Case study research is a systematic inquiry into an issue or series of related issues which aims to describe the phenomenon of interest. Data for case study research can come from multiple sources, such as interviews, observations, document, artifacts, and objective measures. The diversity of data collection sources allows for an accurate and in-depth description of the case or cases being studied. Case studies are also useful for studying issues and events that have more variables and variations than data points. The dynamic and unpredictable nature of mental health treatment lends to the usefulness of case study research. In this case study, the use of narrative family therapy techniques in the treatment of an adolescent male with severe intrapersonal and interpersonal issues will be described, with a focus on application and outcomes. This case study will highlight the implementation of narrative techniques as a key aspect of the family therapy and compliments the work of DeMille and Burdick (2015).

The Program

The OBH program used in this case study is located in the Western United States. Adolescents who are receiving treatment are referred to as *students* while they are in the program; academic credits are earned through completing the education/experiential curriculum. Students also receive weekly individual and group therapy while in treatment. Parents meet with the therapist weekly via conference call. The program uses a continuous flow expedition model (Russell 2003), in which students are immersed in wilderness living and backcountry travel during their entire stay. The backcountry travel is physically demanding; it entails hiking/backpacking expeditions four to five times a week, each trek covering three to five miles. The wilderness living involves setting up and breaking down a campsite using low-impact camping principles (Marion and Reid 2007). Students learn wilderness skills practical for their living situations, such as primitive fire making for warmth and preparing meals.

The program reports that families they work with have "exhausted emotional, familial and community resources" (RedCliff Ascent 2015, p. 7). The overall treatment goal is to disrupt dysfunctional relational and behavioral patterns that are impeding healthy adolescent development and restore clients' age-appropriate functioning. The dysfunction that is impeding healthy adolescent development may come from mental health disorders, trauma, interpersonal problems at home or in the community, and/or substance use. Treatment goals are achieved by integrating evidence-based therapies with clinical expertise in the context of patient characteristics, culture, and preferences (Anderson 2006). In addition, goals are achieved through the use of wilderness living, interpersonal relationships, an experiential curriculum, and a healthy lifestyle (e.g., healthy diet, sleep habits, work and exercise).

Family involvement in the treatment process occurs through different methods, both in person and at a distance. Parents are involved in a series of group and family therapy sessions, with their teen and without them. Families (parents or legal guardians) also participate in an *end of trails* ceremony with their child as part of the treatment process. The end of trails ceremony involves the parents visiting and camping with their teen in the outdoor environment and participating in the concluding family therapy sessions. In addition to the in-person involvement, families also participate in family therapy through a series of narrative writing assignments that the student and family complete when the student is in the backcountry. The narratives are designed to assist the adolescent and the family in telling and retelling their story, identifying problem-saturated stories, and looking for unique outcomes. Sharing and reflection are also fostered through exchanging the narratives. Students are also asked to share their narrative with their peers in group therapy. Parent narratives are shared with the student in therapy, where they are given an opportunity to reflect on their parents' narratives. Following is a description of how narrative family therapy techniques were implemented with Sam in an OBH program.

History and Reason for Treatment

Sam is a 16-year-old male who was referred by his parents for treatment in an OBH program in the Western United States. Parents reported that they sought treatment because of Sam's emotional dysregulation, poor family relationships, and academic problems. Parents described Sam had been *out-of-control* within the home. He was refusing to go to school, refusing to attend local counseling sessions, and refusing to socialize outside of playing interactive video games online. His parents reported that whenever they would attempt to place restrictions or boundaries on his behaviors, Sam would become emotionally volatile and make threats to hurt himself. They also reported that Sam stopped talking with his family, was ignoring everyone in his home, and had refused to engage in outside activities (sports, school, travel, work).

Sam's parents reported that in the past they believed they had a close relationship with their son. They described Sam as being intelligent and academically gifted, athletic, and talented both intellectually and physically. In the past Sam was treated for depression; however, his parents noted it was never very successful. He was also previously in treatment for family problems that emerged around his use of video games, primarily, conflicts that arose when his parents would put limitations on his gaming (see Chaps. 4 and 5). During the last 2 months before entering treatment, Sam had refused to leave the couch, even to bathe. This was reportedly in response to having restrictions placed on his gaming console. Sam's treatment exemplifies what was noted above about matching treatment to the child's problem. Many traditional residential settings are designed to work with conduct disorders adolescents, which is distinct from the types of problems with which Sam presented, making OBH a potentially better match.

Assessment and Therapeutic Goals

When Sam arrived for treatment, his parents identified three goals for their son. First, they wanted him to reengage socially. They wanted him to leave the house, spend time with friends, attend school again, and to start making progress toward independence and adulthood. Second, the parents wanted to improve the family relationships, which had become hostile and dysfunctional for all family members. Finally, they wanted to see more interpersonal flexibility from Sam. They noted that when Sam would set his mind on something he would not back down until he got what he wanted.

When Sam was asked what he wanted to work on in treatment he stated "I want to teach my parents they cannot control me." Sam denied any other treatment needs or past need for treatment. Sam also noted that he was not *depressed* or *addicted* to games and it upset him when people would insist otherwise. Sam acknowledged that his relationship with his family was poor and that he had lost most of his friends.

In response to Sam's adverse reaction to the use of diagnostic labels, a functional approach was taken in Sam's treatment planning. This was done by focusing on functional goals and not the treatment of symptoms associated with diagnoses. The first goal with Sam was to help him actively engage in the treatment process and during the fourth session, Sam collaboratively developed the following goals. The first goal was to engage in appropriate behaviors with peers and authority figures. This included meeting basic expectations, following directives, and being a positive influence on others in his peer group. The second goal was to improve family relationships. This goal included two parts: Sam would start communicating with his parents through letter writing, and he would send and receive narratives with his parents, addressing the problems that he perceived in their relationship.

Narrative Family Therapy

Initially, Sam did not want to engage in therapy or any form of reflective process. As a result, the first three therapy sessions focused on developing a working relationship and helping Sam feel safe. In addition, the first sessions focused on helping Sam develop hope that his life could be different and hope that his relationships could improve. This was a major issue for Sam as he did not believe he or his family could change anything. He felt stuck. Finally, therapy also focused on assisting Sam with adapting to his new contrasting outdoor environment. During the first three sessions Sam was encouraged to reflect on his old environment, relationships, and choices. At first Sam was rigid and did not want to look at his environment, relationship, and choices. However, as Sam spent time in the outdoors and had opportunities to contrast his old familiar environment with his new unfamiliar environment, he began to identify aspects of his life that he did not want to maintain going forward with his life.

In the fourth therapy session Sam acknowledged his new perspective, stating that he wanted to "try something different." He noted that he was not happy with his current situation and current relationships. During that session, Sam set goals for himself and became more open to share his story. Family therapy began with Sam by creating a safe therapeutic environment where he shared about his struggles prior to being placed in treatment in an OBH program. While narrative therapy posits the necessity of creating a collaborative or egalitarian relationship between therapist and client, a therapist in this OBH program has an evaluative and gate-keeping role with the student that makes an egalitarian relationship in therapy unrealistic. The therapist is the gate-keeper of the decision about when the student is ready to transition to a less restrictive treatment environment, and students are aware of this dynamic. Thus, initially in therapy, the goal is to minimize the impact of that dynamic on the treatment process and to create a safe therapeutic environment. To create a safe therapeutic environment with Sam, a collaborative position was taken with him. This involved listening more than questioning, privileging perspective over facts, and taking a collaborative co-authoring position with Sam. An example of this would be when Sam would complain or criticize his parents. Sam was validated and heard through statements such as, "you must have been quite frustrated with your parents during that interaction." This allowed for Sam to know he was being heard without validating or refuting the facts of the stories being told.

In the fourth session, Sam provided the *thin description* of his problem. Sam identified the different areas of his life where the dominant story was imposed upon him. However, Sam described that his problems were not due to his acceptance of the dominate story, but from his resistance to accepting the dominate story. Sam discussed his issues with being described as depressed and addicted. Sam insisted that is not "who he is." Sam also mentioned a professional who labeled him with *Aspergers* and how he never wanted to return to that professional. In addition, Sam identified his struggles with being identified as *smart* and being pressured to attend a prestigious boarding school where he received a scholarship. Through the use of *how* and *when* questions, Sam was challenged in the session to explore in more depth the struggles he was experiencing.

At the end of the session, Sam was challenged to continue to tell his story and retell his story. He was given a few open-ended questions to reflect on and respond to before the next therapy session. This process would continue throughout Sam's entire stay and his answers in the assignments were labeled as Sam's autobiography. The reflection questions Sam was given after the fourth session related to his home, family, authority, and significant events of childhood. Some of the questions included the following: "What did your home look like as a child?" "What did it take to live in your home?" "Who was in charge in your home and what did it take to be in charge?" "What were the most fearful events in your childhood?" In addition, Sam's parents were given open-ended reflection questions similar to Sam's; their answers were called the parent narratives. Those questions included "What did you child's home look like?" "What were the roles and expectations of each family member and how were they communicated?" "What were the most significant events that defined the family?"

In the fifth therapy session, Sam shared his autobiography and the parent narrative was read to Sam. Some of the themes that came out of the parent narrative included an emphasis that the children in the family were expected to "do the best their abilities enabled them to," and to "be polite and respectful." Furthermore, the narrative stated, "We tried to communicate this primarily by example, although we're far from perfect." Some of the significant events that were identified in the parent narrative included significant loss, great academic success in school, and Sam being bullied in school. Sam was asked to reflect on what he read and heard from his parents. He was asked, "How was it to read your story and then hear your parents' story?" "What stood out to you?" and "Was their anything that surprised you?" These questions were intended to produce a *thick description* or *thickening* of Sam's story by allowing him the space to make interpretations.

Sam was asked to identify situations from his parents' narrative that were surprising or that did not fit into his problem-saturated narrative. A few parts of the narrative stood out to Sam. Sam noted that he felt much pressure to be successful because of his physical and academic capacities. His parents did expect him to do "the best his abilities enabled him," and Sam stated how hard that was for him. Sam also noted that he always felt like the problem in the family and he was surprised to hear his parents say, "…although we're far from perfect." Sam also responded to the bullying by saying that he did not think it was as significant of an event as his parents did. Some of the unique outcomes, such as the identified patient story Sam had for himself, were used to begin to reconstruct an alternative story.

At the end of the session, Sam was challenged to continue to *tell and retell his story* and was given new open-ended questions to reflect on before the next therapy session. The questions that Sam was given focused on discipline and self-discipline, such as "Who was in charge of the discipline in your home?" "How was discipline administered and how did you respond to the discipline?" "What areas in your life have you shown self-discipline and what areas are out-of-control?" "How do others know that you are self-disciplined?" Sam's family was also given open-ended reflection questions similar to Sam's. They included, "From where did you derive the method of discipline you implemented in your home?" "Was this different from the kind of discipline you encountered as a child? How so?" "How did your child respond to the discipline you provided?" "What seemed to be successful?" "What would you have changed and why?" "When were you most encouraged by the actions of your child?" These questions were designed to allow the parent to reflect on their personal story, tell their family story, while also looking for unique outcomes in their family story. Finally, at the conclusion of the fifth session, Sam was challenged to share his autobiography with his peer group.

The peer group became the witness to the thickening description and the alternative story. This was done to increase the probability that the alternative story will take root for Sam outside the therapy session and later outside the OBH program. For Sam, sharing his autobiography was usually done in the evening around the camp fire. The peer group would ask questions or share their perspective on the evolving narrative. Witnesses are encouraged to share difficulties that they see for Sam and things to expect as the narrative thickens.

In the sixth session, Sam shared his autobiographies and his parents' new narrative was read to him. After exchanging writings, Sam was asked similar questions to help produce a thick description of the story. Sam noted in this narrative that his parents seemed the most pleased with him when he was interacting and playing with his siblings and not when he was achieving or accomplishing. He was pleased to see that his parents stated, "we are most encouraged by Sam when he was caring with his sisters, honest with us and everyone else, when he showed love to us and to his sisters." Sam noted that he liked the high relational focus of the narratives and the absence of the focus on achievement. The shared beliefs that Sam experienced through telling and retelling his story and hearing his family story highlight the shared values and beliefs within the family.

At the conclusion of the session, Sam was challenged to continue to *tell his story* and *retell his story* and was given new open-ended questions to reflect on and respond to before the next therapy session. Sam's family was also given new open-ended questions similar to Sam's to reflect on and answer. The questions allowed the family to continue to work on the interpersonal theme that emerged in the last narratives. For example, one of the questions provided was, "What events have occurred that indicate you respect yourself and others?" Some other examples of questions for the parents were, "How did you define and teach respect to your child," and "What are examples of when your son demonstrated or rejected your teaching?" Again, Sam was challenged to share his autobiography with his peer group, who witnessed the thickening description and the alternative story. The process of exchanging narratives occurred eight times during the course of treatment while Sam was in the backcountry of an OBH program. Each situation was followed by the group witnessing the process through the sharing of autobiographies with the peer group.

Concluding Therapy and Follow-up

The family narratives concluded with an incorporation practice. On Sam's last day of treatment in the OBH program, Sam shared his alternative story with his family. The alternative story incorporated what he had experienced in the outdoor program, with his peer group, and throughout the narrative therapy process. Sam shared about his new view of his role in the family and not being the problem in the family or *identified patient*. After Sam shared his narrative, Sam's parents were asked to reflect on what they heard and experienced. Parallel experiences were identified and used as bridges for Sam's parents to become a resource for Sam going forward instead of part of the problem.

In an exit interview, Sam reported the most valuable thing he had taken from his time in the outdoors was how it "helped improve my family relationship." This improvement was apparently sustained. One year after Sam had completed treatment he and his family responded to a questionnaire about their experience. Sam noted in his questionnaire:

> I think the most important part of [the program] to me was the space that I found there. I was in the most remote place I had ever been and I didn't feel like I had to be anything. Whereas before I was just whoever my parents thought I was, at [Program] I began to become who I am. I don't think that I could have learnt to be myself had I been at home. I think that learning to sit with myself and being okay with who I am is something that started for me out there.

Sam also noted in the questionnaire about the impact of having his group as a witness:

> The first time I told my group as a whole my life story I cried a hell of a lot because it was the first time that I had told anyone my age about what was going on back home. My friends were extremely helpful and respectful of me, and that experience helped me a lot for a while to feel comfortable with people.

In addition to feedback from Sam, his parents were asked to reflect on their treatment experience in an OBH program. Sam's parents reported:

> [The program] helped us understand [Sam], his concerns, his fears, and his needs. We could not have done this while he was at home as he was unwilling to communicate with us. Removing him from the house for a few weeks gave everyone involved the chance to rethink what was going on and it helped us all get a bit of perspective on the issues [Sam] was dealing with.

The parents continued:

> [The program] made us think about our relationship with our son, and how our role might have had an influence in [Sam's] lack of development. [The program] did this without blaming us and without resentment. Our changes as parents somehow came to us from inside ourselves; [the program] helped us become a better version of ourselves as parents without us noticing, without blame, and without resentment.

Sam's parents were also asked what aspects of the treatment process was the most helpful.

> For us parents, narratives were very helpful in two ways. Firstly it helped us rethink about our relationship with our son, and about how our role might have had an influence on [Sam's] development. Writing the narratives had a huge impact on our way of parenting our kids. Secondly, the parents' narratives made us get involved in [Sam's] improvement, it allowed us play a part in his progress even though he was miles away from home. It was a way of staying in touch with [Sam] while he was staying in the wilderness, a way of working together with him even though we were miles away from him.

Suggestions for Family Therapists

Here, we offer suggestions for family therapists interested in applying these techniques to increase family involvement in OBH or other out-of-home treatments. Therapists should be aware of the nature of the relationship with the client in treatment and power dynamics. O'Connor et al. (1997) found that clients valued the therapists who used the narrative approach because the therapists appeared to respect their perceptions and experiences. Early in treatment this involves a focus on listening over interpreting and focusing on perspectives instead of facts. In addition, the non-punitive physical distance between teen and parents that OBH provides some safety for the adolescent to feel open to discussing problems and challenges without the fear of what happens after the session, as well as the freedom to imagine and create a new narrative. The physical distance should be taken advantage of and can create a sense of safety for describing family problems, while the outdoor setting provides fresh standpoints for taking new perspectives and creating new narratives.

The narrative approach works with the individual parts of the system and with others as an audience to the stories being told in therapy. For family therapists working in OBH, this method of family involvement is very conducive to the treatment setting. The telling of stories and being an audience for stories are practices that can be delivered in an asynchronous format through letters or *two or* structured writing assignments. The asynchronous format provides an opportunity *more* for the family therapist to discuss reactions to the stories separately with families *ospcts/* and adolescents, which may increase a sense of safety and allow the client to more *events* fully develop their *voice*, and then to share their reflections with each other through writing. The asynchronous format also allows for deeper refection and processing, as stories and reflections on received stories are shared with peers and explored with therapists.

Finally, family therapists should use the group as a witness of the alternative story. An advantage of writing the stories is the potential for the stories to be shared and thickened by having a peer group witness the story and then be a witness to the development of the alternative story (see Chap. 16). Witnessing supports the development of the story, and fosters internalization of the alternative story and generalization of the story to new settings such as home environments reentered after treatment.

Conclusion

One of the greatest struggles of out-of-home treatments is the involvement of families in the treatment process. The narrative family therapy techniques described here illustrated how families can be involved in the therapy process, even at a distance. In the case of Sam, a struggling adolescent placed in an OBH program, techniques from narrative family therapy were used to meet the therapeutic goal of improving the family relationship. Specifically, the process of deconstructing the dominant story and reconstructing an alternative story was facilitated by the contrasting outdoor environment offered in an OBH treatment setting. The narrative family therapy integrated into his treatment included techniques of collaboration, identifying unique outcomes, thickening the story, inviting outsiders to witness, and incorporation practices with families. The case illustrates several techniques that family therapists can use to further involve families in inpatient treatment programs, particularly outdoor programs for struggling teens.

References

Anderson, N.B. (2006). Evidence-based practice in psychology. *American Psychologist, 61*(4), 271–285. doi:10.1037/0735-7028.39.6.658

Association of Experiential Education. (2015). *Accreditation for outdoor behavioral healthcare programs*. Retrieved from: http://www.aee.org/accreditation-for-outdoor-behav-health

Becker, S. P. (2010). Wilderness therapy: Ethical considerations for mental health professionals. *Child & Youth Care Forum, 39*(1), 47–61. doi:10.1007/s10566-009-9085-7

Belfer, M. L. (2008). Child and adolescent mental disorders: The magnitude of the problem across the globe. *Journal of Child Psychology and Psychiatry, 49*(3), 226–236. doi:10.1111/j.1469-7610.2007.01855.x

Bettmann, J. E., Russell, K. C., & Parry, K. J. (2012). How substance abuse recovery skills, readiness to change and symptom reduction impact change processes in wilderness therapy participants. *Journal of Child and Family Studies, 22*(8), 1039–1050. doi:10.1007/s10826-012-9665-2

Bray, B. (2014). Going wild. *Counseling Today*. Retrieved from: http://ct.counseling.org/2014/12/going-wild/

Brown, D. W., Anda, R. F., Tiemeier, H., Felitti, V. J., Edwards, V. J., Croft, J. B., et al. (2009). Adverse childhood experiences and the risk of premature mortality. *American Journal of Preventive Medicine, 37*(5), 389–396. doi:10.1016/j.amepre.2009.06.021

Carr, A. (1998). Michael White's narrative therapy. *Contemporary Family Therapy, 20*(4), 485–503.

Cason, D., & Gillis, H. L. (1994). A meta-analysis of outdoor adventure programming with adolescents. *Journal of Experiential Education, 17*, 40–47.

Christenson, J. D., & Miller, A. L. (2016). Slowing down the conversation: The use of letter writing with adolescents and young adults in residential settings. *Contemporary Family Therapy, 38*(1), 23–31.

Clark, J., Marmol, L. M., Cooley, R., & Gathercoal, K. (2004). The effects of wilderness therapy on the clinical concerns (on Axes I, II, and IV) of troubled adolescents. *Journal of Experiential Education, 27*(2), 213–232. doi:10.1177/105382590402700207

Cottrell, D., & Boston, P. (2002). Practitioner review: The effectiveness of systemic family therapy for children and adolescents. *Journal of Child Psychology and Psychiatry, 43*(5), 573–586. doi:10.1111/1469-7610.00047

DeAngelis, T. (2013). Therapy gone wild. *Monitor on Pscyhology, 44*(8), 48–53.

DeMille, S. M. (2015). *Do therapeutic factors and client gender impact treatment outcomes for adolescents participating in outdoor behavioral healthcare treatment? (Doctoral dissertation)*. Minneapolis, MN: Capella University.

DeMille, S. M., & Burdick, M. (2015). A theoretically anchored and multi-modal treatment approach in an outdoor behavioral healthcare program. *Journal of Therapeutic Schools & Programs, 7*(1), 19–30.

DeMille, S. M., Comart, C., & Tucker, A. R. (2014). Body composition changes in an outdoor behavioral healthcare program. *Ecopsychology, 6*(3), 174–182. doi:10.1089/eco.2014.0012

DeMille, S. M., & Montgomery, M. (2016). Integrating narrative family therapy in an outdoor behavioral healthcare program: A case study. *Contemporary Family Therapy, 38*(1), 3–13. doi:10.1007/s10591-015-9362-6

Diamond, G. S., Serrano, A. C., Dickey, M., & Sonis, W. A. (1996). Current status of family-based outcome and process research. *Journal of the American Academy of Child & Adolescent Psychiatry, 35*(1), 6–16. doi:10.1097/00004583-199601000-00007

Epston, D., & White, M. (1992). *Experience, contradiction, narrative and imagination.* Adelaida: Dulwich Centre Publication.

Faddis, T. J., & Bettmann, J. E. (2010). Reflecting teams and other innovative family therapy techniques adapted for outdoor behavioral healthcare. *Journal of Therapeutic Schools and Programs, 1*(1), 57–69.

Faddis, T. J., & Cobb, K. F. (2016). Family therapy techniques in residential settings: Family sculptures and reflecting teams. *Contemporary Family Therapy, 38*(1), 43–51.

Fauber, R. L., & Long, N. (1991). Children in context: The role of the family in child psychotherapy. *Journal of Consulting and Clinical Psychology, 59*(6), 813–820. doi:http://dx. doi.org.library.capella.edu/10.1037/0022-006X.59.6.813

Freedman, J., & Combs, G. (1996). *Narrative therapy: The social construction of preferred realities.* New York: Norton.

Gass, M., Logan, P., Christensen, N., Hallows, G., Liebing, M., Smith, P. … Tierney, S. (2014). *Manual of accreditation standards for outdoor behavioral healthcare programs* (1st ed.). Boulder, CO: Association of Experiential Education.

Gillis, H. L., & Gass, M. A. (2010). Treating juveniles in a sex offender program using adventure-based programming: A matched group design. *Journal of Child Sexual Abuse, 19* (1), 20–34.

Hair, H. J. (2005). Outcomes for children and adolescents after residential treatment: A review of research from 1993 to 2003. *Journal of Child and Family Studies, 14*(4), 551–575. doi:10. 1007/s10826-005-7188-9

Harper, N. J., & Russell, K. C. (2008). Family involvement and outcome in adolescent wilderness treatment: A mixed-methods evaluation. *International Journal of Child & Family Welfare, 1,* 19–36.

Harper, N. J., Russell, K. C., Cooley, R., & Cupples, J. (2007). Catherine Freer wilderness therapy expeditions: An exploratory case study of adolescent wilderness therapy, family functioning, and the maintenance of change. *Child and Youth Care Forum, 36*(2–3), 111–129. doi:10.1007/ s10566-007-9035-1

Jones, C. D., Lowe, L. A., & Risler, E. A. (2004). The effectiveness of wilderness adventure therapy programs for young people involved in the juvenile justice system. *Residential Treatment for Children & Youth, 22*(2), 53–67.

Kieling, C., Baker-Henningham, H., Belfer, M., Conti, G., Ertem, I., Omigbodun, O. … Rahman, A. (2011). Child and adolescent mental health worldwide: Evidence for action. *The Lancet, 378*(9801), 1515–1525.

Lambie, I., Hickling, L., Seymour, F., Simmonds, L., Robson, M., & Houlahan, C. (2000). Using wilderness therapy in treating adolescent sexual offenders. *The Journal of Sexual Aggression, 5* (2), 99–117. doi:10.1080/13552600008413302

Leichtman, M., Leichtman, M. L., Barber, C. C., & Neese, D. T. (2001). Effectiveness of intensive short-term residential treatment with severely disturbed adolescents. *American Journal of Orthopsychiatry, 71*(2), 227. doi:10.1037/0002-9432.71.2.227

Lewis, S. F. (2013). Examining changes in substance use and conduct problems among treatment-seeking adolescents. *Child and Adolescent Mental Health, 18*(1), 33–38. doi:10.1111/j.1475-3588.2012.00657.x

Magle-Haberek, N., Tucker, A., & Gass, M. (2012). The effects of program differences within wilderness therapy and residential treatment center (RTC) programs. *Residential Treatment for Children and Youth, 29*(3), 202–218. doi:10.1080/0886571X.2012.697433

Marion, J. L., & Reid, S. E. (2007). Minimising visitor impacts to protected areas: The efficacy of low impact education programmes. *Journal of Sustainable Tourism, 15*(1), 5–27. doi:10.2167/jost593.0

McLeod, J. (2010). The role of case studies in the development of theory and practice in counselling and psychotherapy. In J McLeods (Ed.), *Case study research: In counselling and psychotherapy* (pp. 1–15). London: SAGE Publications Ltd.

Minuchin, S. (1998). Where is the family in narrative family therapy? *Journal of Marital and Family Therapy, 24*(4), 397–403.

National Building Bridges Initiative. (2007). *Innovative practices for transformation.* Workgroup webinar.

Norton, C. L. (2008). Understanding the impact of wilderness therapy on adolescent depression and psychosocial development. *Illinois Child Welfare, 4*(1), 166–178.

Norton, C. L. (2010a). Exploring the process of a therapeutic wilderness experience: Key therapeutic components in the treatment of adolescent depression and psychosocial development. *Journal of Therapeutic School and Program, 4*(1), 24–46.

Norton, C. L. (2010b). Into the wilderness—A case study: The psychodynamics of adolescent depression and the need for a holistic intervention. *Clinical Social Work Journal, 38*(2), 226–235. doi:10.1007/s10615-009-0205-5

O'Connell, M. E., Boat, T., & Warner, K. E. (Eds.). (2009). *Preventing mental, emotional, and behavioral disorders among young people: Progress and possibilities.* Washington DC: National Academies Press.

O'Connor, T. S. J., Meakes, E., Pickering, M. R., & Schuman, M. (1997). On the right track: Client experience of narrative therapy. *Contemporary Family Therapy, 19*(4), 479–495.

Outdoor Behavioral Healthcare Council. (OBHC, 2015). *About Us.* Retrieved from: https://obhcouncil.com/about/standards/

RedCliff Ascent. (2015). Who do we serve? *The Wilderness Advisor, 1*, 7–8.

Riordan, R. J. (1996). Scriptotherapy: Therapeutic writing as a counseling adjunct. *Journal of Counseling & Development, 74*(3), 263–269.

Russell, K. C. (2006). Evaluating the effects of the Wendigo Lake Expedition Program on young offenders. *Youth Violence and Juvenile Justice, 4*(2), 185–203.

Russell, K. C., & Gillis, H. L. (2010). Experiential therapy in the mental health treatment of adolescents. *Journal of Therapeutic Schools and Programs, 4*(1), 47–79.

Russell, K., & Hendee, J. (2000). *Definition, common practice, expected outcomes, and a nationwide survey of programs (Technical Report 26).* Moscow, ID: University of Idaho.

Russell, K. C. (2003). Assessing treatment outcomes in outdoor behavioral healthcare using the Youth Outcome Questionnaire. *Child and Youth Care Forum. 32*, 355–381. doi:10.1023/B:CCAR.0000004507.12946.7e

Russell, K. C. (2005a). Preliminary results of a study examining the effects of outdoor behavioral healthcare treatment on levels of depression and substance use frequency. *Journal of Experiential Education, 27*, 305–307.

Russell, K. C. (2005b). Two years later: A qualitative assessment of youth-well-being and the role of aftercare in outdoor behavioral healthcare treatment. *Child and Youth Care Forum, 34*, 209–239. doi:10.1007/s10566-005-3470-7

Russell, K. C. (2008). Adolescent substance-use treatment: Service delivery, research on effectiveness, and emerging treatment alternatives. *Journal of Groups in Addiction & Recovery, 2* (2–4), 68–96. doi:10.1080/15560350802081264

Russell, K. C. & Farnum, J. (2004). A concurrent model of the wilderness therapy process. *Journal of Adventure Education and Outdoor Learning, 4*, 39–55. doi:10.1080/14729670485200411

Russell, K. C., Gillis, H. L., & Lewis T. G. (2008). A five-year follow-up of a survey of North American outdoor behavioral healthcare programs. *Journal of Experiential Education, 31*(1), 55–77. doi:10.1177/105382590803100106

Russell, K. C., & Sibthorp, J. (2004). Hierarchical linear modeling of treatment outcomes in outdoor behavioral healthcare. *Journal of Experiential Education, 27,* 176–191.

Safran, J. D., Muran, J. C., & Proskurov, B. (2009). Alliance, negotiation, and rupture resolution. In R. Levy & S. J. Ablon (Eds.), *Handbook of evidence based psychodynamic psychotherapy* (pp. 201–205). New York: Humana Press.

Substance Abuse and Mental Health Services Administration. (2012). *National survey on drug use and health: Mental health findings.* Rockville, MD: Substance Abuse and Mental Health Services Administration.

Stage, S. A. (1998). Predicting adolescents' discharge status following residential treatment. *Residential Treatment for Children & Youth, 16*(3), 37–56. doi:10.1300/J007v16n03_03

Telep, T. (2014). The man who takes troubled youths to therapy camp. *BBC News Magazine.* Retrieved from: http://www.bbc.com/news/magazine-26513805

Tubman, J. G., Montgomery, M. J., & Wagner, E. F. (2001). Letter writing as a tool to increase client motivation to change: Application to an inpatient crisis unit. *Journal of Mental Health Counseling, 23*(4), 295–311.

Tucker, A., Norton, C. L., DeMille, S. M., & Hobson, J. (2016). The impact of wilderness therapy. *Journal of Experiential Education, 39*(1), 15–30. doi:10.1177/1053825915607536

Tucker, A., Smith, A., & Gass, M. (2014). The impact of presenting problems and individual client characteristics on treatment outcomes in residential and wilderness treatment programs. *Residential Treatment for Children and Youth, 31*(2), 135–153.

Tucker, A. R., Zelov, R., & Young, M. (2011). Four years along: Emerging traits of programs in the NATSAP practice research network (PRN). *Journal of Therapeutic Schools and Programs, 5*(1), 10–28.

Walsh, V., & Golins, G. (1976). *The exploration of the outward bound process.* Denver, CO: Outward Bound School.

White, M. (1989). *Select papers.* Adelaide: Dulwich Centre Publications.

White, N. W. (2011). *Stories from the elders: Chronicles and narratives of the early years of wilderness therapy.* Franklin Pierce University.

Wright, A. (1983). Therapeutic potential of the outward bound process: An evaluation of a treatment program for juvenile delinquents. *Therapeutic Recreation Journal, 17*(2), 33–42.

Zelov, R., Tucker, A. R., & Javorksi, S. (2013). A new phase for the NATSAP PRN: Post-discharge reporting and transition to the network wide utilization of the Y-OQ 2.0. *Journal of Therapeutic Schools & Programs, 6*(1), 7–19.

Author Biographies

Steven M. DeMille, Ph.D., LCMHC is Research Director and a therapist for RedCliff Ascent, an Outdoor Behavioral Healthcare program. He specializes in working with struggling adolescents and families. Steven has a Ph.D. in Counselor Education and Supervision and is a Licensed Clinical Mental Health Counselor. Steven's research interests include adolescent interventions, Outdoor Behavioral Healthcare, ethics and effectiveness research. Steven has presented on adolescent interventions at various national and international conferences. His current treatment and research focus is on the impact of nature and the outdoors on adolescent and family therapy.

Marilyn J. Montgomery, Ph.D., LPC is engaged in a lifelong area of scholarship that includes a focus on psychosocial development, particularly the development and revision of one's sense of self through adolescence and adulthood. She has published articles about identity development and conducts research on how individuals change problematic life course trajectories toward more positive and meaningful outcomes through counseling and other helping relationships. She is also interested in exploring how older adults maintain a sense of personal integrity as they face age-related challenges. Additionally, Marilyn studies how counseling interventions provided in outdoor behavioral health settings promote positive development as well as reduce problem behaviors.

Chapter 4
Understanding Video Game Mechanics as a Tool in Creating a Sustainable Relationship with Digital Media

Ryan Anderson

Chapter Highlights

- Specific mechanics in video games utilize principles of behaviorism, such as classical conditioning and operant conditioning, to create addictive potential similar to gambling.
- Internet Gaming Disorder (IGD) and other problematic forms of digital media usage have become a highly disruptive factor in the lives of many people.
- Addictive gaming mechanics and personal biopsychosocial vulnerabilities combine to create the addictive potential of specific video games.
- The addictive potential of digital media appears to be able to be mitigated by enhancing biopsychosocial self-care in combination with an informed and mindful approach to selection of digital media.
- Even digital media with relatively few addictive mechanics can be problematic with sufficient person biopsychosocial vulnerability.

Gaming Evolved

Video games have gone through significant changes in their mechanics in recent years, which in turn has influenced how they interact with the human brain. Many games today are complex masterworks that provide a highly coordinated, sensory rich, neurologically stimulating, and socially involved combination of compelling graphics, social connection, fantasy identity, escapism, constant novelty, accessibility, and meticulously crafted psychological reinforcement. For better or for

R. Anderson (✉)
Telos RTC, 870 West Center Street, Orem, UT 84057, USA
e-mail: ryan@telosrtc.com

© Springer International Publishing AG 2017   49
J.D. Christenson and A.N. Merritts (eds.), *Family Therapy with Adolescents in Residential Treatment*, Focused Issues in Family Therapy,
DOI 10.1007/978-3-319-51747-6_4

worse, each video game in this new breed creates a unique neuro-cyber interface, an ergonomic molding, meshing, and interweaving interface with the various aspects of neurological functioning, including what stimulates and motivates the brain. In combination with the information included in Chap. 5 of this text, understanding how video game mechanics work will provide clinicians and their clients with information that is helpful in creating a strategic approach to a sustainable relationship with digital media.

Gaming Mechanics and Video Game Process Addiction

Video games are evolving not just due to creative progression, but also due to economic pressure. For example, in 2009, *Call of Duty: Modern Warfare 2* PC version had 4.1 million pirated downloads in November and December alone, in contrast to having only 300,000 copies sold in November (Oxford 2010). Given a retail price of $49.99, that is approximately $205 million of stolen goods from a single gaming company in just 2 months, and that is just the value of a single game on the market. An estimated 9.8 million PC games in total were illegally downloaded in the month of December 2009.

Rampant digital piracy has driven game developers to get creative about making games that gamers will be willing to continue to pay increasing amounts of money to continue playing. This allows game developers to continue to increase their profits without having to spend much, or any, time at all, helping to offset a portion of the monetary losses to piracy. Gaming mechanics that produce circular, self-reinforcing sales have become more and more common because they produce economic results—results necessary for the survival of an industry that is at risk of collapsing under the impulsiveness and lack of moral and ethical self-regulation of its own consumer base. Therefore, game developers are strongly economically incentivized to create games with higher addictive potential, whether or not they know that is what they are doing.

The author has conducted an informal qualitative analysis during my years of working with people with video game addictions, and has come upon several patterns that he has found very helpful in explaining why certain video games appear to have a higher addictive potential than others. These observations have held true in his clinical experience, and have proven to be useful as both measures to prevent the development of video game addictions and guidelines to inform recovery from an addictive relationship with video games. The more these specific addictive mechanics are included in a game, and the more prominent each mechanic is, the greater the addictive potential of a specific game appears to be (Anderson 2015).

Addictive Gaming Mechanic #1: Level Grinding

Level grinding is "the playing time spent doing repetitive tasks within a game to unlock a particular game item or to build the experience needed to progress smoothly through the game. Grinding most commonly involves killing the same set of opponents over and over in order to gain experience points or gold. Although other game genres require some grinding, role-playing games (RPG)—specifically massively multiplayer online role-playing games—are the most notorious for requiring this type of time investment from players" (para. 1, Janssen 2014). Video games that require the player to engage in level grinding have them spend a large period of time in tedious tasks to qualify for brief but rewardingly fun gaming moments.

In spite of the fact that level grinding is typically not very fun, it has an influential psychological effect. It creates a sense of emotional investment in the game. At our core, most of us are motivated by what we feel. The more time, energy, and effort we put into something, the more it matters to us (Maer and Braskamp 1986). The more that thing matters to us, the more it becomes a source of motivation for us. This is true of a spouse, a child, an education, a career, or an avatar in an online role-playing game.

Beside emotional investment, level grinding provides a strong intermittent reinforcement pattern, also known as a variable ratio schedule. This is the same psychological reinforcement principle upon which slot machines and other gambling games are based (Miltenberger 2011). Just like those forms of gambling, the player puts in a great deal of time and effort without any real reward, or receiving rewards just large enough to keep the player engaged. However, when the real rewards come, they tend to be large. A player may earn the reward of leveling up and gain new abilities. Now they can cast new spells, wear new armor, enter new realms, or finally kill that monster that has wiped them out dozens or even hundreds of times! The rewards feel like a game changer and provide a new sense of excitement about the game, only to plunge the player into a world where more is needed than they have achieved, setting off another long cycle of level grinding.

This dynamic also provides the game developer with another opportunity to make money by offering *micro-transactions* that allow the gamer to purchase their way up through levels or to buy virtual gear that assists in leveling up—all purchased with real money—thus relieving some of the grinding process for the gamer and artificially accelerating him or her toward the next reward (Jenkins 2014). The player invests time and money, making playing the game increasingly motivating due to that investment and the rewards.

Level grinding tends to be the backbone mechanic of every massive multiplayer online role-playing game. Additionally, social media games and mobile apps often have a strong level grinding element to them, and game designers are integrating level grinding into first person shooters and other action titles as well. This is most likely because it has become a very effective way to keep people playing and to keep people paying for the same game over and over again. Prominent examples of current games with a heavy level grinding mechanic include *World of Warcraft*, *EVE Online*, *Farmville*, *Minecraft*, and *Destiny*.

Addictive Gaming Mechanic #2: Twitch

The second dynamic that can increase the addictive potential of a game is twitch. Technically, twitch refers to high speed gameplay with constant micro-adjustments determining the difference between victory and defeat. Games with high-intensity twitch move along at a heart-pounding pace, and the gamer has to make rapid and accurate adjustments of the controls in order to survive. First person shooters like the *Halo* and *Call of Duty* series are prime examples of twitch gameplay. Twitch gameplay is particularly effective at producing a euphoric adrenaline rush for gamers. It keeps players highly stimulated with immediate, dramatic results of their actions and often involves a rapid sequence of player deaths and respawns. The buzz of simulated velocity and simulated danger make the player feel energized and alive, which makes playing the game an intrinsically rewarding experience, especially for people with Attention Deficit/Hyperactivity Disorder (ADHD) . The mere fact that a game has twitch is not necessarily reason to be alarmed, but when combined with a dumbed down approach to the mechanic, level grinding, and online social guilds, it can be the *hook* that gets the other addictive pieces to sink in.

Addictive Gaming Mechanic #3: Guilds and Leagues

Humans, even introverted ones, have social needs, and therefore are socially motivated. As games have moved online, they have explored various ways of tying social connections into the gameplay experience. Two major ways of doing this are creating leagues, in which gamers enter tiers of competition against each other, and guilds, in which gamers team up to achieve common goals.

The evolution of the culture surrounding guilds in online games has been fascinating to watch. They tend to mirror the organizational dynamics of things like mob families, gangs, or even cults. Groupthink tends to run fairly rampant, and there are often strong hierarchies in social structure. Guilds create and demand a strong sense of social obligation to attend guild activities and raids, and failure to do so can lead to expulsion from the guild. Expulsion feels catastrophic to the expelled gamer, since many online role-playing games cannot be effectively played without being a member of a guild. I have worked with a number of clients who were so devastated by what *banishment* from a guild meant for their social identity in the game that when it happened to them, they attempted to commit suicide in real life. In the guild, it does not matter if it is 2:00 am in the morning for you—if your guild needs you, then you must respond.

The nature of guilds in online games makes it extremely difficult—perhaps nearly impossible—to play a game in a moderate, reasonable manner that can be fit within the *golden mean* of one to three hours of total screen time per day. The average amount of time a person who plays as a guild in a massive multiplayer online role-playing game (MMORPG) is 25 h per week (Griffiths et al. 2004; Smahel et al. 2008). Guild membership and activities become a competing set of priorities for many players of such online games, and I frequently observe that it becomes gamers' predominant priority, hence the growth in the phenomenon known as World of Warcraft Widows or Game Widows. These people describe the degree of their gaming spouse or significant other's emotional and physical unavailability due to their gaming habits to be tantamount to them having an affair or even being dead, and have been observed to go through the same grieving process as people who have lost a spouse through infidelity or death (Benedetti 2007). The phenomenon of Game Widows has become so widespread that they even have online support groups, such as gamerwidow.com.

Leagues, on the other hand, operate quite differently but exert no less of a social pull. One of the predominant examples of leagues in games is the *StarCraft* series. *StarCraft II* features seven hierarchical leagues, each with various divisions, as well as a practice league for newcomers to the multiplayer component of the game. Novices may play up to 50 practice matches in the practice league before they must face evaluation in the form of placement matches. After competing in five official placement matches, players are assigned to a league that fits their current skill level. However, regardless of how brilliantly a new player performs, they must work their way through the various leagues in order to reach the pinnacle Grandmaster League, which is limited to the top 200 players in each region. A player's position in a league and division determines the matches they will be able to compete in. The matchmaking algorithm is designed to give each player an approximately 50% chance of winning each match. To keep players fully engaged, the matchmaking algorithm is also set to *decay*; if a player does not complete any matches in a two week period, their ranking and status will gradually decrease (Liquipedia 2014).

To add further incentive, highly accomplished StarCraft II players become international online celebrities and receive all of the trappings and attention that come along with fame. Aspiring StarCraft contenders are known to spend countless hours studying the gameplay video of highly accomplished gamers, to the point that an excellent StarCraft player can profit considerably from advertisers posting ads on the videos they place online.

This hearkens back to the way a casino works. One slot machine has addictive qualities, but put a thousand of them together in a room so each player can hear when one of them goes off, and those addictive qualities are amplified. Similarly, leagues provide tremendous rewards, both in a sense of accomplishment, status, social recognition, and even fame and money. However, they only provide those rewards for a very small percentage of the people involved. Nonetheless, because some people are getting huge pay offs that are prominently displayed to the whole gaming community, this incentivizes other players to sacrifice and strive to be among the few, the proud, the ones the *gaming gods* smile down upon. To climb the ladder, however, members of leagues must never stop. Besides the decay built into their rating if they do not constantly play, all of the other members of the leagues are constantly working to improve. Thus, trying to play moderately as a part of an online league is a significant challenge. If you are less excessive and obsessive than your competition, you will be left in the dust and remain a mere pawn in the social realm of the leagues. Other games with highly competitive leagues that adhere to the same general dynamic include *DOTA 2, Counter Strike,* and *League of Legends.*

Although many parents comfort themselves about their child's excessive video game time by saying, "At least he or she is being social by playing with other kids on the internet", the online, social element of games—especially when guilds, leagues, or other similar dynamics are at play—frequently contain mechanics that actually significantly increase the addictive potential of a game (Leung 2004; Blinka and Smahel 2011). The addictive potential of the online multiplayer aspects of games appears to be particularly influential when people feel they are more respected, valued, and important in their online gaming group than they do in their lives offline (Smahel 2008).

Addictive Gaming Mechanic #4: Social Status and Achievements

Guilds and leagues are not the only ways in which social status is worked into gamers' experiences. Gaming hubs like *Steam* and *Xbox Live* have found ways to link players together in communities, even when they are not actively playing together online. This is often done in the form of ranking systems based on achievements each player has made in the games they are playing. Achievements can range from predictable tasks such as reaching a certain number of kills to random, mundane events like "I bounced a rock off a rooftop and down a chimney," or "I fell in the water 40 times". Some achievements are known ahead of time and placed as goals for players to strive for, and some are hidden, left to be stumbled upon by accident or by hours of endless experimentation to find hidden achievements. Achievements are used to encourage people to continue playing a game long after the game itself has run out of real content.

These achievements are then publicly tracked and displayed on gaming hubs and are considered a sort of status symbol among gamers. People who are particularly good at chalking up achievements can even become celebrities of a sort. One's prowess based on the achievements they have racked up is often referred to as a gamer's *e-penis*, and it is made larger by playing more games and unlocking more achievements. Additionally, accomplishing achievements often unlocks rewards, such as new levels and items. As a result, many gamers persist in trying to complete achievements, even when they find the achievements unenjoyable. Some gamers report that trying to unlock achievements can become a source of obsession all by itself (Gidari 2013).

Addictive Gaming Mechanic #5: Fantasy Alter Egos

Escapism is not inherently harmful, nor should escapism be seen as something that is unique to video games. Escapism can also be found in stories, music, movies, and other forms of media. Fantasy can and does play a role in healthy lives. It can stimulate the mind to think more creatively. Fantasy play serves a role in the mental, social, and moral development of children. We can find relief and refreshment by connecting for a time with something that is separate from our own life.

On the other hand, when distraction becomes life and life becomes merely a distraction, people begin to fall into a rut in which their real lives begin to atrophy. As important things in their lives decline, they feel a greater need for escapism and bury themselves in it more deeply, wrapping it around them more tightly so as not to let the decay of their real lives perturb them while they are in their fanciful cocoons. Many people who use escapism as an attempted coping skill find that video games are a powerful tool for enhancing and experiencing their fantasy world. Thus, they have the potential to increase both the benefits and the pitfalls of escapism.

Some video games provide players with the ability to assume a predesigned role. Other video games allow players to carefully craft their own character, determining their appearance, characteristics, abilities, allegiances, and so forth. This provides an interesting set of possibilities. Gamers can shape their character to be a sort of virtual compensation for the things they are not, but wish they were. Gamers can try personas entirely different from their own. They can also play out fantasies of being the object of their own desire. All of these options provide numerous possibilities for psychological entanglement, for the game to become more than just a game for the gamer, but an arena in which they are playing out important or vulnerable parts of their own psyche in a way that feels less threatening. There is potential for benefit from this kind of exploration, like a sort of psychodrama being played out in a digital realm with transference, projection, and all manner of subconscious dynamics at play. On the other hand, it can easily become a tool to enhance the debilitating psychological defense mechanisms of displacement or fantasy formation, in which a person only dabbles with their own thoughts and emotions in the safety of fantasy and neglects taking healthy actions in their actual lives (Blinka and Smahel 2011; Turkle 1997; Wolvendale 2006).

People with lower self-esteem and self-efficacy are more vulnerable to developing an addictive relationship with the gaming mechanic of fantasy identities and avatars (Bessiere et al. 2007; Wan and Chiou 2006; Smahel 2008). My clinical experience and informal qualitative analysis indicates that the deeper someone gets into fantasy elements of gaming and the more emotionally and mentally aligned he or she becomes with his or her gaming alter egos—including the degree to which the alter ego is compensatory to any perceived personal flaws—the greater the addictive potential is of a specific game, or any game that the person interacts with in the same manner. Thus, part of learning to have a healthy relationship with video games requires finding real world ways of dealing with our thoughts and emotions besides just taking a break from them through fantasies.

Addictive Gaming Mechanic #6: Long Gaming Epochs and Persistent Universes

A *gaming epoch* refers to the amount of time needed to play before the *status quo* changes from the beginning of a particular gaming episode. One can begin to measure the length of a specific game's epoch by determining how much game time is required before the player is better off than when they started and reaches some sort of satisfactory point of achievement that could reasonably feel like a good place to end a gaming session.

An example of a game with short gaming epochs is *Rogue Legacy*. In this game, a player can select a character, venture into the dungeon, collect gold, die, and pass on their gold to the next character to be used to buy new equipment and abilities in gaming spurts ranging from a few seconds to a few minutes. In Rogue Legacy, an epoch is typically the length of a single *life*. While completing the whole game takes time, a player experiencing one or several epochs will have more of a sense of fulfillment and is less likely to feel like they have been cut off *right in the middle*, before they have been able to complete what they started off to experience. With Rogue Legacy, a player could possibly experience 10, 20, perhaps even 30, or more epochs in an hour of play. Additionally, Rogue Legacy has a finite universe.

On the other hand, the game *Planetside 2* has very long gaming epochs. This online, massively scaled multiplayer first person shooter creates a real time, constantly evolving battlefield. Individual battles can stretch on for days, even weeks. So, the gaming epochs in this game tend to be very long. And, of course, Planetside 2 has a persistent gaming universe, combined with twitch gaming, guilds, social status markers, and fantasy identity elements. As you can see, Planetside 2 is stacked pretty heavily with the addictive gaming mechanics we have discussed to this point.

Games that have a feature that allows the player to save at any time allow the player to artificially shorten gaming epochs. If the player has to save midgame, they may not have completed their goal, but they have also not lost their progress. Thus, their game time was not as satisfying as if they had completed a natural epoch, but it is also not as frustrating as if they had been stopped short of an epoch and thus had lost all of their progress. It has been my experience that people are more likely to play excessively beyond reasonable time constraints (and thus end up missing things like school, work, important family events, and so forth) for games that have long gaming epochs, persistent universes, or both. Therefore, gamers who are engrossed in these types of games are more likely to devolve into pathological patterns of gaming.

Game universes can either be finite or persistent. A finite gaming universe is one that is only active when the game is turned on, and stops progressing in time, plot, and action when the game is turned off. Persistent gaming universes are always on and progressing, regardless of whether the gamer is playing or not. Whereas Mario does not either save the princess or die trying while you are away at work and not playing *Super Mario Galaxy 2*, the world and characters of Planetside 2 and World of Warcraft continue to play on while you are away. By definition, all massive multiplayer online games have persistent universes. With a persistent universe, if you are not there, you literally miss out. Incidentally, this is one of the dynamics that makes social media more addictive: the content of social media continues to evolve when the user is not engaged with it, and they can have a nagging sense that they are *missing out* by not checking in. In a game with a persistent online world, you are actually worse off by not playing—rather than just no better off—because you have fallen behind the development of the gaming world. Persistent universes can cause a sort of *negative gaming epoch* that creates a sense of deficit that the player then feels a need to make up for the next time they play.

Blinka and Smahel (2011) observe,

> This world [of Massively Multiplayer Online games] is consistently in development, disregarding the presence [or absence] of the player, which in a certain sense pressures the player to stay in touch with the virtual world. If players are absent for a longer period of time, they become out of touch with the virtual world and loser their influence and power to affect the world. The player also loses power compared to fellow players who are playing more often and advancing faster (p. 74).

Furthermore, MMORPGs progress in such a way that makes old achievements and equipment obsolete over time, so if gamers do not continue to play and progress, they actually lose ground. Games that require long hours of investment to overcome the status quo and to keep up with an ever evolving gaming world thus hold significant pull toward players to engage in excessive or addictive patterns of gaming.

Addictive Gaming Mechanic #7: Interrupted Flow

The concept of flow in psychology was first put forth by Csikszentmihalyi (1997). Flow is a state reached when a person becomes completely absorbed in an activity in a way that leads to a sense of heightened vitality, awareness, and fulfillment. It is a highly rewarding, resonating state that people experience through many avenues like sports, education, work, service, and meaningful relationships. Flow experiences carry with them common factors, though not all of them need to be present to qualify as a flow experience. These include (Cherry 2014):

1. Having clear goals that are challenging, yet are still attainable.
2. Requiring strong concentration and focused attention.
3. Having aspects of the activity that feel intrinsically rewarding.
4. Providing a sense of serenity, and/or a loss of feelings of self-consciousness. This can be a very anxiety relieving experience.
5. Creating a sense of timelessness or a distorted sense of time. The person feels so focused on the present that they lose track of time passing.
6. Receiving immediate feedback from the experience.

7. Knowing that the task is doable but requires a significant amount of skill and effort.
8. Providing feelings of personal control over the situation and the outcome.
9. Creating a lack of awareness of physical needs. A person feels like they could continue without the need to sleep, eat, etc.
10. The experience allows for a complete focus on the activity itself.

Gamers frequently report experiencing flow in video games, and as a result they experience difficulty tracking their time playing the game due to the time dilation phenomenon in flow experiences (Rau et al. 2006). They also experience greater difficulty disengaging from the game due to the compelling emotional and physiological experience of flow (Rau et al. 2006). A thoughtful game designer can engineer a game so that a gamer is just entering their state of flow when the game is interrupted and the gamer is required to do something to reengage the flow experience. At that point in time, the gamer is highly physiologically and psychologically motivated to do what it takes to get back to that state of flow, which means they are much more likely to be willing to pay in some way in order to continue their flow experience, often in the form of micro-transactions and in-game purchases. The power of interrupted flow is evidenced by the fact that gamers spent $352 million on in-game purchases in console games (Richmond 2014b) and $2.8 billion on micro-transactions in PC games in 2013 alone (Richmond 2014a). Similarly, in just the month of January 2015, users of Apple's App Store spent nearly half a billion dollars on apps and in-app purchases (Kosner 2015). Clearly, flow interruption is an economically compelling form of psychological manipulation and behavioral modification.

A prime example of how flow interruption for monetary gain is done is *Candy Crush Saga*. The game itself is fairly straightforward. Its goals are clear and simplistic, and it provides an achievable challenge. Many people experience a sense of timelessness and loss of self-consciousness while they play it. Candy Crush Saga only allows gamers a set number of tries and failures on a specific level before the gamer must either wait a set amount of time to play again, invite other people to play, or pay to continue. In this way, the game designers have learned to interrupt flow at the most jarring, irritating moment, thus providing incentive for the gamer to either pay to continue, which means more money for the developers, or try to recruit others to the game (via Facebook invitations, for example), which also generates more money for the developers. The cost seems relatively small and worth the effort to the gamer in order to get immediately back to their flow experience. And yet, by the artful use of this psychologically manipulative mechanic, Candy Crush Saga has managed to make so much money that its value at the time of its sale to Activision Blizzard was almost two billion dollars more than the monetary value of the entire *Star Wars* franchise at the time of its sale to the Disney corporation (Morris 2015).

With financial results like that, there is little wonder that this mechanic seems to have become the norm for mobile apps and games. It gets people to pay to continue to play. I have also observed that another, sort of backwards way of going about this is creating *free* games that include intrusive in-game ads. These ads pop up intermittently and interrupt the flow experience. The game then innocently mentions that if the gamers pay a certain amount of money, they no longer have adds intrude upon their flow experience. Overall, by creating the sensation of flow, game developers increase the psychological appeal of the games, and by strategically interrupting flow at critical points, these games produce impulsive and compulsive behavior from game players, which plays an influential role in the development of excessive, obsessive, or addictive patterns of video game playing.

Addictive Gaming Mechanic #8: Infinity

A game's storyline and mission objectives help create a desire to play more. A well-crafted game can be like a well written book, with pacing, tension, plot development, unfolding game elements, and drama weaved skillfully together to create an almost hypnotic influence over the gamer to find out what happens on the next page or after the next gaming epoch. Just as the most natural place to stop reading a book is at the end, the most natural time to stop playing a game is when you reach its completion. After all, it is the end; there is nothing left to be played. By that point in time the objectives have been achieved, the story arch has been completed (or a setup has been made for a sequel), and there is a sense of satisfaction and *coming full circle* that accompanies reaching the end. However, what happens if the game literally has no end? Many games now use open ended, sandbox style gameplay to create games that literally have no end. I have come to refer to this gaming mechanic as *infinity*.

Sandbox gameplay typically provides an open world setting, allowing the player freedom to roam and interact with various parts of the world as they please (Rogers 2014). Some sandbox style games have no real story or plot; they merely create a world and turn the player loose on it. Others provide a main storyline, usually consisting of specific mission objectives or a series of progressive quests or missions that a player can choose to engage in or ignore, as he or she pleases. But, even when the actual plot has come to a finish, the gamer still has full access to the gaming world and can continue playing the game with goals of his or her choosing. Many developers will periodically release expansions (often in the form of DLC, or *downloadable content*) that a player can purchase, adding additional quests, missions, characters, options, or areas in the gaming world. A savvy developer can keep a gamer playing and paying while putting a relatively small amount of work into periodic DLC expansions, thus helping make the developer's business more sustainable in the piracy-drenched environment in which they are trying to make a living.

Infinity is frequently combined with persistent online universes, level grinding, and multiplayer guilds or leagues, providing a gaming experience wherein the gamer is incentivized to play frequently and for extended periods of time to invest in leveling up and being prepared for the next iteration of the game as it expands and to avoid becoming an easy target for everyone else who immerses themselves in the infinity of the game.

Implications

Not all video games have the same degree of addictive potential. Therefore, it is incorrect to lump them all together in the same category. The addictive potential of each video game is a function of the interaction between the specific mechanics of a specific video game (i.e., Gentile 2011) and the individual biological, psychological, and social makeup of a specific human being (i.e., Bessiere et al. 2007; Wan and Chiou 2006; Smahel 2008). While there is a great deal of individualization in the risk each person has to being addicted to specific games, there are also sufficient commonalities between human beings and also within various types of games for certain guidelines to be generally applicable.

Process Addiction and the Biopsychosocial-cyber Interface

The author's informal qualitative analysis, combined with my clinical experience, indicates that the greater the number of addictive gaming mechanics a specific game includes and the greater the magnitude of each of those mechanics, the greater degree of addictive potential that specific video game has. However, it should be noted that for these mechanics to have an effect of increasing addictive potential, the gamer in question has to actively engage with those mechanics. The mere fact that a game contains the dynamics is not what has the effect; it is the gamer engaging with those mechanics that has the addictive effect. The addiction is the result of the biopsychosocial-cyber interface, the connection and intermingling of the pieces of the person and the pieces of the program. For example, a person playing StarCraft II can remove him or herself from two influential, addictive dynamics (i.e., leagues, social status and achievements) by simply not engaging in multiplayer, therefore giving themselves more control over other addictive dynamics based on how they choose to interact with the game (i.e., Lemments and Hendriks 2016). They can artificially shorten gaming epochs by saving at any time, an option which is not available when playing online. They can also reduce social pressure by being able to play when it fits their life, rather than having to shape their life to be able to play when matches are scheduled.

Furthermore, they can use the ability to save at any time without losing progress in the game to manage the intensity of interrupted flow. This ability does not eliminate the sensation of interrupted flow, but it reduces its intensity by not penalizing the player for not continuing to play at any specific moment. A gamer can also have longer gaps between playing sessions without feeling like they are falling behind relative to the other members of the league. The addictive potential of StarCraft II is different for an individual based on whether they play single player, in casual multiplayer matches with friends or family members, or as a part of the competitive StarCraft II leagues. Therefore, a person can help mitigate the addictive potential of StarCraft II by how they choose to play it.

On the other hand, some games are constructed in such a way that a person cannot really play them without engaging in all of the addictive mechanics. One example of this is World of Warcraft. By its very nature, the game is infused with the mechanic of infinity and includes a persistent online universe. Interrupted flow is virtually inevitable as the game itself will always continue when a player logs off. The game plays without the gamer, it does not *ramp down* as an individual's gaming session does, and therefore the separation is always going to be somewhat jarring. Fantasy identity is at the core of a player's experience with the game. The gameplay itself is entirely structured upon level grinding, and therefore one cannot play World of Warcraft without subjecting oneself to an extensive intermittent reinforcement pattern, with its accompanying addictive qualities. Leveling up takes a lot of time and investment, and this necessitates long gaming epochs. These long gaming epochs of leveling up help prepare a player for guild raids, which only compound the issue of long gaming epochs, given that it is not uncommon for a single raid to last three or more hours, depending on the raid objectives. Social status is heavily tied in with a player's level and affiliations. One has to structure his or her life to be present for guild activities.

When we take all of these factors into consideration, there is not really a practical way to play World of Warcraft that significantly reduces its addictive potential. The structure of World of Warcraft makes all of its addictive mechanics inseparable from the experience of playing the game on any level. Therefore, the only move a person can really make to reduce his or her risk of addiction, or at very least an unbalanced, excessive, or otherwise unhealthy relationship with the game, is not to play the game.

There is likely no such thing as a game with absolutely no addictive potential. Therefore, all games merit a degree of thoughtfulness in how they are played. But, to fully evaluate the addictive potential of a game, an individual must to do more than understand the way the game is put together; they also have to understand how they themselves are put together. Any number of things about any given individual could make them more vulnerable to certain mechanics. For example, many people with ADHD resonate very powerfully to the gaming mechanic of twitch, but are turned off by the gaming mechanic of level grinding. Therefore, they are more likely to get addicted to high twitch games, such as the Call of Duty series. On the other hand, many people with Autism Spectrum Disorders resonate powerfully to the level grinding mechanic, but their greater difficulty with fine motor coordination makes twitch less of a *fit* for the way they are put together neurologically. Thus, they are at lower risk for the twitch mechanics of Call of Duty, but are at higher risk for the level grinding mechanics of massive multiplayer online role-playing games or Minecraft. My clinical experience suggests that people who feel lonely or struggle with social connections are likely to be more vulnerable to fantasy identity, social status mechanics, and guilds. Overall, our individual strengths and vulnerabilities, both neurologically and psychologically, help to determine our specific degree of vulnerability to the addictive nature of various gaming mechanics.

This fact can sometimes lead to surprising individual implications that can be hard to discern. Consider the following example of a popular retro game, *Wing*

Commander 3. Wing Commander 3 has no online element at all. It is a cinematic space flight simulator from the 90s and contains twitch gameplay and fantasy identity. The fantasy identity is fixed, as the player assumes the role of Colonel Christopher Blair. However, the player can shape Blair's relationships and fate through making various choices. Blair's wingmen are fleshed out with individual personalities and presented in a way to encourage the gamer to connect with them emotionally, so the game excels at creating some degree of emotional investment by the player. The game is divided into various missions, none of which are overly long, creating naturally short gaming epochs. There are no leagues or guilds, and the closest thing to social standing is a pilot's kill score. But, this is not automatically shared with anyone. To share it, the player would have to overtly tell someone what it is. Overall, Wing Commander 3 is pretty lightweight when it comes to the number and degree of addictive mechanics. The game contains no level grinding and is not built around a mechanic of infinity. On its own merits, the presence and intensity of addictive mechanics would indicate that Wing Commander 3 has a relatively low risk of addiction.

However, individual variations can create a situation where a person could form an addictive relationship with a game that only has low addictive potential. Consider the case of a hypothetical young adult male who has some difficulty with depression. He left home for college and is having a hard time connecting socially there. He is feeling lonely and depressed, and he is stressed out by his workload in his classes. Let us suppose that he starts to play Wing Commander 3 as a way to blow off steam. So far in this example there is no immediate cause for alarm, but there are some risks. By playing when he is depressed, he creates a sort of *slingshot* effect by elevating his crucial neurotransmitters from a low state to a high sate, and the greater the magnitude of the change, the more the brain is motivated to repeat the experience. The characters he interacts with are well portrayed, and he can feel like he is getting some social interaction (even romance) out of his game playing experience. The twitch mechanic helps generate an adrenaline rush and supply the brain with norepinephrine (Skosnik et al. 2000), which can lead him to feel like he is the most alive and vital when playing Wing Commander 3. As he turns to Wing Commander 3 more and more for his social needs and as a way to combat his depression, and as he reduces his efforts to meet those needs in other ways, he can create in himself a much higher risk of addiction from a low-risk game because his predispositions, his lifestyle, and approach to his mental health and wellbeing is high risk.

The addictive potential of a person's relationship with a video game can be conceptualized as the following equation: $f(g + p) = ap$, which indicates that the high-risk, addictive factors of the game (g) plus the person's individual vulnerabilities (p) multiplied by the degree of fit between addictive mechanics and the person's specific vulnerabilities (f) equals the addictive or otherwise pathological potential of the interface between the person and the game (ap). Therefore, a person with less effective self-care and higher personal risk factors can develop an addictive relationship with a relatively low-risk game.

Having a healthy relationship with video games is about much more than limiting screen time, as indispensable a strategy as that may be. It is also about more than making strategic choices about what types of games to play and minimizing exposure to addictive gaming mechanics. First and foremost, having a healthy relationship with video games is about effective, adaptive self-care. To the degree that people are not creating and following purpose in their lives, developing and abiding by a code of ethics and values, building and maintaining good relationships, making meaningful contributions, stimulating and expanding their minds, taking care of their bodies, and engaging in other wholesome and effective forms of recreation, they increase their risk of forming any addiction, including a process addiction to video games. Who people are—their strengths, weaknesses, mindset, and approach to life—is an indispensable part of the equation of both health and addiction. If one finds he or she is struggling with an excessive, obsessive, or addictive relationship with video games, there is a need to step back and examine how well he or she is doing with self-care in all of the areas previously mentioned.

While a process addiction to video games is a problem in and of itself, it often also serves as a signal to call attention to other important needs that should be taken care of in oneself, one's relationships, and one's life. People neglect this call at their own peril, and failing to heed its warnings and attend to the matters it illuminates will make efforts to have a healthier relationship with the cyberworld extremely difficult, prone to constant relapses, and merely superficial improvements.

Strategies

Given that the addictive potential of each video game is a function of the interaction between the specific mechanics of a specific video game, and the individual biological, psychological, and social makeup of a specific human being, there is a significant amount of individual variation on the specific skills and strategies that a clinician, a student, and his or her family can employ to help the student develop a healthy, sustainable relationship with digital technology. That being said, there are a number of strategies that I have found in my clinical experience to be fairly universally applicable.

Time Limits

Time limits by themselves are an insufficient intervention for a person who has developed an excessive, obsessive, or addictive relationship with digital technology. That being said, they are an indispensable part of the overall strategy. The question is then what these time limits should be. There is some variation in what various professionals recommend, but in general the *golden zone* of video games having benefits without significant negative side effects appears to be somewhere between one and three hours per day of total recreational screen time, which includes all use of screens outside of work- or school-related purposes (i.e., American Academy of Pediatrics 2014; Anderson 2015; Cell Press 2013; Gentile 2009; Hoang et al. 2016; University of Texas Medical Branch at Galveston 2012).

Limiting Tech Locations

The near-ubiquitous nature of mobile technology, including smartphones and mobile gaming systems, makes it difficult to regulate technology usage because games, social media, , and the Internet can now literally be always at hand. My clinical experience indicates that people who try to abide by technology time limits, but still try to *nibble* and *graze* at their recreational technology a few minutes at a time as they go about their day are often unsuccessful. It can help to designate a specific time and place for recreational screen time use, and then limit recreational technology use to those specific times and places. It can also be helpful to treat mobile gaming devices as if they were not mobile, and use them only in a designated gaming area.

Limiting Tech Space

Smartphones and mobile gaming platforms allow video games, social media, and Internet to exist anywhere and anytime. This increases the risk of tech becoming intrusive and of people becoming obsessive, mindless consumers of technology. It is helpful to create specific tech-free zones, such as the table during family meals, during family gatherings, in bedrooms (with a special emphasis on not using digital technology in bed), and so forth. I have also found it useful to designate *techno-Sabbaths*, or days in which you refrain from using digital technology for recreational purposes. In general, I would recommend having at least one of these per month, but I would encourage people to consider having one of these per week.

In tech-free zones and during techno-Sabbaths, it is important to not simply mope around, languishing in a technology-free desert of boredom and discouragement, merely waiting for time to pass until digital technology is *legal* to use again. Rather, it is important to use this time to actively engage in other forms of activity, stimulation, communication, and recreation. This helps make tech-free zones a rewarding experience and helps people keep a fresh perspective on why they are trying to have healthy, sustainable limits, boundaries, and standards in their use of digital technology. I have also found that it helps improve people's success rates in shifting from using technology to engaging in other activities days and in times when digital technology is legal to use.

Communicating Intentions

The immediacy of digital technology is part of what makes it convenient and useful. However, culturally we have built up an expectation that we will respond to texts, updates, and notifications instantly, and not doing so can be considered rude. Therefore, when people try to set boundaries around how often they will check and respond to emails, texts, and messages, they often find this places a strain on their relationships with other people who try to contact them digitally.

Therefore, an important part of a strategy for creating a sustainable, nonintrusive relationship with digital communication devices is to have clients communicate their intentions to the people who will try to contact them digitally. It can help to inform their friends and family that they are trying to make their phone less intrusive in their life, and that they will only be checking it every hour or two, and then only for about five to ten minutes at a time. This helps to manage other people's expectations that clients will respond immediately to texts and messages, and often can result in people offering social support for the goal of reducing smartphone usage.

Using Tech Time Tetris

When people use digital technology without time limits, they tend to use it indiscriminately, without really discerning which digital experiences they have are merely stimulating, rather than being compelling and satisfying, and without prioritizing their media use based on this discernment. However, once they have committed to healthy boundaries of space and time regarding digital media usage, people often encounter challenges with figuring out how to make their technology use fit within the time limits while still having a satisfying experience with their digital media. When people have an unsatisfactory experience with their tech time, they are more likely to struggle with maintaining boundaries.

I have developed a strategy which I refer to as *Tech Time Tetris*. The objective of Tech Time Tetris is to help clients have a fun and satisfying experience with digital media within healthy time limits and in the context of a balanced life. To accomplish this, the person must figure out how to arrange their tech time in a way that it is compelling and entertaining, but which allows them to stop in time and successfully transition into other activities.

For those unfamiliar with the game *Tetris*, it is one of the most popular video games of all time. It is a puzzle game that involves a randomized assortment of four-tiled shapes falling from the top of the screen. The player is tasked with rotating the pieces to make them fit in complete lines. When the player makes a complete line, it disappears. But, if the player does not clear lines, the pieces eventually stack up to the top of the screen and the player loses.

Tech Time Tetris approaches time and content management of screen time as if it were a game of Tetris. The *rules* of Tech Time Tetris are:

1. The person must keep their total screen time within the time limit.
2. The person must have fun.
3. The person must be able to walk away feeling like they had a satisfying experience.
4. When they are done, the person must be able to shift their time and attention to other things.
5. When they are not playing, the person cannot just wait around for tech time to arrive again.

Managing tech time so it is both fun and balanced can be a lot like playing Tetris. For example:

1. There is a limited amount of space a person can fill. So, people have to get creative and strategic about how to make the pieces fit.
2. If people do not plan ahead strategically, it can be very easy to let the pieces stack up in a way that does not work and lose the game.
3. Sometimes a piece would not fit if the player has it turned one direction, but if they turn it another way, they can make it fit.
4. When people strategize well, they can have a lot of fun and win the game.

Managing tech time also differs from the game of Tetris in several important ways, including:

1. Unlike Tetris, not all *tech time* items are the same size. For example, it only takes about five minutes to play a round of Rogue Legacy, but the average length of time of a World of Warcraft raid is four hours. Given that the research indicates that a healthy amount of screen time is usually between one and three hours per day, there is no way to make a four-hour gaming experience that cannot be saved part way through fit into the equation.
2. Unlike Tetris, some combinations of gaming mechanics have the potential to *hypnotize* people and make them obsess over the game, thus distracting them from the Tech Time Tetris' objectives of trying to make things fit within the time limits.

There are some individual variations in how people can achieve all five of these objectives. That being said, there are some strategies that tend to be helpful for most people.

1. Whenever possible, pick games that can be saved at any time, rather than having to reach checkpoints or finish rounds.
2. Refrain from playing games with lots of addictive gaming mechanics, or a high intensity of a single addictive gaming mechanic.
3. Be especially mindful of not engaging in games built around the gaming mechanics for which an individual is particularly vulnerable.

4. If the person is playing a round or mission-based game, they should try to pick ones in which they can play at least two rounds within the time limit. For example, if a person has an hour to play, and the average mission on a specific game takes 15–20 min to complete, they could conceivably fit between two and four missions in a playing session. So, even if they only manage to pass one of the missions, they will have had the experience of feeling like they accomplished something and progressed in the game.

5. If an average round takes 15–25 min to play and the person only have 15 min left, they should not try to start another round, since they will likely exceed the time limit. They should choose another tech activity to do with the final 15 min.

6. Clients should allot less tech time on week days then on weekends.

7. On weekends when they have more tech time, it is helpful not to use it all in one block of time. If they have two hours, they should consider breaking it into two one-hour blocks. If they have three hours, they should consider breaking it into two hour-and-a-half long blocks.

8. Every 15–20 min of playing, people should take a break to get up and stretch. This reduces the stress on their body from remaining in a sitting position and also helps prevent them from getting lost in a hypnotic, timeless state.

9. It is helpful to have more than one game that a person is playing at a time, rather than playing a single game exclusively. If they have one game with long mission/round turns, it is helpful to also have a second game with short rounds/turns. That way, if they cannot fit in another round of their longer game, but still have some extra time, they can still play the shorter game with less of a chance of going over the limits.

10. If a person has a portable gaming system, avoid carrying it around with them. If they do, they will be tempted to turn to tech whenever they have an empty moment. Treat portable gaming systems as if they were not portable.

11. People should not use tech time first thing in the morning or as the last thing they do before you go to sleep. They should avoid screen use in the last 45–60 min before going to bed.

12. Whenever possible, play multiplayer games with friends in person rather than over the Internet.

13. When tech time is over, it is over. People's other recreational activities need to be about something other than video games, so spending hours poring over game manuals or planning out gaming strategies does not really count as working on balance.

Conclusion

As clinicians and clients increase their awareness of video game mechanics and how they interact with individual biopsychosocial vulnerabilities, they gain the ability to make informed decisions that facilitate the creation of a sustainable relationship with video games and other forms of digital entertainment. Utilizing a strategy that intentionally reduces and restructures a client's exposure to addictive video game mechanics–especially those to which they have higher levels of personal vulnerability—in combination with developing coping skills and strategies to strengthen clients in their areas of biopsychosocial difficulty can be an effective approach to overcoming excessive, obsessive, and addictive patterns of video game usage.

For clinicians practicing in a residential setting, collecting a client's video game history and exploring specific mechanics included in the games they used problematically can shed light on clients' specific areas of vulnerability. This information can be used to guide the creation of the treatment plan, and can also be helpful in strategically selecting media to include, media to avoid, and guidelines for media usage when conducting the process of carefully reintroducing technology into the client's life (see Chap. 5).

References

American Academy of Pediatrics. (2014). *Media and children*. Retrieved from http://www.aap.org/en-us/advocacy-and-policy/aap-health-initiatives/Pages/Media-and-Children.aspx

Anderson, R. J. (2015). *Navigating the cyberscape: Evaluating and improving our relationship with smartphones, social media, video games, and the internet*. Orem, UT: Author.

Benedetti, W. (2007). Game widows grieve "lost" spouses. *NBC News*. Retrieved from http://www.nbcnews.com/id/20397322/ns/technology_and_science-games/t/game-widows-grieve-lost-spouses/#.VHX6y9LF-So

Bessiere, K., Seay, F. A., & Kiesler, S. (2007). The ideal elf: Identity exploration in world of warcraft. *CyberPsychology & Behavior, 10*(4), 530–535.

Blinka, L., & Smahel, D. (2011). Addiction to online role-playing games. In K. S. Young & C. N. Abreu (Eds.), *Internet addiction: A handbook and guide to evaluation and treatment* (pp. 73–90). Hoboken, NJ: John Wiley and Sons.

Cell Press. (2013). Action video games boost reading skills, study of children with dyslexia suggests. *Science Daily*. Retrieved from http://www.sciencedaily.com/releases/2013/02/130228124132.htm

Cherry, K. (2014). *What is flow? Understanding the psychology of flow*. About.com. Retrieved from http://psychology.about.com/od/PositivePsychology/a/flow.htm

Csikszentmihalyi, M. (1997). *Finding flow: The psychology of engagement with everyday life*. New York: Basic Books.

Gentile, D. (2009). Pathological video game use among youth ages 8 to 18: A national study. *Psychological Science, 20*(5), 594–602.

Gentile, D. A. (2011). The multiple dimensions of video game effects. *Child Development Perspectives, 5*(2), 75–81.

Gidari, C. (2013). Achievements have ruined how I play games. *Kotaku*. Retrieved from http://kotaku.com/achievements-have-ruined-how-i-play-games-510597650

Griffiths, M., Davies, M. N. O., & Chappell, D. (2004). Online computer gaming: A comparison of adolescent and adult gamers. *Journal of Adolescence, 27*(1), 87–96.

Hoang, T. D., Reis, J., Zhu, N., Jacobs, D. R., Launer, L. J., Whitmer, R. A., et al. (2016). Effect of early adult patterns of physical activity and television viewing on midlife cognitive function. *JAMA Psychiatry, 73*(1), 73–79.

Janssen, C. (2014). Grinding. *Technopedia*. Retrieved from http://www.techopedia.com/definition/27527/grinding

Jenkins, D. (2014). How microtransactions conquered the video game industry. *Metro*. Retrieved from http://metro.co.uk/2014/01/28/like-taking-sweets-from-a-gamer-the-numbers-behind-the-hugely-popular-apps-4279836/

Kosner, A. W. (2015). Apple app store revenue surge and the rise of freemium app pricing. *Forbes*. Retrieved from http://www.forbes.com/sites/anthonykosner/2015/01/11/apple-app-store-revenue-surge-and-the-rise-of-the-freemium/

Lemments, J. S., & Hendriks, S. J. F. (2016). Addictive online games: Examining the relationship between game genres and internet gaming disorder. *Cyberpsychology, Behavior, & Social Networking, 19*(4), 270–276.

Leung, L. (2004). Net-generation attributes and seductive properties of the internet of predictors of online activities and internet addiction. *CyberPsychology & Behavior, 7*(3), 333–348.

Liquipedia. (2014). *Battle.net leagues*. Retrieved from http://wiki.teamliquid.net/starcraft2/Battle.net_Leagues

Maer, M. L., & Braskamp, L. A. (1986). *The motivation factor: A theory of personal investment*. Lanham, MD: Lexington Books/DC Health and Com.

Miltenberger, R. (2011). *Behavior modification: Principles and procedures*. Boston: Cengage Learning.

Morris, C. (2015). Is "candy crush" really worth more than "star wars?" *CNBC*. Retrieved from http://www.cnbc.com/2015/11/03/is-candy-crush-really-worth-more-than-star-wars.html

Oxford, T. (2010). The truth about PC game piracy: The figures, the excuses and justifications examined. *Tech Radar*. Retrieved from http://www.techradar.com/news/gaming/the-truth-about-pc-game-piracy-688864/1#articleContent

Rau, P. L., Peng, S. Y., & Yang, C. C. (2006). Time distortion for expert and novice online game players. *CyberPsychology & Behavior, 9*(4), 396–403.

Richmond, B. (2014a). Free-to-play video games earned $2.8 billion last year. *Motherboard*. Retrieved from http://motherboard.vice.com/blog/free-to-play-video-games-earned-28-billion-last-year

Richmond, B. (2014b). Microtransactions are sucking console gamers dry, too. *Motherboard*. Retrieved from http://motherboard.vice.com/read/microtransactions-are-sucking-console-gamers-dry-too

Rogers, S. (2014). *Level up! The guide to great video game design*. Hoboken, NJ: John Wiley and Sons.

Skosnik, P., Chatterton, R., Swisher, T., & Park, S. (2000). Modulation of attentional inhibition by norepinephrine and cortisol after psychological stress. *International Journal of Psychophysiology, 36*, 59–68.

Smahel, D. (2008). Adolescents and young players of MMORPG games: Virtual communities as a form of social group. Paper presented at the XIth EARA conference. Retrieved from http://www.terapie.cz/smahelen

Smahel, D., Blinka, L., & Ledabyl, O. (2008). Playing MMORPGs: Connections between addiction and identifying with a character. *CyberPsychology & Behavior, 2008*(11), 480–490.

Turkle, S. (1997). *Life on the screen: Identity in the age of the Internet*. New York: Touchstone.

University of Texas Medical Branch at Galveston. (2012). Using skills gleaned from video games, high school and college students outmatch medical residents in surgical simulations. *Science Daily*. Retrieved from http://www.sciencedaily.com/releases/2012/11/121115141642.htm

Wan, C. S., & Chiou, W. B. (2006). Why are adolescents addicted to online gaming? An interview study in Taiwan. *CyberPsychology & Behavior, 9*(6), 762–766.

Wolvendale, J. (2006). My avatar, my self: Virtual harm and attachment. Paper presented at the Cyberspace 2005, Brno, Moravia.

Author Biography

Ryan Anderson, Ph.D., LMFT, MedFT received his B.S. degree in Marriage, Family, and Human Development and his M.S. degree in Marriage and Family Therapy from Brigham Young University. He received his Ph.D. in Medical Family Therapy from East Carolina University, and completed his internship at the Duke Comprehensive Cancer Center. He has worked as a family therapist in outpatient practice, in inpatient psychiatric settings, in cancer care, in several other medical settings, as a wilderness therapist and Assistant Clinical Director at Outback Therapeutic Expeditions, and as a therapist at Telos Residential Treatment. His teaching experience includes undergraduate university courses, first year medical students, and community outreach and education programs. He has also been a speaker at various conferences and continuing education events. He is one of the founders and the Clinical Director of Telos U.

Chapter 5
Family Therapy Implications of Electronic Addictions in Residential Treatment

Ryan Anderson

Chapter Highlights

- This chapter begins with identifying the criteria for Internet Gaming Disorder (IGD).
- This chapter details both quantitative and qualitative assessment measures for this disorder.
- Based on the information gained from the assessment, this chapter then discusses guidelines for family systems-based interventions for IGD in the context of residential treatment.
- Building upon the information in Chap. 4 of this text, this chapter then lays out strategies for re-integrating technology into the lives of people with IGD in a sustainable manner.
- Long-term success requires a good follow-up plan after discharge from residential treatment. This chapter ends with a discussion of long-term recovery and sustainability strategies.

Prevalence of Video Game Addictions

This chapter is designed to help clinicians operationalize the information presented in Chap. 4 as a part of a compressive plan for treating Internet Gaming Disorder (IGD) and other problematic forms of digital media usage in residential treatment. Although the fifth edition of the *Diagnostic and Statistical Manual of Mental Disorders* (DSM V) does not yet include Internet Gaming Disorder as an officially

R. Anderson (✉)
Telos RTC, 870 West Center Street, Orem, UT 84057, USA
e-mail: ryan@telosrtc.com

© Springer International Publishing AG 2017   71
J.D. Christenson and A.N. Merritts (eds.), *Family Therapy with Adolescents
in Residential Treatment*, Focused Issues in Family Therapy,
DOI 10.1007/978-3-319-51747-6_5

recognized diagnosis, it has been included as a *condition for further study* (American Psychiatric Association [APA] 2013). Current researchers of this subject have generally agreed upon a proposed set of criteria for Internet Gaming Disorder, which includes a person meeting five or more of the following descriptors over the course of a year:

1. Preoccupation or obsession with video games.
2. Withdrawal symptoms when not able to play video games, including anxiety, irritability, and sadness.
3. A buildup of tolerance, with the person needing to game more in order to reach similar levels of satisfaction.
4. Attempts to cut back or eliminate playing video games have failed.
5. The person has lost interest in other life activities, such as hobbies.
6. The person continues to play video games excessively, even with knowledge that they are disrupting the person's life.
7. The person has lied about the amount or extent of his or her gaming usage.
8. The person uses video games to relieve dysphoric moods.
9. The person has put other important life functions—such as work, school, relationships—at risk as a result of their pattern of gaming (APA 2013).

Problematic use of video games, including video game addictions, is a growing problem across the globe. South Korea is known as the *most wired* nation in the world, and therefore has had a tendency to lead out in trends of cyber issues. South Korean government sources report that approximately 10% of South Korean Internet users (equaling about 2 million people or roughly 4% of their total population) meet their government's definition for online gaming addicts, with a considerable portion of that number spending almost every waking moment playing games (McCurry 2010). A study from Norway revealed that 4.1% of gamers self-reported problematic video game use, but that 6% actually met the criteria for video game addiction (Mentzoni et al. 2011).

In the United States, researchers found that 8.5% of gamers between the ages of 8 and 18 exhibit pathological gaming behavior. Breaking the data down, the average boy gamer tended to clock about 16.4 h of gaming per week (averaging 2.3 h per day, assuming the person is playing 7 days per week), with the average girl getting in just over 9 h of gaming in a week (or approximately 1.2 h per day). The average person who met the criteria for pathological gaming or gaming addiction put in about 24 h per week, or about 3.4 h per day. Twenty-five percent of the surveyed gamers (not just those in the *addicted* category) reported turning to video games in an attempt to escape problems, and nearly as many said they played instead of doing homework. Similarly, 20% of all of the gamers in this study said that their schoolwork had suffered because of the time they spent gaming (Gentile 2009).

The leading author on this research, Dr. Douglas Gentile (2009), points out that gaming addiction is about more than just how much a person plays video games. Rather, a gaming addiction implies that a person's video game usage has become disruptive to their functioning. Although it is true that dysfunction is more likely to be found over a certain number of gaming hours per week, time spent playing is not a complete indicator of addiction. Problems can exist at fewer hours per week than the average of 24 h. In my own practice of working with people experiencing excessive, obsessive, and addictive patterns of gaming, I commonly see people who spend somewhere between 30 and 80 h per week gaming. My current *record holder* in my personal practice was averaging about 100 h per week.

This chapter will provide an overview of how process addictions to digital media, such as video games, smart phones, and the Internet, can be effectively treated in residential treatment. Guidelines for assessment and guiding principles for intervention will be delineated. The approach described here was developed as a result of discussions with other clinicians who treat the same presenting problem, a review of the general literature in the field, my own clinical experience, and the inductive application of a series of informal, unpublished qualitative research projects I have conducted over a number of years.

Assessment in Residential Treatment

Quantitative Screening and Assessment

While the phenomenon of clients reporting a process addiction to electronics as a presenting problem is becoming more common, many clients with electronics addictions do not report these difficulties as a reason for entering treatment. Rather, their chief complaints may be of depression, anxiety, Oppositional Defiant Disorder, Autism Spectrum Disorder, Attention-Deficit/Hyperactivity Disorder (ADHD), family conflict, or other common mental health issues. An excessive, obsessive, or addictive relationship with electronics often only becomes apparent later in the treatment process (Shapiro et al. 2000). These clients may be in active denial that their relationship with electronics has become unhealthy, or they may lack insight because many of their peers also have unhealthy relationships with digital media. As such, waiting for the client or family to self-report problems with digital media is ill advised. Rather, it can be helpful to begin with a general screening instrument, like the Internet Addiction Diagnostic Questionnaire (IADQ) (Young 1998), or the nine item version of the Internet Gaming Disorder Scale (IGD) (Lemmens et al. 2015). Clinicians who wish to have a little more depth in their screening instrument can also use the Internet Addiction Test (IAT), which was the first instrument to be internationally validated for detecting Internet and gaming addictions (Widyanto and McMurren 2004; Ferraro et al. 2007; Khazaal et al. 2008). Clinicians may also consider utilizing the Internet Process Addiction Test (ITAT) (Northrup et al. 2015), which builds upon the foundation of the IAT and adds a greater level of precision regarding different electronic activities.

Qualitative Assessment

In addition to a general quantitative assessment, a can provide rich information about a person's relationship with electronics, including the needs they have been trying to meet through their use of technology, their insight into problems they have with electronics, their current degree of motivation to change, and the way their relationship with electronics fits into the larger context of their lives. This information is useful for refining the assessment done with quantitative measures, but also provides a perspective that can guide the creation of an individualized treatment plan, identifying useful interventions and strategies for helping each individual client find a sustainable relationship with technology. General areas to inquire about include those delineated below.

How much screen time does the client have in the average day and week? Keep in mind that a client may not accurately report this number for one of two reasons. First, he or she may have developed a defense mechanism in which he or she under-reports the amount of time spent on electronics as a way to reduce the concerns that other people have. Second, he or she may genuinely be unaware of how much time he or she is spending, due to the consuming sensory experience he or she has with electronics and due to the fact that portable electronics make it possible for users to constantly *graze* on their electronics consumption without being aware of how much cumulative time they dedicate to the activity.

Therefore, early in the assessment process, it can be useful to utilize a strategy to help people keep track of their screen time. One such strategy involves using an app called *Moment*, which serves the singular purpose of monitoring exactly how much time a person spends on each app and function of his or her smartphone. Another strategy is using a simple tracking sheet to record when they log on to their computer, how much time they spend on it, and how they spend their time while logged on. To augment this, a general mood tracker (e.g., Burns 2009) can be utilized to trace the thoughts and feelings the client has throughout the day, with a focus on thoughts and feelings prior to, during, and after they engage in digital technology.

What games was the client playing? Although it is perhaps easy to lump the experience of playing all video games into a single, monolithic category, doing so is no more accurate than overgeneralizing the experience of playing all sports together into a single category. The experience of playing badminton differs significantly from the experience of playing rugby, just as the experience of playing *Call of Duty: Modern Warfare* is very different from the experience of playing *Braid*. Different game genres—and the individual games within each genre—have variations in their emotional, biological, and social experiences and impact on people (see Chap. 4). Therefore, it is useful to make the evaluation of game time very specific. What games is the client playing? What are those games like? When does the client play them? With whom does the client play games, etc.?

What was the client's actual gaming experience? How a person plays a game changes their experience with it and how it impacts them. For example, a client who plays *Minecraft* only in creative mode has a very different experience than a client playing Minecraft in survival mode on the *Hunger Games* server. Similarly, there is a substantial difference between playing *StarCraft II* in single player mode and playing StarCraft II in the *Diamond League*. Gaming experiences can be complex and filled with variety (like building an empire in *Civilization V*), or they can be highly repetitive (like endlessly clicking cookies in *Cookie Clicker*). Given the variety of experiences a person can have even with a single game, it is important to understand what experiences they are having. Is the client spending their game time committing virtual crimes? Is the client forging alliances as a part of a guild? Is the client absorbed in repetitive tasks of mining and building? This information helps to provide insight into the various aspects of each client's physical and psychological experience of gaming and provides richness to a clinician's understanding of a client's relationship with games. Furthermore, having a detailed conversation about a client's gaming experience helps them to engage in critical thinking about their own patterns of gaming.

What did the client find compelling about the games? Discovering what was most stimulating, compelling, and fulfilling about a client's experience of a particular game provides clues to the various emotional and social needs a client has been trying to meet through their patterns of gaming. Ask about the client's physical and emotional experience while gaming. This information is vital for providing effective treatment, since clients need to find other ways of attending to these needs if they are to be successful in creating a healthier and more sustainable relationship with technology. Furthermore, taking the time to explore clients' fascination with their games in a nonjudgmental fashion helps to build the working relationship between the clinician and the client (Abreu & Goes, in press).

How much time does the client spend thinking about, socializing about, and focused on games when not actually gaming? There are many ways in which a client's digital habits can intrude upon their *real-world* functioning. Some of that is the direct cost of the time, energy, and emotional investment spent during actual game time, and part of that is the indirect cost of the time, energy, and emotional investment placed on games when not actually playing. This includes watching *YouTube* videos of the game being played, talking about the game, daydreaming about the game, or simply being distracted from tasks and relationships by the desire to get to the next gaming session.

Has the client tried to hide or minimize any of their gaming or other electronic activities? Efforts at deception (including self-deception) are strong indicators of an unhealthy relationship. The clinician should place priority on discerning when minimization has been the result of a client trying to downplay their electronics usage, or a client has been so caught up in their use that they have literally lost track of how much they are investing into their games. This is because a lack of awareness and defensiveness require different interventions.

What are the client's patterns of social media usage? Clients who struggle with regulating their gaming frequently have difficulties with other areas of electronics, and vice versa. All of the previous questions are equally applicable to a client's social media use and can be applied in the same fashion. Also, clinicians would do well to recognize that some social media are integrated into some games (e.g., *Steam, Xbox Live, PlayStation Network*), and clients may not realize that the time they spend in these networks qualifies as social media use. Therefore, a clinician should ask about gaming networks explicitly as part of an exploration of a client's social media habits.

Is the client engaged in illegal activities related to their digital media usage (e.g., hacking, piracy, etc.?) Chemical addiction is often accompanied by engagement in illegal behaviors, either to fund the chemical use, or as a result of the general psychological and ethical numbing effect of chemical abuse and dependence. Similarly, illegal activities (including piracy of software, music, or movies, hacking, stealing to fund digital purchase, etc.) often accompany excessive, obsessive, and addictive patterns of digital media usage.

Does the client engage in other high-risk behaviors related to their digital media usage? For example, meeting up with people they met online, texting, engaging in cyber-bullying, online affairs, associating with counterculture or anarchist groups, etc. There is a wide variety of high-risk behaviors that a client can fall into as a part of their relationship with electronics. Many of these have significant potential to be disruptive of client's emotional, physical, financial, and relational well-being, and therefore are worthy of inquiry as a part of a comprehensive assessment.

What are the client's patterns of using internet pornography? Internet pornography has the highest addictive potential of all electronic activities, including gaming and social media (Meerkerk et al. 2006). Its use is extremely widespread, almost to the point of being ubiquitous. In 2008, an estimated 90% of young men and approximately one-third of young women reported using Internet pornography. The average age of first use of Internet pornography is 11 years old. Of special concern is the fact that the average age of the onset of symptoms matching the criteria for addiction is also 11 years old (Carroll et al. 2008). Many clients who struggle with an unhealthy relationship with video games, social media, or the Internet also find themselves in a pattern of compulsive or addictive internet pornography use. Therefore, the clinician should inquire directly about a client's use of Internet pornography, especially since clients are highly unlikely to volunteer any information about their use of Internet pornography without being specifically asked about it.

What are the client's family's patterns of technology use? Related questions include: What have been the family's limits, guidelines, and boundaries relative to digital technology? How were these taught, encouraged, modeled, and enforced? Why were they ineffective? The systemic principle of equifinality indicates that there is more than one way a person can arrive at an unhealthy relationship with digital media (Croft 1996). Sometimes, a client can develop an electronic addiction in spite of a very healthy family and social dynamic with many protective factors. At other times, the client has digital struggles as a natural result of the system in which they live, and thus they function as the identified patient in a system where the presenting problem is prevalent or even ubiquitous. Especially when there are prominent family systems issues that facilitate and enable an electronics addiction, it is vital for a clinician to assess the general relationship the entire family system has with electronics to understand where intervention is needed. Even when family dynamics have not been conducive to an unhealthy relationship with electronics, it is important to seek to understand the mechanism by which healthy family dynamics were overpowered, insufficiently supported, or circumvented.

Has the client perceived any downsides to their use of digital media? Or, have they felt any concerns or have they made any efforts to change in the past? The clinician should assess the client's insight into any negative effects of their gaming. If the client's insight levels are low, it is important to discern whether the lack of insight is due to cognitive difficulties (i.e., low-processing speed, ADHD, executive dysfunction with difficulties in metacognition, autism spectrum disorder, etc.), or whether the client has the ability to be more proactively self-aware, but is utilizing psychological defense mechanisms toward off any conscious awareness of problems related to their use of electronics.

If the lack of insight is due to cognitive difficulties, it can be helpful for the therapist to assume a curious, nonconfrontational approach to examine the situation and help the client *connect the dots* in a patient, unrushed, and emotionally safe manner. Oftentimes, the families of such clients will have had difficulty understanding their processing issues and will have interpreted their lack of understanding to willful ignorance or defiance, often leading to an escalating pattern of emotional reactivity. In such cases, it will be important for the clinician to help the parents stand down from their combative approach, since their child will likely find the emotionally charged nature of their approach so overwhelming that it will preclude his or her willingness to explore whatever problems may be present in his or her relationship with digital media.

If the lack of insight is due to defensiveness, it can be useful to apply the Motivational Interviewing principle of *rolling with resistance* (Miller and Rollnick 2003). In this approach, the clinician does not directly oppose position and avoids lecturing or arguing for change. The clinician invites new perspectives, but does not impose them. The clinician seeks to use the client as the primary resource in finding answers and solutions and considers resistance as a signal to respond differently.

Regardless of whether the client is not displaying insight due to defensiveness or cognitive processing issues, finding ways to build their understanding and acceptance of problems related to their gaming should be identified as an important goal in early treatment, since further progress is unlikely unless this objective is met. If and when the client shows some self-awareness of problems related to their gaming, these areas of insight provide very useful points of entry for building motivation to change.

How functional, healthy, and sustainable is the client in other areas of life functioning? This may concern social interactions, interests, hobbies, mental stimulations, coping skills, work, school, physical self-care, etc. The health of a person's relationship with digital media can only really be understood in the context of their health and functionality in their life as a whole. The mere fact that a person plays video games should not lead a clinician to assume the client has a problematic relationship with video games. Similarly, just because a person plays video games excessively does not mean they are addicted, although excessive video game use is also worthy of attention. Addiction implies disruption to a person's functioning in other key areas of life, such as social relationships, school, work, or maintenance of physical health (Gentile 2009). A thorough biospsychosocial evaluation of a client's life can illuminate if and to what degree the client's video game usage is disruptive of their functioning and development. Treatment should include helping the client reclaim, repair, and redirect the areas of his or her life that are being disrupted by his or her gaming.

Using the Discussion About Electronics to Assess Family Dynamics

In addition to exploring these various areas with the client and his or her family separately, it can be helpful to bring aspects of this discussion into family therapy sessions as a tool to evaluate family dynamics around conflict communication, roles, power dynamics, parenting, structure, alliances, triangulation, boundaries, defense mechanisms, , and so forth. The clinician can use these discussions to help the family begin to think about the process of their communication, and not just the content of it. This is a helpful tool in setting a positive trajectory in family therapy, since effective family therapy intervenes at the process level.

As a part of the assessment of family dynamics, the clinician should evaluate the family culture regarding technology and build an awareness of each family member's electronic habits and attitudes about digital media. Frequently, a shift in the family's culture and mindset about electronics is necessary to help create an environment which is supportive of the client's process while in treatment and conducive of the client's continued recovery following their discharge from residential treatment.

Assess Isomorphic Processes

Isomorphism—or the idea that a person's internal and external configuration tends to lead them to seek out and/or reproduce similar systemic dynamics in different settings and contexts—is a useful concept to inform the assessment process in therapy, including in wilderness and residential settings (Von Bertalanffy 1969). For example, by observing how a young man goes about solving the emotional, physical, and relational problems he encounters when entering wilderness therapy, a skilled wilderness therapist can gain a fairly accurate understanding of that young man's mindset, emotional processes, coping skills, defense mechanisms, relationships, and home system dynamics. Frequently, before learning and applying new skills and adaptations, people in treatment first try to reproduce their maladaptive coping skills to deal with new problems and challenges they find in their residential or wilderness setting. In other words, they try to solve the problems and adapt to the situation using the same approaches that were ineffective in helping them solve problems and adapt to their situations at home. Effective wilderness and residential therapy captures this isomorphism and utilizes it as a medium for intervention, and then applies the gains that emerge from doing so to the client's home system.

Following the principle of isomorphism, a client with a process addiction or otherwise unhealthy relationship with digital media will often reproduce it iso-morphically while in residential care. Even if they do not have access to smart-phones, video games, or the Internet, clients are likely to recreate many or all of the dynamics that existed in their unhealthy relationship with electronics with other systems that have similar features or mechanics. For example, many students with electronic process addictions tend to get sucked into unhealthy obsessions with collectible card or figure-based games such as *Pokemon*, *Magic: The Gathering* or *Warhammer*. This is because these games include many of the same mechanics that contribute to the addictive quality of many video games (Anderson 2015). The relationship that forms between the biopsychosocial vulnerabilities of the client and the addictive mechanics of the nonelectronic games tends to be similar to the dynamics that existed between the client and video games, social media, or whatever their digital addiction was—although the intensity of the dynamic is often somewhat reduced.

General Treatment Principles and Strategies

Digital Detox

A genuine *digital detox* is very difficult to utilize in outpatient settings and indeed may not always be indicated. Depending on the severity of the problem, some outpatient therapists report good results with slowly building up other areas of a client's life, then beginning a *dialing back* process on their digital usage (C. Rowan, personal communication, August 13, 2015). However, as the severity of the issue increases, and as other areas of a client's life are also experiencing significant disruptions, outpatient clinicians may find that a certain percentage of clients will not be successful using a dialing back strategy, and they will require an actual period of abstinence if efforts at treatment are to be successful. That being said, by the time a client's life has become sufficiently unmanageable in their home system to indicate residential treatment, a digital detox is frequently an important beginning step in the process.

Merely providing a period of abstinence from video games—even if it is an extended one—should not be considered adequate treatment for a process addic-tion. The absence of symptoms due to the absence of exposure can sometimes mislead clinicians into thinking the issue has been addressed when in fact the residential setting has temporarily structured away the pathology, only to have it re-emerge with a vengeance upon the client's discharge. Therefore, a digital detox should be considered a step in intervention and a setting for other interventions, but not a complete intervention in and of itself.

Educate

The period of digital detox provides a useful setting for educating the client and his or her family on process addictions in general and digital addictions in particular. A portion of this education can be purely psychoeducational in nature and can cover a range of topics including the nature of process addictions, the prevalence of video game addictions, associated features and comorbidity, the impact of excessive digital usage on emotion and neurological development, and so forth. Additionally, it can be helpful to utilize the client's own process of digital detox as an educational tool, helping him or her be mindful of what he or she was gaining from video games that he or she is now seeking to fulfill in other ways, what he or she lost to video games through direct and indirect cost and what is needed to compensate for those losses, and how his or her excessive digital media usage has shaped and misdirected various aspects of his or her biopsychosocial development, and what he or she can do to redirect his or her developmental trajectory.

Target Individual Vulnerabilities

If the assessment process has been thorough, the clinician should have a clear picture of the client's biopsychosocial strengths and vulnerabilities, as well as the nature of the client's relationship with video games and the needs, roles, and purposes video games have filled in the client's life. Simply trying to reduce a client's electronic habits proves to be an ineffective strategy, since the health of a client's relationship with video games is highly unlikely to exceed their overall general emotional and social health. Therefore, the clinician should use the assessment information to prioritize the most impactful needs and functions that were being addressed through the client's patterns of gaming to build skills, abilities, and supports to help the client meet those needs and fulfill those functions in other, more adaptive ways. These areas could conceivably include such items as increasing emotional regulation, practicing healthy stress relief, making and maintaining social connection and healthy attachments, cultivating autonomy and accountability, developing a sense of self-efficacy, experiencing real-world achievements, managing cognitive distortions, providing mental stimulation, managing ADHD symptoms, learning and practicing effective conflict management, engaging in physical activity, regulating sleep, creating a sense of purpose and contribution, addressing difficulties with executive dysfunction, and so forth.

Rather than utilizing a *shotgun* approach to broadly target all of these areas, a therapist is more likely to be effective by carefully selecting the *big ticket* items for each individual client. Big ticket items are the most salient and influential underlying causes for external symptoms. For example, a client may have an outward symptom of social isolation. Merely thrusting the client out into social situations is unlikely to be an effective treatment approach. If the isolation is driven by social anxiety, the various factors of the anxiety should be addressed (i.e., cognitive behavioral therapy for cognitive distortions, mindfulness for self-soothing, physical self-care, etc.). In that context, a systematic desensitization approach or a mindful completion approach to social exposure could then be effective as a part of a larger understanding of the causes of the symptoms. It is crucial for the therapist to focus on addressing *root* issues rather than just hacking away at symptomatic *branches*.

It is also important for the clinician to be aware of which needs are currently being met by the structure of the residential program (i.e., the client is currently forced to live with peers, so there is much less of a chance of successful social isolation) and to proactively pursue ways to help that client effectively meet those needs once the structure of the residential program has been removed upon the client's discharge.

Neurological Rewiring: Interrupt and Redirect Triggers, Associations, and Sequences

All learning involves neurological restructuring as the repeated paring of stimulus with response creates new and more robust neuronal connection, while neglecting or rejecting specific responses to specific stimuli—thus breaking up stimulus and response pairing—leads to a trimming and rerouting of neuronal pathways (Butler 2010). In gaming addictions, this neurological molding is compounded by the ways in which playing video games influences brain stimulus, functioning, and development. For example, recent experiments have demonstrated that playing logic, puzzle, and platform video games contributes to increases in the size of the entorhinal cortex—the part of the brain that helps with evaluating cause and effect, contextual learning, and perceptual reasoning—while playing role-playing games and action games contributes to decreases in the entorhinal cortex (Kuhn and Gallinat 2014). Similarly, people who play action video games have also been found to have severely less robust striatum nuclei, which is the part of the brain that helps to create internal representations of the external world. This change in brain structure is particularly worrisome, since decreased volume in this part of the brain is associated with the onset of many psychiatric and neurological disorders (West et al. 2015).

Even when not resulting in neurological or psychiatric disorders, excessive video game playing can lead to a sort of *lopsided* neurological development, with significant implications for the biopsychosocial functionality of an individual. Voss et al. (2015, p. 22) described this process with the following analogy,

> Human beings practice who they want to become, and individuals must be careful what they practice and how they program their brains. When a young child spends too much time in Internet gaming or Internet activities, there can be significant problems.
>
> We propose an analogy to clarify how a child's nervous system may develop when exposed to excessive time engaging in Internet gaming or other Internet activities. Observe your left hand. The thumb will represent the cortical areas associated with all the benefits of video gaming: quick analytical skills (but superficial understanding and little research methodologies), improved hand-eye-coordination, and perhaps improved reflexes. The index finger will represent the cortical areas associated with communication skills. The middle finger will represent behaviors associated with social bonding with family and friends. The ring finger will represent the capacity to recognize emotions of both self and others (empathy). Lastly, the little finger will represent the cortical areas associated with self-control. These higher executive functions are all learned behaviors, requiring time and practice. When a child spends an average of seven hours and 38 minutes in front of a digital screen for entertainment, that child is exceeding sevenfold the recommended daily dosage for healthy screen time. Folding the fingers into the palm of your hand represents this situation. As the brain matures, the end product is a young adult who is all thumbs in their thinking: possessing quick analytical skills and quick reflexes with superficial understanding and little research methodologies, but lacking in communication skills, having few bonds with people, exhibiting little empathy, and showing minimal self-control.

Treatment needs to address this lopsided development by identifying the client's deficits in communication skills, deeper thinking and reasoning, long-term problem-solving skills, attachment, empathy, and impulse control and utilizing strategies designed to build and enhance the client's skills in these areas to counterbalance the neurological effects of their excessive gaming. It is helpful to identify each client's triggers, associations and reinforcements through classical and operant conditioning, and *over-learned* sequences. Butler (2010) describes several helpful strategies for re-learning and re-wiring the brain from an addictive state to a healthier state. These strategies include the following:

Identify the client's triggers. Help the client learn when he or she will be vulnerable to the temptation to game in an unhealthy manner. Begin to structure their life in a way to avoid or restructure as many triggers as possible. This includes people, places, and things associated with their unhealthy patterns of use. Overcoming addiction means willingly adopting structure, rules, and limitations that will keep the client safe from triggers where possible and provide the client with the good options for responding effectively to being triggered.

Identify the sequences leading up to a client gaming in an unhealthy way. Identify all the choice points along the way and ways in which the client could redirect themselves at each choice point. This is best accomplished by understanding the needs and functions the client is trying to fulfill at each choice point. Help the client find ways to break the sequence and practice them. It is important not just to learn these rerouting techniques conceptually, the client needs to over-learn and over-practice them in order to counteract addictive sequences that are also over-learned.

Have the client spend time writing, thinking, and talking about the destructive consequences of an unhealthy relationship with electronics. Let their brain develop multiple ways of processing the long-term destructive consequences to counteract the lopsided focus on the immediate gratification that comes from playing games addictively. The client will also benefit from developing a clear vision of what life looks like with a healthy relationship with electronics and actually experiencing the benefits and pleasures of a healthier, more balanced life. Help the client actively and intentionally create rewarding experiences with a more balanced life, then reflect upon these experiences and share them with others on a regular basis.

Help the client create a reliable support system. They cannot rely solely on their own mind and their own willpower because their mind has literally been programmed to use video games in an unhealthy way through their previous decisions. The client will need the assistance of people who can hold them accountable and who can tell them when they are slipping into patterns of thinking and acting that will lead to relapse. The client will benefit from actively utilizing their long-term support system as much as possible while still in residential treatment.

Address Identified Family Dynamics

Just as the health of a client's relationship with video games and other electronics is unlikely to exceed a client's personal emotional and social health, it is also unlikely to exceed the health and functionality of the client's family dynamic. Therefore, family therapy should move beyond parent coaching and education to address a wide variety of dynamics within a family that help gaming addictions thrive, such as problematic dynamics in the parental subsystem, maladaptive family structure and roles, issues with boundaries, poorly defined values and guidelines, ineffective decision-making, destructive attempts at problem-solving, enmeshment, enabling collusion, triangulation, unhealthy power configurations, emotional disengagement, co-dependence, and so forth.

Encourage Intentionality

Intentionality is a helpful principle for biopsychosocial health. When clients identify what matters to them in their lives and determine to *live life on purpose*, proactively putting time, energy, and emotional investment into the things that matter, they are more likely to have fulfilling experiences that continue to motivate them in their efforts to have a balanced and sustainable relationship with technology. This includes creating tech free zones (such as meal times) prioritizing being present with the people they are physically with, actively cultivating deeper personal relationships, learning to wait without needing to be distracted by tech gadgets, and so forth. Therefore, a major focus in therapy is helping the client to determine what he or she truly values, what his or her needs are, what good self-care looks like for him or her, and what characteristics and relationships he or she would like to develop, then creating and applying a proactive strategy to attend to each of these areas. In general, the message and task is for the client to live his or her real-world life intentionally.

However, if the message the clinician is sending the client is only, "We want you to enjoy life besides electronics," this is likely to engender defensiveness in response. If that message is combined with, "We want you to have a satisfying relationship with digital media and gaming within the confines of reasonable boundaries and in the context of a healthy life," that can encourage client engagement. In conjunction with living their real-world lives intentionally, the clinician encourages clients to learn to game intentionally, as well. Although it is true that many clients may have to learn to abstain from their most problematic apps and games, the majority of clients are also able to successfully integrate some degree of gaming back into their lives. Re-engaging in gaming brings with it both opportunities and perils, and clients often need help to learn how to change the way they game beyond merely having time limits.

When clients adopt time limits and boundaries around game time, they are at risk of filling their game time with experiences that do not satisfy them, leaving them empty, craving, and tempted to violate their time limits. They are also at risk of inadvertently exposing themselves to a large number of addictive gaming mechanics in their search to find a fulfilling gaming experience (see Chap. 4). As a result, clients will often need help learning how to thoughtful navigate their gaming choices in order to achieve intentional enjoyment without being snared by psychologically manipulative gaming design. They need to learn what games they can play and how they can play them to give them a satisfying experience in the time they have available.

For example, a typical raid in *World of Warcraft* takes approximately four hours. If a client has a time limit of 2–3 h of recreational screen time per day—which is really the maximum which should be recommended—there really is no practical way for him or her to participate in a World of Warcraft raid, since consistently not being present when raids start or dropping out of raids early would likely lead to expulsion from his or her guild. Therefore, attempting to play World of Warcraft as a member of a guild is likely to be a highly dissatisfying experience for someone trying to maintain a healthier set of boundaries. Therefore, the client is faced with the option of playing without being a member of a guild or choosing to refrain from that specific game. Not being a part of the guild may diminish the play experience for him or her so much that he or she would be happier playing a different game altogether. Furthermore, World of Warcraft is replete with a large number of addictive gaming mechanics present in fairly high levels of intensity. When a client discovers there is not a healthy way for them to play a game they have previously enjoyed but have had an unhealthy relationship with, they often go through a period of mourning. Addressing this emotional process as grieving is helpful.

With the help of the clinician, the client can be assisted to determine what he or she finds enjoyable in a gaming experience, distinguish that from the most addictive and high-risk gaming mechanics, and then choose games to play based on what games offer a gaming experience he or she enjoys which can realistically be played in the bounds of healthy time limits. One indicator that the clinician and client are fulfilling this objective is that the client will be able to leave gaming experiences having had a good time, but also feeling capable of engaging with the other areas of his or her life. If the client is leaving gaming sessions with a sense of apathy about his or her other life activities, and his or her thoughts remain riveted on the next time he or she will be able to game, the right balance of intentional real-world engagement and intentional gaming has not yet been met.

Utilize Isomorphic Processes

Through the process of assessment and treatment, it is likely that most clients will display at least some dynamics that are isomorphic to their process addiction to gaming. The client may turn to isolative reading, obsessive focus on collectible card games like Magic: The Gathering, co-dependent relationships, social withdrawal, excessive focus on fantasy, and so forth. Through doing so, they reproduce portions, or the entirety, of their unhealthy relationship with video games. This is useful to highlight points of personal vulnerability and to discover specific game mechanics that have a particularly addictive pull on each individual client.

Each one of these isomorphic processes provides a useful opportunity to work with the client in real time with his or her process addiction dynamics being manifested in whatever substitute he or she gravitates toward before he or she actually re-engages with technology. This is useful because these isomorphic items are usually not as intense or as entrenched as the client's unhealthy relationship with electronics has become. As a result, these isomorphic items can be used as a sort of prototype for developing and practicing the skills a client will need to use to have a sustainable relationship with technology prior to technology being reintroduced. In other words, by learning their limitations and learning what they need to do to have a healthy relationship with whatever their isomorphic process is—up to and including abstaining from it, if needed—clients gain insight and practice the strategies they will need in order to be effective when confronting technology again. It is helpful for the clinician to make the connection between the work on the isomorphic processes and the direct work on the process addiction extremely explicit.

This has the potential to be far more effective than merely preparing to re-engage with technology in a conceptual and intellectual way. The fact that these isomorphic processes tend to occur relatively early in the course of treatment and in the context of the residential setting allows the clinician to have a much more detailed view of the situation due to the ability to observe it from multiple perspectives, rather than relying upon client self-reports the way an outpatient therapist would have to do. It also opens up opportunities for the therapist and staff to teach, coach, support, and intervene in real time, rather than relying on after-action reports.

Scaffold and Calibrate

Vygotsky's (1978) zone of proximal development suggests that people are capable of achieving greater learning and functionality under the tutelage of a mentor than they are capable of achieving on their own. This involves more than simply imparting information orally or through writing; this process of mentoring involves actions such demonstrating, assisting, giving real-time feedback and encouragement, and so forth. Bruner and his colleagues further developed this idea by introducing the concept of instructional scaffolding (Wood et al. 1976). In scaffolding, a tutor or mentor with knowledge of the various components of a skill or process engages in a teaching approach in which he or she isolates a single sub-component of the skill or process and directly teaches that sub-component in various ways including modeling, explaining, questioning, giving hints, providing feedback, and so forth. In the process of teaching, the tutor has the student actually engage in the skill or process, focusing on only performing the sub-component being taught while the tutor fulfills the functions of the other components of the skill or process. As the student becomes proficient at that particular sub-component, the tutor then expands the process one sub-component at a time until the student is able to perform the entire process on his or her own. Having a healthy and sustainable relationship with video games and other media is a process with many sub-components, including things such as impulse control, emotional regulation, time management, social engagement, and so on. Each of these can be isolated to some degree and focused on sequentially.

This scaffolding process can begin very purposefully at the beginning of treatment by having some initial structure around items that have similar mechanics and thus tend to elicit isomorphic reactions (i.e., card and board games, reading, reclusive activities, overly sexualized talk due to its connections with pornography, etc.), giving real time, direct instruction and coaching over how to regulate these items, and then slowly turning control over the regulation of these items to the client to the degree that he or she shows an ability to do so successfully. It is helpful to directly frame this for the client as practice for going through the same process of scaffolding with digital media.

To help determine the client's readiness at various stages of the scaffolding process, the therapist and staff should consider such indicators as the degree to which the client abides by time limits and schedules for these activities, the degree to which the client obsesses over these actives when not directly engaged in them (i.e., time spend looking at and organizing cards and game pieces, reading through game manuals, etc.), the degree to which the client is able to meaningfully engage in other activities, the client's ability to maintain their performance in school and/or work, the degree to which the client has an identity separate from his or her involvement in these activities, the degree to which the client engages in negative social interactions around these activities (i.e., arguing about rules, getting overly upset upon losing, cheating, stealing cards or game pieces, etc.), and the degree to which the client is able to socialize around things other than these activities.

Throughout the calibration process, there is a gradual reduction in external supports and structure—including modeling, actively assisted completion of tasks, passively assisted completion of task, prompting, redirecting, and so forth—as the client displays the ability to assume more and more personal responsibility for various aspects of self-care and self-regulation of processes isomorphic to gaming and of gaming itself. A guiding principle in this scaffolding process is that new items should be added one at a time. This prevents the errors of giving clients too much to adjust to at once—thus decreasing their chances of success—and of altering too many factors at once, thus clouding the clinician's ability to accurately assess the contributing factors to both positive and negative outcomes of each level of experimentation (C. Rae, Personal Communication, April 28, 2016).

Create the Framework for Long-Term Improvement

Regardless of the progress made through the calibration process while in residential treatment, new challenges in having a healthy and sustainable relationship with technology will likely arise when the time comes for discharge from residential care and reintegration into long-term living conditions. The clinician and client should anticipate that some of the improvements that have occurred in the client's relationship with technology while still in residential care will translate into their new setting fairly directly and smoothly, while other aspects will require a degree of finesse to be transferred into daily living outside of a treatment setting. Full exposure to nontreatment living conditions frequently provides some unanticipated triggers and challenges which benefit from real-time intervention. Therefore, aftercare planning should reflect the need for some continued assistance in this area, especially during the transitional period in which the client is establishing a personal structure, routine, and supports.

The client should be encouraged to begin his or her life outside of residential treatment utilizing a higher degree of external support, and continue the process of gradual scaffolding until they reach a balance point. For example, in the early stages of life after residential treatment, rather than relying simply on willpower and personal accountability, the client may benefit from having monitoring software on their smartphone and computer (with options such as *Phone Sherriff*, *K9 Web Protection*, *Open DNS*, *Norton Online Family*, Moment, *App Detox*, *Offtime*, *Screen Time Control*, *NetSanity*, or *Flipd*) and also having a support team member help them monitor the quantity and content of their screen time.

In the actual transition process out of treatment and back home, it can be helpful to have the client work on establishing and solidifying other important patterns in his or her life (e.g., physical exercise routine, healthy diet, face-to-face socializing, work and/or school, etc.) before adding screen time into their routine, which would include temporary backing down from the screen time usage that he or she calibrated to while still in residential treatment. If clients are unwilling to go that far, they can still find some help in being willing to reduce their screen time usage temporarily to a sub-calibrated level while they get other aspects of their lives up to speed, and only then trying to extend their screen time to their long term limits and boundaries.

Strategies for Sustainability

The following strategies are helpful as the client seeks to create a healthy pattern of real-world engagement and sustainable technology use:

Prioritize self-care and fulfilling biopsychosocial needs in nonelectronic ways. The more effective the client is at constructing a reasonable variety of methods to address self-care, building relationships, providing mental stimulation, and engaging in effective recreation, the less at risk he or she is of relapsing into an unhealthy relationship with electronics.

Eliminate the most problematic games, apps, features, websites, and activities. Each client will have individual limitations as to what electronic activities he or she can engage in without the situation spinning out of control. One general rule of thumb is that if a client had a truly addictive relationship with a game or site before, they are fairly unlikely to be able to establish a healthy relationship with that specific program in the future. In general, games that have the same type of addictive mechanics in the same levels of intensity will have the same addictive potential.

Strategically plan and prioritize specific activities during recreational screen time. The client should prioritize which games, apps, etc., are most satisfying and fulfilling—while steering away from games with high addictive potential —and should purposefully and intentionally use those programs during recreational screen time. This includes choosing gaming experiences which can reach a satisfactory stopping point within the allotted time limits.

Evaluate the excessive and additive potential of apps, games, and sites before using them in order to gain a sense of whether they are low risk, moderate risk, or high risk. Refrain from using high-risk games, and approach moderate-risk games with caution and with oversight from supportive allies and family members in recovery. An explanation of how to evaluate the addictive potential of games is found in Chap. 4 of this volume.

Strategically select how to play games in a way that reduces addictive potential. Whereas completely refraining from a specific game will likely sometimes be necessary, there are other circumstances where changing how a client plays a game can be an effective strategy. Depending on the way certain games are constructed, a person may be able to choose what parts of the game they interact with in order to reduce the addictive potential of it. For example, StarCraft II is constructed in a way that a person can play it at various levels: single player, simple multiplayer, or organized competitive online multiplayer in leagues. It is possible that a person can be successful in having a controlled and balanced relationship with StarCraft II by engaging in the game modes with fewer potentially addictive gaming mechanics. Therefore, rather than playing StarCraft II in the leagues, a person can choose to only play single player.

This type of strategy reduces the risk significantly, since it exposes the player to fewer addictive gaming mechanics. Or, a person may find that with only a little more risk, he or she could try to play online multiplayer with specific friends or family members in one-on-one matches outside of the competitive league structure. Similarly, a client who previously used games as a way to escape depression should not play games while depressed. Rather, he or she should employ other coping methods to relive the depressed state before engaging in gaming.

Once a client has become relatively skilled at identifying addictive gaming mechanics and has developed some insight into his or her specific vulnerabilities, he or she is now in a position to begin to make some educated choices. The first and obvious strategy is to choose not to play games that contain a large number of addictive gaming mechanics. For example, if a person knows they have propensities toward gaming addictions, it would be wise for him or her to refrain from World of Warcraft and other so-called MMORPGs and MMOs, since they tend to have high levels of addictive mechanics by their very nature. The second obvious strategy is to be specifically aware of what gaming mechanics an individual is most vulnerable to, and thus be very cautious about playing any games that may contain high amounts of the gaming mechanic that the individual is most vulnerable to, even if there are very low levels of other addictive gaming mechanics present.

For example, people with ADHD tend to resonate with games that feature *twitch* game play, which involves high speed game interactions. So, a client with ADHD and a history of gaming addictions may really need to rethink whether playing high speed first-person shooters is the right choice for them. Alternately, a client on the autism spectrum may find the level-grinding gameplay of mining resources in Minecraft to be particularly compelling due to his or her neuro-atypical *hardwiring*. As a result, he or she may find that trying to play Minecraft in survival mode without it becoming excessive is unrealistic. However, he or she may find that playing Minecraft in creative mode is more sustainable.

Set and abide by time limits for screen time. There is fairly solid support in the research for limiting total recreational screen time to somewhere between 1 and h per day (i.e., American Academy of Pediatrics 2013, 2014; Cell Press 2013, Gentile 2009; University of Texas Medical Branch at Galveston 2012). Within this range, the various benefits of screen time can be found, but above this range, the problematic effects of screen use are common.

Having clearly defined screen time can also be helpful. Rather than simply playing when they feel like it or when they seem to have some spare time, it can be helpful for clients to create a specific time and place for gaming, and then keep their gaming to those set times in the same manner that they might play golf at a golf course during a designated tee time, rather than pulling out their golf clubs and putting a ball around whenever they seem to have a spare moment.

Utilize allies. When a client's interaction with social media begins to drift into the realm of being excessive, obsessive, co-dependent, or addictive, most of them are fairly ineffective at noticing it by themselves before it progresses to a serious level. Other people around them, especially those that know them well, like members of their family, are prone to notice that they have a problem long before they client recognizes the situation for him or herself. Therefore, I recommend that each client should develop and use a set of allies to help encourage them in their self-care, be available for social interaction, assist in effective emotional coping, act as a source of early warning for relapse behaviors, and offer support on a variety of physical and emotional levels. Family members are particularly useful as allies, especially when family therapy has been used to sufficiently address some of the dysfunctional dynamics discussed above.

Conclusion

In residential treatment, clinicians can combined a number of modalities—including individual therapy, family therapy, group therapy, and various interventions built into the residential milieu, and program structure—to address process addictions to video games and other digital media in a holistic fashion. A systematic, scaffolding approach can be used to extend these residential interventions to the home setting during home visits, and then integrated into a long-term aftercare plan following discharge to help clients establish and maintain a sustainable relationship with digital technology as a part of a healthier, balanced lifestyle following treatment. Working with IGD in residential treatment requires a solid foundation in family therapy since family dynamics have often either contributed to the formation of IGD, have been reorganized around IGD, or both. At the same time, effective work with IGD provides many experiences that illuminate and activate important family dynamics so they can be worked with in real time, which is where some of the most effective family systems interventions can take place.

References

Abreu, C. N., & Goes, D. S. (in press). Structured cognitive psychotherapy model for the treatment of Internet addiction: Research and outcome.

American Academy of Pediatrics. (2013). Cyberbullying rampant among high school students: Nearly one-third of youths also report playing video/computer games for more than 3 h a day. *Science Daily*. Retrieved from http://www.sciencedaily.com/releases/2013/05/130505 073738.htm

American Academy of Pediatrics. (2014). Media and children. Retrieved from http://www.aap.org/en-us/advocacy-and-policy/aap-health-initiatives/Pages/Media-and-Children.aspx

American Psychiatric Association. (2013). *Diagnostic and statistical manual of mental disorders: DSM-5.* Washington, D.C: Author.

Anderson, R. J. (2015). *Navigating the cyberscape: Evaluating and improving our relationship with smartphones, social media, video games, and the internet.* Orem, UT: Author.

Burns, D. D. (2009). *Feeling good: The new mood therapy.* New York: Harper.

Butler, M. H. (2010). *Spiritual exodus: A latter-day saint guide to recovery from behavioral addiction.* Provo, Utah: BYU Academic.

Carroll, J. S., Padilla-Walker, L. M., Nelson, L. J., Olson, C. D., Barry, C. M., & Madsen, S. D. (2008). Generation xxx: Pornography acceptance and use among emerging adults. *Journal of Adolescent Research, 23*(1), 6–30.

Cell Press. (2013). Action video games boost reading skills, study of children with dyslexia suggests. *Science Daily.* Retrieved from http://www.sciencedaily.com/releases/2013/02/130228124132.htm

Croft, G. (1996). *Glossary of systems theory and practice for the applied behavioral sciences.* Freeland, WA: Syntropy Incorporated.

Ferraro, G., Caci, B., D'Amico, A., & DiBlasi, M. (2007). Internet addiction disorder: An Italian study. *CyberPsychology and Behavior, 10*(2), 170–175.

Gentile, D. (2009). Pathological video game use among youth ages 8–18: A national study. *Psychological Science, 20*(5), 594–602.

Khazaal, Y., Billieux, J., Thorens, G., Khan, R., Louati, T., Scarlatti, E., et al. (2008). French validation of the Internet Addiction Test. *CyberPsychology & Behavior, 11*(6), 703–706.

Kuhn, S., & Gallinat, J. (2014). Amount of lifetime video gaming is positively associated with entorhinal, hippocampal, and occipital volume. *Molecular Psychiatry, 19,* 842–847.

McCurry, J. (2010). Internet addiction driving South Koreans into realms of fantasy. *The Guardian.* Retrieved from http://www.theguardian.com/world/2010/jul/13/internet-addiction-south-korea

Meerkerk, G. J., Van Den Eijnden, R. J. J. M., & Garretsen, H. F. L. (2006). *CyberPsychology and Behavior, 9*(1), 95–103.

Mentzoni, R. A., Brunborg, G. S., Molde, H., Myrseth, H., Skouveroe, K. J., Hetland, J., et al. (2011). Problematic video game use: estimated prevalence and associations with mental and physical health. *Cyberpsychology, Behavior, and Social Networking, 14*(10), 591–596.

Miller, W., & Rollnick, S. (2003). Motivational interviewing: Preparing people for change. *Journal for Healthcare Quality, 25*(3), 46.

Northrup, J. C., Lapierre, C., Kirk, J., & Rae, C. (2015). The Internet Process Addiction Test: Screening for addictions to process facilitated by the internet. *Behavioral Sciences, 5,* 341–352.

Shapiro, N. A., Goldsmith, T. D., Keck, P. E., Jr., Khosla, U. M., & McElroy, S. L. (2000). Psychiatric evaluation of individuals with problematic internet use. *Journal of Affect Disorders, 57,* 267–272.

Lemmens, J. S., Valkenburg, P. M., & Gentile, D. A. (2015). The internet gaming disorder scale. *Psychological Assessment.* Advance online publication. Retrieved from http://www.dx.doi.org/10.1037/pas0000062

University of Texas Medical Branch at Galveston. (2012). Using skills gleaned from video games, high school and college students outmatch medical residents in surgical simulations. *Science Daily.* Retrieved from http://www.sciencedaily.com/releases/2012/11/121115141642.htm

Von Bertalanffy, L. (1969). General systems theory and psychiatry—an overview. In W. Gray, F. J. Duhl, & N. D. Rizzo (Eds.), *General systems theory and psychiatry* (pp. 33–46). Boston: Little Brown & Co.

Voss, A., Cash, H., Hurdiss, S., Bishop, F., Klam, W. P., & Doan, A. P. (2015). Case report: Internet gaming disorder associated with pornography use. *Yale Journal of Biology and Medicine, 88*(3), 319–324.

Vygotsky, L. (1978). Interactions between learning and development. *Readings on the Development of Children, 23*(3), 34–41.

West, G. L., Drisdelle, B. L., Konishi, K., Jackson, J., Joliceur, P., & Bohbot, V. D. (2015). Habitual action video game playing is associated with caudate nucleus-dependent. *Proceedings of the Royal Society of London B: Biological Sciences, 282*(180), 20142952.

Widyanto, L., & McMurren, M. (2004). The psychometric properties of the Internet Addiction Test. *CyberPsychology and Behavior, 7*(4), 445–453.

Wood, D., Bruner, J., & Ross, G. (1976). The role of tutoring in problem solving. *Journal of Child Psychology and Psychiatry and Allied Disciplines, 17,* 89–100.

Young, K. S. (1998). Internet addiction: The emergence of a new clinical disorder. *CyberPsychology and Behavior, 1,* 237–244.

Author Biography

Ryan Anderson, Ph.D., LMFT, MedFT received his BS degree in Marriage, Family, and Human Development and his MS degree in Marriage and Family Therapy from Brigham Young University. He received his Ph.D. in Medical Family Therapy from East Carolina University, and completed his internship at the Duke Comprehensive Cancer Centre. He has worked as a family therapist in outpatient practice, in inpatient psychiatric settings, in cancer care, in several other medical settings, as a wilderness therapist and Assistant Clinical Director at Outback Therapeutic Expeditions, and as a therapist at Telos Residential Treatment. His teaching experience includes undergraduate university courses, first year medical students, and community outreach and education programs. He has also been a speaker at various conferences and continuing education events. He is one of the founders and the Clinical Director of Telos U.

Chapter 6
Our Stories of Collaboration Throughout the Therapeutic Wilderness Process

Cynthia Cohen and Lian Zeitz

Chapter Highlights

- The authors share first person knowledge with clinicians about aspects of the experience of families whose children participate in outdoor behavioral healthcare programs.
- Through wilderness therapy, students develop self-efficacy, accountability, motivation, understanding of their own boundaries and how to establish them, and stronger family relationships.
- The process for suggesting wilderness or other alternative residential therapeutic programs starts with the family and the team collaborating to determine the most effective ways to work together and find the best path.
- The family makes the final decision—the consultant has focus on making educated recommendations that are tailored to each individual and family's needs.
- Maximizing dialog and collaboration within each group and among all involved —*referring* clinicians, programs, consultants, parents, and participants—enhances the effectiveness of the work we are all doing.

Every time the phone rings, I think it is the police.

– Spoken by an anonymous, Pathway Partners client several years after his son first went to a therapeutic wilderness program, despite his son's success in college and graduate school.

I finally taught myself to stop answering the phone with 'What's the matter?' whenever my son called. Instead, I learned to accept that all was well and he was living his life independently with strength. I realized that he was handling things competently and I taught myself to see things going well, working out, and to reinforce the image of my son

C. Cohen (✉)
Pathway Partners Independent Educational Consulting, 4 Creamery Road, Great Barrington, MA 01230, USA
e-mail: cynthia@pathwaypartners.info

L. Zeitz
Pathway Partners Independent Educational Consulting, 10507 Streamview Ct., Potomac, MD 20854, USA

© Springer International Publishing AG 2017
J.D. Christenson and A.N. Merritts (eds.), *Family Therapy with Adolescents in Residential Treatment*, Focused Issues in Family Therapy,
DOI 10.1007/978-3-319-51747-6_6

succeeding. I even realized that if he were anxious about something, like writing a paper, I didn't need to fall apart.

– Cynthia Cohen

The prevalence of mental health problems is rising in the United States, as indicated by various sources. The National Center for Children in Poverty found that 20% of adolescents in the United States have a diagnosable mental disorder (Schwarz 2009). According to a recent report from the Substance Abuse and Mental Health Services Administration (SAMHSA), an estimated 2.2 million adolescents aged 12–17 in the United States have had at least one major depressive episode, and there were an estimated 9.6 million adults aged 18 or older in the United States with a serious mental illness (SAMHSA 2013). Environmental challenges that result from school, learning disabilities, turbulent households, lack of community support for mental health treatment, and stigma of mental health issues and illness all exacerbate the problems faced by American youth.

At the same time, prevention and intervention programs are not easy for families to access. Lack of mental health services to support the unique needs of adolescents and young adults, together with emerging data confirming the therapeutic value of wilderness environments have encouraged the spread of wilderness therapy. Wilderness therapy is an extremely effective approach to helping young people who are stuck, suffering, and/or struggling. By combining nature and outdoor activities with psychotherapeutic practices that address participants' psychological problems, emotional distress, failure to thrive and launch, lack of motivation, and substance abuse in a wide range of populations, wilderness therapy has become an effective first step for families seeking help (see Chaps. 3 and 15). Recent years have seen increasing sophistication and diversity among wilderness therapy programs *Wilderness therapy,* as described in this chapter, is consistent with the term Outdoor Behavioral Health care, as described in Chaps. 3, 15, and 16. Though Outdoor Behavioral Health care is a description used increasingly by researchers for this type of treatment, wilderness therapy is still widespread in the common nomenclature. This type of program has a heavy focus on clinical work, and should not be confused with therapeutic wilderness programs, as described in Chap. 23.

Though the use of wilderness therapy traces back to 1874 (Van Hoven 2014), it is only recently that common terminology and theory have been established. During the 1990s, lack of evidence demonstrating the efficacy of wilderness therapy treatments, and associations with boot-camp style programs that tried to break people down in order to build them up, gave rise to serious misgivings about the ethics of wilderness therapy (Russell 2001). In recent years, a rising movement driven by mental health specialists, researchers, wilderness program leaders, and university administrators has worked to ground wilderness therapy in scientific evidence and standardize best practices. In particular, a shift in practice has taken place from more rigid behavioral approaches, including what was sometimes aggressive physical and emotional confrontation, to relationship-based practices, focusing on skill-building in order to engender confidence and foster intrinsic motivation (Russell and Hendee 2000). Self-determination theory, positive psychology, attachment theory, Arbinger Institute philosophy as described in *The Anatomy of Peace* (2015), and adventure-based programming all have become significant theoretical foundations for wilderness therapy (see Chaps. 3, 15, and 16).

Along with these theoretical shifts and the proliferation of alternative education programs, new standards for wilderness therapy and assessing evidence of its effectiveness have arisen. In the article *What is Wilderness Therapy,* Russell (2001), a leader in outdoor behavioral health care and wilderness therapy theory, outlines the key characteristics of wilderness therapy programs. Being licensed by a state agency, having regular sessions with a licensed mental health practitioner (clinical therapist), addressing clinical goals, establishing individualized treatment plans, and pursuing formal evaluations of treatment effectiveness are all typical characteristics of wilderness programs (Russell 2001). One of the strengths of wilderness therapy is that students develop accountability, motivation, self-efficacy, understanding of their own boundaries, and stronger family relationships. Heightened self-efficacy comes about through actual accomplishments. These can include mastery of hiking, such primitive skills as fire building without traditional implements, adventures like rock climbing or mountain biking, self-understanding through participating in initiatives designed to teach insight and new ways of approaching things, and interacting better with peers and adults. Furthermore, living in an outdoor environment helps clients to leave their familiar culture behind in order to have a unique experience that will facilitate meaningful growth.

As can be seen in the content above, wilderness therapy has emerged as an effective approach in helping youths and their families address, and eventually overcome, educational and life struggles. Nevertheless, understanding and clarifying the process of seeking, finding, going through, and moving on with life after wilderness therapy remains a challenge for both families and professionals. In this chapter, we will discuss our experiences as participants in the wilderness process for the purpose of shedding light on some of these challenges and methods to handle them. Of note, an educational consultant can provide guidance to families going through this process.

What Is an Educational Consultant?

Educational consultants work to guide families and students in finding appropriate educational and/or therapeutic placements—schools, boarding schools, colleges, and therapeutic programs. Therapeutic educational consultants, as they are called in this context, are hired by families to help them identify alternative educational and therapeutic programs for young people who are not doing well following traditional routes. They travel nationally or internationally, visiting and assessing these programs.

Educational consultants typically have a variety of backgrounds, from working as admissions counselors, clinicians, educators, and attorneys to coming from other professions, such as business and public health. Thus, a wide range of competencies exists amongst educational consultants. We have found that it is important for educational consultants to be fluent in a variety of disciplines–and to understand the following:

- *Mental health systems* The illnesses people face and what leads to struggles and suffering; developmental psychology; the approaches psychiatry and psychology typically employ to help people; and how to involve and coordinate among an entire team of clinicians, residential staff, and teachers.
- *Educational principles* How to teach students with a variety of learning styles; what is important for high school and college students to develop intellectually; the role of academics in psychological growth and health; what are the elements of a good education; experiential education; progressive education; and online learning. The ability to think critically about the role of the teacher in the process of growth, development, and change.
- *Organizational development* What the factors lead to an effective organization; hiring approaches; professional development; structure of decision-making; team meetings; what is the culture of the program and how is it established and maintained.

The Independent Educational Consultants Association has established criteria for certifying professional educational consultants and offers a training program to develop new consultant competencies. Standards in the field have supported consultant's ability to work families through the arduous process of finding an appropriate placement.

Once clients are participating in a program, consultants work as part of the treatment team alongside educators, clinicians, and parents to help each family select the most effective path for their young person. They work closely with therapists and educators to understand what is going on for each individual—the history, what has worked and what has not, the concerns of the family and therapist, the student's strengths and interests, as well as challenges, etc. They then work together with the therapist to help the family navigate the maze of possibilities. The leadership of the team is ideally shared, with the consultant leading the discussion of placement and the therapist leading the discussion of the client's needs. The collaborative process works differently for different people, so these roles may vary. The bottom line, of course, is that the parents make the decision—the consultant can only make recommendations.

When an adolescents or young adults are participants in a wilderness therapy program, they are often not directly involved in the decision-making process about aftercare. They may provide input or express preferences, but the key conversations usually take place among the therapist, the family, and the educational consultant. However, once the decision has been made to send an adolescent or young adult to a long-term residential program following completion of the wilderness experience, the therapist is typically responsible for coordinating the process by which the adolescent learns of the decision. Because therapists do not have the same knowledge of programs as educational consultants, they work closely together with consultants to understand and clarify the reasons for making specific recommendations, so these can be effectively communicated to the adolescent or young adult.

Our Stories

As noted above, the purpose of this chapter is to share with clinicians some important aspects of the experiences of families whose children go to wilderness therapy. Our perspective, as that of educational consultants who have also participated in wilderness therapy as a parent and a student, is unique. Our perspective provides a broader and deeper lens through which to view the issues families face and enables a better understanding of their responses and reactions. Sometimes families feel comforted to know that we have experienced what they are going through, and sharing our understanding alleviates some of the loneliness and pain that people often feel when they seeking solutions to help their struggling and suffering children. They are more likely to believe that there is hope when they hear that we have also been there.

The combination of our first-hand knowledge of wilderness therapy combined with the things we have observed other families undergoing, and our extensive experience visiting programs and participating in the treatment team has allowed us to develop a richer and deeper understanding of the process. Questions about how growth and change occur, how much of the change is due to being in the wilderness, the role of the therapist, what aspects of a program are most essential to lead to change and growth are all more easily answered by someone who is both a professional and has participated in the experience. Other factors, including the importance of personal growth and change and growth originating from an internal locus of control, the value of positive psychology, and the importance of applying attachment theory can be more clearly defined.

The explorations that follow, of both difficulties and satisfactions, will provide insights for clinicians and educators working with struggling and suffering students and their families, who may often feel frustrated or even hopeless as they begin to contemplate sending an adolescent or young adult to wilderness therapy. Our transparency about the kinds of struggles that families often have in sending their children to therapeutic wilderness programs can make the process less intimidating for families. It can also provide therapists with more specific knowledge to support parents experiencing painful situations and then relief (both of which parents often feel at different times during this process). My perspective (CC) as an educational consultant and parent can help therapists and parents learn how to navigate the path through therapy, which will not be a straight line, without excess worry over every blip in progress. This chapter can be used by educational consultants, families, and therapists alike to better understand the process of wilderness therapy from a holistic perspective.

Our Modified Case Study

We have utilized a modified case study to describe our own experiences as participant-observers in this process. Case studies are used in the field of psychology to provide in-depth investigation of a single person or small group. They are useful for examining processes and development in detail and over a significant period of time. Case studies use interviews and observations to elucidate complex phenomena. For example, Bettman et al. (2011) studied the narratives of 14 adolescents in wilderness therapy to understand their attitudes toward parents. Russell (2001) studied four cases to examine how the wilderness therapy process related to outcomes. Norton (2008) studied one adolescent in wilderness therapy to assess the effects of the program on mood. Case studies like this depict trends. Through our work as educational consultants, we are aware of the universality of some of the experiences we had as family participants. Parents and even siblings share in the experience of young people who participate in wilderness therapy. We explain our experiences here in order to offer therapists and families additional insight into some of what may happen. We also hope to normalize some of the fears and struggles that are part of the process as well as an effort to honor the positive effects of wilderness therapy for the whole family.

Two Families' Stories

We now describe various aspects of the experiences of two families, through the eyes of the mothers of two adolescent boys who were struggling, unhappy, doing poorly in school, and using poor coping strategies. Adam Cohen-Congress (the son of the first author) and Lian Zeitz both went from Northeastern urban centers to wilderness programs, where they developed motivation, accountability, self-confidence, enhanced relationships, and the capacity to flourish. They have become successful young men who are able to push through any challenges and are thriving in all major areas of their lives.

Struggling and suffering. My son, Adam, was struggling during high school—he explains now that in elementary school he began to feel bad about himself, especially in school—he had borderline learning issues and some problems with attention that we did not address adequately. He explains how alone he felt in his lack of success. Then, when he was in middle school, his father and I got divorced —he explains that he became angry then. These feelings continued to develop, and by ninth grade, he ended up being arrested with two friends who were selling marijuana. Although he was unable to take action at that point to change his situation, he now sees that incident as pivotal—a wakeup call. After the arrest, he left his high school and attended two others in New York to complete ninth grade and half of tenth. The last of these schools was a great place, but while Adam always attended class, he was not very involved. The interesting, progressive education, and caring teachers were not enough to draw him in. He was unable to follow through on any interests and kept quitting activities like theater (he had been a successful actor, singer, and dancer in community and children's theater). He was also using/abusing marijuana, though we did not realize the extent of this at the time.

Considering the options. After a year, filled with frustration, feelings of helplessness and quantities of contradictory advice, we finally sent him, at age 15, to a wilderness therapy program. My considerable experience in public health, including in leadership positions in mental health and educational fields, had not led me to knowledge of alternative therapeutic and educational programs at that point. In fact, most of my colleagues, experts in their fields, cautioned me about the dangers and ineffectiveness of such weird interventions, quite far off the grid of Ivy League psychiatry. We were referred to an educational consultant who seemed to see all of what we were going through as minor. She thought Adam was a *soft* kid and thought wilderness would be good for him. Nevertheless, we did not act for several months. The final impetus for us to intervene was Adam's despondence on a family vacation—something that had always been positive for him before. Thus, we sent him off to wilderness treatment in the heart of winter. He did not, however, go willingly. One day Adam had expressed some concern about himself saying "I don't know why I'm not more motivated." I suggested he consider attending one of the therapeutic wilderness programs that have demonstrated effectiveness in helping kids with these issues. He said "no way."

Mindi and Lian. It was a stressful time in the family before deciding to send me (LZ) to wilderness, according to my mother, Mindi Cohen,

> After moving to a new area and putting him in a new school, issues began to arise that we had not expected— he was disconnecting, changing friend groups, selling and abusing pot, and demonstrating large levels of frustration with school. Simultaneously, there were other tensions in the family with other brothers and my relationship with my husband was not its best. It was not until we moved Lian out of the school he was in that we were able to uncover what was actually going on. It was hard on everyone. As well, our older son had struggled when he was younger, but we felt we waited too long with him to get help, especially after learning with him that there are key windows for interventions. So for Lian we decided to address the issues openly and we were able to talk about the process of going through a program.

I was confused about the process, but willing to trust my parents/listen to them. However, before going I think I had a skewed view of what I was going into that made it seem more appealing. I had a love for nature and adventure already, so the thought of going on a big trip was appealing, even though I was wrong about how long I would be going for (I thought I would be gone for a month). Once I got there, my first few letters were hateful—bashing and ranting about how unhappy I was. It was good for my parents to have my therapist explain why I might be sending letters like that because their response was always very considerate and written with conviction.

Getting there. When we were about to send Adam, he refused to consider wilderness even though he had expressed frustration with his lack of motivation. We felt stuck, but proceeded to hire transporters—the process made me so anxious I could not make any of the arrangements or speak with the staff in advance. Our educational consultant remained cheerful throughout all of this—our waking Adam early one morning and handing him over to transporters, his being in wilderness for the winter, working together with his wilderness therapist—a number of things that seemed overwhelmingly difficult for me to handle. Most overwhelming of all was figuring out how to help and support Adam through the process. I was very surprised that once the transporters arrived, I felt supported in a way I had not in years —we were embarking on a path in which we would have help figuring out how to help Adam develop a sense of well-being by dealing with his challenges and embracing his strengths. Adam told us later that he was angry about what was happening, and considered fighting back briefly, but then acceded. Eventually, Adam came to terms with being taken somewhere against his will. He realizes now there was no other way other than for him to have gone to wilderness therapy and that the experience was so important in creating a positive direction in his life and allowing him to push through his challenges. He has at times pointed out the moral dilemma inherent in expecting someone to develop intrinsic motivation to grow and change in the context of being sent somewhere against their will. Although I acknowledge the validity of this point, parents of teenagers sometimes have no better way to set a limit and let their children know that what is going on is not working and that they expect more. It is nevertheless helpful to see the paradox rather than assume that there are no issues inherent in taking such a step.

The program begins. Though I felt relieved that Adam was safe, I remained heavy hearted in his absence for several weeks, participating in every webinar that was available, eagerly reading every suggested resource, anything to feel more connected. I began to feel appreciative that there was someone—a whole entity— taking over the role of *nag* and replacing it with an approach that would help Adam develop motivation and agency. As parents, we had been unable to do that, and now there were people who were able to reach him—a thoughtfully developed program with a history of success. Gradually, Adam became accountable for his behavior and open to growth.

His sister, 5 years older and in college, was reassured that we had taken this step. She had been at home during winter break when Adam left and we gave her and a friend a *gift* of a night in a hotel, so they would not be home when Adam left. When we explained what we had done, she was reassured that we had finally taken action to make a difference in her brother's life. School had always come easily to her; she sailed through largely untroubled (until our divorce, which was traumatic for her as well). However, she recounted to me that she often experienced inadequate attention from us during times when we were preoccupied with how to help her brother. Adam's treatment in wilderness therapy allowed us to refocus on his sister as well.

Adam was required to remain outside of his peer group of students when he arrived at the wilderness program, until he told his life story. His dad and I agreed to speak together with his therapist on weekly calls, something I thought I would never do since we had divorced. We were able to learn to parent together more effectively. We wrote impact letters and read his story. He struggled to be engaged in the process until after a number of weeks. His therapist suggested that he act as if he were engaged and succeeding. This seemed to help him get unstuck. He hiked miles every day, made shelters with his tarp, packed and carried his backpack, had a chance to *bust* a fire—skills he had not had before, though we had spent extensive periods at our country house with him and visited natural settings around the world. He developed connections with the field staff and his peers, as well as participated actively in therapy. His therapist and her intern were continually and increasingly helpful to us and to him—the process became reassuring and hopeful.

Communication by letter was satisfying—as he says, it allowed us to consider our interactions and to respond thoughtfully rather than react immediately. His dad and I flew west to attend a parent seminar at which we met field staff, therapists (not his), and other parents. Somehow it felt okay to be near Adam, but not to see him. We learned communication exercises that he was learning. These entailed dialogs like "I feel _____ when _____ happens," followed by reflective listening "I hear that you feel…" They involved expressing our hope for ourselves, which is within our control—and our hope for the other person, which is out of our control. We felt camaraderie with other parents—they were intelligent, thoughtful and caring, interesting people. It was significant to me to feel part of a group that was *okay*. At home, despite the presence of understanding friends, it was easy to feel alone, as though no one else had been through any difficulties like this. Avoiding the trap of wallowing in isolation is crucial. Over the years, meeting many other parents and attending parent seminars (as both a parent and an educational consultant), processing the teachings of Arbinger Institute (2002, 2015) materials and many other books and articles, I have continued to learn as one active parent among the many active parents doing the best we can to help our children flourish.

Determining what was next. The process of figuring out what would follow wilderness therapy was difficult and brought more uncertainty and anxiety about how to help Adam effectively. I missed him incredibly, but believed the people who insisted that he needed to stay away from home after wilderness. It certainly would have been traumatic for me to bring him home—I would have worried constantly—but it still surprised me a couple of years ago when Adam himself explained that he believes it is best for teenagers not to come home after wilderness therapy because the old triggers are still there in place. I had been sure he would have said he would have preferred to come home and would have handled it well. I have seen a number of students return to settings against advice and they eventually do well—some have struggles and seem to muddle through, but they often arrive in a positive place eventually. For Adam, even though he went to boarding school, it was difficult for me to figure out whether and how to limit his relationships with his old friends, some of whom were stuck in old, self-destructive patterns but who are good people. Adam and his friends all wanted the best for each other, but I worried about the effects of them spending too much time together. By now, however, Adam has worked it out on his own and he is able to be caring, connect with, and see old friends at the same time as he pursues his own life. The friends he has made along the way are also caring, as well as motivated and focused on developing active, productive, and interesting lives. When we were visiting and reviewing follow-up programs (we went to each one suggested), the one we liked the best did not have a space for him. Nothing we saw felt right, and eventually we selected the place closest to home. At that point we were able to plan Adam's graduation from wilderness.

Completing the program. After 93 days, we came to wilderness to stay overnight, for his graduation. It was a wonderful, very touching couple of days. We were impressed with the field staff running the experience and the other two kids. There were three of us—all families whose children were graduating, and we spent 2 days together experiencing some of the wilderness program and participating in transitional rituals and ceremonies to honor our children's work and success. Even writing about it now brings back the intense pride in Adam, appreciation for the opportunity to do some of our own work, and our gratitude to the staff and program. Even the experience of sleeping outside in the now warmer winter—16° Fahrenheit —was amazing. We were impressed with Adam's confidence and easy competence setting up tarps and living in the harsh Utah outdoor winter. The love and caring we all felt toward one another was profound.

The initiatives we participated in were effective in creating situations that we could use to develop insights into our behaviors and responses. The exercise of telling one another things we regretted, respected, and requested was extremely moving and now, five and one half years later, I still remember and continue to work at least some of my behaviors that I learned could be difficult for my son. It seems often that parents change more slowly than their children. Kids in wilderness have the opportunity to have 24 h a day of re-patterning while we have only a couple of hours a week working with the wilderness therapists (see Chap. 14). Over the years, Adam has persisted in reminding me, almost always in a caring and connected way, about some *better* ways of interacting and responding at those times when I am in old patterns.

After wilderness. We left to spend a few days together, and then traveled with Adam across the country to drop him off at the therapeutic school we had selected. It was scary to leave him there, but he helped the separation by telling us, as he met the other students, "These are my friends." He was clearly comfortable with meeting new peers and ready to develop relationships with them. Over the next few months, I was not sure that the fit was right. I did not connect with his therapist, the education seemed too elementary, and there did not seem to be enough activities. Nevertheless, I did not trust myself—my old tendency to rescue might be resurfacing. I finally decided to hire another consultant to assess the situation. She decided that the program was fine, but that our son did not need a therapeutic school, that a traditional supportive boarding school would be good. Adam's dad eventually agreed to go along with the plan to find a new situation for him. We relied on our new consultant's suggestions completely, as we had with the previous person.

The path through the therapeutic world remains unclear to the uninitiated. It is scary to make decisions about what to do because there is no black and white route to well-being. We rely on those who say they know what to do—and I have seen many children and young adults get to better places—but that reliance is a bit tentative because the world is so unfamiliar. But, I learned much from our experience, and that of so many others I have talked with about the variety of effective approaches to helping young people. As a result, I have developed some ideas about which parts of the process are significant and what aspects of programs are the cornerstones of change.

Adam went to another wilderness program, with a different philosophy and different approach, as a transition situation—he was able to leave it for days at a time to visit boarding schools. He selected a boarding school in the West, preferring that part of the country and in order to maintain connection more easily with his wilderness therapist, with whom he continued to work during school. I continued to learn from his therapist—how to identify the ways in which I felt confident in my son's ability to handle things and how to express that confidence to him. I had the opportunity to practice letting him do *it*, whatever *it* was, for himself. I could only be supportive and set some basic limits, which were that he had to do something productive and stay out of trouble. Senior year he was struggling again, thinking of going back to wilderness, because he knew it would be helpful. But then he got involved with people who were not a good influence and activities that were not positive, so the school asked me to send him back to wilderness. Once again, he was transported against his will, but he accepted it. Nevertheless, we both felt upset by the transporters' lack of warmth and caring this time.

Looking back from a successful present. Adam has said that this last trip to wilderness was the most meaningful. I remember I met him there shortly after he arrived. His previous therapist, with whom he had been working on an outpatient basis while in boarding school, was away. The program's clinical director pitched in and in a meeting of the three of us, called me on my unspoken desire to rescue Adam. For one thing, she wanted to make sure everyone knew and saw his strengths. The therapist said to Adam and me, "This is serious. If we don't want Adam to be in a similar place of uncertainty and lack of commitment in his mid-20s, Adam needs to take responsibility for his situation moving forward." We were able to listen, and Adam worked hard. I let him embrace the strength within himself to move forward and to find and pursue his own path. I asked only one thing—that he be productive in some way. He has developed into a person whose values I respect immensely, a leader, able to express his caring and sensitivity in very positive ways to his friends and family. He has also found his academic and intellectual strengths, becoming a very successful student and a deep thinker.

Over the past few years, Adam has worked with me, visiting and assessing programs, consulting with families, suggesting placements. We have spent many hours discussing the wilderness treatment, specific programs, and specific clients and families. His insights are invaluable. He understands the process and can elucidate it in helpful ways. Regarding family involvement, Adam has noted the following, parents who participate in as many activities and programs as possible are likely to be more invested in the process and make the experience more powerful for everyone. Students learn about who their parents are and how to deal with that reality, both the positive and the negative. On the other hand, when parents are not interested or able to make changes, their children have to work through a more difficult process by themselves.

Adam believes that the lack of involvement of his sibling at the time he was in wilderness made it harder to communicate about it. Though he and his sister have a satisfying and close relationship, he sees that her lack of direct participation in the process created a disconnect. He wishes his sister had been able to participate in a family program. Even she, who is glad she did not have to go to wilderness herself, but sees how wonderful an experience it was for Adam, admits that a family intensive would have been helpful. Parents change more slowly than their young people who are in wilderness and experiencing 24 h a day of re-patterning. Our daughter thinks that as a result of our experience with wilderness, we changed somewhat in the way we parented her brother, but not a huge transformation. Children can help parents see certain things, and possibly even change certain behaviors, but they cannot be responsible for creating the change in their parents. It is okay for kids to say to parents "this is what I need from you in our relationship," but it is not appropriate for them to be responsible for their parents changing themselves. At this time, Adam is nearing the completion of a very successful college experience. I have seen how he found ways of calling forth his strengths, of showing up in the arena to push forward, of handling his challenges. At the same time, I have seen how he has been able to enjoy the things that come easily to him —his great social skills, sensitivity, and responsibility toward others, his deep and meaningful relationships. I feel close to him and grateful for our relationship.

Lian and Mindi. I (LZ) have also succeeded socially, emotionally, and academically. I too have developed strong relationships, pursued solid, and good values, and have found academic success. My mother, Mindi, reflected on our family's experience,

> As a family we continued to seek out ways to become stronger. The landmark forum and yoga retreats are things we did to continue the process of family growth and strengthening. The concrete evidence that we have seen as a family is love, positive communication, and continuous growth. Since our son went to wilderness we have made major milestones as a family, such as having three kids right now succeeding in college, passionate children, and Paul and I thriving in our professional endeavors. We feel blessed and privileged to be where we are.

I went to a boarding school and have now graduated college, and am pursuing global mental health as a career. I too am succeeding socially and academically.

What Makes Programs Effective?

There is often urgency for families exploring wilderness therapy. Educational consultants can assist both families and clinicians with access to more accurate information about programs and facilitate the process of identifying appropriate choices for a child or adolescent. I (CC) have been able to continue to appreciate the many benefits of wilderness therapy. It was my experience with Adam that motivated me to become a therapeutic educational consultant in the first place. Over the past few years, I have been able to work with my son and other young people who have had wilderness experiences, review programs, and help place clients' children in appropriate environments. I have seen many people go through the process and have a clear understanding that there are ups and downs along the route to flourishing. I know that the problems are not usually a sign to go back to square one but rather can be a part of the process of healing and growth.

There are divergent opinions about what is the most effective residential treatment. From our experiences and my knowledge, I believe that the most effective growth and development results when an internal locus of control is the focus of change—that each person must change from within, knowing and accepting themselves and their own boundaries. I also believe that the best programs are those that model, as an organization and among staff, the path they want their clients to take—personal growth leading to a sense of well-being and flourishing. Positive psychology is important to create strength-based programs. Of course, sometimes people have great success at programs that follow other approaches. There is no single right answer and people can follow their intuition, once they survey all the information.

Assisting adolescents and young adults, with the help of wilderness therapists, I have learned that three things are needed: each young person has to do *it* himself or herself, while at the same time parents need to set limits. Parents have to expect their child to be productive in some way—and parents need to help young people feel confident in themselves by pointing out their specific successes in handling challenging situations. Part of wilderness therapy is exploring what leads to growth and change for each person in the family. For the child, is it the therapy, the time in wilderness itself, the field staff, the theoretical approach—intrinsic versus extrinsic locus of control—the activities, adventure or primitive skills, or mastery projects? All of these may be significant. For families, is it the break, the therapy, the change in the dynamics of the family system as the person in wilderness changes, the clarity that something needs to be different, learning new strategies or exploring more deeply into one's persona, the psychoeducation—as discussed in Brene Brown's books like *The Gifts of Imperfection* (2012, 2013) or Arbinger Institute materials like *Leadership and Self-Deception* (2002, 2015)? These are all questions about the mechanisms of change that are important to clarify and need to be delineated further.

Working with Educational Consultants

Referring clinicians usually decide that the person with whom they are working is stuck, not making adequate progress, resistant to outpatient treatment, or part of a family that is unable to change. It can be a great benefit for a therapist to work with a consultant who knows about and has assessed programs that are alternatives to typical outpatient treatment and hospitals. When selecting a consultant, it can be useful for the home therapist to determine the consultant's philosophical orientation and approach to vetting programs, style of teamwork, etc., to determine if they are compatible. The process for discussing and selecting wilderness or another alternative residential therapeutic program starts with the family and the team figuring out the best way to work together. Although each situation is different, in general the home therapist determines what the young person needs together with the family and the family makes a choice. Meanwhile, the consultant helps everyone navigate the process. As noted above, the home therapist is the expert on what issues the young person faces, what he or she has responded to in the past, what has not worked, the family relationship, etc.

People often feel like they are jumping into an abyss when they are entering the world of residential therapy—it is unknown to many clinicians and educators. More education about how these programs operate, who the staff are, what their training and professional development includes and how wilderness therapy organizations function would be very helpful for clinicians who are advising families. It is also useful for the therapist to help the family define their goals for their child or young adult so the consultant can help them figure out the best way to help the young person attain those goals. Transporting someone against their will is not anyone's preferred choice. On the other hand, an angry young person almost always arrives less angry when they have been accompanied by someone they do not know rather than by their parents. A good interventionist can help a young person understand why they are being sent to a program and how the program will help them (see Chap. 12). Almost all children who have been transported to programs soon develop an understanding that this was the only way their parents were able to set limits—a young child can have a time out, for a teenager that does not work. They see the benefits of being where they are and understand that there was no other way to get them where they need to be.

Conclusion

It is clear that participants in wilderness therapy have the opportunity to develop motivation and enhance their capacity to lead healthy, productive lives and to flourish despite the continuing need for ongoing and increased research. As therapeutic wilderness programs and other alternative comprehensive residential programs are refined and become increasingly effective, we have also been able to provide more extensive and thoughtful support for parents and family members. In addition, we have identified the importance of honoring student input throughout the process of ongoing support for student alumni. From our perspectives—of public health, of parents of young adults and adolescents, and educational consultants—there are important issues that outdoor behavioral health programs can address. There are several areas which we believe merit emphasis:

- Therapeutic wilderness programs remain unknown to many clinicians, educators, attorneys, clergy, and other professionals working with adolescents and young adults. Therapeutic wilderness programs should be promulgated so that clinicians and others see this as a modality that can effectively address many of the problems their patients face.
- Outdoor behavioral health care should be available on a widespread basis to those who are not able to be self-paying. Hundreds of thousands of dollars a year are spent on each youth in the juvenile justice system in many states, for example. Similarly, young people in underserved communities who are struggling or suffering should have access to these services—the costs compared with the benefits that accrue over a lifetime, including enhanced productivity in society—would make this financially worthwhile.
- Within the field of outdoor behavioral health care, it could be useful to explore the role of the client voice in their own treatment, advanced approaches to research (including studying brain changes after wilderness therapy experiences), and have more information about the factors that actually lead to growth and change. This would immensely benefit the field and beyond.

We are continuing to work together to augment the still limited understanding of clinicians, educators, clergy, attorneys, other professionals, and the general public about the efficacy of alternative educational and therapeutic approaches, such as wilderness therapy. We participate in the field through advocacy efforts, such as appealing to the Outdoor Behavioral Health Council to support education programs for wilderness therapy and by having past clients speak at conferences to share their experience in programs. These endeavors aim to push the educational and health fields to think critically about issues related to collaboration with families during the treatment process, as well as inspire new ways of being that are involved, honest, and founded on trust. In addition, we are addressing the need for access to these services for all young people and to eliminate barriers to providing support to young people in need of alternative models of therapy and education. Maximizing dialog and collaboration among all involved—referring clinicians, educators, programs, consultants, parents, and participants—can enhance the effectiveness of the work we are all doing.

References

Arbinger Institute. (2002). *Leadership and self-deception: Getting out of the box.* Oakland, CA: Berrett-Koehler Publishers.

Arbinger Institute. (2015). *The anatomy of peace: Resolving the heart of conflict* (2nd ed.). Oakland, CA: Berrett-Koehler Publishers.

Bettman, J. E., Olson-Morrison, D., & Jasperson, R. A. (2011). Adolescents in wilderness therapy: A qualitative study of attachment relationships. *Journal of Experiential Education, 34*(2), 182–200.

Brown, B. (2012). *Daring greatly: How the courage to be vulnerable transforms the way we live, love, parent, and lead.* Westminster, UK: Penguin.

Brown, B. (2013). *The gifts of imperfection: Let go of who you think you're supposed to be and embrace who you are.* Center City, MN: Hazelden Publishing.

Norton, C. L. (2008). Understanding the impact of wilderness therapy on adolescent depression and psychosocial development. *Illinois Child Welfare, 4*(1), 166–178.

Russell, K. C. (2001). What is wilderness therapy? *Journal of Experiential Education, 24*, 70–79.

Russell, K. C., & Hendee, J. C. (2000). Wilderness therapy as an intervention and treatment for adolescents with behavioral problems. In *USDA forest service proceedings, 6.*

Schwarz, S. W. (2009). *Adolescent mental health in the United States. National Center for Children in Poverty (NCCP).* Washington, DC: Substance Abuse and Mental Health Services Administration.

Substance Abuse and Mental Health Services Administration. (2013). *Results from the 2012 national survey on drug use and health: Summary of national findings.* Washington, DC: Author.

Van Hoven, L. J. (2014). A systematic review of wilderness therapy: Theory, practice and outcomes. Master of Social Work Clinical Research Papers. Paper 279.

Author Biographies

Cynthia Cohen MSPH has a Master's Degree in Public Health and has had extensive leadership experience in health care, including mental health, and in education. She established an educational consulting practice focusing on alternative therapeutic programs after her entire family experienced the life changing effects of wilderness therapy. Cynthia believes in the power of strength-based programs, with change and growth coming from within each person. She has made it her life's work to support those most in need and has become a leader in the world of educational consulting. She is distinguished for her expertise in supporting families through difficult times, bringing forward discussions of significant issues within the field, and in developing efforts to increase clients' voices in the process of treatment.

Lian Zeitz BASc serves as an Associate at the Global Development Incubator. In his role, he is spearheading efforts to raise the voice of young people in all efforts to address mental health globally. He coordinates local, regional, and international gatherings to develop collective action on mental health and he actively liaises with health policy makers around the world. Lian graduated from Quest University Canada with a degree in Liberal Arts and Science, where he maintained a focus in mental health and international development. Lian is an active speaker at national and international conferences where he talks about the student experience in therapeutic programs and pathways to have successful transitions back into the community. Through working with Pathway Partners, an independent education consulting firm run by Cynthia Cohen, Lian was able to evaluate and connect with over 50 therapeutic and alternative education programs across the US. Lian is a human rights advocate and mental health activist working to dramatically shift mental health out of the periphery and into the mainstream of health priorities.

Chapter 7
A Parallel Process: Home Therapy While the Adolescent or Young Adult is in Residential Care

Heather Hendrickson

Chapter Highlights

- Importance of the parent's engagement in the residential treatment process.
- How to support family while the adolescent is away at treatment.
- How to create and implement a treatment plan for the family.
- Healthy communication and parental influence.
- How to create a safe and supportive environment at home.

Introduction

Most parents never think they will find themselves sitting with their child and professionals in the attempt to find placement in a residential treatment program. They ask themselves, "What happened?" or "How did we get here?" Of countless families I have worked with, most of them feel like they are traveling in a foreign land, not knowing which road to take, which direction to turn, and who to ask for help. As clinicians, we can be the navigational tool for families who feel lost, blindsided, helpless, and overwhelmed. Our role is of a vital nature, beginning with supporting the family in finding the appropriate placement for their child, continuing while the child is in treatment, and ongoing throughout the child's transition home. From the moment a family walks into our office, it is important to recognize the *Parallel Process* that has already been established.

   If you are the clinician that will support the family in finding placement for their young person, it will be imperative to select a program that has a family treatment component that the family can participate in along with their child. In most circumstances, the identified child has become the main focus of the family; dis-

H. Hendrickson (✉)
8337 Sawyer Brown Road, Nashville, TN 3722, USA
e-mail: heatherhendricksonlpc@gmail.com

© Springer International Publishing AG 2017
J.D. Christenson and A.N. Merritts (eds.), *Family Therapy with Adolescents in Residential Treatment*, Focused Issues in Family Therapy,
DOI 10.1007/978-3-319-51747-6_7

tracting a family system from their norm, creating new roles within the family system, and in the end the family members begin to exhibit their own signs and symptoms that something is awry. Our main focus as clinicians during this initial process is to support the family in returning to a sense of balance and a new norm. Often one of the first questions a family asks when their adolescent or young adult enters residential treatment is, "What do we do now?" This undoubtedly is a complex question; however, solutions are available and attainable for the family. This chapter will examine some of the solutions and options available within the context of residential substance abuse treatment. Information throughout this chapter is based largely on my experience in working in residential and private practice settings with families and their adolescent or young adult children that have been impacted by addiction and substance abuse.

Treatment for the Entire Family

When someone enters treatment they begin a process of change that fosters emotional, mental, physical, and spiritual growth. An adolescent or young adult begins to identify and gain awareness of their substance abuse issues, and they gain access to the tools necessary to facilitate change for a healthier and productive life. Equally important during this process is for the family members to identify their part of the process, including their choices, behaviors, and actions that have had and can continue to have a strong influence on the family system and their young person that is new to recovery (Gifford 2013).

What most families have not realized is the similar path that they are walking alongside their adolescent or young adult. The parallel process begins during the adolescent's period of substance abuse and will continue throughout the residential treatment and recovery process. Assisting the family in recognizing the similar path both the child and the other family members walk is both helpful for their understanding of what has occurred as well as beneficial for healing and growth. As clinicians, we can provide much needed direction and support throughout the process, beginning when the child is in residential treatment.

Take a Breath

More often than not, the parent has experienced a time period of total preoccupation with their child prior to establishing residential care for them (Sheff 2008). This preoccupation is the first layer of the parallel process, and typically beneath the preoccupation is a swath of enabling and codependent behaviors. Supporting the family in how to recognize and lessen the tendency for these behaviors while the adolescent is in treatment is essential. A parent's preoccupation and enabling stems from the love for their child and often manifests itself with worry and concern. Quickly the worry and concern will turn to preoccupation in its fullest (Conyers 2003).

During initial sessions with the family, once the child has been placed in treatment, I ask the parents and other members of the immediate family system "How do you believe your life has been impacted and complicated by recent events?" Depending on where the family members are emotionally, you can encounter a wide range of responses. Oftentimes, some family members have the belief that if the identified child would "just get better and stop doing what they are doing" then the family would be okay. It is important at this phase of the parallel process to establish with the family that their family system has no doubt been impacted by substance abuse; however, not solely one person is to blame, nor is one person's change the solution (Barnard 2007). Validate that the child did make their own choices that led to the current circumstances; however, also identify that everyone in the family has their own work to do for healing and forgiveness to take place.

An important note at this point: the family will likely be on an emotional roller coaster ride throughout the therapeutic process, and this is to be expected. Continuing to validate *where they are* mentally and emotionally is imperative, all the while guiding them in a direction that will allow them to continue to let go of resentments, negative feelings, and focus on their own growth process. Resentments, especially from siblings, are a significant area to tackle. Once family members have had the opportunity to share with one another their feelings and how they believe their family system has been impacted, they will likely identify that all of the focus has been on the identified child for a long period of time. This is an opportunity for a clinician to help the family establish some normalcy and self-care for the family system (Conyers 2003).

To emphasize the importance of self-care for the parents, it is often helpful to use the analogy of the airplane and oxygen mask. We all know in case of an emergency on an airplane, we are instructed to place the oxygen mask on ourselves first, and then we are able to help others around us. If we do not follow those directions, we have likely sacrificed ourselves and no longer have the ability to help those around us. The same rule applies to our relationships. If we exhaust ourselves physically, emotionally, and spiritually, we have less energy, ability, and strength to truly support others. Many parents innately feel it has been and is their responsibility to make certain their child is safe, and that is where the preoccupation begins (Sheff 2008). Whether that be following them to determine their whereabouts, or rescuing them from consequences, parents have attempted to control and resolve the problem, and in doing so have established a pattern of self-sacrifice to the point of exhaustion.

It is important to encourage and support the parent by reassuring them their child is in an environment where they are receiving the care and treatment they need. In addition, hearten them to *take a breath* and establish a return to normalcy and routine in their life. Parents often meet these suggestions with resistance, feeling that if they let go and take care of themselves, then they are no longer focusing on the well-being of their child. Prior to residential treatment, parents have likely been operating in overdrive, and typically are highly unaware of the sacrifices they have made for themselves and the rest of the family system. Offer the parent assurance that as a parent they can and will continue to love their child and be involved in their child's life, but in a healthier and supportive way.

After some steps in the direction of self-care the family begins to understand that they have been exhausted and overwhelmed and require much needed rest. Oftentimes this new focus should not only identify activities that the family members enjoy, but also a focus on overall self-care. Identifying and exploring areas of change that will foster emotional, mental, physical, and spiritual growth for the family as a whole will be beneficial for the family system. As the child returns home from treatment, the family system will have established an environment for well-being, both individually and collectively.

Pushing the Family Reset Button

If only it were as easy as unplugging an electronic device or hitting a reset button to reestablish expectations and routines, change the dynamics of their relationships, and help the family find their balance! As a clinician, establishing clear structured goals will be helpful for the family early on in the therapeutic process. The first step is the family allowing themselves to focus on their own self-care, as highlighted above. In a therapeutic setting, developing goals and a plan for self-care is beneficial. Some steps for accomplishing related tasks are outlined below.

Step one. Have the family revisit their hobbies, passions, and interests. It is often helpful to ask each family member to make a list of those things they no longer do or participate in that previously brought them joy, happiness, and balance in their life. Not only does this goal provides a path for a return to self, but also provides an opportunity to develop or revisit activities that provided healthy coping mechanisms. In addition, it is important to support the family in identifying other areas in the home environment that need improvement, such as diet, exercise and spiritual care.

Step two. Challenge the family to participate in something each day that will provide them with a return to self. This can also include activities that the family can participate in together, which leads to step three.

Step three. Reestablish regular communication and family time with the family still at home while the identified family member is away at treatment. Many times parents will disclose they have not been able to focus on other children in their home, due to the overwhelming amount of time and energy they invested in their child that is now in residential treatment. A good guide for assisting the family in learning healthier communication will be reviewed later in the chapter in the section labeled Communication and Feelings.

Step four. Educate the family on establishing ongoing support outside of the therapeutic setting. This support can be accessed by way of attending support groups such as Al-Anon, Alateen, Nar-Anon, and other family programs and support groups often available in most Intensive Outpatient and Residential Treatment Centers. Al-Anon and Nar-Anon have long been known as a place of refuge for families impacted by alcoholism or addiction, and Alateen provides siblings with a place to *speak their truth*. Support groups provide families with a community where they no longer feel alone, an environment that offers a sounding board for their trials, and a place to celebrate growth and change (Sheff 2008).

Typically, when families follow the established goals, they begin to feel relief and renewed energy, and healthier decision-making and awareness soon follows. For example, following an intense family program, a parent shared that in learning to take care of himself he realized that instead of continuing to throw himself between the *moving train* (addiction) and his son, that he can now be a healthy support person for his son and provide stability, positive influence, and encouragement.

Involvement in the Adolescent's Treatment Process

Once a family has had the opportunity to take a breath and receive some initial relief, then it is important to guide them in receiving much needed education on adolescent/young adult substance abuse. Most all residential treatment centers offer a family component as a part of the treatment process. Strongly encouraging the family to participate in the family services is a priority. Studies have long proven that the more family members are engaged and involved in the treatment process, the more positive the results (Liddle 2011). First and foremost a structured family program will provide the family an opportunity to learn about substance abuse, and more specifically the impact of early onset substance abuse. Participating in the treatment process will inform family members what their child is accomplishing while in treatment, which in turn provides more understanding concerning their child's substance use, behaviors, and other possible co-occurring issues. Being involved in the treatment process also provides a good opportunity for family members to practice balance between self-care and support for their child.

Most residential treatment centers for adolescents and young adults establish contact with the family on a routine basis for updates on the progress of their child. Providers need to encourage family to follow the schedule implemented by the treatment center and to limit calls to the treatment staff. This allows family the opportunity to move away from preoccupying and controlling behaviors and practice establishing boundaries with themselves.

It is also important to instruct the family and express the need for their involvement in family services provided by the residential treatment center, whether that is weekly family sessions or participating in a family education program. Family services offer structured therapeutic opportunities for the adolescent and family to begin their healing process. It is also beneficial, if you are the home family therapist, to collaborate with the residential treatment center in order to have a well-rounded spectrum of care for the entire family.

If the residential treatment center does not have a structured family program, then it will be vital as their home therapist to provide the needed education and support. Specifically, provide family members with access to education on early onset adolescent substance abuse and any co-occurring issues that need to be considered for the future of the child's continued care.

Control, Influence, and Healthy Communication

Early on, as experimentation evolves to substance use, and use escalates to substance abuse, and onward on the path to addiction, family members often develop a tolerance for their adolescent or young adult's behaviors, actions, and choices that are all driven by addictive substances. Over time, due primarily to denial, the family becomes accustomed to the change that is created by addiction in the family. They have made adjustments to cope and have developed family roles to deal with the issue at hand (Black 2006). Family members find themselves on a locomotive that is heading toward a train wreck. If we were to draw a locomotive that represents the chain of addiction, you have the engine (drugs/alcohol) , the passenger car (person struggling with substance abuse), and the caboose (the family). The engine pulls the passenger car and the caboose. In addition, the substance controls the addicted, and by succession, the addicted controls the family. Families find themselves attached to the addict, physically, emotionally, and spiritually (Black 2006). However, because of the escalating nature of addiction, at some point, families want off the train. They begin to recognize their exhaustion and hopelessness, and they realize their attempts to control are futile.

Enabling and codependency are terms important for families to learn at this point. Enabling can easily be defined as doing something for someone that they can and should do for themselves. Families often discuss how they did everything they could to try and control the issues, thinking if they helped by paying bills, or taking care of responsibilities for their child, that this would lessen the stress and alleviate the need for their child to abuse substances. In this process with the family, it is important to help them recognize at the root of their attempts to control and their enabling behaviors is love and fear. They love their child and are fearful of the current circumstances, as well as what the future holds if their child continues the path of addiction.

The Illusion of Control

In most situations, the identified adolescent has likely been preoccupied with obtaining substances, using substances, and spending time with using friends. The equivalent for the parent is the parent has likely lived their daily life for some time being acutely watchful of their child's whereabouts, and find themselves engaged in attempts to control their adolescent. Following self-care, assisting the family in identifying their attempts to control (what and how) will support them in the path to continue caring for themselves and provide a healthier influence within the family system. When assisting the family in identifying their own behaviors (responses and attempts to control), it is important to handle this conversation with great care. Parents already typically feel a great sense of responsibility for their child's substance abuse, and often feel they did or did not do something that caused their child's issue. Therefore, reassuring them during the identification process that as parents they have done the best they could with what they have had to work with (prior to getting support and help), and they have done these things out of love and care for their child is important. Below is a common list of areas/items that parents often try to regulate in unhealthy ways as part of their attempts to control their adolescent:

- Attempts to control where their child goes and who they spend time with
- A regular routine of going through the child's room, car, cell phone, computer, etc.
- Following their child or tracking them via GPS devices and checking their locations routinely throughout the day
- Changing plans in order to be available at a moment's notice
- Preoccupying thoughts (e.g., where they are, whether they are okay, whether they are safe)
- Controlling money and controlling wardrobe/clothing
- Calling their child's friends or other parents
- Drug screens (this can be helpful if done in a constructive format)
- Guilt trips
- Bargaining with their adolescent ("If you do this, I'll let you do that")
- Threats ("If you break curfew one more time we will take your car")
- Empty threats
- Yelling, screaming
- Nagging
- Scolding, using guilt and shame
- Statements of comparison (e.g., "Why can't you be like your brother?").

After the family has identified their specific areas of unhealthy control, therapists need to guide them to begin to understand the *why* behind the control. Most importantly, they love their child and they want them to succeed, and when they see that child struggle, fear takes over the parent. Therefore, parents typically begin to make attempts to *fix* the child and the issue, believing all the while that they have the power to do so. Providers should educate the family on the mantra that is well known in Al-Anon: You didn't cause it. You can't control it. You can't cure it (Al-Anon Family Group 2016). This process of change can begin by helping the family learn what they can control, which is themselves.

After the parents have identified their attempts to control, extract the identified components that will remain vital to the adolescent's success when they return home. For instance, it will be important for the adolescent to have structure and routine. Therefore, establish that there will continue to be boundaries and expectations around items such as money, curfew,, and privileges, such as their phone and computer. This type of structured system will help instill responsibility, accountability, and the concept of natural and logical consequences. This information will be vital in establishing the adolescent's *Blueprint for Success* when they return home. (This is covered in detail in the section Blueprint for Success.)

Once the items needed for continued structure are identified, support the family in isolating the unhealthy behaviors and attempts to control and explore them in further detail. For example, if a family identifies that they spent a majority of their time following their adolescent and checking up on them, support the family by providing a structured way of identifying the amount of time each day spent engaged in these preoccupying activities. The goal is to identify the behaviors and the unmanageability it creates for the family, which supports the family members in gaining more insight and awareness of the unhealthy contributions they were unknowingly making during the adolescent's substance abuse.

Influence

Family members, especially parents, often downplay the degree of influence they have on each other. However, revisiting the concept of *action versus reaction* can be helpful. After discussing and processing the attempts to control, ask the family to explore the idea of positive influence. To entertain a process of thought around influence, ask the family members to think of individuals in their life that they have gone to during times of stress, doubt, or uncertainty, or identify individuals that were mentors or leaders that they looked up to. Then ask the family members to write a list of the characteristics identifying what made them so easy to talk to or look up to. Often responses are as follows: wisdom, good listener, calm, trustworthy, caring, nonjudgmental, available, etc. Then request that the family members compare the list of influential traits with their list of controlling behaviors. The most common response is that the two don't match up. For example, is following someone around and checking up on them providing an environment where trust is present? Or, when someone is yelling and screaming can we choose to respond calmly? This process helps the family recognize that they do have a great degree of influence in their family system, and that influence can be positive even in dire circumstances.

The battle between control and influence can be depicted in graph form (Fig. 7.1), identifying that the true ability to control a child begins to diminish from birth, while the ability to influence that child (positively or negatively) increases over time.

What and How I've Tried to Control		Characteristics of Influence

Where they go
Who their friends are
Have them check in frequently
Following them
Checking GPS, texts, phone calls
Going through their room
Going through their things
Statements of Comparison
  "Why can't you be like your sister?"
  "You are going to be a failure like your uncle."
Guilt, Shame
Bargaining/Barter
Yelling, Screaming
Taking away all their privileges
Flush or throw out substances
Rescuing them, bailing them out
Drug Screens
		Trustworthy
		Good Listener
		Calm
		Caring
		Nonjudgmental
		Positive
		Wisdom
		Spiritual
		Uplifting
		Supportive
		Encouraging
		Available
		Grounded
		Equanimity
		Motivating
		Compassionate
		Realistic

AGE: 0 3 6 9 12 15 18 21

CONTROL ➡

INFLUENCE ➡

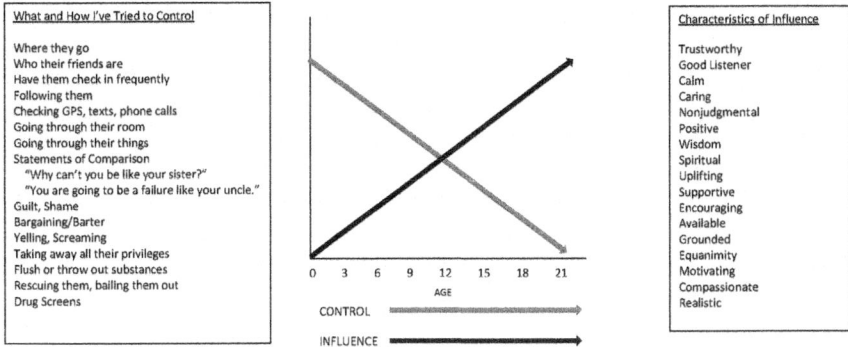

Fig. 7.1 Control versus influence over time

Communication Basics

Those familiar with substance abuse and the impact it has on a family system are highly aware that good communication, or any communication at all, is one of the first things to go (Black 2006) when a child begins to abuse substances. One major area to work on with families is improving communication skills, so that even in the face of difficulties, family members will have the skills to communicate successfully with one another. Revisiting how the family attempted to gain control of their loved one is a good starting point. Identify the verbal means of control: yelling, screaming, statements of guilt, shame, anger/rage, and bribery. After concluding that these types of communication were ineffective, educate the family on healthy communication tools. The basics of healthy communication include good eye contact, mirroring, active listening, using *I-statements*, staying calm, and if necessary, taking a break and coming back to a conversation when all involved can approach the conversation in a healthy manner.

It is essential to have the family explore their own feelings tied to the impact of substance on the family system as well. It can be helpful to create a structured activity to support the family in identifying feeling words, and have the family verbalize those feelings in a therapeutic setting. For example, have each family member list feeling words they experienced while active substance abuse was a part of their family system. Once they have listed those feelings then allow each family to read "When substance abuse was present in my family, I felt _____." Allowing family members to identify and verbally express the feelings can often provide them with a sense of relief, as well as influence healthy communication and sharing of their feelings (Rosenberg 2003). Once family members have read their feelings statements, allow them to have open discussion to further explore the attachment to the identified feelings and how that has impacted their relationship with the family member in treatment.

In addition, educate the family on using I-statements to communicate their thoughts and feelings. In an age where a great deal of our communication is through technology, family members typically struggle with navigating healthy face-to-face communication. Using I-statements in communication provides us with the ability to slow down our thought processes and actually communicate what we are thinking, instead of the *shoulds* or irrational thoughts and beliefs that our brains often present.

When communication is filled with heightened emotions, we have a trap door that closes in our brain, and this trap door can eliminate the ability for our intellect to be utilized in communication. For example, a family member could be feeling overwhelmed and full of fear, but how that might be communicated toward someone might sound like, "Why can't you do anything right, instead of always causing trouble." A healthy option using I-statements might be, "I feel overwhelmed and worried when I haven't heard from you for days." Learning this way of communication takes time; however, it helps facilitate healthy communication and intimacy in relationships because it creates a pattern of sharing feelings and coherent thoughts, versus creating confusion and chaos. As family members begin to harness their emotions, and understand them better, it can vastly improve the quality of not only their communication but also the quality of their relationships within the family system.

Creating a Safe and Supportive Environment

Thus far, we have identified the importance of educating a family in adolescent/young adult substance abuse, supporting family members in identifying their own unhealthy behaviors that have developed in the family system, challenging family members to focus on self-care, identifying areas of enabling and codependency, and lastly improving communication skills within the family system. One of the final areas to focus on prior to a child returning home from residential treatment is establishing a safe and supportive home environment.

Mood Altering Chemicals in the Home

Many parents often ask professionals, "Now that we know our child has a problem with substances, does that mean we need to stop having a glass of wine with dinner?" Short answer is, yes. Not only does removing substances provide a safe environment it also shows support for sobriety. If the parent responds that they do not want to change their life (occasional drinking), then there are obviously complicated issues that need to be addressed prior to the adolescent returning home. This is a good example of control versus influence, and addressing the influence, positive or negative, a parent can have in the home environment, as well as their overall relationship with their child, is required. On the upside, many families do have a positive response to establishing a safe and supportive home environment.

They sometimes take this opportunity as a way for all family members to become healthier physically, emotionally, and spiritually, to improve the overall well-being of the family system, and to develop an attitude of a family in recovery. Also, providers should prompt the parents by letting them know that even if their child comes home and says to the parent, "You can drink, I never did like alcohol anyway," that they need to respond in a supportive way, "We want to support a healthier family and home environment."

Of course, it is typical that there may be other mood altering chemicals in the home that will remain in the home, such as prescriptions that are prescribed to other family members for certain conditions. It is imperative that prescriptions are safe-guarded as much as possible to ensure that the family member returning from treatment cannot gain access to the prescriptions.

Laying the Ground Rules and Expectations

Regardless if you call it guidelines, expectations, or boundaries, families will want to establish these prior to their child returning home. When developing this plan with the family, it is important not to ostracize the child returning home. All family members should have learned by this point that they have many areas they need to change and work on, and all family members need to be included in the expectations and rules in the family home.

A great way to identify, keep track of and implement the expectations is recommending to the family to purchase a white board large enough to include all family members' names, and a list of family rules and expectations. By far, the main purpose behind the expectations and guidelines is to have a structured environment for the family. However, it is also true that the way the expectations and guidelines are implemented prepares a way for family involvement and cohesion, instead of the previous separation that likely occurred during active substance use.

Blueprint for Success

Establishing boundaries and expectations will likely be a two to three therapeutic session discussion. Family members will be at the drawing board as a team, identifying what they would like to see improve in their family system, and developing structure that will lead to that success. Some of the hallmarks of success would include, at a minimum, the following:

Respectful family communication. No cursing, name calling, blaming, etc. This is an area where family members will practice and implement the I-statements, implement good listening skills, respecting and validating one another's feelings, and if someone in the family needs a break from conversation, honoring that request.

Family involvement. Establish a regular time spent together as family. Assist the family in identifying activities that will foster family communication and healthy interactions, such as family meals, family game night, or other activities they can participate in together.

Lending a hand. A sibling in a family I was working with said it best, "We all live under this roof, so we should all lend a hand." Establish within the home that everyone can support one another in maintaining the home. Historically, chores were a part of helping out the entire family, and somehow over generations became a method of punishment or a way for someone to do something to lessen the burden on someone else. The concept of lending a hand can provide opportunities to learn responsibilities; however, it can also be used to improve quality time when joining in these tasks with two or more people involved. For instance, having a family workday where everyone helps out with raking the leaves, trimming the lawn, etc., or having a family cleaning day. This fosters time together as family, and it does not use chores as punishment. It also serves as a time to communicate. Encourage parents to change their way of thinking when it comes to chores. Instead of mom telling daughter to clean the living room, use it as an opportunity for both of them to do it together, with it being a moment they can spend time together and talk to one another. This type of arrangement also provides that moment for a parent to have positive influence.

Family self-care. This is also an area of positive influence for the parents. When a child returns home from treatment, they will likely be expected to continue therapy, attend support groups, and/or meetings. In return, the parents and siblings will need to continue to participate in their support groups, family therapy, etc. When the identified child that returns home from treatment sees the rest of the family engaged in family recovery, this will have a positive influence on them to continue to take care of their own individual recovery.

Leftovers. Some areas where the family will need to determine expectations and boundaries leftover from the discussion above concerns curfew, privileges, school/grades, social activities, etc. It is helpful to establish these expectations based on the initial return home, with the understanding they can be reviewed and changed after 2 weeks, 30 days, and so on, based on needs identified by the treatment center, as well as other clinicians involved.

When the teenager returns home from treatment, and other siblings are in the home, there can be some complications regarding what is fair/unfair. If a parent has a 17-year old returning home that has a twin sibling, how can they establish different curfews without it being an issue? It is important for the parents to have an open and honest conversation that the child returning home will have some different expectations for a while, but that it is not punishment; rather, it is to support them in being successful in their recovery. Understandably, the child may not see it as support and most likely will not; however, it is important for parents to be consistent and not waver on what will be important for their child's continued recovery. When talking about young people, SEC women's basketball coach Pat Summitt used a quote from John Wooten in her book *Sum It Up,* stating, "I don't have to treat them all the same, but I treat them all fairly" (Summit 2013). In establishing

Table 7.1 Example blueprint for success

Boundary	Expectation	Boundary kept	Boundary not kept
Curfew	Sun–Thurs: Home after school daily. Fri–Sat: Home by 9 pm	Increased curfew after 30 days	Loss of night out for 1 week
Nights Out	One night out on weekend	Increase in # of nights out after 30 days.	Loss of night out for 1 week
Grades	No late or missed assignments	Good grades	Loss of good grades and loss of identified privilege
Respectful Family communication	Positive, healthy communication	Good communication with family	Poor relationship and possible loss of privilege

The Following Expectations are to be used to support you in a successful recovery. They will be reviewed after 30 days and changed based on your overall well-being

the expectations, it is important for each item identified (curfew, number of nights out per week, phone/car/computer privileges) that there are clear results if the boundary is kept or not kept. The following, Table 7.1, is a brief example of a Blueprint for Success.

It is important that the child returning home be involved in establishing their Blueprint for Success. If they can participate in establishing the plan, it allows them to have the opportunity to have their voice in the plan, but it also makes them very aware of the expectations, which is helpful when there is a struggle concerning the boundaries.

Family Continuum of Care

When the child returns home, as the home clinician, your work continues. The family will be functioning under new ideas and a new norm; therefore, being a constant for the family will be imperative. Common areas that will need continued work and growth will likely be communication, supporting each other's recovery process, and most importantly, clinicians become a sounding board and *go to* person for initial dilemmas. You will also serve as a mediator for the family, as well as a source of accountability for the new guidelines and expectations established.

Conclusion

As family members receive therapy at home while their loved one is in treatment, there are many areas that can be assessed and a plan developed so that family members receive vital treatment, education, and support themselves while their loved one is experiencing their own individual treatment, change, and growth. Developing a standard plan to work with the families is helpful, not only for the family to have a structured process to walk through emotionally, but it will allow them to also understand what is a priority for them and their . As mentioned throughout this chapter, family members often feel blindsided by the fact they have found themselves in the midst of their current situation and often believe "this shouldn't be happening to us." A good treatment plan for the family will help them slowly detach from those thoughts and allow them to move forward in their healing. A sample standard treatment plan/outline that can be utilized with most families that have a child/young adult in residential treatment is provided in Appendix. As always, collaborating with the child's treatment program throughout the family sessions is essential. This allows the child or young adult to be a part of the process as much as possible. After the child has transitioned home, therapists should continue to support the entire family system in ongoing family therapy as needed.

Appendix

Early Sessions

- Review with the family past and present crises.
    - Explore the family history of behaviors, addiction, and their relationships in general.
    - Map out a structure of the family unit, both historically, and ideal for the future.
- Identify with the family the early warning signs of substance abuse.
- Identify individual and family strengths, as well as healthy coping skills and self-care.
- Identify past unsuccessful strategies/interventions.
- Action Steps:
    - Support family in developing coping skills and focus on self-care.
    - Encourage family to attend family programming offered by the treatment center.

Middle Sessions

- Support family in identifying and communicating their feelings/reactions to substance abuse in their family.
- Assist and educate the family in developing their own sober support system.

- Educational information: following families participation in a family program, continue to discuss the information gained, and if no family program was available, provide needed education through additional family sessions.
- Action Steps:
  - Encourage family members to attend support groups: Al-Anon, Alateen, Nar-Anon, and other family aftercare programs.
  - Completion of a family program, or further education within family sessions.
  - Encourage open and honest communication on thoughts/feelings by asking the family members to participate in daily feelings/thoughts check-in with one another.

Later Sessions

- Focus on personal strengths of individuals in the family, as well as family system strengths.
- Develop short-term goals and long-term goals based on findings throughout therapy sessions.
- Action Steps:
  - Begin developing the family's Blueprint for Success.
  - Identify areas of change for the family system and implement these into the Blueprint for Success.
  - Scheduling appointments for the child returning home. Appointments with an individual therapist and psychiatrist for medication management (if necessary).

References

Al-Anon Family Group. (2016). *The family disease of alcoholism.* Retrieved from http://www.al-anon-sc.org/the-family-disease-of-alcoholism.html

Black, C. (2006). *Family strategies: Practical tools for professionals treating families impacted by addiction.* California: Mac Publishing.

Barnard, M. (2007). *Drug addiction and families.* Philadelphia: Jessica Kingsley Publishers.

Conyers, B. (2003). *Addict in the family: Stories of loss, hope and recovery.* Minnesota: Center City.

Gifford, S. (2013). *Family involvement is important in substance abuse treatment.* Retrieved from http://psychcentral.com/lib/family-involvement-is-important-in-substance-abuse-treatment/

Liddle, H., Rowe, C., Dakof, G., Ungaro, R., & Henderson, C. (2004). Early intervention for adolescent substance abuse: Pretreatment to posttreatment outcomes of a randomized clinical trial comparing multidimensional family therapy and peer group treatment. *Journal of Psychoactive Drugs, 36,* 49–63.

Rosenberg, M. (2003). *Nonviolent communication: A language of life*. California: Puddledancer Press.
Sheff, D. (2008). *Beautiful boy: A father's journey thru his son's addiction*. New York: Houghton Mifflin Company.
Summitt, P. (2013). *Sum it up* (p. 229). New York: Crown Archetype.

Author Biography

Heather Hendrickson, LPC, MHSP, NCC has served in the field of counseling for approximately 10 years in the middle Tennessee area. She is currently the Assistant Director of Treatment Services for The Next Door, a residential treatment center which provides treatment for substance abuse and co-occurring issues for women. She has served as the Director of Family Services for a nationally recognized substance abuse treatment program. In addition, Heather works with individuals, couples, and families in a private practice setting. She has experience working with children, adolescents, young adults, and their families. She has presented at conferences on various issues that impact the adolescent and young adult population including developmental issues, substance abuse, and life transitions. Heather achieved her MA in Professional Counseling from Argosy University-Georgia School of Psychology. She is a National Certified Counselor, Licensed Professional Counselor and a designated Mental Health Service Provider.

Chapter 8
Intentional Separation of Families: Increasing Differentiation Through Wilderness Therapy

Kirsten L. Bolt and Tony Issenmann

Chapter Highlights

- Family systems can become entrenched in unhealthy dynamics that manifest as acute clinical symptoms in adolescent children.
- Increasing differentiation levels and decreasing chronic anxiety are necessary to promote greater wellness for the adolescent and family.
- Intentionally separating the family system and intensely treating the clinical and family system issues can be the most effective way to meet those goals.
- Wilderness therapy provides an environment that can reduce chronic family anxiety by separating the adolescent from the family and treating the family system as a whole.
- Intentional interventions in wilderness therapy can increase differentiation of parents and adolescents by better balancing autonomy and connection, as well as rational thought and emotional experiencing.

I not only have my beautiful boy back, but even better, we've been through the crucible together, and have this amazing shared experience. It's not always been pleasant, or easy, of course, but it is intimate, and ours, and a solid base to continue building a rich, appreciative, and enriching relationship between us.

– Father of an adolescent boy after completing wilderness therapy

Countless stories exist of adolescents who have failed every community-based treatment option, leaving their parents and family members feeling hopeless about the future. How do we best support these adolescents, their parents, and their families when nothing seems to be effective? In some instances, the most effective family treatment is the least expected; namely, separating the family. This is not the solution for the majority of struggling adolescents and families, but rather a particular pop-

K.L. Bolt (✉) · T. Issenmann
Open Sky Wilderness Therapy, PO Box 2201, Durango, CO 81302, USA
e-mail: kirsten@openskywilderness.com

T. Issenmann
e-mail: drtony@openskywilderness.com

© Springer International Publishing AG 2017
J.D. Christenson and A.N. Merritts (eds.), *Family Therapy with Adolescents in Residential Treatment*, Focused Issues in Family Therapy,
DOI 10.1007/978-3-319-51747-6_8

ulation. In families where an adolescent is displaying acute clinical issues, with family system distress, and the adolescent is not responding to typical therapeutic interventions (e.g.,parent coaching, outpatient programming, psychopharmacology, intensive outpatient treatment, short-term hospitalization, or longer term residential treatment), something more drastic and counterintuitive, such as wilderness therapy, can provide the foundation for long-term change (Russell and Phillips-Miller 2002; Russell and Hendee 1999; Russell 2000).

To further clarify the specific population addressed in this chapter, it should be noted these families have typically exhausted local resources, the adolescent seems unable or unwilling to change course and might appear out of control, and the parents are frequently at a loss for what to do next in order to help their child (Russell and Hendee 1999; Russell 2000). Frequently, there exist entrenched, unhealthy patterns in these family systems (Bandoroff and Scherer 1994; Bowen 1978; Harper and Russell 2008; Wells et al. 2004), such as: permissive or authoritarian parenting styles, poor emotional regulation skills, enmeshed or cutoff family relationships, withdrawal and pursuit dynamics between parent and child, parents rescuing and/or enabling their child, invalidation of emotions, and triangulation or other problematic communication patterns.

As aforementioned, it is not only the existence of an unhealthy family system that might warrant therapeutic family separation, but also an adolescent experiencing acute clinical issues who might be at risk of serious harm to self or others, and/or is in a physically or emotionally unsafe environment (Bettmann and Tucker 2011; Russell et al. 2000; Russell and Hendee 1999). A wide variety of clinical issues precede intentional and therapeutic separation of a family. Specific clinical disorders often include: depression, anxiety, emerging personality disorders, Oppositional Defiant Disorder, Bipolar Disorder, and Posttraumatic Stress Disorder (Bettmann and Tucker 2011). Other clinical issues might be related to trauma, adoption and attachment issues, bereavement and loss, gender identity and sexual orientation, and cognitive or other executive functioning issues such as Attention-Deficit/Hyperactivity Disorder (Bettmann and Tucker 2011; Russell et al. 2000). Manifesting from those clinical issues many symptoms tend to exist, such as: alcohol and other drug abuse (Bettmann et al. 2012), self-harm, disordered eating, excessive gaming or Internet use, promiscuity, pornography, aggression, school avoidance, suicidal thoughts or actions, losing oneself in relationships, and family cutoff or enmeshment patterns. (Russell and Hendee 1999; Russell et al. 2000). Typically, adolescents treated in this type of setting are experiencing a combination of these possible presenting problems.

One final note regarding the population of focus in this chapter; these adolescents and families also tend to be stuck in the earliest stages of change (Bettmann et al. 2012; Prochaska and DiClemente 1983). More specifically, adolescents frequently are unaware of the problems that seem so obvious to everyone else at home, or they blame their parents for those problems. At other times, adolescents are aware of the problems, but experience ambivalence about change (Miller and Rollnick 2002), and as such, do not demonstrate significant progress toward change, or even engagement in the change process. These two stages are termed *pre-contemplation* and *contemplation*, respectively, and are the earliest stages of change in the trans-theoretical model (Prochaska and DiClemente 1983). Despite substantial support, effort, and intervention at home, the entire family system can be ambivalent about change; it is not only the adolescent in question. Prochaska and Velicer (1997) found approximately 20% of people are ready for change at any given time. This finding leaves 80% of people who are *not* ready, which might explain the difficulty therapists sometimes experience in trying to create long-lasting family system changes. Accordingly, the importance of resolving ambivalence about change within the entire family system, not only the identified patient, is well documented throughout the literature (Bandoroff and Scherer 1994; Brinkmeyer et al. 2004; Harper and Russell 2008; Wells et al. 2004).

This chapter explores how intentional family separation via wilderness therapy programs can serve adolescents with clinically acute symptoms, and unhealthy and entrenched family relational patterns, who are not responding to more conventional treatment modalities. In the first section below, Murray Bowen's (1978) concepts of *differentiation of self* and *chronic anxiety* are reviewed, as they lay the foundation to understand how intentional family separation in wilderness therapy effectively treats this client population (Bettmann and Tucker 2011; Russell 2000, 2003, 2005; Russell and Hendee 1999). The final section of this chapter examines the various wilderness therapy interventions that facilitate increased differentiation levels in parents and adolescents, both on the individual and relational continuums. The term wilderness therapy, as used in this chapter, is congruent with the term Outdoor Behavioral Healthcare, as described in this Chapter and Chaps. 15, 16, and 18.

Intentional Separation of Family

For severely troubled adolescents and their parents, separating the adolescent from the family can be a fundamental first step, but separation alone is not the solution (Bandoroff and Scherer 1994; Russell and Hendee 1999). The family must be engaged in an intentional therapeutic process to increase *differentiation of self* (Bowen 1978), thereby enabling the alleviation of clinical and family relational symptoms (Bandoroff and Scherer 1994; Bowen 1978; Harper and Russell 2008).

Bowen Family Therapy

Bowen family therapy is based on Bowen theory (1978) and is one of the fundamental approaches to family therapy (Goldenberg and Goldenberg 1996). Murray Bowen, a pioneer in the field of family therapy, developed family systems theory in an effort to leave traditional psychoanalytic approaches, which focused primarily on individual functioning, for an approach that would emphasize the relational dynamics of a family unit (Goldenberg and Goldenberg 1996; Kerr and Bowen 1988).

Differentiation. One of the main concepts fueling Bowen's theory is the concept of differentiation. Kerr and Bowen (1988) state that every human enters the world an infant, completely dependent on others. As the infant grows older, he or she has the task of developing into an increasingly independent person. With this developmental task comes the challenge of differentiating. There are two levels of tasks to balance when striving to differentiate, an individual level and a relational level (Ault-Riche 1986).

Individual level. On an individual level, one is faced with the task of balancing emotional functioning with intellectual functioning (Ault-Riche 1986; Walsh and Scheinkman 1989).

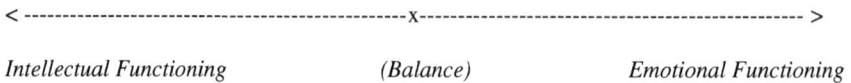

< --x-- >

Intellectual Functioning   *(Balance)*   *Emotional Functioning*

Most individuals are inclined to operate primarily out of one of the two functions (Apter 1990; Chodorow 1978; Knudson-Martin 1994; Lyons 1983; Tannen 1990); however, differentiation occurs when one learns to balance intellectual and emotional functioning. Neither intellectual nor emotional functioning is superior to the other; rather, both are necessary for healthy functioning (Ault-Riche 1986; Kerr and Bowen 1988). The less able one is to balance intellectual functioning with emotional functioning, the more likely one is to experience prolonged periods of anxiety (Kerr and Bowen 1988; Taffel and Masters 1989; Walsh and Scheinkman 1989).

Relational level. The second-level task is relational and involves balancing togetherness and connectedness with individuality and autonomy (Ault-Riche 1986; Bowen 1978; Kerr and Bowen 1988; McGoldrick and Carter 1999; Schnarch 1997; Walsh and Scheinkman 1989).

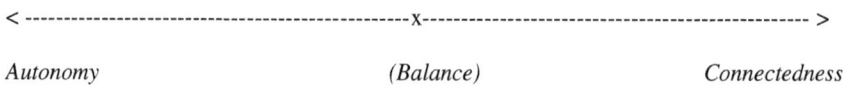

< --x-- >

Autonomy   *(Balance)*   *Connectedness*

The extremes of these two functions are emotional fusion and emotional cutoff. On this level, individuals must evaluate the way they relate with others; increased differentiation comes when one is able to connect with others in meaningful ways without losing oneself in the relationship. As with the individual level, most people have a preferred style of relating to others (Apter 1990; Chodorow 1978; Knudson-Martin 1994; Lyons 1983; Tannen 1990). In regards to relationships, individuals tend to fall on either the cutoff or fused end of the spectrum. When one learns to function out of both sides of the spectrum, one will be less likely to lose oneself in a relationship or to find oneself without meaningful connections (Schnarch 1997). "In a well-differentiated family... people recognize their realistic dependence on one another but are able to be fairly autonomous in their emotional functioning" (Kerr and Bowen 1988, p. 94).

All individuals will experience symptoms of anxiety in situations that produce a high enough level of stress (Bowen 1978; Kerr and Bowen 1988; Titelman 1998). Miller et al. (2004) validated Bowen's theory in finding that *chronic anxiety* in the family system is inversely correlated with differentiation levels (i.e., as differentiation decreases, chronic anxiety increases). Individuals less able to balance the tasks of differentiation are more susceptible to ongoing anxiety and further problem development (Kerr and Bowen 1988; McGoldrick et al. 1989; Schnarch 1997; Taffel and Masters 1989; Walsh and Scheinkman 1989). Those able to balance individuality with togetherness, and balance emotional functioning with intellectual functioning, are better able to handle stressful situations; therefore, they are better able to manage increased levels of anxiety, and they are less likely to experience chronic problems (Bowen 1978; Kerr and Bowen 1988; McKnight 1998; Papero 1990; Titelman 1998).

Until one is able to differentiate, one is likely to experience heightened and continuous levels of anxiety due to the interrelatedness of differentiation and connection with others. One adapts to the environment in which one grows and because many people are not exposed to healthy relationships in childhood, if one is to differentiate one must learn to act differently as one matures (Bowen 1978; Kerr and Bowen 1988; Papero 1990). Kerr and Bowen (1988) suggested that individuals attempt to manage their anxiety via emotionally fused or distant relationships, triangulation of other family members, psychological or physical health issues in oneself or one's children, or acting-out behaviors to distract from the problem. When one adapts to incorporate such strategies into one's individual functioning, one is likely to experience persistent problems.

Basic and functional differentiation. There are two fundamental types of differentiation: basic and functional (Bowen 1978; Gratwick Baker 1998; Kerr and Bowen 1988). One's basic level of differentiation is difficult to change, and is in large part affected by the level of emotional separation achieved from one's family of origin (Gratwick Baker 1998; Kerr and Bowen 1988). Along these lines, the more differentiated a person, the greater the ability to separate the emotional process from the intellectual process (Bowen 1978; Kerr and Bowen 1988; Schnarch 1997; Titelman 1998). Functional differentiation can vary above or below one's basic level of differentiation in response to relationships and life stressors, which makes determining one's basic level of differentiation difficult. It is one's functional level of differentiation that is observable (Gratwick Baker 1998; Kerr and Bowen 1988).

When confronted with stressful situations, individuals with high basic differentiation easily adapt and think of resourceful solutions, whereas individuals with a low basic level can be seriously affected by periods of high anxiety. "When anxiety is low, people are less reactive and more thoughtful" (Kerr and Bowen 1988, p. 99), giving the impression of a higher basic level of differentiation. Therefore, during times of low stress and anxiety, an individual with a low basic level of differentiation can function at a higher level of differentiation, giving the appearance of possessing a higher basic level of differentiation. On the other hand, low levels of functional differentiation are observable when anxiety is high and individuals and systems begin deteriorating. Kerr and Bowen (1988) point out that the higher one's basic level of differentiation, "the more *consistently* high the functional level, and the less the *discrepancy* in the functional levels" (p. 99). Therefore, one with a higher basic level of differentiation experiences an increased capacity to repeatedly handle stressful situations.

Individuation versus connectedness. A Bowen theorist (Bowen 1978) assumes that each person has the deeply rooted desire to develop one's individuality by differentiating from others. Bowen theorists also believe that one possesses the innate desire for connectedness or togetherness (Bowen 1978; Kerr and Bowen 1988). Although this is a personal developmental task, due to the nature of systems, this process can be aided or hindered by familial relationships. Bowen believed that one's level of differentiation is closely related to the level of differentiation of one's parents, as well as to the characteristics of one's relationships with family members (Bowen 1978; Kerr and Bowen 1988; Titelman 1998). Therefore, if one's parents have a low level of differentiation, it is likely that one will also have a low level of differentiation and will engage in many of the same interaction patterns as one's parents.

The higher the level of differentiation, the greater one's ability to differentiate between thoughts and emotions, thus allowing the choice of being directed by one's *head* or *gut*. This is an important skill when considering the struggle to separate from an enmeshed family or the attempt to connect with an emotionally cutoff family, because rather than being unaware of one's actions, one is actively involved in the developing relationship with family members. Individuals with low levels of differentiation and who are enmeshed rely heavily on the opinions of others and thus do not manage well apart from enmeshed relationships (Bowen 1978; Kerr and Bowen 1988; Titelman 1998). Therefore, the more differentiated one becomes, the less reliant one is on others, and the greater one's ability to engage in emotional relationships without being over- or under-involved.

Defining self. Kerr and Bowen (1988) state that complete differentiation exists when one resolves all emotional attachment to one's family. Complete un-differentiation is exactly the opposite, and exists when one does not achieve any emotional separation from one's family. Although these extremes are highly unlikely, if not impossible, to attain, they serve as theoretical guides for measuring one's level of differentiation. If motivated, it is possible to raise one's basic level of differentiation. This is a difficult task that involves a gradual process of "acquiring new knowledge and experience" (Bowen 1978, p. 473). The struggle to define self is sometimes considered a selfish act of avoiding others, and is therefore easily forsaken by individuals not truly invested in the process. Individuals who resign from the differentiating process are usually individuals with a low level of differentiation. Avoidance, however, undermines one's attempts to differentiate. Schnarch (1997) explains that differentiating involves growing closer to others while growing more distinct, rather than distant. The result of differentiating will be an individual who is more self-aware in the midst of emotional relationships with others (Bowen 1978; Kerr and Bowen 1988; Schnarch 1997; Titelman 1998). This does not mean that becoming more differentiated causes one to care less about others, but rather that one's actions are less dependent on those with whom he or she is in an emotional relationship.

Although many people wish to differentiate, or develop a more defined self, there is typically much resistance from others, including spouse, parents, siblings, and close friends (Bowen 1978; Hanes Meyer 1998; Kerr and Bowen 1988). This resistance is attributed to the perceived change in the relationship (Bowen 1978; Kerr and Bowen 1988; Titelman 1998). The loved ones combat the change with efforts to control in hopes of restoring the established ways of relating (Jackson 1957). If one is successful in continuing the pursuit of a higher level of differentiation despite the resistance, one will work not only to define oneself, but also to model effective differentiation for others. "Differentiation is a product of a way of thinking that translates into a way of being" (Kerr and Bowen 1988, p. 108).

Benefits of Differentiating

Raising one's level of differentiation has many benefits, the first of which is the ability to develop intimate relationships. Schnarch (1997) writes "becoming more differentiated is possibly the most loving thing you can do in your lifetime—for those you love as well as yourself" (p. 73). Kerr and Bowen write "the more differentiated a self, the more a person can be an individual *while in emotional contact with the group*" (1988, p. 94). Highly differentiated individuals do not avoid or grow anxious about intimate relationships, but rather embrace such relationships, allowing individuals to have more meaningful connections.

Another benefit of a high level of differentiation is the ability to cope in times of high stress (Bowen 1978; Hanes Meyer 1998; Kerr and Bowen 1988; Titelman 1998). There are several reasons for this. One is that highly differentiated individuals adapt easily to new situations and "require considerable stress to trigger symptoms" (Kerr and Bowen 1988, p. 112). In addition, because one who is well-differentiated is less reactive, one handles stressful situations in a manner consistent with his or her beliefs. Maintaining one's belief system in times of stress may be an indication that one is able to process the situation intellectually rather than reacting emotionally. An additional explanation is that "better differentiated people are more successful in maintaining a network of emotionally supportive relationships" (Kerr and Bowen 1988, p. 118). For these reasons, highly differentiated people are likely to continually experience greater levels of satisfaction than those with lower levels of differentiation.

Differentiation levels also influence parenting styles, which in turn influence the differentiation levels of children (Schwartz et al. 2006; Baumrind 1966, 1967; Bowen 1978, Kerr and Bowen 1988). *Permissive* parents tend to enable and rescue their child, make excuses for poor behavior, and not hold boundaries or provide consequences that allow children to feel safe and to learn healthy parameters (Baumrind, 1966, 1967). These parents might also meet their needs for connection or anxiety-reduction through their children (Bowen 1978). *Authoritarian* parents tend not to attune to their child's emotions and experiences, and in turn, tend to invalidate their child, often resulting in lowered self-worth (Baumrind, 1966; Baumrind, 1967). They might parent from a place of fear and try to instill fear in their child. And they might meet their needs for autonomy through their children. More ideal is the *authoritative* parent who balances warmth and supportiveness, with firm control of actions. (Baumrind 1966, 1967). In order to achieve the tasks of authoritative parenting, one must manage one's own emotional reactivity on the individual level of differentiation, as well as attune to oneself and one's child on the relational level of differentiation.

Another benefit to differentiating includes being able to interrupt intergenerational family patterns so that children are not the beneficiaries of parents' emotional stressors (e.g., a father who was routinely hit by his own father when he made mistakes might parent his own son the same way; or a mother whose parents were emotionally detached might in turn be distant with her own children). Increased differentiation might also enable parents to resolve their own mental health issues (e.g., depression, anxiety, personality disorders, and substance abuse), painful or traumatic experiences (e.g., a family car accident, infertility, or the loss of a child), changes in the family constellation (e.g., due to divorce, remarriage, or blending families), or chronic crisis (e.g., homelessness or poverty), thereby helping decrease chronic anxiety for one's children. Also, working to differentiate can bring greater clarity and resolution to intergenerational experiences of trauma (e.g., Holocaust survivors or families emigrating from war-torn countries) that can impact children generations later despite a current absence of traumatic events.

Lastly, due to the nature of both basic and functional differentiation, as anxiety increases, functional differentiation decreases (Gratwick Baker 1998; Kerr and Bowen 1988; Titelman 1998). In a close family system, this decrease in functional differentiation leads to borrowed functioning, a process in which individuals in a close relationship borrow from the other's functional level as an attempt to alleviate anxiety or symptoms of anxiety (Gratwick Baker 1998; Kerr and Bowen 1988; Titelman 1998). While in a wilderness therapy program, an adolescent has the opportunity to evade, for a period of time, the borrowed functioning of one's family of origin. This brief escape provides one the opportunity to develop new patterns of interacting with others and to increase one's basic differentiation. That separation coupled with the many varying experiences involved with participating in a wilderness program provides the adolescent the chance to evaluate and challenge his or her beliefs, a vital component of defining self (Kerr and Bowen 1988; McKnight 1998; Russell 2000). Norton et al. (2014) found wilderness therapy to be an effective means to facilitate higher levels of differentiation, develop identity complexity, and serve as a bridge between childhood and adulthood. As will be seen more fully below, wilderness therapy can serve as a catalyst for the development of crucial aspects of differentiation, as outlined above.

Increasing Differentiation Through Wilderness Therapy Interventions

Wilderness therapy naturally facilitates the process of differentiation via intentional family separation combined with engagement in intensive individual and family therapeutic processes. When adolescents enroll, they usually join an existing small group of peers of similar age, gender, and clinical issues, which provides an opportunity for communal living, as discussed later. Bettmann et al. (2012) indicated that wilderness therapy is particularly effective with clients in early stages of change (Prochaska and DiClemente 1983), and interestingly, wilderness therapy clients do not need to be ready to change in order to actually create change (Bettmann et al. 2012).

Primary treatment goals for adolescents in wilderness therapy programs include: (1) stabilization; (2) thorough assessment; (3) initial treatment; and (4) long-term planning with specific treatment recommendations (Russell et al. 2000). Therapy exists on multiple levels, which include weekly individual therapy, weekly group therapy, daily therapeutic groups and process groups, milieu therapy, and many forms of family therapy (Harper and Russell 2008; Russell and Hendee 1999). In addition, every component of the wilderness experience is intentionally designed to be therapeutic (e.g., making bow drill fires, carrying one's possessions in a backpack, hiking from point A to point B, living in a peer group, etc.).

Russell (2003) describes key therapeutic factors that illustrate how wilderness therapy is effective: (a) increased *self-efficacy* via *task completion*, in wilderness living, and with natural consequences; (b) *restructuring of the therapist–client relationship*, in which there is greater opportunity for attunement and connection; and, (c) *group cohesion and development* via outdoor and group living. Another benefit and distinction from other traditional forms of therapy is that adolescents in wilderness therapy provide a captive audience, particularly when they are minors and required to remain in the program by their parents. They are not able to run or hide from their emotional discomfort, but instead they must face it every day. Their unhealthy patterns and negative behaviors manifest somehow in wilderness therapy, enabling them to be addressed. As the expression goes: "wherever you go, there you are."

Parents of adolescents in wilderness therapy programs often express a belief that the only way to gain the clarity necessary for change was removing their child from the unhealthy home environment (Harper and Russell 2008). This powerful statement highlights the benefit of intentional family separation. Not only does the physical separation lead to decreased chronic anxiety in the family system, but the intense therapeutic containment and nurturance by the treatment team helps decrease anxiety as well. Adolescents are constantly monitored to maintain physical and emotional safety. They call their names out loud when out of sight of staff members so the staff always knows where they are. To ensure appropriate and emotionally safe conversations in the peer group, treatment staff overhears all conversations. Natural and logical consequences provide clear cause-and-effect experiences. Daily activities support basic structure (e.g., breaking down and setting up camp, hiking, cooking, etc.). And any safety concerns are reported and addressed immediately (e.g., disordered eating, self-harm actions, etc.).

From a humanistic approach (Rogers 1961), adolescents in wilderness therapy are seen as people with inherently good intentions and abilities. They are supported to determine their own values and beliefs, and to be the best version of themselves. Because of this approach and the physical and emotional safety created by treatment staff, adolescents in wilderness therapy are typically able to relax and engage the therapy process, knowing the treatment team will care for them and keep them safe. This level of containment is effective with parents as well in terms of trusting their child is safe and nurtured, but also in knowing that the treatment team will also care for the parents and that the therapist will guide and challenge them to do their own therapeutic work.

As noted above, decreased family system anxiety occurs in many ways in wilderness therapy and lays the foundation for adolescents and parents to differentiate. The next two sections of this chapter will outline how the most common wilderness therapy interventions specifically support increased differentiation, first on the individual continuum, and then on the relational continuum, though it should be noted that there is overlap on both.

Therapeutic Interventions: Individual Continuum

Wilderness and hard skills. The wilderness itself is an essential and powerful component of the therapeutic process. As Richard Louv (2011) writes, "The pleasure of being alive is brought into sharper focus when you need to pay attention to staying alive" (p. 19). Aspects of wilderness that support differentiation are the varied and unpredictable weather conditions, physical terrain, dependence on water sources or shelter, and the inherent need to focus only on the present moment because there is no access to what is happening elsewhere. Because Nature is unpredictable and uncontrollable, these conditions can be particularly challenging. Accordingly, in spite of, and because of, these challenges, adolescents typically increase their tolerance for discomfort and uncertainty. Their parents also frequently have a parallel experience in needing to accept that weather, physical conditions, and access to their child are out of *their* control as much as they are for their children. This lack of control challenges parents similarly to develop tolerance for discomfort.

In order to survive in the unfamiliar wilderness environment, adolescents must develop *hard skills* such as building shelters, creating backpacks with their belongings, starting bow drill fires, learning procedures to protect the land they are roaming, etc. The development of these skills over time fosters self-efficacy (Russell 2003), and in turn supports autonomy. However, adolescents do not learn these hard skills only for survival purposes. The development of these skills typically requires them to also develop emotion regulation skills in order to overcome the frustration of adapting and learning how to live in the wilderness. For example, bow drill fires are typically very challenging to master and require acknowledging one's emotions, while balancing them with rational thought, thereby supporting balance on the individual continuum of differentiation.

Soft skills. In addition to the hard skills, adolescents must also learn and develop *soft skills*, which support the individual and relational continuums of differentiation through effective and healthy coping and communication skills. Specifically, adolescents learn to better tolerate distress (Linehan 1993), identify, express, and regulate emotions, and to communicate assertively. They practice these skills both individually and relationally in person with peers and treatment staff, but also with their parents from afar through various means, detailed in other sections of this book (see Chap. 2). Some wilderness therapy programs might also emphasize mindfulness practices (e.g., meditation, yoga, etc.), which have been shown to increase differentiation, particularly with regards to emotional reactivity (Kim-Appel and Appel 2013). The soft skills clearly support development along the individual continuum as well as the relational continuum of differentiation.

Identity and values development. Adolescents are typically encouraged to explore their autonomy through the identification of their personal values via therapeutic group sessions and individual therapy assignments. In identifying their core values, adolescents can then assess how they have honored or violated their values in events preceding their wilderness therapy placement, leading to motivation to change. Identifying core values also supports them learning how to better honor those values in the future, thereby supporting differentiation and healthier life choices. These adolescents also experience and celebrate rites of passage (e.g., being sent from home to mature, rituals and ceremonies to mark transitions, and solo experiences that support reflection and contemplation as they sit with themselves and Nature). These rites of passage punctuate influential moments and support autonomy. As a former wilderness therapy client said, "I was able to become a young man and change my life."

Safe relapses. Bettmann and Jasperson (2009) suggest that wilderness therapy is an appropriate and beneficial place to explore new patterns and behaviors because of the opportunity for *safe relapses*. These safe relapses can support both the individual and relational continuums, depending on the regressive behavior. For instance, an adolescent with self-harming behaviors, who has been improving emotional regulation and expressing emotions in healthy ways to the peer group and treatment team, might be able to avoid that coping strategies at low-enough levels of anxiety, but as they receive difficult information from parents (e.g., aftercare plans; see Chap. 9), the functional differentiation might decrease and the adolescent might engage in self-harming behaviors to cope. At this point, the treatment team can intervene, highlight this behavior as a relapse, and provide support and coaching to respond differently, while the adolescent is still at a high level of anxiety. As another example, after weeks of only writing letters between parents and children, the therapist might facilitate a family phone call, during which the adolescent might regress into old patterns of communication (e.g., shutting down, hostility, or manipulation). After the call ends, the adolescent and therapist are able to process that experience, and the adolescent has a week to review it and write an intentional letter the following week clearly articulating thoughts and emotions from the call. Of note, this situation can occur as well with parents, as they practice new patterns, make mistakes, and can then review and respond to those mistakes thoughtfully over the next week.

Therapeutic Interventions: Relational Continuum

There are many ways differentiation on the relational continuum is supported during wilderness therapy—both within the adolescent's peer group and with the family, despite the physical distance. It should be noted that wilderness therapy has a less unique impact on parents. While adolescents are immersed in a transformative experience constantly for their two to three months at the program, in contrast, parents still live their regular lives and do not have the benefit of trained professionals available at all times to intervene and offer support or coaching. Accordingly, adolescents at the end of their wilderness therapy programs might have greater gains in differentiation than their parents, and might even be the experts in some areas (e.g., use of communication or emotion regulation skills). Nevertheless, the intentional family separation inherent to wilderness therapy provides many opportunities for intensive and highly effective family therapy, some of which occurs in the peer group through transference experiences and communal living.

Communal living. As aforementioned, adolescents in wilderness therapy live in small groups (typically up to nine or ten people), which naturally creates many opportunities for conflict resolution, as disagreements are common in communal living. The small peer group with treatment team staff replicates a family system and adolescents tend to fall into similar roles in wilderness as they do at home. These patterns provide the treatment team great insight and observations of behaviors. And because the adolescents cannot escape each other (similar to a family), there tends to be more incentive to improve interpersonal skills and conflict resolution. Related to communal living, adolescents have opportunities to improve their sense of autonomy, since an important component of group living is valuing and caring for oneself in order to support others. In a typical wilderness therapy group, some adolescents are people-pleasers, and need support to honor themselves; other adolescents struggle to empathize, and need support to see the needs and feelings of others.

Personal responsibility. Also supporting autonomy and connection are specific opportunities for personal responsibility and leadership. Adolescents are expected to be accountable for past actions that hurt themselves and others, and they have specific assignments to support this process, such as a letter of responsibility (see Chap. 2). Also at a certain point in the wilderness experience, adolescents typically become peer leaders and mentors due to their knowledge and skills-development. This leadership supports differentiation through the necessity of attuning to and managing one's own emotions and thoughts, while also balancing those of each team member and the overall team, thereby also supporting growth on the relational continuum.

Boundary setting. Before, during, and after the wilderness therapy process, parents have opportunities to practice balancing the relational continuum through setting and maintaining boundaries. Just making the decision to enroll their child in wilderness therapy is sometimes the most significant boundary parents establish with their child. Reinforcing that boundary every day their child is enrolled can be powerful, and painful, particularly if the adolescent is writing letters begging to go home, withholding love by not writing, expressing anger and resentment, reporting they feel worse and even suicidal in wilderness, or threatening parents with the loss of their relationship if they don't bring the child home immediately (all of which are common during the first couple of weeks). Parents often have opportunities during wilderness therapy to set boundaries with their children (e.g., "No, I won't tell your friends where you are;" "I will not engage with you when you write to me using curse words and aggression;" "No, I will not contact your boyfriend because I do not believe that is a healthy relationship and I am not going to support it"). The reverse can also be true for some adolescents who need to be assertive or to better set boundaries with their parents (e.g., "Dad, I am not going to continue reading your letters because your words are condescending and hurtful;" "Mom, when you don't write to me every week, I feel hurt. Please write to me"). Toward the end of treatment, parents have additional opportunities to set boundaries related to after-care planning (see Chap. 9).

Direct family involvement. As has been already articulated, it is vital to include the family system directly in the treatment process, intentionally and thoroughly, in order to facilitate long-term change (Bandoroff and Scherer 1994; Brinkmeyer et al. 2004; Harper and Russell 2008). There are a number of ways this can be done, many of which have been detailed extensively in other chapters of this book; accordingly, only a brief overview of each will be provided here, along with a reference to the other chapters. The most obvious expression of family system engagement occurs through their direct communication process, which is primarily, if not solely, done through weekly written letters (Russell 2000). Chapter 2 of this book describes the process and benefits of letter writing in detail. Due to the physical separation and subsequent decrease in chronic anxiety, intentional and directive letter writing enables family members to communicate more deliberately and with less reactivity than historically might have occurred. In addition to the intentional and directive letter-writing process, some therapists might also facilitate one or more intentional therapeutic family phone calls during the treatment process. One reason to engage this type of family contact might be to practice the skills together that they are developing separately (e.g., I-feel statements, reflective listening, validation, etc.). Another reason might be to discuss a particular thera- peutic topic in more depth, or for the therapist to better assess the family dynamics. Often, these calls can help parents and adolescents realize that the other is indeed engaged in treatment and doing their own therapeutic growth, which is sometimes hard to recognize from afar. These calls provide opportunities to practice balancing autonomy and connection, and intellectual and emotional functioning.

Various methods exist to engage parents more deeply in their own therapeutic work as well. Chapters 7, 18, and 19 are entirely devoted to this subject, and the reader should look there for additional information. However, as noted in Chap. 18 intentional workshops can be effective in engaging parents during the wilderness therapy experience. These workshops can be powerful when parents and their children do not actually reunite, and instead the focus is strictly on the parents and their personal growth areas.

Similarly to the parent workshops, weekly homework assignments can be effective in supporting deeper family therapeutic growth by parents doing the same type of work as their child. Assignments can be meaningfully and intentionally designed to highlight particular patterns or teach new topics. They can also mirror the process the adolescents are doing in the field in further defining self, goals, values, etc. (see Chap. 14).

When the wilderness therapist determines a family is ready to reunite and work together in person, an intensive, single-family, therapeutic experience can be created that supports specific and pre-determined goals. These retreats have proven to be very powerful and effective at helping families improve balance on the individual and relational continuums of differentiation. Chapters 17 and 18 provide a substantial amount of information that can be used to learn about this type of intervention.

When combined with a culminating experience at the end of wilderness therapy (e.g., a *graduation* experience), therapeutic family retreats can provide a clear sense of the family's progress during their separation. Part of these culminating experiences is also preparing for the inevitable challenges ahead, knowing it's easier to have done the work of differentiation during the physical separation, and harder to maintain that growth once they are reunited.

Conclusion

This chapter has aimed to demonstrate that, although challenging, it is possible to increase one's basic level of differentiation through decreasing one's chronic anxiety and engaging in an intentional therapeutic process during wilderness therapy. Although it might seem counterintuitive, intentionally separating a family system is sometimes the only way to decrease chronic anxiety in the family system, particularly for adolescents with acting-out or acting-in behaviors that are putting themselves or others in dangerous situations, and/or for family systems with very unhealthy interactional patterns. Wilderness therapy provides the physical separation and intentional therapeutic process necessary to facilitate increased differentiation, which in turn enables healthier relationships with self and others.

It is important to note that wilderness therapy appears to be most effective when paired with structured, intensive therapeutic treatment upon discharge (Russell 2005; Bolt 2016). Wilderness therapy almost always is not the solution itself, but rather an important intervention *toward* the solution, as it takes time to internalize change. Working through pre-contemplation and contemplation in the intensive wilderness therapy environment prepares for the longer term work of *action*, which cannot adequately be done in short-term wilderness therapy programs (Bettmann et al. 2012; Prochaska and DiClemente 1983). Accordingly, most wilderness therapy clients transition to residential therapeutic programs to continue their therapeutic growth (Bolt 2016); thereby protracting the intentional family separation and thus enabling a continued process for family members to further differentiate.

References

Apter, T. (1990). *Altered loves: Mothers and daughters during adolescence*. New York: St. Martin's.

Ault-Riche, M. (1986). A feminist critique of five schools of family therapy. In M. Ault-Riche (Ed.), *Women and family therapy* (pp. 1–15). Rockville, MD: Aspen.

Bandoroff, S., & Scherer, D. G. (1994). Wilderness family therapy: An innovative treatment approach for problem youth. *Journal of Child and Family Studies, 3*(2), 175–191. doi:10.1007/BF02234066

Baumrind, D. (1966). Effects of authoritative parental control on child behavior. *Child Development, 37*(4), 887–907.

Baumrind, D. (1967). Child care practices anteceding three patterns of preschool behavior. *Genetic Psychology Monographs, 75*(1), 43–88.

Bettmann, J. E., & Jasperson, R. A. (2009). Adolescents in residential and inpatient treatment: A review of the outcome literature. *Child and Youth Care Forum, 38,* 161–183. doi:10.1007/s10566-009-9073-y

Bettmann, J. E., Russell, K. C., & Parry, K. J. (2012). How substance abuse recovery skills, readiness to change and symptom reduction impact change processes in wilderness therapy participants. *Journal of Child and Family Studies, 22*(8), 1039–1050. doi:10.1007/s10826-012-9665-2

Bettmann, J. E., & Tucker, A. R. (2011). Shifts in attachment relationships: A study of adolescents in wilderness treatment. *Child and Youth Care Forum, 40*(6), 499–519. doi:10.1007/s10566-011-9146-6

Bolt, K. L. (2016). Descending from the summit: Aftercare planning for adolescents in wilderness therapy. *Contemporary Family Therapy, 38*(1), 62–74. doi:10.1007/s10591-016-9375-9

Bowen, M. (1978). *Family therapy in clinical practice*. New York: Jason Aronson.

Brinkmeyer, M. Y., Eyberg, S. M., Nguyen, M. L., & Adams, R. W. (2004). Family engagement, consumer satisfaction and treatment outcome in the new era of child and adolescent in-patient psychiatric care. *Clinical Child Psychology and Psychiatry, 9*(4), 553–566.

Chodorow, N. (1978). *The reproduction of mothering: Psychoanalysis and the sociology of gender*. Berkeley, CA: University of California Press.

Goldenberg, I., & Goldenberg, H. (1996). *Family therapy: An overview*. Brooks/Cole: Pacific Grove.

Gratwick Baker, K. (1998). Treating a remarried family system. In P. Titelman (Ed.), *Clinical applications of Bowen family systems theory* (pp. 355–380). New York: Haworth.

Hanes Meyer, P. (1998). Bowen Theory as a basis for therapy. In P. Titelman (Ed.), *Clinical applications of Bowen family systems theory* (pp. 69–116). New York: Haworth.

Harper, N. J., & Russell, K. C. (2008). Family involvement and outcome in adolescent wilderness treatment: A mixed-methods evaluation. *International Journal of Child & Family Welfare, 11* (1), 19–36.

Jackson, D. (1957). The question of family homeostasis. *The Psychiatric Quarterly Supplement, 31*(1), 79-90. Presented at the Frieda Fromm-Reichmann Lecture, V. A. Hospital in Menlo Park, January 1954; Also presented May 7, 1954 at the American Psychiatric Association Meeting, St. Louis, MO.

Kerr, M. E., & Bowen, M. (1988). *Family Evaluation: An approach based on Bowen Theory*. New York: W. W. Norton & Co.

Kim-Appel, D. & Appel, J. (2013). *The relationship between Bowen's concept of differentiation of self and measurements of mindfulness*. Presentation at American Counselling Association Conference and Expo, Cincinnati, OH.

Knudson-Martin, C. (1994). The female voice: Application to Bowen's family systems theory. *Journal of Marital and Family Therapy, 20*, 35–46.

Linehan, M. M. (1993). *Skills training manual for treating borderline personality disorder*. New York: The Guilford Press.

Louv, R. (2011). *The nature principle: Human restoration and the end of nature-deficit disorder*. Chapel Hill, NC: Algonquin Books.

Lyons, N. (1983). Two perspectives: On self, relationships and morality. *Harvard Educational Review, 53*, 126–145.

McGoldrick, M., Anderson, C., & Walsh, F. (1989). Women in families and in family therapy. In M. McGoldrick, C. Anderson, & F. Wash (Eds.), *Women ifamilies: A framework for family therapy* (pp. 3–15). New York: Norton.

McGoldrick, M., & Carter, B. (1999). Self in context: The individual life cycle in systemic perspective. In B. Carter & M. McGoldrick (Eds.), *The expanded family life cycle: Individual, family and social perspectives* (3rd ed., pp. 27–46). Boston: Allyn and Bacon.

McKnight, A. S. (1998). Family systems with alcoholism: A case study. In P. Titelman (Ed.), *Clinical applications of Bowen family systems theory* (pp. 69–116). New York: Haworth.

Miller, R. B., Anderson, S., & Keala, D. K. (2004). Is Bowen theory valid? A review of basic research. *Journal of Marital and Family Therapy, 30*(4), 453–466.

Miller, W. R., & Rollnick, S. (2002). *Motivational interviewing: Preparing people for change* (2nd ed.). New York: The Guilford Press.

Norton, C. L., Wisner, B. L., Krugh, M., & Penn, A. (2014). Helping youth transition into an alternative residential school setting: Exploring the effects of a wilderness orientation program on youth purpose and identity complexity. *Child and Adolescent Social Work Journal, 31*(5), 475–493. doi:10.1007/s10560-014-0331-y

Papero, D. (1990). *Bowen family systems theory*. Boston: Allyn & Bacon.

Prochaska, J. O., & DiClemente, C. C. (1983). Stages and processes of self-change of smoking: Toward an integrative model of change. *Journal of Consulting and Clinical Psychology, 51*(3), 390–395. doi:10.1037/0022-006X.51.3.390

Prochaska, J. O., & Velicer, W. F. (1997). The transtheoretical model of health behavior change. *American Journal of Health Promotion, 12*(1), 38–48. doi:10.4278/0890-1171-12.1.38

Rogers, C. (1961). *On becoming a person: A therapist's view of psychotherapy*. London: Constable.

Russell, K. C. (2000). Exploring how the wilderness therapy process relates to outcomes. *The Journal of Experiential Education, 23*(3), 170–176.

Russell, K. C. (2003). An assessment of outcomes in outdoor behavioral healthcare treatment. *Child and Youth Care Forum, 32*(6), 355–381. doi:10.1023/B:CCAR.0000004507.12946.7e

Russell, K. C. (2005). Two years later: A qualitative assessment of youth well-being and the role of aftercare in outdoor behavioral healthcare treatment. *Child and Youth Care Forum, 34*(3), 209–239. doi:10.1007/s10566-005-3470-7

Russell, K. C., & Hendee, J. C. (1999). Wilderness therapy as an intervention and treatment for adolescents with behavioral problems. In A. E. Watson, G. Aplet, & J. C. Hendee (Eds.), *Personal, societal, and ecological values of wilderness: 6th World Wilderness Congress proceedings on research and allocation* (Vol. II). Ogden, UT: USDA Forest Service, Rocky Mountain Research Station.

Russell, K. C., Hendee, J. C., & Phillips-Miller, D. (2000). How wilderness therapy works; An examination of the wilderness therapy process to treat adolescents with behavioral problems and addictions. In S. F. McCool, D. N. Cole, W. T. Borrie, & J. O'Loughlin (Eds.), *Wilderness science in a time of change conference* (Vol. 3). Ogden, UT: USDA Forest Service Proceedings, Rocky Mountain Research Station.

Russell, K. C., & Phillips-Miller, D. (2002). Perspectives on the wilderness therapy process and its relation to outcome. *Child and Youth Care Forum, 31*(6), 415–437. doi:10.1023/A: 1021110417119

Schnarch, D. (1997). *Passionate marriage*. New York: Henry Hold and Company.

Schwartz, J. P., Thigpen, S. E., & Montgomery, J. K. (2006). Examination of parenting styles of processing emotions and differentiation of self. *The Family Journal, 14*(1), 41–48. doi:10. 1177/1066480705282050

Tannen, D. (1990). *You just don't understand: Women and men in conversation*. New York: Ballantine Books.

Taffel, R., & Masters, R. (1989). An evolutionary approach to revolutionary change: The impact of gender arrangements on family therapy. In M. McGoldrick, C. Anderson, & F. Walsh (Eds.), *Women in families: A framework for family therapy* (pp. 117–134). New York: Norton.

Titelman, P. (1998). Overview of the Bowen theoretical-therapeutic system. In P. Titelman (Ed.), *Clinical applications of Bowen family systems theory* (pp. 7–50). New York: Haworth.

Walsh, F., & Scheinkman, M. (1989). (Fe)male: The hidden gender dimension in models of family therapy. In M. McGoldrick, C. Anderson, & F. Walsh (Eds.), *Women in families: A framework for family therapy* (pp. 16–41). New York: Norton.

Wells, M. S., Widmer, M. A., & McCoy, J. K. (2004). Grubs and grasshoppers: Challenge-based recreation and the collective efficacy of families with at-risk youth. *Family Relations, 53*, 326–333.

Author Biographies

Kirsten L. Bolt, MEd, LMFT is a Clinical Therapist at Open Sky Wilderness Therapy, working primarily with adolescent females and their families. Her previous clinical experience also includes working with adolescent boys and young adult men and women. Prior to Open Sky, Kirsten was a Clinical Therapist at Aspen Achievement Academy, as well as a Field Guide. Her undergraduate degree is in Health and Exercise Science from Syracuse University. And her Master's degree is in Couple and Family Therapy from the University of Oregon. She has published articles in Contemporary Family Therapy and the Journal of Therapeutic Schools and Programs. Kirsten has also presented at the annual and regional conferences for the National Association of Therapeutic Schools and Programs, the annual and regional Wilderness Therapy Symposiums, and the International Family Therapy Association's world family therapy conference.

Tony Issenmann, Ph.D, LMFT is a licensed Marriage and Family Therapist who has clinical experience working in a variety of settings including wilderness therapy programs, community agencies, a day treatment center for schizophrenic clients, and family therapy centers. His clinical focus has primarily centered on the adolescent and parent system. He has helped hundreds of students and families as a primary therapist and now serves as the Clinical and Family Services Director for Open Sky Wilderness Therapy. Dr. Issenmann is an accomplished speaker and has presented at regional, national, and international conferences.

Chapter 9
Walking off the Mountain: Planning Aftercare Support for Adolescents in Wilderness Therapy and Their Families

Kirsten L. Bolt

Chapter Highlights

- Additional treatment is necessary after adolescents complete wilderness therapy programs.
- Though counterintuitive, a continued separation of parents and their adolescent children post-wilderness therapy often provides the most benefit for families.
- The post-wilderness aftercare plan is individually crafted with the support of the wilderness therapist and considers many factors.
- Home treatment providers can support families making aftercare decisions post-wilderness therapy.
- Even when longer term treatment is indicated post-discharge, wilderness therapy is often a necessary step to lay the foundation for therapeutic growth and healing within the family system.

There is a common expression among mountain climbers that most accidents occur on the descent. The American Alpine Club (1953) explains that phenomenon as, "Once the summit has been reached, the stimulus for attentiveness becomes less and there is likely to be a relaxation of concentration" (p. 1). That sentiment can be applied to adolescent clients nearing the end of their wilderness therapy journey. After two to three months of exploring one's identity, developing emotional resiliency, and healing fractured family relationships (Russell and Hendee 1999; Russell 2001, 2003), these adolescents frequently describe their pride and sense of accomplishment as though standing atop a mountain peak. They have clarity, wisdom, confidence, and vision. However, they have not yet internalized that vision into reliable action (Russell 2005, 2007). In starting the descent, it becomes more

K.L. Bolt (✉)
Clinical Therapist, Open Sky Wilderness Therapy,
PO Box 2201, Durango, CO 81302, USA
e-mail: kirsten@openskywilderness.com

© Springer International Publishing AG 2017   143
J.D. Christenson and A.N. Merritts (eds.), *Family Therapy with Adolescents in Residential Treatment*, Focused Issues in Family Therapy,
DOI 10.1007/978-3-319-51747-6_9

challenging to maintain that vision and confidence, and adolescent clients are at risk of relapse (Russell 2005, 2007), as are their families. An intentional and comprehensive aftercare plan is paramount for clients transitioning out of residential treatment programs and the need for this plan is well documented (Nickerson et al. 2007; Russell 2005).

This chapter describes the process of developing an appropriate aftercare plan for discharge from a wilderness therapy program by answering the following questions: (1) Why is additional treatment necessary after wilderness therapy? (2) How is the aftercare plan determined and what factors are considered? (3) How can treatment providers support families making aftercare decisions? And, (4) Why is wilderness therapy necessary if longer term treatment is indicated? Throughout this chapter, the term *parents* will be used for ease of reading. However, it is more appropriate to recognize the many people responsible for parenting children, such as grandparents, aunts and uncles, guardians, foster parents, same-sex partners, stepparents, etc.

Why More Treatment? Isn't Wilderness Therapy Enough?

One would not expect a person who experienced a heart attack to leave the Intensive Care Unit and head straight home, returning immediately to the former lifestyle. The American Heart Association (2015) describes the process of preparing patients to return to home life as including treatment, monitoring, rehabilitation, and lifestyle changes, which might include separation from unhealthy triggers (e.g., fatty foods or physical inactivity). Perhaps a parallel can be drawn to wilderness therapy clients post-discharge. Due to the challenging life circumstances or diagnostic complexity they experience prior to enrollment, many adolescents arrive in crisis and as a last resort after many treatment failures (Russell and Hendee 1999; Russell 2000). We cannot expect adolescents leaving a wilderness therapy program, which essentially operates as a therapeutic intensive care unit, to discharge without a solid plan that supports internalization of gains made in the wilderness environment, and changes to unhealthy lifestyles (Nickerson et al. 2007, 2014). Nickerson et al. (2007) indicate that problematic triggers at home are many and include unhealthy family dynamics, negative peer influences, accessibility of substances, and academic stressors, among others.

Strengths and Limitations of Wilderness Therapy

In order to understand why more treatment is needed beyond wilderness therapy, it is necessary to explore the basic strengths and limitations of that setting. For the purposes of this chapter, it is assumed that the reader has at least a cursory understanding of the field of wilderness therapy, sometimes also referred to as Outdoor Behavioral Healthcare (see Chap. 15). Wilderness therapy is designed to be a powerful, intensive, and short-term intervention for adolescents who are struggling in the home environment, and for whom traditional outpatient or other inpatient therapeutic services have proven ineffective (Russell 2000; Russell and Hendee 1999; Bettmann and Jasperson 2009; Ferguson 2009). Typically, these adolescents struggle with issues related to depression, anxiety, disruptive behavior, family relational problems, substance misuse, and other clinical disorders (Behrens et al. 2010; Bettmann and Tucker 2011). Fundamental goals in wilderness therapy include client stabilization, thorough assessment, initial treatment and intervention, and long-term treatment planning (Russell et al. 2000).

Wilderness therapy is designed to be most effective in supporting adolescents working through earlier stages of change (Bettmann et al. 2012; Prochaska and DiClemente 1983). From Prochaska and DiClemente's (1983) writing, one can infer that wilderness therapy will be less effective in supporting growth in the later stages of change that are dependent upon time and proximity to triggering situations, such as unhealthy family dynamics, substances, or unsupportive peer environments. And while there is tremendous benefit to adolescents being separated from their parents during wilderness therapy (see Chap. 8; Bettmann and Tucker 2011; Harper and Russell 2008), families do not have the opportunity to practice new skills together daily.

Taylor (2004) highlights the ethical importance of treating clients within the least-restrictive environment. Perhaps counterintuitive, many parents who choose to send their adolescent child to a residential therapeutic program, at times thousands of miles from home, *are* providing the least-restrictive setting to support change and growth (Bettmann and Tucker 2011; Harper and Russell 2008; Russell 2005). Parents frequently report believing that removing their child from the unhealthy environment was the only way to gain the clarity necessary to create change (Harper and Russell 2008).

According to Prochaska and Velicer (1997), approximately 20% of people in at-risk populations at any given time are preparing to take action to create change. This leaves approximately 80% of these at-risk people needing specialized support to be ready for action. That translates to approximately 80% of at-risk adolescents needing support to accurately identify their problems and work through their ambivalence about change (Prochaska and Velicer 1997; Miller and Rollnick 2002). Miller and Rollnick (2002) highlight the use of motivational interviewing to work with this population. However, for many adolescents, traditional outpatient, and inpatient therapeutic settings have proven ineffective in working through those initial stages of change (Russell 2000; Harper and Russell 2008) and they need a unique approach.

Trans-Theoretical Model: Stages of Change

Prochaska and Velicer (1997) describe the trans-theoretical model (TTM) of health behavior change as consisting of six basic stages: *pre-contemplation,*

contemplation, preparation, action, maintenance, and termination. Chapter 14 of this volume discusses the stages of change as they relate to the adolescent and the parents in detail; therefore, only a cursory overview is provided here. It is important to note that rarely are the adolescent's issues unrelated to the family system. It is essential that parents engage in their own change process alongside their child in order to shift the family homeostasis and allow the adolescent to decrease symptoms (see Chap. 7; Jackson 1957; Brinkmeyer et al. 2004; Harper and Russell 2008). Accordingly, the next several paragraphs offer interventions specific to each stage of change for both adolescents and parents in wilderness therapy.

For many adolescents in the pre-contemplation stage of change, though not all, just being sent to a wilderness therapy program enables them to recognize that a problem exists. Reading impact letters (see Chap. 2) from family members deepens awareness and understanding of the problem. And regular feedback from peers and the treatment team ensures awareness. For parents, the pre-contemplation stage is addressed via the family therapy they are expected to do at home; problem identification during weekly phone calls with the wilderness therapist; completing weekly homework assignments, such as reading specific books, journaling, or watching webinars; attending parent workshops; and reading letters written by their child addressing problematic family dynamics (see Chaps. 8 and 15).

Wilderness therapy interventions for adolescents in the contemplation stage might highlight how they are living incongruently with their personal core values, thereby self-perpetuating a shame cycle. They also explore the pros and cons of changing and not changing. In so doing, motivation to change is fostered. For parents, the same processes occur, though less intensely, as parents are still engaged in their normal daily routines. But parents have many opportunities to explore and potentially resolve their ambivalence about change via intentional letter writing with their child in wilderness (see Chap. 2), family therapy at home, practice of new skills directly with the adolescent via family phone calls or in-person therapeutic experiences, practice of new skills at home, both individually and with others, and other interventions previously described.

Interventions for adolescents in the preparation stage include making a relapse prevention plan, taking full accountability for past actions, and practicing necessary skills amid increased emotional pressure (i.e., using skills *when they count*, such as during the first in-person family interaction). Parents actively develop aftercare plans for their child as well as their own relapse prevention plans. Also, they typically participate in a reunion process that occurs just prior to discharge, helping further develop skills as a family (Ferguson 2009).

These first three stages are what wilderness therapy does best. In fact, Bettmann et al. (2012) state, "…that clients in wilderness therapy do not necessarily need to want to change in order to do so" (p. 1039). In other words, success in wilderness therapy does not mandate being in the action stage of change; rather wilderness therapy often helps clients *prepare for* the action stage of change. Wilderness therapy provides a powerful environment to challenge one's denial that a problem exists because the problems manifest in the wilderness just as they do at home (Russell 2000, 2005). An expression commonly heard in wilderness therapy is, "wherever you go, there you are." As such, clients are able to weigh the pros and cons of change amid daily peer interactions, structured family therapy interventions (e.g., letters or phone calls), frequent and uncomfortable experiences that call for greater emotional resiliency (e.g., living outdoors, being self-reliant, making bow-drill fires), and introspective and reflective time alone such as occurs during solo experiences (Russell 2000). With the support of the treatment team, clients are able to create plans for how to *do* the therapeutic work they have spent the majority of their time in wilderness *discovering* (Russell and Hendee 1999; Russell 2002, 2005, 2007).

Additionally, these first three stages of change are further reinforced in wilderness therapy by the opportunities for safe relapses (Bettmann and Jasperson 2009). An important part of any change process is *relapse*, as relapses help clients resolve ambivalence about changing (Miller and Rollnick 2002). Having opportunities to make safe mistakes in wilderness therapy enables clients to practice new behaviors with minimal to no risk of harm as a result of those mistakes (e.g., as in the cases of substance use, self-harm, disordered eating, sexual promiscuity, or suicide). Adolescents can use their peers, treatment team staff, and parents (from afar) to practice new emotional resiliency and communication skills, and they receive feedback and coaching as they relapse into old patterns (Russell 2002; Bettmann and Jasperson 2009). However, the influence of wilderness therapy typically does not extend far into the fourth, fifth, and sixth stages of change, if at all: *action*, *maintenance*, and *termination* (Prochaska and Velicer 1997).

Reasonable Expectations for Wilderness Therapy Outcomes

Wilderness therapy helps families lay the foundation for long-term growth by directly interrupting unhealthy patterns in relationships, coping strategies, or identity formation. Adolescent clients, also called *students*, typically leave wilderness therapy with awareness of their struggles and the underlying reasons for them, motivation to change, and the skills necessary to support their goals (Russell and Hendee 1999; Bettmann et al. 2012). However, wilderness therapy is designed to be a short-term, intensive intervention, not a long-term solution.

Results from outcome studies demonstrate that adolescents are typically unable to sustain the significant gains made in wilderness therapy without more continued, intensive treatment (Russell 2005, 2007; Becker 2010). Russell (2002) found a few predictable themes from adolescents at the time of discharge from wilderness therapy: "a desire to 'change behavior', a desire to discontinue drugs and alcohol, and a desire to be a 'better person'" (p. 428). These *desires* reflect the first three stages of change (Prochaska and DiClemente 1983): awareness of the problems, motivation to address them, and perhaps even a commitment and plan for how to change. However, *desiring* change does not necessarily lead to *creating* change. The gains made in wilderness therapy programs must be supported by specific and intentional aftercare support, which frequently takes the form of residential therapeutic programs. These schools and programs typically last between one to two years and involve a continued separation of adolescents and their families (Norton et al. 2014).

The notion of continued family separation post-wilderness therapy raises an interesting and frequently asked question about how family engagement, a clear predictor of success (Brinkmeyer et al. 2004; Bandoroff and Scherer 1994; Harper and Russell 2008), can occur when families are far apart. This topic is addressed at length in another chapter within this book (see Chap. 8). To summarize briefly, Kerr and Bowen (1988) indicate that a fundamental goal to create lasting family change is to decrease chronic anxiety within the family system while supporting each family member to further differentiate (Kerr and Bowen 1988). At times, the family system is unable to support these goals while living together due to dangerous behaviors by the adolescent or entrenched dysfunctional family system patterns (McGoldrick and Carter 2001; Norton et al. 2014). Without intentional separation and intervention, families usually revert to unhealthy homeostatic tendencies (Jackson 1957). In Chap. 8, the case is made for intentionally separating a particular population of families, and that chapter is a good resource for those who contest the above made assertions. Simply separating families is not the solution either; rather, therapeutic engagement of the entire family system *amid* physical separation and therefore decreased anxiety can actuate change. And because of the adolescent brain's adaptability, these changes can lead to long-term change as they are reinforced over time (Siegel 2013).

Navigating Aftercare Planning

Aftercare simply refers to whatever type of care comes after the current treatment. Given the typical complexity of issues facing adolescents and their families preceding wilderness therapy (Russell 2002; Bettmann and Tucker 2011), every adolescent and family will need to develop an aftercare plan (i.e., a plan for how to support continued growth post-discharge). Interestingly, only about 80% of wilderness therapy clients report believing that they were adequately prepared for aftercare (Russell 2007). Aftercare planning is fundamental to allow time for the seeds that have sprouted in wilderness to develop and blossom. From the earlier discussion about predictable stages of change as they relate to the wilderness therapy environment, a new question emerges: How do we best support families during the *action* stage of change? Although much of what is discussed below is considered within the context of wilderness therapy, many of the concepts are applicable in any residential setting.

Continuum of Care in Residential Treatment

Continuum of care refers to a multi-level system of delivering health care services of varying degrees of intensity (Evashwick 1989). Evashwick (1989) asserts that ideally, one needing mental health treatment seeks out the least-restrictive setting necessary and then *steps down* in the intensity of support until additional care is no longer needed. As previously described, many families seek help from traditional outpatient therapy, family therapy, skills-focused group therapy, hospitalization, and other inpatient treatment before enrolling their child in a wilderness therapy program (Russell 2000), which frequently is the least-restrictive environment at that time.

Given the intensity of the wilderness therapy treatment approach and the stages of change it is designed to address, stepping down in the level of care is necessary to access the latter stages of change. Post-wilderness therapy, many adolescents continue the treatment process in a residential therapeutic program, such as a therapeutic boarding school or residential treatment center (Norton et al. 2014; Russell 2005; 2007). That treatment is typically followed by a return to the family system (whether in the home, a traditional boarding school, or an independent living option). Upon returning to the family system, it is necessary to incorporate various outpatient treatment services (Nickerson et al. 2007). Due to the tremendous gap in therapeutic support between a wilderness therapy program (i.e., the *therapeutic intensive care unit*) and the home environment (even with outpatient services), long-term residential treatment can be crucial.

Residential, Therapeutic Schools, and Programs

A variety of residential, therapeutic schools exist to fill this need. These schools range from *residential treatment centers*, which serve a population needing more acute clinical focus; to *therapeutic boarding schools* or *emotional growth schools*, which provide clinical intensity more balanced with academic focus (Norton et al. 2014; National Association of Therapeutic Schools and Programs, n.d.). For ease, these environments collectively will be referred to as *residential aftercare*, and more specifically as residential treatment centers (RTC's) or therapeutic boarding schools (TBS's). Chapter 20 of this volume provides an overview of the different types of programs that fall under the title of residential treatment, and it is important to note that most adolescents who leave wilderness programs transfer to client-funded (i.e., private) RTC's and TBS's.

Some essential components of these residential aftercare options are highlighted across the following literature. Norton et al. (2014) describe the intentions for these programs as: (a) developing adolescent emotional growth; (b) strengthening family relationships; (c) supporting academic achievement; (d) improving emotional resiliency; (e) fostering healthy relationships with peers and adults; and, (f) providing structure and positive activities to decrease problematic behaviors. In Russell (2005), the following themes emerged among parents regarding how they believed residential aftercare was effective: (a) family focus; (b) adolescent identity and confidence development; (c) care of treatment staff; (d) addressing deeper therapeutic issues; (e) structure, discipline, personal responsibility; and, (f) a safe, sober environment. Duerden et al. (2010) argue that a strong residential program should incorporate a *positive youth development philosophy*, including these concepts outlined by Eccles and Gootman (2002): (a) physical and psychological safety; (b) appropriate structure; (c) supportive relationships; (d) opportunities to belong; (e) positive social norms; (f) support for efficacy and mattering; (g) opportunities for skill building; and, (h) integration of family, school, and community efforts.

One wilderness therapy program, Open Sky Wilderness Therapy, has unpublished data (2015) indicating that their wilderness therapists recommend 95% of their adolescent clients transition to RTC's or TBS's immediately upon discharge from Open Sky to continue the individual and family growth in the above domains. However, the percentage of families that *choose* residential aftercare programs is only 80%. What accounts for the 15% of families not following aftercare recommendations?

Grief and Emotional Resiliency in Parents

The conversation of aftercare planning tends to be particularly difficult for parents, as most parents *want* their child home with them. However, in many instances, togetherness is not what the child or family *needs*. In addition, there are also significant financial implications in aftercare planning. And because it is counter-intuitive to believe that better family therapy and healing can occur amid physical separation of a family, one can understand why many parents struggle emotionally to choose continued separation from their child.

Frequently, parents worry about placing their child in a residential aftercare program because they expect their child will be sad or angry about the decision and respond in a way that triggers parents' emotional responses, which is due to lower differentiation levels and higher emotional reactivity amid family system anxiety (Bowen 1978; Kerr and Bowen 1988). Parents might fear rejection or angry outbursts from their child or fear their child will feel abandoned by them. Sometimes parents are just starting to feel grief related their child being in wilderness therapy abating when they need to make this difficult aftercare decision, so they have a resurgence of present grief, as well as anticipatory grief. This grief can be compounded in families where the adolescent in treatment is their last child at home and they experience empty-nest grief earlier than expected. Parents who have a pattern of enabling or rescuing their child when both of them feel uncomfortable emotions might respond by not making this hard decision, further perpetuating the enmeshed pattern.

Parents have a unique and powerful opportunity to role model the very things they are asking their child to develop, which are emotional resiliency and differentiation. When a parent makes aftercare decisions from a place of heightened anxiety, rather than a differentiated and grounded balance of rational thought and emotion, they unintentionally reinforce this pattern of responding reactively when emotions are overwhelming. For most adolescents in treatment, that is exactly the underlying problem that brought them to treatment. When parents demonstrate making decisions based on what their child *needs*, as opposed to what they or the child *wants*, parents role model making rational, balanced decisions. It is important for parents to be engaged in their own therapeutic process to increase their levels of differentiation and emotional resiliency, the antidote to emotional reactivity.

When Is Going Home Recommended?

Despite Open Sky Wilderness Therapy's (2015) data that indicates approximately 95% of adolescents are recommended to continue their treatment in a long-term residential setting, this is not an absolute recommendation for every family. Wilderness therapists assess each adolescent and family to determine aftercare recommendations based on the likelihood of relapse if the adolescent returns home (related to the student's progress and predicted stage of change at the time of discharge), the parents' stages of change, the differentiation levels of family members, and the risk to the adolescent and family if relapse occurs at home (e.g., suicide, accidental injury or death, substance use, promiscuity, disordered eating, academic failure, disrupted family relationships, etc.).

In considering whether a student might be successful upon returning home post-discharge, there are a few patterns this author expects to see. First, a student should have no significant risk factors for personal safety (e.g., substantial suicide ideation, self-injury, promiscuity, disordered eating, or substance use). In addition, there should be clear progress in addressing the treatment issues that brought the adolescent to wilderness, evidenced by a decrease in symptoms and a noticeable increase in differentiation and emotional resiliency. Ideally, the student is at least in the preparation stage of change and consistently demonstrating commitment to change. More important than commitment, which is easier to state than create, clear behavioral changes (i.e., action) must be evident to show that the student is actualizing intentions. And the student should be able to demonstrate these actions when under stress (e.g., particularly inclement weather, challenging interpersonal dynamics, difficult family interactions, etc.).

The family's readiness for change is also a significant contributing factor to a student's readiness to return home. Parents should at least be in the *action* stage of change, as they will be setting the tone and structure to support their children upon returning home. Unlike adolescents in wilderness therapy programs, parents are still engaged in their lives at home, with jobs, partners, and other children. Therefore, they have opportunities to practice change in everyday settings and actually engage the action stage of change, thereby demonstrating behaviors that support their stated intentions and commitments. When parents fail to show action in the home environment, it does not bode well for adolescents to implement action upon returning home. Parents should be able to role model emotional resiliency under stress, and they should have a high enough level of differentiation to be able to provide their child appropriate supervision and structure, while balancing that structure with nurturance and autonomy (Siegel 2013). It is not uncommon for parents and children to be at different stages of change at the time of discharge, indicating the importance of family engagement in the treatment process (Brinkmeyer et al. 2004; Harper and Russell 2008). The relationship between parents and children is another factor; if there is substantial relational distress that has not improved or been addressed successfully in wilderness therapy, the likelihood of being successful at home under more relational stress is minimal. We cannot expect families to be more skillful when reunited at home, where more stress exists, than they have been during the wilderness process with less stress.

For families who do bring their child home in conjunction with treatment recommendations, many layers of support should be considered to promote the action stage of change. Nickerson et al. (2007) highlight important considerations in planning residential discharge: (a) outpatient individual, family, and group therapies; (b) couple or co-parenting therapy for parents; (c) intensive outpatient programming for substance abuse support, possibly including 12-step meetings and drug testing; (d) school changes to support academic success, and collaboration with the school; (e) psychiatric support; (f) positive, pro-social activities; (g) service projects and/or employment opportunities; and, (h) peer restrictions; and daily structure and routine. Other considerations for transition planning include: (a) a strong home contract clearly outlining the expectations for the adolescent's behavior at home, and the predicted consequences of meeting or not meeting those expectations; (b) dietary, exercise, and wellness plans; and, (c) a home transition program that can offer coaching, mentoring, and therapy. These recommendations will be individualized to support the adolescent's and family's unique needs.

Another important consideration is the likelihood of the adolescent and family to experience a perceived sense of failure if the adolescent returns home and either the adolescent and/or the family system are unable to sustain the gains made in wilderness. Often, families consider bringing their child home and having a residential aftercare placement as a backup plan in case home proves ineffective. However, if the adolescent is not successful at home, a return to wilderness therapy for a few weeks is often required to restabilize before transitioning to the residential therapeutic school placement, costing the family more money, emotional stress, and prolonging the grieving process. In addition, depending on the reasons for the wilderness placement, relapse at home can be dangerous or even life threatening. And ultimately, the adolescent will then transition to residential aftercare under the (self-imposed) perception of failure, rather than the momentum and pride of completing wilderness therapy and starting the descent from the mountain peak while maintaining clarity, vision, and confidence.

Parents should address the aftercare decision-making process in their weekly appointments with their home therapists. According to Nickerson et al. (2007), it is crucial for the wilderness therapist to collaborate with the home therapist to ensure solidarity in aftercare recommendations and planning for the family. Not all therapists understand the benefit of intentional family separation in supporting long-term change and often struggle with the same counterintuitive process as parents.

Educational Consultant

Many families enter wilderness therapy programs upon the recommendation of an *educational consultant* (see Chap. 6; Wilder 2011; Open Sky Wilderness Therapy 2015) or a *therapeutic placement consultant* (for ease, the former term will be used throughout this section). Other families find wilderness therapy via another healthcare professional, word-of-mouth, or online searches. For these families, a wilderness therapist who is recommending residential placement post-wilderness will usually also recommend that the family hire an educational consultant to make specific recommendations for the schools and programs that will best support the adolescent's and family's needs.

Whereas the wilderness therapist's role is relatively brief in a family's therapeutic journey, the educational consultant (EC) typically works with the family long-term. As such, the EC maintains a broader sense of the adolescent's and family's progress and needs over time. Not only does the EC help a family find residential and wilderness programs, but they also advocate for the family during such placements. The website for the Independent Educational Consultants Association (IECA 2015) indicates, "In times of crisis, parents are often overwhelmed by a barrage of emotions. The confusion and desperation associated with having a troubled teenager or child can be extremely trying. Parents may not be aware of the options available, or may not be able to decide on their own which alternative best meets their situation and the needs of their child" (para. 1).

Although wilderness therapists tend to know various residential, therapeutic programs, it is not within their scope of practice to make recommendations for specific aftercare programs. In contrast, a significant portion of the educational consultant's time is devoted to visiting residential programs across the country (see Chap. 6). Their research informs them of the many programs that exist, which are reputable and accredited, the various treatment approaches of each, the peer milieu at any given time, and the treatment team members (Sklarow 2011). These are components that the wilderness therapist cannot adequately address, and that are even more difficult for parents to discern.

Because of their different skill sets, the wilderness therapist works alongside the educational consultant and provides general recommendations for the type of treatment the adolescent and family will need moving forward. The therapist has comprehensive, daily observations of the adolescent and is therefore able to compile a list of the adolescent's aftercare needs, such as: (a) level of therapeutic care; (b) degree of family engagement; (c) clinical specialization (e.g., trauma or substance recovery); (d) therapeutic modalities (e.g., equine or art therapy); (e) school size; (f) single- or mixed-gender; and, (g) duration. The educational consultant then filters those recommendations through the programs they have critically appraised to generate a list of a few specific programs for the family to then research (Wilder 2011). The EC will help parents narrow their list and explore these options, along with why each was selected.

Getting Safely to Residential Aftercare

Once the decision has been made for an adolescent in wilderness therapy to attend a residential therapeutic school for aftercare, and the program has been chosen, it is important to create an intentional and thorough *transition plan* to get the child safely to the next program. While many metaphors can be drawn to reflect this transitional time, the simple concept of a seedling illustrates the importance of *going slowly* during the transition. While in wilderness, seeds are planted and students and families begin to sprout. They need time, nurture, and structure to blossom. When planting a seedling in the ground, one must be slow, intentional, and gentle. If moving too quickly, the roots become exposed or damaged. For adolescents leaving the wilderness environment that has been their home for two or three months, where they have moved every day at a walking pace, everything tends to be over-stimulating, in a way that people without that experience do not understand.

Probably the most important thing to consider is whether the family should transport the adolescent themselves or hire a transport company that specializes in safely delivering people to their destinations. Although many families do transport their child themselves, at times, it is contraindicated. Situations that warrant the outside help of a transport company might include: (a) when the child has not progressed far enough into the contemplation stage of change and is resisting aftercare placement; (b) when parent-child dynamics are emotionally unsafe; (c) when parents are susceptible to manipulation by their resistant child; or, (d) when physical safety of the adolescent is a concern (e.g., self-harm, running away, and accessing drugs). While many parents struggle with the thought of someone else transporting their child for financial or emotional reasons, sometimes even the adolescent can acknowledge this is the safest plan. A recent study by Tucker et al. (2015) found that students who were transported to a wilderness therapy program via a transport company improved similarly to those whose parents delivered the student themselves, and even showed a greater decrease in symptoms. If emotional or physical safety is a concern, parents should hire outside help.

In the majority of other instances where the family and wilderness therapist believe the family can safely deliver the student themselves, a number of factors are important to consider. First, the time should be kept short (typically two days maximum, and without a visit home during the transition) to prevent increased emotional stress and, in turn, emotional reactivity. Parents need to consider how much, if any, access their child should have to the Internet, electronic devices, phones, television, social media, music, friends and extended family members, different foods, and other types of stimulation. These are things the student typically has missed and will want to access, but each can be problematic in exacerbating grief about the aftercare plan, resentment toward parents, and shame about not being ready to return home, which can trigger emotional overload and reactivity. Despite progress made, under emotional stress people tend not to cope as well as they do under ideal circumstances (Bowen 1978; Kerr and Bowen 1988). The wilderness therapist will guide these discussions with each family and make clear, specific, and individualized recommendations based on the family's particular needs.

One final consideration for this transition period is preparing parents to expect the somewhat predictable pressure from their child to engage old interactional patterns. Upon initially reuniting with each other, parents and adolescents frequently are uncertain about how to relate and interact after so long apart. They each tend to remember their pre-wilderness experiences of each other, which frequently were not positive. As such, they tend to regress quickly into old behaviors and beliefs about each other's intentions. Very quickly, adolescents can start pushing their parents and trying to manipulate regarding situations in which parents have already identified boundaries and the child has agreed (e.g., more time for the transition, use of electronics, calling friends, or even getting a tattoo). Having witnessed these occurrences on many occasions, it seems like adolescents almost cannot help but try old tactics with their parents to get what they want. They might try to make parents feel guilty about their time in wilderness or future aftercare placements; they will pull on parents' heartstrings and parents' grief, and they will test boundaries overtly to see if parents will actually do what they have said they will do. Parents should be prepared ahead of time with a plan of action so they do not buckle under this pressure. It is significantly easier to hold boundaries from afar than to maintain them once in-person with their child.

Aftercare for Aftercare?

Another conversation families will eventually have, when they choose residential aftercare following wilderness, is regarding the transition out of the aftercare placement. One might ask, "Will my child ever be ready to go home?" The process of deciding next steps after residential aftercare will be similar to the aftercare planning done during wilderness therapy. The treatment team will provide recommendations based on assessment of the student and family's levels of differentiation, emotional resiliency, and readiness for change. Then, families will again navigate the aftercare planning process and make the next set of aftercare decisions. Renewed and new issues might arise for parents, such as financial impact, parental grief, fear about transitioning their child home, etc. Aftercare options might include students returning home, stepping down further to a lower level of residential care (e.g., to a therapeutic boarding school after a residential treatment center), or remaining at residential placements until they graduate high school and are ready to transition to college or independent living (Nickerson et al. 2007). The goal is typically to reunify families, and students do often return home with outpatient aftercare support following the initial residential aftercare placement.

Supporting Families Making Aftercare Decisions

Despite a logical presentation by a wilderness therapist or educational consultant outlining how residential placement will best serve the needs of an adolescent and family, it is not often a simple or rational decision for parents, but rather a complicated, confusing, and emotional process. Parents usually need guidance to sort through logical, emotional, financial, logistical, and other aspects of aftercare planning.

Sometimes, parents expect their child's wilderness success to generalize into success at home. These parents often benefit from education. When a child is experiencing success in wilderness, the success needs to be contextualized as occurring in a highly structured and therapeutically supportive environment—significantly more so than what can be achieved at home. With the help of the wilderness and home therapists, parents should answer these questions: (a) Are my child's actions and intentions congruent under stress? (b) Has my child demonstrated repeated successes in difficult conditions? (c) How transferrable will those experiences be to the home environment? (d) How ready am *I* to support my child returning home?

In some instances, parents need to explore multiple aftercare options (e.g., bringing their child home, or selecting a residential therapeutic placement). Considering multiple options can help parents predict the likely outcomes for each setting. Realizing how difficult it will be to continue progress and success if their child returns home post-discharge can help parents make difficult decisions from an informed, rational perspective.

Sometimes highlighting the emotional aspects of the aftercare planning process for parents and validating and empathizing with their emotions is what they need. When they understand the uncomfortable emotions they feel in the context of grief, many parents are able to work through the grief, accept their emotions, and make a decision that is in the best interest of their child and the whole family. These parents tend to have a higher level of differentiation and are able to balance the emotional and rational aspects in order to make a decision that feels painful immediately, but ultimately one they believe will best serve their child and the family in the long-run (Bowen 1978).

In other cases, some parents struggle to stay present with their emotions, looking to decrease their perceived level of anxiety related to the aftercare decision. It is common to hear parents struggling to tolerate emotions related to the grief of not having their child at home, losing their child's senior year of activities they had planned, empty-nesting earlier than anticipated, or feeling unable to manage the anticipatory grief when they have not yet resolved the current grief of having their child in wilderness. At times, families fight logically something that is experienced emotionally. Various therapeutic practices can support these families, such as mindfulness and emotional regulation (Kim-Appel and Appel 2013; Linehan 1993).

It can also be hard to differentiate between the child's wants and needs, or between the parents' wants and the child's needs. Sometimes, parents relapse into denial about the severity of their child's problems pre-wilderness therapy. In other situations, parents' own mental health challenges or low differentiation interferes with the aftercare process. In these situations, the decision can become a means to attack the co-parent, or to make oneself the hero. Sometimes, parents too easily accept aftercare recommendations and do not work through the emotional or logical aspects of the decision, instead following recommendations, but later blaming others for struggles during the treatment process. In some cases, parents make the decision not to bring their child home because they do not want to manage the child at home. While the previous situations might produce the desired outcome for the child, the process of arriving there is flawed. Parents need support making the most appropriate aftercare decision, but they also need to understand, align with, and commit to their decision. That way, families are much better prepared for long-term success and parents are ready to support their child in committing to change.

In the above instances where parents struggle with some aspect(s) of making aftercare plans, the wilderness therapist, educational consultant, and home professionals play a key role in helping parents make decisions that are in the best interest of the child and family by supporting parents' own differentiation processes and helping them progress through stages of change. Ideally, the wilderness therapy program has strong family therapy programming so that parents are a part of the solution and engaged in their own therapeutic growth (Brinkmeyer et al. 2004; Bandoroff and Scherer 1994; Harper and Russell 2008). Through that process, parents' own challenges can be highlighted and then addressed in home therapy. The wilderness and home therapists can support parents to be mindful of their emotions, differentiate the emotions from irrational beliefs, and practice the same skills their child is developing. In doing so, parents demonstrate that they are invested in their own growth and aware that they play a part in the child's problems, and therefore in the solution, which validates their child and expedites the therapy process.

When the therapist sees a clear need for a residential aftercare placement, but parents want to bring the child home, another approach that can help families is *motivational interviewing* (Miller and Rollnick 2002). This intervention helps assess parents' motivation to change, highlight discrepancies between what they state as their intentions and what they demonstrate in their actions, and support self-efficacy in helping them make decisions based on their values, just as their children are learning to do. In other cases, challenging parents to role model the things they are asking their child to do can help them make balanced decisions.

Finally, in some instances, a family is not willing or ready to follow treatment recommendations. In these cases, the therapeutic team can highlight their perceptions of the family's decision-making process and make predictions for what to expect when they bring their child home. Families should also be helped to identify clear behavioral markers that will indicate their home plan is proving ineffective. These markers might include sneaking out, reconnecting with unhealthy peers, violating the behavioral home contract, communicating aggressively, isolating, or many other early warning signs of relapse. Parents should be prepared to engage their backup plan (usually a residential placement, with a possible return to the wilderness therapy program first to restabilize). In predicting the ways parents can expect to see relapse in their child—and in themselves—parents are better prepared to identify those markers and to respond quickly.

If Residential Aftercare Is Necessary, Why Do Wilderness Therapy?

This chapter has examined the importance of ongoing, long-term treatment in the form of residential therapeutic programming. If this level of care post-wilderness therapy is a necessary part of the continuum of care, why participate in wilderness therapy at all? This question warrants an entire book devoted to it, so the answer will remain concise. Wilderness therapy is an intense, short-term, powerful intervention designed to support adolescents and parents to move quickly through the pre-contemplation and contemplation stages of change and enter the preparation stage, in some cases even beginning the action stage. As such, adolescents and families in wilderness therapy have the opportunity to confront and address unhealthy family dynamics, coping mechanisms, and identity. Russell (2005) cites over 80% of parents and at least 90% of adolescents reported positive outcomes when residential treatment was combined with wilderness therapy. The majority of these families indicated two years post-wilderness therapy that they believed they would not have been successful without their wilderness intervention due to the therapeutic intensity of wilderness therapy. No other setting can provide this level of therapeutic intensity because adolescents are not participating in traditional school and are therefore strictly focused on the therapy process, and every component of the program is designed to be therapeutically intense, containing, powerful, and to hasten change. Norton et al. (2014) describe the significance of wilderness therapy in the continuum of care. They say, "Youth need a bridge between these two worlds in order to feel safe and fully engage in a residential, therapeutic educational milieu" (p. 479). They suggest wilderness therapy provides a *transitional space* to help adolescents transition from childhood to adulthood, start a healthy differentiation process, develop identity strength, and prepare for long-term support.

Conclusion

Wilderness therapy is a powerful therapeutic modality for at-risk adolescents and their families that, appropriately, is receiving increased clinical focus and study. A growing body of research has attempted to understand and describe the therapeutic process and benefits of this modality. However, it is difficult to capture in numbers and words the essence of this unique intervention. One must experience wilderness therapy in order to truly understand its power, in order to understand why families express profound gratitude and amazement at the growth they and their child experienced, in order to understand the tenderness families feel in finding connection again, and in order to understand why wilderness professionals can be moved to tears observing these monumental shifts.

Yet, it is important not to lose sight of the mountain climber standing proudly atop the apex, feeling strong and capable, connected to self and others, and to something greater than both. Adolescents and parents frequently feel a sense of completion in the therapy process, which can be a dangerous place to find oneself. Professionals should challenge families with interventions at the end of one's wilderness therapy experience to highlight the ongoing process and to help students and their families start walking off the mountain more grounded and realistic about the work yet to come. As the field of wilderness therapy is still relatively new, it will be interesting to see how future research supports or shifts the current aftercare trends described in this chapter. As new programs emerge that are designed to support the transition of adolescents from wilderness therapy to home environments, new research will need to direct best practices for this industry. Much is yet to be revealed.

References

American Alpine Club. (1953). Accidents in American mountaineering: Sixth annual report of the Safety Committee of the American Alpine Club [editorial]. *American Alpine Journal.* Retrieved from: http://publications.americanalpineclub.org/articles/13195300100/Accidents-in-American-Mountaineering-Sixth-Annual-Report-of-the-Safety-Committee-of-the-American-Alpine-Club-1953

American Heart Association. (2015). *Heart attack recovery FAQs.* Retrieved from: http://www.heart.org/HEARTORG/Conditions/HeartAttack/PreventionTreatmentofHeartAttack/Heart-Attack-Recovery-FAQS_UCM_303936_Article.jsp#.VjT4PaKzFzk

Bandoroff, S., & Scherer, D. G. (1994). Wilderness family therapy: An innovative treatment approach for problem youth. *Journal of Child and Family Studies, 3*(2), 175–191. doi:10.1007/BF02234066

Becker, S. P. (2010). Wilderness therapy: Ethical considerations for mental health professionals. *Child & Youth Care Forum, 39*(1), 47–61. doi:10.1007/s10566-009-9085-7

Behrens, E., Santa, J., & Gass, M. (2010). The evidence base for private therapeutic schools, residential programs, and wilderness therapy programs. *Journal of Therapeutic Schools and Programs, 4*(1), 106–117.

Bettmann, J. E., & Jasperson, R. A. (2009). Adolescents in residential and inpatient treatment: A review of the outcome literature. *Child & Youth Care Forum, 38,* 161–183. doi:10.1007/s10566-009-9073-y

Bettmann, J. E., Russell, K. C., & Parry, K. J. (2012). How substance abuse recovery skills, readiness to change and symptom reduction impact change processes in wilderness therapy participants. *Journal of Child and Family Studies, 22*(8), 1039–1050. doi:10.1007/s10826-012-9665-2

Bettmann, J. E., & Tucker, A. R. (2011). Shifts in attachment relationships: A study of adolescents in wilderness treatment. *Child & Youth Care Forum, 40*(6), 499–519. doi:10.1007/s10566-011-9146-6

Bowen, M. (1978). *Family therapy in clinical practice*. New York: Jason Aronson Inc.

Brinkmeyer, M. Y., Eyberg, S. M., Nguyen, M. L., & Adams, R. W. (2004). Family engagement, consumer satisfaction and treatment outcome in the new era of child and adolescent in-patient psychiatric care. *Clinical Child Psychology and Psychiatry, 9*(4), 553–566. doi:10.1177/1359104504046159

Duerden, M., Widmer, M. A., & Witt, P. A. (2010). Positive youth development: What it is and how it fits in therapeutic settings. *Journal of Therapeutic Schools and Programs, 4*(1), 118–133.

Eccles, J. S., & Gootman, J. A. (Eds.). (2002). *Community programs to promote youth development*. Washington, DC: National Academy Press.

Evashwick, C. (1989). Creating the continuum of care. *Health Matrix, 7*(1), 30–39.

Ferguson, G. (2009). *Shouting at the sky: Troubled teens and the promise of the wild*. New York: St Martin's Press.

Harper, N. J., & Russell, K. C. (2008). Family involvement and outcome in adolescent wilderness treatment: A mixed-methods evaluation. *International Journal of Child & Family Welfare, 11* (1), 19–36.

Independent Educational Consultants Association. (2015). Helping clients with therapeutic needs. Retrieved from: http://www.iecaonline.com/atrisk.html

Jackson, D. (1957). The question of family homeostasis. *The Psychiatric Quarterly Supplement, 31*(1), 79–90. Presented at the Frieda Fromm-Reichmann Lecture, V. A. Hospital in Menlo Park, January 1954; Also presented May 7, 1954 at the American Psychiatric Association Meeting, St. Louis, MO.

Kerr, M. E., & Bowen, M. (1988). *Family evaluation: An approach based on Bowen theory*. New York: W. W. Norton & Co.

Kim-Appel, D., & Appel, J. (2013, March). *The relationship between Bowen's concept of differentiation of self and measurements of mindfulness*. Presentation at American Counseling Association Conference and Expo. Cincinnati, OH. Retrieved from: http://jonathanappel. weebly.com/uploads/5/1/7/0/5170722/the_relationship_between_bowens_concept_of__differentiation_and_mindfulness_3.18.13.pdf

Linehan, M. M. (1993). *Skills training manual for treating borderline personality disorder*. New York: The Guilford Press.

McGoldrick, M., & Carter, B. (2001). Advances in coaching: Family therapy with one person. *Journal of Marital and Family Therapy, 27*(3), 281–300. doi:10.1111/j.1752-0606.2001. tb00325.x

Miller, W. R., & Rollnick, S. (2002). *Motivational interviewing: Preparing people for change* (2nd ed.). New York: The Guilford Press.

National Association of Therapeutic Schools and Programs. (n.d.). *Program definitions*. Retrieved from: http://www.natsap.org/Public/Parents/Definitions.aspx

Nickerson, A. B., Colby, S. A., Brooks, J. L., Rickert, J. M., & Salamone, F. J. (2007). Transitioning youth from residential treatment to the community: A preliminary investigation. *Child & Youth Care Forum, 36*(2), 73–86. doi:10.1007/s10566-007-9032-4

Norton, C. L., Wisner, B. L., Krugh, M., & Penn, A. (2014). Helping youth transition into an alternative residential school setting: Exploring the effects of a wilderness orientation program on youth purpose and identity complexity. *Child and Adolescent Social Work Journal, 31*(5), 475–493. doi:10.1007/s10560-014-0331-y

Open Sky Wilderness Therapy. (2015). *Aftercare data set: 2013–2015*. Durango, Colorado: Unpublished Raw Data.

Prochaska, J. O., & DiClemente, C. C. (1983). Stages and processes of self-change of smoking: Toward an integrative model of change. *Journal of Consulting and Clinical Psychology, 51*(3), 390–395. doi:10.1037/0022-006X.51.3.390

Prochaska, J. O., & Velicer, W. F. (1997). The transtheoretical model of health behavior change. *American Journal of Health Promotion, 12*(1), 38–48. doi:10.4278/0890-1171-12.1.38

Russell, K. C. (2000). Exploring how the wilderness therapy process relates to outcomes. *The Journal of Experiential Education, 23*(3), 170–176.

Russell, K. C. (2002). Perspectives on the wilderness therapy process and its relation to outcome. *Child & Youth Care Forum, 31*(6), 415–437. doi:10.1023/A:1021110417119

Russell, K. C. (2001). What is wilderness therapy? *Journal of Experiential Education, 24*(2), 70–79. doi:10.1177/105382590102400203

Russell, K. C. (2003). An assessment of outcomes in outdoor behavioral healthcare treatment. *Child & Youth Care Forum, 32*(6), 355–381. doi:10.1023/B:CCAR.0000004507.12946.7e

Russell, K. C. (2005). Two years later: A qualitative assessment of youth well-being and the role of aftercare in outdoor behavioral healthcare treatment. *Child & Youth Care Forum, 34*(3), 209–239. doi:10.1007/s10566-005-3470-7

Russell, K. C. (2007). *Summary of research from 1999–2006 and update to 2000 survey of outdoor behavioral healthcare programs in North America.* (Technical Report 2, Outdoor Behavioral Healthcare Research Cooperative). Minneapolis, MN: University of Minnesota.

Russell, K. C., & Hendee, J. C. (1999). Wilderness therapy as an intervention and treatment for adolescents with behavioral problems. In A. E. Watson, G. Aplet, & J. C. Hendee (Eds.), *Personal, societal, and ecological values of wilderness: 6th world wilderness congress proceedings on research and allocation* (Vol. II). Ogden, UT: USDA Forest Service, Rocky Mountain Research Station.

Russell, K. C., Hendee, J. C., & Phillips-Miller, D. (2000). How wilderness therapy works; An examination of the wilderness therapy process to treat adolescents with behavioral problems and addictions. In S. F. McCool, D. N. Cole, W. T. Borrie, & J. O'Loughlin (Eds.), *Wilderness science in a time of change conference* (Vol. 3). Ogden, UT: USDA Forest Service Proceedings, Rocky Mountain Research Station.

Siegel, D. (2013). *Brainstorm: The power and purpose of the teenage brain.* New York: Tarcher.

Sklarow, M. (2011). Why do IECA members travel so much? *IECA's Insights Newsletter.* Retrieved from: http://www.iecaonline.com/PDF/IECA_Why-DO-IECA-Members-Travel.pdf

Taylor, S. J. (2004). Caught in the continuum: A critical analysis of the principle of the least restrictive environment. *Research & Practice for Persons with Severe Disabilities, 29*(4), 218–230. doi:10.2511/rpsd.29.4.218

Tucker, A. R., Bettmann, J. E., Norton, C. L., & Comart, C. (2015). The role of transport use in adolescent wilderness treatment: Its relationship to readiness to change and outcomes. *Child & Youth Care Forum, 44*(1), 671–686. doi:10.1007/s10566-015-9301-6

Wilder, J. (2011). How does an IEC choose a wilderness therapy program? IECA's insights newsletter. Retrieved December 30, 2015 from: https://www.iecaonline.com/PDF/IECA_Library_How-IECs-Choose-Wilderness-Therapy-Pgm.pdf

Author Biography

Kirsten L. Bolt, MEd, LMFT is a Clinical Therapist at Open Sky Wilderness Therapy, working primarily with adolescent females and their families. Her previous clinical experience also includes working with adolescent boys and young adult men and women. Prior to Open Sky, Kirsten was a Clinical Therapist at Aspen Achievement Academy, as well as a Field Guide. Her undergraduate degree is in Health and Exercise Science from Syracuse University. And her Master's degree is in Couple and Family Therapy from the University of Oregon. She has published articles in Contemporary Family Therapy and the Journal of Therapeutic Schools and Programs. Kirsten has also presented at the annual and regional conferences for the National Association of Therapeutic Schools and Programs, the annual and regional Wilderness Therapy Symposiums, and the International Family Therapy Association's world family therapy conference.

Chapter 10
Captaining the Ship: Acting as the Treatment Team Leader

John Hall, Barry Fell, Sam Coates, Nathan Sellers, Ryan Anderson,
Josh Thorn, Drew Davis and Scott Downs

Chapter Highlights

- Achieving powerful second-order change for the entire family system occurs through family programming, modeling in the residential milieu, and intentional intervention from an ecological systems perspective.
- A healthy team dynamic is necessary for delivering quality treatment, which consists of equal value of team members in terms of clinical direction and a culture of collaboration and trust.
- Pertinent categories for evaluation and inquiry include biology, wiring, learned behaviors, character traits, environment, and trauma history.

J. Hall (✉) · B. Fell · S. Coates · N. Sellers · J. Thorn · D. Davis · S. Downs
Telos Residential Treatment, 870 W. Center Street, Orem, UT 84057, USA
e-mail: john@telosrtc.com

B. Fell
e-mail: barry@telosrtc.com

S. Coates
e-mail: sam@telosrtc.com

N. Sellers
e-mail: nsellers@telosrtc.com

J. Thorn
e-mail: josh@telosrtc.com

D. Davis
e-mail: drew@telosrtc.com

S. Downs
e-mail: sdowns@telosrtc.com

R. Anderson
Telos U, 600 S. Geneva Road, Orem, UT 84057, USA
e-mail: ryananderson@telosu.com

© Springer International Publishing AG 2017
J.D. Christenson and A.N. Merritts (eds.), *Family Therapy with Adolescents in Residential Treatment*, Focused Issues in Family Therapy,
DOI 10.1007/978-3-319-51747-6_10

- An effective master treatment plan includes prioritized core issues, measurable and realistic goals, effective intervention, and client skill development.
- A master treatment plan is only effective if it is appropriately delegated, trained, and implemented.
- The progress of treatment must be measured to ensure both effective execution of the plan and to determine the level of effectiveness in meeting treatment goals.
- Continual communication between members of the treatment team is vital for successful implementation of treatment.

For many systems trained clinicians the concept of residential treatment can be concerning due to a priori assumptions that taking a member out of a family system and making changes will not stand up to the test of time due to the re-entry effects, if the system remains unaltered. While it is true that systems will have a strong pull on any member attempting to transcend the established patterns of family dynamics, research being conducted by the National Association of Therapeutic Schools and Programs suggests that residential treatment can actually be a powerful catalyst to help family systems make powerful changes and move from dysfunctional patterns of interaction to functional systems (Hall 2016). On the surface these appear to be contradictory concepts, when in reality they are not disparate, as long as the residential treatment incorporates a healthy dose of family programming. This programming can be designed to help the system change in concert with the changes made by the individual who is enrolled in the treatment setting.

Utilizing the Residential Milieu to Instigate Systemic Change

In order to make the appropriate change in a system the client or family must engage the process of therapy and be motivated for that change (Maier 1985). As many families are in crisis when they send a child to residential treatment, they are often unable to get their child to even attend therapy let alone engage in it at home. Meanwhile the chaos that reigns generally keeps them in management mode, putting out fires, and unable to address issues on a therapeutic level. A key benefit of residential treatment is that when the individual has demonstrated crisis driving behavior, removing them from home and into a stable environment creates an opportunity through space and reduction in chaos (see Chap. 8). This context breaks the day to day interaction cycle and allows a therapeutic inroad through which the whole family can take steps toward making the shifts in structure, family patterns, roles, and rules that were maintaining the existent family dynamics. This space and perspective can allow the therapeutic process the room to shift focus from first order problem solving to psychoeducation and even second-order reframing (Maier 1985), which is critical to systemic change within the family. Each member of the system has an important perspective that contributes to the multiverse of interactional dynamics that maintain the family's current dynamics (Becvar and Becvar 1982). This same multiverse of perspectives can lead to change in the family patterns as individual members gain new perspectives and respond differently to behavior in the current pattern. This leads to a perturbation of current system dynamics, which opens the door for change.

A residential milieu can provide the perturbation necessary to help families make systemic changes by creating a completely new system or residential milieu that is full of novel and powerful experiences for residential clients and their families. Residential treatment is a multi-level intervention. Interventions are relational acts (Fraser and Solovey 2007) in which each new relationship formed between system members, or the whole family with staff members, therapists, or the culture of residential treatment program creates a new and powerful link through which influence on perspective can be accomplished. These interventions can be intentionally and strategically employed through the planned process of residential treatment. Indeed, the process is reciprocal for all parties as the families, individuals, and the treatment program interventionists influence each other constantly, the intervention vitalizing the relationships and the relationships vitalizing the intervention (Fraser and Solovey 2007). Ultimately, the patterns existent within the treatment program can not only provide an intentional model for healthier system dynamics, but through this reciprocal interaction the family can be directly influenced to change family system dynamics as it adjusts to be compatible with the treatment program dynamics.

Second-Order Change

The other concern that can arise in regard to any milieu-based treatment is whether the change is dependent on the structure in that system or upon second-order change, as proposed by the Mental Research Institute (Watzlawick et al. 1974), which is achieved while interacting with the system. The answer, of course, depends on how fully integrated the client or client family becomes with the treatment system or the larger social context (Becvar and Becvar 1982). The principles of second-order change center on creating meta-change rather than mere behavioral change by focusing on changing the principles that underlie the problematic behaviors or interactions. Focusing on these principles leads to intrinsic motivation to change behaviors, which are then maintained beyond any externally reinforcing stimuli (Lyddon 1990). Therefore, residential treatment can employ the same focus on change at a principle-based level rather than using only behavior modification. In this way, any treatment environment that does so enables second-order change to occur.

When residential treatment programs make use of their social construct to enact change, the entire family can be engaged in the construction of a new social paradigm including new principles, rules, patterns of interaction, and behavior. These can be influenced through site visits, correlation of approach, trainings, assigned readings, multi-systemic interaction with the treatment milieu, and of course through intensive family therapy. In recent years options for increasing the power of family therapy have multiplied beyond weekly telephonic therapy and regular visits for in-person session to internet based video sessions that give access to the full range of visual and structural feedback. Using these strategies, the whole family can transcend past patterns and rules by accepting and incorporating the principles and rules encountered in the treatment milieu, which would then allow the family to be transformed and stabilize into a new system (Kern and Wheeler 1977). These principles of change constitute a paradigm shift or core change that resembles a level of enlightened perspective and intentional choices based on an insightfully different state of mind that allows families to transcend the problematic context in favor of the principles learned and known for their value (Bowman and Baylen 1994) through the treatment experience.

Ecological Theory of Systems

Urie Bronfenbrenner (1979) discussed multiple levels of systems that influence individuals and families; microsystems that directly impact the individual on a constant level and the macrosystem of the broader cultural base and the chronosystem of transitional shifts over the life course of the individual. In a milieu-based treatment environment, multiple levels of this systemic ecology can be intentionally utilized to intervene in the development of the child and family. For instance, the residential team, the academic milieu, therapeutic groups and sessions, and even parameters of what types of peers are admitted can have a daily impact on development. On a mesosystem level, the treatment team (comprised of members of the microsystems and in coordination with the family) can direct the interconnected relationships between each of these microsystems according to the clinical needs of the master treatment plan.

The remaining levels of exosystem, macrosystem, and even chronosystem are in large part shaped by the leadership team whose charge it is to maintain a designed therapeutic culture both within the treatment center and in conjunction with determining what external social experiences will be approved, planned, and executed over the course of treatment. This provides a unique and intense ability to shape so many levels of systemic interaction over time and allows for more direct control of the change environment than the short, periodic bursts that outpatient therapy can hope to shape from the position of counseling the individual and family about patterns to develop, without the access or oversight to ensure consistent application of therapeutic recommendations.

To effectively mobilize all of the aspects of the residential milieu, in order to implement effective intervention and achieve systemic change, requires intentional intervention through strong clinical leadership. This leadership from the primary therapist, or *captaining of the ship*, will be detailed in this chapter and will address the process for consistent and intentional transfer of systemic patterns developed and implemented in a residential treatment milieu to the family through training, systemic intervention, and designed opportunities to practice new patterns. This modeling and practicing of the implanted patterns of interaction with the total immersion of the treatment milieu can facilitate the inception of new systemic patterns in families as they gradually transition into the home environment.

Value of the Team

In order to both, model healthy dynamics and create change for clientele, it is critical that the team members (e.g., therapists and line staff) at the treatment center maintain healthy dynamics. Therefore, the establishment and maintenance of a healthy team dynamic must be in place prior to any treatment provided. When working with any team dynamic it is important to acknowledge that as an individual team member we see the world as we are, not as it is. Many factors influence our personal lenses including our upbringing, genetics, as well as society itself. A team that is in conflict often experiences breakdown due to irreconcilable differences. The key to any team success is to reach a state of synergy. Synergistic outcomes are often reached when difference of opinion is valued and encouraged (Covey 1989).

When working in a clinical treatment team the goal is to always put together everyone's views to form a panoramic snapshot of the student being discussed. The three domains that come together to discuss a student's clinical profile are the residential department (the direct care givers), academics, and the clinical department. The treatment team facilitator is the primary therapist whose purpose is to *captain the ship*. Captaining the ship requires a number of skills. The therapist who serves in this capacity needs to be able to rally the team in the process of diagnostic assessment, treatment planning, intervention formation, and measuring treatment plan outcomes. A treatment team has to recognize that no one team member has cornered the market on a student's needs. By valuing the opinions of each team member, the primary therapist can carefully formulate what is driving a student to act the way he or she does and then carve out a plan that operationalizes each department's role in meeting the student's clinical needs.

Turf Guarding

It is common for an organization that has many departments to start guarding their turf. Turf guarding is when unhealthy competition starts to bubble, when one department believes their work objectives surpass those of another department. The byproduct of turf guarding is collusion. Collusion often manifests itself through gossip, backbiting, and the general mistrust of colleagues. A treatment team within the residential setting must maintain a healthy *way of being* in order to best serve its clientele. Team members who strive to cultivate a respect for one another's opinions and have a zero tolerance policy for collusion achieve marvelous results.

Weighted Opinion

Although all opinions are heard within a treatment team, they are not all equally weighted. What tips the balance of power are three factors: (a) experience; (b) education; (c) and level of responsibility. It is typically the professional team members who have higher education and expertise ranging from medical staff like psychiatrists to clinicians who typically hold graduate degrees. It is essential that the professional staff carry themselves appropriately. There is no room for arrogance or haughtiness within a residential treatment team. The team members rely upon one another as each department plays a unique role. It is typically the residential staff who spends most of the week with the student; therefore, they hold key insights into behavioral trends. The residential staff's primary roles consist of gathering information for assessment and executing milieu-based intervention. The academic staff plays a similar role, although the information gathered is more focused on classroom trends like work output and learning challenges that cause distress. The clinicians are key decision makers, but need to express humility in those decisions, recognizing that without the other team member's awareness would be limited.

A Culture of Trust

The opposite of turf guarding is team building. Team building is not necessarily a series of activities, although team building activities can help. Team building is a culture. It occurs when there is a spirit of appreciation, support, recognition, and training. Residential work with at-risk youth is emotionally and mentally taxing. Burnout is high amongst team members; hence, there is an essential need for all caregivers to feel the strength of their colleagues. Residential care is known for high turnover amongst the direct care teams (Mclean 2015). This can be decreased when all three domains show mutual respect for one another. Communicating the *why* behind each treatment plan helps the residential staff feel like they have greater purpose. Treatment centers get greater results when departments are yoked by good communication and a clear understanding of treatment goals (Baron 2008). The benefactors of this type of synergy are the students themselves. There is also a secondary gain when there is a culture of high trust, which is staff retention. A treatment center that has high turnover struggles to maintain continuity of care. Employment research has shown that higher retention is the result of employees feeling like they are a part of a high trust culture (Whipple 2004).

Another contributor to a high trust culture is repetitious training on philosophy, clinical best practices, and maintaining the right *way of being* while serving the students. A culture of training leads to increased competence and greater retention. Additionally, because there are multiple caregivers trying to coordinate their efforts, systems of communication need to be effective and efficient. Collusion rises to the surface when there is infrequent communication or miscommunications among team members. Ultimately, the quality of care is adversely impacted when caregivers are not operating from the same page.

Diagnostic Evaluation Fundamentals

Proper assessment and diagnostic evaluation is the only reliable gateway that can lead us to precise and appropriate treatment. Unless we know how all the puzzle pieces fit together there is no valid way to provide specific, and on target, interventions. A less thorough method of evaluation will likely lead to a *shotgun* approach to treatment. The assessment process must be specific, but also must be seen through a broad enough lens to give us a well-rounded view of the adolescent in question. Pertinent categories for evaluation and inquiry include biology, wiring, learned behaviors, character traits, environment, and trauma history, which are delineated in the bullet points below.

- Biology—Here we are looking for neuropsychological disorders that imply a *chemical imbalance* of brain neurotransmitters. This would include disorders such as Major Depressive Disorder, Bipolar Disorder, ADHD, Schizophrenia, and various anxiety disorders.
- Wiring—This would include information processing problems that are *hard-wired*. This category would include classic learning disorders in reading, writing, and math. It would also include executive dysfunction, low processing speed, working memory deficits, language disorders, and nonverbal learning disorders.
- Learned Behaviors—This area includes issues with low self-esteem, habits, and learned behaviors that appear to be dysfunctional. Examples might include oppositional behavior, avoidance, low resilience, manipulation, and poor emotional control.
- Character Traits—These are learned behaviors that are consolidating into more of a fixed personality style. Examples include traits suggestive of Narcissistic, Borderline, or Histrionic Personality Disorders.
- Environment—Here we are looking for environmental factors that are having an influence on the adolescent's behavior or presentation of symptoms. Examples might include bad influence friends, bullying, school or social stress, family dysfunction, substance use, etc.
- Trauma—This category is closely related to the environmental category, but implies that those environmental stresses have led to a deeper level of impact with longer lasting implications. Examples might include various forms of physical and sexual abuse, divorce, physical illness, accidents, and family deaths.

It is important to utilize multiple resources in order to create a comprehensive evaluation of each of these categories. We rely on data derived from past history, testing, and observation as outlined below. It is important to note that any testing reviewed should be current and applicable to the present treatment process.

Past History

This involves a detailed, exhaustive information gathering process directed toward parents, previous caregivers, schools, and wilderness therapists. Topics to cover include current complaints and symptoms, history of present illness, past medical history, past psychiatric history, family history, substance use history, and developmental history, respectively. It is important to do a comprehensive review of each of these areas. While checklists and diagnostic surveys are helpful, this is a process that requires careful deep and direct questioning of caregivers to ensure accurate and adequate information.

Testing

Good history is supplemented by objective medical and neuropsychological testing. Examples of possible types of testing include physical exam and laboratory testing, genetic testing, IQ and academic testing, personality and projective testing, speech and language evaluations, and tests for memory and executive function. A comprehensive battery of psychological testing provides rich data for use by the treatment team, as will be discussed more fully in the sections below.

Observation

As important as the gathering of past history and testing are in the assessment process, nothing is really confirmed diagnostically until there is a period of adequate observation by those who have trained clinical eyes. The principle of the *proof is in the pudding* applies here. This includes psychiatric mental status examination at admission and ongoing, staff observations by clinical staff, the nursing department, teachers, and residential and recreational staff. Finally, these observations should be made in a variety of environments, including academic, residential, social, and recreational.

The Role of the Treatment Team in Evaluation

All of the above information is necessary and vital to the diagnostic evaluation and treatment process, but it is also just a prelude to the meeting that organizes and gives meaning to that information. Based on our experience and practice, a good and effective treatment team operates on the following concepts we have developed: (a) the humble detective approach; (b) organized reporting; (c) organized analysis of information; (d) prioritization of symptoms; (e) dichotomies; and, (f) diagnostic interventions.

The Humble Detective

The loudest or most confident voice in the room may not necessarily be the most diagnostically accurate voice. Humility in diagnosis implies a willingness to entertain all possibilities. It means that we need to guard against getting locked in too early to a diagnosis that may be based more on *a feeling* or intuition rather than facts. It means being willing to back up and reevaluate your position when new information arises.

The detective is also a relentless fact finder. There is never enough information and all information is useful. He or she works off the premise based on this anonymous quote: "When information is lacking, all choices are hazardous." When practicing this principle, pattern yourself after the legendary television detective, Columbo, who famously stated, "I have just one more question" (Levinson and Link 1971).

Organized Reporting

The treatment team should not be a free for all. A disorganized mass of comments rarely leads to diagnostic precision or consensus. There should be an organized format for reporting that emphasizes an accounting of *facts* rather than serial story telling. In addition, the facts reported should be organized into diagnostic categories that are specific to the issues relevant to the adolescent being discussed. Reports might include summaries by residential staff, clinical staff, and academic staff.

Organized Analysis of Information

All of the facts in the world do not help if we do not know how to organize and make sense of the information. For instance, knowing that an adolescent exhibits symptoms of oppositionality does us little good unless we also understand the source of that oppositionality. Does the root lie in mood, or anxiety, or ADHD, or is it characterological in origin? A good diagnostically focused treatment team always analyzes information in this fashion. They look for the roots of behavior rather than settling on the superficial symptoms.

Prioritization of Symptoms

Once we have separated out the *root* or core issues from the evident symptoms then we want to focus our fact finding, reporting, and analysis on the most disruptive and prominent issues at hand. Plenteous amounts of information can pour into a treatment team, much of it extraneous in nature. Without establishing a clear priority, we can be pulled away from the more important issues. We avoid that pitfall by prioritizing our diagnostic efforts to the three or four most significant areas. We do not ignore other information, but we focus on what is most pertinent and critical to the student's progress.

Dichotomies

Dichotomies represent a simple and organized way of tracking diagnostic symptoms for staff. For instance, if we are tracking the symptom of oppositionality, staff might track the percentage of time a student is compliant versus noncompliant. If an adolescent struggles with social anxiety, the dichotomy tracked might be engaged versus isolating. It is easy to understand and a concrete way of tracking information.

Diagnostic Interventions

Sometimes the best way to test a theory about an adolescent's diagnosis is to create a set of circumstances that will prove or disprove the theory. For instance, does the adolescent avoid cleaning their room because they are oppositional, or because they lack the executive functioning skills to accomplish the task? If we provide help in organizing the task for them, and the resistance melts away, then we have evidence that executive dysfunction was the root of the problem.

Master Treatment Plan Development

The development of a treatment plan follows the processes outlined above and is typically a legal requirement that therapists must fulfill for each of their clients. Unfortunately, a common practice in treatment facilities is to develop a plan within the first 30 days simply to fulfill the requirement, and then archive the plan and give it little attention throughout the course of treatment. Yet, a clear, well-written treatment plan, which is communicated to each invested team member, is a critical aspect of successful residential treatment. A quality plan is broken down into four main points: (a) core issues; (b) goals; (c) interventions; and (d) skills.

Prioritizing Core Issues

Just as with assessment, intervention can lose traction if priorities are not maintained throughout the process. This can be the result of the *loudest* current behavior observed by the staff or therapist. This is detrimental to an effective therapeutic process as these behaviors can either be a distraction from the core issue or simply a symptom of it. Mapping out the underlying core issues from the beginning will help keep treatment on track and treatment team members focused on the most important things.

During the assessment stage of treatment, the therapist should take the time to differentiate the symptoms of the problem from the source of the problem. To draw an analogy, if an arborist wants to get rid of a tree (the problem) he or she does not snip away at the leaves and the branches (symptoms). He or she would know that the tree still has the ability to grow new leaves and branches. However, if the arborist attacks the tree at the roots (core issues) the tree will not be able to grow back. The *root* issues will be the important issues to target in treatment planning, rather than the resultant *leaves and branches*.

Simply labeling the core issue (e.g., depression), while helpful, is typically not sufficient in helping the client, parents, or staff members to know what is being addressed. In the example of depression, there are many ways that it can be manifested, as well as many reasons why it may be a problem. It may be an issue of anhedonia leading to poor school performance, or it could be manifesting as suicidal ideation and self-harm. It is important to clarify how the problem is derived and manifests specifically to give clear focus to invested team members (especially the client).

Once core issues have been identified and clarified, it is important to prioritize which to address first and which are of greatest importance. Often, these problems can be layered within the client. Sometimes a client is too defended or resistant for one reason or another to address a particular problem. Other times they may have developed learned behaviors that prevent them from being able to focus on the deeper issues at hand. Therefore, it is important to decipher what issue needs to have the greatest focus. For example, there may be issues with both anxiety and depression. The anxiety can be stifling and persistent, thereby preventing a client from engaging in school and social interactions with friends which can lead to depression. Addressing the anxiety would likely be a higher priority than the depression due to the underlying nature of the problem. It is also important to understand the client's ability to work on multiple issues at once. There are some clients that may be able to work on five separate issues simultaneously, while some may only be able to do one or two at a time. Recognizing the client's capability will be helpful in maintaining an effective treatment process.

Setting Clear and Measurable Goals

Once the core issues have been identified and prioritized, the therapist can begin writing the treatment goals for each issue. The clarity, accuracy, and direction of the goal are important considerations when it comes to achieving the treatment purpose for each client. A helpful tactic in writing an effective goal is determining why an issue was actually a problem in their life. For some, social skills may be a persistent struggle, but it may not be creating significant problems in their life. For others, it may be dominating their interactions with all their relationships and affecting their ability to perform academically and in a job. It may lead to problems with being bullied. Therefore, starting with how the issue is creating problems in their life is a key starting point.

Next, it will be important to outline the specific behaviors that show how this is manifested at home, at school, and/or in the milieu. This allows all parties to know what specifically is being targeted. After this has been identified, the desired behavior change to be seen can be outlined. It will be important for this to be an observable behavior. For example, with depression, do we want to see a brighter affect or an increased involvement in enjoyable activities?

We must also keep in mind the level of capability of the client. The capacity for insight and ability will greatly determine the effectiveness of certain goals. If a goal is set too high we can set up a client for failure from the beginning. If a client's beginning ability level in school is only turning in assignments 50% of the time and receiving C and D grades, then setting a goal of turning in assignments 100% of the time and having A's and B's will likely be unrealistic. Yet if we work toward a goal of turning in assignments 75% of the time and having B's and C's, this is likely to be more achievable. At the same time, a goal must be challenging enough to stretch the client out of their comfort zone and into the growth zone.

This type of goal setting strategy is an important aspect of SMART goals: Specific, Measurable, Attainable, Results-based, and Time-bound (Conzemius et al. 2005). Without the clarity and focus on measurable outcomes, treatment teams become focused on what *feels* right, without actual evidence of change over time. Often teams will get stuck on the most recent behavior, which in reality may be a false positive or a false negative. The right measurement is essential in determining progress toward the therapeutic goal.

Finding quality measurement strategies can be one of the challenges of residential treatment. It is important to get a read on the most reliable way to measure the observable behavior. There are a few categories of observable behaviors. Two of these are behavioral trends (behaviors seen throughout each day) and isolated behaviors (behaviors that while important to note only happen occasionally). Each of these would be measured in a different way. The behavioral trends can be measured using dichotomies scored by the residential staff each shift. For example, with what frequency did the client exhibit flat or bright affect on a Likert scale of 1 (flat affect) to 5 (bright affect) on a given day? With more isolated behaviors such as an emotional blow-up, measuring how many occurrences per day/week would give a better indicator of change. In addition to these measurements, occasionally a therapist can use self-assessments with students who have good insight and are trustworthy.

Determining Interventions

Once the goal has been set the next step is to determine what interventions will be used to help the client achieve their goal. A therapist must determine between an office-based approach, a milieu intervention, or a combination of the two. Some clients will have good insight levels and are self-motivated. Cognitive work in these cases can be very effective and will largely be done in the office with the inclusion of some therapeutic assignments. However, there are some clients whose behaviors are very ingrained learned behaviors, or they lack insight into their thoughts and interactions. In these cases, interventions must be focused on what is going on in the milieu.

A treatment program can identify a pool of interventions that are most effective within their residential milieu. It is difficult for staff members to constantly have to be learning new creative interventions for each student. If there are too many they become less effective due to staff not knowing how to properly run the intervention (no matter how creative or *perfect* it is).

Therefore, within this pool of interventions the therapist must determine which one will be the most helpful for that particular client in achieving the specific goal. This can be based on learning style, ability level, milieu dynamics, or proven strategies from the client's history.

Once interventions have been determined, delegating assignments for the interventions must be communicated. For example, will the intervention be run in the academic, residential, or clinical portion of the program? This must be clear and well-communicated in order for the intervention to be properly implemented.

Identified Skill Development

During the creation of the treatment plan, it is good to begin with the end in mind (Covey 1989). Parents, clients, and staff should all know the desired result of the intervention. This result often includes proper application of a tangible skill. Skill development is an essential part of residential treatment and a therapist should be mindful what skill is being developed with each intervention. The treatment goal is met when the client is able to be consistent in the use of the new skills or behaviors beyond the completion of the intervention.

Additionally, it should be noted there are hard and soft skills. Hard skills are easily measurable behaviors (e.g., responding to feedback without getting defensive, good eye contact, proactive social engagement, assertive advocating for needs, etc.) Soft skills are more difficult to see immediately because they are internal and lead to external changes in behaviors over time (e.g., positive self-talk, self-soothing, etc.). Skills should be written into the treatment plan and assessed to determine success of interventions in reaching the stated goals (Laker and Powell 2011).

Operationalizing the Treatment Plan

Operationalizing the treatment plan consists of three distinct aspects. These three aspects are (a) delegation; (b) training on interventions; and, (c) the *ramping up* period. Each of these will be discussed more fully below.

Delegation

Once the work to be done has been assessed and effective methods of measurement have been identified, the resultant task is to specifically assign the various parts of the work to individual team members who will take ownership of a clearly defined piece of the intervention. Because of the phenomenon of diffusion of responsibility (Darley and Latané 1968) assigning a task to *everyone* will ensure that no one does it. On the other hand, assigning a task which is clear, concrete, and well communicated to a specific team member, and providing accountability through a process of executing the intervention and then returning and reporting to the treatment team (via daily charting and in person during treatment team meetings) greatly increases the chances that the task will be performed. Utilizing this system facilitates the identification of problems with the intervention and making repairs, since it provides information whether an intervention is happening, how well it is being performed, and how consistently it is being carried out. This can help the treatment team avoid the mistakes of continuing with an intervention that is ineffective or prematurely ending an intervention that could have been effective had it been properly executed or given time to take effect. A mindful treatment team will always examine if they merely need to make an adjustment rather than *reinventing the wheel* when they find that an intervention is not getting results.

Specific tasks should be delegated to various team members based on three major factors: (a) their role; (b) their resources; and (c) their gifts. Intentional delegation weaves together the strengths of various team members in a way that compensates for the weaknesses of individual team members and as such is synergistic in nature. If a program's hiring model is sound, they have chosen team members who have licenses, certifications, and skills that enable them to be effective in their roles and who are passionate and intrinsically motivated about serving students and their families (Collins 2001). In general, asking a team member to operate outside of their role is discouraged, although there are exceptions to this rule. Even highly capable therapists may be merely mediocre tutors and effective administrators may be poor clinicians.

Of the many resources to be considered when delegating tasks to team members, time and energy are among the most vital. Care should be taken not to overload various team members. A program may have a particularly gifted recreational therapist, but if he or she is stretched too thin by asking him or her to do too much, the general effectiveness of all of his or her interactions with all clients and team members is likely to suffer. Employees feeling either burned-out or underutilized can be a warning sign of ineffective delegation (Maslach and Leiter 1997; Leiter and Maslach 2005).

In addition to formal skills and particular roles, team members also have personal gifts. These are separate from their trained skill set and indeed often cannot be taught. These gifts are often the *secret ingredient* of each treatment center and can be a reason to make an exception to the rule of having each team member operating within their formal roles. The treatment team does well to identify the gifts of all of the team members and to carefully select times when utilizing a team member's individual gifts may be called for. This could look like the Mr. Miagi like maintenance man taking a specific student under his wing, or a line staff member with gifts in comforting the grieving spending time with a student during a grandparent's final stages of a terminal illness.

Training on Interventions

Launching a treatment plan begins with training the various team members involved in the specific skills or strategies they will be employing and reporting on. While this is true even if the training is merely a review of an intervention or treatment approach with which the team is already familiar, it is especially true if there are any innovative elements or variations on a more familiar theme. The therapist begins by directly training the residential staff on the milieu-based interventions designated in the treatment plan. Supervision of daily execution of treatment protocols allows for immediate feedback and in-the-moment training. Additionally, the clinician can facilitate ongoing direct training on treatment protocols and work through any difficulties the staff may be encountering as they apply the treatment protocols.

Furthermore, daily charting on interventions by residential staff allows another avenue of accountability for clinical stewardship and supervision by the therapist. As staff report in their charting on the dynamics they observed and how they applied the treatment protocols assigned to them, the therapist can offer affirmations on successes or direction and guidance on both perceiving when to use a treatment protocol and how to help the protocol be more successful. The combination of regular training, daily direct oversight, and a feedback loop with the treatment team on the execution and results helps make sure that treatment plan interventions are occurring as designed, which increases the likelihood of effectiveness.

The Ramping up Period

Even for an experienced clinical team, getting a treatment plan consistently implemented takes some time. It can sometimes require a week or two of training, supervision, and feedback to create enough momentum to consider a treatment plan fully launched. During that time, special attention should be given to making sure treatment protocols are understood, that they are being employed at the right times and under the right circumstances, and that there is as much consistency as possible in the use of treatment protocols between staff.

The practice of having measurable indicators (i.e., target behavior counts, dichotomies, and scales) helps in evaluating if a treatment plan is effectively being implemented. If target behavior counts seem abnormally low, this is usually a good indication that staff still need training and help in perceiving the problematic dynamic when it is active and in applying the assigned intervention. If target behavior counts are excessively high, it can indicate that the staff may still need training in how to utilize the intervention effectively. If target behavior counts feel congruent with what the various members of the treatment team experience from their interaction with the student this usually indicates that a treatment plan has been properly launched and calibrated.

Monitoring the Progress of Treatment

Treatment team reporting ensures that each department involved in the treatment plan for a particular student reports on areas of progress, concerns, possible adjustment, and goal completion. An example of this is the academic representative sharing objective feedback on citizenship, absences, tardiness, grades, and accommodations in the academic setting and/or behavioral concerns in the class-room. The goal listed on the treatment plan may indicate that a student will have no more than two missing assignments for a period of four weeks. The report would consist of stating how many missing assignments the student had over the previous four-week period. The therapist is responsible for maintaining the direction and integrity of the implementation of the treatment plan. He or she is the point person for the treatment team in general and takes the feedback obtained in treatment team meetings and implements it into further treatment progression and goal completion.

This information can be shared with the student in connection with discussing primary issue progress and goal completion.

Having measureable indicators is also very helpful in determining if an intervention is successful. Ideally, target behavior counts, dichotomies, and scales will show a decrease in problematic dynamics and an increase in adaptive coping and functioning over time (Davis and Hall 2015). Tracking the trends in these measurable indictors can help identify complicating factors and give focus to improving the effectiveness of the intervention.

Measurable indicators also help to inform the treatment team about when it is time to make a change. If the indicators for a particular target have reached their goal levels and have held steady over time and in the face of tests and challenges, then the intervention has likely served its purpose, and the treatment team can move on to the next point of focus. Other possibilities that the treatment team is likely to encounter are indicators showing some progress, but then stalling out and plateauing below the goal level, or indicators not showing any progress.

Factors to Consider in Modifying or Changing Milieu Interventions

Resistance is refusal or rejection of the individual to treatment or of their different issues. When resistance of the individual is the issue, using motivational interviewing is a well-known technique to use with the individual to increase their motivation and their accountability (Hettema et al. 2005). If an intervention seemed like it should be a good fit based on a client's clinical presentation, needs, and learning style, but is not gaining traction with that student, the treatment team can conduct a 360 analysis which we developed to assess the obstacle(s). This consists of looking at six different areas: (a) resistance: (b) motivation; (c) insight; (d) competence; (e) questioning the intervention; and, (f) parents. Lack of motivation is a frequent issue in residential treatment. Each individual needs a motivation to move forward with their treatment. In order to work with an individual on motivation, the therapist and treatment team must find and understand what motivates the individual and find an incentive that works with them. At times, a protocol can help with this. An example of this is a token economy.

Lack of insight is when the individual does not understand or is confused about their treatment issues. When a client has a lack of insight, the team must take time to teach and educate the individual about their issues. If a client has a core issue of *rigidity*, but also has low insight, they will resist feedback or treatment for the rigidity due to the lack of insight. Educating, formally and in the moment, is important during this process. Using multiple psychoeducation techniques such as metaphors, stories, or object lessons, may be necessary and/or useful to educate the client.

Competence is the aptitude to do something successfully. When a client struggles with competence it is important for the treatment team to look at the client's skills, as well as what the individual can accomplish realistically. Without realistic expectations, the individual may struggle meet their goal and burn out before achieving his or her potential. For example, if a client struggles socially and understands that this is an issue, but is unsuccessful at making changes certain skills such as social coaching, scripting, and role play can be taught to improve appropriate social interactions.

At times an intervention may not be as productive as another. The treatment team can take a self-assessment in order to determine if the treatment approach may be the obstacle of progress for the client in which case adjustments need to be made accordingly. However, it is also important to recognize that changing too soon can also be detrimental for a client's progress. At times, the intervention may be the correct one, but not in practice long enough to show noticeable progress. It is when the intervention has been in place over a period of approximately three to five weeks that the treatment team should reevaluate the intervention and consider making a change.

The last consideration is the parent's *buy-in*. Parents can struggle to be invested with suggested interventions. Without parents or the family on the same page with the rest of treatment team, the interventions have to potential to be undermined or fail to have success in the family system. This *short circuits* the long-term effectiveness of intervention. In order to help parents buy-into protocols and interventions a collaborative relationship of trust must be established by the therapist and treatment team (Norcross 2002). A therapist who is able to accurately assess behaviors and issues with the client and accurately project the course of treatment will gain a great deal of creditability and trust with the parents. Education may also be needed in order to assist parents to buy-into the work the treatment team recommends.

Treatment teams also need to consider the possibility of either over-programming or over-reaching a client's readiness to engage in activities or situations. There are many different resources that may be used judiciously when implementing interventions or facilitating skill development. Examples of these include sports programs, mentoring, privileges, groups, and adventure-based activities.

Communication and Treatment Coordination

Extra meeting coordination is a vital part of cross communication between departments in residential settings. These are meetings outside of regular or scheduled meetings. You will find that in *nuts and bolts* types of meetings, new ideas, or systems need to be built and operationalized. In order to make this happen the team can assign smaller groups to tackle these issues outside of regular scheduled meetings. This can streamline the discussion and prevent the team from getting bogged down.

Frequent Training of Staff and Teachers

Therapists can meet with the residential team as a whole to train on certain protocols or treatment goals and to reinforce directives discussed in treatment team meetings. This meeting has an agenda. It is not to serve as a dumping ground for problematic behaviors. Rather, it is to follow a system where therapists will continue training on topics repetitiously. This also serves as an opportunity for residential staff to gather background and historical information that may provide insight into a client's behavior.

Teacher training is another integral part of residential treatment. Therapists rotate through the teacher development meetings to conduct clinical trainings. This allows for teachers to broaden their scope of practice and to observe classroom behavior with a clinical eye. Teachers can be very helpful with assessing and reporting back to therapist's issues they may encounter in the classroom. This broadens the systemic purview for therapists (Bronstein 2000).

Clipboard and Email Communication

Communication overload can be experienced by everyone and can easily cause ruptures in the treatment process, though communication is vital to the essence of systemic treatment in residential settings. While an email can be efficient and simple, relying on this form of communication can put at risk the clarity of instructions regarding protocols or treatment plans.

A clipboard is a common tool for ensuring clear and accurate communication of in-the-moment intervention. This can be an electronic and/or physical clipboard that the residential staff have and use throughout their shift. Each client can have a clear list of privileges, protocol, and intervention information on it. Most importantly, it also tells the staff what to chart on, what behavioral trends to look out for and other pertinent clinical information the staff need to know when working with the client. If a supervisor calls in sick and another staff has to fill in, they can refer to this clipboard and know exactly what to look for and chart with any given client. This allows for greater continuity and consistency.

Summary

In order to effectively implement individual and systemic change in residential treatment it is vital that each of the areas discussed above be addressed. Without proper assessment any treatment objectives may be off target. With the right dynamic and approach of a treatment team, led by a clinical captain, the team can effectively develop, implement, and evaluate, individual and family treatment.

The family must be involved in collaboration and communication throughout the treatment process in order to effectively transfer the new dynamics and processes developed in treatment. The therapist is the primary conduit through which family and milieu coordination is directed and accomplished, which is why is it so crucial that therapists understanding and effectively utilize the concepts discussed in this chapter.

References

Baron, N. (2008). *Always on*. New York: Oxford University Press.

Becvar, D. S., & Becvar, R. J. (1982). *Systems theory and family therapy*. University Lanham, MD: Press of America Inc.

Bowman, R. L., & Baylen, D. (1994). Buddhism as a second-order change psychotherapy. *International Journal for the Advancement of Counseling, 17*(2), 101–108.

Bronfenbrenner, U. (1979). *The ecology of human development: Experiments by nature and design*. Cambridge, MA: Harvard University Press.

Bronstein, L. (2000). A model for interdisciplinary collaboration. *Social Work, 48*(3), 297–306.

Collins, J. C. (2001). *Good to great: Why some companies make the leap and others don't*. New York: Random House.

Conzemius, A., O'Niell, J., Commodore, C., & Pulsfus, C. (2005). *The power of SMART goals: Using goals to improve student learning*. Bloomington, IN: Solution Tree Press.

Covey, S. (1989). *The seven habits of highly successful people*. New York: Simon & Schuster

Darley, J. M., & Latané, B. (1968). Bystander intervention in emergencies: Diffusion of responsibility. *Journal of Personality and Social Psychology, 8*, 377–383.

Davis, D., & Hall, J. (2015). *Progress monitoring demonstrates measurable improvement in key diagnostic areas through observation of intermittent dichotomous behavior*. Manuscript submitted for publication.

Fraser, J. S., & Solovey, A. D. (2007). *Second-order change in psychotherapy: The golden thread that unifies effective treatments*. Washington, DC: American Psychological Association.

Hall, J. (2016). *The results are In! research shows that families get better in residential treatment programs that include a focus on the family system [power point slides]*. Retrieved from personal hard drive.

Hettema, J., Steele, J., & Miller, W. R. (2005). Motivational interviewing. *Annual Review of Psychology, 1*, 91–111.

Kern, R. M., & Wheeler, M. S. (1977). Autocratic versus democratic childrearing practices and second-order behavior change in parent-child interactions. *Journal of Individual Psychology, 33*(2), 223–232.

Laker, D. R., & Powell, J. L. (2011). The differences between hard and soft skills and their relative impact on training transfer. *Human Resource Development Quarterly, 22*(1), 111–122.

Leiter, M. P., & Maslach, C. (2005). *Banishing burnout: Six strategies for improving your relationship with work*. San Francisco: Josey-Bass.

Levinson R., & Link, W. (Writer), & McEveety, V., & Frawley, J. (Director). (1971). In executive producer Falk, P. (Executive Producer) *Columbo*. NBC Universal Television.

Lyddon, W. J. (1990). First- and second-order change: Implications for rationalist and constructivist cognitive therapies. *Journal of Counseling & Development, 69*(2), 122–127.

Maier, H. (1985). First and second order change: Powerful concepts for preparing child care practitioners. *Journal of Children in Contemporary Society, 17*(3), 37–45.

Maslach, C., & Leiter, M. P. (1997). *The truth about burnout: How organizations cause personal stress and what to do about it*. San Francisco: Josey-Bass.

McLean, S. (2015). Managing behaviour in child residential group care: Unique tensions. *Child & Family Social Work, 20*(3), 344–353.

Norcross, J. C. (2002). *Psychotherapy relationships that work: Therapist contributions and responsiveness to patients.* New York: Oxford University Press.

Watzlawick, P., Weakland, J. H., & Fisch, R. (1974). *Change: Principles of problem formation and problem resolution.* New York: Norton.

Whipple, B. (2004). *Trust and customer retention.* Retrieved from: http://www.leadergrow.com/articles/530-trust-and-customer-retention

Author Biographies

John Hall, LMFT is the Clinical Director of Research and Development at Telos Residential Treatment. He is also on the board of directors and a partner at Telos Anthem House and a partner at Telos U. He has degrees in Psychology from Brigham Young University and Marriage and Family Therapy from Abilene Christian University and a certificate from the Mental Research Institute. He has published in multiple journals including the Journal of Therapeutic Schools and Programs (JTSP), and is a member of their editorial board, and is currently a guest editor for JTSP. He is on the National Association of Therapeutic Schools and Programs (NATSAP) and the Young Adult Transition Association (YATA) research committees and has given multiple presentations at NATSAP, YATA, and other conferences.

Barry Fell, LCSW is a Licensed Clinical Social Worker who graduated from the University of Utah in 2006. He has worked in the field of Youth Residential Treatment for sixteen years. He served as the Clinical Director of Telos Residential Treatment Center from 2008 through May of 2016. He currently serves as the Executive Director of Telos. Barry's expertise is in inpatient treatment modalities, diagnostic assessment, treatment planning, case management skills, and systems development.

Sam Coates, MD is a Child and Adolescent Psychiatrist and has worked at the Telos Residential Treatment Center for the past twelve years. Dr. Coates is one of the founders of Telos Residential Treatment Center and serves on the program's leadership team. Dr. Coates believes in taking a conservative approach to medication management and spends considerable time making sure that he is addressing the unique needs of each of those with whom he works. Dr. Coates studied medicine at the University of Nebraska Medical School.

Nathan Sellers, LCSW received his Master's in Social Work from Brigham Young University in 2008. He has worked in many residential and wilderness settings as both staff and therapist. He currently works at Telos Residential Treatment Center working with adolescent boys. He helped in the development of effective treatment planning at Telos and has presented at the National Association of Therapeutic Schools and Programs conference on this topic. He has experience in working with students with anxiety, depression, learning and processing disabilities, ADHD, spectrum disorders, substance use, and oppositional defiance. Nathan recognizes the importance of building solid rapport and relationships with clients as a critical element of the effectiveness of residential treatment centers.

Ryan Anderson, Ph.D., LMFT, MedFT received his BS degree in Marriage, Family, and Human Development and his MS degree in Marriage and Family Therapy from Brigham Young University. He received his Ph.D. in Medical Family Therapy from East Carolina University, and completed his internship at the Duke Comprehensive Cancer Center. He has worked as a family therapist in outpatient practice, in inpatient psychiatric settings, in cancer care, in several other medical settings, as a wilderness therapist and Assistant Clinical Director at Outback Therapeutic Expeditions, and as a therapist at Telos Residential Treatment. His teaching experience includes undergraduate university courses, first year medical students, and community outreach and education programs. He has also been a speaker at various conferences and continuing education events. He is one of the founders and the Clinical Director of Telos U.

Josh Thorn, LCSW received his Bachelor degree in Psychology and his Mater's in Social Work from Brigham Young University. Josh has worked in several different mental health settings, and currently works at Telos where he is a primary therapist and manager of the internship program. Josh specializes in substance abuse treatment and enjoys incorporating activity into therapy as a means of helping individuals to gain confidence. Josh is an individual who enjoys the outdoors and trains for competitive triathlons of all distances, including the Ironman. Josh has traveled extensively both domestically and abroad, and spends his free time skiing, boating, reading, and playing with his dog Eliza. Eliza is an English Pointer and accompanies him during race training.

Drew Davis, LCSW is a primary therapist at Telos RTC. He earned his Master's in Social Work at Brigham Young University. Drew has an extensive history of working with youth and families in various capacities including residential treatment, outpatient treatment, public education, and numerous volunteer youth organizations. He has expertise in treating depression, anxiety, learning differences, processing differences, attachment disorders, and is EMDR certified. Numerous experiences throughout his childhood, as well as his natural desire to help others reach their ultimate potential, guided him into a career in the mental health profession. Drew was born in Ohio and takes great pride in his Buckeye roots. Drew is fun-loving, an accomplished pianist, and a great singer. When not helping others at work, he enjoys playing and watching sports, adding to and enjoying his vast library of music and movies, and traveling with his family. Drew has a beautiful wife, who is also a mental health therapist, and two beautiful children.

Scott Downs, LMFT has worked for nine years in clinical settings as a Licensed Marriage and Family Therapist. Scott earned a Bachelor of Science Degree in Psychology and then went on to complete a Master's in Marriage and Family Therapy. Scott's areas of clinical interest and experience include emotional regulation, cognitive restructuring, parent-teen conflict, and attachment injuries, and treating oppositional defiant behaviors. During his nine years of working with adolescents, Scott has developed a style that includes firmness, a high level of empathy, and the ability to rapidly foster a therapeutic alliance with teens. Scott enjoys spending time with his beautiful wife and three children, and hiking, camping, and exercising are some of his favorite activities. During the spring you will find Scott and his daughter taking on the challenges at golf courses in Utah County, Utah.

Part II
Onsite Family Therapy

Chapter 11
Emerging Family Therapy Models Utilized in Residential Settings

Ashley N. Merritts

Chapter Highlights

- There are many methods for engaging families in adolescents' residential treatment that are discussed in recent literature, including but not limited to parent training and support groups, family therapy, therapeutic letter writing, and family workshops.
- Family involvement in residential treatment, including family therapy specifically, has consistently been associated with positive outcomes with adolescents.
- Four emerging approaches currently being used with adolescents in residential treatment and their families include multiple-family group intervention, family-directed structural therapy, narrative family therapy, and experiential therapy.
- There are a number of limitations to family therapy research in residential treatment, which will be discussed in more detail in the chapter.
- The literature pertaining to the use of family therapy in the residential milieu is underdeveloped and there is a need for increased research and integration of family therapy into treatment, including elucidating the specific family therapy approaches that are effective in treating adolescents in this setting and their families.

Researchers have emphasized the importance of family engagement in residential treatment for the last several decades (Báez 2015) as the literature has consistently demonstrated that level of family functioning is associated with successful treatment outcomes in children and adolescents (Sunseri 2004). Furthermore, parental involvement and family support during residential treatment has been found to be a

A.N. Merritts (✉)
Mount Mercy University, 1330 Elmhurst Dr NE, Cedar Rapids, IA 52402, USA
e-mail: amerritts@mtmercy.edu

© Springer International Publishing AG 2017
J.D. Christenson and A.N. Merritts (eds.), *Family Therapy with Adolescents in Residential Treatment*, Focused Issues in Family Therapy,
DOI 10.1007/978-3-319-51747-6_11

significant and consistent predictor not only of the youth's progress during treatment but also his or her ability to adapt following discharge from a residential placement (Frensch and Cameron 2002). Treatment centers are increasingly recognizing that adolescents cannot be understood without also understanding their families (Lyman and Campbell 1996) and that both the adolescents and family members need to identify the influence of their own behaviors on the family system. Additionally, the encouragement of family involvement in residential treatment prepares both the adolescent and the parents for reintegration into the family system (Lakin et al. 2004). New models continue to be developed in order to inform and support residential programs, clinicians, and families with a framework for providing family treatment with adolescents in residential settings (Báez 2015).

Family involvement during adolescent residential treatment is crucial as it has the ability to stimulate necessary and significant changes in the family system and facilitates the transferring of therapeutic gains during placement to the home environment after discharge (Jenson and Whitaker 1987). A review of the literature from the past ten years will highlight significant findings related to treatment efficacy for family therapy in this setting and identify specific family therapy approaches that are being utilized in residential treatment, with a goal of maximizing the quality and quantity of family therapy utilized in the residential setting (Walter and Petr 2008) and improving family treatments for youth with disruptive behavior. First, a general overview of the research will be presented, which will be followed by a specific review on conduct and disruptive disorders. The author will conclude with a discussion of limitations and challenges, implications for practice, and areas that should be given further attention.

Residential Treatment Research Overview

According to the philosophy of care model developed by Stroul and Friedman (Stroul and Friedman 1996), which guides mental health services for children and their families in the U.S., "children with emotional disturbances should receive services within the least restrictive, most normative environment that is clinically appropriate" (p. 8). However, there are times when community-based settings cannot meet the therapeutic needs of a child or adolescent (Hair 2005) and children need to be physically separated from the rest of the family system (see Chap. 8). Residential treatment is typically defined as an out-of-home, therapeutic 24 h facility that allows youth experiencing significant conduct, mood, and/or substance abuse issues to receive a variety of specialized intervention services and support in a less-restrictive setting than inpatient psychiatric care (Hair 2005). According to a 2002 report, there were over 30,000 youth and children living in residential care during the year 2000 (Substance Abuse and Mental Health Services Administration 2002) (SAMHSA). This suggests that residential treatment remains a necessary service for a significantly challenging group of youth (Hair 2005).

It should be noted that there are several types of residential placements available to adolescents, and they all have different ways of structuring treatment and involving the family. This presents methodological challenges in terms of conducting family therapy research in residential placement and evaluating treatment outcomes, which will be further discussed later in the chapter. Program types typically fall within five categories: therapeutic boarding schools, residential treatment centers, client-funded RTCs, government-funded RTCs, short-term programs, and lock-down facilities (see Chap. 20 for an in-depth discussion of these specific program types).

Family Involvement

As has been noted in other chapters, residential treatment has not always embraced a systemic approach. Prior to the unveiling of outcome studies conducted during the 1950s and 1960s, which began pointing to the vital role that family and other systems played in children's success, parents were detached from their child's treatment and viewed as harmful influences (Whittaker 2000). Parental involvement had not been recognized as a necessary component to adolescent residential treatment and the programs were focused solely on treating the child in placement (Laird 1979; Letulle 1979). The field gained increased support for family involvement in the residential milieu as studies began pointing to the positive outcomes associated with family-based treatment. Kemp (1971) was one of the leaders of this movement, advocating for a more active approach to family work and stating that families were no longer *untreatable*. Similarly, Letulle (1979) emphasized that all family members needed to understand that they were part of the treatment process. The Adoption Assistance and Welfare Act passed in 1980 and was a significant factor in the shift from child-centered to family-centered treatment programs (Jenson and Whittaker 1987), which allowed for the introduction of the family into residential life.

The residential field began to define a model of *family-centered practice* as an emerging best practice (Leichtman 2008), a shift from focusing on the individual child to a family systems approach (Cafferty and Leichtman 2001). This called for a shift in culture, including viewing the parents as partners as opposed to adversaries, emphasizing assets and resources of the family, appreciating the importance of culture, and linking children and families with available support systems in their communities. This required the engagement of families in the residential treatment process, as well as a focus on building upon individual and family strengths (Cafferty and Leichtman 2001).

There are currently many methods for engaging families in residential treatment that are discussed in the literature. Family involvement can be defined as "any role or activity that enables families to have direct and meaningful input into and influence on" their adolescent's residential treatment (Kalke et al. 2007, p. 165). Attendance and participation in family therapy is only one component of that involvement. Historically, family involvement has generally been via telephone calls and some in-person visits (as many adolescents are in treatment facilities hundreds of miles away from their families); however, technological advances have allowed for internet-based sessions and interactions which allows for a larger range of visual and structural feedback (see Chap. 19).

Two long-standing methods that have been used with families with adolescents in residential treatment and studied extensively include behavioral parent training and parent support groups (Nickerson et al. 2004). Parent training is focused on teaching parenting skills such as reinforcing behaviors, delivering consequences, and negotiating compromises through the use of instruction, modeling, and role-play (Serketich and Dumas 1996). Family support and education also produces positive results when implemented as an intervention strategy for families of children in residential placement (Nickerson et al. 2004). Martone et al. (1989) developed a four-stage model for support groups of parents with children in residential treatment, which was associated with a shorter length of stay for adolescents. This stage model involves (a) engaging the family in a plan of treatment; (b) providing opportunities for the parents to interact with the child in activities that will enhance family competence; (c) empowering parents to assume caretaking responsibilities during treatment as much as possible; and (d) preparing the child and family for a successful transition back to the home (Martone et al. 1989).

More recently, therapeutic letter writing has been discussed in the literature as a way to involve family members and promote change within the adolescent and family system (Christenson and Miller 2016). This includes the use of impact letters, accountability letters, transactional letters, and strengths letters (see Chaps. 2 and 3). These letters can assist the adolescents and families with moving through the stages of change, teaching communication skills, promoting a systemic view, increasing nurturance, slowing down the conversation, and repairing attachment injuries (Christenson and Miller 2016). The use of therapeutic letter writing is a creative and useful way to maintain a systemic approach in the treatment of adolescents in residential facilities.

The importance of family involvement is reflected throughout the contents of this book. For example, Chap. 17 of this book discusses the use of family workshops as a way to integrate the family into the adolescent's residential treatment and create opportunities for second-order changes in the family system. The author presents a possible structure for these workshops and suggests that they can be an effective way to join with the adolescent's family, help them to develop support networks, teach communication and emotion regulation skills to family members, identify strengths of the family system, and give them opportunities to practice new ways of interacting with one another. Also, Chap. 19 of this book outlines a phase model of treatment for connecting families to what their adolescents are learning in treatment and to support the families in learning new skills to implement during and after treatment. The phase model includes the use of online videos, phone conferencing, and distance family therapy. While these strategies for family involvement are useful, Sunseri (2004) argues that simply encouraging family members to participate in the adolescent's treatment is not the same as "comprehensive family treatment" (p. 48). This highlights the need for an understanding of the specific family therapy approaches that are being used and demonstrate efficacy in treating this population.

Treatment Outcomes

There is a large body of literature demonstrating that child and adolescent psychotherapy results in beneficial impacts on the lives of youth and their families, and four major meta-analyses conducted over the past 20 years have consistently demonstrated that therapy for adolescents outperforms wait-list and placebo conditions (Ollendick and King 2004). Furthermore, there is a strong body of research indicating that certain forms of therapy work better than others and there has been a move to focus on the efficacy of specific treatments for adolescents that present with certain behavioral, emotional, and social problems (Ollendick and King 2004). Reviews conducted by Ollendick and King (2000) and Chambless and Ollendick (2001) identified four well-established treatments for youth with oppositional and conduct issues: behavioral parent training, functional family therapy, multisystemic therapy, and videotape modelling. Several treatments were identified as probably efficacious and included (a) exposure/response prevention; (b) anger control training with stress inoculation; (c) assertiveness training; (d) cognitive-behavioral therapy; (e) delinquency prevention program; (f) parent–child interaction therapy; (g) problem-solving skills training; (h) rational-emotive therapy; and (i) time-out plus signal seat treatment (Ollendick and King 2004).

The current knowledge base related specifically to residential treatment outcomes for youth in a general sense is underdeveloped and mostly based on studies with small nonrepresentative samples and methodological flaws (Bean et al. 2005; James 2011). Several comprehensive reviews conducted between the 1970s and 1990s highlight the methodological difficulties of effectiveness research in the complex setting of residential treatment (Bates et al. 1997; Burns et al. 1999; Chamberlain 1999; Frensch and Cameron 2002; Hair 2005; Pratt and Moreland 1996; Zimmerman et al. 1998). This is partly due to the fact that, from an ecological, systemic perspective individual change and improvement is expected among youth, as residential treatment can provide a consistent, nurturing environment with consistent and predictable expectations that help shape desirable behaviors (Hair 2005; Rosen 1998). For this reason, treatment outcomes are generally measured in terms of symptom reduction (Lyons et al. 2001) and behavioral and socio-emotional functioning (Larzelere et al. 2001) post-discharge in order to examine whether residents are able to maintain therapeutic gains.

In general, the outcome literature indicates that youth with less severe behavior issues, greater capacity for interpersonal relationships, and acute onset of problems tend to have better treatment outcomes (Landsmane et al. 2001; Wilmhurst 2002). Youth with a history of physical or sexual abuse have been found to show more pathology at discharge (Connor et al. 2002) and youth that present with internalizing problems (e.g., anxiety and depression), poor academic achievement, and family difficulties were more likely to need to return to residential treatment (Hair 2005). It is evident that treatment outcomes for youth are also influenced by factors related to the program and level of care they receive. This can include the quality of the intervention services, the level of training of staff, the quality of on-site schooling, the extent to which the family is involved in the treatment process, and the availability of aftercare for the adolescents and their families (McLendon et al. 2012). However, few studies report outcome data related to specific group care models (James 2011).

There are mixed results and very few studies looking at the effectiveness of family therapy on residential treatment outcomes specifically; we know much more about outcomes for outpatient, community treatment, and psychotherapies. The findings of a meta-analysis conducted over twenty years ago found that family therapy led to improved outcomes when compared to those receiving no therapy, but it was no more effective than individual therapy alone (Shadish et al. 1993). However, when broken down by problem type, family therapy was more effective than individual therapy for family-oriented problems, such as parent–child conflict (Shadish et al. 1993). More recently, a study conducted by Landsman et al. (2001) found that an intensive, family-based treatment model was associated with better treatment outcomes for youth as compared to traditional residential treatment. Sunseri (2001) found that youth who did not have home visits during placement were eight times less likely to complete residential treatment and youth with frequent family visits to the residence were six times more likely to finish (see also Sunseri 2004). Another study examining residential treatment outcomes found that participation in family therapy by the resident and his or her family was the only significant predictor of discharge to a less-restrictive setting (Stage 1998). These results were supported by a 1995 meta-analysis of residential treatment outcomes (Hair 2005).

The literature examining family-centered treatments for children and adolescents has "become more specific, looking at the match between particular types of treatments for particular types of problems" (Lakin et al. 2004, p. 39), and although these findings argue for the potential effectiveness on youth outcomes when treatment is family-centered, there are currently no *bestpractices* or broad guidelines in terms of the specific family therapy techniques and interventions that are effective in working with this population (McLendon et al. 2012). Therefore, it seems important to examine the literature more rigorously and integrate findings from a collection of research studies in order to look more specifically at the efficacy of family therapy and the specific approaches and techniques that are being used with adolescents and families in the complex setting of residential treatment.

Review of the Disruptive Disorder Research

Although youth in residential treatment present with a variety of behavioral and emotional issues, this review was limited to those studies examining interventions and outcomes related to youth exhibiting conduct issues and delinquency. An exhaustive computerized search of the literature was conducted in an online data-base, Academic Search Premiere (EBSCO). Search terms included *adolescent*, *residential treatment*, *conduct*, and *family therapy*.

The author reviewed articles that met the following criteria: (a) examined family therapy delivered to adolescents and their families in a residential setting; (b) specifically addressed youth presenting with conduct issues; and (c) were published in a peer-reviewed journal. In order to best identify the recent advances in the research, the author focused this review on studies conducted in the past ten years. Inclusionary criteria initially required that the articles were empirical and included quantitative measures of treatment outcomes; however, the criteria for review were expanded due to limited results.

Due to the lack of findings related to treatment efficacy for specific family therapy approaches utilized in residential settings, the author deemed it helpful to conduct a second review. The focus of this review was to more broadly identify the family therapy approaches that have demonstrated effectiveness in treating youth exhibiting conduct problems in community-based settings and have not yet been tested in order to demonstrate possibly transferring the use of the approach to treatment of adolescents in residential settings.

Findings of the Reviews

The findings of the review indicated a very limited body of empirical outcome data looking specifically at the use of family therapy with youth in residential settings. This is likely due to the methodological difficulties associated with conducting efficacy studies in this setting, some of which include (a) a lack of control or comparison group; (b) small, nonrandomized samples; and (c) subjective judgments of youth outcomes (Hair 2005). However, several articles that highlighted specific family therapy approaches that show probable effectiveness in treating this popu-lation, as well as case studies that illustrated how various family therapy approaches and techniques can be used to further family involvement and promote positive outcomes, were found and reviewed. A brief summary of these approaches and techniques that show probable or possible efficacy in treating youth in residential settings is provided below.

Multiple-family Group Intervention

The multiple-family group intervention was developed to address the need for an effective and affordable treatment for incarcerated adolescents and their families, as their relationships with family members are often not the target of residential treatment (Keiley 2007). The focus of the approach is to alter the negative, coercive interaction patterns of family members from an affect regulation and attachment perspective. The adolescent and family members meet with the facilitators of the intervention for an hour and a half every week to learn the six-step intervention process. The first three steps focus on teaching the adolescent and family members how to manage affect during escalating conflicts and negative affect. The last three steps assist the adolescents and caregivers with expressing their own vulnerable feelings and understanding those vulnerable feelings of one another. The approach also uses video, discussion, and role play (Keiley 2007).

This model was tested in two Indiana juvenile correctional facilities, one for males and one for females (Keiley 2007). The average age of the adolescents was 15.5 and 59% were male. Just over half of the adolescents and 63% of caregivers identified as European American. The 6-month follow-up assessment of these youth indicated a lower recidivism rate as compared to the national average. According to both adolescents and caregivers, there was a decrease in adolescents' externalizing behaviors. The adolescents also reported a decrease in internalizing symptoms as well as alcohol and drug use. Interestingly, the adolescents also reported a significantly stronger attachment to their mothers (Keiley 2007). These findings support short-term effects of this approach. However, further outcome research is needed.

Family-Directed Structural Therapy

One of the emerging approaches to conducting family therapy with youth in residential treatment is family-directed structural therapy (McLendon et al. 2012). Although this is a recently developed model that has not yet been tested against scientific scrutiny, the approach shows promise in working with youth in this complex setting. It is a strength-based, family-driven model that has been developed in the last 20 years. The core concept of the model is tied to the family-directed structural assessment tool, which is a visual depiction of the *family circle*. As stated by two of the founders of the model,

> This circle introduces the concept of an external boundary around the family and helps to establish the idea that adult family members are responsible for the health and well-being of family functioning within the family circle. It also introduces the concept of an internal boundary within the family circle that divides adult level issues from parenting level responsibilities (McLendon et al. 2012, p. 71).

Family members rate family functioning for five core issues: commitment, empowerment, control of self, credibility, and consistency (McLendon et al. 2012). Commitment refers to the willingness of family members to work through their difficulties despite differences and conflict. Empowerment relates to the degree to which family members believe their opinions are valued and respected by one another. Control of self is tied to the ability of family members to change their own behaviors in order to reduce conflict and improve relationships. Credibility refers to the ability of family members to follow through with what they say they will do. Finally, consistency is the ability to be continually predictable. The use of this tool allows families and providers to identify strengths and areas of concern, and the therapist can return to the issues of concern to assess progress and offer tools and specific steps to facilitate positive change. The model provides "a tangible and measurable means by which to initially assess family functioning (from the family's perspective)" (McLendon et al. 2012, p. 73), and higher family functioning has consistently been predictive of an adolescent's positive outcomes post-discharge from residential treatment (Sunseri 2004).

Narrative Family Therapy

A 2016 article by DeMille and Montgomery describes a case study illustrating how narrative family therapy can be used in the treatment of youth and families in outdoor behavioral healthcare (OBH). OBH is another type of out-of-home treatment program for youth presenting with significant emotional, behavioral, or substance abuse issues (DeMille and Montgomery 2016), and it is possible that this approach could transfer to a similar setting such as traditional residential treatment. The basic premise of narrative therapy is that a re-authoring of one's problem-saturated narratives can allow for the externalization of the problems, deconstruction of the narratives, identification of unique outcomes, and the provision of alternative and preferred narratives (DeMille and Montgomery 2016). One of the potential advantages of using this approach in an OBH setting also represents a potential advantage for the use in residential treatment: adaptions can be made to the telling and retelling of the narratives through letter writing, which allows for distant family members to be involved in the process and reflect on stories that are being told (Freedman and Combs 1996) when there are limited opportunities for conjoint sessions. "The use of letter writing as a way for families to tell, retell, and reflect on stories has great potential as a means of integrating the family during the entire treatment" (DeMille and Montgomery 2016, p. 6).

The article discusses a case example that illustrates several techniques that family therapists can use to further involve families in inpatient treatment programs. This includes techniques of collaboration, thickening the story, inviting outsiders to witness, and incorporating the family in reflections on the treatment process (DeMille and Montgomery 2016). The authors discuss that in OBH and residential settings, the therapist often has an evaluative and gate keeping responsibility, which can make it difficult to maintain a true egalitarian relationship. This is important for the therapist to acknowledge, and the therapist should attempt to create a safe place for the adolescent to discuss difficult family issues (DeMille and Montgomery 2016).

An Integrated Family Systems, Narrative, and Experiential Therapy Approach

An article by Faddis and Bettman (2006) outlines an integrated approach and phase model for using narrative and experiential therapy techniques with youth and their families in a wilderness therapy setting. This approach is discussed in more detail in Chap. 16. All of the techniques are rooted in systems theory and are based on the notion that even the smallest shift in one part of the family system will cause shifts in other parts of the system. The intervention of family sculpting is used in this approach in order to allow the adolescent and family members to visually portray one another's roles in the family, to communicate thought and feelings that are difficult to verbalize, and to heighten awareness of family members' behaviors (Faddis and Bettman 2006). Phase 1 of this model includes the adolescent creating a sculpture of his or her family. They are asked to use props that they find outdoors, such as trees or rocks, and to create a meaningful scenario that characterizes how they see themselves and their family members. If family members are unable to be present for the sculpture, a peer sculpture can be used, which "allows adolescents to act out their most troubling family dynamics before exposing themselves to a highly emotional and potentially reactive situation" (Faddis and Cobb 2016, p. 20).

A reflecting team is then used (Phase 2) as it allows the adolescent and family to gain an outsider perspective on their issues and the possibility of seeing things differently (Faddis and Bettman 2006). This fits well within a narrative approach as the focus is on the nonexpert role of the therapist and treatment team and the notion that change happens through finding exceptions to the problem-saturated story and solidification of new stories. While the reflecting team is typically composed of therapists and staff discussing their observations of the family session, the residential treatment milieu provides an opportunity for a peer group reflecting team, which is often a way to push through the typical resistance of the adolescent. Once the adolescent explains his or her family sculpture, the adolescent and family are asked to step away so that the reflecting team can discuss their observations. However, the adolescent and family are located close enough so that they can hear what the reflecting team is sharing. In Phase 3, the therapist and family talk about what they heard and are encouraged to share those comments that were validating, challenging, supporting, and expanding. Phase 4 is a debriefing session where they discuss the three previous interviews as a large group, as well as sharing positive insights they have gained from the experience. Reflecting team members are able to ask more questions and reinforce comments that have the ability to change the problem-saturated story. While this approach highlights the adaptions of experiential and narrative therapy that can be used in the residential milieu, the authors suggest the need for empirical studies investigating how to utilize these approaches and improve the integration of these strategies (Faddis and Cobb 2016).

Promising Approaches

Due to the lack of findings related to treatment efficacy for specific family therapy approaches utilized in residential settings, the author deemed it helpful to conduct a second review. The focus of this review was to more broadly identify the family therapy approaches that have demonstrated effectiveness in treating youth exhibiting conduct problems in community-based settings, but have not yet been tested in order to demonstrate possible efficacy in treating adolescents in residential settings. The majority of the research conducted in the past ten years has focused on three approaches: Brief strategic family therapy (BSFT), multisystemic therapy (MST), and functional family therapy (FFT). However, the author was unable to locate any outcome studies that examined the effectiveness of any of these family-oriented approaches specifically in a residential treatment setting, likely due to the methodological difficulties associated with conducting efficacy research in this setting that have already been discussed in this chapter.

An overview of these three theoretical approaches will be provided. An extensive discussion regarding the specific family therapy techniques and interventions utilized within each approach and any challenges associated with implementing each of these approaches in the complex setting of residential treatment will also be included. The author notes that the intervention strategies of each approach often overlap with one another; however, each approach takes a slightly different perspective on the family processes involved in the youths' behavior problems and the necessary mechanisms for change. Some of the approaches mentioned in this chapter were also discussed in Chap. 13 as they relate to adolescent substance abuse. The reader is referred to that chapter for additional information on that subject.

Brief Strategic Family Therapy. Brief strategic family therapy is an emerging model that has demonstrated effectiveness in engagement and retention as well as the treatment of children and adolescents with conduct problems, oppositional defiant behavior, substance abuse, and other behavioral problems. There have been two controlled effectiveness studies, conducted in community practice settings, that have demonstrated the short-term effectiveness of the therapy model, indicating a reduction in conduct symptoms in youth post-treatment as compared to those in the control condition (Coatsworth et al. 2001; Santisteban et al. 2003). The outcome literature also indicates that families receiving BSFT were more likely to remain in treatment and terminate successfully as compared to control groups (Coatsworth et al. 2001).

BSFT, which draws on structural and strategic therapies, is focused on the assumption that the family is the closest and most influential factor on children's development and behavior (Gehart 2013; Robbins et al. 2002). BSFT recognizes that family relations play a pivotal role in the development of a child's behavior problems and, therefore, should be a target of intervention. The therapist joins with the family, establishes leadership, and tracks needs and goals (Nickerson et al. 2004). Next, the therapist works at identifying and changing problematic family interactions and moves them in a new, more adaptive direction through reframing and shifting alliances (Robbins et al. 2002). A fundamental assumption of this approach is that families enter treatment with natural, systemic networks, which can include friends, extended family members, school, and work (Robbins et al. 2002). BSFT therapists examine these networks in order to identify both potential problems and strengths that can be capitalized on in therapy, with a focus on involving and improving the links to those systems that the client will continue to interact with after treatment in order to maintain therapeutic gains. Another strength of the approach is the development of a specific module focused on bringing reluctant family members into treatment, which has always been a major obstacle in the provision of family therapy services (Robbins et al. 2002).

BSFT is a problem-focused, structured but flexible six-step model, which follows a prescribed process format (Robbins et al. 2002). The average length of treatment is around 12–16 sessions (approximately 3 to 4 months), but continues until the therapist has evidence that the family has achieved the necessary behavioral changes as outlined in the treatment plan. The first step is joining, both with individual family members as well as the family as a whole, with the purpose of having the family connect with and accept the therapist as a person that can be trusted and lead the family through the therapy process. Next, the therapist identifies the problem symptoms and how the family relates to these symptoms. Family members are encouraged to speak with each other about their concerns. From these observations, the therapist identifies the strengths of the family as well as identifying problematic relations related to the child's problem behaviors or the parents' abilities to correct these behaviors. Examples of assessment areas include alliances, effectiveness of conflict resolution styles, and developmental appropriateness of family roles (e.g., responsibilities). The next step includes the development of a treatment plan focused on the family interaction patterns that are directly linked to the behavioral issues (Robbins et al. 2002).

The last step, restructuring, involves implementing changes that are necessary in order to transform these family relationships into effective and supportive interactions. Interventions are focused on current interactions with minimal focus on the past. Some of the interventions implemented in this stage include structural enactments, detriangulation, reframing negativity, working with boundaries and alliances, reversals, and opening closed systems in order to allow for effective expression and resolution of differences (Gehart 2013). There is also a focus on developing and strengthening conflict resolution and behavior management skills as well as fostering parental leadership skills (Robbins et al. 2002).

Multisystemic Therapy.. There is a strong body of evidence for the effectiveness of multisystemic therapy, an intensive family- and community-based model, which was developed for the treatment of serious juvenile offenders (Multisystemic Therapy Services 1998). Although MST has been contraindicated for residential treatment, Nickerson et al. (2004) suggest that "the approach could be adapted within the framework of a family-centered, short-term residential placement" (p. 7). MST draws from strategic, structural, socioecological, and CBT models and places a strong emphasis on the adolescent and family's social networks (Gehart 2013). The model has demonstrated effectiveness in maintaining long-standing changes in youth's antisocial behaviors (Bordoin et al. 1995), and families receiving MST reported increased family cohesion and adaptability post-treatment, as well as increased supportiveness and decreased conflict-hostility (Borduin et al. 1995).

This present-focused, highly individualized, and action-oriented approach addresses both interpersonal and systemic factors that are associated with the adolescent's behavioral problems (Bordoin et al. 1995). The therapist assesses for risks and protective factors in the domains of the individuals, family, peer group, school, and neighborhood and community (Multisystemic Therapy Services 1998) and works with these systems in the adolescent's life in order to develop a strong support network (Nickerson et al. 2004). The approach draws on the strengths of the caregivers and empowers them to serve as change agents for their adolescents. The factors that impede the caregivers' abilities to provide the nurturance, responsiveness, and discipline for their child (e.g., mental illness, substance abuse, stressors) are identified and the MST team identifies the strengths and resources of the caregiver to address these factors (e.g., extended family support).

The overall goals of the approach include (a) decreasing the problematic behaviors; (b) improving family functioning; (c) improving the adolescent's functioning in school and other community contexts; and (d) minimizing out-home placements (Gehart 2013; Multisystemic Therapy Services 1998). There are nine principles of intervention: (1) identifying how the adolescent's problem behaviors fit systemically with their broader social network; (2) emphasizing strengths and potential strengths both in the adolescent and family; (3) increasing responsible behavior, acceptance of responsibility for choices, and promoting parental involvement; (4) focusing on specific and easily defined problems that can be tracked and measured; (5) targeting and modifying sequences of behavior that are problematic; (6) ensuring that interventions are developmentally appropriate and step-wise; (7) ensuring continuous effort from the adolescent and family; (8) continually assessing the effectiveness of interventions and adjusting accordingly; and (9) assisting the adolescent and family with generalizing newly learned skills and abilities to solve future problems (Multisystemic Therapy Services 1998). In order to successfully adapt this approach to work with residential populations, Nickerson et al. (2004) argue that

> Emphasis would need to be placed on the enactment of effective crisis plans, as well as establishment of positive peer/community relations during home visits and planned 'trial runs' within the more naturalistic subsystems to which the youth would return upon discharge (p. 7).

Functional Family Therapy.. Functional family therapy is another empirically validated family therapy treatment for working with conduct disorder and delinquency, which addresses individual, family, peer, and system dynamics both directly and indirectly in order to affect change by helping youth to interact with them differently (Gehart 2013). FFT, when compared to other client-centered family therapy groups and control groups, has resulted in greater positive changes in family process, such as more equality in communication, as well as lower drop-out rates for families of adolescents receiving court-ordered treatment (Alexander and Parsons 1973). FFT integrates cognitive, systems, and learning theories to identify the adaptive function of the problem behaviors (such as avoidance of conflict) (Alexander and Parson 1982). The tasks of the therapist include identifying how the behaviors maintain connection and define hierarchy and finding more effective behaviors to serve the same function. This is accomplished through modifying communication patterns in order to increase clarity and reciprocity (Alexander and Parson 1982; Nickerson et al. 2004).

There are three phases of treatment. The first phase, engagement and motivation, is focused on developing a connection with all family members and assessing the function of the problem behaviors (Sexton and Alexander 2002). During this phase, the therapist uses cognitive techniques to reduce anger, blame, and hopelessness and replace negative characterizations of the child with more positive motives (e.g., experimenting with freedom) (Gehart 2013). The middle phase, Behavior Change, aims to modify beliefs, attitudes, and expectations to assist family members with understanding the interrelation of feelings, thoughts and behaviors and the impact of behavior on others. During this phase, the therapist also works with the parents on skills such as parent training, problem solving, conflict resolution, and communication. During the late phase, Generalization, the focus is on generalizing change to the larger social systems in which the child and family interact (Sexton and Alexander 2002) and encouraging the family to develop and strengthen these positive relations with community systems (Gehart 2013).

Challenges and Opportunities

There are numerous constraints related to conducting research in the setting of residential treatment. This includes fiscal restraints and lack of training, supervision, and implementation by clinical staff (Hair 2005). This can lead to challenges with the reliability and validity of the research findings. There are also participant characteristics that must be considered and notable differences between controlled research and clinical settings. For instance, most residents in placement have severe symptoms and dual diagnoses. There are also demographic factors, such as race and ethnicity, which complicate clinical effectiveness investigations (Hair 2005).

Another challenge in conducting efficacy research in this setting is related to the varying level of involvement of family members in the treatment process (Hair 2005) as well as the impact of other contextual, systemic factors such as parental illness, economic and housing difficulties, academic achievement, school support, and peer networks, to name a few. Although many factors can be controlled, there are numerous others that cannot (Hair 2005).

> In clinical settings the numerous elements of family and agency life weave together with therapeutic intervention and potentially decrease the chance of finding a positive treatment when there is one. Thus outcome research in residential treatment is continually challenged to find ways of demonstrating service effectiveness, particularly since controlled laboratory studies are not possible (Hair 2005, p. 554).

It has been noted in several chapters throughout this book that the literature on family involvement in residential treatment in underdeveloped and there is a need for increased research and integration of family therapy into treatment. Chapter 20 further discusses some of the methodological considerations and covers how qualitative, quantitative, and mixed method studies can be used in this setting in order to better understand and strengthen the place of family therapy in residential treatment. Examples are provided of relevant research questions related to family therapy in this setting, as well as suggestions for how these studies could be conducted.

Implications for Practice and Future Directions

It is evident that family therapy is a key component in residential treatment for troubled youth. However, this review highlights the fact that a systems approach is pertinent to all aspects of an adolescent's residential treatment. "A family systems perspective should guide all interventions, beginning with intake, so that interactions and patterns in families that may serve as barriers to the transfer of skills learned in placement can be addressed in the treatment plan" (Nickerson et al. 2004, p. 12). Family involvement includes more than just attending and participating in family therapy (Fairhurst 1996). It is important that clinicians recognize the importance of other family-oriented interventions other than family therapy. Clinicians can promote and encourage family involvement in all aspects of the treatment process. For instance, clinicians can encourage parents to make phone calls, write letters, and send photos (Fairhurst 1996). If the clinician is still trying to engage the family in treatment, he or she can demonstrate to the family members the importance of their involvement in their child's life. They can assist the family with increasing their community support and include the family in decisions related to treatment. During discharge, the clinician can help them to prepare for the child's return and assist them in obtaining needed services. It is important that the clinician is continually considering the phase of the treatment process and the family's readiness to be involved and change (see Chap. 14; Fairhurst 1996).

With a movement toward common factors research, it is also important to highlight the critical roles of the therapeutic relationship in the treatment process and the significant impact it can have on clinical outcomes for adolescents (Karver et al. 2006). The therapeutic alliance with youth as well as the alliance with the parents and family demonstrated small to moderate relationships with treatment outcomes. Not surprisingly, therapists' interpersonal skills, such as empathy and warmth, were significant predictors of positive treatment outcomes (Karver et al. 2006). Many researchers posit that developing a balanced therapeutic relationship with the adolescent in treatment and family members is especially difficult in this setting due to the multiple relationships and multiple providers involved in the treatment process. It is important that clinicians and researchers seek to further their understanding of how specific aspects of the therapeutic relationship with youth and family are related to positive outcomes, and this research should guide training and intervention efforts. Despite all the future possibilities, one thing in abundantly clear; while family involvement has been found to be a consistent predictor of positive outcomes of children and adolescents in residential placement, there is a need for further research examining specific family therapy approaches and intervention efforts.

References

Alexander, J. F., & Parsons, B. V. (1973). Short-term behavioral intervention with delinquent families: Impact on family process and recidivism. *Journal of Abnormal Psychology, 81*(3), 219–225.

Alexander, J., & Parsons, B. V. (1982). *Functional family therapy.* San Francisco: Brooks/Cole Publishing Company.

Báez, J. C. (2015). Bridging the distance: A clinical phase model of family therapy with adolescent residential treatment. *Families in Society: The Journal of Contemporary Social Services, 96*(1), 41–48.

Bates, B. C., English, D. J., & Kouidou-Giles, S. (1997). Residential treatment and its alternatives: A review of the literature. *Child & Youth Care Forum, 26*(1), 7–51.

Bean, P., White, L., Neagle, L., & Lake, P. (2005). Is residential care an effective approach for treating adolescents with co-occurring substance abuse and mental health diagnoses? *Best Practices in Mental Health, 1*(2), 50–60.

Borduin, C. M., Mann, B. J., Cone, L. T., Henggeler, S. W., Fucci, B. R., Blaske, D. M., et al. (1995). Multisystemic treatment of serious juvenile offenders: Long-term prevention of criminality and violence. *Journal of Consulting and Clinical Psychology, 63*(4), 569.

Burns, B. J., Hoagwood, K., & Mrazek, P. J. (1999). Effective treatment for mental disorders in children and adolescents. *Clinical Child and Family Psychology Review, 2*(4), 199–254.

Cafferty, H., & Leichtman, M. (2001). Facilitating the transition from residential treatment into the community: II. Changing social work roles. *Residential Treatment for Children & Youth, 19*(2), 13–25.

Chamberlain, P. (1999). Residential care for children and adolescents with oppositional defiant disorder and conduct disorder. In H. C. Quay & A. E. Hogan (Eds.), *Handbook of disruptive behavior disorders* (pp. 495–506). US: Springer.

Chambless, D. L., & Ollendick, T. H. (2001). Empirically supported psychological interventions: Controversies and evidence. *Annual Review of Psychology, 52*(1), 685–716.

Christenson, J. D., & Miller, A. L. (2016). Slowing down the conversation: The use of letter writing with adolescents and young adults in residential settings. *Contemporary Family Therapy, 38*(1), 23–31.

Coatsworth, J. D., Santisteban, D. A., McBride, C. K., & Szapocznik, J. (2001). Brief strategic family therapy versus community control: Engagement, retention, and an exploration of the moderating role of adolescent symptom severity. *Family Process, 40*(3), 313–332.

Connor, D. F., Miller, K. P., Cunningham, J. A., & Melloni, R. H., Jr. (2002). What does getting better mean? Child improvement and measure of outcome in residential treatment. *American Journal of Orthopsychiatry, 72*(1), 110.

DeMille, S. M., & Montgomery, M. (2016). Integrating narrative family therapy in an outdoor behavioral healthcare program: A case study. *Contemporary Family Therapy, 38*(1), 1–11.

Faddis, T. J., & Bettmann, J. E. (2006). Reflecting teams and other innovative family therapy techniques adapted for outdoor behavioral healthcare. *Journal of Therapeutic Schools and Programs, 1*(1), 57–69.

Faddis, T. J., & Cobb, K. F. (2016). Family Therapy Techniques in Residential Settings: Family Sculptures and Reflecting Teams. *Contemporary Family Therapy, 38*(1), 43–51.

Fairhurst, S. K. (1996). Promoting change in families: Treatment matching in residential treatment centers. *Residential Treatment for Children & Youth, 14*(2), 21–32.

Freedman, J., & Combs, G. (1996). Narrative therapy. W. W. Norton & Company.

Frensch, K. M., & Cameron, G. (2002). Treatment of choice or a last resort? A review of residential mental health placements for children and youth. *Child & Youth Care Forum, 31*(5), 307–339.

Gehart, D. (2013). *Mastering competencies in family therapy: A practical approach to theory and clinical case documentation.* Belmont, California: Cengage Learning.

Hair, H. J. (2005). Outcomes for children and adolescents after residential treatment: A review of research from 1993 to 2003. *Journal of Child and Family Studies, 14*(4), 551–575.

James, S. (2011). What works in group care? A structured review of treatment models for group homes and residential care. *Children and Youth Services Review, 33*(2), 308–321.

Jenson, J. M., & Whittaker, J. K. (1987). Parental involvement in children's residential treatment: From preplacement to aftercare. *Children and Youth Services Review, 9*(2), 81–100.

Kalke, T., Glanton, A., & Cristalli, M. (2007). Positive behavioral interventions and supports: Using strength-based approaches to enhance the culture of care in residential and day treatment education environments. *Child Welfare, 86*(5), 151–174.

Karver, M. S., Handelsman, J. B., Fields, S., & Bickman, L. (2006). Meta-analysis of therapeutic relationship variables in youth and family therapy: The evidence for different relationship variables in the child and adolescent treatment outcome literature. *Clinical Psychology Review, 26*(1), 50–65.

Keiley, M. K. (2007). Multiple-family group intervention for incarcerated adolescents and their families: A pilot project. *Journal of Marital and Family Therapy, 33*(1), 106–124.

Kemp, C. J. (1971). Family treatment within the milieu of a residential treatment center. *Child Welfare, 50*(4), 229–235.

Laird, J. (1979). An ecological approach to child welfare: Issues of family identity and continuity. In C. B. Germain (Ed.), *Social work practice: People and environments* (pp. 174–209). New York: Columbia University Press.

Lakin, B. L., Brambila, A. D., & Sigda, K. B. (2004). Parental involvement as a factor in the readmission to a residential treatment center. *Residential Treatment for Children & Youth, 22*(2), 37–52.

Landsman, M. J., Groza, V., Tyler, M., & Malone, K. (2001). Outcomes of family-centered residential treatment. *Child Welfare, 80*(3), 351.

Larzelere, R. E., Dinges, K., Schmidt, M. D., Spellman, D. F., Criste, T. R., & Connell, P. (2001). Outcomes of residential treatment: A study of the adolescent clients of Girls and Boys Town. *Child & Youth Care Forum, 30*(3), 175–185.

Leichtman, M. (2008). The essence of residential treatment: III. Change and adaptation. *Residential Treatment for Children & Youth, 25*(3), 189–207.

Letulle, L. J. (1979). Family therapy in residential treatment for children. *Social Work, 24*(1), 49–51.

Lyman, R. D., & Campbell, N. R. (1996). *Treating children and adolescents in residential and inpatient settings*. Thousand Oaks, CA: Sage Publications Inc.

Lyons, J. S., Terry, P., Martinovich, Z., Peterson, J., & Bouska, B. (2001). Outcome trajectories for adolescents in residential treatment: A statewide evaluation. *Journal of Child and Family Studies, 10*(3), 333–345.

McLendon, T., McLendon, D., & Hatch, L. (2012). Engaging families in the residential treatment process utilizing family-directed structural therapy. *Residential Treatment for Children & Youth, 29*(1), 66–77.

Martone, W. P., Kemp, G. F., & Pearson, S. J. (1989). The continuum of parental involvement in residential treatment: Engagement-participation-empowerment-discharge. *Residential Treatment for Children & Youth, 6*(3), 11–37.

Multisystemic Therapy Services. (1998). *Multisystemic therapy*. Retrieved from http://mstservices.com/what-is-mst/nine-principles

Nickerson, A. B., Salamone, F. J., Brooks, J. L., & Colby, S. A. (2004). Promising approaches to engaging families and building strengths in residential treatment. *Residential Treatment for Children & Youth, 22*(1), 1–18.

Ollendick, T. H., & King, N. J. (2000). Empirically supported treatments for children and adolescents. In P. C. Kendall (Ed.), *Child and adolescent therapy: Cognitive behavioural procedures* (2nd ed., pp. 386–425). New York: Guilford Publications.

Ollendick, T. H., & King, N. J. (2004). Empirically supported treatments for children and adolescents: Advances toward evidence-based practice. In P. M. Barrett & T. H. Ollendick

(Eds.), *Handbook of interventions that work with children and adolescents: Prevention and treatment* (pp. 3–25). Chichester, England: John Wiley and Sons.

Pratt, S. I., & Moreland, K. L. (1996). Introduction to treatment outcome: Historical perspectives and current issues. In S. I. Pfeiffer (Ed.), *Outcome assessment in residential treatment* (pp. 1–27). New York: Haworth Press.

Robbins, M. S., Bachrach, K., & Szapocznik, J. (2002). Bridging the research-practice gap in adolescent substance abuse treatment: The case of brief strategic family therapy. *Journal of Substance Abuse Treatment, 23*(2), 123–132.

Rosen, M. (1998). *Treating children in out-of-home placements*. Binghamton: Routledge.

Santisteban, D. A., Coatsworth, J. D., Perez-Vidal, A., Kurtines, W. M., Schwartz, S. J., LaPerriere, A., et al. (2003). Efficacy of brief strategic family therapy in modifying hispanic adolescent behavior problems and substance use. *Journal of Family Psychology, 17*(1), 121.

Serketich, W. J., & Dumas, J. E. (1996). The effectiveness of behavioral parent training to modify antisocial behavior in children: A meta-analysis. *Behavior Therapy, 27*(2), 171–186.

Sexton, T. L., & Alexander, J. F. (2002). Functional family therapy for at-risk adolescents and their families. In F. W. Patterson & T. Kaslow (Eds.), *Comprehensive handbook of psychotherapy: Cognitive-behavioral approaches* (Vol. 2, pp. 117–140). New York: John Wiley and Sons.

Stage, S. A. (1998). Predicting adolescents' discharge status following residential treatment. *Residential Treatment for Children & Youth, 16*(3), 37–56.

Shadish, W. R., Montgomery, L. M., Wilson, P., Wilson, M. R., Bright, I., & Okwumabua, T. (1993). Effects of family and marital psychotherapies: A meta-analysis. *Journal of Consulting and Clinical Psychology, 61*(6), 992.

Stroul, B. A., & Friedman, R. M. (1996). The system of care concept and philosophy. In B. A. Stroul (Ed.), *Children's mental health: Creating systems of care in a changing society* (pp. 3–21). Baltimore: Paul H Brooks Publishing Company.

Sunseri, P. A. (2001). The prediction of unplanned discharge from residential treatment. *In Child and youth care forum* (*30*(5), pp. 283–303). Kluwer Academic Publishers-Plenum Publishers.

Sunseri, P. A. (2004). Family functioning and residential treatment outcomes. *Residential Treatment for Children & Youth, 22*(1), 33–53.

Walter, U. M., & Petr, C. G. (2008). Family-centered residential treatment: Knowledge, research, and values converge. *Residential Treatment for Children & Youth, 25*(1), 1–16.

Whittaker, J. K. (2000). What works in residential child care and treatment: Partnerships with families. In K. Alexander, & P. A. Curtis (Eds.), *What works in child welfare* (pp. 177–186). Washington, DC: CWLA Press.

Wilmshurst, L. A. (2002). Treatment programs for youth with emotional and behavioral disorders: An outcome study of two alternate approaches. *Mental Health Services Research, 4*(2), 85–96.

Zimmerman, D. P., Nansel, T. R., Raines, S., Jackson, D. L., Teal, C. R., Force, R. C., et al. (1998). A survey of residential treatment centers' outcome research practices. *Residential Treatment for Children & Youth, 15*(4), 45–59.

Author Biography

Ashley N. Merritts, Ph.D., LMFT is an assistant professor in the marriage and family therapy program at Mount Mercy University. Dr. Merritts received her BS degree from the University of Iowa in Psychology, with a minor in Human Relations. After graduating from the University of Iowa, Dr. Merritts continued her education and has a Ph.D. in Human Development and Family Studies and a Master of Science degree in the same major, both from Iowa State University. In her Master's degree program, Dr. Merritts specialized in couple and family therapy and is now a Licensed Marital and Family Therapist.

Dr. Merritts has extensive clinical training and has worked with a wide variety of problems in clinical settings. She specializes in working with distressed couples and has advanced training in Trauma Focused Cognitive Behavior Therapy as well. Dr. Merritts has worked with adolescents in residential settings during her career and understands the unique needs of this population. Here clinical interests also include working with childhood behavioral problems, families in crisis, co-parenting and divorce, individual healing, and affairs.

Dr. Merritts is a Clinical Fellow and Approved Supervisor with the American Association for Marriage and Family Therapy. She has also served as a board member for the Iowa Association for Marriage and Family Therapy. Dr. Merritts has published her work in the International Journal of Disability, Development and Education. She has also published in, and has served as a reviewer for, Contemporary Family Therapy: An International Journal. Dr. Merritts' research interests include relationship quality in African American couples and the impact of adverse childhood experiences on parent–child attachment.

Chapter 12
Intervention: The First Step to Recovery from Addiction

Jerry L. Law

Chapter Highlights

- The prevalence of drug and alcohol use in the United States.
- The importance of intervening with a loved one struggling with addiction.
- The bio/psycho/social/spiritual aspects of addiction.
- Models of intervention.
- Early intervention as critical to long-term recovery.

Introduction and Background

An Intervention is a well-planned, structured, highly personalized process where family, friends, or coworkers come together to break through the denial of someone struggling with an addiction to drugs or alcohol, an eating disorder, or other compulsive behavioral problems. The process of Intervention has gained significant notoriety in recent years. Television programs, including talk shows, discussion panels, and *reality* shows, have provided an increased awareness that assistance in guiding addicted individuals into treatment is available. These programs, along with mass media, have elevated awareness about the damage done to society by addictions and compulsive behavior to a new level. The United States alone

J.L. Law (✉)
Intervention Services of Arizona, 1839 S. Alma School Road, Suite 226, Mesa, AZ 85210, USA
e-mail: jerry@interventionaz.com

© Springer International Publishing AG 2017

J.D. Christenson and A.N. Merritts (eds.), *Family Therapy with Adolescents in Residential Treatment*, Focused Issues in Family Therapy,
DOI 10.1007/978-3-319-51747-6_12

sustains billions of dollars in lost productivity, medical costs, and other economic losses annually due to addictions.

The twentieth century was witness to an explosion in treatment options for adults and adolescents addicted to drugs and alcohol. Similar treatment modalities for eating disorders, compulsive gambling, sexual addictions,, and a full range of other compulsive behaviors were developed as therapists began to recognize the successes that addiction treatment programs experienced. While most behavioral health professionals now agree that treatment does in fact work, the stigma attached to treatment, along with the inherent denial that accompanies the types of disorders mentioned above, continue to keep suffering individuals trapped in their addictions.

The word Intervention is widely used in the mental health and behavioral health fields. Dr. Belzman (2003) summarizes one such use of the word well when he refers to, "A counselor client intervention in which the counselor challenges the system of self-deception that upholds the drug or alcohol abusers lifestyle in a one-on-one counseling session or group of sessions" (p. 56). In this context, Intervention is used to describe a wide variety of techniques and methods used in the relationship between counselor and client. The word intervention is also used to describe a very specific process through which friends and family members come together as a united team to confront an addiction or compulsive behavior in the life of a loved one. The express purpose of this type of Intervention is to encourage the suffering individual to engage in some form of treatment. As used in this chapter, the word Intervention shall primarily be used in this later sense and shall be spelled with a capital letter *I* when describing the various models of Intervention commonly practiced. Given that more and more late adolescents and young adults are entering treatment via an Intervention, it is important for therapists to understand this process. This chapter is intended to help fill this gap in understanding.

In order to appreciate the Intervention process, it is crucial to understand the magnitude of the problem at hand. An examination of the economic and health impact of drug, alcohol and tobacco use and abuse highlights the extent of the problem. Although this data does not reflect the additional damage caused by eating disorders, gambling addictions, and other compulsive behaviors, the data does provide clear evidence of the carnage done to society by addiction.

The U.S. Department of Health and Human Services tracks the prevalence of drug, alcohol, and tobacco use and abuse. In a recent report titled *National Survey on Drug Use and Health: National Findings*, statistics were presented (Substance Abuse and Mental Health Services Administration, [SAMHSA] 2014) (SAMHSA). This report is considered by many professionals in the field to be the most accurate and reliable data on the topic currently available. It shall underscore the need for Intervention advocated in this paper. The following information, taken from that report, provides an excellent overview as to the extent of alcohol and illicit drug use in the United States in 2013:

Illicit Drug Use

- An estimated 24.6 million Americans aged 12 or older were current (past month) illicit drug users. This represents 9.4% of the population aged 12 or older.
- Marijuana was the most commonly used illicit drug, with 19.8 million current users aged 12 or older (7.5%). There were 6.5 million nonmedical users of prescription-type drugs (2.5%), including 4.5 million nonmedical users of prescription pain relievers (1.7%).
- There were 1.5 million current cocaine users aged 12 or older, or 0.6% of the population. An estimated 1.3 million individuals aged 12 or older (0.5%) used hallucinogens in the past month.
- An estimated 496,000 individuals aged 12 or older were a current inhalant user, which represents 0.2% of the population. There were about 289,000 current heroin users aged 12 or older, or 0.1% of the population.
- There were 2.2 million adolescents aged 12–17 who were current illicit drug users. This represents 8.8% of adolescents. 7.1% of adolescents were current users of marijuana, 2.2% were current nonmedical users of prescription-type drugs (including 1.7% who were current nonmedical users of pain relievers), 0.6% were current users of hallucinogens, 0.5% were current users of inhalants, 0.2% were current users of cocaine, and 0.1% were current users of heroin.
- There were 22.4 million adults aged 18 or older who currently used illicit drugs. This represents 9.4% of adults. 7.6% of adults were current users of marijuana, 2.5% were current nonmedical users of prescription-type drugs (including 1.7% who were current nonmedical users of pain relievers), 0.5% were current users of hallucinogens, 0.6% were current users of cocaine, 0.2% were current users of inhalants, and 0.1% were current users of heroin.
- Among persons aged 12 or older who used pain relievers nonmedically in the past 12 months, 55.7% reported that the source of the drug the most recent time they used was from a friend or relative for free. Another 19.1% reported they got the drug from just one doctor. Only 3.9% got the pain relievers from a drug dealer or other stranger, and only 0.1% reported buying the drug on the Internet. Among those who reported getting the pain reliever from a friend or relative for free, 80.7% reported in a follow-up question that the friend or relative had obtained the drugs from just one doctor.

Alcohol Use

- Slightly more than half (52.2%) of Americans aged 12 or older were current alcohol users, which translates to an estimated 136.9 million current drinkers. Nearly one quarter (22.9%) of individuals aged 12 or older were binge alcohol users. This translates to about 60.1 million people. Heavy drinking was reported by 6.3% of the population aged 12 or older, or 16.5 million people.

- 11.6% of adolescents aged 12–17 were current alcohol users, representing 2.9 million adolescents. Many of these adolescents reported past month binge drinking (6.2% or 1.6 million adolescents) and 1.2% (293,000 adolescents) were heavy alcohol users.
- 56.4% of adults aged 18 or older were current drinkers of alcohol, which translates to an estimated 134 million current adult drinkers. Nearly one quarter (24.6%) of adults aged 18 or older (58.5 million adults) were binge alcohol users. The percentage of adults engaging in heavy drinking was 6.8% (16.2 million adults).

As alarming as these statistics appear they must be placed in context with the economic damage that accompanies the use and abuse of illicit drugs and alcohol. Though somewhat dated, the information presented in the December 2000 report from the Department of Health and Human Services titled, *Updating Estimates of the Economic Costs of Alcohol Abuse in The United States: Estimates, Update Methods and Data,* provides a clear picture of the damage done to the American economy by the abuse of drugs and alcohol. The economic impact of alcohol abuse consistently mirrors that of drug abuse. In 1998, alcohol abuse cost the economy of the United States nearly $190 billion. This figure represented a 25 % increase over 1992. All indicators pointed to similar trends, which would lead to an estimated impact on the America economy for 2007 at nearly $250 billion (Harwood 2000). Current trends demonstrate that the magnitude of the problem has only worsened since the publication of this report (National Institute of Drug Abuse 2016).

The Impact on Human Suffering

Aside from the prevalence and economic impact of addiction, the suffering experienced by individuals and families nearly defies description. Before moving on to the crux of this chapter, it is necessary to also briefly examine current understanding of the disorder, or disease, called addiction. Behavioral health specialists do not readily embrace a single definition for addiction. Medical doctors bring different points of view to bear on addiction, as do clergy, social workers, and laypersons. Many treatment programs and providers now refer to addiction as a bio/psycho/social/spiritual disorder. All four areas of life are affected by addiction and many believe that all four areas must be dealt with in the treatment of the disorder. What follows is a brief examination of each area and a few of the accepted definitions for addiction that are commonly embraced today.

The biological aspects of addiction are generally addressed in what has come to be known as the medical model for addiction. One of the earliest proponents for the medical model was Dr. E.M. Jellinek. In fact, alcoholism is frequently called Jellinek's Disease. Jellinek, a researcher at Yale University, authored the book, *The*

Disease Concept of Alcoholism and is credited with being the first to define alcoholism as, "...a bona fide disease, a chronic, fatal, progressive disease," (Fitzgerald 2002, p. xii). The now famous *Jellinek's Chart* continues to be used by many professionals as a method for explaining both the downward movement of addiction as well as the upward progression of recovery.

A review of the literature demonstrates a wide variety of books and articles written over the past 50 years that argue on behalf of a medical diagnosis for addiction. In 1957, the American Medical Association formally adopted the disease concept for addiction and began to encourage physicians to take an active role in treatment. One definition for the medical model of addiction is summed up as follows:

> Alcoholism is a primary, chronic disease with genetic, psychosocial, and environmental factors influencing its development and manifestations. The disease is often progressive and fatal. It is characterized by continuous or periodic: impaired control over drinking, preoccupation with the drug alcohol, use of alcohol despite adverse consequences, and distortions in thinking, most notably denial (American Society of Addiction Medicine 2005, p. 1).

Dr. Alan I. Lesher (1997) added, "...the brain has a mechanism that changes from use/abuse to addiction at some point when the *Switch* gets tripped. That is when the disease begins and, as such, meets all the identifiable criteria for a physical condition being truly an illness" (as cited in Fitzgerald 2002, p. 5).

In the book, *Alcoholics Anonymous*, referred to as *The Big Book* by members of Alcoholics Anonymous, the disease concept is also embraced. In the section called, *The Doctor's Opinion*, Dr. William Silkworth states,

> We believe, and so suggested a few years ago, that the action of alcohol on these chronic alcoholics is a manifestation of an allergy; that the phenomenon of craving is limited to this class and never occurs in the average temperate drinker (Alcoholics Anonymous 2001, p. xxviii).

Dr. May (1991), in his pivotal book, *Addiction and Grace*, provides a detailed explanation of the neurological changes that take place in the brain of an individual addicted to drugs or alcohol. In describing the interactions between neurotransmitters and the effects of mood-altering chemicals, May (1991) states, "Foreign chemicals such as caffeine, nicotine, narcotics, and other drugs also reach neuroreceptors through the blood stream and can exert powerful influences on the neurons" (p. 69). He goes on to describe the extraordinary interactions that take place between neurons in the human body and the ways in which drugs and alcohol interfere with the balance, or homeostasis, the body attempts to maintain.

In their book *Beyond the Influence*, Ketcham and Asbury (2000) present a comprehensive review of the biological aspects of addiction. In particular, a great deal of research is presented in the chapter entitled, *The Addicted Brain*. Here the authors empathically argue on behalf of a medical model for addiction. Ketcham and Asbury (2000) offer the following definition of addiction:

> Alcoholism is a progressive neurological disease strongly influenced by genetic vulnerability. Inherited or acquired abnormalities in brain chemistry create an altered response to

alcohol, which in turn causes a wide array of physical, psychological, and behavioral problems. Although environmental and social factors will influence the progression and expression of the disease, they are not in any sense causes of addictive drinking. Alcoholism is caused by biochemical/neurophysiological abnormalities that are passed down from one generation to the next or, in some cases, acquired through heavy or prolonged drinking (p. 46).

The conclusions of these authors may represent the extreme end of the medical model in which addiction is defined *completely* in terms of a physiological disease. Hundreds of additional resources in support of the aspects of addiction are available to the reader.

A psychological definition for addiction is perhaps best summarized by the criteria outline in the *Diagnostic and Statistical Manual of Mental Disorders, Fifth Edition* (*DSM-5*), published by the American Psychiatric Association. The DSM-5 (American Psychiatric Association [APA] 2000) does not refer to addiction but rather defines substance use disorders. The chapter on these disorders begins, "The Substance-Related Disorders include disorders related to the taking of a drug of abuse (including alcohol), to the side effects of a medication, and to toxin exposure" (APA 2000, p. 191). According to the DSM-5 an individual must meet specific criteria to be diagnosed as having a substance use disorder. These disorders are further delineated as mild, moderate, or severe depending on the number of criteria for a given substance use disorder met by an individual. A substance use disorder is often described as a maladaptive pattern of substance use, leading to clinically significant impairment or distress, occurring at any time in the same 12-month period. The manual goes on to present eleven unique psychological or behavioral patterns that are used to identify substance dependence. While recognition of the physiological aspects of substance use disorders is included, the primary focus is psychological and/or behavioral. Most professionals in the drug and alcohol treatment field rely heavily on the DSM-5 criteria for the diagnosis of addiction or alcoholism.

Many believe that drugs and alcohol are used to escape unhappiness in their lives as well. In his celebrated book *Chalk Talks about Alcohol*, Father Joseph Martin (1973) states:

> People use alcohol to escape the unpleasant things in life (or even the pleasant things, as when you have had just about all the pleasure you can stand from your visiting grand-children). I do not mean by escape any deep psychological phenomenon. I simply mean the way ordinary, reasonably happy people with ordinary, normal trials and tribulations simply want to forget it all for a couple of hours (p. 15).

Father Martin presents a compelling case for the use of alcohol to deal with the stresses and strains of life and how such repeated use can and does lead to dependence.

Spickard and Thompson (2005) expressed another example of the psychological implications of drug and alcohol use when they stated:

> The euphoria that compels a heavy drinker to risk embarrassment or serious accident is only a distant memory for the alcoholic. He still depends on alcohol to alter his mood, but now he drinks primarily to numb his pain, not to feel good (p. 15).

In *The Selfish Brain*, Doctor Robert Dupont (1997) spends considerable time detailing the psychological and behavioral implications of addiction. He concludes, "The fundamental explanation for addiction is far more simple, as seen in laboratory experiments with addicting drugs. Human addicts use alcohol and other drugs for the same reasons that laboratory animals do, for the brain-reward effects of the substance use" (p. 7). The psychological and behavioral aspects of addiction are widely researched and clear connections between addiction and the mind have been established over the years.

While a review of the literature does not produce a unique definition for addiction that is purely social in nature, the social aspects of alcohol use can scarcely be overlooked. Whether it is Super Bowl Sunday, girls' night out, a neighborhood cookout, a college fraternity party or a High School prom the presence of alcohol is all but guaranteed. Advertising for alcoholic beverages commands a lion's share of the revenue generated by media, both print and audio/visual. American society would be nearly unrecognizable without the presence of alcohol.

A recent nonscientific review of television programming by this author was quite revealing. During a two-hour span of *typical* television viewing, the number of references to alcohol use, coupled with the number of alcohol-related commercials, as well as the frequency of alcoholic drinks observed were literally impossible to track. The best estimate included seventeen commercials, over thirty references to alcohol use and certainly over one hundred depictions of alcohol being consumed. The use of alcohol has indeed become the norm in our culture. A direct social connection to addiction seems obvious and needs to be part of the definition of the disorder.

Finally, a spiritual or moral connection to addiction must be examined. This shall be looked at from both the traditional religious viewpoint as well as the nonreligious, yet moralistic side. One of the interesting paradoxes of addiction is how the underlying assumption of many religious and nonreligious moralists is very similar, namely that addiction is a matter of choice and in no way a disease. While agreeing on little else, an interesting accord exists between these groups regarding the *myth* of addiction as a *disease*.

One of the most comprehensive and often quoted sources for the moral model of addiction is the book, *The Truth about Addiction and Recovery*. Authors Peele and Brodsky (1991) pull no punches in their insistence that addiction is not a disease and is based in moral choices and behaviors as they state:

> Addiction is an ingrained habit that undermines your health, your work, your relationships, your self-respect, but that you feel you cannot change.... That is, we do not regard addiction of any kind as a disease. Thus we do not recommend that you see a doctor or join a twelve-step organization for one disease or another as a way of dealing with addiction (p. 9).

From this starting point, Peele and Brodsky (1991) develop what they refer to as the *Life Process Program* for recovery, an approach that is entirely based on free will and conscious choice. The disease aspects of addiction are utterly refuted as are religious approaches.

Another advocate for this moral model is Fingarette (1988). In his book, *Heavy Drinking: The Myth of Alcoholism as a Disease*, Fingarette also decries the disease concept of addiction as pure myth. Fingarette (1988) argues that the research on addiction does not support a medical model and states:

> The classic disease concept of alcoholism is unquestionably a hindrance rather than a help in addressing the broad problem of heavy drinking in our society. This is because most individuals in the United States who drink heavily and who get into most of the troubles related to alcohol do not think of themselves as alcoholics and would not be diagnosed as alcoholics (p. 4).

A third source frequently cited by those dismissing the medical model is George Vaillant. During 50 years of longitudinal research, Dr. Vaillant (1995) followed several hundred drinking men that he grouped as the *Core City Men* (*n* = 456), a largely blue-collar group from the Northeastern United States, and a second group known as the *College Men* (*n* = 204). Though Vaillant seldom refutes the disease concept of addiction, his enormous volume of data is frequently quoted to support assertions that define addiction completely in moral terms. Fingarette, mentioned above, often refers to Vaillant's data, as do others who embrace this position. A review of these three books will provide a wealth of information as to the nonreligious moral model for addiction.

The American Association of Christian Counselors, a group claiming membership in excess of 50,000, sponsored the book, *Caring for People God's Way*. In the chapter titled, *Addictions*, authors Clinton et al. (2006) outline a definition for addiction that is both spiritual and biological, stating:

> Addictive behaviors are problems per se, and they are also symptoms of deeper physical, emotional and spiritual issues... Depending on the issues of therapeutic focus, the course of treatment, and the progress (or lack thereof) toward goal attainment, the addiction is best viewed as either symptomatic of the underlying mental disorder or as the primary problem itself (p. 253).

This chapter of the book provides a very good representation of a perspective on addiction that does not view a biological understanding of addiction as being in competition with a spiritual/religious definition. Rather, what is presented is a view that addiction is biological, psychological, and spiritual.

Christian counselor Anderson et al. (2000) also advocate an approach that encourages an understanding of addiction that encompasses the physical, emotional, and spiritual roots of the disorder. In *Christ Centered Therapy*, they state:

> Chemical addictions are long-established habits. They are not easy to break because there is a fleshly craving for your drug of choice. You also have certain, well-established mental flesh-patterns that we are going to flush out during therapy and learn to overcome. To overcome the flesh will require total dependence on God as well as the support of family and friends (p. 304).

As has been demonstrated, a moral or religious definition of addiction is not a simple one and much disagreement exists. It is, however, agreed upon by nearly all of these authors, counselors, and educators that a significant component of addictive behavior is moral in its etiology and must be taken into account when examining this difficult issue.

The data presented makes clear that the need for treatment for those caught in addictions of all types is great. Untold damage to human lives as well as the ongoing harm to the economy makes a solid case for the Intervention process and the need to work toward assisting men and women in reaching out for recovery. Now, more than ever, the need to carry the message of hope and recovery to the suffering addict is upon us.

Current Models of Intervention

As stated earlier, the process known as Intervention has achieved greater notoriety over the past few years. Television programs such as *Intervention* and *Celebrity Rehab* continue to capture a solid share of the viewing audience. Talk show hosts Phil McGraw, Oprah Winfrey, and others frequently spotlight Interventions. Some professional Interventionists have themselves become minor celebrities as a result of this increased awareness about the Intervention process. In reality, these approaches to helping individuals reach out to treatment and recovery is not new. As shall be seen, a clear Intervention protocol was outlined in the New Testament and directly attributed to Jesus Christ (Matthew chapter eighteen). Indeed, it may be argued that Intervention, in a form, was part of the Mosaic Law.

What follows shall be an overview of the four models of Intervention most frequently practiced in the United States. These models are commonly referred to as (a) *Johnson Institute*; (b) *A Relational Intervention Sequence for Engagement (ARISE)*; (c) *Family Systems*; and (d) *Nouthetic*. Each model consists of components similar to one another as well as unique methodology for facilitating an Intervention. All share a common goal: to encourage the suffering individual to accept help in overcoming their disorder while offering hope to friends and family who have either watched the deterioration of a loved one or have participated in the addiction through enabling behaviors or codependency.

Johnson Institute Model

The most frequently practiced approach to Intervention in the United States is the Johnson Institute model developed in the 1960s by Dr. Vernon Johnson. Johnson, a recovering alcoholic, became involved in the treatment of addiction and originated a model for Intervention that bears his name. The term Johnson Institute Intervention Model derived its origin from the treatment program Johnson pioneered (e.g., Liepman 1993). Dr. Johnson outlined his now famous method for intervening in the life of an addict before the individual *hits bottom* knowing that such a bottom may very well be the premature death of that individual.

In 1986, the Hazelden Foundation published Johnson's landmark book, *Intervention—A Step-By-Step Guide for Families and Friends of Chemically Dependent Persons*. This pivotal tome has proven to be a roadmap that is followed, to a lesser or greater extent, by nearly all Interventionists. Though certain aspects of Johnson's model have been modified or even abandoned by some, the basics continue to provide a foundational platform for nearly all Interventions conducted in this country. What follows is a brief summary of the Johnson Institute model for Intervention.

As mentioned, at the core of this model is the belief that waiting for an addict to hit bottom is not only unnecessary it may be perilous. In the Introduction to Johnson's (1986) book, we read:

> If you are like most people, you may believe that there is nothing you can de except wait for the person to 'hit bottom' and then try to pick up the pieces. For more than 25 years, our task at the Johnson Institute has been to prove that just the opposite is true. Waiting is too dangerous. It is also cruel. It allows an already bad situation to be worse. If a friend wanted to jump off a bridge, would you let him do it before you reached out a hand to stop him? Of course not; and neither must you stand by and watch the chemically dependent person plumb the depths of suffering and despair before doing something about it. You don't have to bide your time until your family breaks up, or the person is fired from his or her job—or kills someone in a car accident. You can reach out *now* (p. viii).

From the outset, it may be seen that the Johnson Institute model is based on the concept of breaking through the denial associated with addiction. Critics of the Intervention process argue that it is cruel to confront the addict. Many in Twelve-Step groups also contend that recovery is not an option until the individual hits bottom. Johnson argued that true cruelty lay in standing on the sidelines and watching the addict suffer, or worse yet, participating in that addiction through enabling behaviors.

The Johnson Institute model, therefore, is confrontational. "Intervention is the creation or use of a crisis involving the alcoholic that is so emotionally painful that he/she will stop denying that alcohol/drugs is a problem before he/she has lost everything" (Distance Learning Center 2005, p. 328). Most, if not all, adherents to this approach view addiction as a disease. In comparing addiction to other diseases Johnson (1986) himself wrote that, "We are now able to diagnose chemical dependency in much the same way. A symptomatology—a list of distinct characteristics of the disease—is available, enabling us to recognize its presence and effects" (p. 4). The idea of allowing a disease to run rampant in the life of an individual is untenable to the advocate of this Intervention approach. Similarly, White and Wright (1998) write in support of the Johnson Institute model:

> The process relies heavily on the Disease Model of Alcoholism and Drug Dependence (i.e. chemical dependence) as its foundation. Family and friends of the addicted person are educated regarding the disease and its treatment, trained in the procedures for

nonjudgmental group confrontation, and guided through the actual intervention session by a
qualified professional (p. 7).

The Johnson Institute model for Intervention is frequently portrayed as a single
confrontational event, in which friends and/or family ambush the addict and
threaten punishment if the person does not choose to change. In reality, this model
embraces a process through which an Intervention Team is fully educated about
addiction. The group is prepared for an Intervention in which choices are presented
to the addict. According to Johnson (1986),

> Intervention is a process by which the harmful, progressive, and destructive effects of
> chemical dependency are interrupted and the chemically dependent person is helped to stop
> using mood-altering chemicals and to develop new, healthier ways of coping with his or her
> needs and problems (p. 61).

The process begins with the selection of the Intervention Team, usually friends,
family, or coworkers, who come together to confront the addiction. The key here is
the idea of confronting the addiction, not ambushing the individual. The
Interventionist has the responsibility, at this point in the process, to help Team
members deal with their own misconceptions and insecurities about addiction and
the confrontation that lies ahead. The Johnson Institute model places significant
emphasis on the preparation phase. This approach to Intervention supports the idea
of keeping the Intervention secret from the addict until the very last minute. Many
Team members struggle with the idea of being secretive and view their role as
dishonest. Practitioners of this model spend significant time with the Team members educating them on addiction and helping them understand what is going *inside
the addict* in order to shift their thinking from one of adversary to that of helper.
The goal, once again, is to help the addict choose recovery while there is still time
to do so rather than wait for an inevitable conclusion that may include the death of
the individual or others. Most advocates of the Johnson Institute model consider it
unconscionable to allow addicts to continue to risk their own lives or the lives of
others through tragic events, such as drunk driving accidents or drug-buys gone
wrong. This preparation phase of the Intervention generally consumes more time
than the actual presentation of truth to the addict.

Once the Intervention Team is fully on board with the process, the
Interventionist begins to train and educate Team members as to what will take place
when the addict arrives. Johnson advocated the compilation of two types of data in
preparation for the Intervention. These include facts about the addict's drinking or
drug use and information about treatment options. Practitioners of this model train
the Team members on writing a letter or making lists of specific incidents in the
addict's life that substantiate the concerns being presented. In most cases, each
person is asked to write a letter and to read the letter during the Intervention. The
value of reading the letter is recognizable due to the heavily emotional nature of the
Intervention. The model depends heavily on the Team members staying *on script*
during the presentation of facts to the addict so as to avoid moving off the subject
and/or providing the addict fodder to argue against what is being presented. Team
members are asked to present facts, not conjecture or innuendo.

As mentioned, the Team is encouraged to gather a second type of information during the preparation phase, namely treatment options. Addiction treatment ranges from no-fee programs sponsored by groups such as the Salvation Army to private residential treatment facilities charging as much as one hundred thousand dollars for 30- to 60-day programs. Health insurance options, program types, such as twelve-step based or cognitive behavior therapy, location, family program, gender, sexual orientation, co-occurring disorders and many other issues are examined during the preparation phase. Johnson (1986) argued that it is of little value for the addict to agree to receive treatment as the result of the Intervention only to discover that no plans for treatment have been prearranged.

A rehearsal of the actual Intervention is also an important component of the Johnson Institute model. Jay and Jay (2000), Johnson Institute advocates, state in their book, *Love First,* that there are four reasons for rehearsing the Intervention. The first is to edit and rehearse the reading of the letters. According to Jay and Jay (2000), "Each person reads his or her letter aloud while the group listens carefully to both tone and content" (p. 129). The Jays inform the reader of the importance of removing negative content, to write the letter in the first person, to use first-hand experiences the writer has had with the addict and so on. The second purpose of the rehearsal is to determine the order in which the letters are to be read. Some Interventionists insist on setting the order while others allow a group consensus to make the decision. The Jays' third reason is that the seating order for the actual Intervention needs to be determined in advance. Arranging furniture correctly and positioning individuals in the appropriate seats will go far in making the addict more receptive to what is being said. Finally, the rehearsal allows participants to do everything as they expect to do them on the actual day of the Intervention. As little as possible is left to chance.

The rehearsal also provides opportunity to predict objections the addict may raise against going into treatment. The Team will most likely know what types of objections will be raised and the Interventionist guides the Team on how to best counter these objections as well as determining which Team member is best suited to handle each.

Johnson (1986) outlines six steps for the rehearsal. These include:

- Step one: designate a chairperson.
- Step two: Go over each item on the written lists (letters) that team members have prepared.
- Step three: determine the order in which team members will read their lists during the intervention.
- Step four: choose someone to play the role of the chemically dependent person during the rehearsal.
- Step five: determine the responses that team members will make to the chemically dependent person.
- Step six: conduct the rehearsal (pp. 76–81).

In his book, Johnson (1986) reminds the reader that there may not be such a thing as a *typical* Intervention. It is possible, however, to present a scenario that describes what often happens during the Intervention as the following summary depicts. Once all plans have been finalized and the Team has fully rehearsed the Intervention, it is time to present the truth to the addicted individual. This may be done in a home, an office, a hotel, a church or any number of locations. Through some method, the addict arrives at the destination, where the Intervention Team has already assembled. Either the Interventionist or the Team leader greets the addict and asks the individual to please take a seat in the prearranged location. The Interventionist or leader informs the addict that the group has come together because they love the person and are concerned about the individual. The addict is asked to allow each person to share what they have written and that he or she will have ample time to respond once all Team members have shared their letters. Each team member then reads his or her letter. Once the letters have been read, the Interventionist or leader briefly summarizes the love and concerns that have been presented and asks the addict to go into treatment. Frequently, the impact of the surprise coupled with the profound emotions experienced during the reading of the letters is enough to elicit an agreement to go into treatment. Often the answer is no.

When the addict refuses help the Intervention may enter a negotiation phase in which the Interventionist or leader asks for specific objections to treatment and offers solutions to each objection; the idea being to disarm the individual's apprehension about receiving help and assist the addict in taking ownership of the choice to get help. This phase may last a few minutes or much longer depending on the circumstances in each Intervention. If, after negating the objections, the addicted individual continues to balk at the idea of receiving help, the Team enters the final phase of the Intervention in which each Team member informs the addict of the choices they have made based on the addict's refusal to get help.

Often the addicted person chooses help before this phase is reached. Unfortunately, some individuals are so ensnared by the addiction, that the answer is still no. At this point, the Team members must be prepared to read the consequences they intend to enforce. The key word is consequences, not punishment. If the addicted person chooses not to receive help, the relationship between the addict and each Team member will be forever altered. Team members inform the addict that his or her choice not to receive the gift of life being offered has resulted in individual decisions to change how they interact with the addict and to discontinue any enabling behaviors that have supported the addiction. This phase is often the most difficult portion of the process and the Interventionist who uses the Johnson Institute model spends significant time in the preparation phase addressing this possibility and guiding the Team members on how to present their consequences and why it is necessary.

Advocates of the Johnson Institute model for Intervention generally claim a success rate of eighty to ninety percent when defining success as the addict accepting help that day. Dr. Johnson argues for a one hundred percent success rate when the Intervention is properly done. Johnson (1986) gives two reasons for this claim.

1. The people who do the intervening—the team members—are forever changed. They know that they are not alone. They know that help and support are available to them. Their lives are never the same afterwards.
2. The family unit is also changed—from the immobilized fearful, guilty, shame-ridden group they once were to an entirely new dynamic (pp. 105–106).

Since the publication of Dr. Johnson's (1986) book on the Intervention process, dozens of additional books, and countless articles have been authored in which variations on the theme are advocated. Regardless, the five basic principles as outlined by Johnson continue to underlie nearly all Interventions conducted by those who identify with the Johnson Institute model.

The Johnson Institute model for addiction is advocated as the method most likely to break through the wall of denial and delusion that has been established in the life of the addicted individual. This protocol continues to enjoy a wide following by many professionals and is often the format most recognized by the public.

A Relational Intervention Sequence for Engagement— ARISE Model

A second model for Intervention frequently practiced in the United States is known as A Relational Intervention Sequence for Engagement, commonly referred to by the acronym ARISE. The literature is somewhat vague as to the exact history of this model, however the book titled, *Invitational Intervention*, by Landau and Garrett (2006), sheds light on the beginnings of the ARISE model and the fundamental principles involved. This book, along with several articles posted online by these same authors, will serve as the primary source of information on the model as they do present the most comprehensive outline of the ARISE protocol found in the review of available literature. Those seeking a detailed understanding of the ARISE model are encouraged to read this book as what follows is a brief recap of significant components only.

In the abstract to one of the articles posted online, Garrett et al. (1997) refer to the Albany-Rochester Interventional Sequence for Engagement. In this paper, Garrett et al. describe the ARISE model that was initially developed and implemented at treatment programs located in Albany and Rochester, New York. The model would later be renamed A Relational Intervention Sequence for Engagement and continue to be known by the acronym ARISE.

According to Garrett et al. (1997), "The ARISE model is a three-stage, graduated continuum of intervention designed to utilize the concern of the chemically dependent person's family and friends toward maximizing both engagement, and hopefully, retention in chemical dependency treatment" (p. 238). These three stages shall be outlined in some detail, however, the basic assumptions of the ARISE model must be examined first.

This model for Intervention is built upon seven primary assumptions about addiction and treatment. According to Garrett et al. (1997) these are:

1. Family dynamics look different when viewed from close up rather than when viewed from afar.
2. Systems theory has brought forth the notion that the family is both affected by chemical dependency and affects the course of chemical dependency.
3. Therapists and counselors must realize and appreciate that families are capable of doing much of the therapy work on their own.
4. Families are more powerful that *treaters* in effecting change due to the inherent dynamics within the family system.
5. Many situations do not call for the chemically dependent person to be threatened with consequences as a condition of entering treatment.
6. Outpatient treatment is preferable to inpatient treatment whenever possible for use with an *intervention continuum*.
7. The Intervention Team (or network) benefits from the process regardless of the chemically dependent person's decision to seek treatment.

The practitioner of the ARISE models proceeds from these basic assumptions. Of particular note is the belief that the family system is to be respected as the driving force for guiding the chemically dependent individual toward treatment and that the use of consequences, should the individual not choose treatment, is not always appropriate. Perhaps the most important and even controversial aspect of the ARISE model, verses the Johnson Institute model, is the invitational nature of an ARISE Intervention. When facilitating an Intervention, the ARISE practitioner advocates for the involvement of the chemically dependent person from the outset. The idea of a surprise Intervention, as is the case in the Johnson Institute format, is deemed offensive and counterproductive.

In the book, *Invitational Intervention*, Landau and Garrett (2006) devote an entire chapter to the topic of inviting the chemically dependent person to be part of the Intervention process. They cite their own research in which they studied 350 individuals admitted to an Intensive Outpatient Program. The focus of the study was on the dynamics of what motivated these individuals to enter treatment. According to Landau and Garrett, the lowest completion rate (40%) was for those who self-referred to treatment. Those mandated by court order had a high completion rate (91%) and those coming into treatment as the result of a Johnson Institute Intervention had a completion rate of 55% (Landau and Garrett 2006). From this data, Landau and Garrett conclude that while those entering treatment as the result of a Johnson Institute Intervention started off strong in treatment, they had a high dropout rate. "This finding led the authors to wonder whether the rebellious response and subsequent pattern of relapse noted in the Johnson Intervention group could be avoided using a method that started with an invitation rather than by surprise and coercion" (Landau and Garrett 2006, p. 14).

At the very core of the ARISE model, therefore, we see the concept of an invitational Intervention. Landau, Garrett, and many others who support the ARISE model believe that inviting the chemically dependent person to be engaged in the process from the beginning not only respects the individual, it also provides the greatest opportunity for long term recovery for the addict. Landau and Garrett (2006) list 16 responses to the question of why to use an ARISE invitational Intervention. Among these reasons Landau and Garrett list:

- It is a collaborative process that conveys respect and establishes openness from the very beginning.
- It addresses the addicted individual's biggest complaint, which is one of fear and distrust caused by a surprise Intervention.
- It establishes roles and clarifies the changes to come in treatment.
- It acknowledges the importance of choice at every step of the process (pp. 29–30).

These and many other reasons listed provide the backing for Landau and Garrett's contention that all Interventions should begin with an invitation to the addicted individual to engage in the process.

As previously stated, the ARISE model is a three-stage, or three-level, Intervention process. Stage one is generally referred to as *The First Call* (Landau and Garrett 2006). As the name would indicate, this stage begins the moment a concerned family member or friend contacts a treatment center or Interventionist. During this first level the clinician works toward establishing a relationship with the concerned other (CO) and provides a basis for hope. Often those First Callers have suffered with the disease of addiction impacting their lives for years. Frequently, these CO's are desperate and nearly hopeless. *ARISE* practitioners help establish a *Recovery Message* to be used as a component of the invitation to the addicted individual as well as CO's to engage them in the process. The Interventionist guides the First Caller in how to reach out to those who will be part of the Intervention Network, or Team, and instructs the First Caller on how to establish an initial meeting of the Network.

> Level I, the First Call, ends after the first meeting if the AI (addicted individual) attends and agrees to enter treatment. If the AI does not enter treatment, the Intervention Network goes on to Level II meetings, continuing to invite the AI to each subsequent meeting (Landau and Garrett 2006, p. 2).

Should the chemically dependent individual balk at treatment after the first meeting of the Intervention Network is held, the team moves to level two. At this level, the Intervention Network conducts as many as five face-to-face meetings. The addict is always invited to attend; however, the meetings are held regardless of the AI's participation. According to Landau and Garrett (2006), "During these meetings, motivationalstrategies are developed that are specifically matched to the AI's resistance and his/her reaction to previous attempts to get him/her into treatment" (p. 2). The strategies may include new ways in which each member of the Network will interact with the AI and/or ways in which enabling behaviors shall be eliminated. Landau and Garrett refer to these as meetings of the family's Board of

Directors in which the power of the group is brought to bear on the problem with the single intent of encouraging the AI to receive help.

The third and final stage of the ARISE process, if needed, is a formal Intervention based on the Johnson Institute model. Obviously, the element of surprise, so prevalent in most Johnson Institute Interventions, is missing but the basic format of that method is followed nearly to the letter. By this time, the AI has been given multiple opportunities to engage. The Intervention Network strives to counter continued resistance on the part of the AI. This may include consequences for not entering treatment. The Intervention Network continues to meet, whether the AI enters treatment or not, in order to promote healing and recovery for all who have been impacted by the addiction.

Landau and Garrett (2006) supplement their argument for the ARISE model with the following information:

A recent nonrandomized clinical trial of the ARISE Invitational Intervention showed that following the family initiating the ARISE method 83% ($n = 91$) of 110 severely addicted and resistant alcoholics and substance abusers enrolled in treatment ($n = 86$) or attended self-help meetings ($n = 5$). In cumulative terms, 55% entered treatment in Level I; another 26% were engaged in Level II, bringing the total to 81%. Level III added another 2%, completing the final figure of 83%. The AI's preferred substance did not have any impact on engagement rate, nor did it impact the level of the intervention at which engagement occurred (p. 11).

Although the Johnson Institute model for Intervention continues to be the mostly widely practiced form of Intervention, the literature indicates that the ARISE model enjoys the most published research and hard data.

Family Systems Model

A third type of Intervention frequently practiced in the United States is known as the Family Systems model. This approach, like the Johnson Institute and ARISE models, is recognized by the Association of Intervention Specialists and appears to have a growing number of advocates. A review of the literature does not result in much published material on this model. A good representation, however, can be found on the Internet. Most of this material is to be found on web sites operated by individuals or organizations that follow this approach.

California-based Addiction Recovery Consulting Services (2015) places a brief comparison between the Johnson Institute model and the Systemic Family model (Family Systems) on their web site. The following information is taken directly from the Addiction Recovery Consulting Services (2015, para 1–7) site:

The systemic family intervention (SFI)

SFI differs from the Johnson Model in two important ways, making it preferable in most every case. It is invitational and educational.

1. **Invitational**—Everyone is invited to attend the 2-day family workshop (SFI), including the addict or alcoholic. With SFI, you lead the way to recovery rather than pushing. There are no surprises, no hiding, no sneaking, no deception, and no dishonesty. This difference is critical for everyone involved and a key to the beginning of recovery. Addiction has caused serious damage to family relationships; healing begins with the SFI workshop.
2. **Educational**—SFI is a 2-day educational and interactive family workshop wherein all participants learn about the disease of alcoholism, addiction, codependency, treatment, treatment options and recovery. All participants are helped into recovery thereby addressing their own specific needs and pains.

Intervention model comparison

Johnson model	Systemic family model (SFI)
Focus on the identified patient	Focus on the family system
Focus on individual	Focus on the disease
Goal of treatment for individual	Goal of family (systemic) health
Potentially disrespectful	Gentle and respectful
Confrontational	Invitational
No education	Educational
Professionally directed at intervention	Professional directed at preparation
Impact from shock/power of group	Impact from change in system
Message: YOU need help	Message: WE need help
Fear of failure	There is no failure (win/win)

A review of the above information provides a good snapshot of what is involved in the Family Systems model and, in particular, the differences between this approach and that of the Johnson Institute model according to these advocates of the Family Systems approach.

A second online source for information on the Family Systems approach to Intervention can be found on the website of Julie Kelly & Associates (2015). Kelly adds to what is presented above and further emphasizes a Family Systems approach that is focused on an invitational Intervention that includes a strong education component. According to Kelly, families must engage in a five-stage process in order to begin the process of healing. These five stages are:

1. Inquiry
2. Assessment
3. Preparation
4. Intervention
5. Continuing care

In February of 2006, at the Association of Intervention Specialists semiannual conference, a number of speakers gave presentations on the three models of Intervention reviewed so far in this chapter. Proponents of the Family Systems model included Wayne J. Raiter, Jo Ann Towle, Bill Maher, Kristina Wandzilak, James Tracy and others. Each of the presenters practice Family Systems Interventions and a review of the slides presented at the conference confirms much of what has been previously presented on this approach. In the presentation by Raiter and Towle (2006), the invitational aspect of Family Systems Intervention versus the surprise aspect of the Johnson Institute model is highlighted and these are contrasted as follows:

Surprise event

- Goal is getting the alcoholic/addict to treatment
- Gathering of family, friends concerned others
- Letters are read; *bottom line* stated
- Brief time investment
- *It works* most of the time

Invitation process—systemic family intervention

- Goal is getting help for the entire family/group
- Gathering of family and other love ones
- Alcoholic/Addict is notified, told the truth, invited
- Longer time investment
- Always successful

Wandzilak (2006) advocates Family Systems Interventions on the basis of this approach being:

- Proactive
- Inclusive and invitational
- Family focused

What can be readily deduced from the information presented above is that Family Systems Interventions are invitational in nature. This approach usually entails a two-day workshop, often over a weekend, which is educational rather than confrontational. The focus of the Intervention process is on bringing healing and recovery to the family not just the individual. The role of the Interventionist is largely one of education and facilitation. The underlying belief is that the inherent power of the family can do more than the interdiction of a professional.

Family Systems Interventions are based on the Family Systems Theory. Two key books will be helpful for those wishing a fuller understanding of this theory as it applies to addiction and recovery. In Brown (1985) published her landmark book, *Treating the Alcoholic*. In this book, Brown presented her Developmental Model for the treatment of addiction. After years of applying this approach to treatment, Brown and Lewis (1996), published a follow-up work titled *The Alcoholic Family in Recovery*. In this book, the authors outline how the Developmental Model for the treatment of addiction is applicable to families impacted by addiction. Brown and Lewis (1996) inform us that,

> In a developmental frame, human beings are dynamic, fluid, and changing rather that static.
> So are families. Applied to alcoholism and the alcoholic, abstinence is not an end or a static
> state but the beginning of a new process of development (p. 8).

Throughout the book, Systems Theory, as it applies to addiction is highlighted.

A more contemporary work, *It's Not Okay to be a Cannibal* written by Interventionists Wainwright and Poznanovich (2007) details a *take no prisoners* approach to Intervention in which the health and recovery of the family takes center stage. According Wainwright and Poznanovich, "A proper intervention is a planned realignment of family power, in which power is taken away from the addict and given to the rest of the family" (p. 19). Readers will find a great deal of information regarding the importance of the family system when confronting addiction in this book.

The Family Systems model of Intervention resembles the ARISE model in its insistence on an invitational approach. It differs significantly from the other models in its focus on education, in particular the fact that the process is centered on a workshop designed to educate the family about addiction and treatment options. In fact, the available material on the Family Systems approach seems to be built more upon how it differs from the Johnson Institute model than on its own merit. Advocates of this model would be well served to publish concise, well-researched literature for interested parties to be able to better understand this approach.

Nouthetic Model

A fourth model for Intervention practiced in the United States is one that is built upon Christian biblical principles. The Nouthetic model is not one that is endorsed by groups such as the Association of Intervention Specialists. Although such organizations do not argue against a Nouthetic model, groups that are not decidedly Christian in nature generally do not endorse this approach. In fact, many professional Interventionists are likely not familiar with this approach at all. Nonetheless, this is an Intervention protocol widely practiced by biblical counselors who specifically work with followers of Christ. A review of Intervention protocols that does not include this approach would be very lacking in its thoroughness.

In 1970, Dr. Jay Adams published his book, *Competent to Counsel*. Many counselors cite this work as revolutionizing biblical counseling as it is currently practiced in the United States. Prior to this book and the counseling model built upon it, most Christian counseling was either *pastoral advice* or traditional psychotherapy with some scripture added in; an approach Crabb (1977) calls *Tossed Salad*. Adams brought forth a true counseling system that is grounded in Reformed Theology and built on the concept of *Sola Scriptura*. Christian counseling has never been the same since the publication of *Competent to Counsel*. Though countless adaptations to Adams' work have been proposed over the past 35 plus years, the basic concepts presented by him still stand as the foundation to what has come to be known as *nouthetic* counseling and shall serve as the basis for the Nouthetic model for Intervention as outlined in this paper.

In order to appreciate the Nouthetic model, one must first grasp the fundamentals of Adams' counseling methodology. In *Competent to Counsel*, Adams (1970) builds his case by stating, "Jesus Christ is at the center of all true Christian counseling. Any counseling which moves Christ from that position of centrality has to the extent that it has done so ceased to be Christian" (p. 41). Adams then begins to define nouthetic counseling in great detail, he states:

> The words *nouthesis* and *noutheteo* are the noun and verb forms in the New Testament from which the term "nouthetic" comes. A consideration of most of the passages in which these forms occur will lead inductively to an understanding of the meaning of nouthesis (p. 41).

Adams, a scholar of the Greek language, could not find an English equivalent to the Greek word, nouthetic, and thus chose to use the word as is to describe his counseling method.

From the use of the term nouthetic we may deduce two key points about this type of counseling. First, we see that confrontation is expected. Second, the biblical principle of admonition is to be the characteristic of the confrontation. Biblical admonition is not a reference to punishment. The word admonition, translated from the Greek word *nouthesia*, literally means to instruct or correct. Thus, nouthetic counseling is based on a confrontational approach that has instruction or correction as its goal.

Adams (1970) states that nouthetic confrontation consists of at least three basic elements; first,

> …nouthetic confrontation always implies a problem, and presupposes an obstacle that must be overcome; something is wrong in the life of the one who is confronted. Secondly, an inherent concept in nouthetic counseling is that problems are solved by verbal means. Third, nouthetic counseling has in view the purpose or motive behind the nouthetic activity. The thought is always that the verbal correction is intended to benefit the counselee (p. 49).

As has been shown, nouthetic counseling always uses Scripture in its approach. *Secular* modalities are largely rejected, as the essential aspect of the nouthetic approach is the idea that scripture is more than enough for successful counseling. Key support for nouthetic counseling is to be found in the passage that states, "All scripture [is] given by inspiration of God, and [is] profitable for doctrine, for reproof, for correction, for instruction in righteousness: That the man of God may be perfect, thoroughly furnished unto all good works" II Timothy 3:16–17 (King James Version). The doctrine known as the *sufficiency of scripture* is built on this passage, along with others that teach that God's Word provides all that is necessary for the counseling process. Many biblical counselors rely almost exclusively on passages from the Bible when counseling individuals dealing with a wide variety of issues. A thorough reading of *Competent to Counsel* as well as Adams' later volume entitled, *The Christian Counselor's Manual* will provide a very detailed explanation of the nouthetic counseling modality.

It is important to note that a formal Nouthetic model for Intervention that is tied directly to addiction and compulsive behaviors is not readily available. Rather, the nouthetic counseling approach, in general, *is* a form of Intervention. Nouthetic counselors have written a number of books on overcoming addiction, but few of the authors would advocate for an Intervention process geared toward encouraging an individual to participate in a formal treatment program. Instead, most nouthetic counselors would argue that the nouthetic approach is not only the Intervention, but also the treatment.

Most nouthetic counselors would not consider themselves Interventionists and many, if not most, Interventionists are unfamiliar with the *Nouthetic* model. This brief review of nouthetic principles has shown, however, that nouthetic confrontation of addiction and compulsive behaviors is a form of Intervention that is widely practiced in the United States.

The Johnson Institute, ARISE, Family Systems and Nouthetic models for Intervention may not be the only models practiced in the United States, but are the most well-known and researched. Undoubtedly, numerous variations of each are being practiced and/or developed and many more are likely to come in the future.

Conclusion

The majority of the information on the Intervention process as presented in this chapter is applicable when intervening with an individual in late adolescence who has reached the age of emancipation either chronologically or by court order. One might argue that an Intervention for a 14-year old would look more like putting them in the car and driving them to a treatment program! The chronological age and maturity level of the individual must be taken into account when designing any type of Intervention.

As has been seen, the issues of addiction to alcohol, drugs, gambling, internet pornography, as well as dangerous or deadly compulsive behaviors, such as anorexia, bulimia and a whole host of others, continue to be a scourge to society. The economic impact and human toll is nearly incomprehensible. While great debate continues with respect to agreed upon definitions of exactly what addiction is, much agreement exists that treatment can and does work. For those individuals who have watched loved ones die a little more each day due to their addictions, help in the form of Intervention is available. Treatment modalities, including outpatient therapy, intensive outpatient programs as well as residential treatment have been proven to be effective means of treating these disorders. Once an individual has reached the level of physical and psychological dependency, treatment that is structured, regimented, and evidence based is clearly the protocol of choice. Although it is not the purpose of this chapter to contrast treatment programs, suffice it to say that residential treatment has a proven record of success and the longer an individual remains in this type of treatment, the greater the likelihood of long term recovery.

References

Adams, J. E. (1970). *Competent to counsel.* Grand Rapids, MI: Zondervan.

Addiction Recovery Consulting Services. (2015). *San Francisco interventionists: Intervention models.* Retrieved from: http://www.bayarea-intervention.com/interventionmodels.html

Alcoholics Anonymous. (2001). *Alcoholic anonymous* (4th ed.). New York: Alcoholics Anonymous World Services, Inc.

American Psychiatric Association. (2000). *Diagnostic and statistical manual of mental disorders* (4th ed.). Arlington, VA: Author.

American Society of Addiction Medicine. (2005). *Public policy statement on the definition of alcoholism.* Retrieved from: http://www.asam.org/docs/default-source/public-policy-statements/1definition-of-alcoholism-2-902.pdf?sfvrsn=0

Anderson, N. T., Zuehlke, T. E., & Zuehlke, J. S. (2000). *Christ centered therapy.* Grand Rapids, MI: Zondervan.

Belzman, M. (2003). *Handbook for Christ-centered substance abuse and addiction counselors.* Redlands, CA: Association of Christian Alcohol and Drug Counselors.

Brown, S. (1985). *Treating the alcoholic.* New York: John Wiley and Sons.

Brown, S., & Lewis, V. (1996). *The alcoholic family in recovery.* New York: The Guilford Press.

Clinton, T., Hart, A., & Ohlschlager, G. (Eds.). (2006). *Caring for people God's way: Personal and Emotional Issues, Addictions, Grief, and Trauma.* Nashville: Thomas Nelson.

Crabb, L. (1977). *Effective Christian counseling.* Grand Rapids: Zonervan.

Distance Learning Center. (2005). *Getting ready to test: A review/preparation manual for drug and alcohol credentialing examinations.* Santa Fe, NM: Author.

Dupont, R. L. (1997). *The selfish brain.* Center City, MN: Hazelden.

Fingarette, H. (1988). *Heavy drinking: The myth of alcoholism as a disease.* Berkeley, CA: University of California Press.

Fitzgerald, W. K. (2002). *Alcoholism the genetic inheritance.* Lake Forest, Illinois: Whales' Tale Press.

Garrett, J., Landau-Stanton, J., Stanton, M. D., Stellato-Kabat, J., & Stellato-Kabat, D. (1997). ARISE: A method for engaging reluctant alcohol and drug dependent individuals in treatment. *Journal of Substance Abuse Treatment, 14*(3), 235–248.

Harwood, H. J. (2000). *Updating estimates of the economic costs of alcohol abuse in the United States: Estimates, update methods, and data.* Washington, DC: US Department of Health and Human Services, Public Health Service, National Institutes of Health, National Institute on Alcohol Abuse and Alcoholism.

Jay, J., & Jay, D. (2000). *Love first: A new approach to intervention for alcoholism & drug addiction.* Center City, MN: Hazelden.

Johnson, V. E. (1986). *Intervention: A step-by-step guide for families and friends of chemically dependent persons.* Center City, MN: Hazelden.

Julie Kelly & Associates. (2015). *The joy of recovery.* Retrieved from: http://www.joyofrecovery.com/index.html

Ketcham, K., & Asbury, W. (2000). *Beyond the influence: Understanding and defeating alcoholism.* New York: Bantam Books.

Landau, J., & Garrett, J. (2006). *Invitational intervention: A step by step guide for clinicians helping families engage resistant substance abusers in treatment.* Boulder, CO: Book Surge.

Liepman, M. R. (1993). Using family influence to motivate alcoholics to enter treatment: The Johnson Institute intervention approach. In T. J. O'Farrell (Ed.), *Treating alcohol problems: Marital and family interventions.* New York: The Guilford Press.

Martin, J. C. (1973). *Chalk talks about alcohol.* San Francisco: Harper Collins.

May, G. G. (1991). *Addiction and grace: Love and spirituality in the healing of addictions.* New York: HarperCollins.

National Institute of Drug Abuse. (2016). *Trends and statistics.* Retrieved from: https://www.drugabuse.gov/related-topics/trends-statistics#costs

Peele, S., & Brodsky, A. (1991). *The truth about addiction and recovery*. New York: Fireside.

Raiter, W. J., & Towle, J. A. (2006). *The moment of change*. Nashville, TN: Presentation at the conference for Foundations Associates.

Spickard, A., & Thompson, B. R. (2005). *Dying for a drink*. Nashville: W Publishing Group.

Substance Abuse and Mental Health Services Administration. (2014). *Results from the 2013 National Survey on Drug Use and Health: Summary of national findings*. NSDUH Series H-48, HHS Publication No. (SMA) 14-4863. Rockville, MD: Substance Abuse and Mental Health Services Administration.

Vaillant, G. E. (1995). *The natural history of alcoholism revisited*. Cambridge: Harvard University Press.

Wainwright, A. T., & Poznanovich, R. (2007). *It's not okay to be a cannibal*. Center City, MN: Hazelden.

Wandzilak, K. (2006). *The moment of change*. Nashville, TN: Presentation presented at the conference Foundations Associates.

White, R. K., & Wright, D. G. (Eds.). (1998). *Addiction intervention: Strategies to motivate treatment-seeking behavior*. New York, NY: Haworth Press.

Author Biography

Jerry L. Law, D.Min., MDAAC, CIP is a veteran of 25 years in the corporate world, and his strong leadership and organizational skills lend themselves naturally to the Intervention process. Dr. Law is a Board Certified Professional Christian Counselor, a Board Certified Intervention Professional and a Master Certified Drug Alcohol and Addictions Counselor. Jerry brings compassion and a first-hand understanding about how critical it is to break the cycle of addiction in the professional world as well as within the family. He facilitates Interventions for eating disorders, chemical dependency, and process addictions and has been named one of the Top Ten Interventionists in the United States by quitalcohol.com. Jerry currently serves as Director of Family Education and Leadership Training for Meadows Behavioral Healthcare where he is privileged to support family members while their love one is in treatment. Dr. Law is also nationally known public speaker. Topics include intervention, addiction, marriage and family issues, communication skills, and others. He is a frequent presenter at conferences, treatment facilities, and faith-based organizations.

Chapter 13
Family Involvement in the Treatment of Adolescent Substance Abuse

Whitney Clarahan and Jacob D. Christenson

Chapter Highlights

- The family plays a role in the treatment of adolescent substance abusers and should be included in the treatment process.
- Both the adolescent and the family can benefit from a better understanding of the process of addiction.
- Learning about the neuroscience of addiction can help adolescents and their family members understand why change is difficult with this presenting problem.
- Likewise, the cycle of addiction, when properly understood, provides rich data for designing interventions for adolescent substance abuse.
- Various family-based treatments have been used effectively to treat adolescent substance abuse and should be considered in the design of residential treatment program intervention.

Adolescent substance abuse is increasingly prevalent. This is concerning due to the association between early onset of substance issues and high probability of persistent use in adults (Bertrand et al. 2013). Substance use disorders are progressive diseases that are costly to individuals, families, and communities. There are millions of individuals impacted by the misuse of substances by a relative (Templeton 2009). Addressing these issues early on can prevent a great deal of

W. Clarahan (✉)
Covenant Family Solutions, 3047 Center Point Road NE, Suite B,
Cedar Rapids, IA 52402, USA
e-mail: whitney@covenantfamilysolutions.com

J.D. Christenson
Marriage and Family Therapy Program, Mount Mercy University,
1330 Elmhurst Dr. NE, Cedar Rapids, IA 52402, USA
e-mail: jchristenson@mtmercy.edu

© Springer International Publishing AG 2017   231
J.D. Christenson and A.N. Merritts (eds.), *Family Therapy with Adolescents in Residential Treatment*, Focused Issues in Family Therapy,
DOI 10.1007/978-3-319-51747-6_13

damage in the long-term. During adolescence, peer groups and families are extremely influential. The most effective treatment considers the implication of these relationships and incorporates various domains in which the adolescent participates (National Institute on Drug Abuse 2009). These may include academics, athletics, and employment, among others. Educational functioning is one area that is often impaired by substance use in adolescents. For that reason, guidance counselors at school may be the first point of contact for many youth. The increasing use of technology by teachers and educators allows parents and guardians the opportunity to become better informed of their children's performance. This creates an atmosphere of openness between parents, students, and school professionals. High levels of communication can help to quickly identify academic difficulties resulting from problematic changes in behavior, including drug use. Often it is deemed necessary to provide a referral to an outside specialist. Sometimes the drug use of the adolescent becomes severe enough that inpatient treatment is warranted.

In addition to initially seeking help for the adolescent, family involvement can have a positive effect on the persistence rates of adolescents in treatment. The National Institute on Drug Abuse (2009) identifies dropping out of treatment programs as a major obstacle to tackling addiction. When family members learn how to better communicate with one another it fosters transparency, which leads to the development of trust. One study found that the use of services by parents was correlated with higher self-disclosure and a decline in drug use in adolescents (Bertrand et al. 2013). Learning parenting skills was emphasized as a key factor in supporting adolescents' treatment. Such findings imply that the more involved the parents are in the treatment process, the more substantial the therapeutic gains are. In addition, pressure from family frequently facilitates an individual staying in treatment long enough to take advantage of its full benefits. This is significant because as McWhirter (2008) stated, "Parental perspective can strongly encourage or deter an adolescent's progression through the readiness for change model" (p. 180). Adolescents can fluctuate in their motivation to change their habits and behaviors (see Chap. 14). In addition, Bertrand et al. (2013) stressed, "Empirical evidence shows that various family therapy treatment modalities as well as types of family involvement in the treatment of adolescents are both effective" (p. 29). This may be due, in part, to the family unit beginning to work together in treatment towards mutual welfare.

There are numerous approaches incorporating this idea that are worth considering, and this chapter will discuss and cover four of the more well-known models. As noted below, Chap. 11 in this book also discusses some of the same models, but in that chapter there is a focus on effectiveness in treating conduct disorders. The reader is referred to Chap. 11 for additional information on that particular subject. In this chapter the focus will be on the structure and components of models used to treat adolescent substance abuse. Although it is acknowledged that some of the models discussed herein were specifically developed for use in the community, they can still be adapted and used effectively in residential settings as well. However, before delving into the different models, the first part of the chapter will discuss some of the key concepts that parents and adolescents should understand about addiction.

These concepts are applicable regardless of the model used to treat substance abuse in adolescents and should be deliberately considered in all treatment models. It is our position that an important component missing from all the models described below is direct dissemination of information and education about the nature of addiction. Here we have provided a brief overview of at least two concepts we believe should be integrated into the various treatment models to make them more effective in treating adolescent substance abuse.

The Neuroscience of Addiction

Parents and adolescents often begin the treatment process with little understanding of how addictions develop and what makes them so difficult to combat and overcome. Because of this lack of understanding they often hold beliefs about the addict that are counterproductive to recovery. Among these beliefs might be things like, "He could change if he wanted to, it really isn't that hard." "She should be able to stop cold turkey, that's what my grandfather did." "There's just something wrong with him, if he wasn't so lazy he could overcome this." These types of beliefs ignore the research on the neuroscience of addiction, which elucidates why changing drug related behavior can be so difficult.

What follows is an admittedly simplified discussion of the addicted brain. For those who are interested in a more thorough description, the Institute of Medicine (1997) provides a detailed overview of the neurobiology of addiction. According to Walker (2014) understanding addiction and the brain starts with neurons and neurotransmitters. The neurons are the primary cells of the brain and drive functioning, while neurotransmitters are the chemicals that serve the purpose of communicating across the synapses between neurons. The human brain has billions of neurons and trillions of connections between neurons (Walker 2014). Neurons are grouped together into various structures associate with specific tasks, such as Broca's area (speech) and the prefrontal cortex (complex behaviors, personality).

Walker (2014) and the Institute of Health (1997) point out that the structure most implicated in the addicted brain is the nucleus accumbens, which is one of the structures associated with the *pleasure center* of the brain. All drugs of abuse, as well as a number of addictive behaviors, are associated with a significant influx of dopamine in the nucleus accumbens (Help Guide 2016; Schaefer 2011). This surge of dopamine is self-reinforcing, meaning that the person who experiences it will be motivated to re-experience that feeling. As the nucleus accumbens is flooded with dopamine, the hippocampus creates memories of the pleasurable experience and the amygdala is involved in creating a conditioned response to stimuli associated with drug use (Help Guide 2016).

When these areas of the brain are overloaded on a consistent basis there are also changes in the prefrontal cortex, the area associated with higher level thinking, which leads to drug seeking behaviors that are often inconsistent with the person's values. In this process it is important to consider that the underlying structures linked to addiction (e.g., the nucleus accumbens) are not associated with conscious thought; instead, they are associated with impulses and urges. These impulses and urges push against the higher levels of reasoning associated with the pre-frontal cortex until the addict becomes overwhelmed and gives into drug seeking behavior, as will be described more fully below. In this sense the pleasure center, and associated structures, can be accurately be described as having hijacked the brain of the addict (Help Guide 2016). If the addicted individual were able to change behavior based only on the desires of the prefrontal cortex addictive behaviors would be fairly straightforward to manage. Unfortunately, it is not such a simple undertaking, despite what family members may believe when an adolescent enters treatment. Having a basic knowledge of the way that drugs and alcohol interact with the brain provides a foundation of understanding that can help adolescents and families move away from the belief that character defects or moral flaws are the major contributors to continued substance abuse. This understanding of the addicted brain also sheds light on the addiction cycle, which is considered next.

The Addiction Cycle

The addiction cycle has been written about extensively by those in academics (e.g., Koob and Le Moal 1997, 2005), as well as treatment providers (e.g., Hamrah 2015; Narconon 2016). Though the core components are the same, the terms used and the transition points discussed vary, depending on the person discussing the cycle. What follows is based on the second author's conceptualization of the process through observation of this cycle in his work with those struggling with substance abuse. Although a discrete starting point was chosen for the sake of explanation, it should be noted that those struggling with addiction can be at any place on the cycle in a given moment.

For most addicts, they first become aware of their place on this cycle when they experience a *trigger* (Fig. 13.1). Triggers are those things that bring about thoughts of substance use, most often through one of the senses. For someone who struggles with addiction, almost anything can be a trigger under the right circumstances. They may hear a song that they used to listen to with drug using friends, or pass by an old hangout where they used to get high. Sometimes recognition of a negative internal state is enough to act as a trigger, such as when an addict finds himself or herself feeling sad, angry, lonely, and/or tired. When addicts are reminded of substance use the powerful memories described above may be brought up and become vivid in their mind.

When a trigger takes hold it leads to rumination, which is associated with the activation of the pleasure center of the brain. Once the pleasure center is activated and the addict begins to experience the urge to use they have entered the next stage, *craving*. Craving is a biological process that is uncomfortable for the addict and leads to an internal struggle. When a craving first starts the individual usually will still have a substantial amount ofwillpower available to resist the impulse to use.

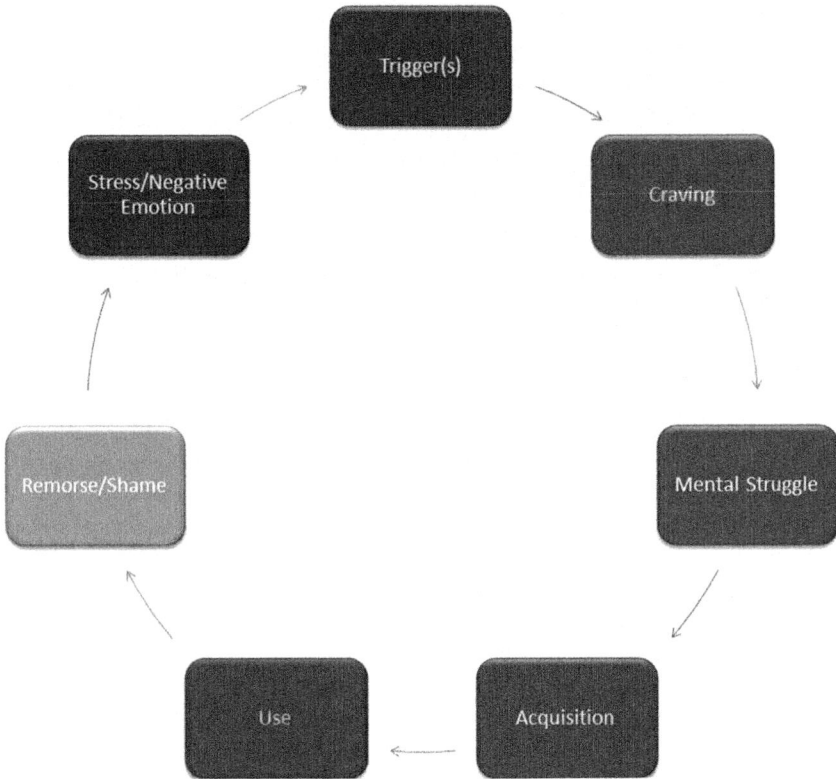

Fig. 13.1 The cycle of addiction

The prefrontal cortex is able to reason that using will lead to long-term pain despite the momentary pleasure. When a craving begins individuals need to make plans to get through it. Since the urge is coming from an area of the brain without conscious thought, it cannot be reasoned with. The addict instead must make plans to block themselves from use and hold on until the craving subsides.

When an addict is not active in managing the craving it will likely build and put more pressure on the prefrontal cortex to acquire a substance or engage in a specific addictive behavior. The *mental struggle* between the part of the person that wants to use and that part that does not becomes intense at this point. Ultimately, the individual becomes aware on some level that they are going to succumb to the urge, which creates a significant internal conflict; the individual knows they should not use, while also knowing that they are probably going to. This dissonance leads to attempts to reconcile the conflicting desires, usually through justification, rationalization, minimization, and denial. Denial is simply refusing to recognize there is a problem. Justification is when a person admits their behavior is incorrect, but sees themselves as having been compelled to participate (e.g., "It was my best friend's wedding, I had to drink"). Minimization occurs when the individual down plays the seriousness of their behavior (e.g., "My wife is overreacting; lots of people use drugs and do just fine"). Finally, a person rationalizes when they tell themselves that the *wrong* thing is actually *right* (e.g., "My doctor said that a glass of wine a day is good for my heart; I'm just trying to stay healthy"). When a person engages in this type of thinking, the ability of the prefrontal cortex to stave off drug use is significantly limited.

Once the decision has been made to use, the individual still has to engage in *acquisition*, meaning that they have to get a hold of a substance or put themselves in a position to engage in an addictive behavior. At this point a person could still make the choice not to use, butwillpower is almost completely absent. The second author of this chapter knew of one individual who was trying to turn her life around who succumbed to a craving and drove three hours to meet her old drug dealer. Clearly, she could have made the choice to turn around, but by that point sobriety was a very low priority. After acquisition comes *use*. Interestingly, early in treatment, when addicts are asked what they could have done to avoid relapse, they identify the moment right before use as the only choice point where they could have stopped.

Although during use there are intense feelings of pleasure, *remorse and shame* quickly come to the forefront when the high subsides. At this point the pleasure center has been satisfied and the prefrontal cortex is able to function properly, which leads to self-recrimination and disgust with oneself. The person's prefrontal cortex might engage in thoughts like, "What is wrong with you; you knew that it was a bad idea. You'll never change; you're a loser." These types of thoughts are intensely unpleasant, so within a short period of time they are often repressed. This leads to the next stage, which is *stressand negative emotions.* Here the underlying distress is ignored and stresses, like what may be experienced at work or home, begin to build. These stresses are compounded by negative emotional states like disappointment, depression, and anxiety. Eventually these build to the point that when the individual encounters a trigger, it has power, which starts the cycle over again.

With this understanding the process of recovery can be conceptually simplified. Basically, individuals who want to recover from substance abuse must fully understand this cycle in their life, and develop methods for countering each stage in the process. Each time the urge to use is successfully resisted the ability to resist the next time is increase. This process is continued until the time between relapse increases to the point that substance use is no longer a significant factor in the person's daily functioning.

As can be seen above in the description of the neuroscience of addiction and the cycle of addiction, there are powerful forces that can keep adolescent substance abusers stuck in their negative behaviors. To compound the issue, adolescents often lack the cognitive sophistication (Dahl 2004) to appreciate the internal forces that make change difficult. Likewise, parents may be stuck in a view of substance abuse/addiction as evidence of character defects or moral flaws. When parents and adolescents do not appreciate the process of addiction there is a tendency for power struggle to develop, which can be detrimental to the recovery process and any family work that is undertaken. On the other hand, when both the family and adolescent understand the information outlined above they are better able to join together in the struggle against addiction. In a sense the addiction becomes the common enemy that both parts of the system can work together against.

Evidence-Based Treatment Approaches

Understanding the neuroscience of addiction and the addiction cycle can serve as a bridge between the individual substance abuse treatment the adolescent receives and the family work that will be described below. It provides a common language that both parents and the adolescent can employ in family therapy. In addition to addressing family dynamics, family work with substance abusing adolescents can aid in the process of developing strategies to help the adolescent respond appropriately in each stage of the cycle of addiction. What follows is a discussion of the major models of intervention, three of which are recognized by the National Institute of Drug Abuse (2009) as useful for adolescent substance abusers. As noted above, it is our position that these types of programs will be enhanced by deliberate incorporation of the addiction related concepts discussed above.

The National Institute of Drug Abuse also recognizes Family Behavior Therapy and Functional Family Therapy as treatments that are appropriate. The reader can find more information about the models not covered in this chapter in the work of Donohue et al. (2009) and Waldron et al. (2005). A fourth model that has been shown to be effective is discussed as well. Families can be supported in a number of ways. According to Templeton (2009), approaches can be divided into three broad classifications. The first targets how to encourage commitment and continuance of abusers in treatment by working with family members. A second approach works jointly with the abuser and family members. A final category entails providing direct support to loved ones. The following is a review of interventions that employ the family system when treating adolescents with substance abuse issues using such methods of engagement.

All of the treatments outlined below would be most effective in short-term community-based residential substance abuse programs for adolescents. These models often require interaction with different systems the adolescent interacts with that are not as accessible in programs located at great distances from the home of the adolescent, such is the case with as Outdoor Behavioral Healthcare programs andtherapeutic boarding schools. Even with close proximity to the adolescent's home, adaptations would need to be made to each of these to make them useful in the residential setting.

Brief Strategic Family Therapy

For some situations, brief treatment may be the most practical option. Templeton (2009) found the development of a structured brief intervention in the United

Kingdom made a considerable contribution to meeting family members' own needs. In addition to efficacy, utilizing a brief method is advantageous because the flexible and adaptable nature makes for a treatment program that is personalized to each unique family. This approach in particular can be used effectively in short-term programs since it is focused on hastening change in the family and the identified patient. Thus, change may be achievable in a shorter amount of time than what may be possible with some of the other models described below.

According to the National Institute of Drug Abuse (2009), Brief Strategic Family Therapy (BSFT) can be applied to an array of settings and modalities, including residential treatment. This approach is one also discussed in Chap. 11 of this book. It may be used as a primary intervention or in a supplementary role with other services. Although BSFT is not solely a residential or day treatment, it can be adapted to use with a wide scope of circumstances and environments. This includes potential use as an aftercare program following residential treatment. The length of treatment is another area in which this approach can be tailored to the specific needs of each family. However, Lindstrom et al. (2015) identified 12–16 sessions as the average duration of treatment.

BSFT focuses on the interaction within families that may reinforce or intensify adolescent substance abuse, in addition to other co-occurring issues. In this approach, the actions of family members (including the substance abusing adolescent) are deemed mutually dependent meaning that the symptoms of any one person reveal, at some level, what else is happening in the family unit (National Institute of Drug Abuse 2009). Lindstrom et al. (2015) outlined three main elements of BFST: joining, diagnosing, and restructuring. The treatment professional's ability to build rapport and form an alliance with each family member, as well as the system as a whole, is central to the process of joining. Diagnosing requires the opportunity to observe familiar patterns of interaction within the family in order to identify characteristics that play a role in challenges with eradicating or diminishing substance abuse issues. Focus is placed primarily on detecting inappropriate alliances, inadequate boundaries, and maladaptive communication styles.

The final component consists of reframing interventions, which are designed to reduce conflict in the family and generate a belief in the possibility for positive change to occur. According to Robbins et al. (2011):

The focus of treatment shifts to implementing restructuring strategies to transform family relations from problematic to effective and mutually supportive, and include (a) directing, redirecting, or blocking communication; (b) shifting family alliances; (c) helping families develop conflict resolution skills; (d) developing effective behavior management skills; and (e) fostering parenting and parental leadership skills. (p. 46)

This technique is appealing not only because it is flexible, but moreover that it centers in on communication patterns within the family that are related to the adolescent's substance abuse. By addressing these dynamics, the patterns can be modified and the relationship strengthened. These are critical elements of a successfully functioning family unit.

Multidimensial Family Therapy

Multidimensial Family Therapy (MDFT) has several delivery options depending on the severity of the substance abuse problem and the functioning level of the family as whole. The level of treatment and setting can vary. One study compared individual Cognitive Behavioral Therapy (CBT) with MDFT. The primary difference between the two was the mode of therapy, individual as opposed to family. Liddle et al. (2008) concluded that MDFT decreased the severity of drug abuse problems more than CBT. MDFT was found to aid in the continuation of changes over time in adolescents treated with this approach. Their results are consistent in that, "treatments involving the family, and focusing upon changing the family environment and parenting practices lead to significant improvement in the youth's substance use problems" (Liddle, et al. 2008).

According to Rowe (2010), MDFT "addresses common root factors underlying a range of emotional and behavioral symptoms that co-occur with adolescent substance abuse, most importantly family relationship factors, parenting practices, family conflict and communication, and parental substance abuse" (p. 4). Both the adolescents and their patents acquire a multitude of skills. Liddle et al. (2008) described MDFT treatment domains: "At various points throughout treatment therapists meet alone with the adolescent, alone with the parent(s), or with the adolescent and parent(s) together, depending upon the specific problem being addressed" (p. 1663). As noted above, this implies that the family be readily available for sessions, which can be a challenge when adolescents are in residential treatment. The notion that adolescents are greatly influenced by their support network is a key factor in the structure of treatment.

Multisystemic Therapy

A behavioral intervention that has demonstrated effectiveness in treating addiction in adolescents is Multisystemic Therapy (MST). Chapter 11 contains additional information about the effectiveness of this approach. The first step in MST is involving the family, which supports the notion that factors pertaining to the family and environment need to be addressed when treating adolescents who abuse substances. According to Swenson et al. (2005), "Engagement is a necessary, but not sufficient, condition for achieving clinical outcomes" (p. 47). This not only allows therapy to start but to progress as well.

There are no predetermined techniques used in MST. Instead, goals are established in consultation with the family members. MST looks closely at family features such as conflict, discipline, and parental substance abuse. When feasible, the caregivers are the ones presenting the interventions to the adolescents in this model (Swenson et al. 2005). This can be an intensive treatment intervention occurring in organic settings such as home and school (National Institute on Drug Abuse (2009), or in residential settings where there is ready access to family members. As a result of the rigorous nature, most participants complete a full course of treatment. The National Institute on Drug Abuse (2009) stated MST "significantly reduces adolescent drug use during treatment and for at least 6 months after treatment" (p. 57). Given the heavy reliance on parent participation and community involvement, this model can be particularly challenging to adapt for use in residential settings; however, the principles used in this type of treatment can guide the development of interventions, even for those separated from their families.

Multiple Family Group Therapy

Multiple Family Group Therapy educates families on how to successfully communicate without blaming or avoiding one another. The environment is a key component as it is non-judgmental in nature due to families being surrounded by other families in distress. The group process can be instrumental in helping loved ones gain a better understanding of substance abuse (see Chap. 16). This can lead to an increased level of empathy and the start of reconciling among family members.

This model also has been modified for use in residential settings (see Chap. 11). One residential therapeutic program developed some strategies to involve families, such as inviting members of the client to the assessment interview and placing emphasis on the participation of family as an element of treatment (Schaefer 2008). "Denial and rationalization are defense mechanisms that stop the family system from changing. One aim of the MFG is to break through these defense mechanisms in order to create an opening for change" (Schafer 2008, p. 93), and this is done through mutual support from the group.

Schaefer (2008) found an advantage of MFGT is that it addresses how members of the family act in response to conflict. Furthermore, it may assist with the gradual reduction of conflict behaviors that are damaging such as "passive aggressive communication, verbal abuse, and conflict withdrawal" (p. 21). In addition to healthier communication patterns, MFGT has been shown to assist with establishing appropriate boundaries and facilitate a higher degree of closeness between substance abusers and their family members (Schaefer 2008).

Conclusion

Many of the therapy approaches examined were discovered to eliminate or reduce substance use at termination of treatment as well as upon follow-up. Parents and other family members often highly motivate this population to enter and remain in treatment. McWhirter (2008) highlighted the importance of educating siblings, in addition to parents, based on the link between older children using and younger siblings following in their footsteps. While not all people who use substances become abusers, the chances of developing a substance use disorder are significantly influenced by genetics. Numerous studies reveal that addiction runs in families. Other factors that contribute to the risk include one's environment. For loved ones, untreated substance-related disorders may have a traumatizing effect on both youth and adults. This leads to a host of problems including relationship difficulties among family members, which can be addressed through family-based treatment.

Additionally, family members are vulnerable to developing high levels of stress when there is an active addiction present. Living in a family affected by substance abuse, many find it difficult to cope with the stress and chaos that can accompany these disorders. It is not uncommon for traditional rituals and routines to be disrupted by the substance-related behavior. Therefore, it is often the case that each person in the family unit can benefit from the support that treatment provides. It is clear that whether an adolescent actively participates in treatment largely depends on the level of support from loved ones. Treatment incorporating family generates long-term gains for adolescents. This process is aided by providing information to the family about the neuroscience of addiction and the addiction cycle. By attending a structured family or group program, family members themselves can exhibit positive change (Templeton 2009). This may lead to healthy boundaries and constructive modeling. By integrating family into substance abuse treatment, each member has the potential to gain.

References

Bertrand, K., Richer, I., Brunelle, N., Beaudoin, I., Lemieux, A., & Menard, J.-M. (2013). Substance abuse treatment for adolescents: How are family factors related to substance use change? *Journal of Psychoactive Drugs, 45*(1), 28–38.

Dahl, R. E. (2004). Adolescent brain development: A period of vulnerabilities and opportunities, keynote address. *Annals of the New York Academy of Sciences, 1021*(1), 1–22.

Donohue, B., Allen, D. A., & Lapota, H. (2009). Family behavior therapy. In D. Springer & A. Rubin (Eds.), *Substance abuse treatment for youth and adults*. New York: John Wiley & Sons Inc.

Hamrah. (2015). *The addiction cycle*. Retrieved from: http://hamrah.co/en/pages/addiction-cycle/

Help Guide. (2016). *Understanding addiction: How addiction Hijacks the brain*. Retrieved from: http://www.helpguide.org/harvard/how-addiction-hijacks-the-brain.htm

Institute of Medicine. (1997). *Dispelling the myths about addiction: Strategies to increase understanding and strengthen research*. Washington, DC: National Academies Press.

Koob, G. F., & Le Moal, M. (1997). Drug abuse: Hedonic homeostatic dysregulation. *Science, 278* (5335), 52–58.

Koob, G. F., & Le Moal, M. (2005). Plasticity of reward neurocircuitry and the "dark side" of drug addiction. *Nature Neuroscience, 8*(11), 1442–1444.

Liddle, H. A., Dakof, G. A., Turner, R. M., Henderson, C. E., & Greenbaum, P. E. (2008). Treating adolescent drug abuse: A randomized trial comparing multidimensional family therapy and cognitive behavioral therapy. *Society for the Study of Addiction, 103*, 1660–1670.

Lindstrom, M., Filges, T., & Klint Jorgensen, A.-M. (2015). Brief strategic family therapy for young people in treatment for drug use. *Research on Social Work Practice, 25*(1), 61–80.

McWhirter, P. T. (2008). Enhancing adolescent substance abuse treatment engagement. *Journal of Psychoactive Drugs, 40*(2), 173–182.

Narconon. (2016). *The vicious cycle of addiction*. Retrieved from: http://www.narconon.org/blog/drug-addiction/vicious-cycle-addiction/

National Institute on Drug Abuse. (2009). *Principles of drug addiction treatment: A Research-based guide*. Washington, DC: National Institute of Health.

Robbins, M., Feaster, D., Horigian, V., Puccinelli, M., Henderson, C., & Szapocznik, J. (2011). Therapist adherence in brief strategic family therapy for adolescent drug abusers. *Journal of Consulting and Clinical Psychology, 79*(1), 43–53.

Rowe, C. L. (2010). Multidimensional family therapy: Addressing co-occurring substance abuse and other problems among adolescents with comprehensive family-based treatment. *Child and Adolescent Psychiatric Clinics of North America, 19*(3), 563–576.

Schaefer, G. (2008). Multiple family group therapy in a drug and alcohol rehabilitation centre. *Australian and New Zealand Journal of Family Therapy, 29*(1), 17–24.

Schafer, G. (2008). Multiple family group therapy in a drug and alcohol rehabilitation centre: Residents' experiences. *Australian and New Zealand Journal of Family Therapy, 29*(2), 88–96.

Shaffer, H. J. (2011). *Overcoming addiction: Paths toward recovery*. Boston: Harvard Health Publications. Retrieved from: http://www.health.harvard.edu/special-health-reports/overcoming-addiction-paths-toward-recovery

Swenson, C. C., Henggeler, S. W., Taylor, I. S., & Addison, O. W. (2005). *Multisystemic therapy and neighborhood partnerships: Reducing adolescent violence and substance abuse*. New York: The Guilford Press.

Templeton, L. (2009). Use of a structured brief intervention in a group setting for family members living with substance misuse. *Journal of Substance Use, 14*(3–4), 211–220.

Waldron, H. B., Turner, C. W., & Ozechowski, T. J. (2005). Profiles of drug use behavior change for adolescents in treatment. *Addictive Behaviors, 30*(9), 1775–1796.

Walker, R. (2014). *The neuroscience of addiction* [*Power point slides*]. Retrieved from http://www.cdar.uky.edu/robertwalker/downloads/Neuroscience%20of%20Addiction%20%20Complete%20Sept%202014.pdf

Author Biographies

Whitney Clarahan, MA, LMHC, NCC, CADC is currently working as a Licensed Mental Health Counselor at Covenant Family Solutions, a private group practice in Cedar Rapids, Iowa. Whitney is well-versed in client issues that range from anxiety and depression to trauma and substance abuse. Whitney is passionate about helping others to identify and reach their goals. She received her Bachelor of Art in Psychology from the University of Iowa and her Master's in Mental Health Counseling from the University of Northern Iowa. Whitney has extensive experience in working with substance abuse issues and is a Certified Drug and Alcohol Counselor. She is also certified by the National Board for Certified Counselors.

Jacob D. Christenson, Ph.D., LMFT is an assistant professor of marriage and family therapy at Mount Mercy University. Dr. Christenson received his Bachelor degree in Psychology from California Polytechnic State University. He then completed his Master's degree and doctorate in Marriage and Family Therapy from Brigham Young University. Before coming to Mount Mercy University Dr. Christenson worked for four years at Aspen Achievement Academy in Loa, UT as a Field Therapist. As a Field Therapist, Dr. Christenson experienced firsthand the challenge of being a systemic marriage and family therapist in the world of residential care.

Over the course of his career Dr. Christenson has consistently been involved in academic research and publication. In addition to numerous presentations at national and international conferences, Dr. Christenson has published a number of articles in peer-reviewed journals such as the Journal of Marital and Family Therapy, Contemporary Family Therapy, and the American Journal of Family Therapy. Dr. Christenson also serves as an editorial board member for the Journal of Marital and Family Therapy and Contemporary Family Therapy.

Dr. Christenson teaches a number of course at Mount Mercy University. The courses he's taught have included, Parents and Children, Micro-counseling, Medical Family Therapy, and Research Methods. Dr. Christenson is also an AAMFT Approved Supervisor, which has enabled him to provide supervision in practicum courses. Dr. Christenson also serves as the Clinical Director for the Gerald and Audrey Olson Marriage and Family Therapy Clinic, which is attached to the marriage and family therapy program at Mount Mercy University. In addition to his work as a professor, Dr. Christenson provides therapy in private practice and is the founder of Covenant Family Solutions, an outpatient therapy group practice in Cedar Rapids, Iowa. When not working, Dr. Christenson enjoys spending time with his family and being active in his community.

Chapter 14
Readiness for Change Within the Family and the Identified Patient

Amber L. Runkel, Jacob D. Christenson, Amanda P. Glunz and Katherine F. Cobb

Chapter Highlights

- Adolescents in residential settings have multiple risk factors and tend to carry negative behaviors with them into treatment.
- An examination of underlying psychosocial factors related to family functioning prior to discharge is important.
- Positive outcomes are associated with increased family involvement.
- The Transtheoretical model, or the Stages of Change model, can be applied to increase engagement in treatment.
- Barriers that inhibit the effective application of the Stages of Change model should be considered as well.

Many researchers agree that adolescence is a considerably challenging and critical period of human development (Buist et al. 2004; Coll et al. 2010). Daniels (1990) stated that this transition appears to be more complicated when adolescents are disconnected from their family. However, youth who exhibit psychopathology

A.L. Runkel (✉)
Sampson Family Therapy Services, LLC, 309 Court Ave., Suite 241,
Des Moines, IA 50309, USA
e-mail: amberm1171@gmail.com

J.D. Christenson · K.F. Cobb
Mount Mercy University, 1330 Elmhurst Dr. NE, Cedar Rapids
IA 52402, USA
e-mail: jchristenson@mtmercy.edu

K.F. Cobb
e-mail: kcobb3118@mustangs.mtmercy.edu

A.P. Glunz
Child Guidance Center, 5776 St. Augustine Rd., Jacksonville, FL 32207, USA
e-mail: aglunz@childguidancecenter.org

© Springer International Publishing AG 2017
J.D. Christenson and A.N. Merritts (eds.), *Family Therapy with Adolescents in Residential Treatment*, Focused Issues in Family Therapy,
DOI 10.1007/978-3-319-51747-6_14

and high-risk behavior are often referred for individual inpatient treatment (Coll et al. 2010). Rosen (1998) explains that residential treatment can provide adolescents a steady, nurturing environment with predictable, persistent expectations that are designed to help produce desirable behaviors and emotional regulation. Nevertheless, it is important to consider how to increase the family's involvement when the adolescent is placed in residential care given the importance of family in the life of a youth.

Adolescents in residential treatment can be a difficult population due to their extreme behaviors and systemic entanglements (Riley et al. 2004). Researchers have identified characteristics such as chaotic behavior, poor impulse control, proneness to harm others, destruction of property, and use of physical threats as those that precede an adolescent being placed in a residential program (Whitaker et al. 1998). Such adolescents have often been exposed to multiple risk factors, such as chronic stress and a chaotic family environment, and tend to carry associated negative behaviors with them into treatment (Green et al. 2001; Zegers et al. 2008). As participating members of a dynamic family system, adolescents' emotional experiences are highly correlated to environmental interactions (McCurdy and McIntyre 2004). Upon discharge from residential treatment the adolescent will often return to their previous environment; therefore, it is important to examine underlying psychosocial factors related to family functioning (e.g., trust and validation) (Coll et al. 2010).

In terms of residential program effectiveness, regardless of gains made during the treatment process, the greatest impact on long-term adjustment is realized when (a) the program is congruent with the post-discharge environment (i.e., the home life of the adolescent); and (b) has continued involvement with the biological family, regardless of placement setting (Whittaker and Maluccio 1989). The importance of family involvement in residential treatment has long been recognized in the literature (e.g., Whittaker 1979; Williamson and Gray 2011). Family involvement has been related to greater satisfaction with residential treatment in adolescents (Palareti and Berti 2010). Additionally, extensive family involvement has been associated with behavioral and academic improvement (Prentice-Dunn et al. 1981), accomplishing a higher percentage of treatment goals (Stage 1999), and maintaining gains after discharge (Hair 2005). Of the numerous variables studied in Stage's (1999) article, only family therapy predicted successful discharge to a less restrictive setting.

Parents are in unique position to help their families considering they have exclusive knowledge of their family's values, overall lifestyle, resources, and available support systems (Collins and Collins 1990; Singh et al. 2000). It is often family members who aid in carrying out interventions; therefore, the family must be collaboratively involved with the treatment team throughout the treatment process (Singh et al. 2000). This chapter seeks to illustrate ways to increase the adolescent's and family's readiness for change and improve family engagement in residential treatment using the lens of the Stages of Change model.

Foundations for Successful Treatment

Adolescents usually enter residential treatment unwilling to change and typically view their parents, their school, and their environment as the problem while seeing themselves as the victim (Fitzgerald 1994). Adolescents in residential treatment typically present with issues related to trust and intimacy and may display aggressive and dangerous behaviors (Sewell and Mendelsohn 2000), which can result in the treatment team emphasizing power or control over youth (Baker et al. 2007; Fitzgerald 1994). However, it is generally recommended that the treatment team focus less on control and more on healing attachment wounds at an individual and family level (McWey 2004).

Similarly, most parents enroll their youth in residential treatment with the mentality that their child is the problem and needs an *attitude adjustment*. Harper and Russell (2008) interviewed 14 families to study the decision making -process. Prior to treatment, most families viewed their circumstances as untenable. "The child's behavior had become the dominant concern in the household and parents believed they may lose their child to substance abuse, mental health issues, criminal or reckless behavior" (Harper and Russell 2008, p. 27). A common theme Harper and Russell found was that most parents felt as if a residential program was their final option. Harper and Russell stated that treatment teams should reconsider the balance of their treatment strategies between youth and families, because families will be better served by increased contact and participation in treatment. It is interesting to note that in Harper and Russell's study no themes reflected the parents recognizing their part in the maintenance of the problem.

As mentioned previously, troubled youth may have experienced and been impacted by familial ordeals. Research has shown when parents are emotionally invalidating, youth have more difficulty regulating their own emotions (Gottman and Katz 2002) and are more likely to learn problematic ways of regulating (Aldo et al. 2010). When parents demonstrate warm and accepting responses to both positive and negative expression of emotions youth are more likely to develop an understanding of their emotional experience, accurately express emotions, regulate emotional reactions, and comply with parental directions (Shenk and Fruzzetti 2014). For these reasons (and others) family involvement is a key element in generating successful outcomes for adolescents in treatment (Singh et al. 2000).

Along with family involvement, the therapeutic alliance is regarded as one of the most important components related to successful treatment outcomes (Lamers and Vermeiren 2014; Shirk et al. 2011). For example, Singh et al. (2000) found that the introduction (i.e., the first set of exchanges between the treatment team and family members) sets the tone for the entire treatment process. A highly benevolent introduction allows the team to build a warm and positive rapport with the family and allows a therapeutic alliance between the family and adolescent to develop (Singh et al. 2000). Hougaard (1994) defines therapeutic alliance as consisting of two components: (a) a personal alliance that is based on interpersonal aspects; and (b) task alliance that is based on an agreement on diagnoses, goals, and treatment planning. A positive therapeutic alliance increases the probability of making progress during the adolescent's residential treatment (Gross and Goldin 2008). In addition, Kazdin et al. (2006) demonstrated that parental alliance with the therapist is correlated with improved parenting skills, greater therapeutic change with the adolescent, and more treatment attendance and retention.

It is widely believed that adolescents with high-risk behavior can benefit from timely and structured residential treatment. The challenge for practitioners is to develop residential treatment that is flexible enough to systemically nurture and support, rather than narrowly or linearly treat troubled adolescents (Small et al. 1991). It is essential for the treatment team to be prepared to meet these adolescents and families where they are at while also motivating them to move toward a more productive stance. By using the Stages of Change model as a framework for intervention (Prochaska et al. 1994), the treatment team can build rapport and better understand where the adolescent and family are at and help them find and maintain the motivation to change mutually destructive behavior.

Readiness for Change

Motivation has received increased attention across therapeutic approaches, seemingly because clients' motivation is a key for treatment effectiveness (Ryan et al. 2011). This is especially important for engagement of families of adolescents in residential treatment (Singh et al. 2000). Coll et al. (2010) found "adolescents who reported low levels of family engagement were also more likely to describe their families as rigid or inflexible…[and this] was significantly related to lower levels of psychosocial functioning with regard to trust and intimacy" (p. 259). Many of the families that place youth in residential treatment feel depleted or paralyzed and struggle with an enormity of family problems that come with raising an oppositional adolescent (Riley et al. 2004). Often the family's low motivation to engage in treatment needs to be resolved in order to move forward and restore stability (Mirkin et al. 1984).

Improved adolescent readiness to change increases their willingness to be engaged in treatment activities, establish a relationship with their treatment team, increase their ability to acknowledge the problem (as well as accept some responsibility), and express a level of commitment to working on the problem (Englebrecht et al. 2008). The adolescents' engagement represents an interrelated set of attitudinal, relational, and behavioral qualities of the adolescent (Yatchmenoff 2005). With respect to behavioral change, it is closely related to concepts such as building rapport, motivation, a working alliance, and compliance (Littell and Tajima 2000). The research literature supports engagement (including motivation for change, therapeutic alliance, and participation in treatment) as a necessary element to achieve treatment success and behavioral change (Coll et al. 2010; Cunningham et al. 2009; Gross and Goldin 2008; Littell and Tajima 2000; Ryan et al. 2011).

It is important to note that clients' motivation for change exists along a continuum of readiness and progresses through stages. In addition, relapse is an expected event that demonstrates dysfunctional patterns can still emerge and families may not progress linearly through stages. "The expectation of a 'cure' in residential treatment implies lack of continuity between preresidential and postresidential environments…A realistic appraisal of the long-term needs of these children and their families will serve them better than wishful expectations of dramatic transformation" (Small et al. 1991, p. 336).

Prochaska et al. (1994) developed one of the most recognized models of change known as the Transtheoretical model, or the Stages of Change model, which is a biopsychosocial model conceptualizing the process of intentional behavior change. These authors identified and defined six stages clients move through with regard to readiness for change. It is through movement along these stages that individuals are able to achieve successful behavioral change (DiClemente and Prochaska 1998). This model can also be quite useful to determine the strategies necessary to support the client's movement through change toward the desired state or behavior.

Several strategies are important to remember when using the Stages of Change model. If the therapist attempts to advance the adolescent and family faster than they are ready, the therapeutic alliance may disintegrate (Miller and Rollnick 2002; Prochaska et al. 1993). Treatment noncompliance can easily result if a therapist attempts to enhance motivation using strategies from a stage other than the current stage of the adolescent or family (Miller and Rollnick 1991). Miller and Rollnick, the creators of motivational interviewing, note that the shaping of client language has been implicated as a causal mechanism that assists in creating readiness for change. It is important for therapists using Prochaska's model to recognize that the stage is related to the specific issue; a client may be at several different stages for several different issues (Steele 2011), which requires flexibility on the part of the therapist.

What follows is a description of each stage in Prochaska's model, along with some of the methods for working with adolescents and families who present in a particular stage (Prochaska et al. 1994). If resistance is encountered at any stage, the therapist must avoid direct confrontation because it will most likely elicit counterproductive defensiveness or further resistance (Britt et al. 2003). Instead, it is recommended that the therapist acknowledge it and hold a curious stance about the resistance. Much of the discussion that follows regarding the specific stages is a combination of the authors own experience and the work of DiClemente and Prochaska (1998), Prochaska et al. (1993), (1994), and Miller and Rollick (1991), (2002).

Precontemplation

When first arriving at residential treatment, the adolescent and family members will most likely be in precontemplation, the first stage in the Stages of Change model. When individuals are in this stage they do not see themselves as part of the problem or solution and are often characterized as resistant and unmotivated. Individuals in precontemplation are unaware of or unwilling to see their part in the problem, expect others to change and have no intention of changing themselves. Often times parents will say, "I don't have the problem, it's all my kid's fault." People in this stage regularly feel that the situation is hopeless. Other indications of this stage include argumentative behavior, interrupting, denial, or ignoring, as well as, avoiding reading, talking, or thinking about the problem.

As noted above, the first set of exchanges between the treatment team and family members sets the tone for the entire treatment process. Building a high quality therapeutic alliance with the adolescent and family will not only enable the treatment team to be more sensitive and compassionate toward a family, but also help family members feel safe enough to express their needs and increase engagement (Alexander and Dore 1999). According to Cunningham et al. (2009), engagement consists of three interrelated factors: (a) client attitudes, (b) client-therapist affective relationship, and (c) client behavioral changes. Only once a family is engaged in the therapeutic process is it safe to gently unbalance the family system and restructure the rules and boundaries that are sustaining the problem (Minuchin 1974; Springer and Orsbon 2002).

During the precontemplation stage, it is important for the therapist to model a curious stance and ask for permission to determine why the adolescent and family have decided on residential treatment. It is important to acknowledge, accept, and normalize the adolescent's and family's thoughts, feelings, fears, and concerns. The practitioner can also help by providing information about the risks and benefits, or pros and cons, of changing their behavior (Rivers et al. 2008). At this point in treatment, the therapist aims to develop discrepancy by helping the adolescent explore the incongruity between their current behavior and the desired outcome or goals (Miller and Rollnick 2012). Miller and Rollnick explain that once this discrepancy is perceived, the adolescent can begin to move toward change. It may also be useful to introduce ambivalence about *recovery* during treatment. For example, explain why it might be a good idea to be present and active during treatment (e.g., to facilitate discharge). Therapists should provide information on the mental health service delivery system and on how parental involvement is an important component for adolescent treatment in the residential setting. Increased knowledge aids in parental empowerment, parent-treatment team collaboration, and enhances the quality of services in residential treatment (Collins and Collins 1990; Curtis and Singh 1996).

In terms of helping parents and adolescents to successfully navigate this stage, it can often be useful to take an indirect approach. In the spirit of strategic intervention, bibliotherapy can be a particularly powerful tool (Heath et al. 2005; Riordan and Wilson 1989) during this stage, especially when integrated with Minuchin and Fishman's (1981) concept of *universal symbols* and Miller and Rollnick's (2012) description of *rolling with resistance*. Minuchin and Fishman argued that therapists can make use of things that *everybody knows* to challenge client's constructions, and Miller and Rollnick encourage providers to avoid directly opposing resistance.

As an example, a bibliotherapy tool that may help in creating motivation is the book *The Anatomy of Peace* by the Arbinger Institute (2015). This book was written to help people soften their interactional position in relation to others and provides specific instruction and tools intended to accomplish this objective. Asking parents to read this text as a means of staying abreast of what their adolescent is learning in the program may be useful in creating motivation for change and parents can be told that the information contained in the book is helpful for anybody. By framing the invitation in this nonthreatening manner, the parents' resistance is bypassed and they may be more likely to act on the recommendation. However, the intended result is for the parents to begin to see themselves in the content as they review the material and begin to incorporate the information into new ways of thinking and behaving.

The same message can also be delivered to the adolescent via an assignment to read the same book his or her parents are reading. Additionally, adolescents can be invited to read books that are focused more on intrapsychic issues. One example of a book that is useful for this purpose is *The Four Agreements* by Ruiz and Mills (2010). This book provides a description of the way distress begins in a person's life and how they can recover and adopt more healthy ways of being. The book is popular with a wide range of people and can be framed as useful even for those with no mental health issues. Even though the principles are outlined in an informal manner, there are close parallels with Cognitive Behavior Therapy. It is useful to then highlight these parallels in a more clinical manner as a means of introducing the need for treatment. Again, it should be noted that when the direct relationship between the concepts in the book and treatment is broached, the therapist should be prepared to roll with resistance if the adolescent is not yet ready to evaluate the need to apply the content.

Another book that can be useful in this process is *Addictive Thinking* by Twerski (1997). Twerski sets out to explore and explain the thinking patterns of those struggling with addiction. However, he does so in a descriptive manner instead of assuming that the individual already identifies as an addict. The therapist can frame this book as an assignment to learn more about addictions with the intent that as the adolescent reads the book he or she will begin to identify with the thinking patterns Twerski outlines. By taking an indirect approach and framing the task as something that is useful for the general population, therapists can facilitate recognition of the problem and encourage the parents and adolescents to move toward the next stage in the model.

A number of chapters in this book complement the information provided above. For example, in Chap. 9 Bolt addresses the precontemplation stage as it relates to wilderness therapy for both the adolescent and parents. For adolescents, Bolt describes that, generally speaking, the act of being sent to a wilderness therapy program by itself can be useful for increasing the awareness that there is a problem. Similarly, in Chap. 15 Tucker, Widmer, Faddis, Randolph, and Gass explain that outdoor behavioral healthcare programs provide a novel environment and require a dramatic change in lifestyle and living conditions, which can initiate processes leading to feelings of hope. Bolt also notes that reading impact letters from family members (see Chap. 2) and daily feedback from peers and the treatment team (e.g., therapists and field staff) can help move an individual out of precontemplation. In regards to parents, Bolt focuses more on where a family's readiness for change can be addressed. In addition to bibliotherapy (as described above), she indicates that weekly phone calls with the wilderness therapist, weekly homework assignments, journaling, watching webinars, and attending parent or family workshops (see Chap. 17) can all be used to work with family members who present in the pre-contemplation stage. During these types of activities family therapists can facilitate hope for change by helping parents move from blaming and justifying to supportive communication. All of these efforts, ideally, move the adolescent and family to an acknowledgment that a problem exists, and therefore toward the next stage of the model.

Contemplation

The second stage in the model is called the contemplation stage. During this stage, individuals may start to acknowledge the existence of a problem and their part in it; however, the individual may still be ambivalent or uncertain regarding a change in behavior. It is important for the therapist to normalize the ambivalence the adolescent and/or the family may feel toward changing behavior. Individuals in this stage may be stalling or waiting for a *sign* to change. Possible indicators of this stage include the adolescent and family meeting the treatment team half way and a willingness to look at pros and cons of changing their behaviors.

During this stage, individuals are traditionally characterized as heedless and time intensive. If the therapist feels frustrated that they are the only one taking re-sponsibility or feeling motivated toward change, it is imperative to acknowledge these feelings, since they may lead to negative or judgmental cognitions or feelings of resentment toward the adolescent and family (Gross and Goldin 2008). If ignored these thoughts and feelings may accumulate and threaten the therapeutic alliance resulting in feeling *stuck* in the treatment process. Many who have worked with adolescents in residential treatment acknowledge the patience this kind of work takes and stress the importance of revealing their frustrations rather than sup-pressing them out of shame or embarrassment (Gross and Goldin 2008).

It may also be helpful during this stage to revisit, discuss, and weigh the pros and cons of a change in behavior (Rivers et al. 2008). In fact, it is sometimes helpful to have the adolescent write out a list of reasons not to change as a way of normalizing their ambivalence (Ryan et al. 2011). Although this seems counterintuitive, this intervention serves two purposes. First, it is consistent with the principle of au-tonomy (Ryan et al. 2011), meaning that clients should be given the option of not changing. Second, this intervention will occasionally produce a paradoxical effect in which the adolescent will recognize that the benefits of the negative behavior are less significant than they had previously thought (Rivers et al. 2008). Listing the so-called benefits may also help illuminate the negative consequences that follow.

As the adolescent becomes more aware of the drawbacks of their behavior, the recognition of the need to change may increase.

Helping adolescents move through the contemplation stage is a crucial task in residential programs, especially in short-term programs whose primary purpose may be preparing adolescents for follow-on services. In Chap. 9 of this book Bolt makes an argument that supports the content in this chapter. She argues that interventions in this stage can be designed to foster readiness and motivation for change by helping adolescents discover how they are living incongruently with their personal core values. Bolt indicates that when adolescents lack an awareness of this type of discrepancy it can perpetuate a shame cycle. In order to uncover this discrepancy, therapist will need to capitalize on a strong therapeutic alliance and ask probing questions that uncover the adolescent's core values. This type of conversation can sometimes be facilitated by asking the adolescents about what kind of person they would like to be in 5 years. This preferred self can then be contrasted with current behaviors.

Despite the utility of specific interventions designed to create forward movement, therapists need to emphasize and empower the adolescent's and family's free choice, responsibility, and accountability of the problem. Singh (1995) defined adolescent empowerment as "a process by which families access knowledge, skills, and resources that enable them to gain positive control on their own lives as well as to improve the quality of their lifestyles" (p. 13). During this stage, the goal of the therapist is to reduce fear of change, as well as elicit self-motivational statements of intent and commitment to change. The therapist may also prompt the adolescent or parents to elaborate on their own perceived self-efficacy, times when they were successful in changing, and expectations regarding treatment (Ryan et al. 2011). These conversations will highlight strengths that can be utilized to help motivate change. The therapist may choose to ask questions that clarify each family member's motivation (e.g., what is important to them and why) or discuss each family members' goals in life and how changing behavior can affect those goals.

In Chaps. 3 and 16 of this book the use of Narrative Therapy is discussed as a way to help adolescents and families deconstruct their problem-saturated stories and externalize the problem to reduce the fear of change. In such an effort, therapists can prompt the adolescent and family to elaborate on times when they were successful at change, and the therapist can utilize these exceptions to the problem to develop thickened narratives that support a client's move toward preparation. Once these new effective narratives are developed, they can be documented (e.g., with letters, certificates, recordings, and artwork) in ways that solidifies the new story (Carr 1998), which aids the treatment process during the stages of change that follow.

Preparation

The third stage in the Stages of Change model is called preparation, which involves getting ready to make changes. During this stage, individuals shift from thinking about behavior change to planning the first steps to change. Indicators of this stage include individuals asking questions, weighing options, and exhibiting openness to a change in behavior. Traditionally, individuals in this stage are characterized as compliant, *coming along*, and *good to work with*. Once a family has reached the preparation stage they are ready to receive and respond to interventions commonly used in therapy.

For example, through role plays family members can probe their relational experiences and discover their primary emotions, as well as strengths and deficits. Role plays can assist adolescents and the family with developing the capacity to experience one's feelings while simultaneously reflecting on their meaning (Fonagy and Target 2006). As an example, Lochman and colleagues (Lochman et al. 1984; Lochman 1992) developed The Angry Coping Program which uses role-playing, peer interaction, and goal-setting to: (a) model speaking an individual's *truth* or perspective as well as problem solving skills; (b) increase awareness of the physiological signs of anger; and (c) increase the range of strategies family members use to deal with conflictual situations. Role plays are often directly contrasted with previous experiences, where one's needs have been misinterpreted, invalidated, or punished, and therefore allow families to explore primary emotions that may be painful and anxiety-provoking (Young et al. 2003).

In order to have productive role plays it may be helpful for the therapist to teach effective communication skills so family members learn to accept what the other person is saying and integrate new information. Discussing examples of when one family member's state of mind was misinterpreted by another family member can often lead to an understanding about misunderstandings between two people. Studies have demonstrated that adolescents benefit from sensitive parenting (i.e., warmth and acceptance), accurate communication, predictability, and the encouragement of autonomy while cultivating supervision (Riggs et al. 2007).

During this stage, it is especially important that the therapist act as a trusted and secure base for family members by affirming and validating their emotions in order to increase their confidence. It is imperative during this stage to support the family's efforts to change, acknowledge the difficulties the adolescent and family overcame in the previous stages, and encourage them to commit to action. During this stage, it is helpful to create a plan of action with the family based on their history and willingness while allowing the family to make decisions. It would also be beneficial for the therapist to clarify goals, identify strategies, and give a clear and consistent message about change with family members.

Action

The fourth stage in the model is called the action stage. During this time, the individual and family actively try to solve the problem, change the environment, and demonstrate steps toward change that lead to positive outcomes. An indicator of this stage is when the individual is receptive to clinical interventions, and treatment compliance is considered normal. Traditionally, clients during this stage are characterized as successful and willing to work with the program. It is important to note that if the individual feels change has failed, cycling back to earlier stages is to be expected, and the therapist should be mindful of the indicators mentioned above for each stage. It may be useful to explain to family members the possibility of a set back and identify risky situations, triggers, and coping strategies that can be used for each.

To be most effective in creating change in their environment, family members should focus on the reinforcement of positive and prosocial behavior (e.g., volunteering to help, completing chores without being asked, following directions, etc.) (Sugai and Horner 2008). During this stage, it is useful to seek commitment to specific behavioral change at each session, as well as to continue to help the adolescent and family identify new methods of reinforcement. In accordance with acting as the safe haven and secure base for the family, the therapist should acknowledge each individual's difficulties, support perseverance despite those difficulties, and affirm even minimal progress. It should be remembered that although the adolescent and family are actively taking steps to change, they have not yet reached a stable state as a cohesive family unit.

Maintenance and Termination

The two last stages of the model are called maintenance and termination. Indicators that the family has entered these stages include when family members are able to sustain treatment goals, have made behavior changes, and practice healthy coping strategies without significant therapeutic support. Once adolescents and the family reach maintenance and termination they have achieved their initial individual and familial goals, such as expressing validation and support toward positive or negative emotional expression, and are now working to maintain gains. Traditionally, individuals during these stages are characterized as *no longer needing treatment*. Therapeutic tools to use during this stage consist of showing support and affirmation for the change in behavior. The maintenance stage involves reviewing and affirming personal growth made during the treatment process as well as long-term goals. Prior to termination, it is useful to rehearse new coping strategies and countermeasures to triggers.

Zimmerman et al. (2000) state that this stage is where clients begin to seek social feedback about the value of their improved behavior. If clients are approached with negative feedback about the changes made, the chances of *slipping* back into old behavioral habits are high. During this stage, it may be beneficial to *predict relapse* in order to increase the ability to anticipate and cope with relapse. "A relapse is viewed as a *transitional process*, a series of events that may or may not be followed by a return to pretreatment baseline levels of the target behavior," (Marlatt and George 1984, p. 263). In that regard, prior to termination it may be beneficial to discuss the possible series of events that may lead to a relapse to old behavioral habits, as well as how to recover when this occurs. The purpose of predicting relapse is ultimately to reduce the likelihood of it occurring and minimize the time spent in relapse should it happen.

A Note on Relapse

As noted above, relapse is an expected event demonstrating that dysfunctional patterns can still emerge and families may not progress linearly through stages. Several things can trigger individuals to a relapse (or slip) to old behavior, including stress, crisis, passiveness, a loss of environmental or emotional support, or frustration from feeling stuck in progress or growth. Discouragement during relapse may cause a hindrance in the process of reengaging in behavioral change and result in the client and family giving up (Zimmerman et al. 2000). However, providing a positive reframe explaining that even though a relapse has occurred they have been presented with the opportunity to learn something new about themselves and the process of changing behavior can help. It is important to normalize relapse and offer empathy and encouragement. For example, a therapist might say, "Yes, maintaining behavioral change is difficult. What other difficult things have you accomplished in the past?" It would be useful to brainstorm with the adolescent and family about possible strategies to overcome barriers and then encourage a commitment to pursue one strategy at a time (Zimmerman et al. 2000). "The goal here is to support [clients] and re-engage their efforts in the change process. They should be left with a sense of realistic goals to prevent discouragement, and their positive steps toward behavior change should be acknowledge" (Zimmerman et al. 2000, p. 1414).

Additional Barriers to Change

Intrapsychic (i.e., from or within the mind or self) conflict or lack of motivation are not the only barriers to successful treatment outcomes in residential treatment for adolescents. As mentioned previously, motivation for change and family engagement are keys to effective residential treatment. However, there are barriers that may render the Stages of Change model ineffective or impractical for particular adolescents. Some examples include limited family availability or involvement in the residential setting due to distance from the family's home, disbelief in the treatment process, death, abandonment, or forced removal of the adolescent from the family. Thus, motivation is not the only barrier to change and family engagement that practitioners should evaluate.

Lack of family involvement in the decision-making process and the overall treatment process is a significant shortcoming of some residential treatment programs (Leichtman and Leichtman 2001). Burns et al. (1999) explain five reasons why families have typically been uninvolved in residential treatment programs, which include (a) *multiple placement* youth who have been removed from their families of origin for a long period of time; (b) parents themselves may be incapable of participating in the treatment process; (c) the residential treatment center may be located in a distant community or state; (d) the family has abandoned the child; or (e) the residential treatment center makes little effort to involve the families.

The distance between a residential treatment facility and the family's residential location is a strong predictor of the frequency of contact as well as the level of family engagement in the treatment process (i.e., greater the distance equals less contact) (Huefner et al. 2014). Upon interviewing staff at a residential facility and parents of adolescents in treatment, Nickerson et al. (2006) found that both parties indicated transportation issues and distance as key factors limiting parental involvement in their adolescent's treatment. Other operational issues ,such as limited service availability, insurance, childcare, and time are also possible factors in parents remaining involved (Herman et al. 2011).

In addition, parents' personal problems and parenting issues have also been identified as a barrier to remaining involved in treatment. This problem reinforces the notion that family stress directly affects parents' resources and availability during the treatment process (Nickerson et al. 2006). Herman et al. (2011) identified that whether or not parents seek treatment for their adolescent is dependent upon their own beliefs regarding the problem's cause, appropriate treatment options, and past experiences with educational and mental health systems. Upon arriving in residential treatment it is often discovered that the adolescent and parents have had multiple interactions with the mental health system, which can influence decisions about parental involvement in treatment (Herman et al. 2011). These negative beliefs can heighten family stress and strain relationships and are often accompanied by decreased involvement. This pattern highlights the importance of moving the mentality about treatment from child-focused to family-centered interventions (Nickerson et al. 2006).

Conclusion

Acknowledging the importance of family involvement in residential treatment allows treatment teams to be more effective in their approaches to working with the adolescent. The main purpose of including parents in adolescent residential treatment is to "alleviate the coercive interchange between parent and child by teaching parents and other caregivers a specific set of skills to address child noncompliance" (McCurdy and McIntyre 2004, p. 148). Hardy (2007) noted that "caregiver involvement in the treatment process…is believed to be an important contributor to positive treatment outcomes" (p. 33). Researchers agree that the most effective programs have moved toward family-focused interventions (Blau et al. 2010; Herman et al. 2011; Nickerson et al. 2006). This modality requires increased parental involvement throughout the treatment process, which leads to a decrease in adolescent externalizing and internalizing behaviors. As highlighted above, research shows that having the family involved in the treatment process increases the likelihood that the adolescent will discharge to a family setting instead of another residential treatment setting. Remembering the Stages of Change model can improve the therapeutic alliance, allow the therapist to join with the adolescent and family, and increase the level of their readiness for change in regard to destructive behavior. The ultimate goal is for families to develop skills and, as they become more confident in their ability to take care of themselves, to learn ways to make themselves feel nurtured and safe individually so they can heal wounds as a family. Residential treatment may not be the best way to construct an ideal family; however, through readiness for change and trust in treatment, it can alleviate family dysfunction and result in family reunification (Carlo and Shennum 1989).

References

Aldo, A., Nolen-Hoeksema, S., & Schweizer, S. (2010). Emotion-regulation strategies across psychopathology: A meta-analytic review. *Clinical Psychology Review, 30,* 217–237. doi:10.1016/j.cpr.2009.11.004

Alexander, L. B., & Dore, M. M. (1999). Making the parents as partners principle a reality: The role of the alliance. *Journal of Child and Family Studies, 8,* 255–270. (doi: l062-1024/99/0900-0255$16.00/)

Arbinger Institute. (2015). *The anatomy of peace: Resolving the heart of conflict* (2nd ed.). Oakland, CA: Berrett-Koehler Publishers.

Baker, A. L., Archer, M., & Curtis, P. (2007). Youth characteristics associated with behavioral and mental health problems during transition to residential treatment centers: The Odyssey Project population. *Child Welfare, 86*(6), 5–29.

Blau, G. M., Caldwell, B., Fisher, S. K., Kuppinger, A., Levison-Johnson, J., & Lieberman, R. (2010). The building bridges initiative: Residential and community-based providers, family, and youth coming together to improve outcomes. *Child Welfare, 89*(2), 21–38.

Britt, E., Blamped, N. M., & Hudson, S. M. (2003). Motivational interviewing: A review. *Australian Psychologist, 38.* doi:10.1080/00050060310001707207

Buist, K. L., Dekovic, M., Meeus, W. H., & van Aken, M. (2004). Attachment in adolescence: A social relations model analysis. *Journal of Adolescent Research, 19,* 826–850. doi:10.1177/0743558403260109

Burns, B. J., Hoagwood, K., & Mrazek, P. (1999). Effective treatment for mental disorders in children and adolescents. *Clinical Child and Family Psychology Review, 2,* 199–254. (doi:1096-4037/99/1200-0199)

Carlo, P., & Shennum, W. A. (1989). Family reunification efforts that work: A three year follow-up study of children in residential treatment. *Child and Adolescent Social Work, 6*(3), 211–216.

Carr, A. (1998). Michael White's narrative therapy. *Contemporary Family Therapy, 20*(4), 485–503.

Coll, K. M., Powell, S., Thobro, P., & Haas, R. (2010). Family functioning and the development of trust and intimacy among adolescents in residential treatment. *The Family Journal: Counseling and Therapy for Couples and Families, 18*(3), 255–262. doi:10.1177/1066480710372082

Collins, B., & Collins, T. (1990). Parent-professional relationships in the treatment of seriously emotionally disturbed children and adolescents. *Social Work, 35,* 522–527.

Cunningham, W. S., Duffee, D. E., Huang, Y., Steinke, C. M., & Naccarato, T. (2009). On the meaning and measurement of engagement in youth residential treatment centers. *Research on Social Work Practice, 19*(1), 63–76. doi:10.1177/1049731508314505

Curtis, W. J., & Singh, N. N. (1996). Family involvement and empowerment in mental health service provision for children with emotional and behavioral disorders. *Journal of Child and Family Studies, 5,* 503–517. (doi:1062-1024/96/1200-0503)

Daniels, J. A. (1990). Adolescent separation-individuation and family transitions. *Adolescence, 97,* 105–117.

DiClemente, C., & Prochaska, J. (1998). Toward a comprehensive transtheorectical model of change. In W. R. Miller & N. Healther (Eds.), *Treating addictive behaviors* (pp. 3–24). New York: Plenum Press.

Englebrecht, C., Peterson, D., Scherer, A., & Naccarato, T. (2008). "It's not my fault": Acceptance of responsibility as a component of engagement in juvenile residential treatment. *Children and Youth Services Review, 30*(4), 466–484. doi:10.1016/j.childyouth.2007.11.005

Fitzgerald, M. D. (1994). Resistant attitudes and behaviors of adolescents in residential care: Considerations and strategies. *Child and Youth Care Forum, 23*(6), 365–375. doi:10.1007/BF02128520

Fonagy, P., & Target, M. (2006). The mentalization focused approach to self pathology. *Journal of Personality Disorders, 20,* 544–576.

Gottman, J. M., & Katz, L. F. (2002). Children's emotional reactions to stressful parent-child interactions: The link between emotion regulation and vagal tone. *Marriage and Family Review, 34,* 265–283. doi:10.1300/J002v34n03_04

Green, J., Kroll, L., Imrie, D., Frances, F. M., Begum, K., Harrison, L., et al. (2001). Health gain and outcome predictors during inpatient and related day treatment in child and adolescent psychiatry. *Journal of the American Academy of Child and Adolescent Psychiatry, 40,* 325–332. doi:10.1097/00004583-200103000-00012

Gross, V., & Goldin, J. (2008). Dynamics and dilemmas in working with families in inpatient CAMH services. *Clinical Child Psychology and Psychiatry, 13*(3), 449–461. doi:10.1177/1359104507088350

Hair, H. J. (2005). Outcomes for children and adolescents after residential treatment: A review of research from 1993 to 2003. *Journal of Child and Family Studies, 14*(4), 551–575. doi:10.1007/s10826-005-7188-9

Hardy, L. T. (2007). Attachment theory and reactive attachment disorder: Theoretical perspectives and treatment implications. *Journal of Child and Adolescent Psychiatric Nursing, 20,* 27–40. doi:10.1111/j.1744-6171.2007.00077.x

Harper, N. J., & Russell, K. C. (2008). Family involvement and outcome in adolescent wilderness treatment: A mixed-methods evaluation. *International Journal of Child & Family Welfare, 1,* 19–36.

Heath, M. A., Sheen, D., Leavy, D., Young, E., & Money, K. (2005). Bibliotherapy: A resource to facilitate emotional healing and growth. *School of Psychology International, 26*(5), 563–580. doi:10.1177/0143034305060792

Herman, K. C., Borden, L. A., Hsu, C., Schultz, T. R., Carney, M., Brooks, C. M., et al. (2011). Enhancing family engagement in interventions for mental health problems in youth. *Residential Treatment for Children and Youth, 28,* 102–119. doi:10.1080/0886571X.2011.569434

Hougaard, E. (1994). The therapeutic alliance—A conceptual analysis. *Scandinavian Journal of Psychology, 35,* 58–67. doi:10.1111/j.1467-9450.1994.tb00934.x

Huefner, J. C., Pick, R. M., Smith, G. L., Stevens, A. L., & Mason, W. A. (2014). Parental involvement in residential care: Distance, frequency of contact, and youth outcomes. *Journal of Children and Family Study, 24,* 1481–1489. doi:10.1007/s10826-014-9953-0

Kazdin, A. E., Whitley, M., & Marciano, P. L. (2006). Child-therapist and parent-therapist alliance and therapeutic change in the treatment of children referred for oppositional, aggressive, and antisocial behavior. *Journal of Child Psychology and Psychiatry, 47*(5), 436–445. doi:10.1111/j.1469-7610.2005.01475.x

Lamers, A., & Vermeiren, R. R. J. M. (2014). Assessment of the therapeutic alliance of youth and parents with team members in youth residential psychiatry. *Clinical Child Psychology and Psychiatry, 1,* 1–17. doi:10.1177/1359104514542304

Leichtman, M., & Leichtman, M. L. (2001). Facilitating the transition from residential treatment into the community: I. The problem. *Residential Treatment for Children and Youth, 19,* 21–27. doi:10.1300/J007v19n01_02

Littell, J. H., & Tajima, E. A. (2000). A multilevel model of client participation in intensive family preservation services. *Social Science Review, 74*(3), 405–435.

Lochman, J. E. (1992). Cognitive-behavioral intervention with aggressive boys: Three-year follow-up and preventive efforts. *Journal of Consulting and Clinical Psychology, 60,* 426–432.

Lochman, J. E., Burch, P. R., Curry, J. F., & Lampron, L. B. (1984). Treatment and generalization effects of cognitive-behavioral and goal-setting interventions with aggressive boys. *Journal of Consulting and Clinical Psychology, 52,* 915–916.

Marlatt, G. A., & George, W. H. (1984). Relapse prevention: Introduction and overview of the model. *British Journal of Addiction, 79*(4), 261–273.

McCurdy, B. L., & McIntyre, E. K. (2004). 'And what about residential...?' Re-conceptualizing residential treatment as a stop-gap service for youth with emotional and behavioral disorders. *Behavioral Interventions, 19,* 137–158. doi:10.1002/bin.151

McWey, L. M. (2004). Predictors of attachment styles of children in foster care: An attachment theory model for working with families. *Journal of Marital and Family Therapy, 30*(4), 439–452. doi:10.1111/j.1752-0606.2004.tb01254.x

Miller, W. R., & Rollnick, S. (1991). *Motivational interviewing: Preparing people to change behavior.* New York: The Guilford Press.

Miller, W. R., & Rollnick, S. (2002). *Motivational interviewing: Preparing people for change.* New York: Guilford Press.

Miller, W. R., & Rollnick, S. (2012). *Motivational interviewing: Helping people change.* New York: Guilford Press.

Minuchin, S. (1974). *Families and family therapy.* Cambridge, MA: Harvard University Press.

Minuchin, S., & Fishman, H. C. (1981). *Family therapy techniques.* Cambridge, MA: Harvard University Press.

Mirkin, M. P., Raskin, P. A., & Antognini, F. C. (1984). Parenting, protecting, preserving: Mission of the adolescent female runaway. *Family Process, 23,* 63–74. doi:10.1111/j.1545-5300.1984.00063.x

Nickerson, A. B., Brooks, J. L., Colby, S. A., Rickert, J. M., & Salamone, F. J. (2006). Family involvement in residential treatment: Staff, parent, and adolescent perspectives. *Journal of Child and Family Studies, 15*(6), 681–694. doi:10.1007/s10826-006-9041-1

Palareti, L., & Berti, C. (2010). Relational climate and effectiveness of residential care: Adolescent perspectives. *Journal of Prevention and Intervention in the Community, 38,* 26–40. doi:10.1080/10852350903393426

Prentice-Dunn, S., Wilson, D. R., & Lyman, R. D. (1981). Client factors related to outcome in a residential and day treatment program for children. *Journal of Clinical Child Psychology, 10,* 188–191. doi:10.1080/15374418109533047

Prochaska, J. O., DiClemente, C. C., & Norcross, J. C. (1993). In search of how people change: Applications to addictive behaviors. *Journal of Addictions Nursing, 5*(1), 2–16. doi:10.3109/10884609309149692

Prochaska, J. O., Norcross, J. C., & DiClemente, C. C. (1994). *Changing for good: A revolutionary six-stage program for overcoming bad habits and moving your life forward.* New York, NY: HarperCollins.

Riggs, S. A., Sahl, G., Greenwald, E., Atkison, H., Paulson, A., & Ross, C. A. (2007). Family environment and adult attachment as predictors of psychopathology and personality dysfunction among inpatient abuse survivors. *Violence and Victims, 22,* 577–598. doi:10.1891/088667007782312159

Riley, D. B., Greif, G. L., Caplan, D. L., & MacAulay, H. K. (2004). Common themes and treatment approaches in working with families of runaway youths. *American Journal of Family Therapy, 32*(2), 139–153.

Riordan, R. J., & Wilson, L. S. (1989). Bibliotherapy: Does it work? *Journal of Counseling and Development, 67,* 506–508.

Rivers, S. E., Reynna, V. F., & Mills, B. (2008). Risk taking under the influence: A fuzzy-trace theory of emotion in adolescence. *Developmental Review, 28*(1), 107–144. doi:10.1016/j.dr.2007.11.002

Rosen, M. (1998). *Treating children in out-of-home placements*. New York: The Haworth Press.

Ruiz, D. M., & Mills, J. (2010). *The four agreements: A practical guide to personal freedom*. San Rafael, CA: Amber-Allen Publishing.

Ryan, R. M., Lynch, M. F., Vansteenkiste, M., & Deci, E. L. (2011). Motivation and autonomy in counseling, psychotherapy, and behavior change: A look at theory and practice. *The Counseling Psychologist, 39*(2), 193–260. doi:10.1177/0011000009359313

Sewell, K. W., & Mendelsohn, M. (2000). Profiling potentially violent youth: Statistical and conceptual problems. *Children's Services: Social, Policy, Research, and Practice, 3*(3), 147–169.

Shenk, C. E., & Fruzzetti, A. E. (2014). Parental validating and invalidating responses and adolescent psychological functioning: An observational study. *The Family Journal: Counseling and Therapy for Couples and Families, 22*(1), 43–48. doi:10.1177/1066480713490900

Shirk, S. R., Karver, M. S., & Brown, R. (2011). The alliance in child and adolescent psychotherapy. *Psychotherapy, 48*, 17–24. doi:10.1037/a0022181

Singh, N. N. (1995). In search of unity: Some thoughts on family—Professional relationships in service delivery systems. *Journal of Child and Family Studies, 4*, 3–18. doi:10.1007/BF02233951

Singh, N. N., Wechsler, H. A., & Curtis, W. J. (2000). Family friendliness of inpatient services for children and adolescents with EBD and their families: Observational study of the treatment team process. *Journal of Emotional and Behavioral Disorders, 8*(1), 19–26. doi:10.1177/106342660000800103

Small, R., Kennedy, K., & Bender, B. (1991). Critical issues for practice in residential treatment: The view from within. *American Journal of Orthopsychiatry, 61*(3), 327–338. doi:10.1037/h0079273

Springer, D. W., & Orsbon, S. H. (2002). Families helping families: Implementing a multifamily therapy group with substance-abuse adolescents. *Health and Social Work, 27*(3), 204–207.

Stage, S. A. (1999). Predicting adolescents' discharge status following residential treatment. *Residential Treatment for Children and Youth, 16*, 37–56. doi:10.1300/J007v16n03_03

Steele, D. J. (2011). *From therapist to coach: How to leverage your clinical expertise to build thriving coaching practice*. Hoboken, NJ: Wiley.

Sugai, G., & Horner, R. H. (2008). What we know and need to know about preventing problem behavior in schools. *Exceptionality, 16*(2), 67–77. doi:10.1080/09362830801981138

Twerski, A. J. (1997). *Addictive thinking*. Central City: Minnesota, Hazelden Publishing.

Whitaker, D., Archer, L., & Hicks, L. (1998). *Working in children's homes: Challenges and complexities*. New York, NY: Wiley.

Whittaker, J. K. (1979). *Caring for troubled children*. San Francisco, CA: Josey-Bass.

Whittaker, J. K., & Maluccio, A. N. (1989). Changing paradigms in residential services for disturbed/disturbing children: Retrospect and prospect. In R. P. Hawkins & J. Breiling (Eds.), *Therapeutic foster care: Critical issues* (pp. 81–102). Washington DC: Child Welfare League of America.

Williamson, E., & Gray, A. (2011). New roles for families in child welfare: Strategies for expanding family involvement beyond the case level. *Children and Youth Services Review, 33*, 1212–1216. doi:10.1016/j.childyouth.2011.02.013

Yatchmenoff, D. K. (2005). Measuring client engagement from the client's perspective in nonvoluntary child protection services. *Research on Social Work Practice, 15*(2), 84–96. doi:10.1177/1049731504271605

Young, J. E., Klosko, J. S., & Weishaar, M. E. (2003). *Schema therapy: A practitioner's guide*. New York: Guilford Press.

Zegers, M. A., Schuengel, C., Van IJzendoorn, M. H., & Janssens, J. M. (2008). Attachment and problem behavior of adolescents during residential treatment. *Attachment and Human Development, 10*, 91–103. doi:10.1080/14616730701868621

Zimmerman, G. L., Olsen, C. G., & Bosworth, M. F. (2000). A 'stages of change' approach to helping patients change behavior. *American Family Physician, 61*(5), 1409–1416.

Author Biographies

Amber L. Runkel, MA, TLMFT works as a provisionally licensed marital and family therapist in a private practice in downtown Des Moines, IA. She specializes in individual, couple, and family therapy, and she strives to help clients gain self-awareness and acceptance, increase mindfulness, and heal wounds that hinder daily functioning, relationships, and life goals. Amber is also a pre-clinical fellow of the American Association for Marriage and Family Therapy and the Iowa Association for Marriage and Family Therapy. Amber received her Master of Arts degree in Marriage and Family Therapy from Mount Mercy University in Cedar Rapids, Iowa, and her Bachelor of Science degree in Psychology at Iowa State University in Ames, Iowa. Amber has published articles in Contemporary Family Therapy as well.

Jacob D. Christenson, Ph.D., LMFT is an assistant professor of marriage and family therapy at Mount Mercy University. Dr. Christenson received his Bachelor degree in Psychology from California Polytechnic State University. He then completed his Master's degree and doctorate in Marriage and Family Therapy from Brigham Young University. Before coming to Mount Mercy University Dr. Christenson worked for four years at Aspen Achievement Academy in Loa, UT as a Field Therapist. As a Field Therapist, Dr. Christenson experienced firsthand the challenge of being a systemic marriage and family therapist in the world of residential care.

Over the course of his career Dr. Christenson has consistently been involved in academic research and publication. In addition to numerous presentations at national and international conferences, Dr. Christenson has published a number of articles in peer-reviewed journals such as the Journal of Marital and Family Therapy, Contemporary Family Therapy, and the American Journal of Family Therapy. Dr. Christenson also serves as an editorial board member for the Journal of Marital and Family Therapy and Contemporary Family Therapy.

Dr. Christenson teaches a number of course at Mount Mercy University. The courses he's taught have included, Parents and Children, Micro-counseling, Medical Family Therapy, and Research Methods. Dr. Christenson is also an AAMFT Approved Supervisor, which has enabled him to provide supervision in practicum courses. Dr. Christenson also serves as the Clinical Director for the Gerald and Audrey Olson Marriage and Family Therapy Clinic, which is attached to the marriage and family therapy program at Mount Mercy University. In addition to his work as a professor, Dr. Christenson provides therapy in private practice and is the founder of Covenant Family Solutions, an outpatient therapy group practice in Cedar Rapids, Iowa. When not working, Dr. Christenson enjoys spending time with his family and being active in his community.

Amanda Glunz, MA works for a nonprofit agency in Jacksonville, Florida as part of their Community Action Team. She provides therapeutic intervention for adolescents and their families who are in need of crisis stabilization in order to deter out-of-home placements, such as foster care, juvenile justice, and residential treatment. After receiving her Bachelor degree, Amanda attended Mount Mercy University and graduated with her Master's in Marriage and Family Therapy. Amanda has been active in researching the relationship between adverse childhood experiences and parent-child attachment, and recently published an article in Contemporary Family Therapy.

Katherine F. Cobb, MA earned a Master's in Religious Studies from the University of Iowa and a Master's in Marriage and Family Therapy from Mount Mercy University. Her research interests concern issues in mental health and religion, attachment, post-modern therapies, and scrupulosity. She recently published articles in Contemporary Family Therapy on working with adolescents in residential settings and will be presenting her own research at upcoming national conferences. She currently works in independent private practice in Iowa City, with a temporary license in marriage and family therapy.

Chapter 15
Engaging Families in Outdoor Behavioral Healthcare

Anita Tucker, Mark Widmer, Troy J. Faddis, Bryan Randolph and Michael Gass

Chapter Highlights

- Outdoor Behavioral Healthcare (OBH) programs are therapeutically based interventions in which clients are involved in outdoor adventure pursuits aimed at creating changes in targeted behaviors, directly focusing on a clear and distinct set of outcomes for each client.
- While research on the impact of OBH on the mental health functioning of youth continues to show evidence of significant changes, research is still growing on its impact on family functioning.

A. Tucker (✉) · M. Gass
Outdoor Behavioral Healthcare (OBH) Research Center, College of Health
and Human Services, University of New Hampshire, 55 College Road,
Durham, NH 03824, USA
e-mail: anita.tucker@unh.edu

M. Gass
e-mail: mgass@unh.edu

M. Widmer
Marriott School of Management, Brigham Young University,
W433 Tanner Building, Provo, UT 84602, USA
e-mail: widmer@byu.edu

T.J. Faddis
Legacy Outdoor Adventures, P.O. Box 400, Loa, UT 84747, USA
e-mail: troy@legacytreatmetncenter.com

B. Randolph
Mountain Valley Treatment Center, 2274 Mt. Moosilauke Hwy, Pike,
NH 03780, USA
e-mail: bryanjrandolph@gmail.com

© Springer International Publishing AG 2017
J.D. Christenson and A.N. Merritts (eds.), *Family Therapy with Adolescents
in Residential Treatment*, Focused Issues in Family Therapy,
DOI 10.1007/978-3-319-51747-6_15

- While a youth is away from home at OBH programs, families may be engaged throughout the therapeutic process through letter writing, phone calls, as well as in person visits.
- Despite the discussion in the literature about the engagement of families within OBH, it is still unclear to what extent individual programs truly engage with families.

Approximately one out of five adolescents in the United States has a diagnosable mental health disorder (Schwartz 2009). These disorders impact youth functioning across all settings including the family, school, and peers. The disorders have significant impact on youth and their families. For example, the associated distress can lead to suicide, the third leading cause of adolescent deaths (Schwartz 2009). Despite the need for services, treatment of children and youth with significant mental health issues is often challenging in an outpatient setting, regardless of access to treatment (Harpaz-Rotem et al. 2004). Harpaz-Rotem et al. (2004) studied outpatient service utilization in children and youth with significant mental and behavioral health issues and found that 55% of children and youth dropped out of treatment in less than one month. In adolescents, it has been argued that attitudes toward mental health treatment are a significant barrier to effective treatment in an outpatient setting (Harpaz-Rotem et al. 2004). Parents of struggling adolescents are then faced with the challenge of finding effective alternatives. In these instances, children are often placed in residential treatment centers (Frensch and Cameron 2002; Zelechoski et al. 2013); however, an increasing number of families are choosing to place their child into an OBH program as an effective treatment option (Russell and Phillips-Miller 2002). The purpose of this chapter is to provide a brief introduction to OBH, discuss the potential benefits of this unique intervention for individuals, and more specifically to highlight the role OBH currently can play in supporting family therapy in building healthy families. Further, this paper seeks to address possibilities for better integrating the role of family therapy within OBH settings.

Outdoor Behavioral Healthcare

OBH, also referred to as wilderness therapy, is a type of adventure therapy. Adventure therapy as a larger field of treatment is defined as "the prescriptive use of adventure experiences provided by mental health professionals, often conducted in natural settings that kinesthetically engage clients on cognitive, affective and behavioral levels" (Gass et al. 2012, p. 1). Adventure therapy interventions can be found in a variety of settings including community-based mental health centers, residential treatment programs, as well as in OBH programs (Norton et al. 2014). OBH programs are therapeutically based interventions in which clients are involved in outdoor adventure pursuits aimed at creating changes in targeted behaviors, directly focusing on a clear and distinct set of outcomes for each client (Russell 2001).

Overview of OBH

In most cases, adolescents are removed from the home and placed in an OBH program (Tucker et al. 2015, 2016a, b, c), essentially removing the individual from the family system (Olson and Gorall 2003). The roots of sending youth away to OBH programs can be traced as far back as the late 1800s; however, the term OBH was not coined until the 1990s. Kurt Hahn's Outward Bound programs, which operated in England in the 1940s and later (1962) in the United States, are recognized as the original programs (Hattie et al. 1997; White 2012). In the 1960s and 1970s, wilderness-based programs were developed to promote personal growth, support struggling students, and as a mental health intervention (Kelly and Baer 1968). The number of *therapeutic* wilderness-based programs in the western United States continued to grow throughout the 1980s and 1990s; however, until the early 1980s traditional clinical processes appear to have been absent from most programs (White 2012). Psychological assessment and individual therapy as part of the wilderness experience became more common in the late 1980s.

In its growth, OBH was marked by a few tragedies widely portrayed in the media. For example, Jon Krakauer's piece in *Outside Magazine*, *Loving Them to Death*, brought public and governmental scrutiny to the industry (Krakauer 1995). In 1996, in an effort to address this scrutiny and promote accountability, a group of leaders from wilderness therapy programs formed the OBH Industry Council (Russell 2003a) and the term OBH was introduced. The OBH Industry Council (see obhcouncil.com) initiated a systematic effort to create and promote safety standards, training, research, and stronger clinical models among wilderness programs (Harper and Russell 2008). For additional information on the OBH Industry Council, see Chap. 3 in this volume.

Most OBH participants spend 6–8 weeks in the wilderness living with limited equipment and supplies. For example, students may learn to build fires without matches, build shelters, learn to identify edible plants, and navigate their way across the land. Although all OBH programs have a component of outdoor group living, not all programs focus solely on expedition and wilderness survival. Other programs use a base camp model from which participants engage in weekly trips that involve adventure activities including backpacking, rock climbing, canyoneering, , and mountain biking (Magle-Haberek et al. 2012). In addition to the experiential and adventure components of each program, participants in all OBH programs engage in weekly individual and group therapy with licensed clinicians.

Recognizing the important role of the family, most OBH programs also include varying family components. Harper's (2005) survey of 10 member programs of the OBH Council found the majority of programs intentionally involved families in the treatment process, including incorporating family goals within treatment plans and providing families with counseling and psychoeducational information. On average families had between 10 and 30 h of contact time with the individual in treatment. Similarly, Russell et al. (2008) in their survey of 65 wilderness therapy programs found that 84.1% of the programs reported offering family sessions and 79.4% reported offering parent sessions with an average of 27 h spent in contact with the family per youth. Additionally, 71.4% offered psychoeducational family groups, 68.3% offered parent/family support groups, 50.8% offered parent seminars, and 38.1% offered online support services (Russell et al. 2008). Clearly, clinicians have a variety of options in OBH settings to engage the family in treatment.

Also, the majority of programs utilized letter writing, therapist–parent phone calls, and direct family participation to keep families involved in programming (Harper 2005). For example, DeMille and Montgomery (2016) highlight how letter writing can help the family "tell, retell, and reflect on stories … as a means of integrating the family during the entire treatment, even when the adolescent is in the backcountry" (p. 6). In addition, Christenson and Miller (2016) described how the use of letter writing can illustrate maladaptive patterns between youth and their family, as well as hold parents accountable for their behaviors. Christenson and Miller and DeMille and Montgomery have both extended their ideas on the subject in Chaps. 2 and 3 of this book as well.

What Does the Research Say?

Research on the impact of OBH programs has been growing over the last 20 years. Similarly, OBH research and theory has identified a number of factors as agents promoting change in clients. These include rites of passage, self-efficacy, positive group living, positive role modeling, beauty and mystery, spirituality, nature as an educator/feedback loop, relationship trust, model fidelity, and solo time (Russell 2000, 2001; Russell and Phillips-Miller 2002). Overall, youth who participate in OBH programs have consistently shown clinical improvements after treatment as measured by both youth and their parents (Bettmann et al. 2013; Norton et al. 2014; Russell 2003b; Tucker et al. 2011). Unlike the weaker methodologies of the past for which the field has been criticized (Hattie et al. 1997), this research tends to employ better measurement instruments like the use of the Youth Outcomes Questionnaires (Y-OQ), a well-established behavioral outcome instrument (Wells et al. 1996) and the collection of longitudinal data which supports lasting improvements in OBH clients (Bettmann et al. 2013; Lewis 2012; Zelov et al. 2013; Tucker et al. 2016c).

Research has been limited, however, by its larger focus on the adolescent client and not the family, despite OBH programs engagement with the family. Only a few studies have specifically looked at the impact of OBH on the family. Harper et al. (2007) evaluated the impact of an OBH program on family functioning, adolescent behavior, and mental issues. At 2 months post treatment, families reported significant increases in family arguments, but also significant improvements in youth's communication with the parents, as well as improvements in youth's success in school and decreases in problem behaviors. Similar to earlier research on client outcomes in OBH, however, the measurement tool was created specifically for the study, hence limiting the validity of these findings. More recently, Harper and Russell's (2008) mixed methods study aimed to evaluate the impact of OBH involvement on the family. Qualitative interviews with 14 families at intake, discharge, and 2 months post-discharge revealed several themes. Families felt that sending their youth to wilderness helped to abate a family crisis or even worse outcomes for their child. In addition, the OBH program provided a needed separation and distance from the youth in order to see the situation with better clarity even though there were mixed emotions about sending their children away. Finally, families saw the experience as providing an opportunity for a new start as a family. Despite these positive themes, quantitative findings suggested minimum impact on family functioning after participation (Harper and Russell 2008). Recently OBH Council member programs have begun to gather data using the Family Assessment Device General Functioning (GF) scale (Epstein et al. 1983) and preliminary research shows significant improvements in family functioning after participation in OBH programs, as reported by the youth; changes that were maintained 6 months post treatment (Tucker et al. 2016c).

An Integrated Model of OBH and Family Therapy

Family therapy's influence in the field of OBH often went unnoticed when compared to wilderness therapy programming early on as the industry attempted to differentiate itself as a newly emerging profession. More recently as family therapy was influencing program development, OBH programs began to use techniques to address family communication and homeostatic patterns of interaction by integrating traditional family therapy techniques into practice (Faddis and Bettmann 2006). A focus on maladaptive patterns within the family was a cornerstone of treatment. For example, impact letters, gratitude letters, letters of accountability, group role-playing, family workshops and seminars, and other communication with parents became standard. Some programs have parents join their child in the wilderness for a number of days, allowing the therapist to help the family learn and practice new healthy behaviors (see Chap. 17).

Despite the increased efforts, for the field of OBH to grow, family therapy needs to be more effectively integrated into the individual and wilderness treatment process. Research consistently demonstrates the efficacy of family involvement in increasing positive long-term outcomes for youth discharged from residential care to stable family contexts (Nickerson et al. 2006; Robinson et al. 2005). Depending on the family structure and support systems in the home, this integration may include work with the primary therapist at the OBH program who can do family therapy, as well as clinicians at home working with the family. To highlight how family therapy can be integrated throughout OBH, each phase of treatment within a typical OBH program is illustrated in the following section. In this chapter, the term family therapist will be used to refer to the home-based therapist, and OBH therapist will be used to refer to the therapist who delivers treatment in the residential program. However, it should be noted that many marriage and family therapists work as OHB therapists, just like many licensed social workers, psychologists, and mental health counselors provide home-based family therapy.

Admission and Intervention

Parents often initiate the admissions phase. Psychological testing is usually completed for an individual client at intake (Bettmann et al. 2014) or even before the decision is made to place an adolescent. This may also include parent interviews and family assessment such as the Family Adaptability and Cohesion Scale and the Dyadic Adjustment Scale. Family therapists may use these reports to help unify the family around common goals and treatment expectations. It can also be used to motivate clients and their families to engage in the process more fully. Family therapists working with a family at home may consider the unique opportunity of OBH and decide to refer a member of the family system. Family therapists may then provide OBH therapists with direction and insight to help direct the treatment phases in an effort to target areas most critical to impacting positive changes in the family.

For example, cognitive, academic, and personality testing may show a high mean scores on perceptual and verbal subscales and low mean scores on working memory and processing speed. This is a common split in scores where a client has strength verbally, but may struggle with production and self-awareness. Sometimes this points to an underlying learning issues and can also indicate the *cognitive dissonance* that occurs with addiction and anxiety. Cognitive dissonance, as used here, is when one overestimates a reward and underrepresents the consequences, thereby encouraging decisions that lead to relapse and use. Similar disconnects occur with anxiety and other mood deregulation problems.

Additionally, personality testing can highlight where low motivation and poor reasoning might be an unconscious personality mechanism. The type of information can be used to help substance abusing clients, for example, see how sobriety can increase processing speeds and effective reasoning, countering the cognitive dissonance. Therapists can then show clients how through deliberate practice one can reshape their reasoning and personality. These two outcomes may be necessary for life goals such as a university education or job training.

As the results are reviewed with a family therapist in an effort to identify areas of concern and treatment goals, it provides parents an opportunity to consider their hopes and expectations for treatment. Parents then discuss treatment options with their child. In addition, Education Consultants are commonly hired at this stage by parents who feel lost in how to find the most appropriate therapeutic setting for their child and his or her needs. Often Educational Consultants are also involved during the admissions process, working with the family to help the OBH therapist recognize and understand the youth and the reason they were referred to the wilderness program in the first place. Hence, the family therapist and Education Consultants who know a lot about the child and family can effectively help with goal identification and in setting appropriate expectations. The admissions process also allows the client to learn about treatment and make a choice with their family.

Often this choice involved family leverage, which also needs to be addressed in treatment. For example, some families may choose to transport their child to an OBH program without the child's knowledge or consent (Tucker et al. 2015), which may impact family attachment, communication, and trust (Bettmann and Tucker 2011). Although some may view this as a potentially damaging step, experts agree,

> Legal interventions and sanctions or family pressure may play an important role in getting adolescents to enter, stay in, and complete treatment. Adolescents with substance use disorders rarely feel they need treatment and almost never seek it on their own. Research shows that treatment can work even if it is mandated or entered into unwillingly (National Institute of Drug Abuse 2015, para. 4)

An adolescent may initially view forcible admission to a treatment program as unfair. This is a typical adolescent response. Although children and young adults with depression or anxiety may feel their parents have violated their trust, children with addictions may respond with even greater resentment and anger, feeling betrayed. Despite this, research suggests that transport for some families is seen as a last resort option and youth transported to OBH programs improve equally as well as those who are not transported (Tucker et al. 2015, 2016a).

Pre-contemplation/Problem Identification Phase

Although some clients are in contemplation stage when entering treatment, most clients are in a pre-contemplation stage of change; therefore, they do not see the need to seek treatment, making out-of-home placement necessary (Bettmann et al. 2013). For a through discussion of this topic see Miller, Christenson, Gluntz and Cobb's discussion in Chap. 14 of this text on readiness to change. OBH programs provide a novel environment, posing a dramatic change in lifestyle and living conditions. This novel environment often serves as a catalyst to initiate processes leading to feelings of hope. The sense of hope creates beliefs and expectations that change is within reach (Miller and Flaherty 2000). Family therapists can capitalize on this hope and belief in change by helping parents move from blaming and justifying communication to supportive communication. In other words, the family therapist at home can use the new environment and sense of hope in the child to move the family from maladaptive to adaptive interactions. Specifically, parents can be coached by the family therapist to write effective impact letters. Christenson and Miller provide an in-depth discussion of letter writing in Chap. 2 of this text, as mentioned above. This is a letter describing how the parent's life has been affected by the child's behavior, writing in direct frank language, but avoiding hostility and blaming. Family therapists may teach parents to repackage the message in a way that it is easier for their child to hear and understand their experience.

For example, parents may describe the impact of constant worry about the health and safety of their child on their lives. They then may describe the experience of seeing their child overdose, rushed to the emergency room, put on a ventilator, and have to be resuscitated. The child then reads the letter to his or her peers around a campfire at night. This process is a vital part of helping change an individual's story about themselves and their relationship with others. Honest and open feedback from peers may be more readily given and accepted in this context, promoting insight and self-awareness (Russell and Farnum 2004; Russell and Phillips-Miller 2002). The child hears her parents differently and is held accountable for her interpretation and response to the letter by peers. Further, this process is supported by the OBH therapist observing the child's response to the letter and to her peers' feedback, and can use techniques such as reframing and circular questioning to help her hear the message, clarify what is said, and begin to see the parent's experience. Later, when the parents visit their child in the program, the child may be invited to share the experience of reading the impact letter and the feedback provided by peers. Ideally, the OBH therapist and family therapist at home work collaboratively so the family therapist is briefed on the process and can then continue work with the parents to build on the experience when they return home.

Since often the child is brought to OBH not by choice, they may arrive with little motivation to change. However, over the course of treatment, regardless of how ready to change they may be, research shows youth improve as much as those who arrive ready to engage in the process (Bettmann et al. 2013). The wilderness setting itself can be a powerful change agent in that it provides multiple opportunities for youth to experience the natural consequences of their behaviors (Tucker 2009). Living successfully in the wilderness requires the acquisition of skills like making fires, building shelters, cooking outdoors, land navigation, as well as long periods of hiking. Resistance to learning new skills can make youth physically and emotionally uncomfortable; hence, the nature of the intervention itself encourages youth to adapt.

Treatment Phase

The treatment phase may include a variety of interventions. Some family therapy techniques have effective application in OBH settings. For example, therapists may use genograms and family mapping to identify family goals for treatment. In addition, Faddis and Bettmann (2006) highlight the potential impact of family sculptures and reflecting. Frequently, a peer group will help another group member with a family sculpture. This peer group also reflects back their own reactions and insights often based in their own family experience and their experience living in the wilderness with their peer. This non-threating insight from others helps OBH participants develop a better understanding of family interactions. Reflecting teams provide opportunities for peers to offer clear and honest feedback. In this process, the OBH therapist can help the child recognize how well they responded to the peer feedback and then have the student compare that response to their parents (Gass et al. 2012). They can then discuss how they can respond more effectively in future conversations with their parents. During group sessions, field guides and peers can provide reflective feedback about their insight on interpersonal effectiveness, coping skills, strengths, and other relational patterns from their experience together in the wilderness. Additional sessions occur between clients, OBH therapists, and field guides, who then create a treatment plan with specific therapeutic goals to take in the field and address throughout the week. This expanding of the treatment team allows for practical application of relational skills in the client's operational world. The expanded team can provide broader support and accountability teams. Faddis and Cobb provide more information on family sculptures and reflecting teams in in Chap. 16.

Adapted modes of additional family therapy practices may also occur in this phase when parents and siblings visit the program and spend time with their child. This includes, but is not limited to, family therapy sessions with a therapist, group therapy with other families, and family sculpture family therapy groups, as well as spending time in the wilderness or engaging in adventure activities as a family (Faddis and Bettmann 2006). One important approach is for the child to lead their parents in an adventure where the child demonstrates gains in self-efficacy as he or she uses skills learned in the program to lead and care for the family. Other opportunities include increased family efficacy, peer modeling of improved relational patterns, psychoeducational groups, and family ceremony and rite of passage. Examples of rites of passage include using a medicine wheel for reunifying a family with their child or using a talking stick to allow family members to address concerns with each other without fear of not being heard.

As children lead their parents in a wilderness context, parents may see their child as an independent and functional person, changing long-held perspectives of their child as a *problem*. The child can adopt the role of servant–caregiver as he or she takes responsibility for the parent's safety and well-being. These experiences and role reversals can provide a completely new narrative and impetus to change for the entire family system. Ideally, the OBH therapist and parents would debrief the experience with the home family therapist. This collaborative relationship provides synergy for the home family therapist to build on these experiences using the new narrative and family efficacy story as they prepare the parents for the child to return home.

Another aspect of the OBH therapy process involves the intense shared wilderness experience of the group including the field guides, peers, and individuals. Wilderness experiences lead to a process of breaking down targeted and inappropriate barriers that individuals create as protective devices in relationships and in society. The process has been called *fractional sublimation* or a peeling away of the protective layers (Taniguchi et al. 2005). It is difficult to maintain facades or images when confronted with the challenges of wilderness living. A unique feature of OBH is peer milieu where the family and individual dynamics are discussed in the peer group and the group reflects these dynamics back to an individual, creating a new communication feedback loop (Harper et al. 2007; Russell and Phillips-Miller 2002). Through this process, OBH participants learn positive communication skills (Tucker 2009). Theory and research suggest open and positive communication is critical for families to overcome dysfunction in family processes (Olson and Gorall 2003). Under the guidance of the OBH therapist, the group living context in the wilderness is a unique mechanism to help participants peel away their facades and approach their interactions and communication differently. As changes are seen in the child, and interpersonal skills are enhanced, these gains are communicated to the parents and home family therapist who discuss how they can support these changes and build a stronger relationship with their child.

The awareness of communication problems can also be brought to the forefront as peers role-play family interactions. Peers are effective actors as they take on and play the role of different family members and reflect the communications patterns of their families. The OBH contexts of wilderness and group naturally lead to fractional sublimation and break down barriers, increasing vulnerability and humility, and leading to greater trust among group members (Taniguchi et al. 2005). It indeed can be a powerful context for the process of self-understanding and reflection to occur. The OBH therapist can use the dynamic interaction of wilderness and peer role-playing as a foundation for continued reflection and self-understanding.

The distance from the family from the OBH group can provide a safe and effective practice space for changing the dynamics with actual family members (see Chap. 8; Harper and Russell 2008). The OBH therapist facilitates the process promoting growth for both the child and the parents. The OBH therapist communicates the child's progress to the parents and home family therapist. In most OBH programs the primary therapist talks with the parents weekly for a period of time, generally an hour. On these phone calls issues of treatment progress, treatment goals, and family progress, as well as aftercare planning are addressed. The home family therapist also communicates the parent's progress to the child, creating hope among family members for healthy interactions when they are reunited, which the home family therapist can foster the development.

In an ideal situation, the home family therapist and program therapist engage in co-therapy. For example, the home therapist may join in on phone calls where the parents are in their home office. In this scenario, updates are given and processed therapeutically based on the parents' reactions. The home family therapist is in a better position to see, interpret, and respond to those reactions. With effective communication between the OBH therapist and home family therapist, the home family therapist may use experiences and interventions from the OBH program as a foundation to continue strengthening the family. The more familiar the home family therapist is with the OBH programs and processes, and the greater the communication between therapists, the more effective this collaboration will be in helping families.

Aftercare Planning Phase

Most OBH programs are designed to be an intermediate level of care. All clients will benefit from follow-up services at some level. Aftercare planning is vital (see Chap. 9). Parents and clients can talk frequently in therapy sessions using a combination of face-to-face, phone, or video conferencing. Effective aftercare planning should include the parents and the home family therapist, and where appropriate, it may involve an Educational Consultant. Along with discussions with the child, decisions regarding aftercare programs can be made together. This allows for information to be gathered, but also gives an opportunity for the client and family to plan together using improved family interactions to create a shared map for the future (Gottman and Silver 2013). As Johnson (2012) describes in her Emotionally Focused Therapy model, attunement of family members creates trust and security in attachment styles. Attunement is a key social skill. It is a couple's, or parent and child's, ability to understand and fully process interactions and move beyond negative emotional interactions and build stronger relationships. This attunement of a shared map in the aftercare process often has a repairing effect on the parent–child relationship. Here again, collaboration between OBH and family therapists may provide synergistic benefits, by guiding both client and parents to a plan that meets therapy needs as well as wants for the future direction in the client's life to build on the experience.

For example, the OBH therapist may initiate aftercare discussions while supporting positive communication and attunement and outline aftercare options. Including the home family therapist in the discussions and gaining their input may serve to support the parents and the child and give them greater confidence to move forward. Effective aftercare planning is an important part of the process. In most cases aftercare allows a lower level of programming to provide a client and the family needed space to develop maintenance skills and give new cognitive schemas the traction to stick, while trying new behaviors on in safer structured life situations. Aftercare options include things such as additional primary care and intermediate or extended outpatient care. In an effort to provide insight into the OBH experience we present below a case representing a typical student.

Andrew: A Case Study

Andrew is a 16-year-old male diagnosed with a moderate substance use disorder. He regularly uses marijuana and alcohol. Andrew was arrested for driving under the influence, was detained at school while drunk, and marijuana was found in his possession. He was suspended from school and referred to juvenile court. In the year preceding his arrest, his school performance dropped from a B average to failing, he quit the tennis team, and was fired from his part-time job. These issues were accompanied by increased conflict with his parents and oppositional behavior at home and school. Andrew refused to follow the family rules. He began engaging in verbally abusive behavior toward his siblings and parents. His parents described him as "feeling entitled" and often angry when they would not provide him with the material possessions his friends had, such as a car, motorcycle, and money to attend concerts. Efforts by his parents to help Andrew produced heightened conflict in their marriage. Consequently, his parents sought help from a marriage and family therapist.

As Andrew's issues intensified, and when he was arrested for driving under the influence, it became apparent the marital and family issues were systematically connected to Andrew's substance abuse. In particular, Andrew and his parents no longer engaged in open communication, and his parents' communication was also disrupted, undermining the family's ability to adapt and deal with Andrew's substance use and maintain cohesive family relationships (Olson and Gorall 2003). In consultation with the family therapist and after discussing different treatment options, Andrew's parents had him transported against his will and admitted to an 8–10 week OBH program in another state. The purpose of the admission was to help Andrew with his substance use and restore and enhance his communication skills. It was also to provide a respite for his parents from the stress and conflict at home in an effort to continue marital therapy.

Part of the OBH program involved his parents attending seminars to help them become more effective parents, which focused on managing conflict and strengthening relationships (Arbinger 2015). With the permission of the parents, the OBH therapist contacted the home family therapist to discuss Andrew's case and to better understand the family dynamics. This was followed by a conference call including both therapists and the parents to discuss key issues and their hopes for Andrew and their family as they began the process of participating in the OBH program. The OBH therapist and home family therapist committed Andrew's parents to engage in the weekly phone sessions with the OBH therapist, attend the parenting seminars and the parent wilderness experience. In addition, they agreed to include the home family therapist in these processes where appropriate.

Andrew was initially angry, resistant, and in denial. His OBH program included living at a base camp and engaging in week-long trips including rock climbing, mountain biking, backpacking, and other activities. He was in a group with seven other young men who had a variety of behavioral and emotional problems. He attended weekly individual and group therapy while at basecamp. He developed strong relationships with his field staff and therapist. Treatment goals were identified each week by his therapist. These goals were communicated to his parents and home family therapist. The home family therapist integrated Andrew's goals into the parent's therapy sessions, focusing specifically on how they can support Andrew in the program and during aftercare in achieving his goals. Then, under the direction of the therapist, the field staff implemented specific techniques focusing on his goals. Most goals focused on issues around substance use and anger management and the development of effective coping skills.

After 3 weeks in his OBH program and without marijuana and alcohol, his level of opposition decreased and he began to express some satisfaction with participation in the program and therapy. He particularly enjoyed mountain biking and was developing excellent mountain biking skills. He enjoyed the feelings of accomplishment and total engagement without being high, as he used his new found skills to take on more and more challenging trials (Csikszentmihalyi 1990). He realized he could find a natural *high* through his newfound skills without drugs and alcohol. He developed a genuine desire to gain knowledge and skills and to continue growing. He also began to miss his parents and siblings and to acknowledge the many comforts his parent provided him. These experiences and growth were shared with his parents and home family therapist. In their therapy at home the family therapist helped them develop strategies to encourage and support Andrew's desire to learn and grow and engage in challenging activities like mountain biking when he returned home.

This specific OBH program was founded on a strength-based approach from positive psychology and Self-Determination Theory (Deci and Flaste 1996; Peterson and Seligman 2004). For example, an emphasis was placed on choice and autonomy, experiencing engagement or *flow* (Csikszentmihalyi 1990), building healthy relationships, finding meaning through service, skill development and achievement. During week 4 of the program, Andrew's therapist directed the field guides to have him engage in a *gratitude letter* intervention. This intervention involves identifying a person who had a positive influence in your life and write a letter describing how he or she impacted you. In this letter, you describe how the person influenced you and express gratitude (Christenson and Miller 2016). Andrew agreed to write a gratitude letter to his parents and describe the important influence they had on his life. Research has shown this intervention increases happiness and life satisfaction, decreases depression, moderates materialism and entitlement, and positively impacts relationships (Lyubomirsky 2008; Emmons and Mishra 2012; Toepfer et al. 2012).

During week 7, Andrew's parents attended the parent seminar. The family was reunited for the first time since he was removed from the home. His parents had been in marriage therapy and they had attended the parenting seminar. Andrew had been living drug free and was facing new and difficult challenges with each week and adventure in the program. In addition, the peer role-playing process described in the treatment phase section provided him with insight about his own role in family conflict and with tools to better engage in positive communication and healthy conflict. Consequently, Andrew's perspective of his parents had changed. His gratitude letter described how angry he was at them when he was sent to the OBH program and how he had vowed never to return home. He then described how over the weeks his world had changed as he read their weekly letters and partici- pated in reflecting teams. He recognized his bad choices and how these choices had affected him and his family. He expressed sorrow and asked for forgiveness. He told his parents how grateful he was for them and for everything they had provided him. He specifically addressed how his mom had always been so caring toward him, and how he loved her cooking and how she decorated the house. He also wrote about how he admired how his father showed honesty, respect, and kindness toward everyone he met. He also expressed his gratitude for their continued concern and love for him. He expressed gratitude for many simple things of life at home, for a bed, for shelter from the weather, for a hot shower, and for his mom's enchiladas. Emotions were difficult to control as he read the letter. Both Andrew and his parent's hearts were touched. For the first time in over a year, they were able to talk without fighting. It was a powerful life changing moment for all of them. With Andrew's permission, his parents shared the gratitude letter with the family home therapist when they returned home. Their family therapist processed the experience with them, and invited them to write a gratitude letter to share with Andrew at their next visit. They then spent time talking about things they were grateful for about Andrew.

In the context of this family situation OBH provided a number of benefits.

The building of self-efficacy around living in the wilderness, doing adventures, and building better interpersonal skills changed Andrew. He developed a love of learning new skills and realized he did not need drugs and alcohol to feel high. In addition, the collaborative work between the OBH therapist and home family therapist allowed the family therapist to process Andrew's experience and capitalize on key insights. It provided energy for marital therapy and strategies to manage conflict around Andrew in their marriage. The OBH context also provided an opportunity to change the parent–child relationship and to strengthen open and positive communication. This laid a foundation to help the family adapt and become more cohesive with the help of the family therapist at home (Olson and Gorall 2003).

OBH provides a unique and potentially powerful venue for affecting individual family members in an effort to strengthen families. It provides a respite from the constant emotional flooding process associated with highly conflicted parent–child relationships. OBH programs also give emotional space to the family. OBH as an intervention engages participants in wilderness where physical movement and a positive peer culture can facilitate decreases in depression, anxiety, and other symptoms while also increasing the physical health of participants (Tucker et al. 2016b). It allows the brain to clear as a client becomes sober (Russell 2001). Most OBH programs require parents to use this space to work with a therapist to heal, develop, and grow. Making change without being in a constant flight or fight response and using letter writing to practice communication patterns is a healthy way to internalize a new homeostatic pattern that can help to strengthen the family. It may also allow the client and family to co-create a healthier narrative for themselves and their shared meaning as a family.

OBH and Family Therapist Collaboration

The power of OBH can be transformative. OBH therapists and children completing the program understand the wilderness experience. It is, however, not something easily described. Both the parents and the family therapist are removed from the wilderness experience and do not have a context to understand what the child is experiencing. A number of factors can help provide a foundation for family therapists to build on the OBH experience. Although this may seem extreme and may not always be practical, first and perhaps foremost, family therapists might consider visiting a program and spending one to three days in the field. The family therapist is likely to come away with a deeper understanding, appreciation, and even enthusiasm for OBH. This can provide a stronger connection to the child and the OBH therapist.

Therapists differ in their approach. Family therapists should feel comfortable reaching out to the OBH therapists to learn about their specific approach to therapy. The family therapist can also share their approach to therapy with the OBH therapist to create a mutual understanding and to look for commonalities to capitalize on. These discussions can provide a strong foundation to a collaborative relationship. Through collaboration, the family therapist can play a meaningful role in helping the parents interpret and integrate their child's experience. This is particularly important in the letters the parent's receive from their child and in the letters they write to their child. These communications can be an opportunity to restructure the relationship in the context of healthy interactions. For example, the family therapist can help the parents be clear on issues around boundaries, conflict, expectations, and their hopes and goals for treatment. Most OBH programs engage parents in family workshops. The family therapist can work to prepare the parents for this workshop and then process and support them when they return.

Further, OBH programs can build stronger collaboration with family therapists by providing details on the intake assessment results and even consultation with the family therapist as an individual program plan is developed. Family therapists should also feel comfortable requesting and receiving weekly progress updates. When this occurs, a spirit of collaboration can be created leading to the exchange of notes and ideas, and a commitment by the OBH therapist to help establish an effective transition from wilderness back to the home environment. The family therapist can serve as a resource to find programs for aftercare, such as Al-Anon, substance abuse groups, and intensive outpatient programs. Beyond theses, they can work to find positive activities for the child to engage in as part of aftercare, such as using the outdoor recreation skills learned in the program to continue to rock climb, bike, or backpack. Successful collaboration requires both parties to engage. Clearly, collaboration can increase the effectiveness of the OBH experience.

Engaging Families Through Activities

In addition to better integrating traditional family techniques into OBH treatment and collaborating effectively with family therapists, it may benefit OBH program clinicians to intentionally engage in adventure activities with families as part of their treatment with more frequency. The use of adventure activities with families as a clinical intervention is not a novel idea (Gass 1993, 1995). Just as mental and behavioral health professionals brought processing and debriefing skills into adventure education, clinicians trained in family systems theories began to explore ways to incorporate family therapy concepts and techniques into adventure experiences (Gass 1993; Gillis and Gass 1993). Adventure therapy with families incorporates the techniques and beliefs of other family therapies, but delivers these practices through the medium of adventure activities.

Lung et al. (2015) stress how adventure activities can be used as agents of change with families, whether this is in a clinical office, a family home, or in an OBH setting. Adventure activities that are chosen intentionally to match the current needs of the family can highlight in real time the current strengths and challenges of families. Families are not asked to role-play but act as they are "in the moment, and to display their typical way of dealing with experiences" (Lung et al. 2015, p. 9). In this model it is the family therapist's job to properly assess the family, choose activities that match the needs of the family based on their assessment, facilitate the activity, guide the learning by providing opportunities for family members to reflect upon their "interactions, thoughts, and behavior in the here and now," and help facilitate the application of their learning to their lives outside of the therapy setting (Lung et al. 2015, p. 10).

In OBH, engaging families more often and intentionally in adventure activities together may provide the benefit of the parents participating in a parallel therapeutic experience to their children, who are engaged in adventure therapy throughout the duration of the program. This may possibly aid in transference in that the youth and the parents both have access to a similar language, created through shared therapeutic adventure activities; that they can together refer back to. Research has shown that living in a camp setting and engaging in activities together, which parents could have access to in OBH programs, can bring personal enlightenment to family members (Haber 2011), provide new opportunities in a technology-free environment to build relationships (Hickmon et al. 1997), and improve family cohesion (McLendon et al. 2009). It may also give the parents better insight into the applicability of their child's experience in OBH.

Just as therapists have worked to integrate family therapy techniques into OBH, family therapists can integrate adventure into home-based therapy. Utilizing adventure activities is not limited to the outdoors, and hence using adventure activities with families at home or in an office setting could provide home clinicians with more active ways to engage families when the youth returns and build upon the foundations created while the youth was at their OBH program. For example, Swank and Daire (2010) describe a model of multiple family adventure therapy groups in which groups of several families meet weekly for two hours to engage in a variety of adventure experiences over the course of several months. In this model, through the use of share adventure activities, which challenged families to solve problems and take risks, families are able to find their commonalities in terms of their family challenges similar to tradition group therapy and support each other and give constructive feedback to help in the clinical growth of the families (Swank and Daire 2010). Utilizing adventure activities intentionally with families regardless of the setting can provide new opportunities for learning and growth while engaging the families in shared experiences, which can also be fun (Lung et al. 2015).

Closing Remarks

The purpose of this chapter was to provide a brief overview of how family can be more thoroughly integrated within OBH programs, including the role of the home family therapist in that process. The current relationship between OBH and family therapy may not, in many instances, fully utilize the potential benefits to help heal individuals and families; hence, more attention must be paid to the important role of treating the family as well as the youth. This includes an active role, if available, by the home clinician in treating both the youth and the family. Clearly, there are risks in separating family members from the system when conducting therapy. In certain situations, however, a need exists to remove a family member as part of the therapeutic process. In these instances, OBH can provide a viable option to impact both the individual and family, and should be considered when removing a child in an effort to support families in crisis. In fact, considering consistent research in which youth report significant clinical improvements after OBH participation, it would only follow logic that as families are more integrated into OBH treatment, these outcomes would strengthen with consistent impacts beyond the youth to the family system.

References

Arbinger. (2015). *The anatomy of peace: Resolving the heart of conflict*. Oakland, CA: Berrett-Koehler.

Bettmann, J., & Tucker, A. (2011). Shifts in attachment relationships: A study of adolescents in wilderness treatment. *Child and Youth Care Forum, 40*(6), 499–519. doi:10.1007/s10566011-9146-6

Bettmann, J., Tucker, A., Tracy, J., & Parry, K. (2014). An exploration of gender, client history and functioning in wilderness therapy participants. *Residential Treatment for Children and Youth, 31*(3), 155–170. doi:10.1177/1053825913518895

Bettmann, J. E., Russell, K. C., & Parry, K. J. (2013). How substance abuse recovery skills, readiness to change and symptom reduction impact change processes in wilderness therapy participants. *Journal of Child and Family Studies, 22*(8), 1039–1050. doi:10.1007/s10826-012-9665

Christenson, J. D., & Miller, A. L. (2016). Slowing down the conversation: The use of letter writing with adolescents and young adults in residential settings. *Contemporary Family Therapy, 38*, 23–31.

Csikszentmihalyi, M. (1990). *Flow: The psychology of optimal experience*. New York: Harper and Row.

Deci, E., & Flaste, R. (1996). *Why we do what we do: Understanding self-motivation*. New York: Penguin. doi:10.1080/15283480903422806

DeMille, S. M., & Montgomery, M. (2016). Integrating narrative family therapy in an outdoor behavioral healthcare program: A case study. *Contemporary Family Therapy, 38*, 3–13. doi:10.1007/s10591-015-9362-6

Emmons, R. A., & Mishra, A. (2012). Why gratitude enhances well-being: What we know, what we need to know (pp. 248–262). In K. Sheldon, T. Kashdan, & M. F. Steger (Eds.) *Designing the future of positive psychology: Taking stock and moving forward.* New York: Oxford University Press. doi:10.1080/17439760.2011.614830

Epstein, N., Baldwin, L., & Bishop, D. (1983). The McMaster family assessment device. *Journal of Marital and Family Therapy, 9,* 171–180. doi: 10.1111/j.1752-0606.1983.tb01497.x

Faddis, T. J., & Bettmann, J. (2006). Reflecting teams and other innovative family therapy techniques adapted for outdoor behavioral healthcare. *Journal of Therapeutic Schools and Programs, 1*(1), 57–69.

Frensch, K. M., & Cameron, G. (2002). Treatment of choice or a last resort? A review of residential mental health placements for children and youth. *Child & Youth Care Forum, 31*(5), 307–339.

Gass, M., Gillis, H. L., & Russell, K. (2012). *Adventure therapy: Theory, research and practice.* New York: Routledge.

Gass, M. A. (1993). The theoretical foundations for adventure family therapy. In M. Gass (Ed.), *Adventure therapy: Therapeutic applications of adventure programming* (pp. 123–138). Dubuque, IA: Kendall/Hunt.

Gass, M. A. (1995). Adventure family therapy: An innovative approach answering the question of lasting change with adjudicated youth. *Alternatives to Incarceration: Prevention or Treatment. Monograph on Youth in the 1990s, 4,* 103–117.

Gillis, H. L., & Gass, M. (1993). Bringing adventure into marriage and family therapy: An innovative experiential approach. *Journal of Marital and Family Therapy, 19,* 275–286.

Gottman, J., & Silver, N. (2013). *What makes love last? How to build trust and avoid betrayal.* New York, NY: Simon & Schuster.

Haber, R. (2011).Virginia Satir's family camp experiment: An intentional growth community still in process. *Contemporary Family Therapy, 33,* 71–84, doi:10.1007/s10591-010-9140-4

Harpaz-Rotem, I., Leslie, D., & Rosenheck, R. A. (2004). Treatment retention among children entering a new episode of mental health care. *Psychiatric Services, 55*(9), 1022–1028. doi:10.1176/appi.ps.55.9.1022

Harper, N. J. (2005). *Family involvement in outdoor behavioral healthcare: A descriptive analysis.* North East Regional Conference of the Association for Experiential Education. Colebrook, CT.

Harper, N. J., & Russell, K. C. (2008). Family involvement and outcome in adolescent wilderness treatment. A mixed methods evaluation. *International Journal of Child and Family Welfare, 1,* 19–36.

Harper, N. J., Russell, K. C., Cooley, R., & Cupples, J. (2007). Catherine Freer wilderness therapy expeditions: An exploratory case study of adolescent wilderness therapy, family functioning, and the maintenance of change. *Child and Youth Care Forum, 36,* 111–129. doi:10.1007/s10566-007-9035-1

Hattie, J., Marsh, H. W., Neill, J. T., & Richards, G. E. (1997). Adventure education and outward bound: Out-of-class experiences that make a lasting difference. *Review of Educational Research, 67*(1), 43–87. doi:10.3102/00346543067001043

Hickmon, W. A., Protinsky, H. O., & Singh, K. (1997). Increasing marital intimacy: Lessons from marital enrichment. *Contemporary Family Therapy, 19*(4), 581–589.

Johnson, S. M. (2012). *Practice of emotionally focused couple therapy: Creating connection.* London: Routledge.

Kelly, F. J., & Baer, D. J. (1968). *Outward Bound schools as an alternative to institutionalization for adolescent delinquent boys.* Boston: Outward Bound Inc.

Krakauer, J. (1995, October). Loving them to death. *Outside Magazine, 20,* 72–80, 82, 142–143.

Lewis, S. F. (2012). Examining changes in substance use and conduct problems among treatment-seeking adolescents. *Child and Adolescent Mental Health, 18,* 33–38. doi:10.1111/j.1475-3588.2012.00657.x

Lung, D. M., Stauffer, G., Alvarez, T., & Conway, J. (2015). *The power of family: An experiential approach to family treatment.* Bethany, OK: Woods N Barnes.

Lyubomirsky, S. (2008). *The how of happiness: A scientific approach to getting the life you want.* New York: Penguin Press.

Magle-Haberek, N., Tucker, A., & Gass, M. (2012). The effects of program differences within wilderness therapy and residential treatment center (RTC) programs. *Residential Treatment for Children and Youth, 29*(3), 202–218. doi:10.1080/0886571X.2012.697433

McLendon, T., McLendon, D., Petr, C. G., Kapp, S., & Mooradian, J. (2009). Family-directed structural therapy in a therapeutic wilderness family camp: An outcome study. *Social Work in Mental Health, 7*(5), 508–527. doi:10.1080/15332980802466425

Miller, N. S., & Flaherty, J. A. (2000). Effectiveness of coerced addiction treatment (alternative consequences): A review of the clinical research. *Journal of Substance Abuse Treatment, 18* (1), 9–16.

Nickerson, A. B., Brooks, J. L., Colby, S. A., Rickert, J. M., & Salamone, F. J. (2006). Family involvement in residential treatment: Staff, parent, and adolescent perspectives. *Journal of Child & Family Studies, 15*(6), 681–694. doi:10.1007/s10826-006-9041-1

National Institute of Drug Abuse. (2015). *Principles of adolescent substance use disorder treatment: A research-based guide*. Retrieved from https://www.drugabuse.gov/publications/principles-adolescent-substance-use-disorder-treatment-research-based-guide/principles-adolescent-substance-use-disorder-treatment

Norton, C. L., Tucker, A., Russell, K., Bettmann, J., Gass, M., Gillis, H. L., et al. (2014). Adventure therapy with youth. *Journal of Experiential Education, 37*(1), 46–59. doi:10.1177/1053825913518895

Olson, D. H., & Gorall, D. M. (2003). Circumplex model of marital and family systems. In F. Walsh (Ed.), *Normal family processes* (3rd ed., pp. 514–547). New York: Guilford.

Outdoor Behavioral Healthcare Council. (2015). *About us*. Retrieved from http://obhcouncil.org/about/

Peterson, C., & Seligman, M. E. (2004). *Character strengths and virtues: Their role in well-being*. Oxford, UK: Oxford University Press.

Robinson, A. D., Kruzich, J. M., Friesen, B. J., Jivanjee, P., & Pullmann, M. (2005). Preserving family bonds: Examining parent perspectives in the light of practice standards for out-of-home treatment. *Journal of Orthopsychiatry, 75*, 632–643. doi:10.1037/0002-9432.75.4.632

Russell, K. C. (2000). Exploring how the wilderness therapy process relates to outcomes. *Journal of Experiential Education, 23*(3), 170–176. doi:10.1177/105382590002300309

Russell, K. C. (2001). What is wilderness therapy? *Journal of Experiential Education, 24*(2), 70–79. doi:10.1177/105382590102400203

Russell, K. C. (2003a). A nationwide survey of outdoor behavioral healthcare programs for adolescents with problem behaviors. *Journal of Experiential Education, 25*(3), 322–331. doi:10.1177/105382590302500306

Russell, K. C. (2003b). Assessing treatment outcomes in outdoor behavioral healthcare using the Youth Outcome Questionnaire. *Child and Youth Care Forum, 32*(6), 355–381. doi:10.1023/B:CCAR.0000004507.12946

Russell, K. C., & Farnum, J. (2004). A concurrent model of wilderness therapy. *Journal of Adventure Education & Outdoor Learning, 4*, 39–55.

Russell, K. C., Gillis, H. L., & Lewis, T. G. (2008). A five year follow-up of North American outdoor behavioral healthcare programs. *Journal of Experiential Education, 31*(1) 55–77. doi:10.1177/105382590803100106

Russell, K. C., & Phillips-Miller, D, (2002). Perspectives on wilderness therapy process and its relation to outcome. *Child and Youth Care Forum, 31*(6), 415–437. doi:10.1023/A:1021110417119

Schwartz, S. W. (2009). *Adolescent mental health in the United States: Facts for policymakers*. Retrieved from http://nccp.org/publications/pdf/text_878.pdf

Swank, J. M., & Daire, A. P. (2010). Multiple family adventure-based group therapy: An innovative integration of two approaches. *The Family Journal: Counseling and Therapy for Couples and Families, 18*(3), 214–247. doi:10.1177/1066480710372123

Taniguchi, S., Freeman, P., & Richards, A. L. (2005). Attributes of meaningful learning experiences in an outdoor education program. *Journal of Adventure Education and Outdoor Learning, 5*(2), 131–144.

Toepfer, S., Cichy, K., & Peters, P. (2012). Letters of gratitude: further evidence of author benefits. *Journal of Happiness Studies, 13*(1), 187–201. doi:10.1007/s10902-011-9257-7

Tucker, A. R. (2009). Adventure-based group therapy to promote social skills in adolescents. *Social Work with Groups, 32,* 315–329. doi:10.1080/01609510902874594

Tucker, A. R., Bettmann, J., Norton, C. L., & Comart, C. (2015). The role of transport use in adolescent wilderness treatment: Its relationship to readiness to change and outcome. *Child and Youth Care Forum, 44,* 671–686.
DOI 10.1007/s10566-015-9301-6

Tucker, A. R., Massey Combs, K., Bettmann, J., Chang, T., Graham, S., Hoag, M., et al. (2016a). Longitudinal outcomes for youth transported to wilderness therapy programs. *Research on Social Work Practice.* doi:10.1177/1049731516647486

Tucker, A. R., Norton, C., DeMille, S., & Hobson, J. (2016b). The impact of wilderness therapy on physical and emotional health: Utilizing an integrated approach in Outdoor Behavioral Healthcare. *Journal of Experiential Education, 39*(1), 15–30. doi:10.1177/1053825915607536

Tucker, A. R., Paul, M., Hobson, J., Karoff, M., & Gass, M. (2016c). Outdoor Behavioral Healthcare: Its impact on family functioning. *Journal of Therapeutic Schools and Programs, 8,* 21–40. doi:10.19157/JTSP.issue.08.01.05

Tucker, A. R., Zelov, R., & Young, M. (2011). Four years along: Emerging traits of programs in the NATSAP practice research network (PRN). *Journal of Therapeutic Schools & Programs, 5*(1), 10–28.

Wells, G., Burlingame, G., Lambert, M., Hoag, M., & Hope, C. (1996). Conceptualization and measurement of patient change during psychotherapy: Development of the outcome questionnaire and youth outcome questionnaire. *Psychotherapy: Theory, Research, Practice, Training, 33*(2), 275–283. doi:10.1037/0033-3204.33.2.275

White, W. (2012). A history of adventure therapy. In M. Gass, H. L. Gillis, & K. C. Russell (Eds.), *Adventure therapy* (pp. 19–48). New York: Routledge.

Zelechoski, A., D., Sharma, R., Beserra, K., Miguel, J. L., DeMarco, M., & Spinazzola, J., (2013). Traumatized youth in residential treatment settings: Prevalence, clinical presentation, treatment, and policy implications. *Journal of Family Violence, 28,* 639–652. doi:10.1007/s10896-013-9534-9

Zelov, R., Tucker, A. R., & Javorksi, S. (2013). A new phase for the NATSAP PRN: Post-discharge reporting and transition to the network wide utilization of the Y-OQ 2.0. *Journal of Therapeutic Schools & Programs, 6*(1), 7–19.

Author Biographies

Anita Tucker, Ph.D., LISCW is an Associate Professor in Social Work at the University of New Hampshire (UNH) where she is the co-coordinator of UNH's dual-degree Master's program in Social Work and Outdoor Education and the Associate Director of UNH's Outdoor Behavioral Healthcare Center. Dr. Tucker has published over 25 empirical articles and four book chapters focused on wilderness and adventure therapy. In addition, she serves on the Board of Directors for the Association for Experiential Education.

Mark Widmer, Ph.D. is a professor of Therapeutic Recreation in the Marriott School of Management at Brigham Young University. He also teaches in the Executive MBA program. His research focuses on the effective use of adventure experiences to promote skills, resilience, and therapeutic outcomes. He regularly publishes his findings in peer-reviewed journals. Mark also develops and runs outdoor adventure programs for families and executive teams in locations around the world including Canada, Spain, Turkey, and New Zealand. These programs focus on skills such as open communication, healthy conflict, effective coping skills, leading strategic change, performance management, and innovation. Recently, he and his partners founded, Ampelis, a consulting company with programs to help families identify, build, and pass on an intentional family culture, to protect the transition of family well-being and wealth.

Troy J. Faddis, MS, LMFT has been working in wilderness therapy since 2001. His clinical experience includes working with adults and adolescents with substance abuse and dual diagnosis. Troy also works with difficult family systems including those impacted by divorce and easily frustrated and chronically inflexible children. He excels in helping clients develop resiliency and self-efficacy skills, and working with clients who have gifted intelligence. Troy worked many years as a field therapist and clinical director for Aspen Achievement Academy. Troy began his studies at Brigham Young University where he graduated with a Bachelor of Science degree in family sciences. He received his Master's of Science in Marriage and Family Therapy from Seattle Pacific University. Troy is a licensed Marriage and Family Therapist and an AAMFT supervisor. Troy was a board member for The Utah Association for Marriage and Family Therapy from 2005 to 2011.

Bryan Randolph, MS, LICSW joined the clinical team of Mountain Valley Treatment Center in 2013 and is passionate about helping others through the use of experiential and adventure activities to promote change. Bryan received a Bachelor degree in Outdoor Adventure Leadership from Ithaca College, after which he went on to complete his Master of Science degree in Outdoor Education at the University of New Hampshire. Bryan is a Licensed Independent Clinical Social Worker in the state of New Hampshire, and he has extensive experience working in adolescent residential programs, including wilderness settings and at a therapeutic boarding school.

Michael Gass, Ph.D., LMFT is a Professor in the College of Health and Human Services and Director of the Outdoor Behavioral Healthcare (OBH) Center at the University of New Hampshire. He began working in the OBH field in 1979 and has published over 150 professional publications and delivered over 300 professional presentations. He has received several awards for his work, including the Distinguished Researcher awards from both the Association for Experiential Education and College of Health and Human Services at the University of New Hampshire.

Chapter 16
Unpacking the Family Story: Family Techniques in Residential Treatment

Troy J. Faddis and Katherine F. Cobb

Chapter Highlights

- Family systems theory,narrative therapy, and experiential therapy can be integrated through the use of a family sculpture reflecting team.
- In this type of residential work, the family sculpture exercise has four movements, and uses peers and their family members as a reflecting team in a group setting.
- As the family is sculpted, and the sculpture is processed from a number of perspectives, families gain new insights into dynamics that maintain their distress.
- A therapist guides this process and works hard to ensure the family being sculpted benefits from the presence of an outsider witness group.
- Recently this intervention has been extended to work with adolescents and young adults while they remain separated from their families.

Over the past 10–15 years significant work has been done within the field of wilderness therapy, also known as Outdoor Behavioral Healthcare (OBH). Wilderness therapy has roots in Outward Bound and other adventure programing, but its development and application in varying contexts has led to much confusion as to what exactly constitutes wilderness therapy. Gass et al. (2012) note that its expansion and adaption by many others may be precisely the reason that wilderness therapy has such a multitude of definitions. Nevertheless, this treatment modality

T.J. Faddis (✉)
Legacy Outdoor Adventures, P.O. Box 400, Loa, UT 84747, USA
e-mail: troy@legacyoutdooradventures.com

K.F. Cobb
Marriage and Family Therapy Program, Mount Mercy University,
1330 Elmhurst Dr. NE, Cedar Rapids, IA 52402, USA
e-mail: kcobb3118@mustangs.mtmercy.edu

© Springer International Publishing AG 2017
J.D. Christenson and A.N. Merritts (eds.), *Family Therapy with Adolescents
in Residential Treatment*, Focused Issues in Family Therapy,
DOI 10.1007/978-3-319-51747-6_16

has become more clinically sophisticated over the course of its development and many have conducted important empirical research within this field (see Gillis et al. 2008 for an overview).

Increasingly, research in wilderness therapy programs has extended beyond the focus on adolescents and has explored the importance of evaluating and involving of family members. As early as 1994, Bandoroff and Scherer found that using a family-as-client as opposed to a child-as-client approach in their wilderness family program led to improved clinical results in family functioning. A growing body of research suggests that involving parents and members of a larger support network in residential treatment facilities increases treatment effectiveness (e.g., Nickerson et al. 2006).

However, as Sunseri (2004) points out, "[e]ncouraging family involvement is not the same as providing effective, comprehensive family treatment" (p. 48). Several programs have taken to incorporating the family into traditional elements of challenge-based recreational therapy, for example, building a fire without the use of matches or effectively working a handcart together (Wells et al. 2004). Other programs make use of ropes courses or balancing activities, all of which promote a sense of collective efficacy and cooperation among family members. This chapter will provide an overview of a four-phase familial sculpting and reflecting inter-vention, as previously outlined by Faddis and Bettmann (2006), which incorporates families into residential wilderness-based therapy through the use of sculpting and reflecting teams. The authors will then review how this intervention and the theories that provide its structure have most recently been adapted for working on family dynamics even when family members cannot be present.

Theoretical Basis

Understanding theory is vital to therapeutic practice in any setting and many have noted its importance in the wilderness and residential settings (Faddis and Bettmann 2006; Hoyer 2004; Russell 2003). Becker (2009) states "[i]n addition to efficiency, theory-informed practice has implications for the way in which treatment may be used efficaciously and ethically" (p. 49). The familial sculpting and reflecting intervention is an integration of different techniques based in the theories of experiential and narrative therapy. In order to provide sufficient background on the intervention and its current adaption some information on the underlying theories is needed

Family Therapy and Systems Theory

In general, systems theory holds that when phenomena are observed together rather than separately, we have the opportunity to understand how these phenomena interact and affect each other (Bateson 1972; Jackson 1965; Keeney 1983; von Bertalanffy 1968). In its application to psychotherapy, systems theory emphasizes observing and intervening at the level of interaction between individuals, rather than with one individual alone (Bateson 1972; Becvar and Becvar 2006; Keeney 1983). In the 1980s, the second wave of systems theory developed the concept of second-order cybernetics, which concerned itself with the connection between the observer and the system being observed. Second-order cybernetics stresses that when working with a family system a therapist cannot help but become part of the system. This theory also holds that because the therapist is now a part of the system, he or she no longer operates in an expert role. Rather than suggest specific changes or behaviors, it is the job of the therapist to set the context for change (Hoffman 1985, 1988).

All of the intervention techniques mentioned in this paper, including those of experiential and narrative therapies, are rooted in systems theory and cybernetics. Those who practice therapy with systems theory in mind hold that changing one thing in the system has the potential to change every other part of the system. Thus, when working with adolescents in residential treatment it is possible to make small changes with adolescents that then create large differences in the family's interactions.

Experiential Family Therapy

Experiential family therapy is based in an understanding of *here-and-now* thinking. Virginia Satir, who was highly influential in its development, was famous for her warmth and empathetic use of self in building relationships with clients. Experiential family therapists focus on affective or emotional interaction sequences both within the family and the individual. The goals of experiential family therapy are twofold in that families should strive to develop effective means of communicating and each individual within the family should strive for increasing their sense of self-esteem and authenticity (Gehart 2013). Often this is accomplished through expressive techniques.

Family sculpting originated as a technique in the work of David Kantor with early contributions from Bunny Duhl, Fred Duhl, and their colleagues at Boston State Hospital and the Boston Family Institute (Constantine 1978; Nichols and Schwartz 1998). This technique originally utilized objects rather than people to represent family members, but on a visit to the Boston Family Institute clinic Satir observed and then adapted the technique to use with actual people. Sculpting can be used as a tool to visually portray the roles of each family member and can heighten family members' awareness of each other's actions. When family members are represented symbolically in the family sculpture, it tends to illuminate unforeseen relational dynamics between family members (Papp et al. 2013).

As will be seen below, sculpting is at the heart of the four-phase familial sculpting and reflecting intervention and its later adaptions. Providing adolescents the opportunity to tell their stories through sculptures gives them power to communicate thoughts and feelings that are often difficult to verbalize. Visually representing the adolescent's point of view within the family creates empathy and understanding among family members. It also helps create witnesses out of the audience members, as well as the family members involved in the sculpture, which enhances the narrative elements of this experiential technique.

Postmodernism

Although postmodernism is a broad movement that spreads across several disciplines, its general philosophical premise is that the act of knowing is subjective and therefore the concept of objective knowledge is disregarded altogether. This then forms the necessary conclusion that unequivocal truth does not exist (Cloete 2001). Consequently, it is the view of postmodernists that reality is a function of the interpretation of the observer. In practice, postmodern family therapy is focused on how individuals are "interpreting, constructing, and storying his or her reality" (Phipps and Vorster 2011, p. 36). These methods soon led to the development of the field of narrative therapy.

Narrative Therapy

Narrative therapy has its origins in the work of Michael White, David Epston, Lynn Hoffman, Harlene Anderson, Harry Goolishian, and others. In their book *Narrative Means to Therapeutic Ends*, White and Epston (1990) outline the basic thesis of narrative therapy: (a) that human beings tend to *story* their experiences; and, (b) in doing so they ascribe significance to the events in their lives as a means of expression. Instead of viewing a person as pathological or defective, narrative therapy holds that persons are essentially separate from their problems. Problems are not viewed as aspects of a person, but rather it is that a problem-saturated story has become dominant in a person's life. When problem-saturated stories come to dominate people's lives, it is the task of narrative therapists to aid their clients in the process of deconstructing and externalizing this problem-saturated story.

Often adolescents enter residential treatment when their behavior has become so extreme and untenable that the parents believe it is their last resort. The parents tend to believe that their child is the problem while the adolescent usually views himself or herself as a victim (Harper and Russell 2008; Fitzgerald 1994). Narrative therapy allows for the deconstruction of these views and externalizing the adolescent's problematic behavior helps both family members and the adolescent reach a new understanding where neither feels persecuted or to blame. Therapists focus on finding exceptions to the problem-saturated story, after which therapists work with clients to develop these exceptions into richer and thicker narratives that support the client's goals. Once these new and preferred narratives have been developed, they can be documented in ways that solidify the story and can serve as potential reminders of it for the clients (see Chap. 3; Epston 1998, 2008; White and Epston 1990). This documentation can come in the form of letters, certificates, announcements, video or audio recordings, poetry, or artwork of many forms. Other methods to solidify these new stories involve incorporating other persons in the form of audiences referred to as *outsider witness groups* in a *definitional ceremony*.

The theory behind this last practice comes from the writings of cultural anthropologist Barbara Meyerhoff (1986) who used the term definitional ceremony to describe her work with elderly Jews who had been displaced from Eastern Europe to Venice, Los Angeles. This community of elderly Jews expressed themselves by painting a set of murals in a community center and subsequently organizing a parade to display these works to their community at large. In doing so they invited the larger community of Californians to witness a representation of a story meaningful in their lives (Combs and Freedman 2012; White 2009). The process of a definitional ceremony will be further elaborated on later in this article with specific reference to working in a residential setting.

Reflecting Teams

The creator of reflecting teams, Anderson (1987, 1991), was influenced by Milan and other forms of therapy but grew tired of its hierarchical nature and was consequently inspired to create a non-hierarchical intervention in the form of reflecting teams. Eventually White (2007) adapted this technique and introduced a structure for the reflecting teams, although he labeled them outsiderwitness groups. This technique usually involves a team of therapists observing a family therapy session behind a one-way mirror. In the middle of the session the reflecting team (composed of therapists) and the family switches places so that the family can observe the reflecting team discuss their observations of the family therapy session. The two groups then switch back and the family is invited to discuss the observations offered by the reflecting team of therapists (Combs and Freedman 1998, 2012). This technique is usually helpful because it allows the families to gather an *external* or *outsider* perspective about their issues and see them in a different light. This kind of technique involves a great deal of transparency and collaboration, which emphasizes the therapist's non-expert role. It is, therefore, well suited for use in narrative therapy.

In residential settings there is an opportunity to not only use therapist and staff as the outsider perspective, but a peer group can also be used to reflect, deconstruct, validate, and expand. This peer group may have already participated in meaningful experiential exercises together, such as technical canyoneering, rappelling, and other challenging events that have built trust and help them in bonding to each other. In this context peers as outside witnesses can be effective in using-meta-communication about the family processes and allow insight to be gained by the client without the typical resistance. In fact, in these situations the safety of the peer group, and the power of the technique, allows for a leaning in opportunity as described by Gottman (2011) and client curiosity about self/family as talked about by Dr. Schwartz (2013).

Reflecting Team Work as Definitional Ceremony

As mentioned previously, the definitional ceremony was a metaphor borrowed by White (2009). White uses this definitional ceremony in order to structure a telling of some of the signature stories of people's lives. There can also be a retelling of these stories when the outsider witness group is present. White (1999, 2009) details the process of how an outsider group can become involved in the use of reflecting teams, which usually occurs over four distinct phases.

First, a person is provided the opportunity to tell a story about a significant event in their life while being observed by an audience of outside witnesses. Second, the outsider witnesses are asked to respond to what they heard. The therapist facilitates this response by asking questions about the parts of the story that they were most drawn to, images evoked by these parts of the story and the ways they have been moved by witnessing the original telling of the story. When doing a more Satir style sculpture, the therapist can ask about specific characters in the sculpture; what they are saying to the client and what the client is saying to them. Using voices, as well as motion, can enhance the experience of the story telling and often evokes emotions that can also be processed. Third, the outsider witnesses retell the story to the original storyteller, now in an audience role, with emphasis placed on elements of the original story that struck him or her as especially important. This act of retelling the original story through an observer's lens links the two groups of people together through shared themes and values. Finally, the original storyteller and the outsider witnesses discuss the first three parts of the definitional ceremony together, which makes for an even more transparent therapeutic conversation.

The entire cycle is designed to create an experience that grounds all participants and resonates within and between individuals as each retelling adds additional layers to the narrative. White states "[i]t is this resonance that contributes to a rich story development, to stronger familiarity with what one accords value to in life and to the erosion and displacement of various negative conclusions about one's life and identity" (White 2009, p. 204). Furthermore, the entire experience provides the foundation upon which all can address the problems in their own lives.

Four-Phase Familial Sculpting and Reflecting Intervention

As previously described, typical reflecting teams can be conducted using four interviews (White 1999, 2000). The following section will provide an overview of how the four-phase reflecting teams in combination with the sculpting technique were adapted for use at a residential outdoor behavioral healthcare setting, as outlined by Faddis and Bettmann (2006). This intervention was typically utilized during the reunion phase when parents or family members came to pick up their child after he or she had spent about 8 weeks in treatment. A few days of activities, which often included the adolescents taking their family members on a hike into the wilderness and setting up camp for a night together, led up to the definitional ceremony, so that families had a chance to reconnect before participating in a therapeutic activity together.

Time spent together prior to the therapy session also provided adolescents with the opportunity to take care of their family members in the wilderness and demonstrate how much they had grown over their time in treatment. This included performing tasks such as setting up a shelter with tarps and rope, making a fire without matches, and cooking over an open fire. In a sense, parents were dependent on their children to provide for their needs over a short period of time. This sometimes would have the effect of *softening* the parent's perception of the child, which often would have a positive effect on the family's experience in the sculpting exercise. The afternoon that the four-phase intervention took place usually began with a short hike into the woods where the families would then be split into groups of three of four families, each with their own facilitating therapist. Conducting this intervention with one family usually took about an hour, so splitting the families into smaller groups was often necessary, in order to keep the experience within a more manageable time frame.

Phase One

In non-residential treatment settings the first interview is performed in *typical* fashion where people discuss core family issues with a therapist. In the residential setting the first interview was replaced by a session in which one adolescent created a family sculpture of his or her family. The adolescent was asked to arrange people and props that they might find outdoors (trees, rocks, cordage, streams, firewood, etc.) to create a meaningful portrait of an event, scenario or dynamic that characterizes his or her perspective of the family. This sculpture represents the dominant story that shapes how each adolescent saw themselves in relation to the rest of the family system. Oftentimes with the teens that attend residential therapy the story is problem-saturated. The adolescent then explained his or her sculpture to the members of the reflecting team while his or her family members are asked to remain silent. When family members are present it is useful to prepare them to use a perceptive that this is their son's or daughter's understanding and that they may not agree with what is said. Additionally they should not challenge the story but they are to listen and validate. This may require significant preparatory work on the part of the therapist, and the therapist may have to redirect the family a number of times throughout the exercise if they are unable to listen without interrupting.

Phase Two

After the adolescent had explained his or her family sculpture, the adolescent and his or her family were asked to separate from the reflecting team while they discussed what they just saw. The reflecting team members sat in a circle and excluded the family who was just sculpted, although the family remained in earshot so that they could hear the feedback from the reflecting team. During this process the family was asked not to respond in any way to the comments they heard, but instead to make notes and remember any statements made that were (1) validating, (2) challenging to hear, and (3) helped them to have a new or better understanding of their family.

The therapist then facilitated a discussion with the reflecting team, who were asked to reflect on the sculpture as if they were at an art gallery and consider the following questions:

1. What about this sculpture are you most drawn to?
2. Do I perceive any metaphors or mental images?
3. What similarities do I share with the story being told in this sculpture?
4. What emotions do I experience as I observe this sculpture?

These questions touch on four categories of inquiry that White (2007) tends to emphasize when interviewing outsider witnesses: what caught your attention (expression), any metaphors that came to mind (images), how the story struck a chord with you (resonance), and the ways in which you have been moved by the story (transport). However, these questions are only starting points for the discussion.

Using a reflecting team composed of peers rather than a team of therapists can be associated with both benefits and risks. Potential benefits include avoiding seeing the therapist as the *expert* while possible risks center on the unpredictable nature of the reflecting team's comments. To avoid these pitfalls therapists can ask the members of the reflecting team to be brief, keep the energy focused on the family's sculpture, and encourage them to concentrate on answering the three questions. Therapist and staff can aid using guiding questions that stimulate conversation about the homeostatic patterns, processes, andmeta-communication regarding the thoughts and feelings within the sculpture. A goal in these conversations is to create non-resistant insight for the client and their family members.

Phase Three

The third phase of this intervention allowed the family that was sculpted and the facilitating therapist to sit inside the circle of the reflecting team, who were once again an audience and remained silent during this discussion. The therapist and the family talked with one another about the comments that they heard. Family members were encouraged to share the comments overheard in phase two that were most validating, challenging, supporting, or expanding and also share how the sculpture and the comments affected them emotionally, physically, cognitively, or spiritually. The therapist facilitated this discussion by asking future-oriented questions or highlighting important comments made earlier by the reflecting team that may have been overlooked by the family. After all of the family members had shared their experiences it was then the adolescent's turn to reflect on the comments made by his or her family members, essentially creating a mini-reflecting team process within phase three. This is also the phase where family members were allowed to discuss the first phase sculpting process, but therapists were usually careful here not to allow too much time so as not to risk family members invalidating or attacking the adolescent's sculpture.

Phase Four

The fourth phase looked similar to a debriefing session in which the family and the reflecting team come together to discuss the three previous interviews as one large group. This was the time for reflecting team members to ask new questions and make strengthening comments that have the potential effect of adding reinforcement to the new story developed through this process. The therapist was also responsible for directing this session. The client and family member were asked to share the greatest impression they took from the experience and what positive insights they gained.

Individuals and their families who participated in the four-phase familial sculpting and reflecting team intervention frequently reported that this was a very powerful experience. The process of hearing multiple perspectives in a safe and non-judgmental environment (when constructed correctly) provided an opportunity for families to *hear* and *see* each other in ways that were not possible through any other intervention. Although the program that originated this method of intervention has since been absorbed by other entities, the intervention developed there remains a potent tool that can be used in any residential program that incorporates family activities and workshops.

The Importance of an Audience

Narrative therapy places a special emphasis on the relational nature of the individual and values the importance of sharing stories through reflecting teams or outsiderwitness groups in that it helps solidify new stories. Three different audiences are employed in the adaption of these techniques to a residential setting: the adolescent's family, the adolescent's peers and their family members, and the therapeutic staff and facilitating therapist. Each has a particular role to play in the formation of a new story. Family members play a significant role in the adolescent's life, and accordingly have a special ability to help challenge old stories and support new ones. Peers and their family members can perform an equally important role by offering reinforcement of new stories and providing empathy when they identify with one another's stories. Peers can be especially impactful when dealing with adolescents who naturally seek connection with and approval from their peers above others. Finally, the therapeutic staff plays a critical role in helping solidify change. In residential and OBH settings the staff and guides interact daily with the teens attending the program and form strong relationships. Given these relationships, comments from the staff have the potential to impact the formation of teens' new stories in a small but dramatic way. Additionally, their insights are often helpful for the facilitating therapists.

Audience Through Art

Art in all its various forms can be an especially useful tool given the significant role that outsiders and observers play in solidifying new narratives. As mentioned previously, it is important to make some documentation of the new story to concretize and reinforce it after the conversations had within therapy are over (Combs and Freedman 2012; White and Epston 1990). Epston (1999) notes that it is most important for persons to have the opportunity to record "knowledge-in-the-making" regardless of the medium or form the documentation takes (p. 149). In the use of the four-phase sculpting and reflecting intervention in residential treatment, clients and their families are sometimes asked to self-record through the use of artwork.

If there is time after all of the families have had their turn at the center of the sculpture and reflecting team, the family is asked to draw their family sculpture. They are also asked to record two or three meaningful comments or lessons they learned through the four-phase process on the back of their artwork. Finally, the family is asked to share the artwork with one another as well as mutually commit to re-sharing and remembering these events by keeping the artwork in an often-visited place with opportunity to develop a shared remembering ritual (Doherty 1999). While the creation and sharing of this artwork is ideal to solidify what took place in the definitional ceremony, often time constrains necessitated that this part of the intervention be omitted.

Recent Advances in the Use of Sculptures and Narrative Techniques

The four-phase intervention is quite an undertaking. Previously, the four-phase intervention was used in an OBH setting on days when multiple families visited their children and required at least three to four hours of group therapy. The therapeutic staff was capable of handling, at most, an average of four families at a time given the complexity of the intervention. At times, additional therapists were called in from the field to help facilitate these groups. In addition, parents and family members were not always able to visit their family members in residential treatment. Lack of parental involvement is one of the most often cited pitfalls in residential treatment (Leichtman and Leichtman 2001). The practical realities of this intervention often make it too difficult to implement. However, techniques similar to those of the four-phase intervention have been further adapted for use in residential OBH settings, even when family members cannot be present. Depending on the skill of the therapist, a family sculpture can be used at any time after the client has stabilized, but is most often used about two-thirds of the way through an adolescent's stay in treatment. In its new adapted form, the intervention focuses on three phases surrounding a sculpture (create, co-create, and debrief) rather than the use of reflecting teams, although these can be used when necessary.

Create

Prior to the actually activity, each person is assigned a week in which they know that they will be the one to sculpt their family. In the create phase, the adolescent at the center of the sculpture selects peers to represent family members and can include as many actors as he or she wants—moms, dads, brothers, sisters, aunts, uncles, or grandparents. They then position their actors in a scene and describe their family members' actions, assigning them emotions and dialog. This practice incorporates elements of drama and experiential therapy in that they act out small but important scenes from the adolescent's life and make family dynamics come alive in the room. Using the context described earlier; the peer group already has a base of trust and a culture of giving feedback. The ability to have peers involved in the process enhances the story experience by having them voice main story themes, as well as act them out. This can create an emotional response that can be addressed, highlighted, and validated.

Co-create

In part two of the sculpting process therapist facilitators become co-creators. Concentrating on each adolescent one at a time provides the therapist space to elaborate on the one person's sculpture in ways not possible due to time constrains in the previous use of the four-phase intervention. The therapist may choose to create deeper meaning by focusing in on a variety of areas within the sculpture. For example, a therapist might attempt to reinforce the client's self-awareness or undiscovered significance of their sculpture through a variety of prompts, including asking which part of the sculpture they were most reluctant to reveal, if there is anyone missing from the sculpture, or what they were most surprised or scared about while sculpting. Identifying important and meaningful parts of the sculpture creates a dynamic discussion of emotions. Labeling emotions underlying relationship dynamics creates clarity and objectivity that can facilitate healing.

Oftentimes, without the family members present, therapists are able to push the adolescent to examine deeper emotions by manipulating body positioning or phrases being used and they frequently ask clients to do things such as yell, point, and other things that would be more difficult to do with actual family members. The distance between the adolescent and the family in these settings can provide an opportunity for the adolescent to do important differentiation work (see Chap. 8). The environment of mutual trust among peers also allows the audience to challenge each other's perspectives and co-create with the person at the center of the sculpture.

Debrief

Phase three of the peer sculpture consists of a group debriefing. Everyone is asked to de-role from their sculpted positions and, in certain circumstances, the therapist facilitator may ask the adolescent to specifically invite each invited family member to de-role with a phrase like, "Mark, you are not my angry mother." The group then engages in a discussion about what it was like to witness or participate in the sculpture that just took place. Each person, whether they were at the center of the sculpture, playing a family member or just watching, is invited to discuss whatever feelings arose while watching or participating in the activity. The majority of the time, everyone present will be able to relate what just took place to their own lives. In this way, the sculpture represents an isomorphic interaction to which everyone present can relate their own experiences. This also provides a reinforcing audience that validates the deconstruction and creates hopeful insights that are then gained by the client. Much like the experiences of the teens who had their story told by author Gary Ferguson in the book on wilderness therapy; *Shouting at the Sky: Troubled Teens and the Promise of the Wild* (2009). In the new afterward in the book, nearly every client written about latter reported that the hope given, and the expectancy created by the hope and positive description about their potential, influenced them to achieve and help others later in life.

Reflecting Team

A reflecting team constitutes an optional fourth phase of this intervention. The purpose of forming a reflecting team is to lower the reactivity toward what was just created in the sculpture. It is a particularly effective technique when bringing together multiple families who do not know one another on a very intimate level or when working with a highly reactive family. When adapting the sculpting exercise in a peer-only setting, adolescents are often intimately familiar with one another and family members are not present for the sculpting process; therefore, there is often no need to deescalate with a reflecting team. However, an adolescent may become too emotionally activated during the sculpting process to engage in self-reflection or have awareness about the interactions in the sculpture. Sculpting can be a particularly challenging task with clients who have personality disorders, serious addictions, mental handicaps, or co-dependent familial relationships. In these situations a reflecting team can be utilized as a fourth phase of the intervention to lower reactivity and enhance self-awareness.

When the facilitating therapist determines that a reflecting team is necessary, he or she asks the audience to form a circle around the sculpture already created. Although the sculpture remains at the center, the therapist asks the client previously at the center of the sculpture to step away and join the outer circle. From here the client is asked to observe and take notes on what the audience says about his or her sculpture. This is analogous to the second phase of the previous four-phase intervention and can also serve as a form of letter writing to self. After everyone has shared their observations, the client previously at the center is then asked to share insights from this process in the form of what he or she wrote down or what he or she heard while observing. Much like the third phase of the previous intervention, this serves as a sort of re-telling and offers the client more authorship of his or her story after having had time to deescalate. The final step, analogous to the fourth phase, consists of a quick debrief with everyone coming together on the same level to ask remaining questions and clarify insights.

Advantages of a Peer-Only Family Sculpture

Some may argue the inability to have family members present for a familial sculpture is a disadvantage; however, there are many aspects of an intervention without family members that are useful. Sculpting one's family before they visit a residential setting allows adolescents to act out their most troubling family dynamics before exposing themselves to a highly emotional and potentially reactive situation. This affords clients in residential settings an opportunity to work through their own emotions independently and also permits them to plan for their family's visit with the therapists' help. The sculpture might also provide clients with certain insights about how their behaviors have changed since the last time they interacted with their family members and highlight what changes they would like their family members to notice in them. This new self-awareness allows for better facilitation of therapeutic sessions with family members when they are able to visit.

Letter Writing

Oftentimes, therapists will encourage adolescents to reflect on the sculpting process by writing down particularly triggering dynamics and how they plan to react when they see their family members in person. Clients can also choose to write letters to their family members to express their feelings in a safe space and choose whether to send them or not. The process of writing letters to family may be reflective, meta-communicative, and co-creative or it may offer a space to start repairing broken trust caused by previous relationship ruptures. When the letters are sent, it opens up lines of communication between adolescent and parents, oftentimes allowing a space to co-create a more positive family story. Letter writing creates an audience while also tying in a narrative perspective to compliment the experiential technique of sculpting. Therapist can also direct parents to write letters focusing mainly the strengths they see in their child countering a misperception that the parents only correct and see negative attributes (see Chap. 2).

Conclusion

Family therapy is a construct of systemic thinking. As a therapeutic modality, systemic family therapy was designed for all family members to be present, but as it grew it was increasingly applied in a variety of settings, including residential outdoor behavioral healthcare, where it is much more difficult to involve family members. Residential and wilderness therapy for troubled adolescents necessarily uses systemic treatment modalities in order to create better functioning family dynamics. As noted earlier, family therapy has shown to be a successful mode of treatment for a variety of issues including maladaptive behaviors as well as addiction and mood disturbances (Nichols and Schwartz 1998). The use of family psychoeducation has significantly improved outcomes in residential treatment settings (Nichols and Schwartz 1998). However, certain obstacles present themselves when adapting family therapy techniques to residential facilities, most notable of which is the inability of family members to directly participate in the therapeutic interventions. While this can be considered an opportunity to work on differentiation, it significantly limits the ability of therapists to deliver traditional family therapy interventions.

This article reviews the theoretical base of both experiential and narrative theories of family therapy, as well as several adaptions of techniques as they have become more widely used in the field. Most notably this article provides an overview of the four-phase familial sculpting and reflecting intervention used in residential settings as previously outlined by Faddis and Bettmann (2006). In the years since its development, this technique that employs sculpting, reflecting, and experiential methods has been adapted for use when parents or family members are unable to attend or participate in treatment sessions in residential settings.

Anecdotal evidence reveals that in lieu of directly involving parents or family members, making use of peers in sculpting exercises and writing letters to parents can actually be more beneficial in certain instances because there is less chance for emotional flooding, ego involvement, or judgment.

Further empirical research is necessary to explore how best to adapt family therapy techniques to residential treatment settings to ensure the best treatment outcomes. It is important to understand how factors related to familial involvement in treatment can enhance or disrupt levels of care for clients, especially when they are highly symptomatic (Karam et al. 2015). In addition, research investigating how to best utilize both experiential therapy elements and narrative therapy techniques may improve the integration of these strategies in residential outdoor behavioral healthcare environments.

References

Anderson, T. (1987). The reflecting team: Dialogue and meta-dialogue in clinical work. *Family Process, 26,* 415–428.

Anderson, T. (Ed.). (1991). *The reflecting team: Dialogues and dialogues about the dialogues.* New York: Norton.

Bateson, G. (1972). *Steps to an ecology of mind: Collected essays in anthropology, psychiatry, evolution and epistemology.* London: Jason Aronson.

Becker, S. P. (2009). Wilderness therapy: Ethical considerations for mental health processionals. *Child & Youth Care Forum, 39,* 47–61. doi:10.1007/s10566-009-9085-7

Becvar, D. S., & Becvar, R. J. (2006). *Family therapy: A systemic integration* (6th ed.). Boston: Pearson Education.

Cloete, M. (2001). *Special tutorial letter: Epistemology and the postmodern challenge.* Pretoria, Gauteng, South Africa: University of South Africa (UNISA), Department of Philosophy.

Combs, G., & Freedman, J. (1998). Tellings and retellings. *Journal of Marital and Family Therapy, 24,* 405–408.

Combs, G., & Freedman, J. (2012). Narrative, poststructuralism, and social justice: Current practices in narrative therapy. *The Counseling Psychologist, 40*(7), 1033–1060. doi:10.1177/0011000012460662

Constantine, L. L. (1978). Family sculpture and relationship mapping techniques. *Journal of Marital and Family Therapy, 4*(2), 13–23. doi:10.1111/j.1752-0606.1978.tb00508.x

Doherty, W. (1999). *The intentional family: Simple rituals to strengthen family ties.* New York: Avon.

Epston, D. (1998). *Catching up with David Epston: A collection of narrative practice-based paper.* Adelaide, Australia: Dulwich Centre.

Epston, D. (1999). Co-research: The making of an alternative knowledge. *Narrative therapy and community work: A conference collection* (pp. 137–157). Dulwich Centre: Adelaide, Australia.

Epston, D. (2008). *Down under and up and over: Travels with narrative therapy.* London: Karnac Books.

Faddis, T. J., & Bettmann, J. E. (2006). Reflecting teams and other innovative family therapy techniques adapted for outdoor behavioral healthcare. *Journal of Therapeutic School Programs, 1*(1), 57–69.

Ferguson, G. (2009). *Shouting at the sky: Troubled teens and the promise of the wild.* Helena, MT: Farcounty Press.

Fitzgerald, M. D. (1994). Resistant attitudes and behaviors of adolescents in residential care: Considerations and strategies. *Child & Youth Care Forum, 23*(6), 365–375. doi:10.1007/BF02128520

Gass, M. A., Gillis, L., & Russell, K. C. (2012). *Adventure therapy: Theory, research, and practice*. London: Routledge.

Gehart, D. (2013). *Mastering competencies in family therapy: A practical approach to theory and clinical case documentation*. Belmont, CA: Cengage Learning.

Gillis, H. L., Gass, M. A., & Russell, K. C. (2008). The effectiveness of project adventure's behavior management programs for male offenders in residential treatment. *Residential Treatment for Children & Youth, 25*(3), 227–247. doi:10.1080/08865710802429689

Gottman, J. M. (2011). *The science of trust: Emotional attunement for couples*. W. W: Norton & Company.

Harper, N. J., & Russell, K. C. (2008). Family involvement and outcome in adolescent wilderness treatment: A mixed-methods evaluation. *International Journal of Child & Family Welfare, 1*, 19–36.

Hoffman, L. (1985). Beyond power and control: Toward a "second order" family systems therapy. *Family Systems Medicine, 3*(4), 381. doi:10.1037/h0089674

Hoffman, L. (1988). A constructivist position for family therapy. *The Irish Journal of Psychology, 9*(1), 110–129. doi:10.1080/03033910.1988.10557709

Hoyer, S. (2004). Effective wilderness therapy: Theory-informed practice. In S. Banderoff & S. Newes (Eds.), *Coming of age: The evolving field of adventure therapy* (pp. 56–72). Boulder, CO: Association for Experiential Education.

Jackson, D. D. (1965). The study of the family. *Family Process, 26*, 331–340. doi:10.1111/j.1545-5300.1965.00001.x

Karam, E. A., Blow, A. J., Sprenkle, D. H., & Davis, S. D. (2015). Strengthening the systemic ties that bind: Integrating common factors into marriage and family therapy curricula. *Journal of Marital and Family Therapy, 41*(2), 136–149. doi:10.1111/jmft.12096

Keeney, B. P. (1983). *Aesthetics of change*. New York: Guilford Press.

Leichtman, M., & Leichtman, M. L. (2001). Facilitating the transition from residential treatment into the community: I. The problem. *Residential Treatment for Children and Youth, 19*, 21–27. doi:10.1037/0002-9432.71.2.227

Meyerhoff, B. (1986). Life not death in Venice: Its second life. In V. W. Turner & E. M. Bruner (Eds.), *The anthropology of experience* (pp. 261–286). Chicago: University of Illinois Press.

Nichols, M., & Schwartz, R. (1998). *Family therapy: Concepts and methods*. Boston, MA: Allyn & Bacon.

Nickerson, A. B., Brooks, J. L., Colby, S. A., Rickert, J. M., & Salamone, F. J. (2006). Family involvement in residential treatment: Staff, parent, and adolescent perspectives. *Journal of Child and Family Studies, 15*, 681–694. doi:10.1007/s10826-006-9041-1

Papp, P., Scheinkman, M., & Malpas, J. (2013). Breaking the mold: Sculpting impasses in couples' therapy. *Family Process, 52*, 33–45. doi:10.1111/famp.12022

Phipps, W. D., & Vorster, C. (2011). Narrative therapy: A return to the intrapsychic perspective? *Journal of Family Psychotherapy, 22*(2), 128–147. doi:10.1080/08975353.2011.578036

Russell, K. (2003). *Definitions, models, and assessing outcomes in outdoor behavioral healthcare*. Paper presented at the Naropa University Wilderness Therapy Symposium. Boulder, CO.

Schwartz, R. (2013) *Evolution of the internal family systems model by Dr. Richard Schwartz* (Ph. D). Retrieved from https://www.selfleadership.org/about-internal-family-systems.html

Sunseri, P. A. (2004). Family functioning and residential treatment outcomes. *Residential Treatment for Children & Youth, 22*, 33–53. doi:10.1300/J007v22n01_03

von Bertalanffy, L. (1968). *General system theory: Foundations, development, applications* (Revised Edition). New York: George Braziller.

Wells, M. S., Widmer, M. A., & McCoy, J. K. (2004). Grubs and grasshoppers: Challenge-based recreation and the collective efficacy of families with at-risk youth. *Family Relations, 53*, 326–333.

White, M. (1999). Reflecting-team work as definitional ceremony revisited. *Gecko: A Journal of Deconstruction and Narrative Ideas in Therapeutic Practice, 2,* 55–82.

White, M. (2000). *Reflecting teamwork as definitional ceremony revisited.* Adelaide: Dulwich Centre Publication.

White, M. (2007). *Maps of narrative practice.* New York: Norton.

White, M. (2009). Narrative practice and conflict dissolution in couples therapy. *Clinical Social Work Journal, 37,* 200–213. doi:10.1007/s10615-009-0192-6

White, M., & Epston, D. (1990). *Narrative means to therapeutic ends.* New York: W.W. Norton & Company.

Author Biographies

Troy J. Faddis, MS, LMFT has been working in wilderness therapy since 2001. His clinical experience includes working with adults and adolescents with substance abuse and dual diagnosis. Troy also works with difficult family systems including those impacted by divorce and easily frustrated and chronically inflexible children. He excels in helping clients develop resiliency and self-efficacy skills, and working with clients who have gifted intelligence. Troy worked many years as a field therapist and clinical director for Aspen Achievement Academy. Troy began his studies at Brigham Young University where he graduated with a Bachelor of Science degree in family sciences. He received his Master's of Science in Marriage and Family Therapy from Seattle Pacific University. Troy is a licensed Marriage and Family Therapist and an AAMFT supervisor. Troy was a board member for the Utah Association for Marriage and Family Therapy from 2005 to 2011.

Katherine F. Cobb, MA earned a Master's in Religious Studies from the University of Iowa and a Master's in Marriage and Family Therapy from Mount Mercy University. Her research interests concern issues in mental health and religion, attachment, postmodern therapies, and scrupulosity. She recently published articles in Contemporary Family Therapy on working with adolescents in residential settings and will be presenting her own research at upcoming national conferences. She currently works in independent private practice in Iowa City, with a temporary license in marriage and family therapy.

.

Chapter 17
Family Workshops in Residential Treatment

Ashlie Lester

Chapter Highlights

- Relevant literature on adolescent residential treatment, family workshops, and family systems theory is reviewed.
- A structure for family workshops, consisting of the preparation, reunion, and separation phases is proposed.
- Each phase is described detail, including therapeutic goals and interventions for each phase.
- Key considerations when developing and delivering a family workshop, including the timing of workshops, family dynamics, and group dynamics is discussed.
- To be effective, efforts must be made to help family members learn communication and emotional management skills, set realistic expectations, and form a supportive relationship with the therapist, as well as develop compassion, look for positive changes in their family members, and practice a new family structure.

Family workshops are an essential aspect of treatment for adolescents in residential therapeutic facilities. Placements in residential treatment have increased substantially since the 1980s (Nickerson et al. 2006), and integrating the family into treatment has been linked to improved treatment outcomes (Cafferty and Leichtman 2001; Slesnick et al. 2006). Therefore, it is imperative to have scholarship that addresses how to incorporate family into treatment. Chapter 11 in this book contains a useful review of the history of family involvement in residential treatment for the interested reader. However, the focus of this chapter is on a single aspect of

A. Lester (✉)
Department of Human Development and Family Science, University of Missouri,
314 Gentry Hall, Columbia, MO 65211, USA
e-mail: lestera@missouri.edu

© Springer International Publishing AG 2017   303
J.D. Christenson and A.N. Merritts (eds.), *Family Therapy with Adolescents in Residential Treatment*, Focused Issues in Family Therapy,
DOI 10.1007/978-3-319-51747-6_17

family involvement, which is family workshops in residential treatment for adolescents.

Residential treatment has long been criticized for focusing primarily on the identified patient and for not purposefully engaging with the family system. Facilities have responded to this criticism by including family elements (e.g., phone calls with parents, parent visits, and parent seminars) into the treatment program; in fact, there has been a significant rise in family involvement in residential treatment in the last two decades (Nickerson et al. 2006). A singular focus or a haphazard involvement of the family, however, may reinforce an unhelpful pattern of blame in the family, prevent successful completion in residential treatment (Nickerson et al. 2006; Sunseri 2004), and inhibit the adolescent's ability to maintain therapeutic gains after discharge (Frensch and Cameron 2002). Indeed, many parents reported that their children displayed problematic behaviors once home (Frensch and Cameron 2002). Because of these criticisms, it is essential that residential treatment programs involve families deliberately and meaningfully into the treatment process.

Despite the research on its importance, meaningful family integration into treatment is challenging. Practically speaking it is difficult to arrange meetings or groups when residential treatment facilities are hours, or states, away and when families are spread throughout different time zones. The cost of frequent travel can be prohibitive, as can the lost wages from days visiting a child in treatment, difficulties finding childcare for other children, and time spent away from other children or family obligations. Emotionally, family treatment can induce significant stress, fear of blame, and anxiety over disrupting a new peace in the household. Perhaps the largest challenge is the perspective that the adolescent is the problem to be fixed, and the residential treatment program is the tool to fix him or her. These barriers, while real and significant, must be overcome for the health of the adolescent and the family system. Chapter 14 of this book contains a discussion of barriers that practitioners face working with adolescents and their families, as well an exploration of the benefits and methods of increasing the identified patient and family's readiness for change.

This book in general details several strategies for meeting these challenges, and successful programs involve parents throughout the treatment process through phone calls, video conferencing, and strategic letter writing (both adolescent to parent, and parent to adolescent; Chaps. 2 and 19). Family workshops can enhance the benefit of these strategies, as the benefits of in-person contact are considerable. "Face-to-face conversations [are]…the most natural, enjoyable, and effective way to fulfill our social needs" (Gatica-Perez 2009, p. 1775). In-person interactions provide significant information, including linguistic, paralinguistic, and nonlinguistic messages that fosters relationships with others; in fact, some refer to face-to-face communication as the *social glue* keeping relationships together (Lakin et al. 2003, p. 145). Family workshops are but a single element, but they are uniquely suited to address the challenges of residential treatment, to integrate families purposefully in treatment, and to create long-lasting change for families. By way of an overview, this chapter will provide a justification for family workshops in residential treatment, describe one possible structure for family workshops, and outline the unique challenges and therapeutic opportunities of family workshops.

Theoretical Justification of Family Workshops

Family systems theory is the oft-used theory to justify family involvement and to explain the correlation of family involvement and successful treatment outcomes (for an overview, see Center for Substance Abuse Treatment 2004). Although this chapter will not discuss the theory in great detail, some understanding of its concepts will be necessary. (For a detailed description of family systems theory and its concepts, please see Nichols 2013.)

First, family systems theory assumes that a family system consists of individual members and of the relationships between and among the members. Together, the system is more than the sum of its parts. Second, the theory assumes family systems seek homeostasis, or a balance, where the family functioning (and therefore the individual members' roles and relationships) is predictable and stable. Predictability and stability, however, does not necessarily equate to health. When the family system, or even a single member in the family is out of balance—that is, not performing the expected role—the system exerts pressure to keep the balance.

Third, the theory assumes all family members are interdependent; that is, that family members exert mutual influence on each other. Change occurring in one family member will necessarily influence both the other individual family members and the relationships one has with the others. Because of the assumption of homeostasis, there is pressure on family members to maintain the equilibrium. In other words, there is an internal pressure to maintain roles and rules of relationships. When one individual changes then the other family members will seek to *correct* it to maintain the equilibrium and maintain their roles and their predictable relationships. If only the adolescent in residential treatment changes, when the adolescent rejoins the family system, the family system will inadvertently work to maintain the old status quo, despite the heartbreak and danger of that previous homeostasis. If, however, parents and (ideally) other key family members can be involved in treatment and change with the adolescent, the family's homeostasis too will be altered. The functioning of the system—its relationships, structure, power, and communication processes—can be reset to a more adaptive equilibrium (i.e., second-order change) , and the system will exert pressure to maintain this new balance. Theoretically, this is why family treatment has been correlated with positive and long-lasting change (Cafferty and Leichtman 2001; Stratton et al. 2015).

Families with adolescents in residential treatment are going through a transition. The previous homeostasis ended when the adolescent entered residential treatment, and the family has not yet created a new balance in the system; it is in the middle space. *This* is where the treatment process occurs. Residential treatment is a bridge from what families have known before to an unknown, hopefully more adaptive, equilibrium.

In-person family workshops, with the benefits that come from direct (not distance-mediated) interaction, can be an essential part of navigating treatment and this transition. Because transitions are stressful, it can be important to have a therapist present to help family members manage the anxiety in the system. Doing so will allow families to establish new, adaptive patterns. Family workshops allow families to practice their new roles and patterns of interaction in person and under the guidance of a mental health professional. Family workshops have the potential to help families reset patterns and realign relationships in a more adaptive way through an intense therapeutic experience.

Purpose of the Family Workshop

In addition to the broad purpose of incorporating the family purposefully into treatment and harnessing the power of the family system in the change process, there are additional goals of the family workshops that directly serve this overall objective. One additional purpose is to build compassion within relationships. Parents and children sometimes have difficulty perceiving each other in a new way, which includes noticing (or believing) any change in the other. Having parents see where their children are living can help them view their children and their children's capabilities differently. In the wilderness therapy setting, for example, the adolescents have lived in a radically different setting and can demonstrate many outdoor and survival skills. Watching their adolescents make fire from sticks and build sleeping shelters—very concrete skills—can help parents become open to other, less tangible changes the adolescents may have made. Having parents live as their adolescents have been living can help parents better understand the experiences of their teens. Having the adolescents become their parents' guides in an unknown (i.e., the residential) setting can help adolescents build compassion for their parents. Compassion can soften formerly rigid perspectives, allowing both parents and adolescents to practice a new way of interacting. It can also introduce warmth into relationships that may have become distant or guarded in the past.

A second additional purpose of the family workshop is to learn skills. Parents can be taught the same communication and emotional management skills that their adolescents learned. Providing a common language of what to do when stressed can be powerful for the family—all members will know what to do, when perhaps before treatment they did not know and used ineffective coping strategies. Also, parents and children can practice these skills together under the supervision of trained staff. Parents and children need a new way of interacting, and these skills allow them to do just this. Although parents are usually provided with information about communication skills and asked to practice while the child is in treatment, it is not uncommon for parents to arrive at a family workshop having spent little time applying the principles they have been taught.

Finally, family workshops allow families in treatment to develop support networks. This can be formal, such as through developing a better relationship with their child's therapist. It can also be informal, through meeting other parents in the same situation, sharing stories, and offering support. Being an active member of a support network benefits both the recipient of the support (e.g., the recipient is soothed emotionally; Cohen 1992) and the giver of the support (e.g., it is rewarding to help others; Brown et al. 2003). It can feel isolating to have an adolescent (or to be an adolescent) in residential treatment, and having a social network with others in a similar position can help.

Timing and Length of Family Workshops

Family workshops can take place at any time during treatment. They can occur upon arrival, during the treatment program, and at the conclusion of treatment. Many of the strategies and processes are the same, with some key distinctions. The timing of workshops may be determined by goals (in addition to integrating families into treatment and creating second-order change) . If an additional goal is to join with parents and increase their buy-in with the program, a workshop may be offered very early in the treatment program. The focus may be more on education about the program itself or the presenting problem. For mid-treatment workshops, an additional goal may be to assess the family's progress and to make new goals for the remainder of the treatment. The focus may be to practice skills and a new way of functioning. For graduation workshops, or workshops that come at the conclusion of treatment, a goal may be to publicly (i.e., in front of other adolescents, families, and staff) celebrate any progress made and to prepare the adolescents and their families for the next step in their treatment, be it at home or at another program. The focus may be more on generalizing skills to a new setting.

The timing of family workshops may also depend on the nature of the residential program itself. Some treatment facilities have family workshops at regular intervals (e.g., every four months), whereas other residential programs (particularly those that are considered short-term intervention programs, like wilderness therapy programs) may have only one workshop. Because families may live far away from the residential treatment facility, it is important to have family workshops be long enough to be meaningful. This is necessary to build a therapeutic alliance, to create or strengthen a support network, and, perhaps most importantly, to have ample opportunity to practice a new way of interacting with the family. On the other hand, workshops must be short enough to not create a hardship (e.g., taking parents away from work). The workshops I have experienced were 3 to 4 days in length, which is typical in this field.

Process of the Family Workshop

Those programs that utilize family workshops often do so in a standardized way, meaning that all families attend and experience similar activities at predetermined time points in the treatment program. They are not visits or impromptu meetings with the family. Family workshops require in-person participation and are directed by the treatment center staff. The regularity of workshops provides treatment providers and families a chance to prepare for the experience, both emotionally and practically (i.e., organizing finances, arranging to take time off work, and arranging childcare), and its structure can reduce anxiety in the family system. Being led by a mental health professional can help make the experience a meaningful integration into families' treatment programs. As a licensed marriage and family therapist, I first worked as a team therapist at a residential treatment facility. In this role, I directed the long-term treatment of a group of 12 females, including weekly individual, family, and group therapy, and quarterly family workshop groups. I also served as the reunion therapist at a wilderness therapy program in rural Utah, during which time I was directly responsible for developing and facilitating the program's reunion family workshop every week. Because the treatment duration was, on average, 8 weeks, each family participated in one workshop at the end of their program. Through both of these experiences, I developed, executed, and refined my process for delivering family workshops. I have found workshops occur in three distinct phases (i.e., preparation, reunion, and separation), and that the therapist's goals and activities must be altered to address the families' needs at each phase. What follows is a synthesis of my experience and a description of my process.

Preparation

Both parents and their adolescents prepare for their workshop experience. This phase is essential in readying the family and the clinician for the workshop, and I have found that those who prepare well tend to have a more meaningful workshop experience. Preparation may occur prior to the workshop during a family therapy phone call, or it may be part of the workshop itself. The former may be more likely with a long-term residential process where parents and children have regular contact. The latter may be more likely in short-term programs, like wilderness therapy programs, where parents and children may not speak to each other (except by letter) until the reunion process. In a situation like this, preparation for the family reunion occurs during the workshop itself in separate, but parallel groups (i.e., parents are in a group at base camp, adolescents are in a group in the field).

   In either situation, though, preparation is a time for family members and clinicians to ready themselves for the upcoming family reunion and to set expectations for the workshop. Emotionally, family members need to prepare to interact with each other again. Parents and adolescents have been separated (sometimes under duress) for a period of time, and the idea of being in each other's presence again may bring up intense and contradictory emotions. Parents can simultaneously express excitement to see their children, fear that their children will be angry or that their children will not have made sufficient progress, shame in sending their children away, and worry for the future. In my work, adolescents reported similar emotions; happiness to be seeing parents, excitement to show off their new skills, fear that parents will not recognize the change in the adolescent, or fear that the parents have not changed. There may be anger about being in treatment, and some adolescents plan to punish the parents by acting out or simply by not helping the parents during the workshop experience. For both parents and adolescents, the underlying emotional current is often anxiety.

According to Bowen (1976), anxiety is the emotion that feeds interaction patterns. Families' previous patterns were often maladaptive (hence, the need for treatment), so the family's anxiety must be reduced in order for the family members to be open to the therapeutic process of the workshop and to interacting with each other in a new way (Winek 2010). Addressing anxiety occurs throughout the workshop and is especially important during preparation in order to build a trusting therapeutic alliance. The relationship a client has with the therapist and the client's hope that the therapist can help have been correlated with better treatment outcomes (Martin et al. 2000). Developing a strong therapeutic alliance before reunion is important in guiding reunited families through the remainder of the workshop, as in-person interaction, while rewarding, can also be quite stressful.

Therapists can help families cope with anxiety using strategies that address individuals' emotional, cognitive, and behavioral experiences. All three aspects are interrelated, thus change in one aspect (e.g., emotional) necessarily alters the other two (e.g., cognitive, behavioral; Hofmann et al. 2010; Swart and Apsche 2014). Emotional interventions directly address the anxiety. Therapists first allow individuals to voice their emotions and concerns. Active listening, validating, open-ended questioning, and reframing legitimizes the families' experiences and are essential in helping family members feel heard and accepted (Miller and Rollnick 1991).

Second, therapists can help families cope with anxiety by building a supportive social network with other families in residential treatment. Adolescents have been in treatment with each other and may already have created a supportive social network. Parents, however, may not have interacted with another parent of an adolescent in residential treatment until the workshop itself. Therefore, the therapist needs to be proactive in helping parents connect. The networking can occur prior to the workshop through online groups hosted by the treatment program or occur in-person during the workshop itself. Parents should be allowed the opportunity to tell their stories to other parents and to hear other parents' stories as well. This can reduce the sense of isolation, failure, and shame many parents feel when they send their adolescents outside the home for treatment. The support group, ideally, will share not only their emotions and experiences, but also their successes and gains so that others may learn from them. Providing support and expertise can be reaffirming to parents of their goodness and competence. Therapists should explicitly identify the strengths in the parents, recognize the collective knowledge of the parent group, and encourage parents to identify the strengths in themselves, each other, and their adolescents. Creating a culture within the parent group of support and strength building can reduce anxiety, empower parents, and model interactions for their children.

Third, therapists can reduce anxiety through psychoeducation. The content of psychoeducation is variable, depending upon the needs of the group or the treatment facility (e.g., understanding the stages of change, process of addiction, the etiology of eating disorders, and the neurobiology of trauma responses). Having knowledge about relevant issues, understanding how and why the family may have experienced what it did, and having a shared vocabulary to discuss these issues with each other have been correlated with a reduction of anxiety in clients in treatment, and to an improvement in functioning 5 years following treatment (Colom et al. 2009). Discussion-based (vs. didactic) psychoeducation groups that blend therapist expertise with client experiences have been associated with positive client outcomes, including destigmatizing of mental health disorders, increased compliance with treatment, and self-acceptance (Poole et al. 2015). Psychoeducation itself may also reduce anxiety as its process can be less personal and less intense than a therapy session.

Fourth, therapists can help families cope with anxiety by teaching skills. These skills may be to reduce anxiety or stress directly (e.g., deep breathing, focusing on the present moment, and identifying the emotion), or they may be other relationship skills, like communication or conflict resolution, that may indirectly reduce anxiety. Those who undergo communication skills training, for example, have reported a reduction in relationship distress and an improvement in their relationship (Blanchard et al. 2009). Adolescents in treatment who undergo skills training have also reported lower substance abuse problems 12 months later (Rohsenow et al. 2001). Families should have opportunities to learn about and practice these skills in a low-risk situation (i.e., with staff or with other parents) before having to implement them with their own family members.

Finally, anxiety can be reduced through setting clear expectations for the workshop experience. Role theory suggests that when individuals are uncertain about expectations for behavior, or when there are inconsistent expectations, individuals are stressed, dissatisfied, and underperform (Kahn et al. 1964). The clinician, therefore, needs to be explicit in the rules and the structure of the workshop. It also sets the therapist as the hierarchical leader of the workshop. Under the guidance of the therapist, family members set their own expectations for themselves and their families during the workshop. This can be formal (e.g., writing out specific objectives family members may have) or informal (e.g., discussing what would be realistic to expect from the experience). Family members are already thinking about what the reunion might be like, or how they want to act during the workshop; providing a space to make these expectations overt helps family members become aware of their cognitions and of how cognitions may be influencing their emotions. It also provides an opportunity for the therapist to help families set expectations that are realistic, under their control, and consistent with longer term treatment goals. As can be seen in the content above, adequate preparation is essential and sets the stage for everything that follows.

Reunion

The moment when parents and their adolescents reunite is an important transition for the family system. Transitions heighten emotions and stress, and they provide an opportunity to see the underlying structure of the family (Nichols 2013). Therapists and staff must be observant and present to help the family use skills to cope and grow. The use of ritual can help this process. This transition allows some time for families just to be together. This moment can be quite emotional and raw.

Introductions. A low-risk multi-family group activity (e.g., introductions and an icebreaker game) can inject an element of fun and can calm a stressed system after the intensity of the initial family reunion. It connects the family to the established support networks (i.e., parents with their parent support group and adolescents with their adolescent support group), which also can reduce the stress on the individual family systems. Introductions and icebreaker games might include having the adolescent introduce his or her parents, or each individual sharing an interesting personal fact or answering a fun question (e.g., If you could travel through time, when would you visit and why?). Other activities may involve a game (e.g., tag or throwing/kicking a ball around a circle and each person who touches the ball must introduce themselves). I have also found that the adolescents in treatment have games they play with each other, and having adolescents teach and play with their parents can be a good icebreaker. After this, the therapist establishes rules for the workshop. These rules may be therapeutic in nature (e.g., commit to using I-feel statements when discussing difficult issues) or they may be practical and unique to the residential treatment program (e.g., do not leave your campsite after dark).

Group Activities and Process. The workshop should provide both structured and unstructured opportunities for families to connect and to establish relationship patterns. Structured opportunities are interventions assigned by the therapist with the express purpose of reestablishing positive patterns (e.g., practicing/using an I-feel statement or activities and process groups). Unstructured opportunities are provided in every other moment of the day (e.g., when cooking food and eating, when sharing stories around the campfire, and when walking from activity to activity).

It can be helpful to introduce a structured activity for all families to practice a key skill learned in the parallel groups described above (e.g., I-feel statements and reflective listening). This is practiced in each family with support and supervision of a staff member. It is important to start the reunited multi-family workshop with practicing skills, as that will set the expectation that new skills will be used rather than relying on old patterns.

After each activity, all families are invited to come together in a process group, focusing on the process of the activity for each family (e.g., How did the family accomplish the goal? What role did each person play in accomplishing the task? How comfortable was this role? Is this a process the family wants to see in the future? Why or why not? How can family members continue this pattern in the future? What can be done differently?). Process groups allow family members to reflect on and communicate about the underlying process, functioning, and structure of their own family. This is important in creating a context for second-order change to occur. In addition to making the family functioning overt, process groups provide opportunities for the participants to identify emotions, struggles, and strengths in a supportive environment with other families. This can allow families to feel validated, to offer support to others, and ultimately to calm anxiety in the family system. Process groups also allow the clinician to intervene as needed. It may be necessary to challenge an old, unhelpful family pattern, to reframe a challenging experience into a growing one, or to address a larger group dynamic.

Many different kinds of activities can be included in the workshop, and each may have a different focus, address a different need, or include different participants. Games, team-building exercises, family sculptures, fishbowl discussion, hikes, or recreational activities may all be appropriate in a family workshop, as can groups specific to a role (e.g., processing groups just for mothers, a group just for adolescents moving on to another treatment facility, or a group just for families who will be taking their adolescent home). For example, if it appears that the adolescents and the parents are having difficulty sharing their thoughts and emotions with each other in their own families, a fishbowl activity might be appropriate. In this activity, parents and adolescents write down their thoughts, emotions, and questions they would like to share; the facilitator reads each anonymous item and allows the entire group to respond. An adolescent might write about her anxiety over going home and that she will not share this emotion with her parents for fear they will put her back into treatment. Parents and adolescents would hear this and start talking—in the safety of a large group—about her predicament. This activity allows parents and children to start communicating and, ultimately, share important information that can alter the underlying structure of the family.

It is important to balance emotionally risky activities with low-risk activities and unstructured leisure time. Family workshops are stressful—individuals are learning and practicing new skills and are being challenged on previous relationship patterns —and it is important to carefully balance the activities so the emotional strain is manageable. Emotionally intense therapy or process sessions followed by leisure time or by a low-risk activity with other families helps them recuperate from stress by getting support from peers or by enjoying each other; this can start relationship repair. Relatedly, activities need to be fun. Pleasure is a valid therapeutic goal; it reduces stress, it provides a new way of interacting for parents and children (who perhaps have not had fun together in a long time), and gives them an enjoyable shared experience to remember for years to come.

Therapy. At some point during the family workshop experience, it is advisable for families to participate in a family therapy session with their primary therapist(s), separate from the other families. This will allow families to work on their treatment goals more directly and to get more individualized attention to process any experiences or intense emotions from the family workshop activities. For those clients who are leaving the program, this session serves as the termination session. See Chap. 11 for a complete review of family therapy approaches and techniques used in residential treatment.

In some residential programs, the family workshop facilitator may not be the family's primary therapist. The primary therapist has been working with the family throughout the program; the primary therapist is often responsible for joining with the family early in the treatment process, assessing the family system, codeveloping the therapeutic goals with the family, and assigning interventions to restructure the system. The workshop therapist is responsible for the facilitation of the workshop itself. The workshop therapist will work together with primary therapists to plan which activities may be most useful to this particular collection of families for enhancing the benefit of the workshop to families. The workshop therapist has the benefit of seeing the family system in a more objective light, and it allows families to add a new person to their support networks. In other programs, however, the primary therapist is also the primary facilitator for the workshops. In this situation, the families may benefit from the therapist's intimate knowledge of the family, and, in this case, the therapist may more easily be able to adjust workshop activities to benefit the families present.

Separation

The conclusion of the family workshop ushers in the separation phase, the last in the family workshop. For family workshops that are mid-treatment, this is the separation of parents and child. For family workshops that are at the end of treatment, this is the separation of the family from the residential treatment center, and if the child is moving to a different residential program, of parents and child. Leaving the center or leaving each other, even for a short time, can be distressing. Families need to be prepared for the separation. Therapists and staff need to be aware of the heightened anxiety transitions bring (along with the potential to resort to old patterns) and to encourage families to use new skills to cope and communicate. It is important to acknowledge when new skills are practiced, and allow opportunities for families to share their emotions and thoughts about the upcoming separation. This can be in a family therapy session, family activity, or multi-family process group focused solely on this topic. Therapists can also reframe the separation as simply another step on the journey of change for families. This can be particularly important for families whose children are coming home; they may believe that once the adolescent is no longer in residential treatment, they have completed their journey. Reframing their experience can help them set expectations that are more realistic. Finally, it can be helpful for each family to spend time alone, without the other families. Doing so allows families to show emotion and affection that may be inhibited when peers (particularly for adolescents) are present.

Special Considerations for the Family Workshop

Family workshopss can be a powerful agent for change, and in order to harness the power of the family in the therapeutic process, clinicians must be deliberate in structuring the process. This section will outline special considerations and common challenges that occur during family workshops in a residential therapy setting.

Family Dynamics

Family dynamics can be quite complicated and entrenched. Old, unhelpful patterns may emerge. Three parent–child patterns common in my experience include: (a) adolescents looking to punish their parents for sending them to residential treatment; (b) both parents and children seeing each other with the old unhelpful lens; and, (c) parents in conflict with each other. These dynamics can be difficult to work with and, in a group setting, can be detrimental to the group process. Clinical work throughout treatment can prevent these dynamics. The primary therapist needs to be active in working with both child and parents to soften their view of the other and to begin a process of forgiveness and coming together. This good clinical work and a strong therapeutic alliance can prevent many difficulties when parents and children see each other again.

In the workshop itself, the therapist can indirectly address the dynamics by working to reduce anxiety in the system that may be perpetuating the unhelpful patterns. The therapist may also directly and explicitly identify, normalize, and validate these dynamics. At the same time, the unhelpful dynamics need to be challenged. The therapist can help the family recognize the pattern's unhelpfulness, can have the family sign a behavioral contract for the duration of the workshop, and can support the family in using new communication skills to talk about their dynamic. Activities in which adolescents must demonstrate new skills can help parents see their children in a new way, and parents willing to engage fully in the residential setting of their children seem to garner more compassion from their adolescents. Furthermore, activities that assign structured roles and rules can also break through rigid family dynamics, as the family is no longer relying on their old roles and rules for functioning. Finally, strong group cohesion can diminish these unhelpful dynamics, as participants may be more willing to engage in the process of the workshop when the other families model more adaptive interaction and show buy-in. Not to mention it appears people are more motivated to present their best selves in social contexts (Jones and Pittman 1982).

Group Dynamics

Ideally, the preparation phase will result in families feeling connected to the group and to the workshop therapist. A common challenge is connecting families from very different backgrounds and experiences. Each family may be dealing with different diagnoses and patterns and may be at different stages of change. When families are very different, they may not relate easily to each other's experiences. The therapist in this instance can identify similarities and strengths, acknowledge the differences, and reframe them. The differences between family systems should be celebrated, as each family will have strength to share with the other families. Families can learn from each other, and that is only possible when they are different. The clinician must be deliberate in his or her attempts to join with all participants in a very short amount of time. Having a group of individuals with widely varying functioning, stages, and issues might present a challenge in activities. The interventions and the activities for families need to be open enough so that they can be helpful to all. The use of metaphor and a focus on process helps make activities relevant and useful for all families, regardless of their level of functioning.

Participants

Although some family workshops invite all family members, it is easier and perhaps more efficient to invite guardians (i.e., parents, stepparents, parenting grandparents, or foster parents) only. They can stay focused on the issues without distraction from younger children; if siblings are invited, they may need to be in their own age-appropriate session. This requires additional staff and preparation. Parents and guardians also tend to have the most power in a system, so they have a greater ability to alter the functioning of a family system (Nichols 2013). It is imperative for the success of treatment, therefore, for the parents to be committed, challenged, and supported in their own change process. This may be easier to accomplish when only parents attend.

Conclusion

Family workshops are an integral aspect of treatment for adolescents in residential programs. The intensive, structured, and in-person nature of workshops make them ideally suited to foster second-order change in family systems, thus improving treatment outcomes in the long-term. These positive treatment outcomes, though, appear to be most likely for those workshops that are purposefully and meaningfully designed (Frensch and Cameron 2002). This chapter described one such family workshop model. In this model, therapists guide families through three phrases of the workshop. In the preparation phase, family members (individually or as a system) are learn and practice skills, set realistic expectations, and create a support network with the therapist and perhaps other families. The therapist's role is to manage the anxiety so that families may have the opportunity to put their new skills into practice.

In the reunion phase, families are come together after a period of separation. The goals for the family members include developing compassion for one another, looking for positive changes in their family members, and interacting in a new, more helpful way. In other words, family members during reunion practice a new structure in the family by communicating differently and by reassigning roles. Clinicians observe and assess the family system and can tailor workshop activities to benefit the families' treatment goals. In the separation phase, parents and adolescents leave each other, leave the program, or both. The transition to separation can produce anxiety, and again the therapist must help families manage it appropriately so that the systems' new structure can be maintained.

The model presented in this chapter is grounded in family systems theory and relevant literature; however, significant research is needed to study the effectiveness of family workshops in both the short- and long-term. Who might benefit most from family workshops? Are family workshops ever contraindicated? When in the treatment process are family workshops most effective? Are family workshops effective for all family members, or only for those who attend? Are particular interventions (e.g., process groups and psychoeducation) more effective than others? Researching these questions will allow clinicians to tailor family workshops, which will result in treatment that is more effective and, ultimately, a better experience for families.

References

Blanchard, V. L., Hawkins, A. J., Baldwin, S. A., & Fawcett, E. B. (2009). Investigating the effects of marriage and relationship education on couples' communication skills: A meta-analytic study. *Journal of Family Psychology, 23*(2), 203–214.

Bowen, M. (1976). Theory in the practice of psychotherapy. *Family therapy: Theory and practice, 4,* 2–90.

Brown, S. L., Nesse, R. M., Vinokur, A. D., & Smith, D. M. (2003). Providing social support may be more beneficial than receiving it: Results from a prospective study of mortality. *Psychological Science, 14*(4), 320–327.

Cafferty, H., & Leichtman, M. (2001). Facilitating the transition from residential treatment into the community: Changing social work roles. *Residential Treatment for Children and Youth, 19*(2), 13–25.

Center for Substance Abuse Treatment. (2004). Substance abuse treatment and family therapy. *Treatment Improvement Protocol (TIP) Series, No. 39.* Rockville, MD: Substance Abuse and Mental Health Services Administration.

Cohen, S. (1992). Stress, social support and disorder. In H. Veiel & U. Baumann (Eds.), *The meaning and measurement of social support* (pp. 109–124). New York: Hemisphere.

Colom, F., Vieta, E., Sánchez-Moreno, J., Palomino-Otiniano, R., Reinares, M., Goikolea, J. M., et al. (2009). Group psychoeducation for stabilised bipolar disorders: 5-year outcome of a randomised clinical trial. *British Journal of Psychiatry, 194*(3), 260–265.

Frensch, K. M., & Cameron, G. (2002). Treatment of choice or a last resort? A review of residential mental health placements for children and youth. In *Child and youth care forum* (Vol. 31, No. 5, pp. 307–339). Kluwer Academic Publishers-Plenum Publishers.

Gatica-Perez, D. (2009). Automatic nonverbal analysis of social interaction in small groups: A review. *Image and Vision Computing, 27*(12), 1775–1787.

Hofmann, S. G., Sawyer, A. T., & Fang, A. (2010). The empirical status of the "new wave" of CBT. *Psychiatric Clinics of North America, 33*(3), 701–710.

Jones, E. E., & Pittman, T. S. (1982). Toward a general theory of strategic self-presentation. In J. Suls (Ed.), *Psychological perspectives on the self* (Vol. 1, pp. 231–262). Hillsdale, NJ: Erlbaum.

Kahn, R. L., Wolfe, D. M., Quinn, R. P., Snoek, J. D., & Rosenthal, R. A. (1964). *Occupational stress: Studies in role conflict and ambiguity.* New York, NY: Wiley.

Lakin, J. L., Jefferis, C. M., Cheng, T. L., & Chartrand, T. L. (2003). The chameleon effect as social glue: Evidence for the evolutionary significance of nonconscious mimicry. *Journal of Nonverbal Behavior, 27*(3), 145–162.

Martin, D. J., Garske, J. P., & Davis, M. K. (2000). Relation of the therapeutic alliance with outcome and other variables: A meta-analytic review. *Journal of Consulting and Clinical Psychology, 68*(3), 438–450.

Miller, W. R., & Rollnick, S. (1991). *Motivational interviewing: Preparing people to change addictive behavior.* New York: Guilford Press.

Nichols, M. P. (2013). *Family therapy: Concepts and methods* (10th ed.). Needham Heights, MA: Allyn & Bacon Inc.

Nickerson, A. B., Brooks, J. L., Colby, S. A., Rickert, J. M., & Salamone, F. J. (2006). Family involvement in residential treatment: Staff, parent, and adolescent perspectives. *Journal of Child and Family Studies, 15*(6), 681–694.

Poole, R., Smith, D., & Simpson, S. (2015). Patients' perspectives of the feasibility, acceptability and impact of a group-based psychoeducation programme for bipolar disorder: A qualitative analysis. *BCM Psychiatry, 15*(1), 1–16.

Rohsenow, D. J., Monti, P. M., Rubonis, A. V., Gulliver, S. B., Colby, S. M., Binkoff, J. A., et al. (2001). Cue exposure with coping skills training and communication skills training for alcohol dependence: 6- and 12-month outcomes. *Addiction, 96*(8), 1161–1174.

Slesnick, N., Bartle-Haring, S., & Gangamma, R. (2006). Predictors of substance use and family therapy outcome among physically and sexually abused-runaway adolescents. *Journal of Marital and Family Therapy, 32*(3), 261–281.

Stratton, P., Silver, E., Nascimento, N., McDonnell, L., Powell, G., & Nowotny, E. (2015). Couple and family therapy outcome research in the previous decade: What does the evidence tell us? *Contemporary Family Therapy, 37*(1), 1–12.

Sunseri, P. (2004). Family functioning and residential treatment outcomes. *Residential Treatment for Children and Youth, 22*(1), 33–53.

Swart, J., & Apsche, J. (2014). Mindfulness, mode deactivation, and family therapy: A winning combination for treating adolescents with complex trauma and behavioral problems. *International Journal of Behavioral Consultation and Therapy, 9*(2), 9–14.

Winek, J. (2010). *Systemic family therapy: From theory to practice.* Thousand Oaks, CA: Sage.

Author Biography

Ashlie Lester, Ph.D., LMFT received her Ph.D. in Human Environmental Sciences, with an emphasis in Human Development and Family Studies from the University of Missouri in 2013. She received her Master of Science in Family Studies and Human Services, with an emphasis in Marriage and Family Therapy from Kansas State University in 2004. As a therapist for adolescents and their families in a therapeutic boarding school, in a wilderness therapy program, and in a private practice setting, Dr. Lester has seen first-hand the strength and resilience of families. She is currently a faculty member at the University of Missouri.

Chapter 18
Expediting Growth: A Call to Measure the Impact of Family Involvement During Wilderness Therapy

Kendall Smith and Tony Issenmann

Chapter Highlights

- A brief history of family involvement in wilderness therapy (WT).
- An overview of current research outlines the strengths and weaknesses of related findings.
- A description of gaps in current research covers the foundational information needed to further research in this field.
- A description of current on-site family programming in WT.
- Recommendations for future family involvement and for research to determine effectiveness of interventions on the student and family system.

Residential treatment facilities for adolescents have followed a similar route of development to that of the counseling field as a whole in terms of how clients experience psychotherapy. Early therapeutic interventions, spearheaded by pioneers in counseling such as Sigmund Freud and Carl Rogers, offered different approaches to treatment with a similar underlying premise, which was that mental and emotional health issues sprung from relational wounds and problems that were best addressed in one-on-one, individual sessions with the identified patient (IP). It was not until the 1950s that psychotherapists began to recognize the potential of working with the entire family system. Leaders in the family therapy movement proposed that relationships and role development in the family system shaped long-term behavior, expectations, and response style to all future encounters (Nichols and Schwartz 1998).

K. Smith (✉) · T. Issenmann
Open Sky Wilderness Therapy, P.O. Box 2201, Durango, CO 81302, USA
e-mail: kendall@openskywilderness.com

T. Issenmann
e-mail: drtony@openskywilderness.com

© Springer International Publishing AG 2017
J.D. Christenson and A.N. Merritts (eds.), *Family Therapy with Adolescents in Residential Treatment*, Focused Issues in Family Therapy,
DOI 10.1007/978-3-319-51747-6_18

Residential and wilderness programs initially adopted the same type of individual-focused intervention; IPs (young members of the family system) were sent away to be *fixed* and then expected to maintain their personal growth and transformation when reunited with a family that had little to no participation in the therapeutic process. When one considers the components of early WT programs, it is clear (similar to any emerging field) there were a wide range of programmatic differences, including, little to no family involvement, lack of integrated theoretical foundations, differences across length of stay, purpose of separation from family, and ultimate goals of the WT intervention. As WT began to define itself, some researchers proposed that it is an intervention based in systems theory with a strong family focus (Russell and Hendee 2000). Chapters 8, 15, and 16 in this book provide additional descriptions of interventions and techniques that can be used in these settings.

The shift from individual to systemic perspective is an evolutionary process and one worth understanding as it creates the framework for continued growth and possibility. It is widely recognized today that treating the entire family in psychotherapy is likely to lead to greater gains and sustained change (Nichols and Schwartz 1998). In this chapter we will identify the need for greater clarity in the WT industry of what constitutes *family involvement* by drawing from research in the larger field of child and family psychotherapy, as well as recognizing the unique opportunity that WT presents for intentional family interventions and measures. This chapter is unique to this book since it represents an attempt to provide research-based conclusions and recommendations for intentional family interventions and programming, while a number of other chapters are focused on describing specific interventions (e.g., Chap. 15) or general methods in current use (e.g., Chap. 16). WT as used in this chapter is synonymous with Outdoor Behavioral Healthcare (OBH).

Family Involvement

In 2001 Burg stated, "Therapeutic adventure with families has grown significantly over the past two decades. It is not uncommon to find residential treatment programs, wilderness programs, and acute care psychiatric hospitals using therapeutic adventure with families" (p. 118). In that article, he made a call to clearly define what level of therapeutic intent programs were employing with families. Burg referred to the work of Gillis et al. (1991) when recommending a four category model of family engagement: *recreation* (fun and short-term), *enrichment* (longer, focus on communication, conflict resolution and development of new skills), *adjunctive therapy* (one family member is IP and all other family members participate in a limited manner), and *primary therapy* (family system is client; principal and sometimes only treatment provided). However, a literature search for family involvement in wilderness and residential programs revealed inconsistent terminology still being utilized to categorize types of family engagement or programming. Unfortunately, advice from early researchers in the field, such as Burg, was not heeded and today we continue to struggle with individual programs employing specific family interventions without the foundation of an overarching model or framework.

In 2003 Keith Russell conducted a nation-wide survey of 86 OBH programs to learn more about various aspects of programming. He found that "responses by program indicate that parent involvement is substantial but not universal" (p. 328). *Substantial* at the time of the article was described as parent involvement in specific curricula developed for caregivers (73% of private placement programs offered parent curricula, while only 32% of adjudicated programs had parent-specific treatment curricula) . Treatment curricula for parents "included suggested readings, parent seminars, meetings with therapists and counselors with their child, attending graduation ceremonies, and suggested outpatient family and marital counseling" (p. 330). Average curricula hours for private placement were more than four times the average hours for adjudicated programs (43 h vs. 9 h). Russell (2003a, b) continued to push the field forward by recommending that future research focus on how much family involvement affects short and long-term outcomes for clients.

It seems the field of OBH is in agreement that family work is an important element of this particular type of intervention (Bettmann et al. 2011; Burg 2001; Harper and Cooley 2007). There is little to no evidence of researchers promoting a narrow focus on the adolescent or young adult experience while excluding the family process. In fact, over the past two decades researchers and practitioners in the field of WT have been proponents for expanding services from the IP to the family system (e.g., Tucker et al. 2016). However, the field has struggled to produce robust, empirically sound research due to a number of conflicts (lack of control group, attrition with longitudinal research, validity and reliability of measurement tools, etc.), and recommendations were made largely based on anecdotal and qualitative research. Current research continues to face challenges and is often based on a small number of case studies; however, it does support the potential for increased efficacy when focusing on the family versus the individual client (Harper and Cooley 2007).

Attachment

Notwithstanding the lack of rigorous research in this area, it is evident that WT can have a substantive effect on family functioning. One profoundly unique benefit of WT is the contained, safe, and prolonged opportunity to provide corrective emotional experiences for adolescents and young adults who have been unable to securely attach to their parents or caregivers. In alignment with family therapists' early claims about the significance of family relational patterns, a qualitative study by Bettman et al. (2011) "demonstrates that most adolescents in WT experience highly conflicting relationships with caregivers and that such relationships appear to color their feelings for all adult relationships" (p. 197). Bettman et al. (2011) found that adolescents in WT often wanted to have a safe foundation and a secure base with their parent or caregiver, but that it was that particular relationship that was causing distress and the necessity for a WT intervention. Because attachment relationships are relatively stable over time, it takes a dramatic shift in the system for them to positively change. Creating a trusting, stable relationship with one's adult psychotherapist while removed from the home environment can alter a young person's attachment style and create fertile ground for new relationship in the family of origin. Success in the restructuring of relationships is only possible when both parties adapt and share common goals for trust, openness, respect, and improved communication. Parent programming in OBH must focus on this skill development in order to provide the IP with a system that is ready to accept his/her changed state.

Family Research in WT

Some of the most influential research in OBH recently has come out of the University of New Hampshire. Tucker et al. (2016) reported on a longitudinal research study concerning the impact of OBH on family functioning. The aim of the report was to respond to the paucity of research on the connection between adolescent outcomes and changes in the family system, as stated in the literature review, "Little research has been done to understand how or why family involvement in OBH treatment contributes to and supports positive clinical change in OBH participants and family functioning" (p. 22).

Tucker et al. (2016) analyzed data from the National Therapeutic Schools and Programs (NATSAP) Practice Research Network (PRN), a consortium of 17 WT programs that began contributing outcome data in 2007. All participating programs conducted research using the Youth Outcome Questionnaire (Y-OQ) at intake, discharge, and 6 months post treatment. Additional data was collected from parents and participants through the Family Assessment Device (FAD) General Functioning (GF) scale at intake, discharge, and six-months post-discharge. This valuable study revealed that:

> As youth improved as reported through their Y-OQ reports, so did family functioning. In addition, youth self-reported Y-OQ total score change was a significant predictor of mothers' mean change in FAD. Specifically, as youth reported improvement in the Y-OQ, mothers' perceptions of family functioning also increased. (p. 31)

Tucker et al.'s (2016) analysis is important in understanding the perceived experience of different family members at the onset of treatment, the close of WT as an intervention, and what the lasting effects may be. However, looking at adolescent outcomes and family functioning alone does not illuminate what kind of family involvement is most purposeful during OBH. The type of family therapy provided over the course of treatment in OBH was not defined, and across 17 different programs the likelihood of consistency in family participation expectations is low.

Defining Family Involvement

Burg (2001) made the astute observation that,

> Over time many programs have realized that for long-term change to occur, the family system must adapt so that the adolescent's problem behavior is no longer supported. But instead of redesigning the intervention program from the beginning, based on family therapy principles, the family intervention component is merely added to the existing program. There may be some efficacy in this type of program, but it is not designed or implemented with the guidance of theory. (p. 121)

As a field, WT has not yet identified what family involvement means, and without interviewing each program in the NATSAP PRN it is impossible to know the range of how parents were being asked to participate in Tucker et al.'s (2016) study. Some programs provide parents with their own family therapist, while others conduct family therapy through the primary therapist that works with the adolescent directly. Some programs have intensive family therapy sessions over the course of several days (see Chap. 17), while other programs use skype (or other video/live chat technology) to conduct distance family therapy on a weekly basis (see Chap. 19). The differences across OBH programs' family therapy components are vast and significant. Today, as a result of not following the advice of early researchers in OBH family therapy (e.g., Burg 2001), we find that although we have had success in collecting longitudinal data on both adolescent and family experience, we do not have clarity on what contributed to the results.

However, WT is not alone in this struggle. The broader field of psychotherapy also struggles to define different levels of family involvement and to clarify what level of parent involvement is best for child and adolescent success in treatment. Haine-Schlagel and Walsh (2015) outlined the difference between attendance and engagement in parents' participation in adolescent psychotherapy. Attendance is required for engagement, but does not equate with actual engagement in the process of therapy. In WT parents may attend a parent workshop or weekly call and thus be in attendance, but without record of their level of participation we cannot determine how engaged they were in the family experience of therapy. Haine-Schlagel and Walsh (2015) define parent participation engagement (PPE) in the following manner:

> PPE includes sharing opinions, asking questions, and providing one's point of view on a problem or solution, as well as participation in therapeutic activities such as games and role plays...PPE also includes parent follow-through with home action plans (referred to here as homework), such as changing one's own parenting behavior (e.g., increasing reinforcement of positive behaviors), serving as a 'co-provider' to continue intervention delivery at home (e.g., working on turn taking when playing games at home), and/or supporting the child's behavior change efforts (e.g., providing reminders to the child to use coping strategies) ... PPE reflects the parent's active, independent, and responsive contribution to treatment, and is a distinct construct from alliance, which represents the relationship between parent and provider (p. 134).

In this article Haine-Schlagel and Walsh (2015) also call for consistent use of terminology to differentiate between engagement and attendance, suggesting the word *participation* and even further requesting that participation activities be clearly defined as clinical interventions. There is also a parent participation engagement measurement in development by these authors which should help further clarify this construct. OBH will be best served to follow suit with greater agreement on terms, measures, and interventions for family therapy. Until we intentionally pursue consensus and common language with regard to what parent participation is in our field, we will likely continue to learn more about individual programs' versions of family involvement and relative success through varied means of incorporating a family systems approach.

Creighton and Mills (2016) provide one such illustration of a residential program's work with parents in their recent article *Family Matters: Engaging Parents in Youth Treatment*. The Pine River Institute (PRI) calls their parent programming *Parallel Process* and use Kristy Pozatek's book by the same name as the foundation for focusing on attunement and boundary setting. Parallel Process is implemented at PRI through "a multitude of events and interventions: Three Day Parent Retreats, Semi-Annual Two-Day Parent Learning Workshops, Weekly Multi-Family Groups, Bi-weekly Parent Groups, Sunday Brunches and Satir Informed Therapy" (p. 53). The intention of Parallel Process is "for parents to behave in new ways based on a higher self-awareness and self-responsibility and ultimately, to facilitate, support, and sustain their youth's treatment gains" (p. 51).

It is not clear if all parents contributing to the research for this article participated in all aspects of the Parallel Process offered at PRI, or what the range of engagement in the process may have been (e.g., Did every participating parent attend all Sunday Brunches? Was there a minimum level of involvement in offered activities to qualify as participating in the Parallel Process?). However, Creighton and Mills (2016) showed results indicating the possibility of decreased treatment duration when parents were engaged throughout the adolescent or young adult's OBH program in their own personal, therapeutic work. Their "findings suggest that, with dedicated family work to increase parent skills, the youth's treatment duration can be reduced by over one month" (p. 57). The level of involvement that PRI suggests is on par with treating the family system versus treating the individual. In the following sections, we will define different levels of parent participation engagement offered through OBH programs. We will also highlight family involvement options at Open Sky Wilderness in particular, as the two authors are currently employed at Open Sky Wilderness and most familiar with this program. We will offer a first review of those varied levels of engagement on perceived adolescent health and family functioning.

Open Sky Wilderness

Open Sky Wilderness is located in Durango, Colorado. According to the Open Sky Wilderness website:

Since 2006, Open Sky WT has been providing the premier family-centered WT experience. The Open Sky approach transcends traditional WT by emphasizing treatment for the whole family not just the adolescent or young adult, and the application of evidence-based clinical modalities with innovative, well-researched holistic healing practices such as yoga, meditation and mindfulness. When a family partners with Open Sky, they embark on a rewarding adventure of self-discovery, and learn a range of strategies that promote lasting success (About Open Sky 2016, para 3).

Description of Current Family Programming

While family program offerings among WT programs vary by name and by activity within each service, there is enough overlap to begin categorizing the services into suggested categories of family programming. After a cursory analysis of leading programs in the industry the following types of services appear to be offered across the field, all of which are deliberately incorporated into the Open Sky experience:

Parent Weekend/Workshop/Seminars. One to three day intensive programs focused on skill development for parents. These workshops typically focus on basic communication skills, including how to identify and express emotion (often in the form of an *I feel...* statement), how to validate others' emotions, and in some cases practice of specific self-regulation techniques. Depending on the skill and certification of facilitators, themes and purpose of these workshops vary. At Open Sky Wilderness (OSW) the intention of parent workshops is to raise parents' awareness about the individual role they play in the family system and the choice they have about how they respond to situations. Different programs focus on different aspects of parenting. Open Sky teaches the most up-to-date, research-informed practices of self-care and emotional regulation, beginning with a focus on the significance of tracking one's own somatic experience. The parent workshop at OSW includes yoga, meditation, psycho-educational presentations, information on theoretical approaches to behavior change, an explanation of the stages of grief, large and small group activities, with time outside and time to share personal stories.

Parent/Child Field Overnights. Some programs invite participatory family members to engage in deep therapeutic work with the IP in the field at some point during the course of treatment. Over the course a few days facilitators conduct family therapy sessions in the setting the student is most used to, the outdoors. Family members camp and eat in a similar manner to that of the student's experience in group. This intervention is an opportunity for each family member to demonstrate how they have positively changed during the time of separation. Family members deliberately practice new ways of being with one another and skills for interrupting old patterns of behavior. Expert facilitators guide families through this experience encouraging them to delve into topics and issues that have long been avoided and need to be addressed in the family system. At Open Sky these intensive family therapy field experiences are called Family Quests (FQ) and are delivered by a Family Therapist and an experienced Wilderness Guide.

The purpose of the FQ is always to improve family relationships and to practice healthy communication; however, they are also tailored specifically to the needs of the individual family. At times, the FQ has been a way to grieve for the death of a family member that was never able to be mourned together, or to process and share about the devastating effects of divorce on the system; sometimes traumas are revealed by the IP, sometimes by parents or siblings. It is a time for a family to be together and carried through a deep process by skilled professionals.

Family Therapist Assigned to the Family. Few OBH programs are currently providing families with a family therapist in addition to the primary therapist that is assigned to a student. When a family therapist works with the family it is a separate, weekly, point of contact with a clinician whose purpose is to facilitate the growth of the family system. Family therapists help parents to manage the swirl of emotions that are inevitable after being in crisis and enrolling a child or young adult in OBH. These therapists assess each parent's current emotional state and begin the coaching process in accordance with a parent's accessibility (emotional), grief state, self-awareness, and understanding of their son or daughter's mental health. Through weekly calls and assignments family therapists engage parents in their own personal work; identifying parenting styles, considering the effects of their own families of origin, learning, practicing, and committing to new ways of communicating, practicing self-care, coming to terms with recommendations and diagnosis from collaborating professionals, and many more healthful, integrative skills that improve the functioning of the entire family.

Graduation Experiences. Graduation ceremonies in WT have traditionally been a significant aspect of programming (see Chap. 15), and this tradition continues at OSW. WT programs often seek to recognize and celebrate milestones for students since many participants in WT have had little to be celebrated and acknowledged prior to the completion of this intense intervention. Graduation is an opportunity to show families how to be in the positive, current experience, regardless of what the next steps may hold. All students who graduate from OBH programs deserve to be celebrated. Living in the wilderness for many weeks is a trying and honorable task that most people in this country will never experience. Also notable is the enormous personal growth that this book and other articles over the past two decades have identified as being directly tied to WT. Graduation is an opportunity for family members to come together to witness the changes in the IP, to share their feelings, and to hopefully experience some well-deserved joy.

Summary. Despite the widespread use of these types of interventions, several of the programs identified as WT on the NATSAP website do not mention anything about family involvement in the descriptive paragraph associated with their program. This does not necessarily mean that they do not provide family programming, as further investigation into individual websites found many with at least some aspect of family programming. However, the authors of this chapter have the most insight and current knowledge of the programming within their own organization, Open Sky Wilderness (openskywildereness.com), and have highlighted that here.

Open Sky provides all of the previously described types of family interventions, and in doing so it transforms the traditional WT model where one family member is the IP and all other family members participate in a limited manner. OSW also conducts research to help identify which interventions, or what combination of interventions is most effective in contributing to long-term change in family systems. Open Sky is in the process of analyzing data that will help to inform what methods of intervention are most successful in creating and sustaining positive growth for the family. Not all families receive all services, so there is an opportunity to compare and contrast experiences with different elements of the family programming that is available. Previous preliminary analysis of research at OSW has revealed that children of parents who participate in Wellness Weekends and Family Quests experience a statistically significant decrease in level of distress (as measured by the Y-OQ) over students whose parents do not participate in family interventions or who only participate in FQs. These results suggest that WT is aided significantly by intensive, skill-building parent workshops and that between the two, intensive, skill-building parent workshops yield better outcomes (as measured by Y-OQ) than parent/child field overnights. Overall, OSW students demonstrated statistically significant change in level of distress regardless of parental intervention; however, it is the students whose parents participate and learn to use the same therapeutic tools as their child who saw the greatest gains.

Need for Additional Research

Despite research indicating improved outcomes with treatment that incorporates family involvement (e.g., Carlo and Shennum 1989) and a history of the field claiming foundations rooted in family therapy, the field is still struggling to implement past calls for a standardized model for family engagement (Burg 2001; Gillis et al. 1991). Also, while the current body of research examining the effectiveness of WT as an intervention for adolescents and young adults is ever-growing, there is a significant gap in the research. Research clearly indicates that participation in a WT program leads to a decrease in symptoms for the student enrolled in the program (Russell 2002, 2003a, 2004, 2005). Recent research (Tucker et al. 2016) has even shown improvements in family functioning as measured by the FAD tied to improvements in adolescent functioning as measured by the Y-OQ. However, given the lack of consistency with family programming in the field of WT, there is no research examining the effectiveness of the specific different types of family involvement.

In 2013, the Outdoor Behavioral Healthcare Council (OBHC) sought to establish an accreditation that would more specifically recognize the unique aspects of its WT programs (OBHC 2014). The OBHC partnered with the Association of Experiential Education (AEE) to create the OBH Accreditation, which is a voluntary credentialing program for OBH providers and a requirement for all OBH Council member programs (OBHC 2014). OBH accredited programs are required to participate in ongoing research. While individual programs maintain some freedom to choose which instrument they use to measure family functioning, programs are required to administer both individual and family measures. The Y-OQ 2.0 and Outcome Questionnaire are commonly used to measure individual functioning (Magle-Haberek et al. 2012; Norton et al. 2014; Russell 2003a, b, 2005; Tucker et al. 2011; Zelov et al. 2013) and the FAD is commonly used to measure family functioning (Tucker et al. 2016). So, while there is variety among WT programs in terms of what family programming they offer, OBH accredited programs are collecting data that, if analyzed appropriately, could shed light on the effectiveness of the types of family programming that are most impactful for the student and family, should those family programming efforts first be clearly defined. Chapter 15 discusses the need for additional family focused research within OBH programs and the reader is referred to that chapter for additional information.

Recommendations

Although there have been increases in family programming in the field of WT, much of the programming has been added as an afterthought rather than an intentional component of the experience (Burg 2001). Additionally, research has largely focused on the student experience (e.g., Russell 2002, 2003a, 2004, 2005). While family programming has been added, and OBH accredited programs are required to measure family functioning, the current body of research fails to parcel out each type of programming to determine how it is impacting the student and family experience.

We support previous recommendations (Burg 2001; Gillis et al. 1991) that call for providers to categorize family programming. While it is important for programs to maintain autonomy, the field would benefit from some categorization of family programming. The OBH programs could use already suggested categories (Burg 2001; Gillis et al. 1991) to provide a framework for the types of family programming currently being offered by their member programs. Once family programming is categorized, researchers would be better able to assess the effectiveness of each type of family program.

Suggestions for which *category* (Burg 2001; Gillis et al. 1991) each major family program offering fits into are as follows:

- *Recreation* (fun and short-term)

  - Graduation

- *Enrichment* (longer, focus on communication, conflict resolution and development of new skills)

  - Parent Weekend/Workshop/Seminars
  - Parent/Child Field Overnight

- *Adjunctive Therapy* (one family member is IP and all other family members participate in a limited manner)

  – Historical WT Model/Base WT Model

- *Primary Therapy* (family system is client, principal, and sometimes only treatment).

  – Family Therapist Assigned to Family

Once categories have been determined, the field would benefit from research examining the effectiveness of family programming on the individual and family experience. Guiding suggestions for future research questions and hypotheses include:

- Do students whose parents participate in family programming while they are in a WT program decrease in levels of distress?
- Do students whose parents participate in one family program offering decrease in levels of distress over students whose parents participate in other family program offerings?
- Do families who participate in family programming improve family functioning as measured by FAD?
- Do families who participate in one family program offering decrease in levels of distress over families who participate in other family program offerings?

Conclusion

It is clear that as a field, WT programming has continued to evolve since its origin. The OBH Council, in conjunction with AEE, has established a unique accreditation to recognize WT, OBH accredited programs are tracking treatment outcomes to demonstrate effectiveness on a student level, and many WT programs are now involving family members more intentionally in the treatment process. However, there is still work to be done. While there is research that generally indicates increased outcome effectiveness when involving family members in the treatment of an adolescent and/or young adult, the field of WT has not yet conducted the research to substantiate that the same is true for WT. Therefore, it is highly recommended that individual WT programs and the OBH Council begin to conduct more specific research examining the impact of diverse family therapy interventions (recreation, enrichment, adjunct therapy, primary therapy) on individual and family functioning. It is only with this type of in-depth research that the field of OBH can move forward with intention.

References

Bettmann, J. E., Olson-Morrison, D., & Jasperson, R. A. (2011). Adolescents in wilderness therapy: A qualitative study of attachment relationships. *Journal of Experiential Education, 34* (2), 182–200.

Burg, J. E. (2001). Emerging issues in therapeutic adventure with families. *Journal of Experiential Education, 24*(2), 118–122.

Carlo, P., & Shennum, W. A. (1989). Family reunification efforts that work: A three year follow-up study of children in residential treatment. *Child and Adolescent Social Work, 6*(3), 211–216.

Creighton, V., & Mills, L. (2016). Family matters: Engaging parents in youth treatment. *Journal of Therapeutic Schools and Programs, 8*(1), 51–58. doi:10.19157/JTSP.issue.08.01.07

Gillis, H. L., Gass, M. A., Bandoroff, S., Rudolph, S., Clapp, C., & Nadler, R. (1991). Family adventure questionnaire: Results and discussion. In C. Birmingham (Ed.), *Association for experiential education: 1991 conference proceedings and workshop summaries book* (pp. 29–39). Boulder, CO: Association for Experiential Education.

Haine-Schlagel, R. H., & Walsh, N. E. (2015). A review of parent participation engagement in child and family mental health treatment. *Clinical Child and Family Psychology Review, 18*(2), 133–150. doi:10.1007/s10567-015-0182-x

Harper, N., & Cooley, R. (2007). Parental reports of adolescent and family well-being following a wilderness therapy intervention: An exploratory look at systemic change. *Journal of Experiential Education, 29*(3), 393–396.

Magle-Haberek, N. A., Tucker, A. R., & Gass, M. A. (2012). Effects of program differences with wilderness therapy and residential treatment center (RTC) programs. *Residential Treatment for Children & Youth, 29,* 202–218.

Nichols, M. P., & Schwartz, R. C. (1998). *Family therapy: Concepts and methods.* Boston: Allyn & Bacon.

Norton, C. L., Tucker, A., Russell, K. C., Bettman, J. E., Gass, M. E., Gillis H. L., Behrens, E. (2014). Adventure therapy with youth. *Journal of Experiential Education, 37*(1), 46–59.

Open Sky Wilderness. (2016). About Open Sky. Retrieved from http://www.openskywilderness.com

Outdoor Behavioral Healthcare Council. (2014). Accreditation: OBH accreditation. Retrieved from https://obhcouncil.com/accreditation

Russell, K. C. (2002). Does outdoor behavioral healthcare work? A review of studies on the effectiveness of OBH as an intervention and treatment. *Journal of Therapeutic Camping, 2*(1), 5–12.

Russell, K. C. (2003a). Assessing treatment outcomes in outdoor behavioral healthcare using the youth outcome questionnaire. *Child & Youth Care Forum, 32*(6), 355–381.

Russell, K. C. (2003b). A Nationwide survey of outdoor behavioral healthcare programs for adolescents with problem behaviors. *The Journal of Experiential Education, 25*(3), 322–331.

Russell, K. C. (2004). Two years later a qualitative assessment of youth-well-being and the role of aftercare in outdoor behavioral healthcare treatment. Technical Report 1, Outdoor Behavioral Healthcare Research Cooperative, School of Health and Human Services, University of New Hampshire, Durham NH.

Russell, K. C. (2005). Two years later: A qualitative assessment of youth-well-being and the role of aftercare in outdoor behavioral healthcare treatment. *Child & Youth Care Forum, 34*(3), 209–239.

Russell, K. C., & Hendee, J. C. (2000). Outdoor Behavioral Healthcare: Definitions, common practice, expected outcomes, and a nationwide survey of programs. In *Proceedings on personal, societal, and ecological values of wilderness from the Sixth World Wilderness Congress on Research, Management, and Allocation* (Vol. II, pp. 136–141), October 24–29, 1998. Bangalore, India. (Proc. RMRS-P-14).

Tucker, A. R., Paul, M., Hobson, J., Karoff, M., & Gass, M. (2016). Outdoor behavioral healthcare: Its impact on family functioning. *Journal of Therapeutic Schools and Programs, 8*(1), 21–40.

Tucker, A., Zelov, R., & Young, M. (2011). Four years along: Emerging traits of programs in the NATSAP Practice Research Network (PRN). *Journal of Therapeutic Schools and Programs, 5*(1), 10–28.

Zelov, R., Tucker, A. R., & Javorksi, S. (2013). A new phase for the NATSAP PRN: Post discharge reporting and transition to the network wide utilization of the Y-OQ 2.0. *Journal of Therapeutic Schools & Programs, 6*(1), 7–19.

Author Biographies

Kendall Smith, MA, LPC is dedicated to working with families and individuals as they pursue improved health and more meaningful relationships. She received her MA in Transpersonal Counselling Psychology with an emphasis in Wilderness Therapy from Naropa University and has been utilizing holistic, integrated interventions with clients for the past decade. She has over 750 h of training in yoga specifically designed for mental, emotional, spiritual, and physical well-being. She is currently the Family Services Supervisor at Open Sky Wilderness and hopes to continue to make family work an essential aspect of all child and adolescent therapy.

Tony Issenmann, PhD, LMFT is a licensed Marriage and Family Therapist who has clinical experience working in a variety of settings including wilderness therapy programs, community agencies, a day treatment center for schizophrenic clients, and family therapy centers. His clinical focus has primarily centered on the adolescent and parent system. He has helped hundreds of students and families as a primary therapist and now serves as the Clinical and Family Services Director for Open Sky Wilderness Therapy. Dr. Issenmann is an accomplished speaker and has presented at regional, national, and international conferences.

Chapter 19
Connecting the Family: Short-Term Residential Treatment and Telemental Health

Johanna Creswell Báez

Chapter Highlights

- Short-term residential work has shown to be effective, but there is a lack of prior research studies and more research is needed.
- Wediko Children's Services will be described along with its commitment to applied research.
- The Wediko Summer Program provides a short-term residential model for providing family interventions using telemental health, such as online videos, phone conferencing and distance family therapy.
- A phase model of treatment will be described that connects families with what their children are learning in the residential setting.
- The use of technology to provide remote interventions has advanced rapidly over the last 10 years and has been shown to be effective.

As is noted throughout this book, studies have shown that family involvement in residential treatment is correlated with improved outcomes post-discharge and that family environment post-discharge is significantly associated with child outcomes (Hair 2005; Merritts 2016). However, literature on family work and short-term residential programs is scarce. Short-term residential programs are intensive programs with stays far shorter than traditional residential programs, around 1–3 months. Treatment is based on principles common to short-term therapies with a focus on supporting children and families to learn skills and then continue to

J.C. Báez (✉)
Wediko Children's Services, 122 West 27th St, 10th Floor, New York,
NY 10001, USA
e-mail: jcreswell@wediko.org; jcreswellbaez@utexas.edu

J.C. Báez
The University of Texas at Austin, School of Social Work, 1925 San Jacinto Blvd.,
Austin, TX 78712, USA

© Springer International Publishing AG 2017
J.D. Christenson and A.N. Merritts (eds.), *Family Therapy with Adolescents
in Residential Treatment*, Focused Issues in Family Therapy,
DOI 10.1007/978-3-319-51747-6_19

practice these skills at home. Very few outcome studies exist on short-term residential programs, but several have found clinical improvements in youth with severe psychiatric problems that had not responded to a range of interventions, including brief hospitalizations and extensive outpatient treatment (Leichtman et al. 2001) and in youth with learning disabilities and psychosocial problems (Michalski et al. 2003). Further, a summer treatment program for youth diagnosed with Attention-Deficit/Hyperactivity Disorder (ADHD) found that almost all participants benefited from the program as reported in parent, staff, and self-ratings (Sibley et al. 2011).

There are discrepancies in the residential literature regarding the optimal time in treatment for youth in residential treatment; however, one recent study found that the most drastic changes happen between 1 and 6 months of treatment. Up until 6 months, there is a strong positive predictive relationship between a longer time in treatment and a greater improvement in overall functioning at school, home, behaviors toward others, and moods/emotions (Strickler et al. 2016). However, there is no literature on short-term residential programs and the use of technology to support family work. This chapter will provide an overview of Wediko Children's Services and the short-term Wediko Summer Program, with a focus on the family program and the use of telemental health as a phase model intervention where families and children are learning skills in parallel.

Wediko Children's Services

Established in 1934, Wediko's continuum of mental health and therapeutic programs helps children develop skills and mastery to support healthier lives. Wediko's comprehensive services span four distinct programs including the Wediko School (year-round residential program for boys ages 11–21), Wediko Summer Program (short-term residential program for boys and girls ages 9–19), Wediko School-Based Programs (in Boston and New York), and Wediko Community Programs. Wediko uses the slogan, "Four Mental Health Programs with One Goal" to emphasize the importance of providing this continuum of care that includes in-home services, school-based services, and residential treatment (Wediko 2016a, para 1).

The Wediko Summer Program

In the early 1930s, Dr. Robert Young recognized that children with emotional and psychiatric needs were often institutionalized away from family and loved ones and that there was a strong need to support these children in a fresh air experience they called a "therapeutic camp program" (Young et al. 1951, p. 819). The program was designed so that children could go to summer camp instead of psychiatric wards to get treatment and enjoy the outdoors. More than eight decades later, the Wediko Summer Program continues to serve children who face repeated obstacles in their lives such as abuse, violence, trauma, depression, bipolar disorders, Autism, anxiety, and loss (Wediko 2013a).

The Wediko Summer Program is located in New Hampshire on a 450-acre lakefront campus with cabins for students and staff. The summer program is a short-term, 45-day residential treatment program serving boys and girls ages 9–19 with social, emotional, and behavioral challenges. The children who come to Wediko are referred by schools, educational consultants, and clinicians from across the country with around 50% paying privately and/or with support from their local school district. The summer program has approximately 125 students annually and offers a 1:2 staff to student ratio for individualized support. Further, the program has a strong emphasis in training the next generation of mental health workers (undergraduate and graduate students in mental health and education fields), providing a week-long training before staff arrive as well as a week-long reorientation after the children leave. Wediko staff includes social workers, psychologists, special education teachers, activity staff, and direct care staff.

At Wediko, children are supported in becoming the best versions of themselves, rather than being defined by their diagnoses or challenges. To support students in success, Wediko's structured summer program includes group therapy, academic instruction (10 h per week), daily experiential outdoor activities, and lots of individualized support. Counselors work with students throughout the day in moment to moment clinical interactions, using a primarily cognitive behavioral approach that engages students to think about their behaviors and recognize success in the clinical milieu. Staff can be seen talking with students when difficult emotions arise, working with several students to promote social skills, or tracking progress on set clinical goals, among many other daily therapeutic interventions. Overall, "Wediko students build social–emotional competence, confidence, and resilience in order to get along with others, make and keep friends, fulfill their personal needs, and succeed in school and in life" (Wediko 2016b, para 2).

For Summer 2016, a blog posting by the Summer Program Director, Mik Oyler, M.Ed., outlined the five key program values that embody the work of the Wediko Summer Program: fun, honesty, grit, Ubuntu, and safety (Oyler and Luddy 2016). The concept of *Ubuntu* was introduced to the Summer Program by former Summer Program Director, Dr. Tod Rossi, who learned this concept during his work in South Africa with the Truth and Reconciliation program. "Ubuntu, a Nguni Bantu term, is loosely translated as 'A person is a person through other persons'" (Wediko 2016c, para 2). At Wediko, Ubuntu is a key word used to support others in helping each other, using empathy, and creating a strong culture of kindness and understanding.

Research at the Wediko Summer Program

Research at Wediko began early in the mid-1950s when Dr. Robert Young and colleagues evaluated treatment techniques in the summer program (Young et al. 1951), and Dr. Howard J. Parad examined the need for uniform recording practices to translate clinical experiences from a residential treatment setting to family, school, and clinical providers (Parad and Young 1953). In the 1980s, there was a shift toward evaluating behavior change and outcomes (Parad 1983) and understanding personality and social development in a residential setting (Wright 1983). Dr. Harry W. Parad, past Executive Director, continued for three decades to support research, along with direction from Dr. Jack Wright of Brown University and Dr. Audrey Zakriski at Connecticut College, who focused on understanding how the students' behaviors varied by context and how best to provide interventions based on different contextual factors, such as different student peer groups or skill levels of staff (Cardoos et al. 2015; Hartley et al. 2011; Zakriski et al. 2005, 2006).

Dr. Parad has helped support Wediko's current research including, most recently, looking at phases of family therapy treatment with an adolescent in residential treatment (Báez 2015) and evaluating the behavioral data tool used in the summer program (Wediko 2016d). Further, Wediko's Executive Director, Dr. Amy Sousa, recently published on parental involvement and raising children with developmental disabilities (Sousa 2015). Overall, Wediko's research has shown that understanding contextual factors are important in residential treatment, using daily behavior checklists with students is a helpful clinical intervention tool (Reiger 2014), and implementing phase models in family therapy treatment supports residential programming. Wediko is continually investing in scholarly and applied research with a range of publications, dissertations, and presentations based on data from Wediko (2016d).

Currently, research in the summer program has continued to assess positive outcomes for students and how to best support parents. In 2016, students, teachers, and parents will complete the Behavioral and Emotional Rating Scale–Second Edition (BERS-2) which measures the personal strengths and competencies of children (Epstein and Sharma 1998). The following is the schedule for administering the BERS-2: (1) Pre-summer parents and youth will complete the assessment; (2) during the summer supervisors will fill out the assessment; and, (3) post-summer parents and youth will fill out a final assessment. The data on these outcomes of the Wediko Summer Program will be published in future publications.

Wediko's Summer Program Family Model

Wediko sees parents and guardians as important partners in the therapeutic process and as the cornerstone of Wediko's work with students. Wediko views the work done with families as laying the groundwork for the student's successful return home (Wediko 2013b). Further, building the therapeutic alliance is viewed as essential to support the family clinical work and promote successful treatment outcomes (Báez 2015). For Wediko, building the therapeutic alliance begins at the initial contact with a comprehensive family interview process in which all active members of the family participate, and family successes and challenges are noted. During the interview, a family contract is signed with co-created goals and a commitment to work weekly with a Wediko family therapist.

Moving away from a Psychodynamic, Structural, and Cognitive–Behavioral family therapy model that was used in the Summer Program previously, the current family therapy model uses Solution-Focused family therapy with an emphasis on behavioral psychoeducation in teaching Positive Behavioral Supports (PBS) and Collaborative Problem Solving (CPS) (Oyler and Luddy, personal communication, April 6, 2016). The shift in family therapy models came out of the need to have a model that fit better within a 6-week timeframe, the reality that many of the families were already in outside family therapy, and the evidence around effectiveness of skills training programs for parents (Kaminski et al. 2008). A Solution-Focused family therapy model is a strength-based and time-limited family therapy approach that works with families to take small, active steps in the directions of their set goals (Gehart 2014). A PBS approach provides structure on giving positive feedback, intervening before a problem starts, providing clear structures around expectations at home, and reinforcing consequences (Hieneman et al. 2006). Collaborative problem solving (CPS) teaches parents how to empathize and proactively identify issues with their children and models how children and adults can collaboratively solve problems together (Pollastri et al. 2013).

The Summer Family Program has an emphasis on providing skill-based psychoeducation for parents using technology to connect families with the treatment of their children and therapeutic support for the families. Starting in summer 2016, the key family program components include the following *weekly* services: (a) Self-paced online videos for families with a focus on skill building; (b) parent support groups via phone conference facilitated by a family program therapist with other parents in the child's cabin; (c) individualized family phone or video sessions by an assigned family program therapist; and (d) family homework on topics covered in the videos. Further, this model includes collaboration and consultation with schools and involved services providers and the above outlined evaluation measures (see Fig. 19.1 outlining Wediko's Summer Family Program model).

This model was developed based on feedback from families who had participated in the Wediko Summer Program. The overall model is run by one family program manager and three family program therapists, all who have master's degrees or higher in social work or other related mental health fields. The family program therapists each work with around 35 families to provide the weekly support groups and individual sessions. The family program therapists also work with the clinical supervisors to get weekly updates on children and collaborate via phone calls, emails, and session/intervention notes in an online, HIPAA compliant database system called BestNotes (BestNotes 2016).

Central Components
1. Psycho-Educational Videos (weekly): Selected topics sequentially build and expand parent education and skills, self-paced.
2. Group Discussion Calls (weekly): Facilitated by the Family Program Manager, families review video material, connect with other participating parents, and apply skills to individualized scenarios, one hour via phone conference.
3. Family Check-In/Sessions (weekly): Family therapist provides solution-focused family therapy sessions, individualized for each child, 30 minutes via phone or videoconferencing.
4. Family Homework (weekly): Select readings on related topics in addition to education related to Wediko's program structures and interventions.
5. Collaboration and Consultation with Schools and Involved Service Providers (ongoing): Wediko staff provides extensive information about successful interventions, behavior plans, and ongoing challenges to maximize gains and transfer skills when students return home.
6. Program Evaluation and Outcome Measurement: Wediko uses parent satisfaction surveys, staff feedback, and performance measures for program monitoring and to evaluate client success.

Fig. 19.1 Six central components of the Wediko Summer Family Program model

Anecdotally, parents are saying that they enjoy the weekly parent support groups and connecting with other parents around similar challenges and successes, but would like the family therapists to have a better understanding of the unique challenges that their children are struggling with and how they are doing in the residential setting. Currently, clinical supervisors have the role of directly providing families with weekly updates on their children's individual progress via phone or email and then having the weekly update check-ins with the family therapist. As the model continues to develop, Wediko can look toward ways for family therapists to be better integrated into what is also happening in the residential setting. Some initial ideas include having family therapists spend periodic days throughout the summer with the cabin groups to better understand the children and having a smaller caseload.

The Summer Family Program and Telemental Health

A key approach to the Summer Family Program is the use of technology to connect children and families and to support families in making changes too. The use of technology to provide remote interventions has advanced rapidly over the last ten years and has been shown to be effective and comparable to in-person mental health care (Hilty et al. 2013). The American Psychological Association defines *Telepsychology* or *Telemental Health* as the provision of psychological services using telecommunication technologies, such as providing mental health services remotely via telephone, internet websites, or videoconferencing (APA, 2013).

Asynchronous or delayed telehealth technologies, such as prerecorded videos and online activities, have shown preliminary efficacy in supporting youth mental health outcomes and augmenting in-person interventions (Myers and Comer 2016). Further, several different articles have begun to note the benefits of using telemental health in residential treatment (Alicata et al. 2016; Goldstein and Glueck 2016; Kramer and Luxton 2016).

Phase Model: Wediko's Psychoeducational, Skill-Building Videos

With the known benefits of telemental health, Wediko created a model of family treatment using telemental health that parallels the different phases of what students are learning in the residential program. Phase models of treatment have been a key component in generalist family therapy practice to frame the therapy or family work in a series of segments (e.g., beginning phase, the assessment phase, the intervention phase, and the termination phase) with corresponding treatment interventions (Nichols 2013). Phase models are viewed as a useful framework in psychotherapy (Hilsenroth et al. 2001), especially in organizing phase-specific interventions. Currently, the Summer Program is using a phase framework for families that parallels what the students are learning about in terms of behavioral supports and collaborative problem solving. See Báez (2015) for a discussion on phase models in families with an adolescent in residential treatment and the year-round Wediko school phase model.

The following phases are used in Wediko's weekly telemental health online videos for parents and correspond to what children are working on in the residential setting during the summer: (1) Getting Ready—preparing for common concerns that come up in having your child in short-term residential care; (2) What's Going On—understanding routines and structures at Wediko and introducing PBS and how to use these strategies in your home; (3) Routines and Habits—understanding how consistency and predictability helps children succeed; (4) Collaborative Problem Solving Part 1—learning about motivation, rewards, and consequences; (5) Collaborative Problem Solving Part 2—prioritizing what to work on and identifying skills that kids struggle with; and (6) Transitions and Continued Practice —celebrating successes and continuing to use the skills learned in the summer program at home (see Fig. 19.2).

The online videos were created to address the common themes occurring each week in the clinical milieu, for Wediko staff to share strategies that are being used, and to provide opportunities for parents to practice skills while their children are away and then after they return home. At the end of each video, there are homework activities and a section for families to type in questions that help support the weekly group discussions and individual sessions led by Wediko family program therapists. The phases are flexible and dynamic with the videos being self-paced, noting the

Weekly Online Video Modules
Before Programming (June 19-June 28) Introduction: The focus of this week will be to introduce the Family Program model and to review expectations for the Family Program.
Session 1 (June 28-July 4th, Students arrive July 5th) Getting Ready: The theme for this week is to help the parents and child prepare to transition to the Wediko Summer Program. Overall logistics will be discussed to help the family prepare for Child Arrival Day as well as discussing common concerns.
Session 2 (July 5th- 11th) What's Going On: Introduce basic programmatic concepts, "kids will do well if they can and if they know how" and how to teach the behaviors you want, including an overview on PBS.
Session 3 (July 12-18th) Routines and Habits: Introduce theory behind supporting consistency and predictability in using schedules.
Session 4 (July 19-25th) Collaborative Problem Solving 1: Teach parents about motivation, rewards, and behavior. Provide examples of how they could use these principles in their parenting.
Session 5 (July 26-Aug 1st) Collaborative Problem Solving 2: Support parents in prioritizing what they would like to work on and identifying skills that their children struggle with.
Session 6 (Aug 2nd- Aug 8th): No video. Focus will be on skills learned during sessions with the family therapist and clinical supervisor of the child.
Session 7 (Aug 9th-Aug 15th) Transitions: The importance of transitions will be discussed and the different types of transitions that families often experience. Strategies will be discussed for continuing to practice the skills learned in the summer program.
Session 8 (Aug 15th and beyond) Now What: Support will be provided around continuing gains made in the summer program and collaboration with key support in the child's community.

Fig. 19.2 An example of scheduled weekly psychoeducational, skill building videos at Wediko

need for families to move back and forth and to build upon stages during treatment (Báez 2015). Further, the videos continue to be accessible after the students go home to help families continue building support after their children are back home. See Fig. 19.3 for a screenshot of one of the introduction videos on the Wediko family website.

Conclusion and Implications for Practice

Overall, short-term residential treatment can be an effective means of teaching children and parents' therapeutic skills. The Wediko Summer Program provides a model for how short-term residential programs can support family work, in parallel with what children are learning in the residential milieu. The Summer Family Program includes using telemental health with families via online videos, phone

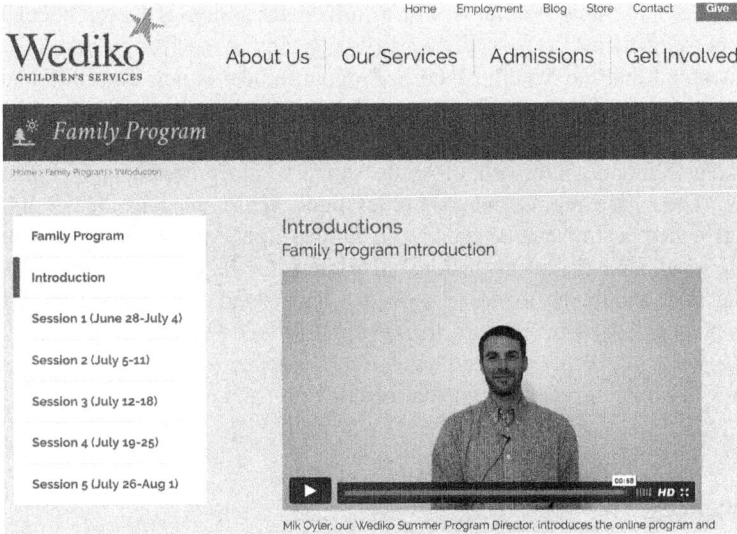

Fig. 19.3 Introduction video screenshot on the family web site

conferencing, and distance family therapy, to support a phase model of treatment that begins with how to support the transition into a residential program and ends with ways to continue the skills gained at home and involve local mental health providers. A skills based approach was used because of evidence around effectiveness of skills training programs for parents (Kaminski et al. 2008). It is clear that involving family in treatment and the family environment post-discharge is associated with improved child outcomes (Merritts 2016).

Further, the use of telemental health has been noted to support residential programs (Alicata et al. 2016; Goldstein and Glueck 2016; Kramer and Luxton 2016), but there is no research focusing specifically on this topic. Wediko will publish future evaluation research on this topic in supporting families (Robinson 2016). Studies have shown that telemental health is equally effective as traditional face-to-face treatment for symptom reduction and patient satisfaction (Springer et al. 2016). Telemental health makes accessibility to treatment easier and bridges the gap in bringing the families along as their children are learning valuable skills. Providing remote interventions is becoming an increasingly convenient method of providing psychological treatments to clients in need (Yuen et al. 2012). However, it is important to consider *when, under what circumstances*, and *for whom* telemental health formats may be most indicated (Myers and Comer 2016). Use of telemental health needs to have thoughtful attention to how residential service providers are building and maintaining the therapeutic relationships, supporting engagement, and connecting the direct work happening in the residential setting to the distance family work. Telemental health also presents service providers with a wide range of clinical, technical, and ethical challenges that need to be considered when developing new programs. For a further discussion of these challenges, see Yuen et al. (2012).

It is noted that the Wediko Family Program model is new for 2016 and that it will continue to develop and be assessed for effectiveness. Wediko hopes this model can support other short-term residential programs, clinicians, and families in using phase models and technology to support family treatment in a residential setting. The phase model helps families build skills alongside their children to support better post-discharge outcomes. Further, the experiences of families, children in residential treatment, residential administrators, family therapists, and residential staff should be explored to better understand how using this telemental health phase model works in practice. Overall, Wediko's family program strives to instill a sense of competency and hope, a best practice for engaging and supporting families of children receiving mental health care (McLendon 2009).

References

Alicata, D., Schroepfer, A., Unten, T., Agoha, R., Helm, S., Fukuda, M., … Stanton, M. (2016). Telemental health training, team building, and workforce development in cultural context: The Hawaii experience. *Journal of Child and Adolescent Psychopharmacology, 26*(3), 260–265.

Báez, J. C. (2015). Bridging the distance: A clinical phase model of family therapy with adolescent residential treatment. *Families in Society: The Journal of Contemporary Social Services, 96*(1), 41–48.

BestNotes. (2016). About BestNotes. Retrieved from: http://www.bestnotes.com

Cardoos, S. L., Zakriski, A. L., Wright, J. C., & Parad, H. W. (2015). Peer experiences in short-term residential treatment: Individual and group-moderated prediction of behavioral responses to peers and adults. *Journal of Abnormal Child Psychology, 43*(6), 1145–1159.

Epstein, M. H., & Sharma, H. M. (1998). *Behavioral and emotional rating scale: A strength based approach to assessment.* Austin, TX: PRO-ED.

Gehart, D. (2014). *Mastering competencies in family therapy: A practical approach to theories and clinical case documentation* (2nd ed.). Belmont, CA: Brooks/Cole.

Goldstein, F., & Glueck, D. (2016). Developing rapport and therapeutic alliance during telemental health sessions with children and adolescents. *Journal of Child and Adolescent Psychopharmacology, 26*(3), 204–211.

Hair, H. J. (2005). Outcomes for children and adolescents after residential treatment: A review of research from 1993 to 2003. *Journal of Child and Family Studies, 14*(4), 551–575.

Hartley, A. G., Zakriski, A. L., & Wright, J. C. (2011). Probing the depths of informant discrepancies: Contextual influences on divergence and convergence. *Journal of Clinical Child & Adolescent Psychology, 40*(1), 54–66.

Hieneman, M., Childs, K., & Sergay, J. (2006). *Parenting with positive behavior support: A practical guide to resolving your child's difficult behavior.* Baltimore, MD: Brookes Publishing Company.

Hilsenroth, M. J., Ackerman, S. J., & Blagys, M. D. (2001). Evaluating the phase model of change during short-term psychodynamic psychotherapy. *Psychotherapy Research, 11*(1), 29–47.

Hilty, D. M., Ferrer, D. C., Parish, M. B., Johnston, B., Callahan, E. J., & Yellowlees, P. M. (2013). The effectiveness of telemental health: a 2013 review. *Telemedicine and e-Health, 19* (6), 444–454.

Kaminski, J. W., Valle, L. A., Filene, J. H., & Boyle, C. L. (2008). A meta-analytic review of components associated with parent training program effectiveness. *Journal of Abnormal Child Psychology, 36*(4), 567–589.

Kramer, G. M., & Luxton, D. D. (2016). Telemental health for children and adolescents: An overview of legal, regulatory, and risk management issues. *Journal of Child and Adolescent Psychopharmacology, 26*(3), 198–203.

Leichtman, M., Leichtman, M. L., Barber, C. C., & Neese, D. T. (2001). Effectiveness of intensive short-term residential treatment with severely disturbed adolescents. *American Journal of Orthopsychiatry, 71*(2), 227.

McLendon, T. (2009). Best practices for engaging parents of children receiving mental health services. In C. G. Petr (Ed.), *Multidimensional evidence-based practice: Synthesizing knowledge, research, and values* (pp. 108–131). New York: Routledge.

Merritts, A. (2016). A review of family therapy in residential settings. *Contemporary Family Therapy, 38*(1), 75–85.

Michalski, J. H., Mishna, F., Worthington, C., & Cummings, R. (2003). A multi-method impact evaluation of a therapeutic summer camp program. *Child and Adolescent Social Work Journal, 20*(1), 53–76.

Myers, K., & Comer, J. S. (2016). The case for telemental health for improving the accessibility and quality of children's mental health services. *Journal of Child and Adolescent Psychopharmacology, 26*(3), 186–191.

Nichols, M. (2013). *Family therapy concepts and methods* (10th ed.). Upper Saddles River, NJ: Pearson Education Inc.

Oyler M., & Luddy, J. (2016). What's the deal with the 2016 Wediko Summer Program? Retrieved from: http://www.wediko.org/our-blog/whats-deal-2016-wediko-summer-program

Parad, H. W. (1983). *Behavioral consistency and change in children during and after short-term residential treatment: A multiple perspectives approach.* Unpublished Doctoral Dissertation: University of North Carolina at Chapel Hill.

Parad, H. J., & Young, R. A. (1953). Recording practices in a therapeutic camp. *American Journal of Orthopsychiatry, 23,* 358–368.

Pollastri, A. R., Epstein, L. D., Heath, G. H., & Ablon, J. S. (2013). The collaborative problem solving approach: Outcomes across settings. *Harvard Review of Psychiatry, 21*(4), 188–199.

Reiger, C. (2014). *Summer program research coordinator report.* Boston, MA: Author.

Robinson, W. (2016). *Exploring parenting self-efficacy among parents of children in residential treatment: Evaluating a combined psychoeducational intervention.* Unpublished Doctoral Dissertation Proposal: Boston University School of Social Work.

Sibley, M. H., Pelham, W. E., Evans, S. W., Gnagy, E. M., Ross, J. M., & Greiner, A. R. (2011). An evaluation of a summer treatment program for adolescents with ADHD. *Cognitive and Behavioral Practice, 18*(4), 530–544.

Sousa, A. C. (2015). "Crying doesn't work": Emotion and parental involvement of working class mothers raising children with developmental disabilities. *Disability Studies Quarterly, 35*(1).

Springer, P. R., Farero, A., Bischoff, R. J., & Taylor, N. C. (2016). Using experiential interventions with distance technology: Overcoming traditional barriers. *Journal of Family Psychotherapy, 27*(2), 148–153.

Strickler, A., Mihalo, J. R., Bundick, M. J., & Trunzo, A. C. (2016). Relationship between time in residential treatment and youth outcomes: Results from a cross-site 5-year analysis. *Journal of Child and Family Studies, 25*(6), 1860–1870.

Wediko Children's Services. (2013a). *Fiscal Year 2013 Annual Report.* Boston: Wediko Children's Services.

Wediko Children's Services. (2013b). *Wediko school family handbook.* Boston: Wediko Children's Services.

Wediko Children's Services. (2016a). Our services. Retrieved from: http://www.wediko.org/our-services/continuum-of-care

Wediko Children's Services. (2016b). Summer program. Retrieved from: http://www.wediko.org/our-services/wediko-summer-program/overview

Wediko Children's Services. (2016c). At Wediko, we tackle problems together—In Ubuntu. Retrieved from: http://www.wediko.org/our-blog/wediko-tackle-problems-together-ubuntu

Wediko Children's Services. (2016d). Expertise in multiple fields of study. Retrieved from: http://www.wediko.org/about-us/research

Wright, J. C. (1983). *The structure and perception of behavioral consistency.* Unpublished Doctoral Dissertation: Stanford University.

Young, R. A., Miller, L., & Verven, N. (1951). Treatment techniques in a therapeutic camp. *American Journal of Orthopsychiatry, 21,* 819–826.

Yuen, E. K., Goetter, E. M., Herbert, J. D., & Forman, E. M. (2012). Challenges and opportunities in internet-mediated telemental health. *Professional Psychology: Research and Practice, 43*(1), 1.

Zakriski, A. L., Wright, J. C., & Parad, H. W. (2006). Intensive short-term residential treatment: A contextual evaluation of the "stop-gap" model. *The Brown University Child and Adolescent Behavior Letter, 22*(6), 1–6.

Zakriski, A. L., Wright, J. C., & Underwood, M. K. (2005). Gender similarities and differences in children's social behavior: Finding personality in contextualized patterns of adaptation. *Journal of Personality and Social Psychology, 88*(5), 844.

Author Biography

Johanna Creswell Báez Ph.D., LCSW, Co-Founder and Research and Grants Manager, Wediko Children's Services, New York. Johanna has been working with the nonprofit Wediko Children's Services since 2000, from Direct Care Counselor to Senior Clinical Supervisor, including ten summers in the Wediko Summer Residential Program. Since 2007, Johanna has worked in the New York City public schools with different nonprofits in the role of Director, most recently co-founding the Wediko New York School-Based branch providing social and emotional services that is now in over 20 different schools. Further, Johanna has maintained an evening individual and family therapy private practice and teaches Master's level social work classes online and has taught courses in family therapy, trauma and resilience, financial management, and direct practice with the University of Texas at Austin School of Social Work and the Columbia University School of Social Work. Beyond her clinical background, she has experience in program evaluation, program development, staff training, grant writing, and financial management. She holds a Ph.D. from Smith College in Clinical Social Work, an MS from Columbia University in Social Work, and a BS in Neuroscience from Colorado College.

Part III
Research and Outcomes

Chapter 20
Investigating Family Therapy with Qualitative, Quantitative, and Mixed Methods in Adolescent Residential Treatment Programs

Jacob D. Christenson and Dumayi M. Gutierrez

Chapter Highlights

- Family involvement has long been associated with positive outcomes for adolescents in residential treatment.
- Different types of treatment settings are described to aid in the discussion of research methods.
- Research conducted in residential settings has the advantage of easy access to participants and assessments.
- Qualitative, quantitative, and mixed methods can all be utilized effectively in these settings to promote family therapy.
- Research on family therapy should consider both the clinical aspect and financial aspect of treatment.

The majority of the research on adolescents in residential settings over the last three decades has been focused on outcomes at the program level (e.g., Hair 2005; Leichtman et al. 2001; Lyons et al. 2001), and has largely ignored the specific role of family therapy, other than to indicate it was part of the milieu. Given that between 50,000 and 200,000 children and adolescents are placed in residential treatment each year (Government Accountability Office 2008; Vaughn 2005) family therapists should be actively engaged in producing research that supports their inclusion in this field of care. Family therapy providers within adolescent residential

J.D. Christenson (✉)
Marriage and Family Therapy Program, Mount Mercy University,
1330 Elmhurst Dr. NE, Cedar Rapids, IA 52402, USA
e-mail: jchristenson@mtmercy.edu

D.M. Gutierrez
Couple and Family Therapy, University of Iowa,
N310 Lindquist Center, Iowa City, IA 52242, USA
e-mail: dumayi-gutierrez@uiowa.edu

© Springer International Publishing AG 2017
J.D. Christenson and A.N. Merritts (eds.), *Family Therapy with Adolescents in Residential Treatment*, Focused Issues in Family Therapy,
DOI 10.1007/978-3-319-51747-6_20

programs need to understand the importance of producing their own findings to support their work, which can be accomplished by employing the scientist–practitioner model.

The purpose of this chapter is to provide an overview of research methods that are available for use in such settings and how these methods can be applied to strengthen the place of family therapy in residential treatment. This broad discussion also provides a prelude to the next three chapters of the book, which give detailed examples of some of the methods discussed here. It is hoped that after reading these four chapters together those new to conducting research in this field will feel more empowered to do so, as well as obtain some of the practical knowledge that will be needed to be successful in such endeavors. Within the field of residential care for adolescents there are two areas that require concerted research focus. The first is the clinical aspect of the work, meaning the treatment that is delivered to the adolescents. The second aspect is the financial aspect, which concerns the costs and benefits of providing this type of treatment. Accordingly, the discussion of methods below will be broken down by aspect where possible.

Types of Residential Placement

One of the challenges of doing family therapy research with adolescents in residential treatment is that there are various types of placements available, and each of them has different ways of organizing treatment, involving the family, and delivering program content. Program types within five broad categories are described below. Definitions are based on the literature and the experience of the authors in working with adolescent residential programs.

Therapeutic Boarding Schools

Therapeutic boarding schools are residential programs focused on the emotional growth and development of the adolescent, while also preparing them for academic success (National Association of Therapeutic Schools and Programs [NATSAP], n. d.). These programs typically have fewer restrictions placed on the adolescent and have stricter admissions requirements. Commonly, therapeutic boarding schools operate on a level system that provides the adolescent with more freedoms and opportunities as they move up to higher levels. They are designed to provide therapeutic support to those students who have mental health issues, in such a way that they can be academically successful. One such program is the Oakley School located near Park City, Utah (www.oakley-school.com). Adolescents who participate in these programs typically stay for at least one year and sometimes up to 2–3 years.

Residential Treatment Centers

The term residential treatment center (RTC) is used to describe a wide range of programs and services designed to work with troubled adolescents, which has led to confusion about what exactly constitutes an RTC (Lee 2008). However, in general, residential treatment centers (RTCs) are inpatient programs designed to serve adolescents who are suffering from significant psychiatric, behavioral, or co-morbid disorders. RTCs focus on behavior modification and psychiatric management, and usually will have medication management services on-site. Though RTCs will also sometimes use a level system, the opportunities for increased privileges are fewer than what would be expected in a therapeutic boarding school. The quality of these types of programs varies greatly throughout the United States, with at least one survey showing that 27% do not offer any type of therapy services to adolescents in their care (Hockenberry et al. 2009). RTCs can be further broken down into two subtypes, client-funded RTCs and government-funded RTCs. Lee and Barth (2011) indicated that a program's funding source is an important factor in defining types of programs.

Client-funded RTCs. These programs operate on funds paid by the family of the adolescent (Behrens and Satterfield 2006) are often run by for-profit organizations, and may admit adolescents from all over the country. They usually have admissions standards that specify their target client and there is a heavy focus on providing quality therapeutic services. Some client-funded RTCs also have a strong academic component, which serves to facilitate entrance into top tier universities. An example of this type of program is Cedar Ridge RTC located in Roosevelt, Utah (www.cedaridge.net). Since clients in this type of program come from geographically diverse locations, family therapy opportunities are limited to phone therapy and infrequent family workshops. At higher levels in the program, opportunities may also be provided for the adolescent to participate in home visits.

Government-funded RTCs. Government-funded RTCs will typically accept adolescents from the surrounding areas, are set up to operate under a mandate of the state. As the term implies, these program are publically funded (Behrens and Satterfield 2006). As an example, in Iowa adolescents can be placed in a Psychiatric Medical Institute for Children (PMIC). Four Oaks in Cedar Rapids, Iowa is typical of the type of organization that provides this type of services (www.fouroaks.org). Adolescents placed in a PMIC unit have to demonstrate a pattern of severe behavioral disturbance over time before being admitted due to high demand for services and long wait lists. Family members live closer to the facility, so opportunities for in-person family therapy are more readily available, though family engagement is a consistent challenge.

Short-Term Programs

The two primary types of programs that fall under the category of short-term treatment are substance abuse programs and wilderness therapy. Substance abuse programs are usually based on a 12-step recovery model and are similar to those designed for working with adults (e.g., Ouimette et al. 1997). These programs are more likely to want the adolescent to have some desire to change, even if the desire to change is largely being driven by external factors (e.g., a family intervention; Callaghan et al. 2005). Wilderness programs, on the other hand, do not require the adolescent to have any desire to change and most adolescents arrive resistant to treatment. Wilderness programs make use of backcountry travel (NATSAP, n.d.), usually last between six and eight weeks, and offer little direct contact between family members during the expedition phase, with the exception of letters, and ongoing contact with the program's clinical staff (e.g., Red Cliff Ascent; www.redcliffascent.com). At the end of the program there is usually a *reunion* phase that spans a few days and provides opportunities for face-to-face family therapy. It should be noted the amount of contact between family members depends on the model used by a particular wilderness program. In fact, some wilderness programs require the family to be present for the duration of the adolescent's stay (e.g., Bandoroff and Scherer 1994).

Lockdown Facilities

Lockdown facilities are those that take high risk adolescents who may be a danger to themselves and others. One example of this type of setting is a psychiatric hospital where adolescents are committed as a result of a high risk of suicide. Another example is correctional facilities for those with conduct disorder and severe criminal behavior (Lee 2008). The length of stay at lockdown facilities varies and may be as short as a few days in the case of suicidality. Lockdown facilities are much more focused on controlling behavior and preventing harm than academic preparation or providing space for emotional growth.

Without a clear understanding of what each program type entails it is difficult to create, execute, and evaluate a meaningful research program (Lee 2008). While we acknowledge there continues to be a significant amount of disagreement regarding definitions (e.g., Lee 2008; Lee and Barth 2011), the definitions offered above will be used throughout the remainder of the paper to facilitate the present discussion. In the discussion that follows, a brief description of each method will be presented before examining ways to use it in research in adolescent residential programs. This overview will be followed by a brief review of research literature wherein the specific method had been utilized. After this brief review, studies that could be conducted using the methods are outlined, with specific focus on the clinical and financial aspects, as described above.

Qualitative Methods

Qualitative methods are most often used to explore and understand the meaning individuals and groups assign to their lived experience (Creswell 2009). Some of the more popular methods are phenomenology, ethnography, narratology, grounded theory, action research, and the Delphi method (Creswell 2009; Sprenkle and Piercy 2005). Qualitative research on family therapy with adolescents in residential treatment is sparse. However, one example is Demmitt and Joanning (1998), who used focus groups with parents to determine their impression of the treatment process. Similarly, Spencer and Powell (2000), as well as Springer and Stahmann (1998), reported on feedback from parents about their role in treatment and what they found to be helpful during the process. In Chap. 23 of this book, Liermann and Norton provide a description of a phenomenological study they conducted in one of the Outward Bound programs. In their study they interviewed parents of adolescents who had participated in the program and asked about their relationship with their child. One of the unique things about this qualitative study was that they collected data at discharge, 3 months post-discharge, and 6 months post-discharge, and the program did not depend on licensed therapist to deliver the skills training the adolescents received. Their results showed that parents consistently reported their communication with the adolescent had improved, and that this change was present even after 6 months. Although Liermann and Norton's work adds to the literature, there is still a scarcity of qualitative research with families of adolescents in residential treatment, which is unfortunate since such methods often provide a foundation for additional quantitative inquiry and there are ample opportunities to draw a sample without adding undue strain on families or staff.

Clinical Aspect

As noted above, the clinical aspect of treatment is concerned with how therapy is delivered and what makes it effective. Researchers could use qualitative methods to address questions pertaining to the treatment process. Some possible research questions include: What actions do therapists take to include parents in the treatment process? What did parents perceive as the most helpful aspect of family involvement? How did they change their behavior during the treatment process and what led to that change? How did their perceptions of the adolescent change over the course of treatment? What factors were most influential in taking responsibility for their own behavior and working on their part of the relationship? How did the relationship change with siblings and other family members who were not the focus of treatment? How well are therapists communicating about the therapeutic process and what could they do better?

As previously highlighted, therapists in government-funded RTCs often have difficulty promoting engagement in therapy, notwithstanding the proximity of the program to the family. Family members of adolescents in government-funded RTCs may feel like the mental health care system is set up in opposition to them, even though the stated goal is usually for the child to return home to the family. Action research could be applied to this problem and used to generate solutions and methods for engaging the family. According to Mendenhall and Doherty (2005) action research is particularly amenable to situations where there is a need to correct an oppressive arrangement and understand the context of a particular system. One of the greatest strengths of action research is that the findings are immediately applicable to the local situation since the researchers are also participants in the system (Hambridge 2000; Mendenhall and Doherty 2005).

As described by Lewin (1958) action research involves first establishing an understanding of the problem and recognizing the need for collaboration in solving the problem. With regard to engaging families in residential treatment, therapists could sit down with a group of parents and discuss concerns and issues around family involvement. Adolescents could be brought into this conversation as well to get their perspective. During these initial meetings the democratic nature of the process and the need to avoid taking a one-up position would be emphasized. Therapists, parents, and adolescents could then be asked to work collaboratively to identify areas of concern and barriers to family involvement. During the second phase of the research process, the group would work together to establish methods that would be effective at promoting involvement and actively engaging families in the therapeutic process. The group would then come up with plans for implementing the ideas, followed by determining the required action steps. As the solutions and ideas are put into practice the group would meet often to determine how well the solutions are working and determine what changes are needed. During the third phase of action research, solutions are solidified into concrete processes that will be used by the group to promote a sustainable change in behavior. The therapists, parents, and adolescents would again gather data and feed it back into the system to determine how they will move forward in a way that keeps families engaged.

Although action research has a number of strengths that make this approach appealing, there are also some weaknesses that should be considered. First among the criticisms is that the findings are not generalizable beyond the setting in which the research takes place. This makes one of the methods greatest strengths also one of its greatest weaknesses. Because the solutions discovered through action research are specific to problems in a particular setting, with its own particular circumstances, it is unlikely that the solutions will be transferrable to other settings. Additionally, because of the lack of rigorous methods used to conduct this type of inquiry (Rose et al. 2014) some researchers may find it is difficult to publish action research in peer-reviewed journals. Notwithstanding these criticisms, action research remains appealing because of the opportunity to effect positive change during the research process.

Another problem that could be addressed through qualitative research is the lack of an agreed upon set of best practices for family therapy in adolescent residential settings (McLendon et al. 2012). A study using the Delphi method could potentially address this deficit in the clinical treatment approach for this population. The Delphi method was developed to provide a group of experts the opportunity to share ideas in a way that reduced the likelihood of *group think* influencing the process (Dalkey 1969; Dalkey and Helmer 1963). In order to conduct this type of study a researcher could first identify a group of experts in the field who possess extensive conceptual and practical knowledge about family therapy within adolescent residential settings (Jenkins and Smith 1994). One possibility for accomplishing this would be to look for presenters at national conferences, such as those held by the National Association of Therapeutic Schools and Programs. Once the panel is determined, the researcher would send out a survey with open-ended questions to the panelists about what they believe constitutes best practices programs should follow with regard to family therapy. The researcher would then collect the responses and use them to create a well-structured questionnaire that is sent back out to the panelists (Hsu and Sandford 2007). The questionnaire would consist of the statements from the first round and require that the panelists rate their agreement with each one. The research would then analyze and summarize the findings from the questionnaire, and send it back out for a final review by the panel. Following this process would allow the panel to reach a greater level of consensus about best practices with each round of data collection and analysis. Best practices generated through this method could then be disseminated to accrediting bodies and used to guide intervention and research.

One difficultly that could be encountered doing this type of research is different program types may have contradictory practices that contribute to positive outcomes. For example, wilderness programs may rely on stress and challenge to create a situation where change can occur, such as when adolescents participate in mountain biking or rappelling. For this type of program considering how to make these types of experiences effective may be an important part of the best practices in this industry. Conversely, lockdown facilities that accept those demonstrating high levels of suicidality may be set up to purposefully reduce or avoid stress and challenge that could exacerbate symptoms. Because of the different needs and purposes evident in different programs, Delphi research as described here may need to first be conducted within a single program type, or at least within similar program types (e.g., therapeutic boarding schools and client-funded RTCs).

Financial Aspect

As health care costs have increase dramatically there has been a call for less expensive forms of treatment. To complicate matters, there are studies showing that outpatient treatment of adolescents is effective and costs less than residential programs (e.g., Schoenwald et al. 1996). Residential programs have been slow to respond to this challenge. Cost-effectiveness will be established primarily through quantitative analyses, but qualitative studies could be used to set the stage. For example, researchers could conduct qualitative interview with parents to determine their decision making process given the high cost of client-funded RTCs and therapeutic boarding schools. This type of inquiry may prove valuable in distinguishing between those who would benefit from placement in this type of setting more than outpatient therapy alone. It is possible that the combined therapeutic and educational benefits of a residential placement outweigh the cost of the program in the minds of parents. Conversely, researchers could work with parents whose children have been placed in government-funded RTCs to determine how they and their families are affected as a result of participation. How much time are they spending complying with the requirements of the program? How much do they spend on treatment related activities, such as traveling to the program for session? How does this affect their work productivity? How has their own mental health been affected by the child's placement? The findings from these types of studies could prove useful to researchers trying to quantify the costs and benefits of adolescent residential treatment, as will be discussed later in this chapter.

Another way qualitative methods could be used to investigate the financial aspect of adolescent residential treatment would be to interview different stakeholders in focus groups (Hesse-Biber and Leavy 2010). For example, researchers could conduct focus groups with insurance company decision-makers to determine their thoughts about coverage for residential services and how family therapy fits into this form of treatment. Gaining insight into the thought processes of third-party payers could prove invaluable in increasing reimbursement rates and extending coverage to alternative treatments. Programs could use related findings to develop a response and address any revealed concerns. Another group that could be interviewed through the use of focus groups is policymakers who have a role in funding programs. The responses provided by policymakers could be helpful in the process of crafting legislation aimed at supporting the use of family therapy in residential settings.

Quantitative Methods

There are four main categories of quantitative research; namely, descriptive, correlational, quasi-experimental, and experimental (Creswell 2009). Quantitative designs are most often used to test conceptual models and understand the relationships between variables, establish the effectiveness of a particular treatment, or measure the opinions or views of a particular group. Examples of quantitative research on family therapy in adolescent residential placements are more readily available. For example, Stage (1999) examined factors affecting the placement of a youth in a less restrictive environment (e.g., home) after discharge. Stage found that the use of family therapy was the only factor that significantly predicted discharge to a less restrictive environment for these adolescents. Lakin et al. (2004) studied the effect of parental involvement on post-discharge functioning. These authors found that those adolescents whose parents actively participated in phone calls, home visits, and family therapy had higher functioning at discharge. In Chap. 22 of this book, Preyde, Furtado, Tran, and Currie discuss their efforts to conduct self-report based survey research with adolescents. They studied the coping strategies of adolescents accessing day and residential programs and found that the two coping strategies most often used were *learning to live with it* and *doing an activity alone*. They also found there was a strong relationship between risky coping behavior and psychological difficulties. Their findings provide family therapists with insight into how to approach struggling adolescents and what the family can do to support them.

Clinical Aspect

The methods outlined below could be used by researchers to further establish the importance of family therapy in the treatment process for adolescents in residential settings. Although some past research has shown that adolescents do better when their families are involved, the methods have not always been rigorous and questions remains unanswered. Quantitative research on the clinical aspect of treatment will help researchers to better understand whether family therapy is effective, and more importantly, what makes it effective. Different programs use different approaches to involve the family and little to no research has been conducted to determine if any one approach is better than the others. These methods can be used to begin to address this gap in the literature.

Not all quantitative research in adolescent residential settings needs to be overly complicated to promote the use of family therapy. Even a descriptive study on the characteristics and views of those whose participation in family therapy is low could provide insight to programs and help them to develop better methods of engagement. Although a pre-experimental design does not allow for the determination of causality, such studies can still be useful in promoting the inclusion of family therapy through the accumulation of positive findings. One thing that makes this design so appealing is that most programs can easily collect data without adding a significant burden to staff or therapists. Many programs already have an assessment packet that adolescents and families complete when a child enters the program. In order to carry out a single group pre-test/post-test study, the program would only need to evaluate the packet to make sure it contains all the measures of interest and readminister the measures at the end of the program.

However, it should be noted that a weakness of a single group design is the lack a comparison group. Without a comparison group the attribution of the effect being caused by the intervention becomes more tenuous. The prevalence of this type of study in the literature is likely due to the use of retrospective data to determine the effect of family involvement on outcomes. One possible way to begin to address this deficit would be to use a prospective nonequivalent control group design. In a nonequivalent control group study there is no randomization controlled by the researcher. Instead, participants self-select into a treatment and control group (Bryk and Weisberg 1977). In an adolescent residential program with a family therapy component a researcher could split participants into two groups. The first group would consist of those whose family members are actively involved in the treatment process, as evidence by the frequency of phone calls, arrangement of home visits, and participation in weekly family therapy. The second group would consist of those whose parents are not actively involved and regularly miss phone calls or refuse to participate in family therapy sessions. Differences in outcomes between the adolescents in these two groups could then be determined by comparing pre-test scores and post-test scores. One drawback of this approach is a threat to internal validity through selection bias; however, this could be mitigated by evaluating the pre-test scores of the individuals in both groups to determine similarity.

Although the non-equivalent control group design represents an improvement over single group designs, in order to determine causality prospective research with randomization is needed. This type of research could be conducted, for example, using the existing structure within a wilderness therapy program. The adolescents in these programs are usually placed within a specific group that has little to no contact with other groups throughout the expedition phase of their stay. Adolescents could be randomly assigned to different groups that receive different treatments. One group could receive the standard level of care with basic family involvement (e.g., reunion participation only). A second group could then receive the standard level of care and enhanced family involvement (e.g., reunion, home therapy, psychoeducation, etc.). The ability to randomly assign the participants would allow the researcher to determine if the treatment is causing the observed effect. Internal validity would also be strengthened since the researcher would be able to ensure that the treatment effects are not being transported to other groups; though to accomplish this they would need to ensure that the same staff consistently works with the same group. Additionally, the researcher could test different models of family involvement against one another by adding a third group. For example, the researcher could add family therapy via satellite phone on a weekly basis to the treatment of this third group and see if this increases effectiveness beyond what is observed with the enhanced family involvement approach alone.

Another unique design that could be applied to establish the utility of family therapy in these settings is the ABAB single subject design. Within this design baseline functioning is established, after which the intervention is applied. After the intervention is delivered it is then withdrawn again, though it is reintroduced a final time afterward (Creswell 2009). This type of design could be used without difficulty in an RTC where the adolescent is expected to remain for at least one year. The researcher could have the adolescent participate in treatment without any family therapy for the first 3 months, followed by three months with family therapy. This process could then be repeated by having the adolescent again experience the *no family therapy condition* for 3 months, followed by three months of family therapy before discharge. Adolescent and family functioning would be measure through the year to determine the effect of treatment on variables of interest. Use of this experimental design would allow the researcher to determine the effect of adding family therapy to the treatment approach.

Financial Aspect

As highlighted above, there is a significant need to evaluate the cost of treating adolescents in residential settings. This is especially true when one considers the number of articles arguing that some outpatient therapies produce better results and are more cost-effective (e.g., Klietz 2007; Shoenwald et al. 1996). However, it is not entirely certain that outpatient therapy is superior to inpatient programs in terms of outcomes or costs. This is due in large part to the very few studies that have directly compared inpatient and outpatient programs. In one of the few studies that directly compared the two, Grizenko and Papineau (1992) found there was no difference in outcomes, though the outpatient program was much less expensive than the residential program. However, this study stopped at evaluating cost-effectiveness and did not incorporate the benefits of treatment. Given the intensive treatment adolescents receive in residential settings it is entirely possible that additional benefits are realized that would further offset the cost.

In order to fully evaluate the financial aspect of adolescent residential treatment, researchers will need to conduct cost–benefit analyses. Cost–benefit analysis is a research method that involves the use of actual costs and economic estimates to determine the value of participation in a program. The first step in conducting a cost–benefit analysis is to determine the cost of treatment. Christenson and Crane (2014) recommend assessing both direct and indirect costs associated with treatment. Direct costs would include things such as staff pay, supplies, operational expenses, etc. Indirect costs are associated with lost resources, such as a parent having to take time off work to participate in a family workshop. In this case the parent's lost wages would be added in as one of the costs. In terms of benefits, researchers can include both direct and indirect benefits. An example of direct benefits would be increased wages available to the parent since they are spending less time being called away from work once their child is in a residential placement. Another benefit that could likely be quantified is the increase in earning potential that an adolescent gets from the quality education provided in a client-funded RTC or therapeutic boarding school. Indirect benefits are those that are gained by avoiding a particular outcome, such as incarceration or hospitalizations (Christenson and Crane 2014).

Once all of the potential costs and benefits have been calculated, the researcher can use mathematical formulas to factor in the effectiveness of the intervention and determine the value of the intervention in terms of total savings. Given that Klietz et al. (2010) were able to show a total savings of $199,374 for Multisystemic therapy, it is not at all unlikely that a client-funded RTC or therapeutic boarding school could similarly show a savings associated with placement in their program. Therapeutic boarding schools, given their focus on academic achievement, are in a solid position to show that participation in their programs results in overall savings. However, to date this type of research has not been conducted extensively within the industry.

Mixed Methods

Mixed methods research combine both qualitative methods and quantitative methods within a single study. Creswell (2009) notes there are six common mixed method designs (some of which will be discussed more fully below). These six designs are: (a) sequential explanatory, (b) sequential exploratory, (c) sequential transformative, (d) concurrent triangulation, (e) concurrent embedded, and (f) concurrent transformative. Harper and Russell (2008) used this method to investigate perceptions of family involvement in a wilderness therapy program. These researchers used a concurrent triangulation design in their study. This specific design is characterized by collecting qualitative and quantitative data at the same time, and then comparing the two databases to determine how well one set of data concurs with the other (Creswell 2009).

Harper and Russell's (2008) study was intended to demonstrate that including the family in treatment improved outcomes and reduced the risk of mistreatment. These authors interviewed 14 families during the qualitative phase and surveyed 50 parents and 35 adolescents during the quantitative phase. Although the authors intended to evaluate the role of family involvement, the interviews produced data focused more on the parent's perception of their child's treatment and their own experience while the child was away. The quantitative phase of the study produced only one significant result, which was that the adolescents rated the family's functioning as better after the program compared to when they entered the program.

In this book, Chap. 21 contains a report on the efforts of McConnell and Taglione to use mixed methods to investigate outcomes associated with the Relational Re-enactment Systems Approach to Treatment model. This model includes *clinical consultation*, which consists of regularly scheduled contact between the adolescents, the parents or guardians, and the treatment team to discuss issues and possible solutions. They found that youth with fewer consultations per month had poorer outcomes than those who had a greater number of consultations per month. They also found that youth who were involved with child protective services had less favorable outcomes. When they discussed this with therapist in the qualitative portion of the study, one thing they found was that therapists noticed those who had less favorable outcomes wanted to go home to their families, but were told that was not an option that would work. This finding shed light on the outcomes discovered in the quantitative potion.

Clinical Aspect

Mixed methods research has been growing in popularity over the last decade and can be used effectively to promote family therapy in adolescent residential settings. Using a mixed methods approach provides a means to gain a greater understanding than is available through either qualitative or quantitative methods alone. A number of possibilities exist for utilizing this method. For example, the qualitative study described above regarding best practices could be modified to include a quantitative component. In such a study the researcher would employ a sequential exploratory design by first using the Delphi method to arrive at a set of best practices. After determining a set of best practices, the researcher would work with a program to adopt the best practices and gather quantitative data aimed at showing increased effectiveness.

Another possibility could be to conduct a sequential explanatory study, wherein the researcher first collects quantitative data about family participation during their child's stay. This would include descriptive data covering family member demographics, frequency of attending sessions, and compliance with treatment recommendations. The data would be further analyzed to determine if certain groups have lower participation than other groups. These groups would then be targeted for qualitative inquiry to determine barriers to participations. The action research methods described above could also be used to generate solutions. Likewise, a researcher could address the qualitative component by conducting an ethnographic study wherein they embed themselves within a program and observe interactions between the staff, therapists, administrators, and the low participation families. They would also conduct interviews with the key individuals involved in the program, such as the therapist and the members of the low participation family. Interviews would be augmented with field notes obtained through direct observation of clinical meetings, as well as conversations in the hallway and at the front desk (Mendenhall et al. 2014). This type of data would then be used to explain the observations that were made during the analysis of the quantitative data.

Financial Aspect

To date, mixed method approaches have not been applied to costs related to adolescent residential treatment. However, this type of analysis could be conducted rather easily and might offer even more support for the inclusion of family therapy in adolescent residential settings. Because mixed methods are an extension of the methods already outlined above, the methods for conducting a cost analysis would be the same as what has already been described. As Christenson and Crane (2014) noted in their paper, researcher can begin to advance cost evaluations by simply adding cost data to what they are already doing. As a brief example a researcher could conduct a sequential exploratory study, wherein qualitative data is first gathered about parent perception of treatment and outcomes. The researcher might even consider including some of the questions outlined above concerning decision-making around costs. This could be followed by a quantitative analysis of outcomes. During the process the researcher could gather and report cost data, and even employ some of the cost analyses described above. As has been highlighted, it is anticipated that the benefits of providing the treatment would more than offset the costs incurred.

Summary

It is evident that family therapy researchers, with clear knowledge of treatment programs and qualitative, quantitative, and mixed methods designs, will have a significant role in investigating treatment outcomes for adolescent residential treatment. This has important ramifications for those who practice family therapy, since such research can be used to promote family therapy's inclusion in this area of practice. Furthermore, increased research and integration would ultimately strengthen the place of family therapy in adolescent residential settings. This effort will sometimes require the use of a scientist–practitioner approach, with emphasis on the clinical and financial aspects of the work.

Despite the research that has been done, the literature on family therapy in adolescent residential settings is underdeveloped and can be advanced through the application of the methods outlined above. Researchers should use the information in this chapter as a starting point for developing well thought out studies that will further advance the use of family therapy in adolescent residential settings. This could be accomplished by first conducting qualitative studies to help generate research questions, though this is not a required first step since there are already numerous unaddressed researcher questions that can be answered with quantitative methods.

Researchers would do well to see research in this field as a cumulative effort. As noted above, there are a number of studies that have been executed with each of these methods, but each of them has weaknesses that affect the utility of the findings. This does not mean the research that has been done on this topic should be disparaged. Instead, it is important to remember that all of the research that has been done can be used as a foundation from which researchers can build more rigorous studies that avoid the problems encountered by those who have come before. As the amount of research on family therapy in adolescent residential settings continues to expand the use of related techniques should become not only more effective, but efficient as well.

References

Bandoroff, S., & Scherer, D. G. (1994). Wilderness family therapy: An innovative treatment approach for problem youth. *Journal of Child and Family Studies, 3,* 175–191.

Behrens, E., & Satterfield, K. (2006). Report of findings from a multi-center study of youth outcomes in private residential treatment. In *Proceedings of the Annual Convention of the American Psychological Association* (pp. 1–21). New Orleans, LA: American Psychological Association.

Bryk, A. S., & Weisberg, H. I. (1977). Use of the nonequivalent control group design when subjects are growing. *Psychological Bulletin, 84*(5), 950. doi:10.1037/0033-2909.84.5.950

Callaghan, R. C., Hathaway, A., Cunningham, J. A., Vettese, L. C., Wyatt, S., & Taylor, L. (2005). Does stage-of-change predict dropout in a culturally diverse sample of adolescents admitted to inpatient substance-abuse treatment? A test of the transtheoretical model. *Addictive Behaviors, 30*(9), 1834–1847.

Christenson, J. D., & Crane, D. R. (2014). Integrating costs into marriage and family therapy research. In R. B. Miller & L. N. Johnson (Eds.), *Advanced methods in family therapy research: A focus on validity and change* (pp. 420–436). New York: Routledge.

Creswell, J. W. (2009). *Research design: Qualitative, quantitative, and mixed methods approaches* (3rd ed.). Los Angeles: Sage Publications.

Dalkey, N. (1969). An experimental study of group opinion: The Delphi method. *Futures, 1*(5), 408–426. doi:10.1016/S0016-3287(69)80025

Dalkey, N., & Helmer, O. (1963). An experimental application of the Delphi method to the use of experts. *Management Science, 9*(3), 458–467.

Demmitt, A. D., & Joanning, H. (1998). A parent-based description of residential treatment. *Journal of Family Psychotherapy, 9*(1), 47–66. doi:10.1300/J085V09N01_04

Government Accountability Office. (2008). *Residential facilities: State and federal oversight gaps may increase risk to youth well-being: Testimony before the committee of education and labor.* Washington, D.C.: U.S. House of Representatives.

Grizenko, N., & Papineau, D. (1992). A comparison of the cost-effectiveness of day treatment and residential treatment for children with severe behaviour problems. *Canadian Journal of Psychiatry, 37*(6), 393–400.

Hair, H. J. (2005). Outcomes for children and adolescents after residential treatment: A review of research from 1993 to 2003. *Journal of Child and Family Studies, 14*(4), 551–575. doi:10.1007/s10826-005-7188-9

Hambridge, K. (2000). Action research. *Professional Nurse, 15,* 598–601.

Harper, N. J., & Russell, K. C. (2008). Family involvement and outcome in adolescent wilderness treatment: A mixed-methods evaluation. *International Journal of Child & Family Welfare, 1,* 19–36.

Hesse-Biber, S. N., & Leavy, P. (Eds.). (2010). *Handbook of emergent methods.* New York: Guilford Press.

Hockenberry, S., Sickmund, M., & Sladky, A. (2009). *Juvenile residential facility census, 2006: Selected findings.* Washington, D.C.: U.S. Department of Justice, Office of Justice Programs, Bureau of Justice Statistics.

Hsu, C. C., & Sandford, B. A. (2007). The Delphi technique: Making sense of consensus. *Practical Assessment, Research & Evaluation, 12*(10), 1–8.

Jenkins, D. A., & Smith, T. E. (1994). Applying Delphi methodology in family therapy research. *Contemporary Family Therapy, 16*(5), 411–430. doi:10.1007/BF02197902

Klietz, S. J. (2007). *Cost-benefit analysis of multisystemic therapy with serious and violent juvenile offenders* (Unpublished doctoral dissertation). University of Missouri, Columbia, MO.

Klietz, S. J., Borduin, C. M., & Schaeffer, C. M. (2010). Cost—Benefit analysis of multisystemic therapy with serious and violent juvenile offenders. *Journal of Family Psychology, 24*(5), 657.

Lakin, B. L., Brambila, A. D., & Sigda, K. B. (2004). Parental involvement as a factor in the readmission to a residential treatment center. *Residential Treatment for Children and Youth, 22* (2), 37–52. doi:10.1300/J007v22n02_03

Lee, B. R. (2008). Defining residential treatment. *Journal of Child and Family Studies, 17*(5), 689–692. doi:10.1007/s10826-007-9182-x

Lee, B. R., & Barth, R. P. (2011). Defining group care programs: An index of reporting standards. *Child & Youth Care Forum, 40,* 253–266. doi:10.1007/s10566-011-9143-9

Leichtman, M., Leichtman, M. L., Barber, C. C., & Neese, D. T. (2001). Effectiveness of intensive short-term residential treatment with severely disturbed adolescents. *American Journal of Orthopsychiatry, 71*(2), 227. doi:10.1037/0002-9432.71.2.227

Lewin, K. (1958). *Group decision and social change.* New York: Holt, Rinehart, and Winston.

Lyons, J. S., Terry, P., Martinovich, Z., Peterson, J., & Bouska, B. (2001). Outcome trajectories for adolescents in residential treatment: A statewide evaluation. *Journal of Child and Family Studies, 10*(3), 333–345. doi:10.1023/A:1012576826136

McLendon, T., McLendon, D., & Hatch, L. (2012). Engaging families in the residential treatment process utilizing family-directed structural therapy. *Residential Treatment for Children & Youth, 29,* 66–77. doi:10.1080/0886571X.2012.643679

Mendenhall, T. J., & Doherty, W. J. (2005). Action research methods in family therapy. In D. H. Sprenkle & F. P. Piercy (Eds.), *Research methods in family therapy* (2nd ed., pp. 100–118). New York: Guilford Press.

Mendenhall, T. J., Pratt, K., Phelps, K., Baird, M., & Younkin, F. (2014). Advancing medical family therapy through qualitative, quantitative, and mixed-methods research. In J. Hodgson, A. Lamson, T. Mendenhall, & D. R. Crane (Eds.), *Medical family therapy: Advanced applications* (pp. 241–258). New York: Springer.

National Alliance of Therapeutic Schools and Programs. (n.d.). *Program definitions.* Retrieved September 24, 2015, from: http://www.natsap.org/for-parents/programdefinitions/

Ouimette, P. C., Finney, J. W., & Moos, R. H. (1997). Twelve-step and cognitive-behavioral treatment for substance abuse: A comparison of treatment effectiveness. *Journal of Consulting and Clinical Psychology, 65*(2), 230.

Rose, S., Spinks, N., & Canhoto, A. I. (2014). *Management research: Applying the principles.* New York: Routledge.

Schoenwald, S. K., Ward, D. M., Henggeler, S. W., Pickrel, S. G., & Patel, H. (1996). Multisystemic therapy treatment of substance abusing or dependent adolescent offenders: Costs of reducing incarceration, inpatient, and residential placement. *Journal of Child and Family Studies, 5*(4), 431–444. doi:10.1007/BF02233864

Spencer, S., & Powell, J. Y. (2000). Family-centered practice in residential treatment settings: A parent's perspective. *Residential Treatment for Children and Youth, 17*(3), 33–43. doi:10.1300/J007v17n03_06

Sprenkle, D. H., & Piercy, F. P. (2005). *Research methods in family therapy* (2nd ed.). New York: Guilford Press.

Springer, A. K., & Stahmann, R. F. (1998). Parent perception of the value of telephone family therapy when adolescents are in residential treatment. *The American Journal of Family Therapy, 26*(2), 169–176. doi:10.1080/01926189808251096

Stage, S. A. (1999). Predicting adolescents' discharge status following residential treatment. *Residential Treatment for Children and Youth, 16*(3), 37–56. doi:10.1300/J007v16n03_03

Vaughn, C. F. (2005). Residential treatment centers: Not a solution for children with mental health needs. *Clearinghouse Review Journal of Poverty Law and Policy, 39*(3–4), 274.

Author Biographies

Jacob D. Christenson, Ph.D., LMFT is an assistant professor of marriage and family therapy at Mount Mercy University. Dr. Christenson received his Bachelor degree in Psychology from California Polytechnic State University. He then completed his Master's degree and doctorate in Marriage and Family Therapy from Brigham Young University. Before coming to Mount Mercy University Dr. Christenson worked for 4 years at Aspen Achievement Academy in Loa, UT as a Field Therapist. As a Field Therapist, Dr. Christenson experienced firsthand the challenge of being a systemic marriage and family therapist in the world of residential care. Over the course of his career Dr. Christenson has consistently been involved in academic research and publication. In addition to numerous presentations at national and international conferences, Dr. Christenson has published a number of articles in peer-reviewed journals such as the Journal of Marital and Family Therapy, Contemporary Family Therapy, and the American Journal of Family Therapy. Dr. Christenson also serves as an editorial board member for the Journal of Marital and Family Therapy and Contemporary Family Therapy. Dr. Christenson teaches a number of course at Mount Mercy University. The courses he have taught have included, Parents and Children,

Micro-counselling, Medical Family Therapy, and Research Methods. Dr. Christenson is also an AAMFT Approved Supervisor, which has enabled him to provide supervision in practicum courses. Dr. Christenson also serves as the Clinical Director for the Gerald and Audrey Olson Marriage and Family Therapy Clinic, which is attached to the marriage and family therapy program at Mount Mercy University. In addition to his work as a professor, Dr. Christenson provides therapy in private practice and is the founder of Covenant Family Solutions, an outpatient therapy group practice in Cedar Rapids, Iowa. When not working, Dr. Christenson enjoys spending time with his family and being active in his community.

Dumayi M. Gutierrez, MA is currently a second year doctoral student at the University of Iowa Couple and Family Therapy (CFT) program in Iowa City, Iowa. She works as a research assistant studying sibling relationships in foster care and as a CFT program graduate assistant. Dumayi is involved in multiple research projects involving adverse childhood experiences, minority stress in lesbian, gay and bisexual families, same sex parenting, support systems of Latina lesbians, and roles of minority women in academia. Her personal research involves oppression and resiliency of sexual and racial minority women. She currently sees clients in the CFT LGBTQ clinic and does hormone replacement therapy and gender reassignment surgery mental health assessments. Dumayi is also a member of the Latino Graduate Student Association and Graduate Diversity Committee on campus.

Chapter 21
Mixed Methods Research on Clinical Consultation Within the REStArT Model in Residential Treatment

Catherine McConnell and Patricia Taglione

Chapter Highlights

- This chapter reviews the principles of the REStArT model related to its core family intervention: clinical consultation.
- Components of clinical consultation—its format and function—are presented.
- A case study is provided to demonstrate the application of the principles and process of clinical consultation.
- Both quantitative and qualitative results were used to examine trends in outcomes.
- Youths' involvement with state child welfare was found to be related to the process of treatment and stability of discharge placement.

Although the importance of working with families is accepted, the nature of this involvement is still being investigated. Family therapy is only one method of involving families in their child's treatment and has evolved in some cases to better meet the needs of families (Huefner et al. 2015). For example, in order to make services accessible to families, therapy by phone has been used (Robst et al. 2013). Letter writing as a family intervention also provides a unique form of contact between family and youth. Christenson and Miller in Chap. 2 of this volume discuss the use of letter writing in depth. The options appear broad for facilitating a family's role in its youth's care. Given this breadth of possibility, there is question about what makes family involvement optimally successful. While there is some evidence that almost any involvement—even if it is not specifically therapeutic—is beneficial, the need to provide therapeutic interventions to families and other caregivers

C. McConnell (✉) · P. Taglione
Allendale Association, PO Box 1088, Lake Villa, IL 60046, USA
e-mail: cmcconnell@allendale4kids.org

P. Taglione
e-mail: ptaglione@allendale4kids.org

© Springer International Publishing AG 2017
J.D. Christenson and A.N. Merritts (eds.), *Family Therapy with Adolescents in Residential Treatment*, Focused Issues in Family Therapy,
DOI 10.1007/978-3-319-51747-6_21

who will remain in the lives of youth with mental health challenges seems crucial (Lakin et al. 2004).

The Relational Re-Enactment Systems Approach to Treatment (REStArT) is a model for residential treatment that seeks specifically to address the challenges inherent in engaging families in their youth's care. While the introduction of this intervention at one agency precipitated improvements in outcomes broadly (McConnell and Taglione 2012), the study described in this chapter was intended to explore the aspects of treatment in aggregate, either case characteristics inherent to particular subsets of youths and their families or program dynamics, that differentiated youth who were successful in the program. This exploration included an examination of both the frequency of family participation and the process of the family involvement. By studying the characteristics of successful cases, we hoped to better understand the factors that encourage or possibly impede family involvement as a catalyst for positive youth outcomes.

The purpose of this chapter is twofold. First, the chapter will provide the reader with an example of a study conducted with a specific study methodology, which can help those beginning a research career to better understand the process. Second, the chapter will report the results of our study and improve understanding of the REStArT model and related outcomes. The study described in this chapter used a mixed methods approach to investigate outcomes. A mixed methods approach to research on family interventions in residential treatment potentially augments the research process, as Christensen and Gutierrez discuss in Chap. 19 of this volume. This study used qualitative methods to expand our understanding of our quantitative results and thus provides an example of the ways that one method can enhance the other.

Quantitative results, especially in exploratory studies and those without specific hypotheses that are being tested, may not be sufficient to explain results. Qualitative components then can be used to provide depth in the form of possible explanations for the results found. These process-oriented results, in turn, can help shape hypotheses for future research. Qualitative and quantitative components also augment one another in a specific way; the empirical findings allow for results which, although not free from bias, capture a more global phenomenon than participant observation. Qualitative material, however, breathes life into these broad results by giving voice to those who are experiencing the clinical work, either as client or provider. A mixed methods approach is most successful when approaches are given equal importance rather than viewing one as secondary to the other. In this current study, for example, our interest in exploring the impact of different client variables on outcomes came without specific hypotheses to direct our empirical analyses, and the ethic of transparency calls on the research to be clear that such results were generated without direction. However, such descriptive analyses are of limited value. When a difference is found, the meaning of this difference is less likely discovered through further empirical study, but rather by returning to those who did the actual work, which in this case meant turning to the therapists who worked with the clients and their treatment teams to assess their understanding of our empirical results.

The REStArT Model and Clinical Consultation

Before describing the study and results, some background information on the REStArT model and clinical consultation will be provided to put the research described below into greater context. The REStArT model originated at a multi-service agency for youth and their families that provides residential treatment. Within the agency's residential program, the *high-end* treatment units are unlocked, but considered the most restrictive level of care for youth whose behavior can no longer safely be addressed in the community. High end in the context of residential treatment, as used in this chapter, refers to level of care. It is a not a locked facility; however, the youth in care require a higher level of supervision and structure (due to the severity of their behaviors or symptoms) than that which can be provided by a less-intensive residential or group home program. Since the model's implementation in 2007, youth at this agency increasingly saw positive outcomes and movement to less-restrictive levels of care (McConnell and Taglione 2012). The model provides a coherent yet flexible approach to treatment that is informed by research on trauma-based treatment, attachment and developmental theories, systems theory, and object relations (Taglione et al. 2014). Thirteen guiding principles articulate the tenets of the model and provide the basis for training (see Appendix). Additionally, the principles are congruent with the model's primary intervention for working with families, which is clinical consultation.

Principles of the Model

Presented here is a very brief overview of some of the model's principles that are most relevant to working with families. The REStArT training manual (Taglione et al. 2014) includes a broader description of the model's principles, core concepts, and interventions than the scope of this chapter allows (the manual is available from the authors upon request). The first principle of the model and the one most central to consultations is the treatment providers' therapeutic alliance with youth and their families. The therapeutic alliance is often defined not simply as the quality of the relationship between clinician and client but as agreement on the goals of treatment as well as the process of obtaining those goals (e.g., Norcross and Wampold 2011). Developing a balanced therapeutic alliance in family treatment is difficult, even outside the residential treatment setting, due to the multiple relationships in the treatment process (Hogue et al. 2006; Robbins et al. 2003). But the therapeutic alliance is further complicated in residential treatment by not only multiple family members participating in treatment, but also multiple providers, sometimes from multiple agencies. The training and ongoing supervision involved in the model's implementation utilizes decision trees that guide providers through the process of assessing the alliance with youth and their families.

Sometimes, even when clients have articulated goals for themselves and appear committed to those goals—for example, to return to their family of origin or to move on to independence—they may still have ambivalence. In residential treatment, much like family work in other therapeutic settings, ambivalence is sometimes expressed through clients acting in ways that elicit a response in treatment providers to *take the other side* of the ambivalence (Miller and Rollnick 2013). The emphasis in the model on ongoing feedback provided by supervisors and colleagues allows therapists and other treatment providers to be cognizant of the pull to persuade family members. As a result of this reflection, providers can be aware of what factors may be motivating both sides of the family's ambivalence and give them the space in the family work to resolve the ambivalence in ways that are authentic to them. In doing this, therapists and others also activate the principle of the model that asks providers to expect health from youth and their families.

Being aware of how youth or their families may be engaging us in the process of avoiding their ambivalence is only one of the ways that self-reflection is used in the REStArT model. The model extends the work of Wood and Long (1991) in using *conflict cycles* to better understand the re-enactments that occur between youth and adults. The conflict cycle provides a unique understanding of each youth by identifying their individual stressors and their individual ways of emotionally and behaviorally responding to those stressors. The conflict cycle also includes the adults' ways of responding to youth behaviors. Often these adult responses inadvertently maintain the youth's conflict cycle either by amplifying the original stressor (a counter-aggressive response) or by protecting the youth from the stressor (a counter-indulgent response). Both counter-responses interfere with the youth's opportunity to develop new and more adaptive ways of responding to their own stressors.

The understanding of an individual youth's conflict cycle requires treatment providers to be aware of their counter-response, which may be indulgent (that is, feeling overly empathic and excessively externalizing the youth's presenting problem) or aggressive (such as feeling frustrated with lack of progress). Due to the histories of trauma that most of the youth in residential treatment have and the conduct disordered behavior that has then precipitated their placement, many of the children and adolescents in treatment present with a *control-sensitive* conflict cycle; that is, one in which they may alternately view themselves as victims or aggressors. They may elicit complementary feelings in the adults working with them that, in turn, can result in overly permissive or excessively controlling approaches to working with the youth. The understanding of re-enactments as conflict cycles, managing counter-response, and developing plans to interrupt the cycle are the focus of three of the model's principles.

These principles as described above closely inform the process and content of the REStArT model's family intervention, clinical consultation. While consultation has traditionally involved providers as experts informing family members about their youth, these principles create a clinical consultation process that is systems-oriented and inclusive. The purpose of the clinical consultations is driven by the principles in that the quality of the therapeutic alliance that the treatment team has with the youth and their family is assessed after every consultation. During the consultations, the therapist and other team members work with family member and the youth to help them understand the youth's conflict cycle. And ambivalence, often a barrier to successful residential treatment if left unaddressed, can safely be explored as team members allow the family to determine the course of treatment and discharge.

Clinical Consultation

Clinical consultation was originally developed to address deficits in engaging families in their youth's care. Clinical consultation involves regularly scheduled collaborative contact between members of the youth's treatment team, the youth, and their family. Caseworkers from funding sources, as well as other collaterals, are also encouraged to participate in the process. Especially for youth who have funding through a state child welfare agency, the external caseworker for that youth is considered an integral part of the consultation process because of the youth's legal standing with the state. Consultations are scheduled at the convenience of the family and more often than not take place via telephone in order to accommodate work schedules and travel distance. Unlike a more traditional approach to consultation, clinical consultation does not position the treatment providers as the authorities and the family as recipients of the providers' expertise and direction. Nor are these contacts an opportunity for staff simply to inform family members or collaterals about the youth's progress. Rather, consultations are intended to address multiple principles of the model.

On center stage during the consultation process is the assessment of the therapeutic alliance between youth, family, and treatment providers. As mentioned above, the alliance between family and providers is even more complex in residential treatment than it may be in a traditional family therapy setting. Families encounter many providers within milieu treatment. It is this complex system that clinical consultation seeks to balance, in part by addressing in each clinical consultation the goals for discharge that the youth and their family have identified, even if those goals differ from what the providers think they should be. Additionally, clinical consultation removes the compartmentalization of relationships between family members and different providers within the agency that may make it more likely for splits to develop. Therapists and other providers are asked to look for evidence of the strength of the alliance in each consultation meeting.

Clinical consultation also provides a forum to address ambivalence about treatment and discharge goals that youth or families may be experiencing. Clinical consultation requires providers who are facilitating the consultation to be aware of this ambivalence and watch for ways that it may be acted out rather than explicitly communicated. Because progress toward discharge is a regular focus of clinical consultation, providers have the opportunity to consistently assess and bring to the attention of youth and families discrepancies between their stated goals and their progress toward those goals.

The importance of the youths' conflict cycles in clinical consultation cannot be overstated. The conflict cycle provides the opportunity for therapists, caseworkers, and family members to create a shared understanding of the youth. This shared understanding also addresses a criticism sometimes leveled at residential treatment providers by families, that family members feel blamed by their youths' providers (c.f., Walter and Petr 2008). Additionally, the conflict cycle offers a rationale for the ongoing structure that youth may need when they return to a less-restrictive environment, which helps families see the importance of this. Because the clinical consultation process is nuanced and can seem abstract to those who are not familiar with the process, we have included a case example below that is intended to illustrate some of the components of this type of intervention.

The REStArT Model: A Case Example

A case that illustrates the implementation of REStArT model and its family intervention is that of Carlos, a 15-year-old Latino adolescent who came to residential treatment following many years of out-of-home placements such as psychiatric hospitalizations, state mental health hospitals, and group homes. He had a history of aggression against other children and adults, including a security guard at a hospital. He also engaged in self-harm that included ingesting foreign objects. Additionally, he made what were deemed to be false accusations against others. Carlos' medical history was complex, leading him at times to claim that he needed hospitalization even when it was not necessary. Furthermore, Carlos' brother had died when Carlos was young and he appeared to be re-enacting the trauma of this loss, as well as fears about his own mortality, through his repeated medical hospitalizations. Clinical consultations included the treatment team as well as Carlos, his mother, and the caseworker from his funding source. At the time he was admitted, Carlos' mother was identified as his discharge resource, but his funding source did not agree with this goal.

Despite wanting to be discharged from residential treatment, Carlos often made allegations against others and requested hospitalizations. During consultation, the treatment team started to point out the ambivalence that was emerging. On the one hand, he wanted to return home to his mother and have more freedom, but another part of him may have sought the structure that was provided by the hospital and acted out in ways that ensured he would stay in residential care. Carlos' mother also appeared to be ambivalent about having him return home. The treatment team identified that Carlos and his mother sometimes avoided addressing their ambivalence about one another by joining together in conflict with treatment providers. Interventions to address this ambivalence started with the team's awareness of ways in which they felt pulled to either indulge requests made by Carlos and his mother in order to avoid conflict or to withhold reasonable requests out of frustration with their many demands. By interrupting this cycle of conflict, Carlos and his mother were then able to engage with the treatment team in their alliance of working together to have Carlos safely discharged. This process also helped Carlos and his mother see ways that he would need to continue to have structure in place even if he was no longer in treatment.

As his acting out subsided, however, his funding source still did not support his placement with his mother, but rather wanted him to step down to a group home. Although staff were aware of their wish to take on this battle for Carlos and his mother, and maybe try to convince the funding source that Carlos should return home, the team instead sought a more balanced response that allowed Carlos and his mother to work with the funding source more realistically. Carlos, wanting to leave even if he didn't go home, eventually agreed to go to the group home. This step down was, therefore, technically a positive outcome, but was not sustained. Soon after being placed in the group home, Carlos ran away from treatment. But rather than running to the hospital as he had in the past, he ran to his mother. He remains stable and with his mother over two years later.

Quantitative and Qualitative Methods of Exploration

As noted above, research in residential treatment is inherently complex (Curry 2004). As such, our approach to our questions about family interventions and outcomes was exploratory in that we assumed family involvement would be an important factor in successful treatment, but did not have specific hypotheses about the nature of this relationship. We used a mixed methods approach in which we began with aggregate descriptive data to look at group differences in outcomes. We then sought qualitative descriptions of successful and unsuccessful cases from therapists in order to create a more three-dimensional look at youth and family's experiences in the program. This type of design is often referred to as a sequential explanatory mixed method design. The processes for both the quantitative and qualitative components of the study are as follows.

Youth Sample

The agency involved in this study is a comprehensive treatment facility for youth and their families. The high-end residential program—that is, the most restrictive of the residential programs—has a capacity of approximately 130 youth at any given time. We selected as our sample all youth who were discharged in the fiscal year 2014 from the high-end treatment program. The youth in this program either have a conduct disorder diagnosis or have exhibited behaviors that are related to conduct disorder that cannot be contained in a less-restrictive environment. These behaviors are the precipitants to placement, although additional diagnoses may include mood disorders, Post-Traumatic Stress Disorder, autism spectrum disorders, and border-line personality disorder. The selection of this particular group allowed for a sample that was recent enough to reasonably reflect the current implementation of the model, but also allowed for a sample from which we would have information on whether discharges that were favorable had been sustained for 6 months.

In this current sample, there were 100 discharged youth who ranged in age from 13 years old to 21 years old, with an average age at discharge of approximately 17 years ($M = 16.76$, $SD = 1.51$). Most of the youth discharged were boys (68%) and the majority of the youth were African American (56%). An additional 34% of the youth identified as White, 7% as Latino/a, and 3% as bi-racial. The Department of Child and Family Services (DCFS) was the funding source for and, therefore, also the legal guardian of 66% of the youth. The remaining 34% had an alternative funding source and a guardian who was either a biological family member or adopted family. These clients had state School Board of Education funding (ISBE) (18%), Department of Human Services funding (DHS) (13%) or funding through a neighboring state (e.g., Wisconsin) (3%).

Therapist Participants

Six therapists were asked to participate in the qualitative portion of the study and all six agreed to participate. All were therapists at the agency during the fiscal year 2014 in which the youth for this study were discharged. They had all received ongoing training on the implementation of the REStArT model. Therapist training in the principles and practice of the REStArT model is multifaceted. When therapists first join the agency, they receive didactic training that covers the model's principles, the purpose and process of clinical consultation, the trauma-informed components of the model, and working with control-sensitive youth. On an ongoing basis, therapists have multiple opportunities to observe others practicing the model and to get feedback on their implementation of the model. Therapists and case workers complete a checklist following clinical consultation designed to provide a self-report of their fidelity to the intervention. Four of the six therapists were female. They had an average of 4.8 years of experience, with a range of 3 to 8 years as therapists at the agency. Each therapist worked primarily with a single residential unit and they provided individual therapy to the youth in this unit. Therapists also facilitated the clinical consultation intervention with the cooperation of the youth's agency caseworker.

Variables

Discharge outcome as a dependent variable was assessed both at the time youth exited the program and also after 6 months. A *favorable* discharge was one in which the youth left the high-end residential program for a less-restrictive level of care including a group home (this program's or another's), family home, foster care, a transitional living program, a more moderate residential program, independence, or a less-restrictive adult mental health facility. Lateral discharges to other residential programs or psychiatric hospitals, as well as more obviously negative outcomes such as detention and running away, were considered *unfavorable* discharges.

The agency routinely offers aftercare consultation to youth and their families or caretakers following program discharge, and this also allows us to track whether youth have maintained their placement. For this study, we measured sustained outcomes at 6 months. Because we consider youths' ability to maintain their placement as a measure of our alliance with the youth and their family, for the purposes of this study, we delineated our sample as follows: *positive* outcomes were those that were favorable and sustained at 6 months and *negative* outcomes were those that were either unfavorable at the time of discharge or were not sustained for 6 months. This was conceptually congruent for our model, but it also allowed for *oversampling* of unfavorable discharges as our favorable results proportion at the time of discharge is high and would create uneven sub-samples.

Independent variables that we examined for their relationship to discharge status included rate of consultations (average number of consultations occurring in each month of stay), length of stay, and funding source. The rate of consultations was selected in order to determine whether frequency of this particular form of family contact influenced outcomes. Although it is not clear from previous research if length of stay is associated with deleterious effects for the youth in treatment, it was selected as a variable due to recent increased focus on its impact on treatment (James et al. 2012). Length of stay was measured by the number of months the youth was placed in the agency's high-end program. Funding source was divided between youth who were funded by the Department of Children and Family Services and youth funded by all other sources, which included the DHS and the state School Board of Education. This variable stands in for the different case dynamics present in working with youth whose families are their legal guardians compared to youth for whom the state is their guardian.

Data Analysis

Quantitative analysis. Consultation rate, length of stay, and funding source were all assessed for their relationship to outcomes 6 months post-discharge. Separate two-tailed t tests assuming unequal variance were conducted to measure the difference between the mean consultation rate by outcome type and between the mean length of stay by outcome type. As an exploratory study, we were interested in their independent relationship with outcomes rather than their combined explanation of variance. A chi-square test was used to assess the difference between the proportion of positive and negative discharges by funding source. Because this chi-square test produced the only significant relationship between one of the variables (funding source) and outcomes, we also conducted t tests for the mean consultation rate and mean length of stay by funding source.

Qualitative analysis. Because, with few exceptions, the negative outcomes in this sample were youth who were funded by DCFS, we also conducted a qualitative review of the model's implementation across selected cases. Residential therapists of the units whose youth were included in the discharge sample were asked to provide recollections about the process of consultation with DCFS youth and their families. In particular, we were interested in exploring the ways in which the model's primary family intervention, clinical consultation, impacted differential outcomes. Therapists were provided with a list of DCFS youth who had discharged in the fiscal year 2014. Therapists selected two cases to discuss, one with a positive and one with a negative outcome, based on their ability to recall details about the process of the youth's treatment in those cases. Written responses were requested because the schedules of both the researchers (who also provide direct care) and the residential therapists made it difficult to schedule face-to-face interviews without disrupting services to clients. The culture of the agency is one in which the process of treatment is discussed often, so therapists were knowledgeable about how to respond to an open-ended request for their reflections on this. They were asked to respond to the question, "What aspects of treatment, especially related to consultation, did you notice seemed to help or hinder the case?" The therapists were instructed to focus on the process of clinical consultation because we were specifically interested in their reflections on family involvement. The written responses from therapists were separated into groups by discharge outcome. Narratives were assessed for themes related to REStArT model principles and were considered salient if they occurred across a majority of respondents.

Understanding Youths' Outcomes

The results of the quantitative and qualitative components contributed to our understanding of outcomes for the youth in this study. It is useful, however, to start with a view of the quantitative findings that then led to our qualitative questions. Most youth discharged in fiscal year 2014 had a favorable outcome at the time of discharge (82%, $n = 82$). Although it is difficult to compare outcome studies to one another given different populations and methodologies, this rate of favorable discharges appears comparable to other favorable studies (c.f., Hair 2005; Thomson et al. 2011). Most favorable discharge outcomes for the youth in this sample were either to a family home or to a group home (25 and 31% of total discharges, respectively). The remaining favorable discharges were to transitional living programs (10%), moderate residential treatment (7%), foster care (6%), adult mental health programs (2%), or independence (1%).

Youth with DCFS funding accounted for 48% of the discharges to family homes and this represented 18% of all DCFS-funded discharges. Alternately, 34% of youth without DCFS funding returned home. The unfavorable outcomes at the time of discharge included runaways (11% of total discharges), detention (5%), and lateral moves to other high-end residential programs (2%). All of the discharges that were

Table 21.1 Discharge distribution by funding source

	Total N = 100	DCFS n = 66		Non-DCFS n = 34	
		At discharge	Sustained at 6 mos.	At discharge	Sustained at 6 mos.
Favorable discharges	82	49	38	33	30
Group home	31	14	12	17	16
Family home	25	12	9	13	12
TLP	10	9	5	1	0
Moderate residential	7	7	6	0	0
Foster care	6	6	5	0	0
Adult mental health	2	0	0	2	2
Independence	1	1	1	0	0
Unfavorable discharges	18	17		1	
Runaway	11	11		0	
Detention	5	5		0	
Lateral residential	2	1		1	

due to runaways and detention were youth who had DCFS funding. Table 21.1 contains discharge type by funding source.

Of the 82 favorable discharges, 83% ($n = 68$) were sustained at 6 months. Therefore, from the original sample of 100 discharges, 68% were positive at 6 months. The remaining 32% were negative, meaning they were either unfavorable at discharge ($n = 18$) or were not sustained or unknown at 6 months ($n = 14$). Of the discharges that were not sustained, four of 25 discharges to family homes disrupted, three of 31 group home discharges disrupted, and half of discharges to transitional living program disrupted (five of 10). Three of the favorable discharges were considered negative outcomes at 6 months because their disposition was unknown. These included one foster care discharge and two discharges to family homes.

As the primary family intervention, clinical consultation is offered to all families. In the current sample, 95% of the youth and their families participated in clinical consultation during their treatment. Youth who had positive outcomes had, on average, fewer consultations per month ($M = 1.17$, $SD = 0.69$) than youth with negative outcomes ($M = 1.26$, $SD = 0.87$). This difference in rate of consultations was not statistically significant, nor was it practically meaningful. See Table 21.2 for differences between outcomes.

Both youth with positive outcomes and those with negative outcomes were participating in approximately one to two consults for each month they were in treatment. Although there was a statistically significant difference between rates of

Table 21.2 Differences between positive and negative outcomes

	Positive outcome at 6 months			Negative outcome at 6 months				
	n	M	SD	n	M	SD	t	p
Length of stay (in months)	68	13.47	7.41	32	12.56	5.78	0.67	0.51
Rate of consultations (consults per month)	68	1.17	0.69	32	1.26	0.87	−0.48	0.63

Table 21.3 Differences between funding sources

	DCFS			Non-DCFS				
	n	M	SD	N	M	SD	t	p
Length of stay (in months)	66	14.14	6.23	34	11.32	7.85	1.82	0.07
Rate of consultations (consults per month)	66	1.00	0.64	34	1.58	0.81	−3.63	0.000

consultation for DCFS youth and non-DCFS ($t = -3.63$, $p < 0.001$), the actual difference was an average of half a consultation a month ($M = 1.00$, $SD = 0.64$ and $M = 1.58$, $SD = 0.81$, respectively). While this may represent a larger issue about how DCFS youth were approached, the actual difference is small. See Table 21.3 for differences between funding sources.

It was somewhat surprising to find that there was no relevant difference in the amount of time spent with families related to discharge outcomes considering previous research that has found such a link (Huefner et al. 2015). This suggests that the agency was equally involving youth and their families in treatment regardless of outcomes, implying that variables other than simply the amount of treatment were at play in the relationship between family contact and the maintenance of favorable discharges. Notably, of the five youth who did not participate in any family intervention during their stay, three youth were discharged due to running away from the program.

The average length of time in treatment for all clients was 13.18 months ($SD = 6.92$), with a minimum stay of 6 months and a maximum stay of over three years (39 months). Length of stay did not differ between positive and negative outcomes ($M = 13.47$ months, $SD = 7.41$ and $M = 12.56$ months, $SD = 5.78$ respectively). The length of stay for youth with DCFS funding was 14.14 months ($SD = 6.23$) and the length of stay for youth with an alternative funding source was 11.32 months ($SD = 7.85$). The difference between these two groups was not statistically significant ($t = 1.81$, $p < 0.07$); however, the difference may still be meaningful in that DCFS youth were spending almost 3 months more in treatment. Longer lengths of stay have not always been associated with an actual need for a longer stay, but rather the absence of a post-discharge placement option (James et al. 2012).

The proportion of positive and negative discharges varied significantly by funding source, X^2 (1, $N = 100$) = 9.69, $p < 0.01$ (see Table 21.4). Youth with

Table 21.4 Proportion of positive discharges by funding source

	n	Positive outcome at 6 months (%)	N	Negative outcome at 6 months (%)	Total
DCFS funding	38	57.6	28	42.4	66
Non-DCFS funding	28	87.5	4	12.5	32

DCFS funding represented two-thirds of the youth discharged, but were just over half of the sustained positive discharges. On the other hand, only four of the 34 youth without DCFS funding had negative discharges (meaning, discharges that were either unfavorable or not sustained at 6 months). Certainly some of this difference is apparent in how many returned to a family home. Of the 68 DCFS-related discharges, 12 returned to a family home (18%), and nine of these youth were still in that home at 6 months. On the other hand, 13 of the 34 youth without DCFS funding (38%) returned home and only one was not sustained at 6 months.

While the lack of a family resource seems the obvious source of difference between working with the youth and families with DCFS funding, discharges to *step-downs* in level of treatment (i.e., group homes, transitional living programs, and more moderate residential care) also resulted in disrupted favorable discharges. This lack of continuity in placement suggests that in some way, the REStArT model's treatment was differentially effective for youth with different funding sources even though both sets of youth and their outside resources took part in family-oriented consultations at rates that were, practically speaking, very similar.

The qualitative component of our study allowed us to add texture to our understanding of these differential outcomes for youth with and without DCFS involvement. Across examples of unsuccessful DCFS cases, therapists noted that youth often wanted to live with a family member, but were discouraged from doing so. Youth were either informed by a DCFS caseworker that their chosen family members were not appropriate as a discharge resource or the youth and their family members perceived barriers with family members that interfered with the youth being placed in their care. Sometimes therapists spoke of this broadly, such as a case in which a therapist noted, "The youth had other family in state, but there was little momentum from the system to pursue those avenues." In other cases, the therapist's view of the youth's barrier was more specific: "The expectation was that they [any identified family member] come visit him on campus several times and then she [the DCFS caseworker] would talk about home visits." In both of these cases the youth ran away from treatment to be with family. Another therapist discussed a case in which a youth was detained by corrections, which resulted in his discharge. "After dealing with his legal issues, he went to live with family."

Therapists commented on cases in which the initial discharge was favorable, a group home or transitional living program, but ultimately the placement was not sustained. One therapist observed,

Sometimes DCFS youth remain [in treatment] for years, and so when a group home is finally suggested....the client is just desperate to leave, and agrees to the goal...in reality they were hoping all along they could go to [a] parent.

In a specific example of this, one therapist reflected on a case in which a client wanted to return to family in a different part of the state. When a group home was offered, the youth agreed with the expectation that the group home would be closer to his family. It was not, and his behaviors deteriorated once he was placed in the group home. The first principle of the REStArT model is the development of a working therapeutic alliance with the family and youth that includes youth- and family-driven goals. These examples suggest that, at times, it is possible that the model was not being implemented as intended in that the goals identified by the youth and family were not accepted by treatment providers or collaterals.

Therapists also reflected on factors internal to the agency that may impact the success of DCFS-funded cases. The theme that emerged was one in which fidelity to the model's emphasis on the recognition of ambivalence during consultation may be abdicated when DCFS is involved. Therapists and other treatment providers may see the responsibility of finding an appropriate discharge as the DCFS caseworker's responsibility. One therapist observed that "we come up against a natural split with DCFS" in which DCFS staff may advocate one discharge plan and treatment providers may advocate another. In the process, the youth's treatment needs tend to get overlooked because families may simply choose to align with whoever will support their discharge goal. If this split is left unacknowledged in the consultation process, the discharge is less likely to be stable. In another case, a youth was discharged to a former foster home, but then soon re-hospitalized. The therapist thought that "maybe we were pushing too hard and not hearing her [the foster mother] or her concerns and that is why there was not as good as a partnership as there could have been in the treatment process." Therapists seem to be identifying ways in which the principles of *finding imbalances in the system* and *working with ambivalence* were neglected in these cases.

Not surprisingly, for DCFS cases that were successful, therapists noted that agency providers were able to work cooperatively with DCFS caseworkers, the youth's biological family, and the youth. In particular, they observed that the youth were given the opportunity *to drive that conversation*. In one case described by a therapist, a youth was encouraged to find a family member who "was willing to participate in treatment and the youth was discharged to them." This resonates with other studies that have emphasized more than simple contact between youth and families, but rather the development of collaboration and partnerships between providers and families in order to work toward their goals (Geurts et al. 2012; Scarborough et al. 2013; Sharrock et al. 2013).

The lack of emphasis on finding family members by an agency such as DCFS that is charged with protecting children from potential unsafe family situations is understandable. It is notable, however, that the average age of discharge for these youth was just under 17. One of the therapists shared the case of a youth who stated that he intended to leave treatment when he was 18 in order to reunite with family, whether or not his move was supported by treatment providers. As a recent literature review suggests (Collins et al. 2008), the developmentally appropriate focus on knowing one's place with family is a significant aspect of adolescence, so treatment that acknowledges and preserves those relationships seems likely to be successful in a more enduring way. The successful cases therapists noted appeared to preserve these family relationships, which is consistent with the model's principle that asks providers to *expect health* from youth and their families.

Summary

In investigating outcomes related to family involvement and the REStArT model, we were interested in answering the question, "Do youth and their families benefit from treatment when they leave and is that benefit enduring?" Most of the youth who left the agency's residential program were older adolescents living in a less-restrictive placement. The durability of the treatment's impact, however, varied depending on the youth's guardianship. Those youth whose families were involved with DCFS were much more likely to leave without completing treatment or to have favorable discharges that disrupted. When therapists' reflected on the process of individual cases, both positive and negative, they suggested that the model's implementation was challenged in a number of ways, such as the development of a therapeutic alliance in which youth and their families were given ownership over their goals. These results suggest on the one hand that, in response to the need for family-driven treatment to improve residential outcomes, the REStArT model offers one way of successfully responding to families' needs. But the results also suggest that families with DCFS involvement may not be receiving the same benefits of the model's efforts at collaboration.

Limitations, Implications, and Research

A number of limitations need to be acknowledged that temper the interpretation of these results. While it appears that the model's emphasis on family involvement has differential effectiveness based on the family's relationship with DCFS, this study examined only 1 year of discharges, so it is possible that this sample of youth with DCFS guardianship is different than other years. Indeed, previous research (McConnell and Taglione 2012) found more comparable results, at least at the time of discharge, even in returns to family homes between youth with different funding sources. However, the previous study did not consider the sustainability of favorable outcomes.

One possible hypothesis for why relatively equal frequency of family interventions was less successful with DCFS-funded youth relates to the implementation of the model. The therapists interviewed speculated that the fidelity of the model was compromised in cases that included DCFS involvement. Another limitation then of this current study is that it did not contain a fidelity check that would allow us to see if, in fact, therapists and other treatment providers were not implementing the model as it is intended, despite providers being trained to monitor fidelity (as described above). Without such a check, it is unclear if the model was implemented accurately, but was less effective in these cases or if the model was not being used as intended.

This study looked only at whether discharges that were favorable at the time of discharge were sustained. A number of therapists observed anecdotally that DCFS-funded youth sometimes ran away from treatment and returned to live with family in response to being limited in their family contact by treatment providers, DCFS, or the courts. An additional limitation then of this study is that there may be youth who were able to return successfully to family homes despite external prohibitions.

The need for family involvement in residential treatment has been soundly supported by research and increasingly accepted by residential treatment programs. However, the effectiveness of family interventions will remain limited if providers and the larger system working with youth remain ambivalent about youth returning to their families. There is some research to support therapists' assumption that youth sometimes return to their families when they are old enough to make their own choice (Collins et al. 2008). The REStArT model asks treatment providers to help youth and families address their ambivalence about their relationships with one another but likely needs to do more to address the ambivalence in the larger system.

This chapter shows that mixed methods can be effectively used in residential settings serving adolescents. In the study described here, the mixed methods approach allowed the researchers to understand empirically the characteristics that differentiated outcomes and also to bring some depth to that understanding by looking at the treatment process that may explain those results. In other words, the qualitative results provided a possible explanation for the quantitative data: perhaps clinical consultation was differentially effective because its application varied depending on the youth's guardianship. With that hypothesis in hand, future studies may be conducted to further assess the accuracy of this. For example, empirical studies could examine whether the two groups, DCFS-funded and non-DCFS-funded youth, varied in any other ways that may play a mediating role in the correlation between clinical consultation participation and quality of outcomes. Another benefit of a mixed methods approach is its accessibility to providers. Empirical results at times can seem remote and disembodied from daily practice. The narrative lens can help providers make sense of quantitative outcomes by understanding the process at play behind the numbers.

Appendix: Principles: The Relational Re-enactment Systems Approach to Treatment (REStArT)

    I. **Developing a Working Therapeutic Alliance**: Client, family, and service providers agree on the goals and tasks of treatment. These goals and tasks need to be youth and family driven.

   II. **Relational Re-Enactment**: Identify youth's attachment style through the ways in which the youth re-enacts it in their behavior with others (i.e., identify the conflict cycle).

  III. **Managing Counter-Response**: Identify the adult counter-response (feelings and subsequent behavior) within that youth's particular conflict cycle; identify the adult's unpleasant reality (related to the youth's conflict cycle) that is being avoided by the adult; face the adult's unpleasant reality and the adult's feelings so that they are not driving the adult's behavior (counter-response).

  IV. **System-Oriented**: Identify all the adults involved with the youth and have them come together to develop a shared understanding of and way of approaching the youth.

   V. **Finding the Imbalance in the System**: Identify polarities in youth's behavior and subsequent polarities in adults' counter-response (i.e., splits/divisions within the system).

  VI. **Seeing the Whole Youth**: Identify ways in which our view of the youth has been compartmentalized (i.e., sees the youth in a particular way). Work together and dialogue so that all parties see both sides of the youth—the adaptive side and the maladaptive side.

 VII. **Restoring the Balance**: Use dialogue and consensus to restore balance in developing a plan to interrupt the youth's conflict cycle (integrate both extremes of the adults' counter-response reactions in order to arrive at a more balanced response).

VIII. **Interrupting the Conflict Cycle**: Implement a plan that interrupts the way the youth typically responds to stressors which provides an opportunity for the youth to respond in a new more adaptive way.

  IX. **Working with Ambivalence**: Be aware of and identify examples of ambivalence toward the current circumstance in the family and the youth so that this can be verbalized instead of expressed through behavior.

   X. **Expecting Health**: Trust the youth's ability to determine their own goals, tolerate disappointments, and repair relational disruptions.

  XI. **Ownership at Every Part of the System**: Create investment in the model across the entire system and support each part's contribution to the plan, which promotes responsibility and accountability.

XII. **Evidence-Based**: Use concrete data about the youth to determine conflict cycle and plan development and to evaluate effectiveness and outcomes.

XIII. **Dynamic and Reflexive Process**: Establish a continuous process of looking at our own responses/reactions and evaluating whether the plan is effective.

References

Collins, M. E., Paris, R., & Ward, R. L. (2008). The permanence of family ties: Implications for youth transitioning from foster care. *American Journal of Orthopsychiatry, 78,* 54–62. doi:10.1037/0002-9432.78.1.54

Curry, J. (2004). Future directions in residential treatment outcome research. *Child Adolescent Psychiatric Clinics of North America, 13,* 429–440. doi:10.1016/S1056-4993(03)00127-5

Geurts, E. M. W., Boddy, J., Noom, M. J., & Knorth, E. J. (2012). Family-centred residential care: The new reality? *Child and Family Social Work, 17,* 170–179. doi:10.1111/j.1365-2206.2012.00838.x

Hair, H. J. (2005). Outcomes for children and adolescents after residential treatment: A review of research from 1993 to 2003. *Journal of Child and Family Studies, 14,* 551–575. doi:10.1007/s10826-005-7188-9

Hogue, A., Dauber, S., Stambough, L. F., Cecero, J. J., & Liddle, H. A. (2006). Early therapeutic alliance and treatment outcome in individual and family therapy for adolescent behavior problems. *Journal of Consulting and Clinical Psychology, 74,* 121–129. doi:10.1037/0022-006X.74.1.121

Huefner, J. C., Pick, R. M., Smith, G. L., Stevens, A. L., & Mason, W. A. (2015). Parental involvement in residential care: Distance, frequency of contact, and youth outcomes. *Journal of Child and Family Studies, 24,* 1481–1489. doi:10.1007/s10826-014-9953-0

James, S. S., Zhang, J. J., & Landsverk, J. (2012). Residential care for youth in the child welfare system: Stop-gap option or not? *Residential Treatment for Children & Youth, 29,* 48–65. doi:10.1080/0886571X.2012.643678

Lakin, B. L., Brambila, A. D., & Sigda, K. B. (2004). Parental involvement as a factor in the readmission to a residential treatment center. *Residential Treatment for Children & Youth, 22,* 37–51. doi:10.1300/J007v22n02_03

McConnell, C., & Taglione, P. (2012). Collaborating with clients and improving outcomes: The relational re-enactment systems approach to treatment model. *Residential Treatment for Children and Youth, 29,* 103–117. doi:10.1080/0886571X.2012.669252

Miller, W. R., & Rollnick, S. (2013). *Motivational interviewing: Helping people change* (3rd ed.). The Guildford Press.

Norcross, J. C., & Wampold, B. E. (2011). Evidence-based therapy relationships: Research conclusions and clinical practices. *Psychotherapy, 48,* 98–102. doi:10.1037/a0022161

Robbins, M. S., Turner, C. W., Alexander, J. F., & Perez, G. A. (2003). Alliance and dropout in family therapy for adolescents with behavior problems: Individual and systemic effects. *Journal of Family Psychology, 17,* 534–544. doi:10.1037/0893-3200.17.4.534

Robst, J., Rohrer, L., Armstrong, M., Dollard, N., Sharrock, P., Batsche, C., et al. (2013). Family involvement and changes in child behavior during residential mental health treatment. *Child & Youth Care Forum, 42,* 225–238. doi:10.1007/s10566-013-9201-6

Scarborough, N., Taylor, B., & Tuttle, A. (2013). Collaborative home-based therapy (CHBT): A culturally responsive model for treating children and adolescents involved in child protective service systems. *Contemporary Family Therapy: An International Journal, 35,* 465–477. DOI 10.1007/s10591-012-9223-5

Sharrock, P. J., Dollard, N., Armstrong, M. I., & Rohrer, L. (2013). Provider perspectives on involving families in children's residential psychiatric care. *Residential Treatment for Children & Youth, 30,* 40–54. doi:10.1080/0886571X.2013.751807

Taglione, P., Shahbazian, M., & McConnell, C. (2014). *Relational re-enactment systems approach to treatment (unpublished training manual).* Lake Villa, IL: Allendale Association.

Thomson, S., Hirschberg, D., & Qiao, J. (2011). Outcomes for adolescent girls after long-term residential treatment. *Residential Treatment for Children & Youth, 28,* 251–267. doi:10.1080/0886571X.2011.605051

Walter, U. M., & Petr, C. G. (2008). Family-centered residential treatment: Knowledge, research, and values converge. *Residential Treatment of Children & Youth, 25,* 1–16. doi:10.1080/08865710802209594

Wood, M. M., & Long, N. J. (1991). *Life space intervention.* Austin, Texas: pro-ed.

Author Biographies

Catherine McConnell Ph.D. has been at the Allendale Association for almost 20 years, having been drawn there initially as a pre-doctoral intern because of its reputation for self-reflective psychodynamic work with children and adolescents who have experienced trauma. Catherine McConnell holds a Ph.D. from the University of Wisconsin-Madison and is a licensed clinical psychologist. In addition to providing therapeutic services to children and their families across a variety of settings within Allendale, Dr. McConnell has had the opportunity to work with staff across the agency in developing and conducting research on the agency's treatment model: the Relational Re-Enactment Systems Approach to Treatment.

Patricia Taglione Psy.D. is a licensed clinical psychologist and the Senior Vice President of Clinical and Community Services at the Allendale Association. Dr. Taglione holds a Psy.D. from the Forest Institute. She has over 30 years of experience working directly with youth and their families, as well as supervising trainees and psychologists. As a founding developer of the agency's Relational Re-Enactment Systems Approach to Treatment model, she has developed and conducted dozens of innovative trainings and presented in multiple forums to help all levels of staff who work with traumatized children and families.

Chapter 22
Youth with Emotional and Behavioral Disorders: Coping and Psychological Difficulties

Michèle Preyde, Jessica Furtado, Amy Tran and Victoria Currie

Chapter Highlights

- Utilizing a cross-sectional survey to discover self-reported strategies and difficulties the youth perceived appears feasible in residential mental health settings.
- Greater use of active strategies was associated with lower psychological and interpersonal difficulties.
- Greater use of risky strategies was related to greater psychological difficulties, while passive/depressive strategies were not associated with psychological difficulties.
- Adult mentors regularly engaging with youth to facilitate and model coping strategies and to guide youth through difficulties may be beneficial.
- Findings suggested it may be beneficial to help youth develop a repertoire of active and passive coping skills to improve their ability to flexibly enhance well-being.

M. Preyde (✉)
Department of Family Relations and Applied Nutrition, University of Guelph,
Guelph, ON N1G 2W1, Canada
e-mail: mpreyde@uoguelph.ca

J. Furtado
Factor-Inwentash Faculty of Social Work, University of Toronto,
246 Bloor Street West, Toronto, ON M5S 1V4, USA
e-mail: jessica.furtado@mail.utoronto.ca

A. Tran
Department of Psychology, University of Windsor, 401 Sunset Avenue,
Windsor, ON N9B 3P4, USA
e-mail: trana@mail.uoguelph.ca

V. Currie
Speech-Language Pathology, 500 University Ave #160, Toronto, ON M5G 1V7, USA
e-mail: victoria.currie@mail.utoronto.ca

© Springer International Publishing AG 2017   385
J.D. Christenson and A.N. Merritts (eds.), *Family Therapy with Adolescents
in Residential Treatment*, Focused Issues in Family Therapy,
DOI 10.1007/978-3-319-51747-6_22

Learning how to cope with and adapt to stress and adversity is critical for one's health and well-being. It is also a central task for children and adolescents, many of whom have difficulty coping. Coping is a multidimensional concept (Compas et al. 2001; Eisenberg et al. 1997; Lazarus and Folkman 1984) that refers to the processes employed to adapt to perceived stress. There are a wide range of coping strategies employed and any individual can employ various strategies for various stressors. Though the success of any given strategy is dependent on the individual and the situation, active coping strategies, in general, are viewed as more adaptive than passive or risky strategies. Coping is distinct from competence; Competence refers to the youths' ability to employ resources or strategies to adapt successfully. Coping and adapting in youth with emotional and behavioral disorders (EBD) may be even more challenging than for the average youth. There is scant research on the coping strategies employed by youth with EBD who are accessing residential mental health treatment. These youth may have limitations in coping and be vulnerable in their adaptation to the stresses of life. The purpose for this chapter is to describe the use of self-reported questionnaires with youth accessing residential and day treatment programs to discover the coping strategies they endorse and to provide an example of a specific methodology (i.e., survey research; see Chap. 20) with an exploration of the association between self-reported coping and psychological difficulties.

Survey methods involve a systematic approach to gathering data from individuals who represent a certain group of people (Aldridge and Levine 2001). The purpose of survey research is to elicit participants' perspectives such as attitudes and opinions, but also about their behaviors and emotions in order to understand something about them as a whole. The intent is to produce results that are representative of the population from which the participants were sampled. A questionnaire is developed to capture a variety of data including information (such as age and gender), standardized measures of the relevant constructs (e.g., coping strategies endorsed), and sometimes open-ended questions are asked (e.g., did you find the support helpful?) where the answer is expected to be somewhat brief. Standardized measures are frequently used in survey designs; they have been tested through research to ensure that they are both valid and reliable. An example of a standardized measure is the Beck Depression Inventory (Beck et al. 1961, 1988) for which participants rate their feelings (e.g., sadness) and behaviors (e.g., how often they cry) on 21 items about depression. An example of an item is how much sadness they feel on a scale of zero (I do not feel sad) to four (I am so sad and unhappy that I can't stand it). These types of standardized measures that participants complete reflect self-reported data; that is, it is the participants' subjective perspective as opposed to objective standardized measures that a therapist or doctor or researcher might use to rate a participant. In the present study, standardized measures were used for which the participants (i.e., youth with EBD) rated the amount of psychological difficulties and interpersonal difficulties they were experiencing, and they rated how frequently they used various coping strategies. It is our hope that the application of survey research/self-reported data methods as described in this chapter will provide a useful example of how to conduct this type of research.

Adolescent Functioning and Coping

The prevalence estimates of mental health disorders in adolescents range from approximately 14 to 25% (Briggs-Gowan et al. 2003; Kessler et al. 2005; Waddell et al. 2002). Levels of comorbidity are also high (Costello et al. 2003; Rutter 2003) which contributes to the complexity of providing effective care for children and adolescents (Preyde et al. 2011a, b). The etiology of EBD appears to be complex. Biological, genetic, social, psychological, and environmental factors have been shown to contribute to the onset of EBD (Angold and Costello 1995; Rutter 2003). Investigators have identified risk factors underlying EBD to include parenting characteristics (e.g., coercive parenting), child characteristics (e.g., difficult temperament), negative interactions, and social stressors such as unstable family composition and inadequate incomes (Baker et al. 2007). Furthermore, adolescents with EBD may have families who experience a range of challenges including parental mental illness, economic hardship, and family conflict. In addition, some adolescents may have interfaced with the child welfare system and have thus potentially experienced maltreatment or family violence (Angold and Costello 1995; Baker et al. 2007; Waddell et al. 2002). Therefore, trends show that adolescents with moderate to severe EBD may have experienced adversity or negative life experiences in addition to the EBD, and may have family relationships that are less than ideal.

Day and residential treatment programs are designed to meet the mental health needs of children and youth with moderate to severe EBD. A wide range of services are offered including individual and family therapies, symptom management, skills building, and academic assistance. The number of adolescents accessing mental health services has increased over the past few decades (Connor et al. 2004; Griffith et al. 2009). The youth accessing residential and day treatment programs usually present with externalizing behaviors with conduct disorder as most prevalent and internalizing behaviors such as anxiety or depression (Baker et al. 2007; Briggs-Gowan et al. 2003; Child Welfare League of America 2005; Preyde et al. 2011a, b). Each youth presents a unique set of complex mental health challenges.

Coping refers to an individual's ongoing behavioral and cognitive efforts to manage the internal (person) and external (environment) demands that are appraised as stressful or as exceeding the person's resources (Lazarus and Folkman 1984). The coping resources and strategies adolescents adopt may play a role in their levels of stress as well as provide insight into the adjustment of these adolescents. Compas (1987) suggested that both the resources available to cope and the strategies which adolescents recruit are important factors influencing growth and development. Coping strategies, including access to social support, are thus thought to aid youth with mental health challenges and could have a positive impact on their outcomes and life trajectories.

Types of Coping

Traditionally, theoretical foundations of stress and coping have characterized coping strategies into two general categories: problem-focused coping (active) and emotion-focused coping (passive) (Carver et al. 1989). Problem-focused coping encompasses strategies which are aimed at mitigating the stress by problem solving or altering the source of stress. Emotion-focused coping strategies are used in an attempt to alleviate or manage the emotional distress elicited by the source of stress. Another type of passive coping can be categorized as depressive or learned hopelessness (Compas et al. 2001). Although the distinction between these strategies is an important one, the same person can use a mix of strategies that includes both. Nonetheless, the use of active coping strategies is often regarded as superior to the use of passive ones. However, any coping strategy is not inherently good or bad because it depends on the youths' appraisal of the situation and the resources they possess to manage the stress (Lazarus and Folkman 1984). However, risky coping strategies such as consuming alcohol or drugs to deal with stress may be physically and socially harmful. Moreover, risky coping strategies have been associated with family conflict (Plunkett and Henry 1999) and parent conflict (Steinberg et al. 2006).

Coping strategies endorsed by individuals have been found to be contingent upon the appraisal of the situation (Lazarus and Folkman 1984). For example, labeling a situation as amenable was associated with active coping strategies, such as planning and seeking social support for instrumental reasons. In contrast, subjects who characterized their situation as immutable reported using passive coping, such as denial and acceptance (Carver et al. 1989). Carver et al. (1989) indicated several strategies such as behavioral and mental disengagement that might be considered as dysfunctional coping as they impede the individual's adaptive coping abilities.

It is apparent that both problem- and emotion-focused coping contribute to effective coping strategies and that each strategy is neither exclusively adaptive nor maladaptive (Lazarus and Folkman 1984). Coping with stress is a central component of human development and is moderated by individual and situational differences. The most effective coping strategies are most likely characterized by adaptive flexibility and change to meet environmental demands. In light of the complexity of coping dispositions, exploring the coping styles endorsed by adolescents has been recognized as an important area of study given its mediating role between stress and illness or conversely health. Researchers have noted that the development of a large repertoire of coping strategies during this time is crucial for immediate and future stress management. The coping styles adopted when faced with novel stressors during this time may dictate coping styles employed later in adulthood (Garnefski et al. 2002).

Coping theorists Lazarus and Folkman (1984) noted that a greater sense of control facilitates problem-focused coping, as opposed to emotion-focused coping, which is endorsed when one perceives no control over his/her environment.

Additionally, a greater sense of mastery over an environment is linked to successful adjustment and to coping with stress (Ben-Zur 2003; Lipschitz-Elhawi and Itzhaky 2005). However, youth enrolled at residential treatment facilities often come from impoverished environments characterized by stress and a lack of role models to provide a sense of mastery over their surroundings (Herman-Stahi and Peterson 1996; Preyde et al. 2011a, b). Youth may be uncertain about their ability to influence and control their environment.

The limited studies exclusively focused on at-risk adolescent populations with EBD bolsters the rationale for exploring coping strategies youth employ during residential care and the relationship between coping and well-being (Barendregt et al. 2015; Greve et al. 2001). The exact nature of the relationship between psychopathology and problem-focused strategies (i.e., effortful strategies) is unclear. In a sample of youth with EBD accessing residential treatment, Singer et al. (2000) found a positive relationship between psychopathology and the use of effortful disengagement. Furthermore, the youth who adopted problem-focused strategies, such as problem solving, cognitive restricting, and positive thinking, reported maladjustment similar to youth who adopted disengagement strategies (Singer et al. 2000). The authors provide a possible explanation for this discrepancy; the psychological problems experienced by this population may be contributing to the failure of effectively adopting problem-focused strategies in a manner that results in successful coping (Singer et al. 2000). No other studies on coping strategies used by youth accessing residential or day treatment programs were located.

The Role of the Family in Adolescent Distress and Coping

Through the process of interpersonal co-regulation, attachments are developed as caregivers respond to the needs of their child, and the child learns to trust the parent and how to regulate emotions (Ainsworth et al. 1978). When an infant is distressed and the caregiver is unresponsive to his/her needs, this situation can affect the quality of attachment which can have implications for emotional regulation and relationship quality later in life (Sroufe 2005). Temperament of the child is also a contributing factor to coping but is dynamic and can be altered (Fox et al. 2005; Gunnar and Cheatham 2003; Rutter 1983). Intrapersonal self-regulation begins in toddlerhood and is scaffolded by significant adults who teach and model how to appraise and confront stressful situations (Power 2004; Zimmer-Gembeck and Locke 2007). Middle childhood brings changes in cognition that allows children to co-ordinate coping strategies with others (Skinner and Zimmer-Gembeck 2007). As cognition develops in adolescence, young people can use more sophisticated meta-cognitive strategies to consider and select coping strategies (Skinner and Zimmer-Gembeck 2007); however, ineffective coping can make adolescents vulnerable to psychopathology (Compas et al. 2014). Thus, the development of coping in children and adolescents is dependent on many intersecting factors.

Stress experienced by families can increase intra-family strain (Lavee et al. 1987). Moreover, family process variables have been shown to significantly affect an individual's distress (Rosman and Baker 1988). In particular, conflict within the family can be a significant source of stress for adolescents (Auerbach and Ho 2012). Many youth with EBD have faced adversity throughout their lives and have often experienced greater family conflict and family stress compared to their general cohort. Notably, the disadvantaged background experienced by these youth may have thwarted their acquisition of successful coping strategies or influenced their propensity for strategies that exacerbate the source of stress. Additionally, disadvantaged youth with severe EBD who are admitted to residential treatment centers may also have to deal with the stress that is provoked by the admission to a new and restrictive environment (Barendregt et al. 2015).

Though it is common for families to experience stress, the development of coping strategies is complex. Genetic and personality factors are modest contributors to an individual's coping styles (Jang et al. 2007); however, coping in children is substantially influenced by the child's environment (Wang et al. 2005) where the family context offers the avenues for social learning (Bandura 1977) of various coping strategies. For example, adolescents with a secure attachment pattern have been shown to employ more functional coping strategies than youth with insecure patterns (Kraaij et al. 2003). Thus, having an understanding of the coping strategies employed by youth with EBD and how coping relates to key clinical features such as the severity of psychological difficulties can aid family therapists in their work with this vulnerable population.

In sum, there is a dearth of research on coping in youth with EBD accessing residential and day treatment programs, and the relationship between coping strategies and psychological difficulties is unclear. The purpose for the study reported in this chapter was to explore the self-reported strategies youth with moderate to severe EBD endorse when coping with stress. The authors also explored the association of self-reported active, passive/depressive and risky coping strategies with psychological difficulties as well as the association between active, passive/depressive, and risky coping strategies with self-reported interpersonal difficulties.

These explorations are part of a larger survey on the characteristics of youth with EBD accessing residential and day treatment programs. Data used in the larger survey were collected from two community mental health agencies in Ontario, Canada providing both day and residential treatment services for males and females ranging from 12 to 18 years of age. A mental health team manages the treatment for these youth and delivers strength-based, cognitive behavioral, and anger management interventions. The treatment team is made up of psychiatric nurses, social workers,, and youth workers. Each youth is provided with educational opportunities on-site, though some may continue in their community school. Whenever possible, family members and parents are included in the treatment process. The day program portion of the setting operates from 8:30 am to 2:30 pm, and children in this part of the program return to their families or guardian(s) at the end of the day. More specific and detailed information can be found in the work of DiCroce et al. (2016) and Furtado et al. (2016).

Procedures for Recruitment and Collection of Self-reported Data

Institutional ethics clearance was obtained from the University of Guelph. To protect privacy, an administrative staff member at each agency first contacted the parents or guardians of youth 15 years old or younger and staff contacted youth 16 years old and older to determine interest in hearing about an opportunity to engage in a study. For those interested, the research assistant then provided further details. Parent/guardian consent was first required for individuals 15 years and younger, and then assent was obtained from these youth. Informed consent was obtained from youth who were 16 years old and older. The Health Canada Research Ethics Board (Health Canada 2009) has indicated that children 16 years old are capable of consenting provided they have been counseled and have sufficient maturity to understand the nature, purpose and potential impacts of participating in the research. Furthermore, in this case youth were already in a secure, residential mental health center with professional mental health expertise on-site. The research assistant administered a survey containing self-reported standardized measures to each participant in a private room in the day or residential treatment setting, and only research personnel had access to participant data. Individuals received a $10 gift card for their participation.

Measures

The youths' psychological difficulties were assessed with the Strengths and Difficulties Questionnaire (SDQ; Goodman et al. 1998). The SDQ is a 25-item self-report behavioral screen comprised of five subscales: emotional symptoms, conduct problems, hyperactivity score, peer problems, and prosocial behaviors. Items are scored on a three-point scale ranging from zero to two; 'not true' (0), 'somewhat true' (1), or 'certainly true' (2). Greater scores on the SDQ indicate overall greater difficulties with the exception of the prosocial behavior subscale where higher scores reflect greater prosocial behavior. A total sum score of difficulties (i.e., not including prosocial behavior) can range from zero to 40. The normal range is considered between zero and 14, the borderline range is 15–19, and the abnormal range is 20–40. The SDQ has demonstrated both high discriminant validity and cross-informant correlations (Goodman et al. 1998).

Interpersonal difficulties were measured with the short version of the Inventory of Interpersonal Problems (IIP) developed by Barkham et al. (1994). There are 32 items, which are scored on a five-point scale from 'not at all' (0) to 'extremely' (4). The short form IIP is comprised of eight subscales, paired to create four major constructs: problems relating to competition (hard to be assertive vs. too aggressive), socializing (hard to be sociable vs. too open), nurturance (hard to be supportive vs. too caring) and independence (hard to be involved vs. too dependent). The IIP has been used by psychotherapists or researchers as an outcome measure (Barkham et al. 1994). This measure has demonstrated sensitivity to change, good reliability, and high face validity (Horowitz et al. 1988). Higher scores indicate greater interpersonal problems.

The strategies youth use to cope with stress were captured with the Youth Stress and Coping Questionnaire (YSCQ; Cloutier et al. 2008; Kennedy et al. 2009) which was based on the "How I Deal with Stress Questionnaire" (Heath and Ross 2002) and the Brief COPE (Carver 1997). For the YSCQ, youth rated the frequency of using each strategy on a four-point scale ranging from zero (never used this way of dealing with stress) to three (frequently used this way of dealing with stress). Subscales are reported below. The YSCQ has been used successfully in research with adolescents (see Martin et al. 2013).

Data Analysis

Data were entered into The Statistical Package for Social Sciences (SPSS). Demographic data and psychosocial characteristics were analyzed using descriptive statistics. A composite of active, passive/depressive, and risky coping strategies were computed with mean scores. In previous research with adolescents (Barendregt et al. 2015), depressive responses such as crying were categorized as passive. Regression analysis was used to explore the association between active, passive, and risky coping with psychological difficulty while controlling for gender. Assumptions of regression were met. In a secondary exploration, regression analysis was used to explore the association between each of the three strategies and interpersonal problems while controlling for gender. The relatively small sample size is indicative of the numbers of youth with this severe expression of EBD who access intensive mental health treatment; the small size limited the number of statistical analyses that could be performed (i.e., only being able to include one control variable in the regression).

Findings

Of the 47 youth who were accessing programs at the time of the study, 30 adolescents consented to participate in this study (Response Rate = 64%). Ten youth refused participation and for seven youth there were difficulties in obtaining guardian consent. Youth reported a mean age of 15.3 years (SD = 1.6), and the majority identified as female (n = 21, 70%; Table 22.1).

Youth reported employing a number of strategies when attempting to manage stress (Table 22.2). Youth reported the greatest frequency of use of acceptance (M = 2.41, SD = 0.87), doing an activity alone (M = 2.41, SD = 0.95), talking with someone (M = 2.18, SD = 1.12), and crying (M = 2.10, SD = 0.84); of these four, three involve passive or depressive types of responses.

Table 22.1 Youth
characteristics

	$n = 30$
Age (years), $M(SD)$	15.30 (1.64)
Gender, n (%)	
Male	9 (30)
Female	21 (70)
Grade, n (%)	
7–8	6 (21)
9–10	9 (31)
11–12	14 (48)

In terms of the regression analysis, the correlation matrix appears in Table 22.3. Results indicate that gender did not contribute to psychological difficulties. Active ($F = 4.10$, $p = 0.029$, adjusted $r^2 = 0.19$) and risky behavioral ($F = 3.71$, $p = 0.018$, adjusted $r^2 = 0.29$) strategies were significantly associated with psychological difficulties. Specifically, increased use of active strategies was associated with lower self-reported psychological difficulties, and increased use of risky strategies was associated with greater psychological difficulties. There was no association between passive strategies and psychological difficulties.

The beta-coefficients (Table 22.4) reveal that both active and risky strategies were statistically significant in their relationship with psychological difficulties.

In the final exploration the results were mixed. Active coping ($F = 9.44$, $p = 0.001$, adjusted $r^2 = 0.39$) strategies were negatively associated with total interpersonal difficulties. While risky coping strategies were significantly correlated with interpersonal difficulties (Table 22.5), the beta-coefficients (Table 22.6) suggest that active and passive strategies were statistically significant in their relationship with interpersonal difficulties. Thus, there is some confidence that increased use of active strategies was associated with fewer interpersonal problems. The exact role of passive and risky coping strategies is not clear.

Implications of the Findings

As mentioned above, the findings for this study were revealed using self-reported data in a residential setting and therefore show the utility of survey research in these settings. As can be seen in the discussion below, despite the limitations of this approach to generating research data, self-report can provide rich information that can be used to guide clinical intervention. In the present study, youth reported employing a range of coping strategies when dealing with stress, and there was a strong, negative correlation between the reported use of active strategies and psychological difficulties and interpersonal difficulties. Conversely, there was a positive association between risky behavioral strategies and psychological difficulties. That is, lower psychological and interpersonal difficulty was associated with increased use of active strategies, and higher psychological difficulty was associated with increased use of risky coping strategies.

Table 22.2 Coping strategies

Strategy used	n	M (SD)
Acceptance		
Learn to live with it[b]	29	2.41 (0.87)
Distraction		
Do an activity by myself	29	2.41 (0.95)
Do an activity with others	29	1.83 (1.04)
Chat online	29	1.41 (1.35)
Play violent video games	30	1.20 (1.27)
Mediate or do relaxation exercises	30	1.03 (1.07)
Play online interactive fantasy games	29	0.62 (1.08)
Using emotional support		
Talk to someone[a]	28	2.18 (1.12)
Venting		
Cry[b]	30	2.10 (0.84)
Express my upset feelings[b]	29	1.83 (1.07)
Active coping		
Try to solve the problem[a]	29	2.00 (0.93)
Do something about the situation[a]	30	1.93 (0.87)
Reframing		
Tell myself it doesn't matter	30	1.97 (1.07)
Convince myself the stress isn't there	29	1.14 (1.09)
Disengagement		
Give up on dealing with the situation[b]	30	1.97 (1.13)
Instrumental support		
Get help from other people[a]	30	1.90 (1.18)
Humor		
Make jokes about the problem	28	1.75 (1.21)
Make fun of the situation	30	1.37 (1.10)
Positive reframing		
Find the positive in situation	29	1.48 (1.09)
Vent behaviorally		
Hit someone[c]	30	1.47 (1.20)
Argue with people[c]	30	1.37 (1.16)
Self-harm		
Hurt myself on purpose[c]	30	1.40 (1.25)
Risky behavior		
Smoke cigarettes[c]	30	1.30 (1.32)
Do risky things[c]	30	1.20 (1.16)
Do drugs[c]	30	1.07 (1.23)
Drink alcohol[c]	30	0.80 (1.06)
Gamble[c]	29	0.21 (0.68)
Religion		
Pray	29	0.67 (1.01)

[a]Active coping strategies; [b]Passive/depressive coping; [c]Risky behavior

Table 22.3 Correlation matrix total difficulties

Measure	1	2	3	4
1. Total difficulties	–	–	–	–
2. Gender (M/F)	0.14	–	–	–
3. Active coping	−0.50**	−0.37*	–	–
4. Passive coping	−0.10	0.36*	0.20	–
5. Risky coping	0.41*	0.21	−0.10	0.19

Note $*p < 0.05$, $**p < 0.01$

Table 22.4 Summary of hierarchal regression analysis total difficulties

Variable	Model 1		Model 2	
	B	Beta	B	Beta
Gender (M/F)	1.73	0.14	−1.83	−0.15
Active coping			−4.15	−0.52*
Passive coping			0.72	0.07
Risky coping			3.49	0.38*

Note $*p < 0.05$, $**p < 0.01$; B = unstandardized coefficient, $Beta$ = standardized coefficients

Table 22.5 Correlation matrix interpersonal difficulties

Measure	1	2	3	4
1. Interpersonal difficulties	–	–	–	–
2. Gender (M/F)	0.38*	–	–	–
3. Active coping	−0.63**	0.34*	–	–
4. Passive coping	0.26	0.36*	0.20	–
5. Risky coping	0.35*	0.21	−0.10	0.19

Note $*p < 0.05$, $**p < 0.01$

Table 22.6 Summary of hierarchal regression analysis interpersonal difficulties

Variable	Model 1		Model 2	
	B	Beta	B	Beta
Gender (M/F)	0.61	0.38	−0.58	−0.04
Active coping			−7.12	−0.70**
Passive coping			0.46	0.37*
Risky coping			0.25	0.21

Note $*p < 0.05$, $**p < 0.01$; B = unstandardized coefficient, $Beta$ = standardized coefficients

The severity of psychological and interpersonal difficulties was negatively associated with active coping among youth with EBD. Given the current state of knowledge, it appears logical that this relationship exists. In their theory, Lazarus and Folkman's (1984) included the idea that youth who had an internal locus of control, or felt they had some control over their difficulties, used a greater number of problem-focused (compared to emotion-focused) strategies. Higher self-esteem and an internal locus of control have been associated with greater use of functional coping strategies (Dumont and Provost 1999). Dumone and Provost (1999) suggested that those with higher self-esteem perceive stressors to be within their control and believe they have the competence to execute actions that will solve their problems. In contrast, those with lower self-esteem choose avoidant and often risky behaviors. Such strategies may be ineffective in mitigating stress by dealing with the issue itself and therefore leave youth vulnerable to further psychological stress. Similarly, Kraaij et al. (2003) found that securely attached adolescents tended to employ active coping strategies, whereas insecurely attached youth used strategies such as rumination, catastrophizing,, and self-blame, which were associated with negative outcomes. However, the concept of coping flexibility, as first conceptualized by Cheng (2001), refers to cases where individuals can both adapt their cognitions as well as their behaviors to fit a given situation. Inflexibility with either cognitive appraisals or coping behaviors was theorized to have negative outcomes. It seems that youth who use active strategies can also recruit passive strategies when required, thus the adaptive strength lies in flexibly drawing from a range of possible strategies depending on the situation and not the strategies themselves. The implication for family therapists suggests that helping youth develop a repertoire of active and passive coping skills and helping youth learn when to apply various strategies is warranted. Family therapists may also consider attending to attachment, locus of control, and self-esteem.

The second notable finding of this study is the positive correlation between the use of risky behavior as a strategy for coping with stress and psychological difficulties. As expected, the greater one's use of risky behavior, the greater the psychological difficulty. This finding is consistent with other studies (Fergusson et al. 2002; Lahey et al. 2005). Some of these risky coping strategies may be considered maladaptive such as hitting, arguing with others and self-harming. It is understood from Lazarus and Folkman's (1984) theory that any particular strategy is not inherently good or bad because it depends on the person's situation; that is, the person's appraisal of the stress and of the resources available, including his or her ability to cope. However, risky behaviors may result in harm to self or others and might be considered inherently maladaptive. It is possible that some youth accessing residential and day programs were never taught, nor learned, effective coping strategies. Given that many of these youth may have experienced adversity in childhood, it is plausible that youth may have attachment issues with caregivers (Sroufe 2005), which is known to affect a child's ability to self-regulate their emotions (Compas et al. 2014) and also affect the development of effective coping behaviors (Kraiij et al. 2003).

Bowlby's (1969) seminal work on attachment and internal working models may bring understanding to youth in this population who may believe that they are incapable of modifying themselves or changing their environment. Piko (2001) found that youth who used risky coping strategies fell into a cycle of avoidance and perceived this behavior as sensation-seeking, not as coping, thus failing to recognize the harm the behaviors may cause. Thus, for family therapists, facilitating the development of a range of strategies and facilitating the development of insight in the youth and family members may be beneficial. This finding has implications for building coping skills and resiliency for youth but also for engaging these youth in a therapeutic context. Since some of the strategies youth employ may have been learned, the whole family may benefit from treatment designed to expand the repertoire of strategies. Further exploration of this topic may help professionals understand specific needs with regard to adolescents with EBD and the influence these issues may have on coping and adaptation for youth accessing intensive treatment in residential or day settings.

One surprising finding was that passive/depressive strategies were not associated with psychological difficulties. It seems intuitive that youth who report crying and giving up on the situation as strategies commonly employed when dealing with stress would report greater psychological difficulties. However, this finding may be viewed with the lens provided by Lazarus and Folkman (1984) who suggested that strategies in and of themselves generally do not indicate positive or negative outcomes. It may be that accepting certain situations as stressful could be adaptive for some stressors in certain situations for certain people.

Implications for Practice

When considering the findings in the context of family therapy, it seems important for therapists to begin the work by seeking to understand concerns and solutions from their clients' perspectives (Bogo 2006). Healthy family relationships may be important for modeling effective coping and maintaining coping strategies. Therefore, it is important to include parents or other significant adults in the therapeutic process. Family therapists may consider helping the caregivers to develop and model a range of strategies, help them to socialize and shape their children's coping strategies, and in particular help children to develop a range of strategies. Thus, while the youth is accessing residential care, a parallel process of engaging families in the home can occur simultaneously (see Chaps. 7 and 14). Some of these youth may not have a healthy relationship with an adult who can provide guidance for managing stress and act as a role model (Rabley et al. 2014) and having a positive relationship with an adult has been shown to protect youth from adverse outcomes (Masten 2006). Thus, linking these youth with an informal mentor who has regular and frequent contact with the youth should be considered in cases where no such person exists in the youths' network. A mentor could help youth develop a repertoire of strategies and help youth analyze their effectiveness in the moment rather than waiting for the next appointment.

From a strengths' based perspective, much of the family therapy with these youth could be devoted to focusing on positive interactions and reviewing positive coping; however, these youth also have considerable internalizing and externalizing problems and employing intervention strategies that target these behaviors may also be warranted. Lochman and Wells (2003) targeted both parents and children in a classroom-based intervention for children with aggressive behaviors. The program, which included a cognitive-behavioral component for children, was found to produce long-term changes in processing social information, locus of control, temperament, and their perceptions of parental consistency (parents received behavioral training) (Lochman and Wells 2003). Most relevant to the current study were decreases in risky coping strategies that were then associated with decreased psychopathology. Similarly, Kowalenko et al. (2005), used a school-based group intervention to address depressive symptoms in adolescents also using a cognitive-behavioral model addressing "thinking and feeling, challenging unrealistic thinking, realistic thinking in the face of conflict, social skills training, recognizing achievement and rewarding self, learning assertiveness skills, dealing with conflict, interpersonal negotiation skills and problem solving" (Kowalenko et al. 2005, p. 500). Those offered the program had statistically significant decreases in depressive symptoms and improvements in active coping skills (as well as decreases in non-productive coping) as compared to a waitlist control group (Kowalenko et al. 2005). In terms of interventions specific to conduct disorder, three approaches, Brief Strategic Family Therapy, Multi-Systemic Therapy, and Functional Family Therapy, have been shown to be effective (see Chap. 11 for a review). Using such strategies, family therapists could consider building resiliency in youth with EBD for treatment of current disorders and to equip them with the coping skills to manage future adversity.

In fact, several family therapy strategies and interventions have been linked to improved outcomes for youth and their families that should be considered for this population. Steinberg et al. (1997) revealed that child-focused family therapy was effective for reducing parent-reported child behavior problems and depression—addressing these two symptoms may be particularly important for these youth with severe EBD. Similarly, family psychoeducation for families of children and youth with mood disorders was shown to improve family climate (Fristad et al. 1998) which may be essential for creating a climate for therapeutic change. In this family therapy protocol, there were emphases on the development of cohesion among family members and awareness of mood disorders. Another potential family therapy intervention that could have significant impacts for this population post-discharge is home-based family therapy (Thompson et al. 2007; Zarski and Fluharty 1992) in which family therapists first build an alliance with the youth, which then facilitates the building of a shared alliance among family members. These family therapy strategies could be harnessed to help youth develop and increase their repertoire of active or functional coping strategies which in the present study was associated with decreased psychological difficulties and decreased interpersonal difficulties.

Implications for Research

There are implications for research in family therapy. The small but significant results this study contributes to the body of research in the mental health field suggest several avenues for further clinical research (see Chap. 20). Further exploration of the relationship between coping and motivation to change would be useful to better understand adolescents accessing residential treatment and their needs. Better understanding the way in which youth desire and need support will help professionals create adequate intervention/prevention programs. In the future, investigators might explore longitudinally the effect of teaching youth a range of coping strategies with guidance for flexibly using them on perceived emotional difficulties and interpersonal problem severity. Also, investigators should explore the effect of establishing a supportive mentor for youth on mental health outcomes. The development of a supportive mentor would require establishment of long-term, healthy relationships between youth and a supportive adult who can model various strategies for coping. Understanding an individual's psychological difficulties and interpersonal problems may inform the development of an effective coping strategy toolkit along with building the necessary resources that can be one aim of family therapy. Another direction for future clinical research would be to discover which of the family therapy strategies reviewed above or combination of strategies is most effective for assisting youth in developing adaptive coping strategies and improving overall health.

There are also implications for clinical research in residential settings. The reliance on self-reported measures permitted youth to interpret their own coping behaviors and psychological and interpersonal statuses. This methodology appears to be feasible for this population as supported by the response rate of 64%. Youth reported many risky strategies alongside active and passive ones. They also reported significant difficulties, both psychological and interpersonal. Many of these youth with significant EBD engaged in this project.

Although this study makes important contributions to the mental health field in terms of support seeking and the difficulties experienced by youth with EBD, the results should be interpreted with a view to the study's limitations. Sample size, social desirability, and a lack of self-awareness could have potentially had an impact on the findings. Recruitment in this research study was affected by a few factors. The multistep recruitment process may have created barriers to participation. Following ethical principles, particularly with respect to privacy, agency staff members were required to initiate contact to determine if the youth's name/contact could be given to the research assistants. This step may have placed added burden on agencies that are already strapped for resources. It is also common for some of these youth with EBD to be involved in the child welfare system, thus the child welfare workers were contacted (whom are also working under enormously stressful conditions).

Also, the culture and specific youth characteristics within some settings may have had an impact on engaging youth. For example, at one site for male adolescents, recruitment was very low. These youth were extraordinarily difficult to engage at all and were not motivated by the gift card. The inability for researchers to engage youth at this site affected the gender balance of the study. In previous research with five similar sites, the sample included 75% males (Preyde et al. 2011a) versus the 30% included in this chapter. The overall relatively small sample size ($N = 30$) may be appropriate when considering the small percentage of youth who access residential and day treatment; however, the small sample size was a limitation for some statistical analyses and the representativeness of the sample. Nonetheless, this study presents useful results that amplify the need for further inquiry on adolescents with EBD and their coping with stress. Those who conduct this type of research in a treatment setting often face similar problems in terms of making sure they have a sample large enough to have sufficient power in the statistical analysis. One suggestion for increasing the sample size is to pool data from a number of similar programs. As described in Chaps. 3 and 15 of this book, the Outdoor Behavioral Healthcare Council has begun doing this across various wilderness therapy programs, which has provided that group with large data sets that have been used to increase the power of related statistical analyses.

Conclusion

The youth in this study reported significant levels of difficulties, both psychological and interpersonal, and many reported using risky coping strategies. To understand their experiences, youth completed questionnaires for which they rated the intensity of their own psychological difficulties and interpersonal difficulties, and they rated the frequency of employing various coping strategies. In research, there is always a concern that participants are afraid to provide candid responses for fear of potential consequences, such as being perceived negatively by others or that penalties will be applied (e.g., reduced privileges if staff find out that the youth employed risky strategies to cope such as using drugs). That is, social desirability may affect the way youth complete self-rated measures. There is also a concern that youth with EBD may not be able to read social cues as accurately as their unaffected counterparts and may have other awareness deficits (Landrum et al. 2003) that could influence their ability to rate their experiences. At the same time, it is important to gain youths' perceptions because it is their reality. Moreover, the youth in this study did endorse a number of risky behaviors suggesting that many responses may not have been overly affected by social desirability. Thus, it is important to keep in mind that this study is about youths' perceptions of their difficulties and how they are related to various types of coping strategies they endorsed using.

In this chapter's study, it was demonstrated that youth with EBD who accessed residential and day treatment programs reported using a wide range of coping strategies. Moreover, increased use of active coping strategies was found to be associated with decreased psychological difficulties, and increased use of risky strategies was found to be associated with increased psychological difficulties. Surprisingly, there was no association between the use of passive/depressive coping strategies and psychological difficulties. Finally, only increased use of active coping strategies was associated with decreased interpersonal difficulties. Further clinical research is needed to explore whether family therapy can serve as an effective avenue for the development of active coping strategies in youth and their families, and whether employing these active coping strategies would result in improved clinical and interpersonal well-being.

Acknowledgements The authors are grateful to the youth who participated in the study and took the time to share their personal challenges and experiences. We also have great appreciation for the staff that facilitated the study.

References

Ainsworth, M. D. S., Blehar, M., Waters, E., & Wall, S. (1978). *Patterns of attachment*. Hillsdale, NJ: Erlbaum.

Aldridge, A., & Levine, K. (2001). *Surveying the social world*. Philadelphia: Open University Press.

Angold, A., & Costello, E. J. (1995). Developmental epidemiology. *Epidemiology Review, 17*, 74–82.

Auerbach, R. P., & Ho, M. R. (2012). A Cognitive-interpersonal model of adolescent depression: The impact of family conflict and depression-genic cognitive styles. *Journal of Clinical & Adolescent Psychology, 41*(6), 792–802. doi:10.1080/15374416.2012.727760

Baker, A. J. L., Kurland, D., Curtis, P., Alexander, G., & Papa-Lentini, C. (2007). Mental health and behavioral problems of youth in the child welfare system: Residential treatment centers compared to therapeutic foster care in the Odyssey Project population. *Child Welfare, 86*, 97–123.

Bandura, A. (1977). *Social learning theory*. Englewood Cliffs, NJ: Prentice Hall.

Barkham, M., Hardy, G. E., & Startup, M. (1994). The structure, validity, and clinical relevance of the Inventory of Interpersonal Problems. *British Journal of Medical Psychobiology, 67*(2), 171–185.

Barendregt, C. S., Van Der Laan, A. M., Bongers, I. L., & Van Nieuwenhuizen, Ch. (2015). Stability and change in subjective quality of life of adolescents in secure residential care. *The Journal of Forensic Psychiatry & Psychology, 26*(4), 493–509.

Beck, A. T., Ward, C. H., Mendelson, M., Mock, J., & Erbaugh, J. (1961). An inventory for measuring depression. *Archives of General Psychiatry, 4*, 561–571.

Beck, A. T., Steer, R. A., & Carbin, M. G. (1988). Psychometric properties of the Beck depression inventory: Twenty-five years of evaluation. *Clinical Psychology Review, 8*(1), 77–100.

Ben-Zur, H. (2003). Happy adolescents: Subjective well-being, internal resources, and parental factors. *Journal of Youth and Adolescence, 32*, 67–79.

Bogo, M. (2006). *Social work practice: Concepts, processes, and interviewing*. New York: Columbia University Press.

Bowlby, J. (1969). Attachment and loss: Attachment (Vol. 1). New York: Basic.

Briggs-Gowan, M. J., Owens, P. L., Schwab-Stone, M. E., Leventhal, J. M., Leaf, P. J., & Horwitz, S. M. (2003). Persistence of psychiatric disorders in pediatric settings. *Journal of the American Academy of Child and Adolescent Psychiatry, 42*(11), 1360–1369.

Carver, C. S. (1997). You want to measure coping but your protocol's too long: Consider the Brief COPE. *International Journal of Behavioral Medicine, 4*, 92–100.

Carver, C. S., Scheier, M. F., & Weintraub, J. K. (1989). Assessing coping strategies: A theoretically based approach. *Journal of Personality and Social Psychology, 56*(2), 267.

Cheng, C. (2001). Assessing coping flexibility in real-life and laboratory settings: A multimethod approach. *Journal of Personality and Social Psychology, 80*(5), 814–830.

Child Welfare League of America. (2005). *The Odyssey Project: A descriptive and prospective study of children and youth in residential group care and therapeutic foster care*. Washington, D.C.: Author.

Cloutier, P., Kennedy, A., & Glennie, E. (2008). *Coping behaviours and intensity of non-suicidal self-harm in Canadian adolescents presenting to emergency mental health services*. Abstract from the 3rd Annual Meeting of the International Society for the Study of Self-Injury (ISSS), Harvard University, Cambridge, MA.

Compas, B. E. (1987). Coping with stress during childhood and adolescence. *Psychological Bulletin, 101*(3), 393–403.

Compas, B. E., Connor-Smith, J. K., Saltzman, H., Thomsen, A., & Wadsworth, M. E. (2001). Coping with stress during childhood and adolescence: Problems, progress and potential theory and research. *Psychological Bulletin, 127*(1), 87–127.

Compas, B. E., Jaser, S. S., Dunbar, J. P., Watson, K. H., Bettis, A. H., ... & Williams, E. K. (2014). Coping and emotion regulation for childhood to early adulthood: Points of convergence and divergence. *Australian Journal of Psychology, 66*(2), 71–81.

Connor, D. F., Doerfler, L. A., Toscano, P. F., Volungis, A. M., & Steingard, R. J. (2004). Characteristics of children and adolescents admitted to a residential treatment center. *Journal of Child and Family Studies, 13,* 497–510.

Costello, E. J., Mustillo, S., Erkanli, A., Keeler, G., & Angold, A. (2003). Prevalence and development of psychiatric disorders in childhood and adolescence. *Archives of General Psychiatry, 60*(8), 837–844.

DiCroce, M., Preyde, M., Flaherty, S., Waverly, K., Karki-Niejadlik, N., & Kuczynski, L. (2016). Therapeutic engagement of adolescents with emotional and behavioral disorders. *Child and Adolescent Social Work Journal, 33*(3), 259–271.

Dumont, M., & Provost, M. A. (1999). Resilience in adolescents: Protective role of social support, coping strategies, self-esteem, and social activities on experience of stress and depression. *Journal of Youth and Adolescence, 28*(3), 343–363.

Eisenberg, N., Fabes, R. A., & Guthrie, I. (1997). Coping with stress: The role of regulation and development. In J. N. Sandler & S. A. Wolchik (Eds.), *Handbook of children's coping with common stressors: Linking theory, research, and intervention* (pp. 41–70). New York: Plenum.

Fergusson, D. M., Horwood, L. J., & Swain-Campbell, J. B. W. (2002). Cannabis use and psychosocial adjustment in adolescence and young adulthood. *Addiction, 97*(9), 1123–1135.

Fox, N. A., Henderson, H. A., Marshall, P. J., Nichols, K. E., & Ghera, M. A. (2005). Behavioral inhibition: Linking biology and behavior within a developmental framework. *Annual Review of Psychology, 56,* 235–262.

Fristad, M., Gavazzi, S., & Soldano, K. (1998). Multi-Family Psychoeducation Groups for childhood mood disorders: A program description and preliminary efficacy data. *Contemporary Family Therapy, 20*(3), 385–402.

Furtado, J., Tran, A., Currie, V., & Preyde, M. (2016). Exploration of coping strategies of youth accessing residential and day treatment programs. *Contemporary Family Therapy, 38,* 108. doi:10.1007/s10591-015-9372-4

Garnefski, N., Van Den Kommer, T., Kraaij, V., Teerds, J., Legerstee, J., & Onstein, E. (2002). The relationship between cognitive emotion regulation strategies and emotional problems: Comparison between a clinical and a non-clinical sample. *European Journal of Personality, 16,* 403–420. doi:10.1002/per.458

Goodman, R., Meltzer, H., & Bailey, V. (1998). The strengths and difficulties questionnaire: A pilot study on the validity of the self-report version. *European Child and Adolescent Psychiatry, 7,* 125–130.

Greve, W., Enzmann, D., & Hosser, D. (2001). The stabilization of self-esteem among incarcerated adolescents: Accommodative and immunizing processes. *International Journal of Offender Therapy and Comparative Criminology, 45*(6), 749–768.

Griffith, A. K., Ingram, S. D., Barth, R. P., Trout, A. L., Hurley, K. D., Thompson, R. W., et al. (2009). The family characteristics of youth entering a residential care program. *Residential Treatment for Children and Youth, 26,* 135–150.

Gunnar, M. R., & Cheatham, C. L. (2003). Brain and behavior interface: Stress and the developing brain. *Infant Mental Health Journal, 24,* 195–211.

Herman-Stahl, M., & Peterson, A. C. (1996). The protective role of coping and social resources for depressive symptoms among young adolescents. *Journal of Youth and Adolescence, 25*(6), 733–753.

Health Canada's Research Ethics Board Ethics Review of Research Involving Humans. (2009). *Administrative Policy and Procedures Manual*. Retrieved from: http://www.hc-sc.gc.ca/index-eng.php

Horowitz, L. M., Rosenberg, S. E., Baer, B. A., Ureno, G., & Villasenor, V. S. (1988). Inventory of interpersonal problems: Psychometric properties and clinical applications. *Journal of Consulting and Clinical Psychobiology, 56,* 885–892.

Jang, K. L., Thordarson, D. S., Stein, M. B., Cohan, S. L., & Taylor, S. (2007). Coping styles and personality: A biometric analysis. *Anxiety Stress Coping, 20*(1), 17–24.

Kennedy, A., Cloutier, P., Glennie, E., Gray, C. (2009, June). *Coping in youth who present to pediatric emergency mental health services.* Poster presented at the Canadian Psychological Association's 70th Annual Convention, Montréal, Québec.

Kessler, R. C., Berglund, P., Demler, O., Jin, R., Merikangas, K. R., & Walters, E. E. (2005). Lifetime prevalence and age-of-onset distributions of DSM-IV disorders in the National Comorbidity Survey Replication. *Archives of General Psychiatry, 62,* 593–602.

Kowalenko, N., Rapee, R., Simmons, J., Wignall, A., Hoge, R., Whitefield, K., et al. (2005). Short-term effectiveness of a school based early intervention program for adolescent depression. *Clinical Child Psychology and Psychiatry, 10,* 493–507.

Kraaij, V., Garnefski, N., de Wilde, E. J., Dijkstra, A., Gebhardt, W., Maes, S., & ter Doest, L. (2003). Negative life events and depressive symptoms in late adolescence: Bonding and cognitive coping as vulnerability factors. *Journal of Youth and Adolescence, 32*(3), 185–193. doi:0047-2891/03/0600-0185/0

Lahey, B. B., Loeber, R., Burke, J. D., & Applegate, B. (2005). Predicting future antisocial personality disorder in males from a clinical assessment in childhood. *Journal of Consulting and Clinical Psychology, 73*(3), 389–399.

Landrum, T. J., Tankersley, M., & Kauffman, J. M. (2003). What's special about special education for students with emotional or behavioral disorders? *Journal of Special Education, 37,* 148–156.

Lazarus, R. S., & Folkman, S. (1984). *Stress, appraisal and coping.* New York: Springer.

Lavee, Y., McCubbin, H. I., & Olson, D. H. (1987). The effects of stressful life events and transitions on family functioning and well-being. *Journal of Marriage and the Family, 49,* 857–873.

Lipschitz-Elhawi, R., & Itzhaky, H. (2005). Social support, mastery, self-esteem and individual adjustment among at-risk youth. *Child & Youth Care Forum, 34*(5), 329–346.

Lochman, J. E., & Wells, K. C. (2003). Effectiveness of the coping power program and of classroom intervention with aggressive children: Outcomes at a 1-year follow-up. *Behavior Therapy, 34*(4), 493–515.

Masten, A. (2006). Promoting resilience in development: A general framework for systems of care. In R. Flynn, P. Dudding, & J. Barber (Eds.), *Promoting resilience in child welfare* (pp. 3–13). Ottawa, ON: University of Ottawa Press.

Martin, J., Cloutier, P. F., Levesque, C., Bureau, J. F., Lafontaine, M. F., & Nixon, M. K. (2013). Psychometric properties of the functions and addictive features scales of the Ottawa self-injury inventory: A preliminary investigation using a university sample. *Psychological Assessment, 25*(3), 1013–1018.

Piko, B. (2001). Gender differences and strategies in adolescent's ways of coping. *The Psychological Record, 51,* 223–235.

Plunkett, S. W., & Henry, C. S. (1999). The parent-adolescent relationship: Sociological perspectives (Part II). *Sociological Inquiry, 69*(4), 599–620.

Power, T. G. (2004). Stress and coping in childhood: The parents' role. *Parenting: Science and Practice, 4,* 271–317

Preyde, M., Frensch, K., Cameron, G., White, S., Penny, R., & Lazure, K. (2011a). Long-term outcomes of children and youth accessing residential or intensive home-based treatment: Three year follow up. *Journal of Child and Family Studies, 20*(5), 660–668.

Preyde, M., Frensch, K., Cameron, G., Hazineh, L., & Riosa, P. B. (2011b). Mental health outcomes of children and youth accessing residential programs or a home-based alternative. *Social Work in Mental Health, 9*(1), 1–21.

Rabley, S., Preyde, M., & Gharabaghi, K. (2014). A survey of adolescents' perceptions of their relationships with nonparental caregivers in group home settings: An attachment perspective. *Children and Youth Services Review, 40*, 61–70.

Rosman, B. L., & Baker, L. (1988). The "psychosomatic family" reconsidered: Diabetes in context —A reply. *Journal of Marital and Family Therapy, 14*, 125–132.

Ross, S., & Heath, N. (2002). A study of the frequency of self-mutilation in a community sample of adolescents. Journal of Youth and Adolescence, 31(1), 67–77.

Rutter, M. (1983). Stress, coping, and development: Some issues and some questions. In N. Garmezy & M. Rutter (Eds.), *Stress, coping, and development in children* (pp. 1–41). Baltimore, MD: Johns Hopkins University Press.

Rutter, M. (2003). Categories, dimensions, and the mental health of children and adolescents. *Annals of the New York Academy of Science, 1008*, 11–21.

Singer, A., Glenwick, D., & Danyko, S. (2000). Stress responses of adolescents in residential treatment: A research note. *Residential Treatment for Children & Youth, 17*(4), 67–82.

Skinner, E. A., & Zimmer-Gembeck, M. J. (2007). The development of coping. *Annual Review of Psychology, 58*, 119–144.

Sroufe, L. A. (2005). Attachment and development: A perspective, longitudinal study from birth to adulthood. *Attachment & Human Development, 7*(4), 349–367.

Steinberg, S. J., Davila, J., & Fincham, F. (2006). Adolescent marital expectations and romantic experiences: Associations with perceptions about parental conflict and adolescent attachment security. *Journal of Youth and Adolescence, 35*(3), 333–348.

Steinberg, E. B., Sayger, T. V., & Szykula, S. A. (1997). The effects of strategic and behavioral family therapies on child behavior and depression. *Contemporary Family Therapy, 19*(4), 537–551.

Thompson, S. J., Bender, K., Lantry, J., & Flynn, P. M. (2007). Treatment engagement: Building therapeutic alliance in home-based treatment with adolescents and their families. *Contemporary Family Therapy, 29*(1), 39–55.

Waddell, C., Offord, D. R., Shepherd, C. A., Hua, J. M., & McEwan, K. (2002). Child psychiatric epidemiology and Canadian public policy-making: The state of the science and the art of the possible. *Canadian Journal of Psychiatry, 47*(9), 825–832.

Wang, X., Trivedi, R., Treiber, F., & Snieder, H. (2005). Genetic and environmental influences on anger expression, John Henryism, and stressful life events: The Georgia Cardiovascular Twin Study. *Psychosomatic Medicine, 67*(1), 16–23.

Zarski, J., & Fluharty, L. (1992). Treating emotionally disturbed youth: A comparison of home-based and outpatient interventions. *Contemporary Family Therapy, 14*(4), 335–350.

Zimmer-Gembeck, M. J., & Locke, E. M. (2007). The socialization of adolescent coping: Relationships at home and school. *Journal of Adolescence, 30*, 1–16.

Author Biographies

Michèle Preyde Ph.D., Dr. Preyde's research is centered on three main themes: the psychosocial impact of mental and physical illness, practitioner–researcher collaboration, and intervention effectiveness research. Dr. Preyde engages in collaborative research efforts with clinicians including family therapists, physicians, social workers, nurses, and psychologists. Her research activity in children's mental health includes a focus on children and youth who have accessed intensive mental health treatment, the short- and long-term outcomes, family dynamics, the continuum of care in the community, and access to social support. The hope is that this research may lead to improvements in the long-term adaptation of children and youth with serious emotional and behavioral disorders.

Jessica Furtado BASc, MSW Candidate completed her undergraduate degree in Child, Youth, and Family Studies at the University of Guelph. During this time, she completed an honors thesis under the supervision of Dr. Michèle Preyde exploring bullying and victimization of adolescents in residential treatment centers. She has recently completed her Master of Social Work at the University of Toronto, continuing her focus in the Children and their Families stream, and conducting clinical and research work in pediatric rehabilitation. Currently, Jessica is the Social Work Fellow at the Hincks-Dellcrest Center, completing advanced training in child and family therapy.

Amy Tran BA Honours, graduated from The University of Guelph with a major in psychology. Her research explored how students with mental illness cope with stigma-related stress. During her time in Guelph, she was actively involved in the community as an advocate for mental health by participating in several programs designed to ease the student experience for individuals with mental health concerns. She is currently attending The University of Windsor in the Child Clinical Psychology program where her current research focus explores how mobile media use by children (e.g., smart phones, tablets, etc.) influence parent–child interactions and developmental outcomes in youth. Amy is also interested in how individuals with mental illness use the Internet as well as interventions designed to encourage help-seeking.

Victoria Currie M.Sc. Candidate completed her undergraduate degree at the University of Guelph and completed a thesis under the supervision of Dr. Michèle Preyde, conducting research with adolescents in residential treatment centers/facilities. Since then, Victoria has become a registered Speech-Language Pathologist and is pursuing doctoral studies at the University of Toronto with the goal to become a clinician scientist in the health care field. Victoria has already had success in this regard and has seen some of her work published in an international journal.

Chapter 23
Communication as a Positive Relationship Outcome with Families Participating in a Therapeutic Wilderness Program

Christine Norton and Katie Liermann

Chapter Highlights

- Phenomenological research is a useful approach for collecting and analyzing in-depth qualitative data from interviews and surveys to examine connectedness, trust, and communication in families that participated in an Outward Bound Intercept course.
- Therapeutic wilderness programs can be a beneficial intervention for families struggling with communication .
- Providing adolescent and parents with communication tools is shown to be effective in improving family communication.
- Parental involvement in a therapeutic wilderness programs adds to the effectiveness and positive family outcomes.
- Therapeutic wilderness programs can diminish adolescent's negative behaviors such as truancy, drug use, anger, and low motivation.

When youth experience negative family dynamics, such as poor communication, anger, and distrust they may require intervention through family therapy. Though a wide range of systemic family therapy interventions exist (Cottrell and Boston 2002), research has shown that therapeutic wilderness programs in particular can improve both youth and family functioning (Harper and Cooley 2007; Harper and Russell 2008). According to Norton (2007), there is a continuum of therapeutic

C. Norton (✉)
LCSW, School of Social Work, Texas State University,
San Marcos, TX 78666, USA
e-mail: cn19@txstate.edu

K. Liermann
LMSW, School of Social Work, San Jose State University,
1 Washington Square, San Jose, CA 95192, USA
e-mail: kdliermann@gmail.com

© Springer International Publishing AG 2017
J.D. Christenson and A.N. Merritts (eds.), *Family Therapy with Adolescents in Residential Treatment*, Focused Issues in Family Therapy,
DOI 10.1007/978-3-319-51747-6_23

wilderness interventions, from experience-based therapeutic wilderness programs (such as the one described in this chapter), which include nonclinical staff, to Outdoor Behavioral Healthcare (OBH), which involves clinical staff administering therapeutic interventions, specifically targeting issues identified on a client's treatment plan (see Chaps. 3, 8, 15, and 16). Overall programming, field staff training, and the type of youth served is often similar, and both types of programs play a key role in serving youth and families, but key differences as identified above should be noted. Though the program reported on in this chapter is not a traditional Outdoor Behavioral Healthcare program, the risk factors of youth in this program are similar to those in OBH programs (Norton 2010); therefore, related research is deemed applicable and relevant to the larger category of OBH research.

Regardless of the level of clinical services provided, most therapeutic wilderness programs utilize adventure-based activities in the outdoors to implement therapeutic interventions for adolescents who are struggling with behavior issues, as seen by parents, schools, and/or the courts (Berman and Davis-Berman 2008). Traditionally, it is has been thought that these programs only treat the adolescent who attends the wilderness program (Harper and Cooley 2007). In fact, it was not until the late 1980s that wilderness programs saw the opportunity to involve the family in the adolescent's recovery (Bandoroff and Scherer 1994). However, research on therapeutic wilderness programs has begun to show the need for "more intentional and direct involvement of families in the change process … to help families address issues preventing effective family functioning" (Harper et al. 2007, p. 126).

Therefore, more wilderness programs are involving the entire family system, such as Outward Bound's Intercept program for struggling teens, which incorporates the family into the adolescent's experience (Outward Bound 2013a). Every year approximately 130 families participate in the Intercept program at the Voyageur Outward Bound School in Ely, Minnesota. Intercept is a 28-day therapeutic wilderness program for struggling teens and their families. Preprogram data collected show that families participate in this program because they are concerned about the loss of trust, poor communication, and/or other high-risk behaviors they are experiencing with their children. Though significant research demonstrates the positive impact of therapeutic wilderness interventions on youth functioning (Clark et al. 2004; Norton et al. 2014), more research is needed on the impact on the parent/child relationship and how families are functioning once they leave a program.

This chapter is intended, in part, to fulfill the need for more research by providing the results of a research study that examined the positive relationship outcomes that emerged between parent(s) and their adolescent child after participation in the Outward Bound Intercept program. A secondary purpose of this chapter is to provide an example of qualitative research methods that can be effectively used to study adolescents and outcomes in residential settings. In this particular study, a phenomenological approach was used to study nine families who had participated in the program. A basic discussion of phenomenological qualitative research methods is included to help orient the reader and provide some basic information on how to conduct this type of study in residential programs. However, before discussing the method and the results, an overview of the literature on this type of intervention will be provided.

Therapeutic Wilderness Programs as a Family Systems Intervention

After a family makes the decision to change their family dynamics by sending an adolescent child to Outward Bound, the Intercept program staff first work with the adolescent to create goals for the expedition that are transferable to home life, gain insight as to why they were sent to this program, and what they and their parents can change to create a more positive home life (Norton 2007). Though it is the adolescent that participates in the wilderness expedition, the parent plays an important role in the program's outcomes as well. While the adolescent is engaged in the wilderness program, it is the parents' responsibility to evaluate their parenting style and relationship with their child, by completing weekly homework assignments, writing a letter to their child and participating in a Parent/Guardian Seminar at the end of the wilderness phase of the program. The letter is guided by restorative, strengths-based questions to help the parent reflect on what they love about their child and what they hope for in their relationship with them upon their return home. It is given to the youth the night before youth are reunited with their families.

The strategy of using letter writing in family therapy is not a new one. Christenson and Miller (2016) discussed how letter writing can be used to slow down the conversation between parents and adolescents and provide an opportunity for practicing skills that improve communication in families. They also argued that letter writing among family members can promote a more systemic view of the family in which members can take responsibility for their actions and develop a greater acceptance of the need for positive change in the family system. Chapter 3 in this book also contains a discussion of how providers in one particular Outdoor Behavioral Healthcare program used letter writing within a narrative framework to promote change in a program participant and his parents.

Along with letter writing, during the Parent/Guardian Seminar, parents and child have a conference to determine what positive changes they would like to sustain in the home environment. The Intercept instructors work with the family to transfer learning that has occurred over the past month for both the parents and the child. This conversation includes setting goals and expectations upon their arrival home (Norton 2007). Intercept instructors who are trained in family systems theory facilitate this therapeutic conversation, but are not licensed family therapists. The conversation is intended to help families connect, to provide appropriate space for autonomy, and to help families work on regulating their emotions by applying new skills. It is also a time to coach the family in how to use the new skills they learned in the program upon their return home. This model of family intervention is similar to Doherty's (1995) family life education approach, which "provide[s] family members with information, skills, experiences, or resources intended to strengthen, improve or enrich their family experience" (National Council on Family Relations 2014, p. 11). Often, these conversations lead families to be more open to the idea of participating in formal family therapy upon their return home.

Prior Research on Family Involvement in Outdoor Behavioral Healthcare

In addition to youth functioning, research on wilderness programs (i.e., OBH) has also looked at the impact and role of the family in treatment, as well as impact on attachment. Many wilderness programs have a requirement of family involvement in the treatment process and research has shown mixed results on the impact of wilderness therapy on family functioning (Harper and Cooley 2007; Harper and Russell 2008). The evaluation of a one day pretreatment and one day posttreatment multifamily program, in addition to wilderness therapy, showed significant impacts on youth's behaviors post-discharge; however, it had limited impact on family functioning (Harper and Cooley 2007). A mixed methods study looking at the involvement of family and the impact of wilderness on family functioning found only one out of four areas impacted in terms of functioning, yet qualitative interviews revealed families felt a stabilizing effect from wilderness therapy involvement (Harper and Russell 2008). The results from the qualitative interviews in Harper and Russell's (2008) study show how mixed methods research can provide rich data from which to draw broader conclusions (see Chap. 20). These findings point to the complexity of family relationships, further highlighted by research, as described below, showing the mixed impacts of wilderness treatment on attachment in youth participants.

Bettmann (2005) explored the impact of wilderness treatment on youth and parent attachment and found adolescents improved attachment relationships in terms of decreased anger and increased emotional connection; yet, there were also increases in problems of trust or communication with parents at discharge. In a similar study, Bettmann and Tucker (2011) found mixed results in terms of increases in connection, but decreases in trust and communication, as well as both positive and negative growth in attachment with peers. These trends may be reflective of the nature of out-of-home treatment, which makes family involvement difficult due to distance and expense and has the adolescent as the main focus of the treatment. Attachment may also be negatively affected by the high rate of youth who go on to some form of aftercare after participating in OBH. Different than most OBH programs, in which 60% of clients go on to some form of aftercare (Russell and Hendee 1999), most youth attending Outward Bound's Intercept program return home; therefore, the program presents an ideal climate in which to research the impact on family functioning post-program since youth are back in the home environment and the family has more opportunity to use the tools that they gained in the program.

An Introduction to Phenomenological Research

A phenomenological, qualitative approach was used in the study described in this chapter. This was done in order to gain in-depth, descriptive information regarding the lived experiences of families who participate in the Intercept program. One of the reasons why this chapter is included in this book is to provide the reader with a demonstration of the use of this type of research approach in residential settings. Here we provide a brief introduction to phenomenological research for readers who are unfamiliar with this method, which is intended to provide foundational information that will aid in understanding the description of the study below. According to Waters (2016), "the goal of qualitative phenomenological research is to describe a 'lived experience' of a phenomenon" (para. 1). Open-ended interviews, surveys and questionnaires are often used in phenomenological research as a means of collecting qualitative data that highlights the participants' voices and subjective experiences. Though non-generalizable, phenomenological research often yields detailed data from which to analyze emergent themes (Waters 2016). Furthermore, data is collected and analyzed with the purpose of getting at the essential meaning of the experience. According to Waters (2016), "these are essential aspects 'without which the experience would not have been the same,' discovered through a thoughtful engagement with the description of the experience to understand its meaning. The meanings can be implicit, and need to be made explicit with thematic analysis"(para. 4).

Once the data has been collected, phenomenological researchers engage in a process called *abstracting the themes* (Waters 2016). This process entails a detailed content analysis and thematic analysis of all qualitative data that yields both collective themes (those that pertain to the whole sample) and individual themes (those that pertain only to certain individuals). In the study described below, collective themes around communication, trust, and connectedness were identified. These themes revealed the essential meaning of these families lived experiences with the Outward Bound program and its felt impact on family functioning. Both the lead researcher and the co-author of the study reviewed the data for collective themes, as a way of double checking the data, and also utilized negative case (or *deviant*) analysis in which the researcher intentionally looks for outliers in the study data that go against the prevailing evidence in the majority of the data. According to Roller (2016), "This analysis compels the researcher to develop an understanding about why outliers exist, leading to a greater comprehension as to the strengths and limits of the research data" (para. 3). This type of analysis was conducted to increase the trustworthiness and accuracy of the results, both of which are important to attend to when conducting qualitative research. Nevertheless, because the analysis of the data is also subjective, it is once again important to reiterate that it cannot be generalized. For this reason, phenomenological research results add specific, non-generalizable data to the body of knowledge, while identifying important areas for future research.

The Intercept Program Study

Our phenomenological study queried nine families through open-ended pre-post course questionnaires administered to parents one-week prior and 6 months after the program, as well as in-depth phone interviews with parents conducted 3 months post program. Both the questionnaires and the interviews sought to answer the following research questions:

- How has the parent/child relationship been impacted since participating in the Intercept course?
- What, if any, aspects of the Outward Bound Intercept curriculum had a positive impact on the parent/child relationship?

The open-ended questions utilized in the questionnaire and in the qualitative interviews focused on how the parent–adolescent relationship has changed since participating in the Intercept course, especially in regard to communication, trust, and connectedness. Questions asked also examined what aspects of the Intercept course were beneficial in improving the parent–adolescent relationship, with a focus on the specific skills the family has used since participating in the program. The following are a sample of the interview questions asked to the parents who participated in the Outward Bound Intercept course:

- What can you tell me about the improvement in your relationship with your son/daughter in regard to connectedness, trust, and communication?
- What can you tell me about the frustrations that exist in your relationship with your son/daughter in regard to connectedness, trust, and communication?
- What parts of the Intercept curriculum did you find useful?
- What components of the Parent/Guardian Seminar have been helpful in improving the relationship with your son/daughter?

Additional Program Details

This phenomenological study conducted research with families who participated in Outward Bound's Intercept program to better understand the impact of the program on family relationships and communication. Outward Bound is an adventure-based organization that operates in 33 countries around the world, with nine wilderness programs alone in the United States. Every year approximately a quarter of a million youth and adults participate in an Outward Bound course worldwide, with almost 33,000 of those participants attending expeditions in the United States (Outward Bound International 2012). Significant to all Outward Bound courses are wilderness expeditions in which participants move through three phases: (a) training; (b) main expedition; and (c) final expedition. At each phase the group gains more autonomy such as they would in life (e.g., infancy, adolescence, adulthood).

All students also participate in a solo experience where they spend a predetermined amount of time away from the group, supervised by an instructor, in which to reflect on their lives and connect with the natural world. In particular, Outward Bound's Intercept courses for struggling teens believe in the ability of the wilderness to impart confidence and strength to the adolescent, which can become the building blocks for a healthy adulthood experience (Outward Bound 2013a). An Outward Bound Intercept course also includes parent involvement in a three day Parent/Guardian Seminar at the end of the 28-day wilderness expedition. At the Voyageur Outward Bound School the seminar is divided into the following components: (a) facilitated multi-family group discussions on course curriculum and adolescent development; (b) a parent conference with the Intercept instructor that provides parents with information on how their teen performed on the wilderness expedition; (c) group presentations by the students to the parents in which youth show a slide show with photos from their trip and discuss highs and lows; (d) sharing tools they learned to take home and try to help parents experience what they experienced; and, (e) the parent/child conference, a facilitated, therapeutic conversation between parents and their teen. Through these components the parents learn the skills their teen learned and utilized on their wilderness expedition. These skills are related to communication, trust, and other needs specific to each family.

Analysis of Data

All of the parent qualitative survey questions were administered online using San Jose State University Qualtrics survey software and specific steps were taken to systematically analyze the data. The survey data were first coded and analyzed thematically using a constant comparative method of sequential coding (Strauss and Corbin 1990) in which emergent themes were identified. The interview responses were recorded (with consent), transcribed, coded, and thematically analyzed using the same data analysis methods. Consistent with qualitative phenomenological data analysis procedures as described by Creswell (2013), data in the form of participant statements from the questionnaires and interview transcripts were coded and categorized using open, axial, and then selective coding methods. Throughout this process, the researcher became immersed in the data in order to effectively interpret and understand the essential meaning of participants' experiences. To minimize bias, one researcher, who had no contact with the families, also examined the data to assure consistent interpretations across analysts. This particular process was also somewhat described above in the introduction to phenomenological research.

According to Auerbach and Silverstein (2003), it is important to exercise reflexivity when conducting qualitative research through the active self-examination of the researcher's biases and participation in the research process in order to verify the accuracy of the qualitative findings. In this study, the researcher and the second author have also worked as instructors for Outward Bound and value the therapeutic adventure approach. Therefore, it was particularly important for us as the researchers to recognize and own our personal views, values, and biases throughout the research process. We instituted efforts to maximize our plan to elicit parents' views of the therapeutic adventure approach and not impose our values on them. These reflexivity efforts included discussions with other clinical, research, and teaching professionals, keeping notes throughout the research process, and prioritizing an awareness of parents' feedback about the program. Furthermore, a phenomenological explorative research design was selected in order to prevent or restrict the researchers' bias (Groenewald 2004).

Study Findings

This study used open-ended questions on all surveys (preprogram, one-week, and 6-month post-program) and parent interviews at 3-month post intervention. Throughout the multiple sources of qualitative data collected, communication stood out as a positive theme from preprogram to 6-month post-program data, which supports its significance in this research.

Preprogram Survey Themes

Communication and Trust. The preprogram survey highlighted themes of improved communication and trust as desired outcomes of the Intercept course, as evidenced by this parent quote: "I would like to see trust in the relationship. I have lost trust in my son after repeated and compulsive lies to the point I am skeptical about anything that he says." A father expressed comparable frustrations with truthful communication as the root of the problem,

> I would like to see improved communication. I would like for my son to be truthful with us and with everyone so that when we speak to each other it is based on substance rather than something made up...to leave him alone.

The need for open and honest communication was a common theme among parents sending their youth to Outward Bound. Families reported feeling stuck in avoidant or confrontational patterns of communication, which negatively affected levels of trust.

One-Week Post-program Survey Themes

Communication. At one-week post program, the parent survey data specified less argumentative communication, having a common language, and desire of listening to their teen more. One parent commented, "The communication is more open. We have a common language now that helps us understand each other. I think he appreciates what I do for him more and shows it. He says how he feels more often." Another parent reported,

> We are communicating better on both sides. I am more patient as is he. He smiles more. I think we both can see the other's perspective better. We have been using rules for fair-fighting and have been taking time outs (breaks) like we did at Outward Bound.

One area of frustration for several of the parents was comprised of mothers' desire for their sons to be more emotionally expressive. This was revealed several times, as in the following comments: "I wish he would express himself more; let us know what he is feeling and thinking." "He still seems to not want to talk to me and is easily frustrated with much of the communication with me." "I don't know how he really is feeling, but it is not as bad as it was in the past."

Course Components. When asked what the most important components of the Intercept course were, a prevalent theme emerged for parents. They reported that the parent/child conference and workbook were most beneficial for improving their relationship with their teens because it got them involved in their child's treatment process. Parent's thorough attention to the workbook over the course of the month when their teen was in the program helped them be more reflective, as evidenced by this parent quote: "The workbook questions forced me to think through things in advance that I would not have done."

The parent/child conference was significant to parents because of the staff that lead the conference. One parent said, "The leadership is so professional and compassionate. Even though [instructor] was not a counselor, we got so much out of the meeting because she really knew our son." Another parent commented: "Hearing how staff approached issues with [my son], how they helped him develop skills, was beneficial in improving this relationship." Another parent similarly reported,

> The parent/child conference was very beneficial. In particular, there was a[n] un-biased third party facilitating the conversation who was the same individual, the field instructor, that spent the past four weeks with my child; this was someone that my child trusted to be the one facilitating the conversation.

Three-Month Post-program Interview Themes

At 3 months post program, parents were interviewed over the phone. The interviews were transcribed and coded for themes in parent/child relationship and components of the Intercept course that were reported as being beneficial. Again, the main theme that emerged was improved communication, which triangulates the findings from the survey data. Course components that parents found helpful were related to the Parent Seminar weekend, specifically, information on the adolescent brain and the group presentations presented by the teens to the parents.

Communication. Qualitative data collected showed three aspects that contribute to improved communication between the parents and their teen: improved listening, taking *time-outs*, and using specific communication skills taught at Outward Bound. A father stated: "One of the things that is good is that we are both listening, I mean not just [wife] and I but [son] is listening to each other." Another parent reflected on how improved listening creates more understanding in his relationship with his teen,

> I do think it's been [a] helpful thing with our relationship too that I see his side a little bit more than, gosh darn why is he doing this and I think it makes these moments not quite as bad...knowing and understanding on both sides.

Taking time-outs added to improved communication because when family members noticed the conversation spiraling into an argument or that they were not listening to each other, then a time-out was suggested, with the stipulation to come back in a certain timeframe and finish the conversation. Several parents identified this as an important element. The two quotes below show this was the case

(1) It is the idea if you are frustrated or something is bothering [you], step away for a moment and go collect yourself. He [son] use to just storm off sometimes, I mean like slamming doors and all that. Now when he gets upset, he does walk away, but he does it in a much more cool collected way and then able to come back and move forward.

(2) The time-outs have helped out a lot, if one of us feels like the discussion is going in a really negative direction, then one of us will say 'okay, we need to take a break,' and we will come back to this at another time, you know like 15 or 20 min later and that has been really beneficial as well, instead of being angry and saying the same thing over and over again.

Finally, communication skills such as using assertive communication strategies enabled families to work together in solving problems, as per this example

> We communicate a little bit better; I think there is a little less heat in our conversations. I think because of the skills we all learned at the Intercept course on communication have come in handy for us, I think we all fall back on them quite a lot which is awesome, but remembering what we learned, this isn't [the] way we should be digressing into an argument, we should be talking about this conservatively and appropriately, so I think that has been a really great thing. I think that [my son] feels more comfortable speaking his mind... and we are all communicating better. We are more assertive in our communication.

Course Components. Parents reported specific aspects of the Parent Seminar as helpful to their relationships with their teens. These included information they received about the teenage brain and the teen's group presentation to their parents. Learning about adolescent brain development was useful information to parents as they were able to recognize why their teen may be making the choices they make. These two comments speak to the impact of this information on parents' ability to better understand their teens: "His [son] brain isn't working like ours is, but that conversation with [facilitator] to kind of reset us to expectation was very useful."

"When the [facilitator] talked about the teenage brain, I learned how stunningly wonderful it is, even though it is big into risk taking."

The parents were equally impressed with the group presentation and their teens' part in it. One parent said,

> Coming from them and seeing the interaction between them, I don't know it was just really, really moving and it gave me a feeling of unusual camaraderie that...I was sort of unaware that it could exist with teenagers because you hear so much about all the social stuff that goes on with bullying and caddy remarks and heartbreak and people being mean.

Another mother was impressed with her son's role in the group presentation,

> When I sit here and reflect on it when the kids were all presenting together...listening to [my son] stand up in front of that room and talk, I was in tears because he has never been that confident and that assured speaking in front of people and feeling comfortable in his own skin, that was huge I was on the verge of tears multiple times throughout that whole thing...to see that transition in my child.

Six-Month Post-program Survey Themes

Communication. At 6 months post program, parents reported that the communication skills they gained were still useful. They reported continued relationship improvements, such as, increased trust and a better understanding of each other, often supported by the use of time-outs. One parent stated: "We take step backs when emotions run too high. We forgive and try to start anew. We have learned to communicate better, take time- outs, and regroup." Another said: "We have a greater level of honesty and trust. He [son] has taken on more responsibility and I have tried harder to listen and understand his point of view."

However, despite these positive results, there remained frustrations with continued lying and a struggle to get schoolwork completed. One mother said about her son: "He continues to lie to get out of doing something or to get out of trouble." Another parent recognized that her son is trying, but knows that he can do better in his schoolwork: "Still schoolwork, while improved, he still does not put forth his best effort. At least he is now doing enough to get by, but just that."

Course Components. At 6 months post program, parents continued to report that the Intercept course was beneficial because of the parent/child conference. This was once again evidenced by the following comments: "The parent/child conference was helpful, because it forced [my son] to open up to not only his own feelings, but also to see how he affects his family." "The [parent] seminar was helpful, because we were able to share ideas among the parents."

Overall, parents observed the positive impact the experience had on their child, even 6 months later, as measured by the 6-month post-program survey. One parent reflected on this by stating: "What stays with me at this point in time is my respect for what my daughter accomplished on her OB journey, which was so much more than I knew she was capable of." Parents also commented on witnessing an increase in their teens' confidence and the positive impact the wilderness expedition had on their teen. According to parents, youth gained a sense of pride from the physical and emotional rigors of the wilderness expedition, as indicated by this quote, "Looking back, it's a marker for how good he can feel about himself. He gained self-confidence."

Implications of the Findings

This phenomenological study collected multiple sources of qualitative data from parents in order to explore positive relationship outcomes between parent(s) and their adolescent child after a therapeutic wilderness course. Across all of the qualitative data collected, improved family communication emerged as a theme for parents. This remained true immediately after the therapeutic wilderness intervention and was sustained 3 and 6 months later. This is especially positive, as this was a main point of concern for families going into the program. The communication skills the parents found to be beneficial in improving the relationship were having a *common language* and listening to their teen. By demonstrating listening skills, parents began modeling the behavior they want to see in their teen. Parents and teens also learned to communicate more assertively, and take time-outs to manage themselves and better resolve conflict. All of these improvements in communication brought about increased trust and better relationships.

Though this study focused on improvements in family communication and relationships, parents also noticed positive behavioral changes in their teens, similar to findings from other studies showing improvements in youth functioning post-wilderness program (Norton 2008, 2010; Russell 2000). In Russell's (2000) study, adolescents articulated finding success in improving their family relationships, increasing abstinence from drugs and alcohol, and improving performance in school. Likewise, in Norton's (2008, 2010) research, similar positive results were found in school improvement, improved family relationships and increased self-confidence in the teens. This study validated this prior research; however, more research needs to be conducted on youth functioning following a therapeutic wilderness experience.

This study also examined which aspects of the program helped improve positive relationship outcomes within the family. In this study, the families found the skills taught during the expedition and the Parent Seminar contributed to improvements in family relationships. The parallel process of parents and teens learning the same skills and tools was highly beneficial for creating lasting change in the family system. The group presentations at the end also gave youth an opportunity to teach some of these skills to their parents, taking a leadership role in improving family functioning. Furthermore, though the wilderness intervention targeted the teen as the main participant, the program found ways for parents to be fully engaged in the process as well. The parents spent the first 25 days of the program writing in the workbook in order to reflect on their relationship with their teens and address their parenting style. Then, they attended the Parent Seminar to experientially learn and practice the interpersonal skills their teens were taught. In many cases, this learning came directly from their teen and the Outward Bound staff, which was very empowering. The final parent/child conference provided an opportunity to bring these skills together to have a conversation with other families about how to use what was learned in the program at home. The outcomes of this study reflect the continued use of these skills at home.

Limitations

The families in this study reported improved family communication and enhanced quality of their relationships with each other. This qualitative study offers descriptions of the ways in which these families were impacted by their partici- pation in the therapeutic wilderness program. The study gained parent perspectives on changes in the family system, and found that these changes were sustained 6 months post program. However, consistent with qualitative findings, especially with such a small sample size, we cannot provide causal connections regarding the findings, and we cannot generalize the findings to other populations or even to other families who participate in Outward Bound Intercept courses. Additional studies of this nature are needed to clarify and extend our findings, and studies of a quanti- tative nature will provide the causality and generalizability so important for a complete picture of the efficacy and importance of therapeutic wilderness programs for youth-at-risk and their families (see Chap. 20). Furthermore, future studies should also include the adolescent participants' perspectives on changes in family functioning post-program.

Implications for Clinical Practice

Despite these limitations, several implications for family therapy have emerged as this study unfolded. First, we know that a therapeutic wilderness program that engages both youth and parents can be a positive intervention for families strug- gling with communication. This is in contrast to earlier research, which found that communication among family members diminished somewhat after wilderness treatment (Bettmann and Tucker 2011). Understanding the reason for this dis- crepancy was beyond the scope of this study; however, it may be related to the aforementioned fact that many youth in wilderness treatment (vs. Outward Bound) often go on to some form of residential aftercare instead of going home to live with their families, which may impact communication.

Truancy, anger, defiance, low motivation, and risky behaviors such as drug and/or alcohol use are also reasons families may send their adolescent children to a therapeutic wilderness program (Outward Bound 2013b). Findings from this study show that this type of program may also have a positive impact on these issues. Based on these findings, as well as prior research showing the documented benefits of family participation in an adolescent's treatment (Harper et al. 2007), family therapists who work with families struggling with similar challenges may refer them to this type of program. Having parent involvement in this type of program increases positive outcomes, as parents have the opportunity to reflect on their parenting and family relationships, and then practice the skills and reflect on their parenting. Likewise, the psychoeducational information provided to parents during the Parent Seminar at the end of the Outward Bound course helped build a sense of parental efficacy by giving them tools to help better cope with their child's struggles. Based on earlier research showing that family-based psychoeducation effectively reduces relapse rates (Fristad et al. 1998), this may allow for the therapeutic wilderness experiences to have more lasting effects. Both parental involvement and family-based psychoeducation are especially important components of family therapy in residential treatment settings. Although youth are often the primary client of residential programs, the findings from this study reinforce earlier research findings which argue for a family-centered approach to residential care (Walter and Petr 2008).

Given that this type of program has such a positive impact on family communication and relationships, it may also be an effective tool for family therapists to utilize in order to promote treatment engagement. Research on treatment engagement has examined the relationship between family dynamics and treatment participation. For example, negative parent interactions with youth have been shown to predict treatment disengagement (Fernandez and Eyberg 2009). Recent research also indicates that families are most at risk of dropout due to family difficulties (Burns et al. 2008). Similarly, problems with family dynamics are related to the highest proportion of families who drop out of treatment (Johnson et al. 2008). If a therapeutic wilderness program can help a family improve communication and family relationships, then perhaps families will experience more cohesion, and be better equipped to resolve potential conflicts between parents and youth by finding common treatment goals. According to Gopalan et al. (2010) these variables are important for promoting engagement, which may mean that therapeutic wilderness programs have utility in increasing treatment retention.

In order to further assess this assertion, as well as to support families who have participated in therapeutic wilderness programs, follow-up is needed. This could include individual and/or family therapy to help maintain the communication skills that families learned in the program. In the interviews, parents who participated in this study commented on the need for follow-up after the Intercept course. Family therapists could play an integral role in helping implement follow-up programming in the community. Even early studies of Outward Bound programming stated the importance of providing community-based programs that have adventure challenges, community service, alternative education, and counseling (Kaplan 1979). Norton (2007, 2008) also supports the need for follow up in her prior research on the Intercept program. After all, the most important aspect of family therapy is creating lasting change in the family system, long after treatment has ended.

Closing Thoughts

Families in crisis need access to meaningful opportunities for growth and change. Along with ongoing family therapy, youth may need an out-of-home intervention that allows the family to experience a meaningful separation in which both the youth and parents learn new skills. Outward Bound's Intercept program is one such program, which focuses on skill-building in the areas of communication, connectedness, and trust between parents and their adolescent child.

Using a phenomenological approach, this research study was able to explore families' lived experiences through this kind of program, and gained insight into the positive relationship outcomes in the above areas. This chapter shows that phenomenological methods can be effectively employed in residential settings that serve adolescents. Qualitative measures, which included both surveys and interviews, showed that communication remained the strongest positive outcome. Specific tools that were beneficial to family functioning included taking time-outs, improved listening, and other specific communication skills. Other positive key findings affecting outcomes included course components, such as the parent workbook, education from the parent seminar, and the parent/child conference.

Though many programs may teach these skills, Outward Bound's unique methodology of teaching youth and families these skills in an outdoor, experiential setting kinesthetically engages family members on cognitive, affective, and behavioral levels, adding to the intervention's effectiveness. Though this research is not generalizable to the larger population, this study has important implications for how the use of adjunctive, therapeutic, outdoor adventure experiences can improve family functioning.

References

Auerbach, C. F., & Silverstein, L. B. (2003). *Qualitative data: An introduction to coding and analysis.* New York: University Press.

Bandoroff, S., & Scherer, D. G. (1994). Wilderness family therapy: An innovative treatment approach for problem youth. *Journal of Child and Family Studies, 3*(2), 175–191. doi:10.1007/BF02234066

Berman, D., & Davis-Berman, J. (2008). *The promise of wilderness therapy.* Boulder, CO: Association for Experiential Education.

Burns, C. D., Cortell, R., & Wagner, B. M. (2008). Treatment compliance in adolescents after attempted suicide: A 2-year follow-up study. *Journal of the American Academy of Child and Adolescent Psychiatry, 47*(8), 948–957. doi:10.1097/CHI.Ob013e3181799e84

Bettmann, J. E. (2005). *Shifts in attachment relationships: A quantitative study of adolescents in brief residential treatment.* Doctoral dissertation, Smith College School for Social Work, Northampton, Mass.

Bettmann, J. E., & Tucker, A. R. (2011). Shifts in attachment relationships: A study of adolescents in wilderness treatment. *Child & Youth Care Forum, 40*(6), 499–519.

Christenson, J. D., & Miller, A. L. (2016). Slowing down the conversation: The use of letter writing with adolescents and young adults in residential settings. *Contemporary Family Therapy, 38*(1), 23–31.

Clark, J. P., Cooley, R., Gathercoal, K., & Marmol, L. M. (2004). The effects of wilderness therapy on the clinical concerns (on axes I, II, and IV) of troubled adolescents. *Journal of Experiential Education, 27*(2), 213–232. doi:10.1177/105382590402700207

Cottrell, D., & Boston, P. (2002). Practitioner review: The effectiveness of systemic family therapy for children and adolescents. *Journal of Child Psychology and Psychiatry, 43*(5), 573–586. doi:10.1111/1469-7610.00047

Creswell, J. W. (2013). *Qualitative inquiry and research design: Choosing among five traditions.* Thousand Oaks, CA: Sage.

Doherty, W. J. (1995). Boundaries between parent and family education and family therapy: The levels of family involvement model. *Family Relations, 44*, 353–358. doi:10.2307/584990

Fernandez, M. A., & Eyberg, S. M. (2009). Predicting treatment and follow-up attrition in parent–child interaction therapy. *Journal of Abnormal Child Psychology, 37*(3), 431–441. doi:10.1007/s10802-008-9281-1

Fristad, M. A., Gavazzi, S. M., & Soldano, K. W. (1998). Multi-family psychoeducation groups for childhood mood disorders: A program description and preliminary efficacy data. *Contemporary Family Therapy, 20*(3), 385–402. doi:10.1023/A:1022477215195

Gopalan, G., Goldstein, L., Klingenstein, K., Sicher, C., Blake, C., & McKay, M. M. (2010). Engaging families into child mental health treatment: Updates and special considerations. *Journal of the Canadian Academy of Child and Adolescent Psychiatry, 19*(3), 182–219.

Groenewald, T. (2004). A phenomenological research design illustrated. *International Journal of Qualitative Methods, 3*, 1–26.

Harper, N., & Cooley, R. (2007). Parental reports of adolescent and family well-being following a wilderness therapy intervention: An exploratory look at systemic change. *Journal of Experiential Education, 29*(3), 393–396. doi:10.1177/105382590702900314

Harper, N., Russell, K. C., Cooley, R., & Cupples, J. (2007). Catherine Freer wilderness therapy expeditions: An exploratory case study of adolescent wilderness therapy, family functioning, and the maintenance of change. *Child & Youth Care Forum, 36*, 111–129. doi:10.1007/s10566-007-9035-1

Harper, N. J., & Russell, K. C. (2008). Family involvement and outcome in adolescent wilderness treatment: A mixed-methods evaluation. *International Journal of Child & Family Welfare, 1*, 19–36.

Johnson, E., Mellor, D., & Brann, P. (2008). Differences in dropout between diagnoses in child and adolescent mental health services. *Clinical Child Psychology and Psychiatry, 13*, 515–530. doi:10.1177/1359104508096767

Kaplan, L. (1979). Outward bound: A treatment modality unexplored by the social work profession. *Child Welfare, 58*, 37–47.

National Council on Family Relations (2014). *Family life education* [*PowerPoint slides*]. Retrieved from: https://www.ncfr.org/sites/default/files/downloads/news/fle_cfle_2016.pdf

Norton, C. L. (2007). *Understanding the impact of wilderness therapy on adolescent depression and psychosocial development.* Dissertation abstracts international: Section A. Humanities and Social Sciences, 68(4-A), 1661.

Norton, C. L. (2008). Understanding the impact of wilderness therapy on adolescent depression and psychosocial development. *Illinois Child Welfare, 4*(1), 166–178.

Norton, C. L. (2010). Exploring the process of wilderness therapy: Key therapeutic components in the treatment of adolescent depression and psychosocial development. *Journal of Therapeutic Schools and Programs, 4*, 24–46.

Norton, C. L., Tucker, A., Russell, K. C., Bettmann, J. E., Gass, M. A., & Behrens, E. (2014). Adventure therapy with youth. *Journal of Experiential Education, 37*(1), 46–59.

Outward Bound. (2013a). *What is an Outward Bound course?* Retrieved from: http://www.outwardbound.org/wilderness-expeditions/outdoor-trips/outdoor-education-courses/

Outward Bound. (2013b). *Intercept for struggling youth.* Retrieved from http://www.
    outwardbound.org/intercept/intercept/
Outward Bound International. (2012). *Outward Bound International Annual Report 2012.*
    Retrieved from http://www.ceskacesta.cz/useruploads/files/obi_2012_annual_report.pdf
Roller, M. (2016). *Verification: Looking beyond the data in qualitative data analysis.* Retrieved
    from: https://researchdesignreview.com/2014/04/30/verification-looking-beyond-the-data-in-
    qualitative-data-analysis/
Russell, K. (2000). Exploring how the wilderness therapy process relates to outcomes. *Journal of
    Experiential Education, 23*(3), 170–176. doi:10.1177/105382590002300309
Russell, K. C., & Hendee, J. C. (1999). Wilderness therapy as an intervention and treatment for
    adolescents with behavioral problems. In *Personal, Societal and Ecological Values of
    Wilderness: 6th World Wilderness Congress Proceedings on Research and Allocation (Vol. 2).*
    US Department of Agriculture, Forest Service, Rocky Mountain Research Station.
Strauss, A. L., & Corbin, J. M. (1990). *Basics of qualitative research* (Vol. 15). Newbury Park,
    CA: Sage.
Walter, U. M., & Petr, C. G. (2008). Family-centered residential treatment: Knowledge, research,
    and values converge. *Residential Treatment for Children & Youth, 25*(1), 1–16. doi:10.1080/
    08865710802209594
Waters, J. (2016). *Phenomenological research guidelines.* Retrieved from: https://www.capilanou.
    ca/psychology/student-resources/research-guidelines/Phenomenological-Research-Guidelines/

Author Biographies

Christine Norton Ph.D., LCSW received her Ph.D. in Social Work from Loyola University
Chicago. She has a Master of Arts in Social Service Administration from the University of
Chicago and a Master of Science in Experiential Education from Minnesota State
University-Mankato. She is a Licensed Clinical Social Worker and a Board Approved
Supervisor in the State of Texas. She has over 20 years of experience working with youth and
young adults in a variety of settings including therapeutic wilderness programs, juvenile justice,
schools, mentoring and campus support programs. She has taught as adjunct faculty at The
University of Denver, Prescott College, and Naropa University. Her areas of practice and research
interest and expertise are in positive youth development; innovative interventions in child and
adolescent mental health; adventure therapy; outdoor behavioral healthcare; experiential education; foster care support in higher education; and international social work. Dr. Norton is a
Research Scientist with the Outdoor Behavioral Healthcare Center and she helped launch Foster
Care Alumni Creating Educational Success (FACES) at Texas State. She is the Foster Care Liaison
Officer to the Texas Higher Education Coordinating Board, and is the founder of the Foster Care
Adventure Therapy Network, an international group of programs and practitioners who utilize
adventure therapy with current and former foster care youth and young adults. Dr. Norton has over
25 peer-reviewed journal articles, has edited three books, and has authored over ten book chapters.
She has secured over $3,162,154 in internal and external research funding as principal investigator
and co-investigator, and is a leading social work scholar who has presented her research nationally
and internationally. Dr. Norton is active in study abroad and is also a Fulbright Scholar, teaching
adventure therapy in the Department of Civic Education and Leadership at National Taiwan
Normal University.

Katie Liermann LMSW is a mental health social worker at Veterans Affairs in Little Rock,
Arkansas. She received her Master's in Social Work at San Jose State University in San Jose,

California. Prior to becoming a social worker she spent several years working for Outward Bound in Minnesota as an instructor, trainer, and course director. Her experience at Outward Bound and as an inner city elementary school teacher is what led her to a career in social work. Despite now spending most of her days in an office, she still pursues outdoor adventures through trail running, canoeing, mountain biking, and winter sport activities when given the opportunity.

Chapter 24
Program Evaluation for Health and Human Service Programs: How to Tell the Right Story Successfully

Michael Gass, Edward G. Foden and Anita Tucker

Chapter Highlights

- Program evaluation can help protect clients' and families' well-being, justify costs, and monitor effectiveness.
- Program evaluation is only as effective as its ability to follow several critical standards/guidelines in its process, which are utility, feasibility, propriety, and accuracy.
- The primary focus of program evaluation performance is on needs assessment, feasibility study, process evaluation, outcome evaluation, and cost–benefit analyses.
- Needs assessment measures the gap between *what is* and *what could be*.
- For family therapy in residential treatment, feasibility studies examine the areas of therapeutic, financial, and systemic feasibility.

More than 50,000 children in the United States alone are placed into residential treatment programs annually (Vaughn 2005; Warner and Pottick 2003). Estimates that are more recent suggest an even greater increase in enrollment (up to 80,000) in residential care annually (Substance Abuse and Mental Health Services Administration [SAMHSA] 2012), and the need for treatment extends beyond just

M. Gass (✉) · A. Tucker
Outdoor Behavioral Healthcare (OBH) Research Center,
College of Health and Human Services, University of New Hampshire,
Durham, NH 03824, USA
e-mail: mgass@unh.edu

A. Tucker
e-mail: anita.tucker@unh.edu

E.G. Foden
College of Health and Human Services, University of New Hampshire,
Durham, NH 03824, USA
e-mail: Edward.Foden@colorado.edu

© Springer International Publishing AG 2017
J.D. Christenson and A.N. Merritts (eds.), *Family Therapy with Adolescents
in Residential Treatment*, Focused Issues in Family Therapy,
DOI 10.1007/978-3-319-51747-6_24

these clients. Using a nationally representative sample, Merikangas et al. (2010) found that 49.5% of adolescents will be diagnosed with a mental health disorder at some time over the course of their lifetime. Additionally, 27.6% are diagnosed with a disorder causing *severe impairment* (Merikangas et al. 2010, p. 984). Mental illness and behavioral disorders in children and adolescents exact a serious toll, affecting five million American children and their families, and costing 10.9 billion dollars per year (Davis 2014).

Failure to properly address these issues can compound problems, resulting in costly and long-term treatment issues. For example, in an effort to address serious and alarming behavioral health needs (e.g., substance abuse, overdose deaths, and child abuse) the State of New Mexico enacted several waves of intervention over the past 20 years (Program Evaluation Unit, Legislative Finance Committee 2014). However, many of these interventions were not effective and lacked processes that could inform decision-makers and provide appropriate oversight. The result has been several ineffective (and sometimes abusive) treatments at a cost of over half a billion dollars passed on to state taxpayers (Program Evaluation Unit, Legislative Finance Committee 2014).

Although program evaluation is typically used by internal stakeholders to examine an existing program (Williams-Reade et al. 2014), the implications of effective evaluation extend far beyond internal program functions. At a micro-level (involving the client and the client system) and macro-level (involving an entire healthcare system), program evaluation helps protect the clients' and families' well-being, justify costs, and monitor effectiveness. Treatment providers receive accurate appraisals of their program by analyzing processes and outcomes. Funding sources ensure their money is well spent through accurate cost–benefit analyses. Consultants gain insights on program effectiveness, them to better match families with programs. When done correctly, program evaluation can benefit all stakeholders in the landscape of residential treatment.

Program evaluation is "a systematic study using research methods to collect and analyze data to assess how well a program is working and why" (United States Government Accountability Office 2012, p. 3). The W. K. Kellogg Foundation's Evaluation Handbook (2004) outlines several key components of evaluation. These are to "strengthen projects, use multiple approaches, and design evaluation to address real issues, create a participatory process, allow for flexibility, and build capacity" (pp. 2–3). Program evaluation allows for a deeper understanding of the specific responses to treatment provided in an agency. For example, a myriad of studies demonstrate the effectiveness of substance abuse treatment. However, the modality and program often vary in effectiveness depending on the population served, the precipitating factors leading to treatment, challenges arising from dual diagnoses, etc. It is important to effectively match clientele with treatment. "The surest way to make this determination is through rigorous evaluation of treatment modalities, treatment programs, and patient outcomes" (McCaffrey 1996, para 3).

It should be noted that program evaluation is only as effective as its ability to follow several critical standards/guidelines in its process—*utility, feasibility, propriety*, and *accuracy* (Center for Disease Control [CDC] 1999; Williams-Reade et al. 2014). The standard of utility relates to the worth of evaluation findings. Proper utility in evaluation ensures that findings are useful to stakeholders. On the other hand, a poorly timed evaluation that produces irrelevant information demonstrates weak utility, and is relatively useless to stakeholders. The standard of feasibility refers to the realistic, prudent, diplomatic, and cost effective nature of the evaluation (CDC 1999; Williams-Reade et al. 2014). Proper feasibility ensures that program evaluation is not overly burdensome to human and financial resources, whereas weak feasibility results in evaluation that is irresponsible, tactless, or impracticable. The standard of propriety is the assumption of appropriate ethical and legal practices. Proper propriety in program evaluation entails decent, respectful, and apt evaluative measures, whereas weak propriety results in potentially offensive, irregular, or illegal evaluative measures. The standard of accuracy implies that the evaluation must "demonstrate scientific rigor and convey appropriate information" (CDC 1999; Williams-Read et al. 2014, p. 285). Proper accuracy ensures that evaluations are objective, correct, and applicable, whereas weak accuracy results in misleading or inapplicable evaluation. Sound evaluation design, valid and reliable information, and justified conclusions and decisions all relate to the accuracy of the evaluation. When applied diligently, the standards of utility, feasibility, propriety, and accuracy guide evaluators to worthwhile results.

The purpose of this chapter is to provide a general understanding of the rationale, purposes, and methods of program evaluation. Specific attention will be given to the role of family therapy in residential treatment. The primary focus of this discussion on program evaluation will be on needs assessment, feasibility study, process evaluation, outcome evaluation, and cost–benefit analyses. Each evaluation type will be discussed in detail, with particular attention paid to how these types of evaluation are currently being used in the field of residential treatment. Proper program evaluation of residential treatment programs results in the promotion of practices that lead to proper treatment, as well as the maintenance of a program's productivity and profitability.

Types of Program Evaluation

Program evaluation can take on several different forms, each with a unique purpose. The five major categories, into which most all other types of evaluation fit, are (a) needs assessment, (b) feasibility studies, (c) process evaluation, (d) outcomes evaluation, and (e) cost–benefit analyses (Rossi et al. 2003; United States Department of Health and Human Services [DHHS] 2010). There is critical overlap between a client's evaluation process through a program and the timing of each evaluation (see Fig. 24.1). Each type of program evaluation is utilized to answer various and specific questions relating to the treatment process. When used effectively evaluation can delineate functional and dysfunctional aspects of a program, demonstrate effectiveness to funders, identify program strengths and weaknesses, and contribute insight into family therapy in residential treatment (Gass 2014). The

Program Evaluation

Intake	Discharge	PD6[a]	PD12 (etc.)

`- - - --------I-----------------------------------------I----------------------I-------------------------I--- - - -`

Needs Assessment

Feasibility Study

      Process Evaluation

           Outcomes Evaluation → (Ongoing)

Cost Analyses (prior to placement)   Cost Analyses (post treatment)

[a]Post Discharge, Six Months

Fig. 24.1 Program evaluation timeline

timeline in Fig. 24.1 illustrates when the types of program evaluation are actually implemented, which are used to search for knowledge and answers during that time in the program. Note the overlap between certain forms of program evaluation.

The timeline above provides context for *when* each of the following evaluation types are most relevant. Much of this is intuitive, but preparation and planning are essential for proper evaluation (Gass 2014). What follows is a brief introduction to the five categories of evaluation, posing relevant questions for each. In essence, answering the following questions is the process of program evaluation.

Needs Assessment

- What level of care does the client need?
- How can we determine the right program for a specific client?
- How can we reach the desired outcome for families?

Feasibility Study

- Is family therapy technically feasible?
- Is it financially feasible?
- Can we construct a family system that will answer its organizational needs?

Process Evaluation

- Does the process meet accreditation standards? Is it evidence-based? How is risk properly managed?
- Does the actual process align with the intended process?
- Is the program working for the client? What alterations are necessary for the client's success?

Outcomes Evaluation

- Did the client experience success in the program?
- Has the client maintained positive change over time?
- What are the success rates?

Cost–Benefit Analysis

- What direct and indirect costs are involved in the treatment decision?
- What is the benefit, effect, utility, and efficiency of treatment?
- In consideration of the above, is the program worth the cost?

Needs Assessment: What Are the Clinical Objectives?

Needs assessment is intended to measure the gap between *what is* and *what could be*. What is refers to the present state of affairs and what could be refers to the desired target state that a family would like to reach. This type of evaluation is not always included in texts pertaining to program evaluation. However, client assessment is important in the landscape of residential treatment as it can inform the greater evaluation process (Ellis et al. 1984). An initial assessment also determines a client's appropriate level of care. If residential placement is considered the most prudent course of action, clients and their families need help in specific program selection. Some considerations are quality, restrictiveness, and appropriateness. Another possible consideration involves past outcomes with similar clients. Results of a needs assessment are used to understand the context of the enrollment and to establish a treatment plan. In short, needs assessment determines an individual or family's current level of functioning, and provides direction on how to reach desired outcomes (Ellis et al. 1984).

The first step in a client's treatment is contact with an admissions representative. There is an initial *screening* or determination of fit between the client and the residential program. This process informs both consumer and provider of the needs of the client, allowing for the initial evaluation to begin. After screening, there is typically a series of early evaluations of both client and family needs. A conversation with a clinician (perhaps the clinical director or the client's individual therapist) will ensue. This may happen before or upon arrival. Once enrolled in the program, ongoing assessment guides treatment.

One example of a screening tool utilized in determining client *need* is the Youth Outcome Questionnaire (or Y-OQ). This is a 64-question self-report diagnostic tool designed for parents to assess their child's level of function/dysfunction (OQ Measures 2014). There is also a self-report form of the Y-OQ written for either adolescent or young adult clients themselves. These surveys are useful as both initial and ongoing assessment tools, collecting information from both the parents' and the clients' perspectives. The questionnaire presents a *critical items scale*, examining certain risk factors. High scores on this scale denote that a client's needs are best met in a residential setting (OQ Measures 2014). Following the initial assessment, the Y-OQ can also be used mid-treatment or post-discharge, to evaluate client process and outcome, respectively.

When deciding on residential treatment, close analysis of client needs is imperative for accurate placement. There are myriad modalities and program models that cater to the wide variety of needs exhibited by former, current, and future clientele. Psychological and academic testing by trained professionals is an additional level of needs assessment. Professionals such as educational consultants (see Chap. 6), who are well versed in program options and specialties, are also a valuable resource in matching clients with the most appropriate program.

Once enrolled, needs assessment becomes a matter of treatment planning. Upon their son or daughter's arrival at many residential treatment programs, parents complete a Y-OQ. At this juncture in the treatment process, the Y-OQ provides information to begin treatment planning. The Y-OQ can also identify parent–child reporting discrepancies, which is potentially useful in understanding the family system (OQ Measures 2014). One particular advantage of the Y-OQ is that it can be offered at intake, mid-point, discharge, and post-discharge (OQ Measures 2014). Using the Y-OQ at these intervals can inform every part of practice, providing longitudinal data to improve a client's treatment and analyze their post-treatment experience.

Another needs assessment utilized in family therapy treatment planning is the Family Assessment Device, or FAD. This self-survey examines family function levels based on six sub-scales: problem solving, communication, roles, affective responsiveness, affective involvement, and behavior control (Ryan et al. 2005). The FAD also provides a general functioning measurement. Administered to every family member over the age of 12, the 60-question FAD is a comprehensive assessment of the family system (Ryan et al. 2005; Yingling 2012). The FAD was built on the McMaster Model of Family Functioning, which assumes an interrelated family system lies at the core of family success or failure (Ryan et al. 2005; Yingling 2012). Clinicians using the FAD follow the belief system that the *client* is the family system and the issues are only explained through familial transaction and interaction (Ryan et al. 2005; Yingling 2012). Initially designed as a screening tool, the FAD has also been utilized as a multiphasic instrument, alongside the Y-OQ, measuring process and outcome, as well as intake needs.

As one can see, needs assessment is vital in identifying what level of care a client's needs, what program will provide the best fit, and what presenting aspects to address while in treatment. The Y-OQ and FAD are two specific examples of needs assessment instruments. Although self-reported measures are subjective in nature, they can provide potent information, especially when utilizing multiple sources of data (e.g., parents/guardians, clients, siblings). Cross-referencing can uncover poignant family dynamics that must be addressed in order to establish family success. Needs assessment, in general, is a critical component in evaluating family therapy, as it sets the stage for appropriate and effective treatment.

Feasibility Study: How Will It Be Facilitated, Funded, and Managed?

For family therapy in residential treatment in particular, feasibility studies examine the areas of therapeutic, financial, and systemic feasibility (Gass 2014). Special attention is often paid to the best use of resources (e.g., staff, equipment, finances, space, and time). Therapeutic feasibility examines how particular interventions or modalities will be chosen, implemented, and tracked. Financial feasibility refers to funding for staff, materials, space, and additional services. Systemic feasibility needs include professional training, management, collaboration, and oversight. In a departure from solely examining client-centered needs, feasibility studies focus on programs, looking specifically at facilitation, funding, and management. Feasibility studies consider the factors of long-term intervention, looking to determine capability and lasting effectiveness.

Client success depends upon many factors. One of them is facilitation, or the type of therapeutic modality or intervention employed in their treatment. Selection, implementation, and documentation of treatment will have a profound effect on efficacy. Prescriptive treatment design is ideal, as certain forms of treatment will better match certain presenting symptoms. Correlations between therapeutic modality and symptoms are well researched. Clinicians increase efficacy by considering historical treatment effectiveness with similar clients. Evaluating the process of selection and implementation can inform stakeholders of the prescriptive nature of their subjected program. Both selection and implementation are reinforced through documentation. Whether approaches prove successful or not, the knowledge provided in assessment is valuable. Treatment must be documented, not only from an ethical standpoint, but also to inform associated treatment professionals and to track client progress. Having systems for selection, implementation, and documentation in place will provide structure that enhances therapeutic efficacy.

An assessment of financial feasibility is a programmatic cost evaluation. Questions pertinent to finances include the following: Who will conduct family therapy? Are they internal or external to the organization? What resources will they need? Where will they meet their clients? Are there any additional services necessary for families or their children? Will the cost of family therapy be included in tuition, or will it be an additional cost? A thorough program design will generate clarity in terms of financial feasibility.

Along with therapeutic and financial assessments, the systemic needs of family therapy must be addressed. Questions of management, certification, oversight, and collaboration all relate to the feasibility of a program. In one residential program the authors are familiar with, the family therapists primarily work remotely, flying in to attend parent workshop weekends. As licensed psychotherapists, they serve in this role as adjunct staff. Family therapists work with the client's individual therapist to provide holistic family therapy that synchronizes the client's process with their parent's parallel process (see Chap. 7). Family therapists also coordinate with operations staff to schedule family workshops. Due to the specific program design, it is common that clients will be on adventure therapy experiences, so scheduling and transportation are integral in the planning process. Physical space where the workshop will take place is another consideration. The Clinical Director, to ensure quality and consistency, typically oversees the work of family therapists. As evidenced above, organizational considerations are paramount in the overall treatment process and integral in the feasibility conversation.

Process Evaluation: How Does It Work?

Process evaluation measures program propriety, fidelity, and effectiveness (Gass 2014). Measuring propriety, or adherence to standards of conduct, can include accreditation assessment, risk management analyses, and the level of congruence with program models. Measuring fidelity, or the accuracy of implementation to program design, helps ensure consistency between intended and actual programming. Measuring process effectiveness entails mid-treatment assessment, informing decisions about maintenance, alteration, or termination of treatment. Findings from fidelity, propriety, and effectiveness studies are used to increase program consistency, excellence, and potency.

Stakeholders of all kinds stand to benefit from propriety assessment. Consumers look for quality programs, program directors compete for clientele, and organizations are charged with ensuring appropriate therapeutic conduct. Even evidence-based practices and adequate risk management depend on the propriety of process. Accreditation and licensure are two types of comprehensive evaluation. Depending on the type of program, different accreditation or licensure standards apply. Program directors may join an organization aligned with similar programs. Some professional organizations require members to adhere to certain standards and professional practices through a systematic accreditation process. For example, members of the Outdoor Behavioral Healthcare Council (OBHC) have an accreditation process specific to their organization. Designed with input from their own membership and with support from outside experts, members of the OBHC created industry standards that ensure a focus on best practices, the health and best interests of clients, and the promotion of quality, well-managed programs. Such a process examines the way risk is managed, the types of clients served or excluded, and the related therapy provided.

Fidelity and effectiveness are also important factors in process evaluation. One useful tool for measuring fidelity and effectiveness is a logic model (Kellogg 2004). When establishing a program model, they provide a clear vision to guide implementation. Once the vision is made tangible, fidelity can be assessed through comparison between a program model and actual implementation. To assess effectiveness, such models provide a road map for reaching desired outcomes. A basic logic model for a program is outlined below:

Needs/Input/Resources → Strategies/Activities → Immediate
Outcomes/Output → Intermediate Outcomes → Final Outcomes/Impact

An example of a well-developed logic model is that of the Soltreks Wilderness Therapy Program (see Fig. 24.2). Founded in 1997 by Lorri Hanna and Doug Sabo, this wilderness program offers prescriptive adventure expeditions for adolescents, young adults, and older adults who are seeking healthy growth and change (Gass et al. 2012). Note the potential for fidelity and effectiveness study in the figure recreated below.

A logic model can measure program fidelity in several ways. For example, a survey of Soltreks' staff might uncover that they are consistently working on family roles, but are inconsistently encouraging parent and sibling participation in assignments. These are two standard categories of intervention outlined in the logic model, part of the *intended* process. Because the vision of the program is so clearly laid-out, assessment of fidelity is easier to conduct. With knowledge of the

Needs	Strategies/Activities	Immediate Outcomes	Intermediate Outcomes	Final Outcomes
Adolescents, ages 13-17 that have difficulty coping with the challenges of life (e.g. depression, learning challenges, low self-esteem, anxiety, underachieving) Supported by their parents and siblings (as appropriate) Individual experiences Restore family relationships (family involvement required) Need for emotional regulation,	Specially designed trips of appropriate trek length: 4-7 days (specialty) or 6-8 weeks (small group or one-on-one). Emotionally safe settings based on structure, consistency, and accountability through group norms, daily routine, mindfulness practices, experiential education, ceremony, and rituals Individual therapist with each student to create individual Personal Development Plan Develop and practice strategies for effective communication and	Independence, patience, assertiveness, self-reliance, and maturity Experience emotional and physical safety, healthy habits, intentionality, reflection, validation, and empathy Goal-setting skills (e.g. Personal Development Plan) Demonstrate outdoor living skills Support peers in skill development Practice	Improve stress management skills Willingness to take emotional and physical risks (e.g. speak the truth) Address negative and limiting thoughts Increase emotional regulation (e.g. waiting until group to share emotions, appropriate expression of emotions) Identification of unhealthy behaviors and coping skills	Positive significant changes in school performance, leisure activities, accountability, respect of boundaries Increased communication with family members Positive results from Youth Outcome Questionnaire (Y-OQ) Obtain academic credit Improved parent-child communication and relationship

Fig. 24.2 Logic model of the Soltreks Wilderness Therapy Program

Increased self-awareness, responsibility and accountability of behavior	problem solving Use appropriate curriculum activities, including: art therapy, initiatives, leader of the day, letter writing with parents	sharing, cooperation, language of power Improve coping and social skills base	Develop healthy boundaries Increased self-efficacy (e.g. socially, academically)	Increased motivation Desire to do new leisure activities Decrease in family conflict
Reclaim or develop personal power and true potential	Identify thinking and behavior patterns, limiting and empowering personal characteristics	Value of healthy nutrition and personal care	Ability to receive and give appropriate feedback	Less social isolation Demonstration of new, healthy habits
Rites of passage opportunity				
Intervention to determine level of care/transition (e.g., boarding school, therapeutic environment, home)	Identify role in family and social settings Individual and group therapy Academic work Adventure experiences Parent and sibling participation in assignments Transition Planning: goals and action steps, home agreement, continuity of care		Demonstrate responsibility Improve motivation	Healthy structure developed in home Increased self-assurance and confidence

Fig. 24.2 (continued)

discrepancy between intention and implementation, Soltreks' leadership was provided with a clear direction for reestablishing fidelity (Gass et al. 2012).

In another example regarding effectiveness measurement in program evaluation, a client was demonstrating a mixed degree of success and failure in meeting his established *immediate outcomes*. Using the logic model, the client's therapist examined the areas contributing to these mixed results and adjusted treatment accordingly. The Y-OQ and the FAD are useful tools in process evaluation as well. As mentioned previously, using the Y-OQ and the FAD as multiphasic tools allows a therapist to reflect on the variable success of particular interventions. The purpose of evaluating process effectiveness is to guide ensuing treatment. Moving forward, therapists synthesize information gathered from the past, the client's readiness in the present, and the desired future outcome. Evaluating the process of going from *here* to *there* helps to operationalize the therapeutic process for all involved.

Outcome Evaluation: How Well Did It Work?

Outcome evaluation gauges the extent to which clients achieve therapeutic objectives. Post-treatment functioning, recidivism statistics, and consumer satisfaction are all examples of variables used to evaluate program outcomes. Such assessment, if utilized effectively, leads to program improvements and informed policy decisions. There are certain instruments, like the Y-OQ and the FAD, that help determine both global and specific functioning in the individual and family. Recidivism statistics and associated analyses can offer a broader scope of effectiveness, helpful in assessing data from programs, modalities, or entire symptom populations. There are also measures of consumer satisfaction, like the National Association of Therapeutic Schools and Programs (NATSAP) Parent-Discharge Questionnaire (PD-Q), used to track parent satisfaction levels following their child's treatment (NATSAP 2015).

As mentioned earlier when highlighting needs assessment and process evaluation, the Y-OQ and FAD can also be used to measure outcomes. For example, Y-OQ and FAD scores are commonly collected by many residential programs at intake, discharge, and 6- and 12 months post-discharge. Durability measurement, like 12-month post-discharge data, increases validity and improves understanding of the client's long-term success. The NATSAP data pool allows individual programs to compare the outcomes of their clients to the national average. Figures 24.3 and 24.4 depict examples of comparative data (from an anonymized NATSAP member program) that reflects the NATSAP average. Notice the rise in dysfunctional reporting at the 6-month interval. This rise might be alarming to consumers, clients, and program staff alike. However, the levels decline once again, approaching the low exhibited at discharge. Such information is valuable to all stakeholders, helping to explain trends in outcomes reporting.

The two previous graphs include student-reported Y-OQ and FAD scores.[1] The clinical cutoff defines clinically significant dysfunction. As seen in the figures, post-discharge measurement provides important context, at both 6- and 12-month intervals. The client and family may have experienced the most growth while the client was enrolled in therapy, but the change appears to be lasting, as reported at 12 months post-discharge. The above graphs depict global functioning, demonstrating a decrease in overall dysfunction in the identified client (Y-OQ) and the family as a whole (FAD).

The Y-OQ and the FAD are useful in evaluating specific outcomes as well. Examining self-reported symptom severity in particular areas can help identify

---

[1]Student-generated responses were chosen due to high attrition rates in parent post-discharge data.

YOQ 2.0 SR Mean Scores at Intake, Discharge, PD6 and PD12

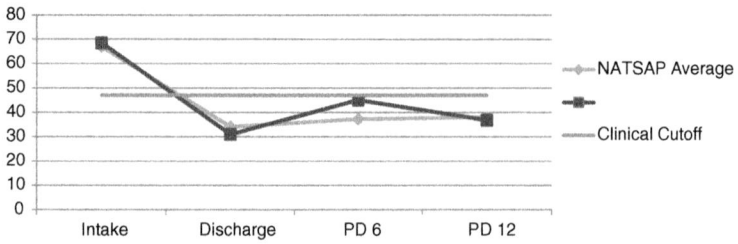

Fig. 24.3 Youth outcome questionnaire (Y-OQ) self-report results indicating functional change occurs at discharge and continues to show positive trends after one year of treatment

FAD Youth Report Mean Scores at Intake, Discharge, PD6, and PD12

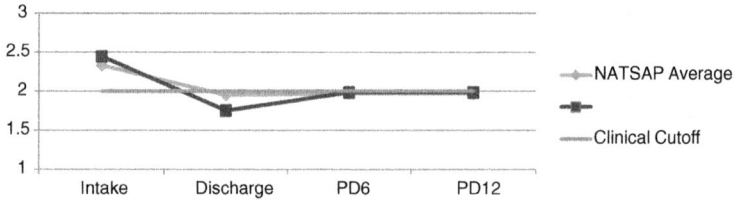

Fig. 24.4 Family assessment device (FAD) scores indicating significant change in treatment that is maintained for at least one year after discharge

potential weak points for program staff to address. In cases of inconsistent behavioral functioning, those areas that remain below target may take priority in future program planning. For example, perhaps a client and their family, through the FAD, report better functioning in behavior control, but remain the same in affective communication (Ryan et al. 2005). These findings will empower program staff to address such discrepancies when working with future clients.

Recidivism statistics are often used as an outcome measurement of behavioral effectiveness as well, examining the extent to which clients repeat maladapted behaviors. For example, Calley (2012) examined the risk factors for recidivism and found that offender type was a significant factor in predicting recidivism. More specifically, outcome statistics suggest that the applied treatment is more effective for one type of offender (sex offenses) than others (violent or substance-involved). Statistics on recidivism can also aid in policy decision-making.

A comparative study of treatment programs for juvenile offenders in Georgia showed considerable outcome discrepancy depending on treatment modality. Figure 24.5 was created using data from this study and demonstrates this discrepancy. For a 3-year comparison of Behavior Modification through Adventure (BMtA), other therapeutic programs (OTP), and a youth *boot camp* model (YDC), the BMtA program yielded a lower recidivism rate than the other two programs (Gillis et al. 2008). In this way, recidivism statistics can help policymakers decide on funding allocation based on program effectiveness.

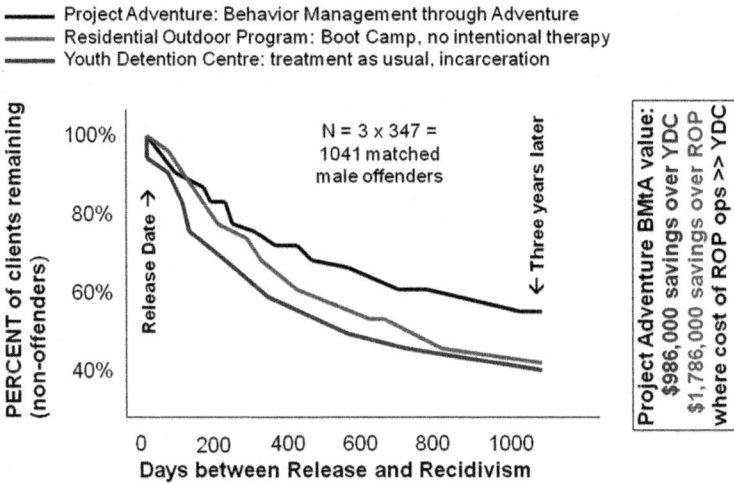

Fig. 24.5 A 3-year comparison of different treatment programs and their outcomes

Finally, there are outcome measurements of consumer satisfaction. Using the NATSAP Parent Questionnaire at Discharge (PQ-D) and 6 months post-discharge (PQ-PD) researchers assess parental satisfaction regarding their child's treatment (NATSAP 2015). Parent satisfaction is largely a function of expected therapeutic outcomes (e.g., overall family growth, affective and behavioral change, and skills acquisition). With the PQ-PD, parents are asked a series of questions regarding the functioning of their child. After reviewing such topics as school GPA, involvement with the legal system, and recently prescribed medication, parents are asked how satisfied they are with their child's treatment (NATSAP 2015). This type of outcome evaluation incorporates both objective and subjective data for measuring and comparing objective client outcomes and subjective consumer perceptions of effectiveness.

Cost–Benefit Analysis: Is It Worth the Financial Burden?

Cost analyses seek to answer three basic questions: What are the costs? What are the benefits? Is it worth the money? The costs can seem simple at first, examining tuition, travel expenses, additional testing, etc. However, there typically are hidden costs incorporated in treatment and evaluation (see Chap. 20), many of which are associated with the decision to postpone or avoid therapy or evaluation altogether. The second factor relating to cost–benefit analyses are the effect, utility, and efficiency of a program. These factors represent the process and outcomes of a program, compared through a monetary denominator. The conclusion is whether the therapeutic outcomes are valued more than the monetary inputs. For parents and policymakers alike, selection among various treatment options is largely dependent upon the cost–benefit evaluation.

Tuition, travel expenses, academic and psychological evaluation, and secondary placement considerations account for the bulk of what families and insurance companies spend on residential treatment. Tuition alone can be financially burdensome. For example, residential treatment for a client struggling with an eating disorder costs an average of $956 per day, with an average stay costing $79,348 (Evaluating Residential 2006). Some programs have parent workshops, weekends, or visits. These are often impactful interventions, but may be cost prohibitive for a family already stretched by the price of tuition. These direct costs are perhaps more readily apparent in a family's treatment decision-making, and can be calculated during a program evaluation.

There are indirect costs savings (also referred to as benefits) related to effective treatments that are also considered. Aos et al. (2006) created a system of understanding the indirect aspect of cost analyses. With regard to a cohort of non-sexual juvenile offenders, the cost of recidivism per offender, per offense, was $61, 985. When examined in another way, this number represents the tax revenue saved for each previous offender who did not recidivate. Aos et al. (2006) used five categories in calculating this figure: savings in police costs, criminal filings and conviction processes, prison costs, crime victims in terms of monetary out of pocket costs, and savings by crime victims in terms of quality of life issues. For parents of non-offender at risk youth, impending hospital, judicial, or post-treatment costs may factor into a current evaluation.

On the other side are the effects, utility, and efficiency provided in treatment. Like those examined through the FAD, this may relate to an increase in family functioning. Effects or changes in parent–child relationships may provide greater understanding or openness toward one another (e.g., better affective communication). Utility relates to the practical ways in which therapy can aid a family system. This could be in the form of skill building, goal setting, consensus on placement decisions, or as simple as acceptance of one another. Efficiency relates to the process of these aspects, done in the most productive way at the lowest cost. Improvement in functioning can then be monetized and combined with the types of data described above in the final cost–benefit calculations.

The final question, then, is whether the effects of treatment are worth the price. The effects of treatment outcomes on a family system, or society at large, are hardly explained in monetary terms. However, effective, comprehensive evaluation of costs and benefits will yield the most accurate assessment. Policymakers often have more time to run such comprehensive evaluations, but often face challenging bureaucratic forces resisting change in therapeutic or penal modality.

Treatment decisions for families may also entail other challenging factors. For many families such decisions are made in a time of crisis, not allowing for comprehensive investigation. In any case, experts are incredibly helpful. Education consultants are familiar with programs, their typical clientele, processes, and outcomes. Guidance counselors may also know what options are available for youth in their school system. Researchers are available for testimony concerning macro decision-making. The bottom line is that the tools to make the most cost-wise decision for consumers, policymakers, and supporting professionals are available. Although important, a thorough description of how to conduct cost–benefit analysis is beyond the scope of this chapter. For those who are interested in learning more, Christenson and Crane (2014) provide an in depth description of how to conduct cost–benefit analysis with family therapy.

Utilization of Findings

It is the purpose of evaluation to incorporate related findings, whether directly, conceptually, or persuasively, into the treatment decisions facing stakeholders (Williams-Reade et al. 2014). Program staff directly implement findings when they alter a client's course of treatment based on Y-OQ or FAD mid-stay data. Policymakers conceptually utilize findings when they consider cost–benefit analyses, and marketers persuasively apply findings when creating promotional materials. These represent three ways to utilize evaluation findings. Perhaps the greatest use, however, is the increase in oversight, leading to better programs, better policy, and healthier clients.

Conclusion

Program evaluation is the intersection of research and practice. The behavioral health sector lags behind the broader health industry in its use of evidence-based practices. If done effectively, evaluation can provide evidence for program outcomes, benefitting all involved. The basic types of evaluation are needs assessment, feasibility study, process evaluation, outcomes evaluation, and cost analysis. Evaluations serve providers, consumers, policymakers, funding sources, and consulting professionals. By evaluating our current and future programs, we are ensuring the healthy growth of our clients, programs, and field at large.

References

Aos, S., Miller, M., & Drake, E. (2006). *Evidence-based public policy options to reduce future prison construction, criminal costs, and crime rates*. Olympia, WA: Washington State Institute for Public Policy.

Calley, N. G. (2012). Juvenile offender recidivism: An examination of risk factors. *Journal of Child Sexual Abuse, 21*(3), 257–272. doi:10.1080/10538712.2012.668266

Centers for Disease Control and Prevention 1999. Framework for program evaluation in public health. MMWR; 48 (No. RR-11)

Christenson, J. D., & Crane, D. R. (2014). Integrating costs into marriage and family therapy research. In R. B. Miller & L. Johnson (Eds.), *Advanced research methods in family therapy research: A focus on validity and change* (pp. 420–436). New York: Taylor and Francis.

Davis, K. E. (2014). *Expenditures for treatment of mental health disorders among children, ages 5–17, 2009–2011: Estimates for the U.S. civilian noninstitutionalized population*. Retrieved from http://meps.ahrq.gov/mepsweb/data_files/publications/st440/stat440.shtml

Ellis, R. H., Wilson, N. Z., & Foster, F. M. (1984). Statewide treatment outcome assessment in Colorado: The Colorado client assessment record (CCAR). *Community Mental Health Journal, 20*(1), 72–89.

Evaluating Residential Treatment Programs. (2006). *Eating Disorders Review, 17*(3). Retrieved from http://eatingdisordersreview.com/nl/nl_edr_17_3_7.html

Gass, M. (2014). *Program evaluation: Critical factors for measuring client change*. A workshop presented at the 2014 Northeast Conference for Experiential Education. The Berkshires, MA. April 17, 2014.

Gass, M., Gillis, H., & Russell, K. (2012). *Adventure therapy theory research and practice*. New York: Taylor and Francis Group.

Gillis, H. L., Gass, M. A., & Russell, K. C. (2008). The effectiveness of project adventure's behavior management programs for male offenders in residential treatment. *Residential Treatment for Children & Youth, 25*(3), 227–247.

Merikangas, K. R., He, J., Burstein, M., Swanson, S. A., Avenevoli, S., Cui, L., et al. (2010). Lifetime prevalence of mental disorders in U.S. adolescents: Results from the National Comorbidity-Study Adolescent Supplement (NCS-A). *Journal of the American Academy of Child and Adolescent Psychiatry, 49*(10), 980–989.

McCaffrey, B. R. (1996). *Treatment protocol effectiveness study*. Retrieved from https://www.ncjrs.gov/ondcppubs/publications/treat/trmtprot.html

National Association for Therapeutic School and Programs. (2015). *NATSAP PQ-D (Parent Questionnaire-Discharge)*. Bethesda, MD.

OQ Measures. (2014). *What can the Y-OQ tell you about your younger clients?* Retrieved from http://www.oqmeasures.com/measures/youth-adolescent-measures/y-oq/

Program Evaluation Unit, Legislative Finance Committee. (2014). *Results first: Adult behavioral health programs*. Retrieved from http://www.nmlegis.gov/lcs/lfc/lfcdocs/resultsfirst/Evidence-Based%20Behavioral%20Health%20Programs%20to%20Improve%20Outcomes%20for%20Adults.pdf

Rossi, P. H., Lipsey, M. W., & Freeman, H. E. (2003). *Evaluation: A systematic approach*. New York: Sage Publications.

Ryan, C., Epstein, N., Keitner, G., Miller, I., & Bishop, D. (2005). *Evaluating and treating families*. New York: Taylor and Francis.

Substance Abuse and Mental Health Services Administration. (2012). *National survey on drug use and health: Mental health findings*. Rockville, MD: Substance Abuse and Mental Health Services Administration.

United States Department of Health and Human Services. (2010). *The program managers guide to program evaluation* (2nd ed.). Retrieved from http://www.acf.hhs.gov/sites/default/files/opre/program_managers_guide_to_eval2010.pdf

United States Government Accountability Office. (2012, January). *Designing evaluations*. Retrieved from http://www.gao.gov/assets/590/588146.pdf

Vaughn, C. F. (2005). Residential treatment centers: Not a solution for children with mental health needs. *Clearinghouse Review Journal of Poverty Law and Policy, 39*(3–4), 274.

W. K. Kellogg Foundation. (2004). *W. K. Kellogg Foundation evaluation handbook*. Retrieved from https://www.wkkf.org/resource-directory/resource/2010/w-k-kellogg-foundation-evaluation-handbook

Warner, L. A., & Pottick, K. J. (2003). Nearly 66,000 youth live in US mental health programs. Latest findings in children's mental health (Policy Report submitted to the Annie E. Casey Foundation). New Brunswick, NJ: Institute for Health. *Health Care Policy, and Aging Research, Rutgers University, 2*(1), 1–2.

Williams-Reade, J., Gordon, B., Wray, W. (2014). A primer in program evaluation for MedFTs. In Hodgson, J., Lamson, A., Mendenhall, T., & Russell, C. (2014). *Medical family therapy: Advanced applications* (pp. 283–299). Switzerland: Springer International Publishing.

Yingling, L. C. (2012). Parent-child and family assessment strategy and inventories. In Sperry, L. (Ed.), *Family assessment: Contemporary and cutting-edge strategies.* (2nd ed., pp. 203–229). New York: Routledge.

Author Biographies

Michael Gass Ph.D., LMFT is a Professor in the College of Health and Human Services and Director of the Outdoor Behavioral Healthcare (OBH) Center at the University of New Hampshire. He began working in the OBH field in 1979 and has published over 150 professional publications and delivered over 300 professional presentations. He has received several awards for his work, including the Distinguished Researcher awards from both the Association for Experiential Education and College of Health and Human Services at the University of New Hampshire.

Edward G. Foden BA, with experience working as direct care staff in both wilderness and residential therapy, is now attending the dual-degree program in Social Work and Outdoor Education at the University of New Hampshire. While at the University of New Hampshire, Edward has been assisting research faculty in the Social Work department and the Outdoor Behavioral Healthcare Center.

Anita Tucker Ph.D., LISCW is an Associate Professor in Social Work at the University of New Hampshire (UNH) where she is the Co-coordinator of UNH's dual-degree Master's program in Social Work and Outdoor Education and the Associate Director of UNH's Outdoor Behavioral Healthcare Center. Dr. Tucker has published over 25 empirical articles and four book chapters focused on wilderness and adventure therapy. In addition, she serves on the Board of Directors for the Association for Experiential Education.

Chapter 25
Expanding Our Understanding of Family Therapy in Residential Treatment

Ashley N. Merritts and Jacob D. Christenson

Chapter Highlights

- One of the major criticisms of residential treatment for youth has been that treatment gains are not maintained post-discharge.
- A strength-based, family systems approach throughout treatment is crucial in order to increase the likelihood of adolescents maintaining treatment gains when they return to their homes and communities.
- This book highlighted emerging approaches and foundational techniques for engaging adolescents and family members in the treatment process and providing effective family therapy services.
- The authors addressed inherent clinical and methodological challenges to conducting research in this setting and provided practical suggestions for conducting studies and applying results in order to strengthen the place of family therapy.

There is clear evidence in the literature, as presented throughout this book, of a long-standing discontinuity between the mental health needs of troubled adolescents and the services that they are receiving, especially as it relates to residential treatment. This is partly due to the fact that it was not until the last few decades that researchers began to review and evaluate mental health services for children and adolescents. Since then, intense debates have arisen regarding the need for residential treatment and whether or not adolescents would be better served in community-based and family settings (Nickerson et al. 2004).

A.N. Merritts (✉) · J.D. Christenson
Mount Mercy University, 1330 Elmhurst Dr. NE, Cedar Rapids, IA 52402, USA
e-mail: amerritts@mtmercy.edu

J.D. Christenson
e-mail: jchristenson@mtmercy.edu

© Springer International Publishing AG 2017
J.D. Christenson and A.N. Merritts (eds.), *Family Therapy with Adolescents
in Residential Treatment*, Focused Issues in Family Therapy,
DOI 10.1007/978-3-319-51747-6_25

One of the concerns about residential treatment is the consistent finding that adolescents' treatment gains are not maintained after discharge (Curry 1991). There are many explanations that have been suggested in the literature, but most come back to the fact that the traditional goal of residential treatment, which is to provide a protected and regulated environment that will prevent adolescents from engaging in oppositional and aggressive behaviors, is foundationally counterproductive when it comes to efforts to transition them back to their previous home and community environment (Nickerson et al. 2004), where there is often problematic triggers, unhealthy family dynamics, negative peer influences, accessibility to substances, and chronic stressors (Nickerson et al. 2007). This highlights the importance of alleviating family dysfunction, addressing other environmental influences, and teaching the parents new skills for addressing their adolescent's behavior issues prior to the reunification and return of the adolescent to their home environment (McCurdy and McIntyre 2004).

Historically, services have been focused on the individual adolescent in residential treatment and have looked identical regardless of the adolescent's developmental level and type of need (Lyons 1998). More recently, there has been a movement to adopt a more systemic approach to assessment and treatment that incorporates contextual dynamics both directly and indirectly. Cafferty and Leichtman (2001) have suggested five changes that must happen in the culture of the residential milieu, specifically with treatment team members, in order to increase the likelihood of adolescents maintaining treatment gains when they return to their homes and communities, and each of these principles have been reflected in the various chapters contained in this book:

- Shifting to a family systems orientation versus focusing solely on the adolescent in treatment.
- Viewing the parents as partners instead of adversaries.
- Emphasizing assets and strengths of the adolescent and family rather than pathology.
- Understanding and appreciating the role of culture.
- Connecting the adolescent to available support systems in their communities.

Nickerson and colleagues suggest that it comes down to two basic requirements: (1) engaging the families of the adolescents that are in treatment and (2) building on the strengths of these adolescents and their families (2004). The importance of family involvement has been well established in the literature, and in this book, and treatment centers are recognizing that adolescents cannot be understood without also understanding their families. It is evident that family therapy is a key component in helping the adolescent and family members to identify the influence of their own behaviors on the family system and make necessary second-order changes. Therefore, it is surprising that the literature lacks any broad guidelines or best practices for conducting family therapy in this setting. This makes it especially difficulty for clinicians that are providing these services to know where to turn in terms of professional development. The purpose of this book was to provide therapists and researchers with a solid groundwork related to engaging families, using family therapy, and conducting research in the residential setting in order to increase the use and the quality of family-oriented services.

Nearly all of the chapters in this book reinforce the importance of adopting a strength-focused, family systems approach throughout the entire treatment process, from the initial decision that the family makes to initiate treatment, to supporting and engaging the family during the treatment process, to aftercare planning. Chapter 12 outlined four approaches to delivering *Interventions*, and focused not only on the role of the family in encouraging the adolescent to seek treatment, but also the importance of supporting the family members throughout the process of recovery. Chapter 6 offered personal narratives of families' experiences with sending their child to treatment, which included a discussion of their own valuable engagement in their child's treatment.

The importance of *joining* with family members was emphasized throughout the book and several strategies for building a strong therapeutic alliance with families were highlighted. Chapter 14 provided readers with a framework for engaging parents using a stages of change approach, and the authors suggested that if the family's motivation to engage in treatment is low, it must be resolved in order for the adolescent's treatment to progress. Research has consistently shown that parental alliance with the therapist is associated not only with improved parenting skills and treatment attendance, but also with greater therapeutic change with the adolescent (Kazdin et al. 2006).

Several chapters focused on specific techniques and approaches that can be used to engage families in the adolescent's treatment process, as there are unique challenges to accomplishing this in the residential setting. These challenges include, but are not limited to, the distance from treatment centers, the family's perceived relevance of their involvement in treatment, the quality of the therapeutic relationship between therapist and family, and family members' resistance to change (Fairhurst 1996). The use of letter writing was presented in Chap. 2 as a way to not only engage adolescents and families in the treatment process, but also as way to move them through the stages of change, promote a systemic view, slow down the conversation, teach communication skills, and increase nurturance and repair of attachment injuries.

A discussion regarding how to engage the family in developing a comprehensive aftercare plan was discussed in Chap. 9, which is crucial to the maintenance of therapeutic gains as mentioned throughout this chapter. The authors of this book highlighted how the conversation of aftercare planning can be especially difficult for the parents of the adolescents as they want their child home, but also fear relapse occurring at home. The authors also emphasized the importance of parents engaging in their own therapeutic process in order to work through their feelings of grief and increase their levels of differentiation and emotional resiliency. A more detailed description of this parallel process was outlined in Chap. 7.

Although researchers have suggested that there are a multitude of family therapy approaches that can be adopted for use in treating adolescents and families in residential settings, a recent review of family therapy models being used highlighted the fact that the field has not yet identified specific models that demonstrate efficacy in this setting (see Chap. 11). Some of the emerging models of family therapy being used were discussed in this book, including Multiple Group Family Intervention, Family-Directed Structural Therapy, Narrative Family Therapy, and Experiential Family Therapy. The book also includes a discussion of three approaches that show promise in treating youth and their families in this setting: Brief Strategic Structural Therapy, Multi Systemic Therapy, and Functional Family Therapy.

The authors of this book sought to provide readers with practical tools, techniques, and systemic approaches that can be used to promote change within the adolescent and the family system. For example, Chap. 3 described how a narrative approach could be used to make the family the audience to the storying and re-storying of the adolescent's personal narratives, highlighting the use of therapeutic letters. In Chap. 16, family sculptures and reflecting teams are presented as interventions that can be helpful to the adolescents and families in terms of gaining insight into the dynamics that are maintaining their distress.

A significant portion of the book was reserved for discussion of some of the fundamental issues that clinicians need a working knowledge of when treating an adolescent population with emotional and behavioral issues in this era. This included a discussion of the rising problem of video game addiction and the implications of this problem when this is a significant issue for the adolescent in treatment. Chapter 13 provided readers with an understanding of adolescent substance abuse, which is increasing at an alarming rate, and included a review of the major models being used to treat substance abuse in this setting.

Throughout the book, the strengths and resources of the adolescents and their families were emphasized. Youth in residential treatment also possess abilities and strengths that can be developed and reinforced, "although these competencies are typically not recognized, given these students' histories of maladaptive and aversive social behaviors" (Nickerson et al. 2004, p. 8). Some of the recommendations for drawing on adolescents' and families' strengths and resources that are offered in this book include the use of strength letters (where parents highlight the positive qualities that they see in their adolescent); supporting family members to develop healthy coping skills with a focus on self-care; using reframing interventions "to transform family relations from problematic to effective and mutually supportive" (Robbins et al. 2011, p. 46); assigning role-plays to highlight strengths of the families' interactions; having staff and peers provide reflective feedback during which they share their insights and perceptions of strengths during group therapy sessions; and having the adolescents and parents reflect on their own self-efficacy and times when they were able to make positive changes in their lives. Specific strength-based approaches to treatment that have been suggested for work with this population were also discussed in this book, such as wilderness therapy (Nickerson et al. 2004). There is solid agreement that these strength-based techniques and approaches should be integrated into residential treatment.

A final purpose of this book was to address many of the inherent challenges associated with conducting traditional family therapy with adolescents in residential treatment. This includes an inadequate amount of effectiveness research to support the use of specific family therapy models despite the understanding that family involvement with adolescents in residential treatment leads to more successful outcomes post-discharge (Hair 2005). The last part of this book provided readers with practical suggestions for conducting qualitative, quantitative, and mixed methods studies that could promote the use of family therapy in this setting. The various authors made the argument not only for more research related to the clinical aspect of residential treatment (i.e., program delivery and treatment outcomes), but also the financial aspect. The cost of residential programs is often very high and there is little research demonstrating the cost effectiveness of residential placements. It is our hope that researchers and clinicians will feel compelled to advance the literature on family therapy in residential settings through applying the research methods outlined in Chap. 20.

Conclusion

Although family involvement has been found to be a consistent predictor of positive outcomes of adolescents in residential placement, this book sought to fill a gap in the literature through highlighting the emerging approaches and techniques for engaging families in residential treatment, as well as helping clinicians to navigate some of the inherent challenges associated with providing services to adolescents in this setting. It is clear that a strength-focused, family systems perspective should direct all aspects of the adolescent's residential treatment "so that interactions and patterns in families that may serve as barriers to the transfer of skills learned in placement can be addressed in the treatment plan" (Nickerson et al. 2004, p. 12). We are hopeful that readers obtained a greater understanding of how to work effectively with adolescents and their families in this setting, as well as an appreciation for the importance of further research in this area in order to better establish the place of family therapy in residential treatment.

We are also hopeful that the contents of this book can be used to improve the quality of training in marriage and family therapy graduate programs. Most, if not all, training in these programs is based on an assumption that the relevant members of the system will be locally available for participation in sessions. Training programs need to expand their training to include techniques for working with families that are separated and in distress. As marriage and family therapy programs take up this challenge the quality of their graduates will improve and they will better able to meet the needs of their employers in an ever changing health care market. There remains much to be done, but it is our belief that the contents of this book will make a significant contribution to furthering discussion on this topic.

References

Cafferty, H., & Leichtman, M. (2001). Facilitating the transfer from residential treatment into the community: II. Changing social work roles. *Residential Treatment for Children and Youth, 19,* 13–25.

Curry, J. F. (1991). Outcome research on residential treatment: Implications and suggested directions. *American Journal of Orthopsychiatry, 61,* 348–357.

Fairhurst, S. K. (1996). Promoting change in families: Treatment matching in residential treatment centers. *Residential Treatment for Children & Youth, 14*(2), 21–32.

Hair, H. J. (2005). Outcomes for children and adolescents after residential treatment: A review of research from 1993 to 2003. *Journal of Child and Family Studies, 14*(4), 551–575.

Kazdin, A. E., Whitley, M., & Marciano, P. L. (2006). Child-therapist and parent-therapist alliance and therapeutic change in the treatment of children referred for oppositional, aggressive, and antisocial behavior. *Journal of Child Psychology and Psychiatry, 47*(5), 436–445.

Lyons, J. S., Libman-Mintzer, L. N., Kisiel, C. L., & Shallcross, H. (1998). Understanding the mental health needs of children and adolescents in residential treatment. *Professional psychology: Research and Practice, 29*(6), 582–587.

McCurdy, B. L., & McIntyre, E. K. (2004). 'And what about residential…?' Reconceptualizing residential treatment as a stop-gap service for youth with emotional and behavioral disorders. *Behavioral Interventions, 19,* 137–158.

Nickerson, A. B., Colby, S. A., Brooks, J. L., Rickert, J. M., & Salamone, F. J. (2007). Transitioning youth from residential treatment to the community: A preliminary investigation. *Child & Youth Care Forum, 36*(2), 73–86.

Nickerson, A. B., Salamone, F. J., Brooks, J. L., & Colby, S. A. (2004). Promising approaches toengaging families and building strengths in residential treatment. *Residential Treatment for Children & Youth, 22*(1), 1–18.

Robbins, M. S., Feaster, D. J., Horigian, V. E., Rohrbaugh, M., Shoham, V., Bachrach, K., et al. (2011). Brief strategic family therapy versus treatment as usual: Results of a multisite randomized trial for substance using adolescents. *Journal of Consulting and Clinical psychology, 79*(6), 713.

Author Biographies

Ashley N. Merritts, Ph.D., LMFT is an assistant professor in the marriage and family therapy program at Mount Mercy University. Dr. Merritts received her BS degree from the University of Iowa in Psychology, with a minor in Human Relations. After graduating from the University of Iowa, Dr. Merritts continued her education and has a Ph.D. in Human Development and Family Studies and a Master of Science degree in the same major, both from Iowa State University. In her Master's degree program, Dr. Merritts specialized in couple and family therapy and is now a Licensed Marital and Family Therapist. Dr. Merritts has extensive clinical training and has worked with a wide variety of problems in clinical settings. She specializes in working with distressed couples and has advanced training in Trauma Focused Cognitive Behavior Therapy as well. Dr. Merritt's has worked with adolescents in residential settings during her career and understands the unique needs of this population. Here clinical interests also include working with childhood behavioral problems, families in crisis, co-parenting and divorce, individual healing, and affairs. Dr. Merritts is a Clinical Fellow and Approved Supervisor with the American Association for Marriage and Family Therapy. She has also served as a board member for the Iowa Association for Marriage and Family Therapy. Dr. Merritts has published her work in the International Journal of Disability, Development and Education. She has also published in, and has served as a reviewer for, Contemporary Family Therapy: An International Journal. Dr. Merritts' research interests include relationship quality in African American couples and the impact of adverse childhood experiences on parent–child attachment.

Jacob D. Christenson, Ph.D., LMFT is an assistant professor of marriage and family therapy at Mount Mercy University. Dr. Christenson received his Bachelor degree in Psychology from California Polytechnic State University. He then completed his Master's degree and doctorate in Marriage and Family Therapy from Brigham Young University. Before coming to Mount Mercy University Dr. Christenson worked for 4 years at Aspen Achievement Academy in Loa, UT as a Field Therapist. As a Field Therapist, Dr. Christenson experienced firsthand the challenge of being a systemic marriage and family therapist in the world of residential care. Over the course of his career Dr. Christenson has consistently been involved in academic research and publication. In addition to numerous presentations at national and international conferences, Dr. Christenson has published a number of articles in peer-reviewed journals such as the Journal of Marital and Family Therapy, Contemporary Family Therapy, and the American Journal of Family Therapy. Dr. Christenson also serves as an editorial board member for the Journal of Marital and Family Therapy and Contemporary Family Therapy. Dr. Christenson teaches a number of course at Mount Mercy University. The courses he have taught have included, Parents and Children, Micro-counseling, Medical Family Therapy, and Research Methods. Dr. Christenson is also an AAMFT Approved Supervisor, which has enabled him to provide supervision in practicum courses. Dr. Christenson also serves as the Clinical Director for the Gerald and Audrey Olson Marriage and Family Therapy Clinic, which is attached to the marriage and family therapy program at Mount Mercy University. In addition to his work as a professor, Dr. Christenson provides therapy in private practice and is the founder of Covenant Family Solutions, an outpatient therapy group practice in Cedar Rapids, Iowa. When not working, Dr. Christenson enjoys spending time with his family and being active in his community.

.

Index

© Springer International Publishing AG 2017
J.D. Christenson and A.N. Merritts (eds.), *Family Therapy with Adolescents in Residential Treatment*, Focused Issues in Family Therapy,
DOI 10.1007/978-3-319-51747-6

451

Printed by Printforce, the Netherlands